Don Jones

VBScript, WMI, and ADSI

Using VBScript, WMI, and ADSI to Automate Windows® Administration

UNLEASHED

SAMS | 800 East 96th Street, Indianapolis, Indiana 46240 USA

VBScript, WMI, and ADSI Unleashed

ISBN-13: 978-0-321-50171-4
ISBN-10: 0-321-50171-3

Library of Congress Cataloging-in-Publication Data:

Jones, Don, 1971-

  VBScript, WMI and ADSI unleashed : using VBSscript, WMI, and ADSI to automate Windows administration / Don Jones. — 1st ed.

    p. cm.

  ISBN 0-321-50171-3 (pbk. : alk. paper) 1. VBScript (Computer program language) 2. Microsoft Windows (Computer file) 3. Directory services (Computer network technology) I. Title.

QA76.73.V27J67 2007

005.13'3—dc22

                     2007008741

Printed in the United States on America

First Printing May 2007

Trademarks

Warning and Disclaimer

Bulk Sales

Sams Publishing offers excellent discounts on this book when ordered in quantity for bulk purchases or special sales. For more information, please contact

U.S. Corporate and Government Sales
1-800-382-3419
corpsales@pearsontechgroup.com

For sales outside of the U.S., please contact

International Sales
international@pearsoned.com

 ### This Book Is Safari Enabled

The Safari® Enabled icon on the cover of your favorite technology book means the book is available through Safari Bookshelf. When you buy this book, you get free access to the online edition for 45 days.

Safari Bookshelf is an electronic reference library that lets you easily search thousands of technical books, find code samples, download chapters, and access technical information whenever and wherever you need it.

To gain 45-day Safari Enabled access to this book:

· Go to http://www.samspublishing.com/safarienabled

· Complete the brief registration form

· Enter the coupon code 8UEX-JHLG-KG9J-7WFE-62B7

If you have difficulty registering on Safari Bookshelf or accessing the online edition, please email customer-service@safaribooksonline.com.

Editor-in-Chief
Karen Gettman

Acquisitions Editor
Joan Murray

Managing Editor
Gina Kanouse

Senior Project Editor
Kristy Hart

Copy Editor
Karen Annett

Indexer
Brad Herriman

Proofreader
Williams Woods
Publishing, LLC

Cover Designer
Gary Adair

Composition
Bronkella Publishing

Contents at a Glance

Table of Contents

About the Author

Don Jones is an internationally recognized scripting guru, speaker, and author. He serves as the Director of Projects and Services for SAPIEN Technologies, where his primary job is to drive the development of new products and services for Windows administrative scripting. Don is the founder of ScriptingAnswers.com, the web's friendliest community for Windows scripting. Don has written more than 30 books on information technology, including *Managing Windows with VBScript and WMI* (Addison-Wesley; the first edition of this book), *Windows Administrator's Automation Toolkit* (Microsoft Press), *Advanced VBScript for Windows Administrators* (Microsoft Press), and *Windows PowerShell: TFM™* (SAPIEN Press). Don heads SAPIEN Technologies' Las Vegas office, speaks at a half-dozen technical conferences each year, and contributes monthly content to Microsoft *TechNet Magazine*.

Dedication

To Alex and Ferdinand: Thanks for having me.

Acknowledgments

Book projects always go more smoothly with an experienced team—and of the major publishing houses, let me tell you that Pearson (Addison-Wesley and Sams) has consistently had the best teams. I'm indebted to them for the opportunity to produce this new, revised edition of my original scripting book.

I would also like to thank my technical review panel made up of Dan Cazzulino, Jim Christopher, Doug Ellis, Jeffery Hicks, Bob Reselman, and Rob van der Woude. Without their valuable commentary and feedback, the book would not have been what it is today.

Support on the home front is important, too: Thanks to Chris for being wonderfully patient, and thanks to Alex, Ferdinand, Spoon, and Margaret for giving me the time to work on this lengthy revision. Thanks also to my ferrets, Pepper, Patch, and Nutmeg, who were wonderfully understanding—not—when "daddy" couldn't play right then because he was typing.

And thanks, perhaps most of all, to Microsoft, for realizing at long last how important VBScript is to the community of Windows administrators, for deciding to continue to include it in future versions of Windows, and for giving the TechNet "Scripting Guys" full-time permission to produce samples, answer questions, and, in general, really promote administrative scripting to the world.

Don Jones

SAPIEN Technologies

May 2007

We Want to Hear from You!

As the reader of this book, *you* are our most important critic and commentator. We value your opinion and want to know what we're doing right, what we could do better, what areas you'd like to see us publish in, and any other words of wisdom you're willing to pass our way.

You can email or write me directly to let me know what you did or didn't like about this book—as well as what we can do to make our books stronger.

Please note that I cannot help you with technical problems related to the topic of this book, and that due to the high volume of mail I receive, I might not be able to reply to every message.

When you write, please be sure to include this book's title and author as well as your name and phone or email address. I will carefully review your comments and share them with the author and editors who worked on the book.

E-mail: consumer@samspublishing.com

Mail: Mark Taber
          Associate Publisher
          Sams Publishing
          800 East 96th Street
          Indianapolis, IN 46240 USA

Reader Services

Visit our website and register this book at www.samspublishing.com/register for convenient access to any updates, downloads, or errata that might be available for this book.

Introduction

Microsoft introduced Visual Basic, Scripting Edition—commonly known as VBScript—in the mid-1990s, positioning it as a native replacement for Windows' aging command-line batch language, which was based on Microsoft's earliest operating system, MS-DOS. VBScript was intended to be easy to learn, powerful, and flexible. The language was included as an add-on to Windows 95 and Windows NT 4.0, was an optional installation component included in Windows 98, and was included in all editions of Windows Me, Windows 2000, Windows XP, and Windows Server 2003.

Software developers immediately seized upon VBScript for web programming, particularly in Active Server Pages, Microsoft's rapid-development programming framework for the web. However, Windows administrators—one of VBScript's initial target audiences—were left cold. VBScript seemed to be much more complicated than administrators' beloved MS-DOS-based batch language, and many didn't see the need to learn an entirely new batch language.

When Windows 2000 and Active Directory came along, however, administrators found that Windows administration had become a great deal more complex. Suddenly, administrators were searching for Resource Kits and other utilities that offered automated administration, especially for repetitive tasks. Active Directory enabled the use of VBScript for logon and logoff scripts, which seemed to promise more advanced-use environment manipulation. At around the same time, Microsoft's naiveté in releasing a powerful language like VBScript with absolutely no security controls resulted in a huge wave of high-impact VBScript-based viruses, forcing administrators to lock down their environments and remove VBScript as an option both for viruses and for administrative tools.

As a regular speaker at some of the country's top technical conferences that focus on Windows technologies, including TechMentor, the past few years I've given half- and full-day sessions on VBScripting for Windows administrators, and the sessions have been incredibly popular. In these sessions, I try to provide just enough VBScript experience to make scripting possible, and then concentrate on accomplishing common administrative tasks with VBScript. I also cover the security concerns of VBScript and provide administrators with the means for safely using VBScript in their environments. This book is essentially a written form of those sessions, greatly expanded with more coverage of Windows Management Instrumentation and other advanced topics, and with more coverage of VBScript security issues and resolutions.

I'm not out to turn you into a programmer. In fact, one of the real successes of VBScript is that you don't *need* to be a programmer to use it. Most of what you'll be doing in this book involves using VBScript to tell Windows to do things for you; you'll be able to ignore much of VBScript's complexity, using it as a sort of electronic glue to combine various operating system functions.

It's been four years since the original edition of this book, published as *Managing Windows with VBScript and WMI*. At the time, Windows administrators were really just discovering scripting and its potential to automate administrative tasks; since then, scripting and automation have taken off in a big way. Managers—not just administrators—realize that automation makes better use of skilled technical professionals, freeing them up from boring, repetitive tasks for new projects. That realization has led to the word *scripting* being added to many a high-end job description, and scripting is emerging as one of the most important differentiators between entry-level technicians and experienced professionals.

In the past four years, I've done a tremendous amount of work to promote scripting and education. I produced more than a dozen free Webcasts for Microsoft TechNet (which are still viewable; links can be found on http://www.ScriptingAnswers.com), launched a web community for administrative scripting called www.ScriptingAnswers.com, created two complete series of training videos for scripting (viewable at http://www.ScriptingTraining.com), designed a web search engine specifically for scripting resources (http://www.SearchScripting.com), and wrote nearly a half-dozen books on Windows scripting and automation (including two free ones from http://www.Realtimepublishers.com). Scripting is here to stay.

Who Should Read This Book?

The only assumption I have about you is that you already know how to administer some version of Microsoft Windows. You'll find that most of the material in this book is suitable for Windows NT, Windows 2000, Windows Server 2003, and (as it's known as of this writing) Windows "Longhorn" Server environments (that includes the client versions of these operating systems, such as Windows XP and Windows Vista), and it will continue to be useful through future versions of Windows. I do not assume that you have any background in programming, and I'm not going to give you a programming background.

You should have a desire to learn how to use what I call "the batch language of the twenty-first century" and a desire to move away from clumsier—and often more complex—batch files based on the MS-DOS batch language. Although some folks like to refer to batch files as scripts, I don't; and when you see how easy and flexible VBScript is, you'll understand why!

How to Use This Book

You can read this book in order from the Introduction to the Appendix. However, if you already have some experience with VBScript, or if you just want to dive right in to the more complete sample scripts, you can skip around as much as you want. This book is organized in the same way that I organize my live VBScripting sessions at conferences, so you might feel that it's some time before you really get into the meat of scripting. I assure you, though, that each example in this book—starting in Chapter 1—is focused on Windows administration. You'll get your feet wet right away!

To help you decide where to start, the following sections provide a brief overview of each chapter.

Part I: Introduction to Windows Administrative Scripting

Part I serves as an introduction to the world of scripting and provides you with a methodology for approaching administrative tasks from a scripting standpoint. One of the most difficult parts about producing new scripts from scratch is the "Where do I start?" factor, and this part provides you with a framework for figuring that out every time.

Chapter 1: Scripting Concepts and Terminology

As implied previously, administrative scripting isn't hard-core programming. Instead, it's using VBScript as a sort of electronic glue to secure various bits of the Windows operating system together. This chapter introduces you to those various bits and sets the stage with some basic terminology that you'll use throughout this book.

Chapter 2: Running Scripts

Writing a script isn't much fun if you can't run the script! This chapter focuses on the technologies used to execute scripts. You might be surprised to learn how many different Microsoft products support scripting. This chapter shows you how far your scripting skills can really take you and also introduces you to some scripting tools that can make writing and debugging scripts a bit easier.

Chapter 3: The Components of a Script

This chapter presents a complete administrative script and then breaks it down line-by-line to explain its various components. Although this chapter isn't necessary to learning administrative scripting, it will help you write scripts that are more reliable and easier to troubleshoot.

Chapter 4: Designing a Script

As mentioned previously, one of the toughest aspects about scripting can be figuring out where to start. This chapter provides you with a framework that you can use as a starting point for every new scripting project. This chapter also introduces you to some concepts that many scripting books ignore, such as planning for errors and creating a useful "resource kit" of script components that you can reuse throughout your scripting projects.

Part II: VBScript Tutorial

Part II serves as your official crash course to the VBScript language: just enough to make administration via script a possibility! The best part is that this part doesn't use the trite "Hello, world" examples that books for software developers often start out with. Instead, every example is useful to you as a Windows administrator. This means you'll produce simple, useful scripts at the same time you're learning VBScript. What could be better?

Chapter 5: Functions, Objects, Variables, and More

This chapter shows you the basic building blocks of any script and introduces you to some sample scripts that use each building block in a particular administrative task. This is really the meat of administrative scripting, and you'll be able to write useful scripts when you're finished with this chapter.

Chapter 6: Input and Output

You can make your scripts more flexible by adding the ability to dynamically change computer, user, and domain names, along with other information. This chapter shows you how your script can collect information it needs to run and dynamically alter itself to take advantage of that information.

Chapter 7: Manipulating Numbers

This chapter explains how scripts can manipulate numbers, making it easier to create scripts that work with numeric data, such as user account data. It also introduces you to VBScript's numeric data handling and conversion commands, putting you on the path to some great scripting techniques.

Chapter 8: Manipulating Strings

Strings—a fancy word for text data—are at the heart of most scripting tasks. This chapter shows you how VBScript deals with strings and how you can easily integrate them into your scripts.

Chapter 9: Manipulating Other Types of Data

Aside from text and numbers, your scripts might need to deal with dates, times, bytes, and other forms of data to accomplish specific administrative tasks. This chapter shows you how VBScript handles these other data types and how you can use them in your own scripts.

Chapter 10: Controlling the Flow of Execution

The best administrative scripts can respond to changing conditions with internal logic, called control-of-flow. This chapter shows you how your scripts can be made to evaluate various conditions and respond accordingly, perform repetitive tasks, and much more.

Chapter 11: Built-in Scripting Objects

Much of VBScript's power comes from its capability to join various operating system objects, and this chapter introduces you to your first set of those objects. You'll learn how to manipulate network information, map drives, and much more—pretty much everything you need to write effective logon scripts.

Chapter 12: Working with the File System

A common use of scripting is to manipulate files and folders, and this chapter introduces you to the VBScript `FileSystemObject`, which provides a complete object model for working with the file system. You'll learn to build a utility that scans Internet Information Services (IIS) log files for error messages, a useful script for any environment!

Chapter 13: Putting It All Together: Creating Your First Script from Scratch

This is where you put everything from Part II together. You'll create a script that rotates IIS log files, keeping the past 30 days worth of files in a special archive folder. This chapter guides you through the complete process of designing, writing, testing, and troubleshooting the script. In fact, it deliberately introduces some logic errors into the script so that you can see the debugging process in action.

Part III: Windows Management Instrumentation and Active Directory Services Interface

With the glue of VBScript under your belt, this part dives into the two most powerful technologies for administering Windows: Windows Management Instrumentation (WMI) and the Active Directory Services Interface (ADSI). These technologies provide administrative access to, and control over, nearly every aspect of the Windows operating system, from Windows NT to Windows Server 2003.

Chapter 14: Working with ADSI Providers

Despite its name, ADSI isn't just for Active Directory. This chapter shows you how ADSI can be used to interface with NT, Active Directory, Novell NDS, Exchange Server, and other types of directory services. This chapter provides some basic examples of the types of tasks you can perform with ADSI to get you started.

Chapter 15: Manipulating Domains

With the ADSI basics out of the way, this chapter focuses on manipulating domain information in a script. You'll learn how to query domain information, modify domain policies such as password length, and much more.

Chapter 16: Manipulating Users and Groups

This chapter shows you how to write scripts that query and modify user and group information. This is one of the most common tasks you'll perform with VBScript, and this chapter includes plenty of useful examples.

Chapter 17: Understanding WMI

WMI provides a hook into just about every portion of the Windows operating system, making it an incredibly useful tool for administrative scripts. This chapter introduces you to WMI and shows you a preview of what you can use it for in your environment.

Chapter 18: Querying Basic WMI Information

Do you want to find out which users in your organization have a Pentium 4 computer? This chapter shows you how to write your own basic WMI queries, including those that involve remote machines. You'll also learn basic WMI manipulation, which lets you modify local and remote machine settings from within a script.

Chapter 19: Querying Complex WMI Information

Some WMI queries are more complex, such as querying the IP addresses from multiple network adapters in multiple remote computers. This chapter provides clear examples of these more complex WMI tasks, helping you learn to write enterprise management scripts.

Chapter 20: Putting It All Together: Your First WMI/ADSI Script

This is where it all comes together. This chapter walks you through the process of designing, writing, testing, and debugging a complete WMI/ADSI script from scratch. You'll finish this chapter with a concrete example of the administrative capabilities of these technologies, and then you'll be ready to start writing your own scripts.

Chapter 21: Testing and Debugging WMI and ADSI Queries

Getting the perfect WMI or ADSI query is critical to the success of your scripts, so this chapter focuses on tools you can use to develop those queries more interactively, test your queries, and have them fully refined before pasting them into your scripts.

Part IV: Advanced Scripting Techniques

As you become a more experienced scripter, you'll be ready to start saving time and be more secure, with advanced techniques like script encryption, scripting components, script security, and so forth. This part of the book gives you a comprehensive look at each of these technologies and shows you how to put them into use in your own environment.

Chapter 22: Modular Script Programming

If you find yourself cutting and pasting code—or worse, retyping it—this is the chapter for you. This chapter introduces you to modular scripting concepts, which make it easier to reuse code between various scripts, saving you time and effort! By way of example, this chapter starts with a complex script that contains lots of useful code and then breaks it down into easily reused modules.

Chapter 23: Scripts Packaging and Protection

Are you worried that others will peek into your scripts and steal your ideas? Script packaging and other techniques help protect your scripts from both Peeping Toms and potential misuse, so this chapter shows you how to set up, deploy, and use script packages within your environment.

Chapter 24: Scripting Security

Some folks think Microsoft made a huge mistake when it included VBScript in the Windows operating system, but others disagree. Properly configured, scripting can be as safe as any other type of application. This chapter explains scripting security concepts and introduces you to the tools that can make scripting a safe and valuable part of any computing environment.

Chapter 25: Introduction to HTML Applications

HTML Applications, or HTAs, provide a way to mix VBScript and Hypertext Markup Language (HTML) code to produce graphical scripts that look almost like full Windows applications. They're a great way to produce tools that you plan to share with less-experienced users or administrators. This chapter gives you a quick start in building HTAs, along with an explanation of how they differ from more traditional VBScript projects.

Chapter 26: Debugging Tips, Tools, and Techniques

By now, you'll have seen your fair share of script bugs, and so this chapter shows you how to prevent them from happening, find them quickly when they do happen, and squash them just as quickly so that you can get on with your scripting.

Part V: Ready-to-Run Examples

This part is a great way to wrap up the book—with a whole section on ready-made sample scripts that you can start using in your own environment. In addition, these scripts—like every other script in this book—have complete, line-by-line explanations, making them a perfect reference guide as you start to create your own scripts from scratch.

Chapter 27: Logon and Logoff Scripts

This chapter presents more complex logon and logoff scripts and gives you some ideas for how scripting can make these important scripts more effective. Of course, the line-by-line explanations make each script a useful reference for customizing your own scripts.

Chapter 28: Windows and Domain Administration Scripts

Automating domain administration is probably one of the big reasons you started looking at scripting in the first place, so this chapter presents a number of examples of tasks that scripts can perform. The detailed explanations with each script will help you rip them apart and customize them for your own use.

Chapter 29: Network Administration Scripts

Network administration is ideally suited for scripting, and this chapter provides a handful of examples that show you what's possible. The line-by-line explanations make it easy to put these into use in your own environment.

Chapter 30: WMI and ADSI Scripts

These can be the toughest scripts to write because of the complexity and flexibility of WMI and ADSI. This chapter provides you with several ready-to-use scripts for common tasks, such as querying WMI, creating users and groups, and more. These scripts can be easily modified and incorporated into your own scripts, saving you scripting time!

Appendix

Appendix: Administrator's Quick Script Reference

One of the toughest parts about VBScript is that it contains so much functionality. It's usually pretty easy to figure out what you want a script to do; the tough part is often figuring out how to make VBScript do it! This appendix provides an alphabetical list of common tasks and gives the VBScript commands that perform each task. You can use this reference along with the VBScript documentation to make designing and writing scripts much easier.

Preparing to Use This Book

Before you dive in, you should make sure that your computers are ready for VBScript. Fortunately, any computer with Windows 2000 or later is ready to go out of the box, and this book assumes that you're doing your development work on either a Windows 2000–, Windows XP–, or Windows Server 2003–based computer.

Typographical Elements

Books on programming can benefit a great deal from easy-to-understand typestyles and elements like the ones explained here. These typestyles and elements are designed to make the text easier to follow and to call your attention to special concerns.

Monospaced type will be used to set off material that should be typed into the computer. For example, "select `Run` from the Start menu, type `wbemtest`, and click `OK`" sets off the menu selection, and what you need to type onscreen.

Blocks of code and code lines that appear within the text appear in a monospaced font, as in, "To change the contents of a variable, you can use `Var1 = Trim(Var1)`."

TIP

Tips provide shortcuts and other "insider advice" about scripting that you'll find valuable.

NOTE

Notes provide cautions and other clarifications that will help you avoid problems or further clarify complex concepts.

You'll also be directed to material that more thoroughly explains particular concepts, VBScript commands, and so forth. Although you might not be a big fan of flipping back and forth through a book, these cross-references allow you to remain focused within each chapter and guide you to more detailed explanations, when appropriate.

Finally, there are times when it is necessary to present an extended explanation of something that isn't critical to the task at hand. In those cases, a sidebar is included. A sidebar is a cue that the information is useful, but it's not really key to the main text; you're welcome to skip the sidebar and come back to it later.

Sidebars

Sidebars make it easier to cover slightly off-topic information without distracting you from the main text.

Sample Scripts

Obviously, a book on scripting is going to have many code listings. To make these as useful as possible, each sample script is presented in a listing by itself with no comments.

LISTING P.1   A Sample Script

```
'Get the user's name
sName = InputBox("What is your name?")

'Display the user's name
MsgBox "Your name is " & sName
```

After each script, any changes you might need to make to get the script running in your environment, such as changing computer or domain names, are presented. You'll find each complete script included on the CD that accompanies this book. Each chapter has a separate folder and the script files are named with their listing number for easy reference.

Sample Scripts—Explained

For each script in this book, a line-by-line explanation of the script is included, so that you understand exactly what's going on. For example:

First, the sample script displays a dialog box where the user can type his name. By default, this dialog box includes an OK and Cancel button; this script does not provide any way to detect the Cancel button, so it is assumed the user will type something and click OK.

```
'Get the user's name
sName = InputBox("What is your name?")
```

Finally, the script uses the `MsgBox` statement to redisplay the user's name. Notice the use of the ampersand operator (&) to tack on the contents of the variable `sName`, which stores whatever the user typed into the input box.

```
'Display the user's name
MsgBox "Your name is " & sName
```

Walk-throughs like this one will help you become more familiar with VBScript, what each command does, and exactly how each sample script works.

PART I

Introduction to Windows Administrative Scripting

IN THIS PART

CHAPTER 1

Scripting Concepts and Terminology

In the past few years, scripting has become increasingly popular with Windows administrators. Visual Basic, Scripting Edition—commonly known as VBScript—has become especially popular because of its ease of use and incredible flexibility. Unfortunately, most books on scripting seemed to be focused toward developers, or at least toward Windows administrators with a strong software development background. The result is that most administrators think that scripting is too complex for them, which simply isn't true. In this book, I'll introduce you to scripting from a purely administrative standpoint, starting with this chapter, where I'll explain exactly what I mean by "scripting," and how it all fits into Windows administration.

Overview of Scripting

Scripting means different things to different people. Some folks, for example, define a *script* as any series of computer commands that are executed in a sequence, including so-called scripts written in the MS-DOS batch language. These batch files were the mainstay of administrative automation for many years, and many administrators still rely heavily upon them today. Other people define scripts as small computer programs written in a high-level scripting language, such as VBScript.

Nobody's really wrong, and scripting can mean all of these things. In fact, I've recently changed my opinion on the subject, and agree that batch files are, in fact, scripts. They're scripts in the most literal sense because when you run a batch file, it's exactly as if you were manually typing every character in the script—the script just does so faster.

VBScript is, in fact, an *interpreted language*, which is somewhat more complicated than a mere script. It's all splitting hairs, though! You can call all of them *scripts* and get away with it.

For the purposes of this book, *scripting* refers to the act of creating, executing, and utilizing small computer programs that are written in a high-end scripting language, specifically VBScript.

Script Hosts

Scripts start out life as simple text files. Try this: Open Windows Notepad on a Windows XP computer, and type the following text:

```
Set objWMI = GetObject("winmgmts:\\" & _
 ".\root\cimv2")
Set colOS = objWMI.ExecQuery("SELECT " & _
 "* FROM Win32_OperatingSystem")
For Each objOS In colOS
    MsgBox "Serial number: " & _
     objOS.SerialNumber
Next
```

> **NOTE**
>
> In the production of this book, I tested each and every sample and script fragment on my computer (running Windows XP), and they all worked at the time unless otherwise noted in the text. If a script isn't working for you, first double-check your typing—VBScript doesn't tolerate typos! Next, ask for help. I've set up a special forum on my site, www.ScriptingAnswers.com, where you can ask questions about the scripts and samples in this book. I'll do my best to help, but keep in mind, however, that sometimes things like your environment's configuration, security policies, and other external factors might make a script impossible to run.

Save the file as `SampleScript.vbs`. Be sure to include the filename in double quotation marks, or Notepad will append a `.txt` filename extension. Now, locate the file in Windows Explorer. Make sure it has a `.vbs` filename extension and double-click it. Provided you're running Windows XP and VBScript hasn't been disabled on your computer, you should see a small dialog box containing the serial number of your operating system. Congratulations, you've just scripted!

> **NOTE**
>
> For the time being, you don't need to worry about how this script does what it does. In later chapters, I'll explain what each of these four lines of code accomplishes. If you just can't wait, jump to Chapters 17 through 19, where I demonstrate how to use Windows Management Instrumentation (WMI) to retrieve serial numbers and other operating system information.

What actually happens when you double-click the VBS file? You can find out easily enough. From any Windows Explorer window, select *Folder Options* from the Tools menu. Select the File Types tab and locate VBS in the list. As shown in Figure 1.1, the .vbs file-name extension is associated with the Microsoft Windows Script Host. Whenever you double-click a VBS file, Windows fires up the Script Host, tells it which script you double-clicked, and lets the Script Host run the script. It's similar to what happens when you double-click a DOC file: Windows fires up Microsoft Word, tells it which file to open, and your document appears.

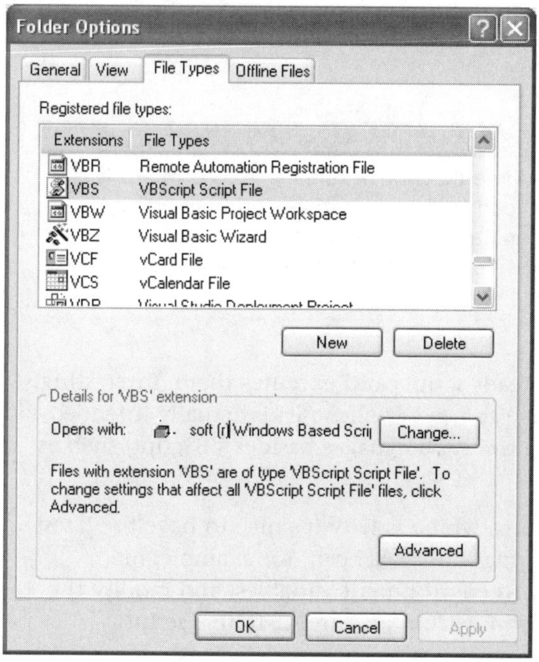

FIGURE 1.1   File association for the VBS file type.

The Windows Script Host (WSH) is a built-in component of Windows 2000, Windows XP, Windows Server 2003, Windows Vista, and later versions of Windows. In fact, it's under Windows File Protection for those operating systems, meaning you can't delete or remove the WSH executable, Wscript.exe. WSH is also included with Windows Me, is an optional installation component in Windows 98, and can be added to Windows NT 4.0 and Windows 95 through a free download from http://www.Microsoft.com/scripting.

TIP

As of this writing, the latest version of WSH is 5.6, and you can download it for free from http://www.Microsoft.com/scripting. WSH is packaged in a Windows Installer file (MSI), so you can easily deploy it to your client computers via Windows Group Policy.

WSH is present in many Microsoft products, in various versions. Here's where you can find WSH, along with the default versions:

► Windows 98 (optional), v1.0

► Windows NT 4.0 Option Pack, v1.0

► Windows 2000, v2.0

► Windows XP, v5.6

► Windows Server 2003, v5.6

► All later versions, including Windows Vista, v5.6

> **NOTE**
>
> For the purposes of this book, I'll always assume that you're running v5.6 of WSH. If you aren't, you can upgrade for free by downloading the newest version from http://www.Microsoft.com/scripting. To check your installed version, locate `WScript.exe` in the `\Windows\System32` folder, right-click it, select Properties, and examine the Version tab.

WSH is simply a Windows application that reads scripts and executes them. Interestingly, VBScript is *not* implemented right within `WScript.exe` itself. WSH is actually intended to be extensible, and it supports a number of scripting languages besides VBScript, such as JScript.

WSH does have a number of built-in functions, which is why it's nice to have the latest version—newer versions and more built-in functions. WSH can, for example, map network drives, connect to printers, work with environment variables, and modify the Registry—all useful things to be able to do from within an administrative script.

> **NOTE**
>
> Other applications—such as Microsoft Internet Explorer, Exchange Server, SQL Server, and IIS Active Server Pages—can serve as script hosts, too. The nice part about learning to create Windows administration scripts in VBScript is that you can quickly learn to create Structured Query Language (SQL) scripts, Exchange scripts, or even Active Server Pages, all using the same scripting language.

ActiveX Scripting Languages

VBScript is just one of many *ActiveX scripting languages*. These languages are written to a specification developed by Microsoft, and scripts written in these languages can be executed by WSH. Each ActiveX scripting language is implemented by a *scripting engine*. Usually, this dynamic link library (DLL) file interfaces with `WScript.exe` to interpret scripts, one line at a time, so that WSH can execute them. Microsoft maintains two

ActiveX scripting languages: VBScript and JScript. JScript is the Microsoft implementation of ECMAScript, which is the industry-standard version of Netscape's JavaScript scripting language.

> **NOTE**
>
> Ignoring company copyrights, trade names, and other legal matters, JScript, ECMAScript, and JavaScript are more or less interchangeable terms.

The scripting engines are maintained separately from WSH and carry their own version numbers. However, both the latest version of VBScript and JScript are included with the basic WSH installation, so you don't need to worry about getting them individually.

Other companies have produced ActiveX scripting languages, too. For example, VideoScript is an independent scripting language that works with WSH (http://www.videoscript.com). PerlScript and LiveScript are other popular ActiveX scripting languages.

Scripting languages all have a few common characteristics.

- They are *interpreted*. This means the scripting engine reads each line of script, one at a time, and then executes it. Execution requires the WSH to translate the scripted instructions into native Windows application programming interface (API) calls. Interpreted languages are slower than *compiled* languages like Visual Basic 6.0, where the compiler translates the entire program into native Windows code all at once, saving time later when the program is executed.

- They are *text based*. In other words, you can create scripts with a simple text editor like Notepad. The downside is that anyone can read your script with Notepad, too. Most software applications' code is compiled into a native binary format, making it very difficult for end users to read the code. Microsoft does offer an encoding utility (discussed in Chapter 27, "Logon and Logoff Scripts") that allows you to protect your source code from prying eyes.

- They are *native*. In other words, your scripts only execute on Windows because WSH itself only executes on Windows. Contrast this with languages like Java, which can be compiled and executed on any platform for which a Java Virtual Machine (JVM) is available.

- They are *easy to deploy*. Unlike compiled Visual Basic 6.0 applications, scripts don't usually require a bunch of DLLs and other files that you have to deploy, register, and so forth. Scripts can generally be copied from one computer to another and executed as is.

Perhaps the most powerful feature of VBScript is its capability to interface with the Microsoft Component Object Model (COM).

VBScript and .NET: What Does the Future Hold?

I'm often asked how the release of VB .NET and the .NET Framework affect VBScript. After all, you don't hear much mention of "VBScript.NET!"

It's a complicated question. The easy answer is this: Microsoft invested a lot of time and money getting administrators to use VBScript, and administrators are using it. WSH will be included in new releases of Windows for some time to come, even if Microsoft doesn't do any further development. In fact, Microsoft wrote a number of command-line tools in VBScript, and includes them with Windows!

The Component Object Model (COM)

Software developers have always been encouraged to develop reusable code. Imagine that you created some piece of code that retrieves the TCP/IP settings of a remote computer. Many administrators might want to use that code again. So how do you make your code available to them in an easy-to-use way?

Microsoft's answer is COM, the Component Object Model. COM is a specification that describes how code can be packaged into *objects,* making them self-contained, easy (relatively speaking) to deploy, and easy for other developers to use. Physically, COM objects are usually implemented in DLL files—which, if you check out the contents of a Windows computer's System32 folder, should tell you how pervasive COM is!

VBScript is completely capable of utilizing COM objects. That's a powerful feature because most of Windows' functionality—and most other Microsoft applications' functionality—is rolled up into COM components. Working with email, Active Directory, Windows Management Instrumentation (WMI), networking, the Registry, and more is all possible through COM components, and, therefore, through VBScript. I'll cover objects in more detail, including examples of how to use them in scripts, beginning in Chapter 5, "Functions, Objects, Variables, and More," and Chapter 11, "Built-In Scripting Objects," shows you how to really take advantage of them.

VBScript is even capable of creating COM components. This means that you can use VBScript to create your Internet Protocol (IP)–retrieval software, package that software as a COM component, and distribute it to other administrators. This feature of scripting is called *Windows Script Components.* However, it's a pretty advanced topic and, frankly, not many administrators find it useful, so I won't be covering it in any detail. You can, however, obtain more information at http://www.ScriptingAnswers.com.

Critical Scripting Security Issues

Sadly, Microsoft implemented VBScript without much thought for the consequences. Windows XP and Windows Vista, Microsoft's most recent client operating systems, ship with full scripting capability built-in and enabled by default. The power of VBScript can be used not only for beneficial administrative tasks, but also for malicious hacking, and many viruses are based on VBScript or another ActiveX scripting language.

Administrators have reacted to the security threat of scripts in a number of ways:

▶ Deleting `WScript.exe`. Unfortunately, this doesn't work on Windows 2000 or later because `WScript.exe` is protected with Windows File Protection. If you delete it, it just comes back.

▶ Disassociating the VB, VBS, JS, and other WSH file extensions, or reassociating them to simply open in Notepad rather than in WSH. This effectively disables scripting.

▶ Deploying antivirus software, such as Norton AntiVirus, which detects script execution and halts it.

Regrettably, disabling scripting usually disables it for good, meaning you can't use scripting for logon scripts, administrative tasks, and other beneficial purposes. There's a middle road that you can take, however, which authorizes only certain scripts for execution. This middle road helps protect you against scripts written by hackers, but still allows scripts to be used for administrative and logon purposes.

Fortunately, Microsoft came to the table with security improvements that can make scripting safe again, and Chapter 24, "Scripting Security," is devoted to the topic of scripting security.

VBScript Versus Windows PowerShell

In late 2006, Microsoft launched an all-new tool for Windows administrative automation: Windows PowerShell. Immediately, Windows administrators started asking, "Do I need to learn this?" and "Will this replace VBScript?" The answers to those questions are a bit complicated.

First, let me make very clear that I *love* Windows PowerShell. I think it's a great tool with some amazing capabilities, many of which parallel capabilities found in VBScript. That said, though, Windows PowerShell *is just a tool*. It isn't a religion or a spouse, which you would normally only have one of—you can have as many tools as you want! While I think you should absolutely learn Windows PowerShell—I even coauthored a book, *Windows PowerShell: TFM*, on the topic—I also think you should learn VBScript.

VBScript was introduced around 1996, but it took nearly 5 or 6 years before Windows administrators really started using it. Now that Windows administrative automation is a bigger deal, Windows PowerShell will enjoy a much faster adoption rate, but it'll still be a few years. Also, because Windows PowerShell is so new compared to VBScript, you won't yet find the wealth of free community resources, examples, and so forth that VBScript has behind it. Also, Windows PowerShell is a long-term strategic investment for Microsoft. Windows "Longhorn" Server, for example, won't be built primarily on Windows PowerShell, meaning VBScript will still be a big tool. In fact, the "Server Core" version of Longhorn relies heavily on a command-line tool written in VBScript by Microsoft! So, VBScript has a long life ahead of it, and you should plan to use both VBScript and Windows PowerShell as complementary parts of your administrative arsenal.

Here's another interesting fact: Microsoft isn't developing VBScript any further. Yes, that's right, folks, you're about to learn how to use the *only Microsoft product that's finished*, and still in production! No new versions, no upgrades, no changes to worry about—it's done! That's literally the reason Microsoft isn't developing it further: They feel it's feature-complete and doesn't require any additional work. That should come as a huge relief to you because it means what you'll learn from this book will remain the same for years to come. Of course, one of my jobs at SAPIEN Technologies is to think of clever new ways to give VBScript more capability and functionality, so don't regard VBScript as some old, deprecated, stagnant technology—it's still very much alive and relevant!

Summary

VBScript is one of many available ActiveX scripting languages. The scripts that you write are executed by the Windows Script Host (WSH), which is physically implemented as WScript.exe and available for (or included with) all 32-bit Windows operating systems. VBScript—like other ActiveX scripting languages—is especially powerful because it can interface with COM, the Microsoft Component Object Model. COM allows VBScript to be infinitely extended to perform other functions, including the majority of the Windows operating system functions. In fact, COM integration sets VBScript apart from other so-called scripting technologies like old MS-DOS-style batch files.

However, VBScript does bring up some important security issues that you'll need to learn to deal with in your environment. Microsoft's regrettable lack of planning when it comes to scripting has resulted in a huge number of script-based viruses, making scripting a tool for both good and evil. Nonetheless, you can learn to configure your environment so that only approved ("good") scripts run, allowing you to use the power and flexibility of script-based administration, while protecting your environment from malicious scripts.

CHAPTER 2

Running Scripts

Suppose you have several scripts ready to run—what do you do with them? Do you load them into Visual Basic and compile them? How do you distribute them to your users for use as logon scripts? What about when you're ready to start writing your own scripts? What tools are available, and how well do they work? This chapter is designed to introduce you to your scripting toolbox—the tools you'll need to write, run, edit, and debug your administrative scripts.

Windows Script Host

The most common way to run scripts is to use `WScript.exe`, the graphical version of the Windows Script Host (WSH), which I introduced in Chapter 1, "Scripting Concepts and Terminology." WScript is registered to handle common scripting file extensions, so simply double-clicking a `.vb` or `.vbs` file normally executes `WScript.exe` and then asks it to execute the double-clicked script.

To see WScript in action, follow these steps:

1. Right-click your desktop and select New; then point to Text File.

2. Rename the new text file to **Sample1.vbs**.

3. Right-click the file and choose Edit. By default, Windows registers Notepad as the handler for the Edit action, so a blank Notepad window opens.

4. Type **WScript.Echo "Displaying Output"** and save the file.

5. Close Notepad.

6. Create another new text file on the desktop, and name this one **Sample2.vbs**.

7. Edit Sample2.vbs and enter the following:

```
Wscript.Echo "Here we go!"
Dim V
V = InputBox("What is your name?")
MsgBox "Hello, " & V
```

These aren't terribly complex scripts, but they serve to illustrate some important concepts. To run this script, follow these steps:

Double-click Sample1.vbs. If your system is properly configured, you'll see a dialog box similar to the one shown in Figure 2.1.

Click OK on the dialog box to dismiss it and end the first script.

Double-click Sample2.vbs. It starts with a similar dialog box, as shown in Figure 2.2.

As shown in Figure 2.3, you are prompted to enter your name.

FIGURE 2.1   Basic graphical dialog box from a script.

FIGURE 2.2   Starting dialog box.

FIGURE 2.3   Prompting you for your name.

Finally, Figure 2.4 shows the final dialog box, which addresses you by name.

FIGURE 2.4   Addressing you by name.

> **TIP**
>
> What you've just seen is the sum total of VBScript's user-interface capabilities. If you were hoping to use VBScript to create complex dialog boxes and graphical controls, forget about it! Not by itself, at least—Chapter 25, "Introduction to HTML Applications," introduces you to HTML Applications (HTAs), which combine VBScript with Hypertext Markup Language (HTML) to produce scripts with greater graphical capabilities.

What does all this buy you? First, you've experienced the type of graphical user interface (GUI) that VBScript can provide: simple input and output. You can get a tad more complex and create dialog boxes with Yes and No buttons, or Abort, Retry, and Ignore buttons, but that's about the extent of it.

This script is simple enough that you should be able to figure out exactly what each line of code is doing. `Wscript.Echo` obviously displays a dialog box with some text in it, and was used in both scripts. `Dim V` creates a new variable named `"V"` (more on variables in Chapter 5, "Functions, Objects, Variables, and More"), and the `InputBox` function collects some information and places it into the variable. Finally, `MsgBox` seems to duplicate `Wscript.Echo`, displaying some specified information in a dialog box.

The big question on your mind is probably, "What's the difference between this `Echo` and that `MsgBox`?" There *is* a difference, although it's subtle.

Command-Line Scripts

Most of the time, you'll likely use `WScript.exe` to execute your scripts, and when I refer to WSH I'll generally do so as a nickname for WScript. However, WSH consists of one other executable, `CScript.exe`, which is used to execute scripts on a command line.

The difference with CScript is that it doesn't provide any nongraphical means of collecting user input. In other words, although you can use a CScript script to display command-line output, you can't use it to get input from the command-line window. Follow these steps to see what I mean about how CScript works:

1. Open a command-line window.

2. Change to your Desktop folder.

3. Enter **CScript sample1.vbs**.

You should see something like Figure 2.5: a basic command-line prompt, with "Displaying Output" shown in the command line. That's the work of WScript.Echo: When executed by WScript.exe, Echo creates a dialog box. When executed by CScript.exe, Echo outputs to the command line. This allows you to create scripts that can be run graphically or from a command line. Scripts written with this technique appear to be natively written for each environment.

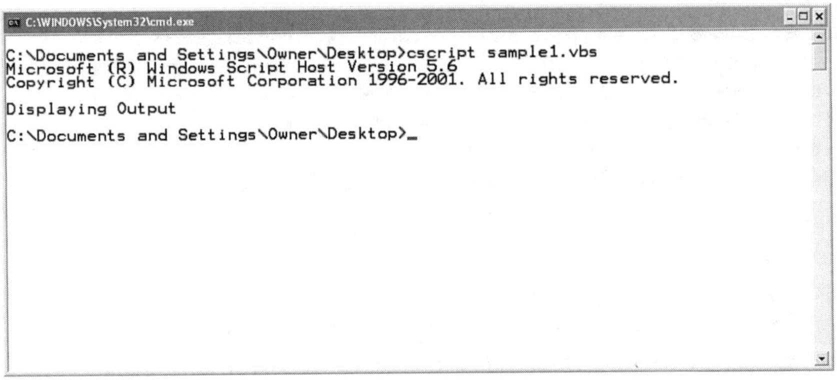

```
C:\WINDOWS\System32\cmd.exe

C:\Documents and Settings\Owner\Desktop>cscript sample1.vbs
Microsoft (R) Windows Script Host Version 5.6
Copyright (C) Microsoft Corporation 1996-2001. All rights reserved.

Displaying Output

C:\Documents and Settings\Owner\Desktop>_
```

FIGURE 2.5   Executing Sample1.vbs with CScript.exe.

Now try the same thing with Sample2.vbs. At first, you'll notice a command line like the one shown in Figure 2.6, simply displaying the output of WScript.Echo as in the previous example. However, when CScript hits the InputBox function, it switches into graphical mode, as shown in Figure 2.7, just like WScript did. Finally, the MsgBox command also forces CScript to display a dialog box, as shown in Figure 2.8 and exactly as WScript did— only WScript.Echo is *dual mode*, working differently in WScript or CScript. Everything else defaults to a graphical mode of operation.

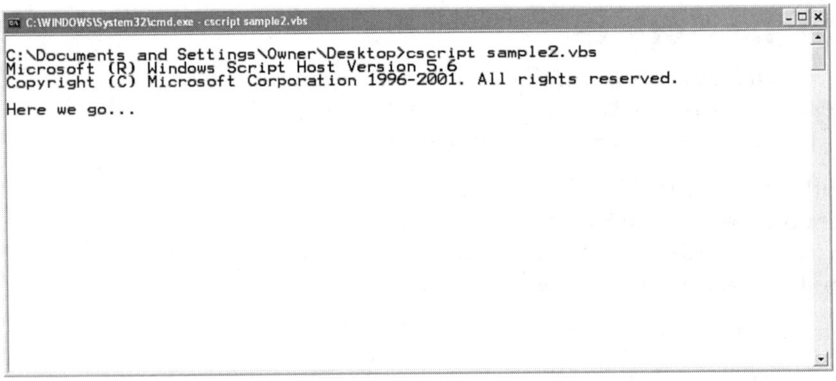

```
C:\WINDOWS\System32\cmd.exe - cscript sample2.vbs

C:\Documents and Settings\Owner\Desktop>cscript sample2.vbs
Microsoft (R) Windows Script Host Version 5.6
Copyright (C) Microsoft Corporation 1996-2001. All rights reserved.

Here we go...
```

FIGURE 2.6   Command-line output of WScript.echo.

FIGURE 2.7   Switching to GUI mode for `InputBox`.

FIGURE 2.8   `MsgBox` is also GUI-only.

Why should you care about the differences? Someday, you might want to write scripts that can be scheduled for background execution using Task Scheduler or some other tool. It's always a good idea to have scripts display some kind of output so that you can see what they're doing while you debug them. If you use `Wscript.Echo` for that output, and run your scripts with WScript, you'll see each output message and have to click OK to have the script continue. When you schedule the script for background execution, you can use CScript instead. Your output still displays (even though you don't see it), and the script doesn't wait for you to click OK. Had you used `MsgBox`, CScript would throw up a dialog box, and your script would stop running until you clicked OK. Because the script would be running in the background as a scheduled task, nobody would ever be *able* to click OK, and the script would "hang" forever or until you killed Task Scheduler.

The big question now is how to ensure your scripts run with CScript and not WScript! You can set one of them to be the default. Windows comes preinstalled with WScript as the default, but if you can open a command-line window, you can change that:

```
CScript //h:CScript
```

To switch back to WScript as the default, use the following:

```
wscript //h:wscript
```

Notepad and Script Editors

When it comes time to write your scripts, you'll probably take the path of many administrators before you and start with Notepad. It's free, easy to use, and did I mention that *it's free*?! Eventually, you might come to a point when you realize that Notepad is making you work too hard, and it is time to look at some professional alternatives.

Bare Bones: Notepad

Notepad, shown in Figure 2.9, is a basic text editor that makes a passable script editor. The biggest problem with Notepad that you'll notice right away is a lack of line numbering. When you get a VBScript error, it refers to a specific line number. Notepad does have a Go to Line Number feature that lets you type in the offending line number and jump straight to it, but it isn't as satisfying as if Notepad displayed a line number on every line of text.

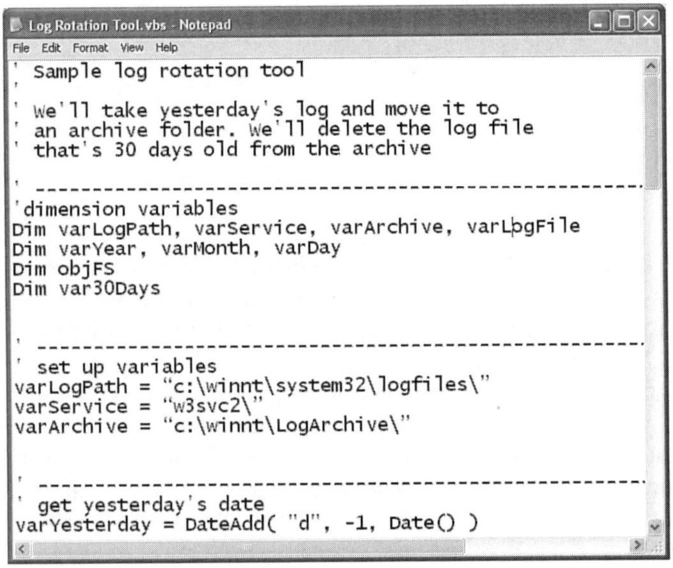

FIGURE 2.9   Notepad as a script editor.

Notepad also lacks any kind of color-coding, which can make scripting *much* easier, especially for long scripts.

A Step Up: Programmer's File Editor

Programmer's File Editor, or PFE, is a decent step up from Notepad. As shown in Figure 2.10, PFE can be configured to show line numbers on each line, making it easy to zip straight to the line of code that's causing errors.

PFE doesn't include any VBScript-specific functionality, however, such as color-coding of comment lines, strings, commands, and so forth. It also doesn't provide any kind of debugging integration, which is a nice thing to have for longer, more complex scripts.

PFE is a free tool, although it's no longer under development for new versions. You can download the latest version, 1.01, from http://www.lancs.ac.uk/staff/steveb/cpaap/pfe/. It's compatible with all 32-bit Windows platforms, and there's even a version for Windows 3.1 (if you find that this link has gone stale, hop on http://www.download.com and search for PFE instead).

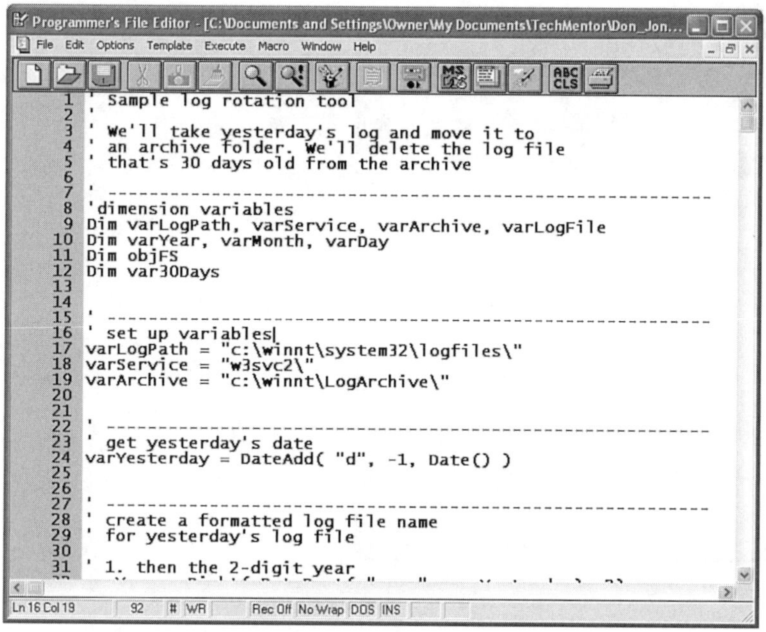

```
 1  ' Sample log rotation tool
 2  '
 3  ' We'll take yesterday's log and move it to
 4  ' an archive folder. We'll delete the log file
 5  ' that's 30 days old from the archive
 6  '
 7  ' --------------------------------------------------
 8  'dimension variables
 9  Dim varLogPath, varService, varArchive, varLogFile
10  Dim varYear, varMonth, varDay
11  Dim objFS
12  Dim var30Days
13
14
15  ' --------------------------------------------------
16  ' set up variables|
17  varLogPath = "c:\winnt\system32\logfiles\"
18  varService = "w3svc2\"
19  varArchive = "c:\winnt\LogArchive\"
20
21
22  ' --------------------------------------------------
23  ' get yesterday's date
24  varYesterday = DateAdd( "d", -1, Date() )
25
26
27  ' --------------------------------------------------
28  ' create a formatted log file name
29  ' for yesterday's log file
30
31  ' 1. then the 2-digit year
```

FIGURE 2.10   Programmer's File Editor.

Script-Specific: VBScript Editors

A few VBScript-specific editors exist on the market. One entry-level mode, VbsEdit (http://www.vbsedit.com), provides functionality that's very specific to VBScript and Windows administrative scripting. There's an important distinction, there: Some VBScript editors are designed more for Dynamic HTML (DHTML) editing, and they don't work very well for administrative scripting. At around $50, VbsEdit (shown in Figure 2.11) provides good, basic functionality, including the following:

▶ Color-coding of syntax, meaning comment lines, commands, and other types of script show up in different colors

▶ Line numbering

▶ Drag-and-drop editing, much like Microsoft Word

▶ Auto-capitalization of VBScript commands; this doesn't improve your scripts, but it does make them easier to read

VbsEdit also includes a degree of IntelliSense-like functionality. For example, when working with objects, you can type the object's name and a period, and VbsEdit displays a list of properties and methods for that object. I haven't discussed objects in VBScript yet, but trust me when I say that this is a handy feature to have! (I'll get to objects in Chapter 5.)

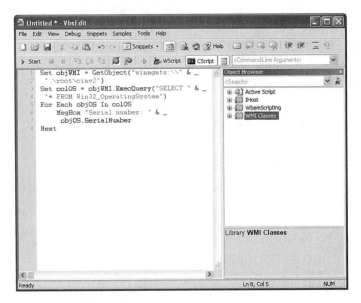

FIGURE 2.11   VbsEdit

Finally, VbsEdit has a built-in script debugger. This handy feature lets you run scripts one line at a time, checking variable values and seeing what's going on "under the hood." This is a great way to quickly debug scripts. VbsEdit even allows you to hover your mouse pointer over a variable while the script is running, and it pops up the value of that variable in a ToolTip. It's a great way to see what your script is doing as you try to track down bugs. Figure 2.12 shows VbsEdit's debugger.

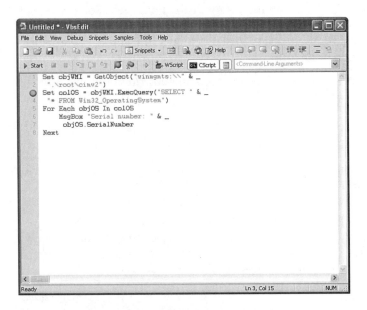

FIGURE 2.12   VbsEdit's debugger.

All-Inclusive: VBScript IDEs

An editor is really just a dressed-up version of Notepad; an Integrated Development Environment (IDE) provides not only strong editing capabilities, but also a wealth of other utilities and tools, built right in, that make scripting faster. The "big gun" of VBScript IDEs is PrimalScript, which costs around $200 for a single-computer license of the entry-level version, and close to $400 for the full-fledged Enterprise edition (http://www.primalscript.com). PrimalScript, shown in Figure 2.13, offers the usual VBScript editor frills, like color-coding, line numbering, and so forth. However, as shown in Figure 2.14, PrimalScript offers a true VBScript-specific clone of the Microsoft IntelliSense technology from Visual Studio. For example, as you type language keywords, a ToolTip appears displaying the proper syntax for the keyword. This handy pop-up saves you from constant round-trips to the VBScript documentation, serving as a quick reminder of which parameters come in which order. You also get pop-up lists of object properties and methods, as in VbsEdit, automatic capitalization for prettier scripts, and so forth.

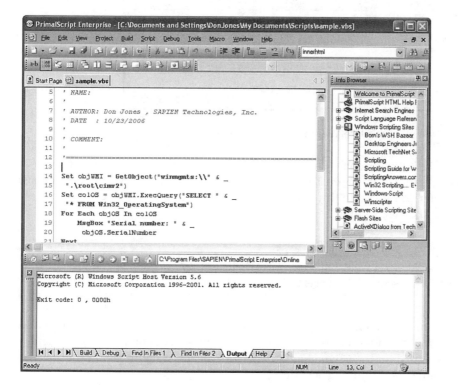

FIGURE 2.13   PrimalScript.

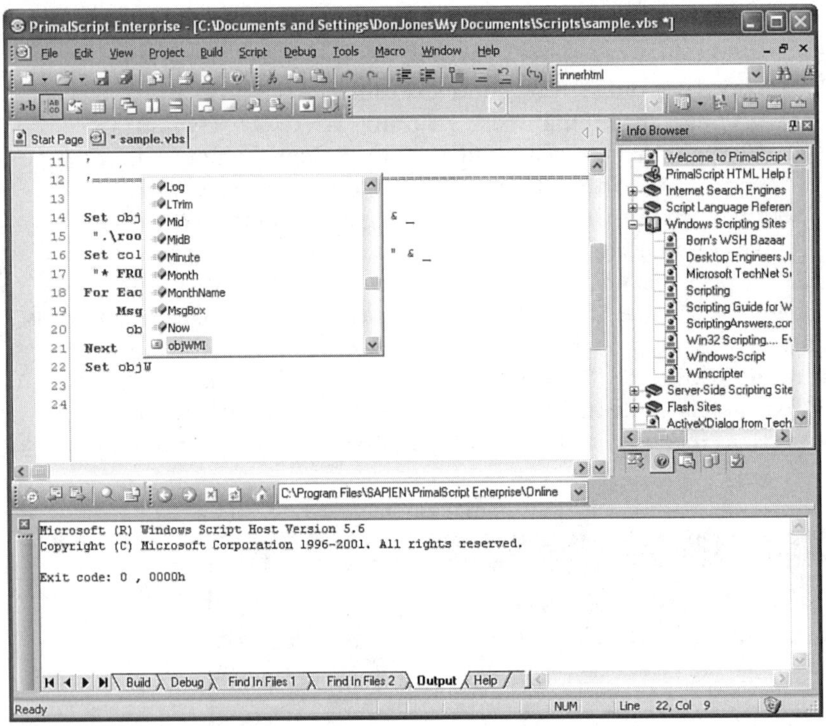

FIGURE 2.14   PrimalScript's IntelliSense-like syntax help.

Finally, PrimalScript's Professional and Enterprise editions include a custom debugger, called PrimalScope, shown in Figure 2.15. This handy tool, which I'll cover in more detail later in this chapter, lets you step through scripts one line at a time, making it easier to pinpoint errors and correct coding issues.

> **NOTE**
>
> PrimalScript also supports WinBatch, Ruby, ASP, HTML, PHP, JSP, Windows PowerShell, and a bunch of other scripting languages—it's not VBScript only.

PrimalScript also integrates script signing, which is a key function of secure scripting environments. By digitally signing scripts, you can instruct your client computers to execute only your scripts, based on their signed identity. (I'll cover script signing and other security topics in Chapter 24, "Scripting Security.")

I'm obviously partial to PrimalScript—after all, in mid-2005, I started working for SAPIEN Technologies, the company that produces PrimalScript. It's sometimes difficult for folks to understand why I'm so attached to a product that costs close to $400, when another editor out there only costs $50. Without making this into a sales pitch—I honestly don't get paid commissions—I want you to understand why a good VBScript IDE is a valuable tool to have.

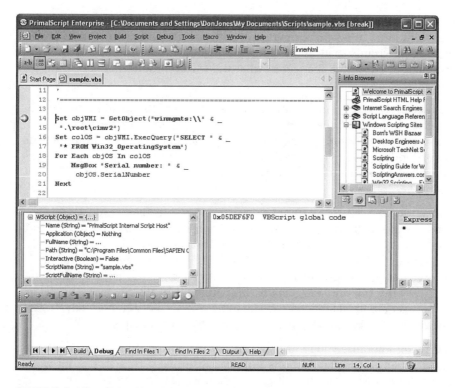

FIGURE 2.15   PrimalScript's debugger is built right in to the product.

Drop by a construction site sometime and watch as they're framing a new building. You don't see a lot of claw hammers on the job site because they're too slow. Instead, the framers are using pneumatic nail guns, and they probably work 10 times faster that way. That's exactly what a good IDE is to you: a pneumatic nail gun for scripting. Since I wrote the first edition of this book in 2003, I've probably written over two thousand scripts, and saving time and effort became very important to me. Here are some ways in which a good IDE—no matter which one you choose to buy—can make scripting better:

▶ **Reusable code**—I try to *never* write the same code twice. When I get a chunk of script code working properly, I highlight it in PrimalScript, right-click the block, and select Save as Snippet from the context menu. The next time I need that code, I can just drag it into my script—all tested, debugged, and ready to go. These days, I have so many Snippets ready, writing a script is more like assembling the various bits than actually scripting (you can obtain packs of my Snippets from http://www. ScriptingOutpost.com, under the Add-Ins category).

▶ **Bug prevention**—PrimalScript, like a script editor, color-codes the script syntax, so that keywords, variables, and other elements appear in different colors. This helps me spot typos: If I type something and it doesn't color-code correctly, I know to look more closely. PrimalScript also has live syntax checking for VBScript, which works a bit like automatic spell-checking in Microsoft Word: Suspect lines of code get a red underline, calling my attention to them.

▶ **Code wizards**—I don't like working with complex technologies in scripts because they take a long time to research, figure out, and debug. A good IDE, however, comes with code wizards that can produce templates for more complex scripts. I can often just make a few minor changes to what the wizard produced and be on my way in much less time.

▶ **Oops resilience**—I make plenty of mistakes when I'm scripting, and being able to recover quickly keeps me more productive. PrimalScript, for example, retains "undo" information between editing sessions, so I can open up a file from months ago and start undoing changes, if need be. It also maintains a file history, which allows me to roll back to a previous version of a file whenever I need to, or even compare two versions.

▶ **Tools, tools, tools**—A lot of the things I do with my scripts require tools, and I'd rather have good ones built in to my IDE than have to run around assembling individual tools on my own. For example, I use File Transfer Protocol (FTP) a lot, and PrimalScript has a built-in graphical FTP client. I also need to deploy a lot of my scripts as executables, so I use my built-in script packager a lot. I write a lot of scripts that save information to databases, and my built-in Visual Query Builder and Database Browser are invaluable to me. The tools you need depend entirely on the type of work you do—but always make sure you get tools to help you!

▶ **Edit everything**—Because you're just starting with VBScript, it probably seems sufficient to just get an editor that supports VBScript. Eventually, though—and it won't be long—you're going to want to edit more. You'll want Windows PowerShell capabilities, and support for HTAs. You'll want to work with advanced Windows Script Host formats like `.wsf` and `.wsc`. And you'll want to work in those formats using graphical tools that help manage their complex formatting requirements—not just open them up and edit the raw Extensible Markup Language (XML). A big reason I've grown accustomed to PrimalScript (which happened long before I joined the team at SAPIEN) is because it supports *everything*, and does so using specialized support for each. It's not just a big, generic editor that treats all files the same—each file type gets appropriate features and tools that make working with *that specific file type* faster and easier.

Okay, I'm off my soapbox now. In the interests of full disclosure, the following is a list of editors (and IDEs) that I'm currently aware of, and which provide support for administrative scripting in VBScript:

▶ PrimalScript (http://www.primalscript.com)

▶ VbsEdit (http://www.vbsedit.com)

▶ Admin Script Editor (http://www.adminscripteditor.com)

▶ OnScript (http://www.onscript.com)

Just one more word of advice: All of these products are available as free trial editions, ranging anywhere from 15 to 45 days. *Try them* before you commit money to one. And remember that you really do get what you pay for: If you're looking at two products with vastly different prices, and you can't figure out how they're different, rest assured that *they are different.* Spend a bit more time on their websites investigating those differences. Post in the forums on http://www.ScriptingAnswers.com and ask other users for their opinions. Look at each company's technical support offerings and decide which one will be able to help you most if you get stuck, or have a feature request. And bear in mind that, as you learn more about scripting, your needs will change and grow—try to select a product that can grow with you.

Writing Your First Script

Because I don't expect you to plop down money to start scripting, I'm going to assume that you're either using Notepad or PFE as your script editor. I do highly recommend that you at least get PFE, because it's free and provides the all-important line numbering capability to your scripts. If you've decided to purchase another script editor, great! You shouldn't have any problems following along. Keep in mind, though, that most of the script editors I've mentioned offer free trials. Why not download them, and try them out as you learn scripting? You'll quickly notice which ones are making the actual scripting process easier on you, and because you won't have picked up any bad habits from working in Notepad yet, you can really leverage the capabilities of the editor (or IDE) to make your scripting education smoother.

For your first script, I've selected a sample that will tell you which user or users, if any, have a particular file open through a shared folder on a file server. This can be a handy tool to have when you're trying to get to a file that's partially locked because someone else has it open. Listing 2.1 shows the complete script; you can type it into a text file and save it as WhoHas.vbs.

LISTING 2.1   WhoHas.vbs Displays the User or Users Who Have a File Open

```
' first, get the server name we want to work with
varServer = InputBox ("Server name to check")

' get the local path of the file to check
varFile= InputBox _
 ("Full path and filename of the file on the " & _
 "server (use the local path as if you were " & _
 "at the server console)")

' bind to the server's file service
set objFS = GetObject("WinNT://" & varServr & _
 "/lanmanserver,fileservice")

' scan through the open resources until we
```

LISTING 2.1   Continued

```
' locate the file we want
varFoundNone = True

' use a FOR...EACH loop to walk through the
' open resources
For Each objRes in objFS.Resources

        ' does this resource match the
        ' one we're looking for?
        If objRes.Path = varFile Then

                ' we found the file - show who's got it
                varFoundNone = False
                WScript.Echo objRes.Path & _
                  " is opened by " & objRes.User
        End If
Next

' if we didn't find the file open, display a msg
if varFoundNone = True then
        WScript.Echo "Didn't find that file opened " & _
          "by anyone."
end If
```

NOTE

In the preceding listing, you'll notice several lines that end in an underscore (_) character. The underscore is referred to as a *line continuation character,* meaning that the line of script is continued on the next line simply because it doesn't all fit on the first line. When you type this script, you can type the underscore exactly as shown.

Also, note that I've had some problems with this script under newer versions of Windows. Try it on a Windows XP computer, if nothing else, and regard it more as an illustration of a scripting technique than as a tool you'll always be able to use in production.

You shouldn't have to make any changes to this script to get it to run in your environment, especially if you're running it on a Windows 2000 or Windows XP computer (the script does use Active Directory Services Interface [ADSI], which is on 2000 and XP by default).

> **NOTE**
>
> Normally in this book, I'll follow each script with a detailed, line-by-line breakdown of what it does. Because this script is just meant to be an example of editing and debugging scripts, I'm going to forgo that explanation this time. I'll be using this script again later, though, so you'll still get that line-by-line explanation.
>
> Remember that all of the longer scripts in this book are also on the accompanying CD-ROM, so you don't need to type them from scratch. Each chapter has its own folder on the CD, and the script filenames match the listing numbers (2.1 in this case).

If you're using a scripting IDE like PrimalScript, take a moment to browse through the script. Notice how comment lines (those that begin with a single quote) appear in a different color, helping you to focus on them when you want an explanation of what the script is doing. Also, notice the coloring for statements and commands, and for strings of text that appear in dialog boxes. Get used to how your script editor works and you'll become a much more efficient scripter—as I mentioned earlier, becoming sensitive to incorrect color-coding is a great way to quickly spot typos before they turn into bugs!

Running Your First Script

Double-clicking WhoHas.vbs should execute it in WScript. First, you'll be asked which server you want to connect to. Provide the server name, making sure you have administrative permissions on that server (the script will use your user credentials to access the server). Next, provide the complete path and filename of the file you want to check.

For example, suppose a folder on the server, named D:\Shares\Sales, is shared as Sales. A user is accessing a file named \\Server\Sales\SalesGoals.doc, and you want to find out which user it is. You'd type D:\Shares\Sales\SalesGoals.doc because that's the server-local path to the file.

When you click OK—whoops! There's an error on line 11 (or another line, depending on how you typed the script)! That's not good! Looks like you're ready to start debugging your first script.

Debugging Your First Script

Microsoft offers a free script debugger from http://www.Microsoft.com/scripting; many script editors integrate this debugger into their environment, and IDEs like PrimalScript often have more powerful debuggers built in. After you download and install the debugger (or a trial edition of an IDE with a built-in debugger), it is available for the scripts that you write. In Figure 2.16, I've started the debugger in PrimalScript. As you can see, the first line of code is highlighted with an arrow, meaning the debugger is waiting to execute that code (it automatically skipped the very first line of text, which is just a comment line).

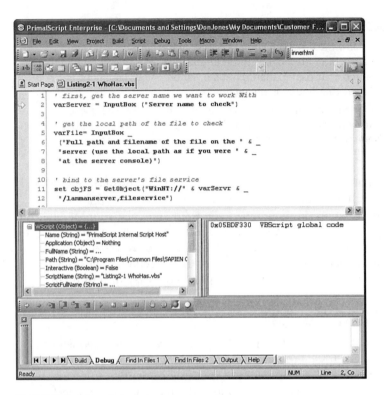

FIGURE 2.16 Debugging WhoHas.vbs.

At this point, I can press F11 to execute *just* the highlighted line of text. Doing so displays an input box requesting the server name; after I provide that and click OK, the debugger jumps to the next line of text. A distinct disadvantage of the Microsoft Script Debugger is its lack of access to variable contents; in the PrimalScript debugger, I can see all the variables and their values at the bottom of the window.

I can keep pressing F11 to execute each line of code, one at a time, until I run into the error again—as I do on line 11. It is time to look at line 11 more carefully.

The problem, in fact, is the variable varServr. It should be varServer, as referenced on line 2. Correcting that lets the script continue normally.

Often, the debugger is the best way to see what "path" VBScript is taking. For example, your script might be behaving unexpectedly because you entered an incorrect logical comparison, perhaps typing ">" instead of "<" in a numeric comparison. These types of mistakes don't necessarily generate errors—at least, not ones you can track down easily—but using the debugger can let you "walk" through a script one line at a time as it executes and spot the location where the script's logic begins to go wrong.

Summary

VBScript is easy to execute because WScript.exe has been included with every major release of Windows since Windows 98. And, in Windows 2000 and later, WScript is even under Windows File Protection, ensuring that your users can't accidentally delete it. After you've taken precautions to ensure that only your scripts will execute (something I'll address in Chapter 24), you'll be ready to run!

Editing scripts can be a bit less satisfying. Windows doesn't come with any built-in tools specifically for editing scripts, and Notepad is a poor substitute. An advanced text editor like Programmer's File Editor makes things easier, and you can acquire some well-designed editors designed specifically for VBScript. And the most powerful scripting IDEs actually compare with the convenience and flexibility of professional software development tools like Visual Studio.

CHAPTER 3

The Components of a Script

Every good book has a structure. This book, for example, includes an introduction and some introductory chapters. Most of the book is taken up with explanatory chapters and examples. There's an appendix, an index, and a table of contents. These elements work together to make the book useful for a variety of purposes, including learning, referencing, and so forth.

Scripts have a structure, too. The main body of the script is a bit like its table of contents, organizing what the script will do. Functions and subroutines are the chapters of the book and perform the actual work. Finally, the comments and documentation act as an index and help provide cross-references and meaning to the actual script code.

Do you really need to know these things to pump out a useful administrative script? Not at all. In fact, if your goal is to start programming as quickly as possible, skip ahead to the next chapter. However, understanding the structure of a good script can help make scripting easier, make your scripts more useful, and save you a lot of time and effort in the long run.

A Typical VBScript

Listing 3.1 shows the sample script I'll be using in this chapter. This is actually a sneak preview; you'll see this script again in various forms in the next chapter. For now, don't worry much about what the script does or how it works; instead, just focus on what it looks like. The goal here is not to understand how this script works, but rather to focus on the various elements of a script.

LISTING 3.1   *LoginScript.vbs* Sample Logon Script

```vbscript
'Display Message
MsgBox "Welcome to SAPIEN. You are " & _
 "now logged on."

'Map N: Drive
If IsMemberOf("Domain Users") Then
 MapDrive "N:","\\Server\Users"
End If

'Map R: Drive
If IsMemberOf("Research") Then
 MapDrive "R:","\\Server2\Research"
End If

'Map S: Drive
If IsMemberOf("Sales") Then
 MapDrive "S:","\\Server2\SalesDocs"
End If

'Get IP address
sIP = GetIP()

'Figure out 3rd octet
iFirstDot = InStr(1,sIP,".")
iSecondDot = InStr(iFirstDot+1,sIP,".")
iThirdDot = InStr(iSecondDot+1,sIP,".")
sThirdOctet = Mid(sIP, iSecondDot+1, _
 Len(sIP)-iThirdDot)

'Map printer based on octet
Select Case sThirdOctet
 Case "100"
  MapPrinter "\\NYDC\HPColor3"
 Case "110"
  MapPrinter "\\LADC\HP6"
 Case "120"
  MapPrinter "\\TXDC1\LaserJet"
End Select

'-----------------------------------------
' FUNCTIONS
'-----------------------------------------

Sub MapDrive(sLetter, sUNC)
```

LISTING 3.1   Continued

```
 Set oNet = _
  WScript.CreateObject("WScript.Network")
 oNet.MapNetworkDrive sLetter, sUNC
End Sub

Function GetIP()
 Set oWMI = GetObject("winmgmts:" & _
  "\\.\root\cimv2")

 Set myObj = oWMI.ExecQuery _
  ("select IPAddress from " & _
  "Win32_NetworkAdapterConfiguration" & _
  " where IPEnabled=TRUE")

 'Go through the addresses
 For Each IPAddress in myObj
  If IPAddress.IPAddress(0) <> "0.0.0.0" Then
   LocalIP = IPAddress.IPAddress(0)
   Exit For
  End If
 Next
 GetIP = LocalIP
End Function

Sub MapPrinter(sUNC)
 Set oNet = WScript.CreateObject("WScript.Network")
 oNet.AddWindowsPrinterConnection sUNC
 oNet.SetDefaultPrinter sUNC
End Sub

Function IsMemberOf(sGroupName)
  Set oNetwork = CreateObject("WScript.Network")
  sDomain = oNetwork.UserDomain
  sUser = oNetwork.UserName
  bIsMember = False
  Set oUser = GetObject("WinNT://" & sDomain & _
   "/" & sUser & ",user")
  For Each oGroup In oUser.Groups
    If oGroup.Name = sGroupName Then
      bIsMember = True
      Exit For
    End If
Next
  IsMemberOf = bIsMember
End Function
```

Remember that this script isn't designed to run as is (skip ahead to the next chapter to find out what it does and what needs to change to make it execute properly in your environment). Instead, it's just intended to represent the structure of a good script. Oh, and one caveat: I've written this script to assume an IP address that has three digits in the third octet (such as 192.168.123.4); if that's not the case in your environment, you might need to make some adjustments to it.

Functions

Functions are one of the workhorses of any script. They perform operations of some kind, and return some kind of result back to the main script. For example, VBScript has a built-in function called Date() that simply returns the current date.

There are built-in functions and custom functions that you write. The only difference between them, of course, is that Microsoft wrote the built-in functions and you write your custom ones. The sample login script has a couple of custom functions.

```
Function GetIP()
 Set oWMI = GetObject("winmgmts:" & _
  "\\.\root\cimv2")

 Set myObj = oWMI.ExecQuery _
  ("select IPAddress from " & _
  "Win32_NetworkAdapterConfiguration" & _
  " where IPEnabled=TRUE")

 'Go through the addresses
 For Each IPAddress in myObj
  If IPAddress.IPAddress(0) <> "0.0.0.0" Then
   LocalIP = IPAddress.IPAddress(0)
   Exit For
  End If
 Next
 GetIP = LocalIP
End Function

Function IsMemberOf(sGroupName)
  Set oNetwork = CreateObject("WScript.Network")
  sDomain = oNetwork.UserDomain
  sUser = oNetwork.UserName
  bIsMember = False
  Set oUser = GetObject("WinNT://" & sDomain & _
   "/" & sUser & ",user")
  For Each oGroup In oUser.Groups
    If oGroup.Name = sGroupName Then
      bIsMember = True
```

```
      Exit For
    End If
Next
  IsMemberOf = bIsMember
End Function
```

You'll notice that these all begin with the declaration `Function`, followed by the name of the function. They can include a list of input parameters, as the `IsMemberOf` function does. All of them return some information, too. Notice that the last line of each function sets the function name equal to some other variable; this action returns that other variable's value as the result of the function.

For now, make sure you can recognize a function at 30 feet by the keyword `Function`. Also remember that functions are designed to perform some task, and that functions are meant to be *modular*, meaning they can be easily copied and pasted into many different scripts that need to perform the task that the function handles. I cover functions in more detail in Chapter 5, "Functions, Objects, Variables, and More."

Why use functions? Well, in the case of intrinsic functions, they perform a very valuable service, providing information like the date and time, and allowing you to manipulate data. Custom functions do the same thing. Custom functions, however, can be a lot more useful in the end. Take the `IsMemberOf` function as an example: That function identifies whether the current user is a member of a specific domain user group. It took me a couple of hours to figure out how to perform that little trick. In the future, though, I can just paste the function into whatever script I need, and I'll never have to spend those couple of hours again. Bundling the task into a function makes it easily portable between scripts, and allows me to easily reuse my hard work.

Subroutines

The sample script has two custom subroutines, too. These are just like functions, except that they just do something; they don't return a result afterward.

```
Sub MapDrive(sLetter, sUNC)
 Set oNet = _
  WScript.CreateObject("WScript.Network")
 oNet.MapNetworkDrive sLetter, sUNC
End Sub

Sub MapPrinter(sUNC)
 Set oNet = WScript.CreateObject("WScript.Network")
 oNet.AddWindowsPrinterConnection sUNC
 oNet.SetDefaultPrinter sUNC
End Sub
```

These subroutines are declared with the word Sub, followed by the name of the subroutine. Like a function, these two subroutines each accept some input parameters. Unlike a function, they never set their name to some value, which is why they don't return a value.

VBScript has intrinsic (built-in) subroutines, only they're called *statements*. A simple statement, like Dim, simply sets up a new variable—it doesn't do anything visually interesting, or return any data.

Subroutines serve the same purpose as a function: Although mapping a drive or a printer obviously isn't difficult (taking only two or three lines of code), there's no reason I should have to type those lines of code over and over. Encapsulating the functionality into a subroutine means I can reuse the code repeatedly in one script, and easily paste it into other scripts, saving myself work. In fact, once I got these subroutines—and their friends, the functions—working correctly, I turned them into Snippets within my scripting Integrated Development Environment (IDE), such as PrimalScript. Doing so means that, from now on, I can add these routines to a script simply by dragging and dropping them, or pressing a keyboard shortcut.

Main Script

The main script performs a good bit of work: The main script does act as a sort of table of contents, organizing the flow of the overall script. For example, notice where the MapDrive and MapPrinter subroutines are used, and where the IsMemberOf() and GetIP() functions are used. The main script also utilizes some of VBScript's intrinsic functions, such as InStr() and Mid(). The main script acts as a sort of conductor, orchestrating the flow of the tasks that need to be completed, and calling on specialists—the functions and subroutines—to perform specialized tasks. The following is the main script in its entirety:

```
'Display Message
MsgBox "Welcome to SAPIEN. You are " & _
 "now logged on."

'Map N: Drive
If IsMemberOf("Domain Users") Then
 MapDrive "N:","\\Server\Users"
End If

'Map R: Drive
If IsMemberOf("Research") Then
 MapDrive "R:","\\Server2\Research"
End If

'Map S: Drive
If IsMemberOf("Sales") Then
```

```
  MapDrive "S:","\\Server2\SalesDocs"
End If

'Get IP address
sIP = GetIP()

'Figure out 3rd octet
iFirstDot = InStr(1,sIP,".")
iSecondDot = InStr(iFirstDot+1,sIP,".")
iThirdDot = InStr(iSecondDot+1,sIP,".")
sThirdOctet = Mid(sIP, iSecondDot+1, _
 Len(sIP)-iThirdDot)

'Map printer based on octet
Select Case sThirdOctet
 Case "100"
  MapPrinter "\\NYDC\HPColor3"
 Case "110"
  MapPrinter "\\LADC\HP6"
 Case "120"
  MapPrinter "\\TXDC1\LaserJet"
End Select
```

> **TIP**
>
> Notice that the script uses subs and functions for some things, but uses inline code for other things, such as determining the third octet of an IP address. A general rule is to use functions and subs whenever you think the code will be useful elsewhere, or will be used more than once. Otherwise, just use inline code in the main script.

In the next few sections, I'll point out specific portions of the main script to which you should pay attention. Don't worry much about what these do or how they work; focus for now on the overall structure of the script and how the different pieces fit together. In Chapter 4, "Designing a Script," you'll see how this script went together and what each line does.

Using Custom Functions and Subroutines

Where does the main script call on custom functions and subroutines? I've boldfaced the custom bits in this version of the script:

```
'Display Message
MsgBox "Welcome to SAPIEN. You are " & _
 "now logged on."
```

```
'Map N: Drive
If IsMemberOf("Domain Users") Then
 MapDrive "N:","\\Server\Users"
End If

'Map R: Drive
If IsMemberOf("Research") Then
 MapDrive "R:","\\Server2\Research"
End If

'Map S: Drive
If IsMemberOf("Sales") Then
 MapDrive "S:","\\Server2\SalesDocs"
End If

'Get IP address
sIP = GetIP()

'Figure out 3rd octet
iFirstDot = InStr(1,sIP,".")
iSecondDot = InStr(iFirstDot+1,sIP,".")
iThirdDot = InStr(iSecondDot+1,sIP,".")
sThirdOctet = Mid(sIP, iSecondDot+1, _
 Len(sIP)-iThirdDot)

'Map printer based on octet
Select Case sThirdOctet
 Case "100"
  MapPrinter "\\NYDC\HPColor3"
 Case "110"
  MapPrinter "\\LADC\HP6"
 Case "120"
  MapPrinter "\\TXDC1\LaserJet"
End Select
```

You can see how using custom functions and subs save a lot of typing and a lot of room. For example, without the custom function IsMember(), the script would be a lot longer, with a lot of repeated code. The script is a lot easier to read when the repeated code is pulled into a custom function. Also, the function makes the script easier to maintain; if you find a bug, you only have to fix it in the function. If you haven't used functions, you have to go fix the bug everywhere you used the code. For example, suppose I'd used the wrong syntax for For Each oGroup in oUser.Groups. In the original script, I'd just have to fix it in the IsMemberOf() function. Without the function, I'd have to make the fix three separate times.

Using Intrinsic Functions and Statements

Where is the script using built-in functions and statements? I'll boldface them to call them out.

```
'Display Message
MsgBox "Welcome to SAPIEN. You are " & _
 "now logged on."

'Map N: Drive
If IsMemberOf("Domain Users") Then
 MapDrive "N:","\\Server\Users"
End If

'Map R: Drive
If IsMemberOf("Research") Then
 MapDrive "R:","\\Server2\Research"
End If

'Map S: Drive
If IsMemberOf("Sales") Then
 MapDrive "S:","\\Server2\SalesDocs"
End If

'Get IP address
sIP = GetIP()

'Figure out 3rd octet
iFirstDot = InStr(1,sIP,".")
iSecondDot = InStr(iFirstDot+1,sIP,".")
iThirdDot = InStr(iSecondDot+1,sIP,".")
sThirdOctet = Mid(sIP, iSecondDot+1, _
 Len(sIP)-iThirdDot)

'Map printer based on octet
Select Case sThirdOctet
 Case "100"
  MapPrinter "\\NYDC\HPColor3"
 Case "110"
  MapPrinter "\\LADC\HP6"
 Case "120"
  MapPrinter "\\TXDC1\LaserJet"
End Select
```

You can spot the built-in functions and subroutines because they don't have a corresponding Function or Sub statement later in the script. If you're curious about what these do, check out the VBScript documentation, or flip through Chapters 8 and 10 ("Manipulating Strings," and "Controlling the Flow of Execution," respectively).

> **NOTE**
>
> Notice that the intrinsic and custom functions and statements look identical. The only way to tell them apart is that the custom ones are defined somewhere in the script by the Function or Sub keywords. Right now, you just need to be adept at spotting the differences between the two.
>
> For a custom function or sub, the only way to tell how it works is to read the corresponding Function or Sub block and figure out what's going on. For intrinsic functions and statements, you can look them up in the VBScript documentation to see how they work.

Making Decisions in a Script

Sometimes, you need a script to do something different based on a set of circumstances. The sample script makes a decision about what printer to map based on the third octet of the client's IP address. It makes that decision by using a Select/Case construct:

```
'Map printer based on octet
Select Case sThirdOctet
 Case "100"
  MapPrinter "\\NYDC\HPColor3"
 Case "110"
  MapPrinter "\\LADC\HP6"
 Case "120"
  MapPrinter "\\TXDC1\LaserJet"
End Select
```

The Select/Case construct is making a decision, mapping a different printer based on the third octet of the user's IP address. Select/Case is a special kind of intrinsic VBScript statement—one that helps your script react to changing conditions automatically by building some kind of logic into the script. For more information on Select/Case, see Chapter 10.

Comments and Documentation

Documenting your scripts is always a very good idea. Although the script makes perfect sense now, you might not be able to remember what it's doing in a year, or even in a couple of months.

For example, examine the script in Listing 3.2. See if you can figure out what the various portions of the script are doing.

LISTING 3.2   *AddUsersFromXLS.vbs.* Creates users from an Excel spreadsheet.

```
Set oCN = CreateObject("ADODB.Connection")
oCN.Open "Excel"
Set oRS = oCN.Execute("SELECT * FROM [Sheet1$]")
Set oDomain = GetObject("WinNT://NT4PDC")
Set oFSO = CreateObject("Scripting.FileSystemObject")
Set oTS = oFSO.CreateTextFile("c:\passwords.txt",True)
sHomePath = "\\iridis1\c$\users\"
Do Until oRS.EOF
sUserID = oRS("UserID")
sFullName = oRS("FullName")
sDescription = oRS("Description")
sHomeDir = oRS("HomeDirectory")
sGroups = oRS("Groups")
sDialIn = oRS("DialIn")
sPassword = Left(sUserID,2) & DatePart("n",Time) & _
DatePart("y",Date) & DatePart("s",Time)
Set oUserAcct = oDomain.Create("user",sUserID)
oUserAcct.SetPassword sPassword
oUserAcct.FullName = sFullName
oUserAcct.Description = sDescription
oUserAcct.HomeDirectory = sHomeDir
If sDialIn = "Y" Then
oUserAcct.RasPermissions = 9
Else
oUserAcct.RasPermissions = 1
End If
oUserAcct.SetInfo
Set oUserAcct = GetObject("WinNT://NT4PDC/" & _
 sUserID & ",user")
oTS.Write sUserID & "," & sPassword & vbCrLf
sGroupList = Split(sGroups, ",")
For iTemp = 0 To uBound(sGroupList)
Set oGroup = GetObject("WinNT://NT4PDC/" & _
sGroupList(iTemp) & ",group")
oGroup.Add oUserAcct.ADsPath
Set oGroup = Nothing
Next
Set oFolder = oFSO.CreateFolder(sHomePath & sUserID)
Set oUserAcct = Nothing
oRS.MoveNext
Loop
oRS.Close
oTS.Close
WScript.Echo "Passwords have been written to c:\passwords.txt."
```

It's a bit tough to follow, isn't it? Now look at Listing 3.3.

LISTING 3.3   *AddUsersFromXLS.vbs.* Creates users from an Excel spreadsheet.

```
' PART 1: Open up the Excel spreadsheet
' using ActiveX Data Objects
Dim oCN
Set oCN = CreateObject("ADODB.Connection")
oCN.Open "Excel"

Dim oRS
Set oRS = oCN.Execute("SELECT * FROM [Sheet1$]")

' PART 2: Get a reference to the
' Windows NT domain using ADSI
Dim oDomain
Set oDomain = GetObject("WinNT://NT4PDC")

' PART 3: Open an output text file
' to store users' initial passwords
Dim oFSO, oTS
Set oFSO = CreateObject("Scripting.FileSystemObject")
Set oTS = oFSO.CreateTextFile("c:\passwords.txt",True)

' PART 4: For each record in the recordset,
' add the user, set the correct user
' properties, and add the user to the
' appropriate groups

' create the necessary variables
Dim sUserID, sFullName, sDescription
Dim sHomeDir, sGroups, sDialIn
Dim sPassword, oUserAcct, oFolder
Dim sGroupList, iTemp, oGroup

' define the base path for the home
' directories to be created in
Dim sHomePath
sHomePath = "\\iridis1\c$\users\"

' now go through the recordset one
' row at a time
Do Until oRS.EOF

   ' get the user information from this row
   sUserID = oRS("UserID")
```

LISTING 3.3   Continued

```
sFullName = oRS("FullName")
sDescription = oRS("Description")
sHomeDir = oRS("HomeDirectory")
sGroups = oRS("Groups")
sDialIn = oRS("DialIn")

' make up a new password
sPassword = Left(sUserID,2) & _
 DatePart("n",Time) & _
 DatePart("y",Date) & DatePart("s",Time)

' create the user account
Set oUserAcct = oDomain.Create("user",sUserID)

' set account properties
oUserAcct.SetPassword sPassword
oUserAcct.FullName = sFullName
oUserAcct.Description = sDescription
oUserAcct.HomeDirectory = sHomeDir

' set RAS permission
If sDialIn = "Y" Then
  oUserAcct.RasPermissions = 9
Else
  oUserAcct.RasPermissions = 1
End If

' save the account
oUserAcct.SetInfo

' get a reference to the new account
' this gets us a valid SID & other info
Set oUserAcct = GetObject("WinNT://NT4PDC/" & _
 sUserID & ",user")

' write password to file
oTS.Write sUserID & "," & sPassword & VbCrLf

' PART 4A: Add user account to groups
' use the Split function to turn the
' comma-separated list into an array
sGroupList = Split(sGroups, ",")

' go through the array and add the user
```

3

LISTING 3.3   Continued

```
' to each group
For iTemp = 0 To uBound(sGroupList)

  ' get the group
  Set oGroup = GetObject("WinNT://NT4PDC/" & _
   sGroupList(iTemp) & ",group")

  ' add the user account
  oGroup.Add oUserAcct.ADsPath

  ' release the group
  Set oGroup = Nothing

Next


  ' PART 4B: Create the user's Home Directory
  ' (append UserID to the Home Path variable)
  Set oFolder = oFSO.CreateFolder(sHomePath & _
   sUserID)

  ' PART 5: All done!
  ' release the user account
  Set oUserAcct = Nothing

  ' move to the next row in the recordset
  oRS.MoveNext

Loop

' PART 6: Final clean up, close down
oTS.CloseoRS.Close
WScript.Echo "Passwords have been written to " & _
 "c:\passwords.txt."
```

> **NOTE**
>
> Neither of the scripts in Listings 3.2 and 3.3 is intended for you to run; you're missing some of the components the scripts require. But you'll see them again later, and have a chance to try them at that time.

The scripts in Listings 3.2 and 3.3 will execute and do the exact same thing, but the one in Listing 3.3 is much, much easier to figure out. Here's why:

- ▶ Comment lines (those beginning with the ' character) are included throughout, explaining what each section of the script is doing.

- ▶ The lines of code are indented, making it easy to see which blocks will be repeated in loops.

- ▶ Whitespace in the form of blank lines is used to help break up the script and make different sections stand out more readily from one another.

As you can see from these examples, documentation and commenting isn't required, but it sure is nice. VBScript doesn't care about documentation and commenting, but you sure will if you ever have to work with a script that doesn't have it!

Summary

This chapter, I tried to illustrate some of the different components of a good script. You've seen what functions, statements, and subroutines look like, how a main script ties them all together, and how comments and documentation make them easier to read and maintain in the future. Keep all these new concepts in mind as you move through the rest of the book. Try to spot intrinsic functions and custom ones, and watch for comment lines and other types of code documentation. Try to use these standards in your own scripts, and you'll find yourself becoming more efficient and more capable very quickly.

Designing a Script

Suppose you want to do a tune-up on your car, and you don't want to hire a mechanic to do the job for you. It's easy enough to run down to the hardware store and acquire the necessary tools, and you can even buy some books that explain how to use those tools. If you're like me, though, none of that will help you get the tune-up done. Where do you start? What should it look like? Which tools do you use, and when?

I've found that's how many administrators feel about scripting. Sure, the VBScript documentation is available, and there are plenty of examples on the web. But where do you start when it comes time to write your own scripts? Much of this book will be focused on the tools, like VBScript and programming objects, that you'll need to do the job. In this chapter, I want to share some of the tips and techniques that I use to actually get started in designing a new script.

It'll be easier to see how my design process works with a meaningful example. Because logon scripts are a popular administrative use of VBScript, I'll use a logon script as an example. I want to write a logon script that maps three network drives based on the user's group membership, and then maps a printer based on the user's DHCP-assigned IP address. That way, I can assign a printer that's local to wherever the user logged on. I also want to display a welcome message, and I want the script to run on Windows NT Workstation 4.0 (Service Pack 6a or later), Windows XP Professional (Service Pack 2 or later), Windows 2000 Professional (Service Pack 4 or later), and Windows Vista.

Creating a Task List

The first thing to do in the design process is to create a task list. This is essentially an English-language version of the script you plan to write. In the list, you must break down the various things you want the script to perform in as much detail as possible. I often go through several iterations of the task list, adding a bit more detail each time through. Listing 4.1 shows what my first pass might look like.

LISTING 4.1   *Logon script task list.* Your first task list should just summarize what you want the script to do.

```
Logon script task list

Display a logon welcome message.
Map the N: drive based on group membership.
Map the R: drive based on group membership.
Map the S: drive based on group membership.
Map a printer and make it the default. Base the printer selection on the user's
physical location at the time.
```

> **NOTE**
>
> Programmers call this kind of a task list *pseudocode* because it sort of looks like programming code but isn't. It's a great way to lay out what a script is supposed to do without having to look up the exact VBScript syntax of every command. Plus, you can throw around phrases like, "I just finished pseudocoding that script, and boy was it tough," and you'll impress the software developers in your company.

After you've got your first task list completed, look at what detail might be missing. For example, "based on group membership" is vague. What specific parameters will be used to determine where the N: drive is mapped? Will the N: drive always be mapped, or will it be mapped only if the user is in one or more specific groups? Pretend you're explaining how the script will work to the least technical person you know, and add the level of detail they'd need to understand what the script should do. Listing 4.2 shows a second, more detailed attempt.

LISTING 4.2   *Logon script task list v2.* Adding detail makes the task list more useful.

```
Logon script task list v2

Display a logon welcome message:
"Welcome to SAPIEN. You are now logged on."

Map the N: drive:
If the user is a member of the Domain Users group.
```

LISTING 4.2   Continued

```
Map the drive to \\Server\Users.

Map the R: drive:
If the user is a member of the Research group.
Map the drive to \\Server2\ResearchDocs.

Map the S: drive:
If the user is a member of the Sales group.
Map the drive to \\Server2\SalesDocs.

Map a printer:
Examine the third octet of the user's IP address. If it is 100, map the printer
\\NYDC\HPColor3. If the third octet is 110, map the printer to \\LADC2\HP6. If the
third octet is 120, map the printer to \\TXDC1\LaserJet. Make the mapped printer
the default on the user's system.
```

This new script provides much more in the way of detail. However, it's still lacking the feel of a procedure. For example, suppose you were going to manually perform the tasks in this script. How would you perform the drive-mapping task? You'd have to open the Domain Users group and see if the user's account was listed there. Rewrite the task list with that level of procedural detail because that's what the computer executing the script will need to know. Look at Listing 4.3, which tries to make the task list even more detailed and procedural.

LISTING 4.3   *Logon script task list v3*. Making the tasks a procedure will help translate the list to a script later.

```
Logon script task list v3

Display a logon welcome message:
"Welcome to SAPIEN. You are now logged on."
Wait until the user clicks OK to dismiss the welcome message.

Map the N: drive:
Obtain a list of Domain Users group members. See if the user is in the list. If
they are, map the drive to \\Server\Users.

Map the R: drive:
Obtain a list of Research group members. See if the user is in the list. If they
are, map the drive to \\Server2\ResearchDocs.

Map the S: drive:
Obtain a list of Sales group members. See if the user is in the list. If they are,
map the drive to \\Server2\SalesDocs.
```

LISTING 4.3   Continued

Map a printer:
Get the user's IP address. Look at just the third octet. To find it, look for the
last period in the IP address, and then the next-to-the-last period. The third
octet is between the two periods. If the octet is 100, map to \\NYDC\HPColor3. If
it's 110, map to \\LADC\HP6. If it's 120, map to \\TXDC1\LaserJet. Then make the
mapped printer the default.

Now take one last pass through the list and think about the underlying technologies. For
example, what information is really contained within a Windows domain user group? It's
not a list of usernames; it's a list of security identifiers, or SIDs. So, when you're checking
group membership, you might need to get the user's SID and then check the groups' SID
list. You don't necessarily need to modify your task list with this information, but make a
note of it. That way when you start to write the script in VBScript, you'll remember what
it is you really need the computer to do for you.

Selecting the Appropriate Tools

Now comes what is truly the most difficult part of administrative scripting: selecting the
right tools. You know what you want your script to do, and you know VBScript can do it
(or at least you hope it can), so you just need to figure out *how* to make it work.

Software developers do this all the time. Typically, they know so much about the tools
they have to work with, though, that they select the right ones without even thinking
about it. As an administrator, I'm more likely to have to do some research first.

Looking at the task list, there are really six types of tasks I need the computer to perform:

1. Displaying a message

2. Mapping a drive

3. Checking group membership

4. Mapping a printer

5. Getting the local IP address

6. Getting the third octet from the IP address

I'll show you how I research each of these tasks to figure out how they can be
accomplished.

> **TIP**
>
> The Appendix of this book is a Quick Script Reference. It's designed to list common
> administrative tasks and briefly describe what VBScript tools you can use to accom-
> plish them. This reference should make it easier for you to figure out which tools to
> use when you write your own scripts.

Displaying a Message

I always start my research in the VBScript documentation. You can find it online at http://www.microsoft.com/scripting, and there's even a downloadable version that you can use offline. You can also find the documentation in the MSDN Library. That's available online at http://msdn.microsoft.com/library, or you can receive it on CD or DVD as part of a yearly subscription. In either case, I find an offline version of the documents to be more convenient.

TIP

At the very least, download the offline VBScript documentation. Go to http://www. microsoft.com/scripting and look for the appropriate link. The actual download uniform resource locator (URL) changes from time to time, so you're better off starting at the main scripting page and locating the link.

When I need to search the VBScript documentation, I usually start with the alphabetical list of available functions and commands. That's just an easy way for me to scan through the documents and spot likely looking tools. In this case, down in the M section of the function list, I ran across MsgBox. Even if you know nothing about VBScript, MsgBox certainly sounds as if it displays a message box. Looking into the details of the function, I see that it does, in fact, display a dialog box with a message in it. I can specify the message, the title of the dialog box, and which buttons and icons appear on the dialog box. It sounds perfect for my welcome message.

There's no need at this point in the design process to actually start writing script. However, MsgBox appears to be a simple command.

```
'Display welcome message
MsgBox "Welcome to SAPIEN. You are now logged on."
```

Suppose you don't want to browse through the VBScript documentation (and you don't have this book handy). First, I definitely recommend the browsing method because it exposes you to a lot of other functions and commands that might be useful later in life. Still, if that's just not your way of working, you can always fall back on my favorite search engine, Google.

Go up to http://www.google.com and enter a search phrase. Here are some tips.

▶ I always use "VBScript" as my first search term because it narrows down Google's billions of web pages to those that deal with VBScript.

▶ I always include "-browser" in the phrase. Doing so eliminates a lot of pages that talk about using VBScript in Dynamic HTML (DHTML) web pages, which isn't what I'm usually looking for.

▶ Finally, include a term that describes what you're trying to do. In this case, "display message" should do the trick.

NOTE

Use quotes carefully in a search phrase. For example, if you type **display message**, you'll get hits that include both words, and hits that include just one of the two words. If you include **"display message"** in quotes, you'll only get hits that have the entire phrase "display message" in the page. That might not be helpful in this case; it's more likely the pages will contain something like "display a message" or "display the message." Using **display** and **message** outside of quotes will find these pages; using **"display message"** in quotes won't.

You can also use a more specific search engine. For example, I created http://www.SearchScripting.com, and hand-selected about two dozen sites that only offer resources related to Windows administrative scripting. It's a lot easier to get good results from such a targeted search engine.

With the Google search phrase "vbscript display message –browser," my first hit is a website on GeoCities that describes how to use the VBScript MsgBox function. Farther down the first page of hits is a page titled "VBScript MsgBox Function," which could work, too.

Google's great for finding sample scripts that do what you want, and I'll be using it a lot more as I try to figure out how to perform more complicated tasks.

I'll show you how to use the MsgBox function in more detail in Chapter 6, "Input and Output."

Mapping a Drive

Speaking of more complicated tasks, this one's a bit more difficult. There are plenty of command-line programs that can map a drive, including the easy-to-use net command, but that's cheating. I'm looking for a way to do it in VBScript.

Running through the VBScript documentation doesn't provide any help, either. I don't see any commands with "map" or "drive" anywhere in them. I do see something about a Drive object, but that seems to have something to do with accessing drives. I need to map it before that'll be possible.

Back to Google. Searching for "vbscript map drive –browser" doesn't return anything helpful in the first page of hits, so I'll need to be a little more creative. Searching for "vbscript "maps a drive" –browser" gets me a promising article in the first page of hits. Clicking on the first hit, I find myself at MyITForum.com (http://www.myitforum.com/articles/11/section.asp?w= 2&au=lduncan). There's a list of articles here by Larry Duncan, and there are actually two that look useful: "How Do I Retrieve the IP Address Using VBScript," and "How Can I Map a Drive Using WSH?" WSH, VBScript, whatever. It's worth a look.

TIP

The terms VBScript, ADSI, WSH, and WMI are interchangeable when you're looking through search results. They're all more or less a part of the larger world of administrative scripting.

Larry's article is actually a short snippet of VBScript code that uses just two lines of code. It uses the `WScript.Network` object, which seems to have a command called `MapNetworkDrive` associated with it. No need to go into more detail right now; this is the information I was looking for. I'll bookmark the URL for later reference and go on to the next task.

I'll cover the `WScript.Network` object, too; look in Chapter 11, "Built-In Scripting Objects."

Checking Group Membership

This task also seems complicated. This time, I'm not even going to bother with the VBScript documents because I've been through them twice already and I don't remember seeing anything even remotely related to group membership. On to Google, where I search for "vbscript group membership –browser." The first hit is titled "Detecting Group Membership using VBScript." Perfect!

The link takes me to http://www.sanx.org/tipShow.asp?articleRef=66. The article in question provides a sample script. It's actually a complete function, where I just provide the name of a group, and the function tells me whether the currently logged-on user is a member of that group. Great! Another bookmark in the browser, and I'll come back to the example when it's time to start writing the script.

> **NOTE**
>
> Obviously, as times change, the hits you get on Google won't be the same as mine. Go with the flow: It's likely that whatever hits are showing up by the time you read this are even better than the ones I found.

Mapping a Printer

This is a place where a little logic can save some time. I already discovered this `WScript.Network` thing, which maps drives. Surely, it also maps printers, right? Searching the MSDN Library for `WScript.Network` takes me to the documentation for that object, which does in fact include an `AddWindowsPrinterConnection`. I also find that it can set the default printer for the current user, which means it's exactly what I need. No need to perform a more complicated search than that, and I can review the documentation later to figure out how to use it. Right now, it's enough to know that it'll do what I need it to do.

Getting the Local IP Address

I already found out how to do this, based on the list of Larry Duncan articles I ran across when looking for drive mapping techniques. Larry's article is at http://www.myitforum.com/articles/11/view.asp?id-3340, and it's a brief example of how to get the local IP address from within a script. At the very end of the script is the command `MsgBox Line`. I know that `MsgBox` displays a message, so it appears as if `Line` is a variable that contains the IP address I'm looking for. Keep in mind that I need to work with that IP address a little bit, so it's important for me to adapt Larry's script to my purposes.

Larry's script seems to be able to list all of the IP addresses associated with a computer. That's an important thing to understand! Remember that a computer usually has multiple network adapters. One of them might be a FireWire port, another might be a wireless network card, and still another might be an Ethernet card. Even if none of them is connected, they all have an IP address—even if it's 0.0.0.0.

This makes my task a bit more complicated. I was thinking I just had to pull out the IP address, but, in fact, it looks like I have to pull *all* of the IP addresses, and then look for one that isn't 0.0.0.0. Looking again at Larry's example, it might be worth taking a quick guess at what my own IP address script might look like. Listing 4.4 shows an example. I don't know if this is perfect yet, but it's a guess.

> **TIP**
>
> You'll see some code in the next few examples that won't make much sense. Remember: You're only on Chapter 4! I'm using this example because it's something you can use immediately in your environment. I promise you'll see these again in later chapters, where I'll also explain what each line of code is doing.

LISTING 4.4 *Retrieve IP Address.vbs.* I'll need to test this script later and figure out more about how it works so that I can make sure it'll work in my logon script.

```
Set oWMI = GetObject("winmgmts:" & _
 "\\.\root\cimv2")

 Set myObj = oWMI.ExecQuery _
 ("select IPAddress from " & _
 "Win32_NetworkAdapterConfiguration" & _
 " where IPEnabled=TRUE")

 'Go through the addresses
 For Each IPAddress in myObj
  If IPAddress.IPAddress(0) <> "0.0.0.0" Then
   LocalIP = IPAddress.IPAddress(0)
   Exit For
  End If
 Next
 GetIP = LocalIP
```

Larry's script was saving all of the IP addresses, so I just looked for the section of his script that seemed to be pulling the IP address out of the computer. I added an If/Then section to grab the first IP address that isn't 0.0.0.0. I'll try it later to see how it works.

I'm getting a little ahead of myself, but if you want to check out using `If/Then`, turn to Chapter 10, "Controlling the Flow of Execution." I'll cover variables in Chapter 5, "Functions, Objects, Variables, and More," and the rest of this script uses WMI, which I'll introduce in Chapter 17, "Understanding WMI."

Anyway, it looks like I'll have a variable named `LocalIP` that contains my local IP address, which is exactly what I wanted.

Getting the Third Octet from the IP Address

With my IP address in a variable, I need to figure out how to get just the third octet. Now, this seems like it could be harder than it looks. I can't just grab the ninth, tenth, and eleventh characters from the IP address, because in an address like "10.123.52.4," that wouldn't be right. What I need to do is what I put into my task list: Look for the location of the second and third periods, and then grab everything in between.

Back to the VBScript function list. It turns out there are two functions that might work: `InStr()`, which returns the specific location of a specific character, and `Mid()`, which grabs characters out of the middle of a string variable. These two look like they'll do the job, so I'm not going to worry too much about exactly how they work. I know I need to do something like this:

- ▶ Use `InStr()` to get the location of the first period. This way, I'll know that the *next* one is the second one.

- ▶ Use `InStr()` to get the location of the second period.

- ▶ Use `InStr()` to get the location of the third period.

- ▶ Use `Mid()` to grab everything in between the second and third periods.

All Tasks Accounted For

It was a bit of work, but I think I know how to do everything I need my script to do. Hopefully, this helps you see how I go about figuring these things out; it's certainly not as easy as just sitting down and starting to type lines of VBScript! A little bit of up-front research is necessary, although it's not usually too hard. The web, fortunately, is loaded with examples (as is this book), and you can usually find something that does what you want, or at least points you in the right direction.

Creating Modules to Perform Tasks

After you've got your task list nailed down, and you've figured out how to perform each of the tasks in the script, you can start designing the modules of the script. I often have to spend a lot of time figuring out how to do things like look up IP addresses or connect to domain controllers; after I've spent that time, I don't ever want to have to do it again. In other words, I want to *modularize* my scripts, so that difficult or commonly used tasks can be easily cut and pasted into future scripts.

VBScript provides a way for you to write your own functions and statements, making it easy to modularize your code. Most of the time, the tasks your script accomplishes—in this case, mapping drives, getting IP addresses, and so forth—can be easily written as functions and subroutines, which can be easily cut and pasted into future scripts.

For a quick overview of functions and statements, see Chapter 5. You can see how they fit into a script in Chapter 3, "The Components of a Script." Finally, I provide more detail on modular script programming in Chapter 22, "Modular Script Programming."

Probably the best way to see how these tasks can be modularized is with an example of the completed logon script.

The Logon Script   Listing 4.5 shows what the various functions for the logon script might look like, and also shows how the main script might be written to call on each of these functions.

> **NOTE**
>
> Don't worry for now about how this script actually works. You'll be seeing all of these features again in later chapters, where I'll provide explanations that are more detailed. For now, just focus on how the various things are broken into modules that make them easier to reuse throughout the main script.

LISTING 4.5   *LogonScript.vbs.* This script includes a main script as well as functions, making a modular script.

```
'Display Message
MsgBox "Welcome to SAPIEN. You are " & _
 "now logged on."

'Map N: Drive
If IsMemberOf("Domain Users") Then
 MapDrive "N:","\\Server\Users"
End If

'Map R: Drive
If IsMemberOf("Research") Then
 MapDrive "R:","\\Server2\Research"
End If

'Map S: Drive
If IsMemberOf("Sales") Then
 MapDrive "S:","\\Server2\SalesDocs"
End If

'Get IP address
```

LISTING 4.5   Continued

```
sIP = GetIP()


'Figure out 3rd octet
iFirstDot = InStr(1,sIP,".")
iSecondDot = InStr(iFirstDot+1,sIP,".")
iThirdDot = InStr(iSecondDot+1,sIP,".")
sThirdOctet = Mid(sIP, iSecondDot+1, _
 Len(sIP)-iThirdDot)


'Map printer based on octet
Select Case sThirdOctet
 Case "100"
  MapPrinter "\\NYDC\HPColor3"
 Case "110"
  MapPrinter "\\LADC\HP6"
 Case "120"
  MapPrinter "\\TXDC1\LaserJet"
End Select


'-----------------------------------------------
' FUNCTIONS
'-----------------------------------------------


Sub MapDrive(sLetter, sUNC)
 Set oNet = _
  WScript.CreateObject("WScript.Network")
 oNet.MapNetworkDrive sLetter, sUNC
End Sub


Function GetIP()
 Set oWMI = GetObject("winmgmts:" & _
  "\\.\root\cimv2")


 Set myObj = oWMI.ExecQuery _
  ("select IPAddress from " & _
  "Win32_NetworkAdapterConfiguration" & _
  " where IPEnabled=TRUE")


 'Go through the addresses
 For Each IPAddress in myObj
  If IPAddress.IPAddress(0) <> "0.0.0.0" Then
   LocalIP = IPAddress.IPAddress(0)
   Exit For
  End If
```

4

LISTING 4.5   Continued

```
Next
 GetIP = LocalIP
End Function

Sub MapPrinter(sUNC)
 Set oNet = WScript.CreateObject("WScript.Network")
 oNet.AddWindowsPrinterConnection sUNC
 oNet.SetDefaultPrinter sUNC
End Sub

Function IsMemberOf(sGroupName)
  Set oNetwork = CreateObject("WScript.Network")
  sDomain = oNetwork.UserDomain
  sUser = oNetwork.UserName
  bIsMember = False
  Set oUser = GetObject("WinNT://" & sDomain & _
   "/" & sUser & ",user")
  For Each oGroup In oUser.Groups
    If oGroup.Name = sGroupName Then
      bIsMember = True
      Exit For
    End If
Next
  IsMemberOf = bIsMember
End Function
```

Of course, you'll need to modify this script to suit your environment before you can use it. The universal naming conventions (UNCs), for example, will need to reflect ones that exist in your environment.

The Logon Script—Explained   I'll walk through this script line-by-line and explain what it does. This is the format I'll use for most longer examples in this book: Presenting the script in its entirety first, and then again with line-by-line explanations. Because I haven't yet covered most of the concepts this script is using, I'll provide cross-references where appropriate. That way, you can jump straight to more detailed explanations if you want.

The script starts off by using MsgBox to display a simple message. Notice the comment line, which begins with a single quotation mark. You should use comments to help describe what your script is doing; I'll be sure to do that in all the examples I show you.

For details on MsgBox, see Chapter 6.

```
'Display Message
MsgBox "Welcome to SAPIEN. You are now logged on."
```

Next, the script maps the three drives according to the user's group membership. Notice that each is using the `IsMemberOf()` function to check the group membership, and the `MapDrive` subroutine to actually map the drive. Both of these are modules I created; I'll cover how they work in a bit.

For details on `If/Then`, see Chapter 10.

```
'Map N: Drive
If IsMemberOf("Domain Users") Then
 MapDrive("N:","\\Server\Users")
End If

'Map S: Drive
If IsMemberOf("Research") Then
 MapDrive("R:","\\Server2\Research")
End If

'Map R: Drive
If IsMemberOf("Sales") Then
 MapDrive("S:","\\Server2\SalesDocs")
End If
```

Next, the script uses the custom `GetIP()` function to get the local IP address. Then, I use the `InStr()` and `Mid()` functions to pull out the third octet. `GetIP()` is a function I created, not one that's built in to VBScript.

For details on `InStr()` and `Mid()`, see Chapter 8, "Manipulating Strings."

```
'Get IP address
sIP = GetIP()

'Figure out 3rd octet
iFirstDot = InStr(1,sIP,".")
iSecondDot = InStr(iFirstDot+1,sIP,".")
iThirdDot = InStr(iSecondDot+1,sIP,".")
sThirdOctet = Mid(sIP, iSecondDot+1, _
 Len(sIP)-iThirdDot)
```

Finally, I use the custom `MapPrinter` command to map a printer based on the third octet.

For details on `Select/Case`, see Chapter 10.

```
'Map printer based on octet
Select Case sThirdOctet
 Case "100"
  MapPrinter "\\NYDC\HPColor3"
 Case "110"
  MapPrinter "\\LADC\HP6"
```

```
Case "120"
  MapPrinter "\\TXDC1\LaserJet"
End Select
```

Next come the parts of the script that actually do all of the work. First is the MapDrive routine, which simply maps a network drive.

For details on the Network object, see Chapter 11.

```
Sub MapDrive(sLetter, sUNC)
  Set oNet = WScript.CreateObject("WScript.Network")
  oNet.MapNetworkDrive sLetter, sUNC)
End Sub
```

Next, the GetIP() function retrieves the local IP address by using Windows Management Instrumentation (WMI).

For an introduction to WMI and lots of examples, turn to Chapter 17.

```
Function GetIP()
  Set oWMI = GetObject("winmgmts:" & _
   "\\.\root\cimv2")

  Set myObj = oWMI.ExecQuery _
   ("select IPAddress from " & _
   "Win32_NetworkAdapterConfiguration" & _
   " where IPEnabled=TRUE")

  'Go through the addresses
  For Each IPAddress in myObj
   If IPAddress.IPAddress(0) <> "0.0.0.0" Then
    LocalIP = IPAddress.IPAddress(0)
    Exit For
   End If
  Next
  GetIP = LocalIP
End Function
```

MapPrinter works similarly to MapDrive, only it also sets the mapped printer to be the default.

```
Sub MapPrinter(sUNC)
  Set oNet = WScript.CreateObject("WScript.Network")
  oNet.AddWindowsPrinterConnection sUNC
  oNet.SetDefaultPrinter sUNC
End Sub
```

Finally, the IsMemberOf() function checks to see if the current user is a member of the specified user group.

```
Function IsMemberOf(sGroupName)
  Set oNetwork = CreateObject("WScript.Network")
  sDomain = oNetwork.UserDomain
  sUser = oNetwork.UserName
  bIsMember = False
  Set oUser = GetObject("WinNT://" & sDomain & _
   "/" & sUser & ",user")
  For Each oGroup In oUser.Groups
    If oGroup.Name = sGroupName Then
      bIsMember = True
      Exit For
    End If
  Next
  IsMemberOf = bIsMember
End Function
```

That's it! The new logon script is ready for testing and debugging.

Validating User Input

This sample logon script doesn't have any user input, but some of your scripts might. For example, you might write a script that asks for a server name, and then does some operation on that server. Any time you're asking for user input, you need to validate that input to make sure it's within the range that you expected.

For example, suppose you have a script that shuts down a remote server. You might have the script ask for the server name, and then ask for a shutdown delay in seconds. After accepting that input from the script's user (who might even be you), the script should check to make sure the server name was valid (perhaps it must start with two backslashes), and that the delay was within an acceptable range (maybe 5–30 seconds).

You can generally use If/Then constructs to validate user input. Why bother? Validation ensures that your scripts are working with proper input, and can help prevent the scripts from running into errors or performing unexpected actions.

Chapter 10 introduces If/Then.

If users provide incorrect or unexpected input, your script can display an error message and end, or even give users another chance to enter the necessary information.

TIP

Plan to add user validation to all scripts that accept input from a user. The examples in this book don't always include input validation; I've deliberately left it out in many cases to help focus on what the script is supposed to accomplish. Scripts used in the real world, however, should always validate user input.

Planning for Errors

Errors occur. There are actually a few different types of errors, with specific ways of dealing with each.

- ▶ **Syntax errors**—These are simple typos that you introduce when writing a script. You'll generally catch these when you test your scripts.

- ▶ **Logic errors**—These design flaws make the script behave unexpectedly or incorrectly. Again, these are usually your fault, and you'll find them as you test the script.

- ▶ **Conditional errors**—These errors occur because something in the script's operating environment was other than what you planned for when you wrote the script. For example, a domain controller might be unavailable, or a user might have typed a server name that doesn't exist.

Syntax and logic errors often crop up in scripting, and you'll find them as you test and debug your scripts. Conditional errors, however, are generally beyond your control. Your scripts should try to anticipate these errors, however, and handle them gracefully. For example, suppose you're using the WScript.Network object to map a network drive, and the server happens to be unavailable at the time. The basic script might look like this:

```
Set oNet = WScript.CreateObject("Wscript.Network")
oNet.MapNetworkDrive "S:", "\\Server2\SalesDocs"
```

If Server2 isn't available, the script will fail when executing the second line of code. That means the script will display an error message and won't execute anything else in the script. You can make the script a bit more resilient by anticipating the problem and adding *error-handling* code.

```
Set oNet = WScript.CreateObject("Wscript.Network")

On Error Resume Next
oNet.MapNetworkDrive "S:", "\\Server2\SalesDocs"
If Err <> 0 Then
 MsgBox "Server2 was unavailable; your S: drive was not mapped."
End If
On Error Goto 0
```

This modified script starts out by telling VBScript, "Look, if an error occurs, it's OK, I'll handle it. You just resume execution with the next line of script." That's done by On Error Resume Next.

After trying to map the drive, an If/Then construct checks the value of the special variable Err. If it's zero, the drive was mapped. If not, a friendlier error message is displayed to the user letting him know something went wrong. Finally, error checking is turned off with On Error Goto 0. From then on, errors will result in a VBScript error message and the script will stop executing.

If/Then is introduced in Chapter 10. Variables are covered in Chapter 5. I'll cover error handling in more detail throughout the book.

NOTE

As you can see, error trapping and handling can add bulk to a script. To help keep the examples in this book focused on the task, I'll usually omit error handling. However, all scripts meant to run in the real world should include error handling wherever something might go wrong.

Error handling needs to be something you plan for in your initial script design. Listing 4.6 shows how you might make a note of possible conditional errors in your original task list.

LISTING 4.6   *Identifying possible errors.* Anticipating errors in your design will show you where to add error-handling code to your script.

```
Logon script task list v3 with error notes

Display a logon welcome message:
"Welcome to SAPIEN. You are now logged on."
Wait until the user presses OK to dismiss the welcome message.
* Can't think of any potential errors here.

Map the N: drive:
Obtain a list of Domain Users group members. See if the user is in the list. If
they are, map the drive to \\Server\Users.
* Server might be unavailable, need to handle this.

Map the R: drive:
Obtain a list of Research group members. See if the user is in the list. If they
are, map the drive to \\Server2\ResearchDocs.
* Server might be unavailable, need to handle this.

Map the S: drive:
Obtain a list of Sales group members. See if the user is in the list. If they are,
map the drive to \\Server2\SalesDocs.
* Server might be unavailable, need to handle this.

Map a printer:
Get the user's IP address. Look at just the third octet. To find it,
      look for the last period in the IP address, and then the next-to-the-last
period. The third octet is between the two periods. If the octet is 100, map to
\\NYDC\HPColor3. If it's 110, map to \\LADC\HP6. If it's 120, map to \\TXDC1\Laser-
Jet. Then make the mapped printer the default.
* Printer or server might be unavailable. Need to handle this if it occurs.
```

Anticipating errors and handling them within the script is definitely the mark of a careful, experienced scripter. Plan for errors in every script you write and you'll definitely be more appreciated by the folks who use your scripts. Of course, I haven't anticipated every possible error in the preceding listing. For example, I haven't accounted for a situation where the N: drive is already mapped; you'll need to determine on a case-by-case basis what errors are possible and how you'll choose to deal with them.

Creating Script Libraries

After you've created some useful functions, you can save them into a script library. That's nothing any fancier than a collection of useful scriptlets, which you can reuse in various scripts that you write. For example, you might pull out all of the functions and subroutines from the logon script you wrote, saving them into a separate file. That'll make it easier to reuse those useful bits of code in the future. In fact, better commercial script editors and IDEs (Integrated Development Environments) provide a feature that lets you create reusable chunks of script code, called Snippets, right within the editing environment. I use PrimalScript, which lets you highlight a section of code and right-click it to save a new Snippet; you can then drag Snippets right into the editing window to reuse them. This saves a ton of time, and really reduces debugging effort, because you don't save a Snippet until it's fully debugged and tested.

By carefully modularizing your code, you'll quickly build a library of useful scripts, making it easier to write new scripts in the future.

Summary

In this chapter, I tried to provide you with a look at how I go about designing and writing scripts. I don't just sit down and start typing; instead, I create a list of tasks I want the script to accomplish, and then I try to do some research and find out exactly how to perform each of those tasks in a script. The VBScript documentation, Google, and other web resources are useful for finding examples and information, and before long I usually find everything I need to know. Next, I try to modularize the script, so that I can reuse my hard-earned information in other scripts that I might write in the future.

If you approach script design and development with this methodical approach, you won't need to be an expert developer to write great scripts. You can build on the work of those who came before you, and quickly start writing scripts that are useful in your environment.

You're ready to start learning VBScript, and your crash course begins in the next chapter. Don't worry; you're not going to be turned into a programmer! Instead, you'll be learning just enough VBScript to have some powerful tools at your disposal as you start scripting.

PART II

VBScript Tutorial

IN THIS PART

Functions, Objects, Variables, and More

Scripting is, of course, a form of computer programming, and computer programming is all about telling a computer what to do. Before you can start ordering the computer around, though, you need to learn to speak a language that it understands. VBScript is one such language, and in this chapter, I'll introduce you to the VBScript *syntax*, or language.

Almost all computer programming languages, including VBScript, have a few things in common:

▶ They have built-in commands that tell the computer to perform certain tasks or calculate certain kinds of information.

▶ They have a means for tracking temporary information, such as data entered by a user or collected during some calculation.

▶ Windows-based programming languages generally have a means for interacting with objects because objects form the basis of Windows' functionality.

NOTE

The capability to interact with objects is *not* the same thing as being an object-oriented programming language. It's like the difference between knowing how to start a car and being able to build a car. Although the concepts and benefits of object-oriented programming are beyond the scope of this book, suffice to say that VBScript isn't object oriented, despite its capability to interact with objects created in other languages.

VBScript implements these common programming elements through variables, functions, and statements, and through an object interface.

▶ *Variables* act as storage areas for different types of data.

▶ *Functions* are VBScript's way of performing calculations or tasks and providing you with the results; *statements* simply perform tasks. You can even create your own functions and statements to customize VBScript's capabilities.

▶ VBScript includes a complete *object interface* based on the Microsoft Component Object Model, or COM. Essentially, an *object* is a piece of external functionality, usually in a dynamic link library (DLL) file; an *interface* is just the way that VBScript "talks" to the DLL. I'll cover objects and interfaces in more detail as we go.

In this chapter, you'll learn how to use each of these elements within scripts.

NOTE

I've never liked programming books that provide short, useless snippets of script as examples, even as early in the book as you are right now. Sometimes, I have to use that type of snippet to make a point, especially early on when using a complete script would just be too much; but for the most part I'll try and use fully functioning scripts that you can actually use in your environment. Of course, to make them fully functioning, they have to include some things that you won't learn about until later chapters. Hopefully, that's OK with you; I'll point out the parts of the scripts that are important for now, and as you read through the next few chapters in Part II, you'll learn more and more about how these scripts operate.

Variables Defined

Variables are temporary storage areas for data. You might even remember them from algebra: $x + 5 = 10$, solve for variable x. Of course, in those situations, x wasn't really a variable because it always equaled some fixed amount when you solved the equation. In scripting, variables can change their contents many times.

Sample Script   Listing 5.1 shows a sample script. It's a fully functional script that will connect to a domain, locate any inactive user accounts, and disable them.

NOTE

Once more, I'm showing you a script that uses some advanced features. This lets me show you functional, useful scripts rather than dumbed-down examples, but for now I'm just going to explain the bits that are important for this chapter. I promise you'll get to the rest later!

LISTING 5.1   *DisableUser.vbs.* We'll use this script as a running example throughout this chapter.

```
Dim sTheDate
Dim oUserObj
Dim oObject
Dim oGroupObj
Dim iFlags
Dim iDiff
Dim sResult
Dim sName
Const UF_ACCOUNTDISABLE = &H0002

' Constant for Log file path
 Const sLogFile = "C:\UserMgr1.txt"

' Point to Object containing users to check
Set oGroupObj = _
 GetObject("WinNT://MYDOMAINCONTROLLER/Users")

On Error Resume Next
For Each oObject in oGroupObj.Members

 ' Find all User Objects Within Domain Users group
 ' (ignore machine accounts)
 If (oObject.Class = "User") And _
  (InStr(oObject.Name, "$") = 0) then Set oUserObj = _
  GetObject(oObject.ADsPath)

  ' get last login date
  sTheDate = UserObj.get("LastLogin")
  sTheDate = Left(sTheDate,8)
  sTheDate = CDate(sTheDate)

  ' find difference in weeks between then and now
  iDiff = DateDiff("ww", sTheDate, Now)

' if 6 weeks or more then disable the account
 If iDiff >= 6 Then
  iFlags = UserObj.Get("UserFlags")
 End If

 ' if the account is not already disabled...
 If (iFlags And UF_ACCOUNTDISABLE) = 0 Then

  ' disable account
```

LISTING 5.1   Continued

```
  oUserObj.Put "UserFlags", iFlags Or UF_ACCOUNTDISABLE
  oUserObj.SetInfo

   ' Get user name and write a log entry
   sName = oUserObj.Name
   sResult = Log(sName,iDiff)

  End If

 End If
Next

' Release object
Set oGroupObj = Nothing

Function Log(oUser,sDate)

' Create a FileSystemObject
 Dim oFS
 Set oFS = CreateObject("Scripting.FileSystemObject")

 ' Create a TextStream object
 Dim oTextStream
 Set oTextStream = objFS.OpenTextFile(sLogFile, 8, True)

 ' Write log entry
 oTextStream.WriteLine("Account:" & vbTab & oUser & vbTab & _
 "Inactive  for:" & vbTab & strdate & vbatb & "Weeks" & _
 vbtab & "Disabled on:" & vbTab & Date & vbTab & "at:" & _
 vbTab & Time)

 ' Close file
 oTextStream.Close

 ' Release objects
 Set oFS = Nothing
 Set oTextStream = Nothing

 Log = True

End Function
```

CAUTION

Please don't try to run this script right now. To begin with, there are some things you will need to make it work, and there are some things actually wrong with it that I want to point out as I explain what it's doing.

NOTE

Note the use of the underscore (_) character at the end of some lines of text. Because the pages of this book are only so wide, I can't include very long lines of code. Instead, I break those lines up by using the underscore character. When you type this code, you can just skip right over the underscore and type the code as one long line. However, VBScript understands that the underscore is a *line continuation character*, so if you do type the underscore and keep the code on multiple lines, VBScript will understand perfectly. Try it both ways and see which method you like; I prefer to keep the underscore because it means I don't have to scroll to the right in my script editor to see the entire line of code.

This script logs on to the domain using the user credentials of whatever user runs the script; for it to work, however, that user needs to be a member of the Domain Admins group. The script locates all users who haven't logged on for at least six weeks, disables their accounts, and writes an entry to the specified log file for your review. However, you should keep in mind that this script is primarily just a *demonstration*; it'll run very slowly in a large Active Directory domain. For now, just treat the script as an example, not as something you want to rush into your production environment!

NOTE

There's a lot going on in this script that I won't be explaining right away. I'll be using this script, along with a couple of others, as a running example through the next few chapters. Eventually, I'll explain everything in it. In the meantime, though, feel free to use it both as a working tool in your environment and as a great example of administrative scripting.

Declaring Variables

One of the first things you see in the DisableUsers script is the variable declarations:

```
Dim sTheDate
Dim oUserObj
Dim oObject
Dim oGroupObj
Dim iFlags
Dim iDiff
Dim sResult
Dim sName
Const UF_ACCOUNTDISABLE = &H0002
```

The Dim statements tell VBScript that you're defining, or declaring, a variable. Actually, Dim is short for *dimension,* a term that hearkens back to the early days of computing. Following each Dim statement is a variable name. Each of these statements tells VBScript to set aside room in memory for the variable and to remember the variable's name.

Variable names must follow a few basic rules:

- ▶ They are not case sensitive. For example, sTheDate and sthedate are treated the same.

- ▶ They must begin with a letter or an underscore (_) character.

- ▶ They can contain letters, underscores, and numbers.

- ▶ VBScript allows quite long variable names (up to 128 characters), but, practically speaking, they shouldn't be more than a dozen characters or so, or your script will become difficult for other people to read.

You might also notice the Const statement, which is short for *constant.* Constants are like variables in that they assign a meaningful name to an arbitrary value. In this case, the constant name UF_ACCOUNTDISABLE is a bit easier to remember than the hexadecimal value 02. However, unlike variables, constants—as their name implies—don't change. If you try to assign a different value to UF_ACCOUNTDISABLE during the course of the script, you'll receive an error message. Notice that I typed the constant name in all uppercase letters: Although that's a common practice (I wouldn't call it a *best* practice, just a common one), VBScript doesn't care. Apart from the literal strings that you put inside double quotation marks, VBScript is not case sensitive.

> **NOTE**
>
> Constants and variables are the two types of data storage that VBScript utilizes. Constants are simply names for fixed values, whereas variables are names that represent values which can change as your script runs.

You need to understand that VBScript doesn't *require* you to define variables up front. In fact, you could delete every single Dim statement from this script and it would still work the same. So why bother?

One of the biggest causes of bugs in scripting is simple mistyping. For example, consider the following snippet of code from the DisableUsers script:

```
' get last login date
sTheDaet = UserObj.get("LastLogin")
sTheDate = Left(sTheDate,8)
sTheDate = CDate(sTheDate)
```

Notice anything peculiar? In the second line of code, I changed sTheDate to sTheDaet. Because VBScript doesn't require me to declare my variables up front, this line of code won't generate an error. Instead, VBScript will dynamically create a brand-new variable named sTheDaet on the fly. Of course, the third line of code assumes that the second line of code put some data into sTheDate, not sTheDaet, and so the third line of code won't work correctly. It still won't generate an error, but sTheDate will contain no data. Finally, the last line of code *will* generate an error—despite the fact that there's nothing wrong with the last line of code. The problem is all the way back in the second line of code where a simple typo created a new variable and introduced a serious logic error into the script.

Typos like this are easy to make and are all too common. Because they throw a wrench into your script but don't generate an error, you'll usually wind up with an error else-where—even though the actual *code* where the error occurs might be fine. To help combat these devious errors, VBScript provides Option Explicit, a command you can add to the beginning of your script.

```
Option Explicit
Dim sTheDate
Dim oUserObj
Dim oObject
Dim oGroupObj
Dim iFlags
Dim iDiff
Dim sResult
Dim sName
Const UF_ACCOUNTDISABLE = &H0002
```

With Option Explicit in place, VBScript will *require* all variables to be declared before they can be used. Now suppose I were to rerun the script with the typo in the variable name:

```
' get last login date
  sTheDaet = UserObj.get("LastLogin")
  sTheDate = Left(sTheDate,8)
  sTheDate = CDate(sTheDate)
```

VBScript would generate an error on the second line of the script because I'm attempting to use a variable that hasn't yet been declared. That's exactly where I want VBScript to generate an error, too, because it's the line of script that actually contains the error.

TIP

Always include Option Explicit in your scripts. For brevity, I won't always include the line in the sample scripts in this book, but it's a great way to avoid spending hours tracking down a typo.

Understanding Data Types

If you've worked with other programming languages, you might be familiar with the concept of *data types*. Simply put, there are different kinds of data in the world around us: numbers, letters, dates, huge numbers, pictures, and more. Most programming languages need to understand what kind of data a variable will contain, so that the language can treat the variable appropriately. For example, it wouldn't make sense to try to subtract the word *Hello* from a picture of a flower, and so most programming languages won't allow you to perform mathematical operations with anything but numeric variables. Languages that care about the type of data a variable will hold are called *strongly typed* languages.

VBScript, on the other hand, is *weakly typed*. You'll notice that none of the variable declarations include any hint as to the data type each variable would hold:

```
Dim sTheDate
Dim oUserObj
Dim oObject
Dim oGroupObj
Dim iFlags
Dim iDiff
Dim sResult
Dim sName
Const UF_ACCOUNTDISABLE = &H0002
```

Actually, there *is* a clue because I've set the first letter of each variable name to be a reminder of what data type I want the variable to contain: "s" for strings, "o" for objects, "i" for integers, and so forth. However, that's not a clue VBScript can recognize, and you're certainly not required to use that kind of variable-naming scheme. VBScript doesn't care what type of data is in each variable because VBScript only has one data type: variant. The variant data type can hold any kind of data, and that data type can even change to a different type as your script runs. For example, the following snippet of code is perfectly valid in VBScript:

```
Dim vData
vData = 1
vData = "Hello"
vData = Date()
```

You might think that this weakly typed stuff is great. After all, you can just pop any kind of data you want into a variable and VBScript doesn't care. In some ways, that's true; not having to worry about data types can be a time-saver. On the other hand, as you'll see shortly, it can also be a real pain in the neck.

Assigning Data to Variables

You've already seen several examples of how to assign data to a variable. The following is a section of the `DisableUsers` script, with the data assignment lines highlighted in bold. Note that I fixed my earlier `sTheDaet` typo.

```
' get last login date
sTheDate = UserObj.get("LastLogin")
sTheDate = Left(sTheDate,8)
sTheDate = CDate(sTheDate)

' find difference in week between then and now
iDiff = DateDiff("ww", sTheDate, Now)
```

This actually looks a lot like the old algebra class, right? The variable name appears on the left side of the equal sign (=), which is referred to as the *assignment operator.* Whatever you want inserted into the variable appears on the right side of the assignment operator. In all four of these examples, the variable is being filled with the results of a function, which I'll cover later in this chapter.

The right side of the assignment operator can include any kind of operation that results in a single value. So all of the following commands are legal:

```
Dim vVariable
vVariable = 1
vVariable = 1 + 1
vVariable = "Hello"
vVariable = Date()
```

Variables can also be assigned to each other. This makes sense if you consider variables as simply a representation of a value; assigning one variable to another simply copies the value.

```
Dim vVar1
Dim vVar2
vVar1 = 1
vVar2 = 2
vVar1 = vVar1 + vVar2
```

After running this brief chunk of script, vVar1 will contain the value 3.

Data Coercion

As I've already mentioned, VBScript doesn't much care what kind of data you put into a variable. However, certain operations only support certain data types, so you can run into trouble. For example, consider the following operations and see if you can predict their output:

```
Dim vVar1
Dim vVar2
Dim vVar3
vVar1 = 1
```

```
vVar2 = "1"
vVar3 = "2"

MsgBox vVar1 & vVar2
MsgBox vVar1 + vVar2
MsgBox vVar1 - vVar2
MsgBox vVar2 + vVar3
```

NOTE

The `MsgBox` statement will display a small dialog box with the result of whatever operation you've given it. It's an easy way, in an example like this, to see how VBScript treats each operation.

If you type this script in and run it, you'll get four message boxes. They might not be what you expect! You should see an 11, a 2, a 0, and a 12. Can you guess why?

When you assign data to a variable, VBScript actually does care. It keeps track of what it *thinks* the data type is, based on what you gave it. For example, any number not included in quotes is definitely numeric data, without question. Anything in quotation marks is text, called a *string*. However, if the text is all numeric, VBScript acknowledges that it could be numeric data, not a string. Here's what happens:

1. The first operation uses the concatenation operator (the ampersand). This operator is only used to tack one string onto another string. VBScript knows this, and so it *coerces,* or temporarily converts, vVar1—which was a numeric value—into a string so that the operation will work. The result is a 1 being tacked onto another 1, for a result of 11. This coercion occurred entirely because of the operator that was in use: The ampersand is *only* used for string concatenation, so VBScript *had* to treat both values as if they were strings.

2. The second operation seems to be adding a numeric value and a string. This doesn't make sense, of course. However, in this case, because the string contains a numeric digit, VBScript can coerce the string data into a number, and it does so. The addition operation works smoothly from that point, with the result of 2.

3. The third operation requires a similar coercion to complete the subtraction operation and arrive at the correct result of 0.

4. The fourth operation is more interesting. Back before Microsoft added the ampersand as a concatenation operator, the plus (+) operator did double duty: For numbers, it was addition. For strings, it handled concatenation. Modern VBScript knows this, so when it sees two string values being "added" together, it concatenates them instead, giving you a result of 12.

Order isn't important to how VBScript tries to coerce data. For example, let's modify our sample script as follows:

```
Dim vVar1
Dim vVar2
Dim vVar3
vVar1 = 1
vVar2 = "1"
vVar3 = "2"


MsgBox vVar2 & vVar1
MsgBox vVar2 + vVar1
MsgBox vVar2 - vVar1
MsgBox vVar3 + vVar2
```

Rerun the script. Do you see any differences in the results? You shouldn't. VBScript prefers to use + as an addition operator, so it will try to do so when any of the involved values is numeric. However, in the last operation, where both values were set up as strings, VBScript gives in and performs concatenation.

What can you do to make sure VBScript treats your data the way you want?

▶ Keep track of the data types you put into variables. I do this with the first letter of the variable name: s tells me it's a string, i is for integers, d is for dates, b is for Boolean values (True or False), and so forth. You can use my naming scheme or make up your own. Microsoft popularized a variable naming scheme called *Hungarian notation*, where "str" was used to prefix the names of string variables, "int" for integers, and so forth; you'll see a lot of folks using that naming scheme if you peruse sample scripts on the Internet.

▶ VBScript includes data-conversion functions, which you'll learn about in Chapter 7, "Manipulating Numbers." These functions can force data into a specific data type.

▶ Avoid using the ambiguous + operator for concatenation. Instead, use the dedicated ampersand (&) and save the + operator for addition. You'll read more about concatenation in Chapter 8, "Manipulating Strings."

Functions Defined

Functions are a way to perform a task and get something back. For example, VBScript has a function named Date(), which simply looks up and provides the current date according to your computer's internal clock. Functions are used to perform special calculations, retrieve information, look up information, convert data types, manipulate data, and much more.

Input Parameters

Functions can include one or more *input parameters,* which give the function something to work with and usually are a major part of the function's output. Not all functions need input, however. For example, the Date() function doesn't need any input parameters to function; it knows how to look up the date without any help from you.

Other functions might require multiple input parameters. For example, the InStr() function is used to locate a particular character within a string. Here's how it works:

```
Dim sVar
Dim iResult
sVar = "Howdy!"
iResult = InStr(1, sVar, "w")
```

After running this short script, iResult will contain the value 3, meaning the Instr() function located the letter *w* at the third position within the variable sVar. InStr() requires three input parameters:

▶ The character position where the search should start

▶ The string in which to search

▶ The string to search for

NOTE

Of course, I haven't necessarily memorized InStr()'s input parameters. The script editor I use, PrimalScript, reminds me of the correct syntax as I'm typing, so I don't need to look it up. Some other script editors provide similar "syntax reminder" functionality. After you use a function a few times in scripts, you'll remember its parameters without looking them up, but I don't use InStr() very often, so I always need that little hint.

Now that you know what a function looks like, refer to this section of the DisableUsers sample script to see if you can spot the functions (I've boldfaced them to make it easy):

```
' get last login date
sTheDate = UserObj.get("LastLogin")
sTheDate = Left(sTheDate,8)
sTheDate = CDate(sTheDate)

' find difference in week between then and now
iDiff = DateDiff("ww", sTheDate, Now)

' if 6 weeks or more then disable the account
If iDiff >= 6 Then
 iFlags = UserObj.Get("UserFlags")
End If

' if the account is not already disabled...
If (iFlags And UF_ACCOUNTDISABLE) = 0 Then

  ' disable account
```

```
oUserObj.Put "UserFlags", iFlags Or UF_ACCOUNTDISABLE
oUserObj.SetInfo

' Get user name and write a log entry
  sName = oUserObj.Name
  sResult = Log(sName,iDiff)

  End If
```

> **NOTE**
>
> I try to keep my scripts nice and pretty by capitalizing function names, but VBScript couldn't care less. DateDiff() and datediff() or even DaTediFf() are all the same as far as VBScript is concerned.

You might wonder why I didn't boldface Get(), which looks for all the world like a function. It is, sort of, but it's more correctly called a *method* because it's associated with an object. It works just like a function, though, and if you think it should be called a function, go right ahead. Most folks will know what you're talking about.

Output Values

All functions return some kind of value to your script. The VBScript documentation can tell you what type of data that is (numeric, date, string, and so on), but you need to decide what to do with it. The most common action is to assign the result to a variable.

```
' get last login date
  sTheDate = UserObj.get("LastLogin")
  sTheDate = Left(sTheDate,8)
  sTheDate = CDate(sTheDate)
```

In this case, variable sTheDate is being used to hold the results of a function. In fact, the function is performing an operation with the old value of sTheDate and returning a new value to be stored into sTheDate, overwriting the old value.

The results of a function can also be fed as the input parameter to another function. For example, consider the following few lines of code:

```
Dim sVar1
sVar1 = "Transcription"
MsgBox Left(Right(sVar1, 9), 6)
```

The result will be a message box containing "script" and an OK button. Here's what's happening:

1. VBScript executes functions from the inside out. In other words, it looks for the most deeply nested function and starts with that one, and then works its way out.

2. The `Right()` function is executed first and returns the rightmost nine characters of whatever is in sVar1. The result, of course, is "scription".

3. The `Left()` function then takes the leftmost six characters of whatever the `Right()` function returned, resulting in "script".

4. The `Left()` function's results are passed to the `MsgBox` statement, which displays the results.

Nesting functions can make your script difficult to read and troubleshoot, although VBScript itself doesn't mind. You can make your scripts easier to read by breaking each function out into its own line of code.

```
Dim sVar1
sVar1 = "Transcription"
sVar1 = Right(sVar1, 9)
sVar1 = Left(sVar1, 6)
MsgBox sVar1
```

This revised snippet takes a bit more typing, but it's clearer what the script is doing.

Intrinsic Versus Custom Functions

So far, the functions I've introduced have been *intrinsic* functions, which means they're built in to VBScript. You can look them all up in the VBScript documentation to see how they work. However, you can build your own custom functions. For example, suppose you want a function that writes entries to a log file. That would be a useful function to have, and you could probably use it in any number of different scripts. In fact, the `DisableUsers` sample script contains a custom function that writes log file entries:

```
Function Log(oUser,sDate)

 ' Constant for Log file path
 Const sLogFile = "C:\UserMgr1.txt"

 ' Create a FileSystemObject
 Dim oFS
 Set oFS = CreateObject("Scripting.FileSystemObject")

 ' Create a TextStream object
 Dim oTextStream
Set oTextStream = objFS.OpenTextFile(sLogFile, 8, True)

 ' Write log entry
 oTextStream.WriteLine("Account:" & vbTab & oUser & vbTab & _
 "Inactive  for:" & vbTab & strdate & vbatb & "Weeks" & _
 vbtab & "Disabled on:" & vbTab & Date & vbTab & "at:" & _
```

```
 vbTab & Time)

 ' Close file
 oTextStream.Close

 ' Release objects
 Set oFS = Nothing
 Set oTextStream = Nothing

 Log = True

End Function
```

This function is defined by the `Function` statement, and all of the code within the function falls between `Function` and `End Function`. The `Function` statement has several important components:

- ▶ The `Function` statement itself
- ▶ The name of the function, in this case `Log`
- ▶ The function's input parameters, `oUser` and `sDate`

Note that the two input parameters aren't specifically declared anywhere. This can be one of the big confusing things about functions, in fact, so I want to explain what's going on. Technically, `oUser` and `sDate` aren't variables—they're *input parameters*. Inside the function, you use them just as you would use variables—functionally speaking, there's no difference. It's just that you don't declare them using the `Dim` keyword. Another way to think about it is that parameters don't get declared by using the `Dim` keyword because they're declared as part of the `Function` statement itself.

This function is called from within the main script just as if it were an intrinsic function. I've passed two variables as the input parameters: The *values within these variables* will be copied into the input parameters, `oUser` and `sDate`, enabling those values to be utilized within the function.

```
' Get username and write a log entry
   sName = oUserObj.Name
   sResult = Log(sName,iDiff)
```

The last line of code in the function is `Log = True`. This is a special line of code because it uses the function's name on the left side of the assignment operator. This line of code tells VBScript that the function's return value will be `True`. In a custom function, you use this technique to return a value to whatever called your function—assign the return value to the function's name. You must generally do so in the last line of code before `End Function`.

However, this is really a *bad* example of how to write a custom function. It works perfectly, but it's doing a few things that you don't normally want a function to do:

▶ The function doesn't return a useful value. You can tell because the calling script doesn't do anything with the value; it just stores it in a variable. If the return value isn't useful, why have it at all? This function could have been written as a *subroutine,* which doesn't return a value. I'll be covering subroutines in the next section. However, VBScript is the only language where functions should always return a value; in nearly any other language, subroutines don't exist and functions are used regardless of whether they return a value. So if you're writing functions that don't return values—don't worry. Probably nobody will yell at you.

▶ The function is relying on data that was defined outside of itself. Specifically, the sLogFile variable was defined in the main part of the script, not the function. Generally, functions should be entirely self-contained, making them easier to transport from one script to another without modifications. Listing 5.2 shows a modified script that passes the log filename as an input parameter because input parameters provide a legitimate way of getting information into a function.

LISTING 5.2   *DisableUser2.vbs.* This script has been modified to have a better-written function.

```
Dim sTheDate
Dim oUserObj
Dim oObject
Dim oGroupObj
Dim iFlags
Dim iDiff
Dim sResult
Dim sName
Const UF_ACCOUNTDISABLE = &H0002

' Point to Object containing users to check
Set oGroupObj = GetObject("WinNT://MYDOMAINCONTROLLER/Users")

On Error Resume Next
For Each oObject in oGroupObj.Members

  ' Find all User Objects Within Domain Users group
  ' (ignore machine accounts)
  If (oObject.Class = "User") And _
   (InStr(oObject.Name, "$") = 0) then Set oUserObj = _
   GetObject(oObject.ADsPath)
 ' get last login date
   sTheDate = UserObj.get("LastLogin")
   sTheDate = Left(sTheDate,8)
```

LISTING 5.2   Continued

```
  sTheDate = CDate(sTheDate)

  ' find difference in week between then and now
  iDiff = DateDiff("ww", sTheDate, Now)

  ' if 6 weeks or more then disable the account
  If iDiff >= 6 Then
   iFlags = UserObj.Get("UserFlags")
  End If

  ' if the account is not already disabled...
  If (iFlags And UF_ACCOUNTDISABLE) = 0 Then

   ' disable account
   oUserObj.Put "UserFlags", iFlags Or UF_ACCOUNTDISABLE
   oUserObj.SetInfo

   ' Get username and write a log entry
   sName = oUserObj.Name
   sResult = Log(sName,iDiff,sLogFile)

  End If

 End If
Next

' Release object
Set oGroupObj = Nothing

Function Log(oUser,sDate,sLog)

 ' Constant for Log file path
 Const sLogFile = "C:\UserMgr1.txt"

 ' Create a FileSystemObject
 Dim oFS
 Set oFS = CreateObject("Scripting.FileSystemObject")

 ' Create a TextStream object
 Dim oTextStream
 Set oTextStream = objFS.OpenTextFile(sLog, 8, True)

 ' Write log entry
 oTextStream.WriteLine("Account:" & vbTab & oUser & vbTab & _
```

LISTING 5.2   Continued

```
"Inactive  for:" & vbTab & strdate & vbatb & "Weeks" & _
vbtab & "Disabled on:" & vbTab & Date & vbTab & "at:" & _
vbTab & Time)

' Close file
oTextStream.Close

' Release objects
Set oFS = Nothing
Set oTextStream = Nothing

Log = True

End Function
```

The boldfaced code indicates what has changed. Now, the function is much more appropriate and will be easier to reuse in other scripts. It still isn't returning a useful value, so in the next section I'll show you how to convert it into a subroutine.

Statements and Subroutines Defined

Here's where VBScript's terminology gets a bit complicated, and for no good reason: Aside from the terms themselves, statements and subroutines are actually quite straightforward. A *statement* is an intrinsic command that accepts zero or more parameters and returns no value—instead of returning a value, it just does something. A *subroutine* is simply a custom statement that you write yourself. Intrinsic and custom functions are both called functions; why custom statements are called subroutines (or *subs* for short) is a mystery from the depths of VBScript's past.

Functions, Without the Output

Statements (and subroutines) always perform some kind of task. Unlike a function, statements cannot return a value to your script, so they *just* perform a task. One of the simplest VBScript statements is Stop, which stops the script's execution (not in a good way, though; you should only use the statement when you're actually debugging your script). It takes no parameters, returns no value, and performs one task.

A Custom Subroutine   You might want to create custom routines that perform a task but return no value. For example, suppose you're writing a script and you want your computer to display some specific message when it encounters some specific condition, such as an error or a full hard disk. You could just list multiple MsgBox statements each time it happened, but it would be more efficient to use a custom subroutine. Listing 5.3 shows an example.

LISTING 5.3   *ErrorMsg Subroutine*. This subroutine can be used to make the computer display a fixed error message.

```
Sub ErrorMsg()
      MsgBox "A file error occured."
End Sub
```

You can use the `ErrorMsg` subroutine from anywhere in the main portion of your script.

A Custom Subroutine—Explained   The `ErrorMsg` subroutine actually uses VBScript commands I haven't introduced yet, but I'll focus for now on the parts that define the subroutine. First, all subroutines include a `Sub` and an `End Sub` statement, in much the same way that custom functions use `Function` and `End Function`:

```
Sub ErrorMsg()
End Sub
```

As with a custom function, note that the parameters are defined in the `Sub` statement. In this case, there are no parameters—this subroutine can run without any input. If there were parameters, they'd be in the parentheses following the sub's name.

Everything else in the subroutine is your custom code.

```
      MsgBox "A file error occurred."
```

> **TIP**
>
> Notice in Listing 5.3 that I indented the line of the script between `Sub` and `End Sub`. Indenting is a common programming practice that helps keep your code easier to read. The indent serves as a visual cue that the code is within some other routine or construct.

Now it's time for a really important difference between using functions and subroutines. Take a look at these three lines of code:

```
Dim sResult
sResult = MyFunction(5)
MySub 5
```

In the second line of code, I'm calling the function `MyFunction`, passing it the value 5 as an input parameter. I'm taking whatever `MyFunction` returns and storing it in the variable `sResult`. On the third line of code, I'm calling the subroutine `MySub` and passing it the value 5 as an input parameter—notice anything different? First, subroutines return no values, so I'm not assigning anything equal to `MySub`, as I did with `MyFunction`. Second, the values passed to `MySub` are not in parentheses! This is an arbitrary difference that VBScript is very strict about. If I had put `MySub(5)` instead, I would have gotten an error telling me that I can't call a sub using parentheses. You have to be very careful to observe this difference when writing your scripts!

Leading a Dual Life

A few of VBScript's built-in functions lead a double life as statements. The most common example is MsgBox. As a statement, it displays a message box, complete with whatever icons and buttons you want. When the user clicks one of those buttons, the message box goes away and your script continues.

However, MsgBox() can be a function, too. In this guise, it still displays the same type of message box, but it also returns a value indicating which button the user clicked. For example, this allows your script to ask Are-you-sure?-type messages with Yes and No buttons and act appropriately based on which button the user clicks.

There's only one real difference in the way you use MsgBox as a statement or a function. As a statement, there's no return value, so you can use MsgBox on a line of script by itself, as in MsgBox "Hello!". However, as a function, MsgBox() returns a value, which you'll need to assign to a variable, as in iResult = MsgBox("Are you sure?").

You'll see a lot more of MsgBox, both as a function and a statement, throughout this book and especially in Chapter 6, "Input and Output."

Objects Defined

I've already made a big deal about how VBScript lets you access operating system functionality because VBScript is object based, and Windows exposes much of its functionality through objects. So, you might be wondering, "What the heck is an object?"

Bear with me for the 10-second synopsis. You might have heard of COM or COM+, two versions of Microsoft's Component Object Model. The whole idea behind COM is that software developers can package their code in a way that makes it easily accessible to other applications. For example, suppose some poor developer spent a few years developing a cool way to interact with email systems. If the developer wrote that code according to the rules of COM, every other developer—or scripter—would be able to take advantage of that email interaction. In fact, a bunch of developers did exactly that! You might have heard of the Microsoft Messaging Application Programming Interface, or MAPI. It's what Microsoft Outlook uses to access an Exchange server, for example. MAPI is an example of COM in action; any programmer—including you—can use MAPI to access a mail server because MAPI is written to the COM standard.

Therefore, an *object* is simply a piece of software that's written to the COM standard. VBScript can use most objects that are written to the COM standard; most of Windows' functionality is written to the COM standard, and that's what makes VBScript so powerful. What makes objects relatively easy to work with is that they're a kind of "black box," meaning you don't need to know a lot about what goes on inside the object: You can just use the buttons on the face of it—*interfaces*, in COM lingo—to tell the black box—or COM object—to do whatever it does.

To be fair, the word *object* is pretty overused in the world of software programming. Most software developers would argue that my definition isn't entirely complete. That might be; however, for our purposes it's complete enough. So long as you understand that, in the world of VBScript, an object is some external functionality, usually bundled up into a DLL, you're fine.

Properties

Most software requires some kind of configuration to use it, and COM objects are no exception. You configure an object by setting its *properties*. Properties are simply a means of customizing an object's behavior. For example, an email object might have properties for setting the mail server name, setting the user's name and password, and so forth.

Properties can also provide information to your script. A mail object might include a property that tells you how many new messages are available or how much space is left in the mailbox.

In your scripts, you'll generally use a variable name to represent an object. I use variable names that start with the letter o, so that I know the variable is really an object reference. To refer to an object's properties, simply list the property name after the object name. For example, suppose you have a mail object referenced by the variable oMail. To set the mail server name, you might use oMail.ServerName = "email.sapien.com". The period in between the object variable and the property name helps VBScript distinguish between the two. Here's a real-world example of an object in use:

```
oFile.Name = "Testfile.txt"
```

If oFile represents a file object, then this line of code is changing the filename of the file.

Methods

You already know that functions, statements, and subroutines exist in VBScript. Objects have functions, statements, and subroutines too, but they're called *methods*. Suppose your fictional mail object provided a statement named GetMail, which retrieved mail from the mail server. You could then simply include oMail.GetMail in your script to activate the statement and retrieve the mail.

Like functions and statements, some methods accept input parameters. For example, oMail.GetMail(1) might retrieve the first message in the mailbox. Other methods might work as functions—sMessage = oMail.GetMail(2) might retrieve the second message and store the message body in the variable sMessage.

How do you know what methods an object supports? Check the documentation. Also, I'll introduce you to several useful objects in Chapters 11 and 12, "Built-In Scripting Objects" and "Working with the File System," respectively.

Something that's very important to remember is that objects' methods are basically just functions and subs, as I've suggested earlier in this chapter. Methods follow *the same rules as functions and subs* when they're used. For example:

```
Dim sResult
sResult = objMail.GetMail(5)
objMail.DeleteMail 5
```

Here, I'm using the GetMail() method—which, because it returns a value, works like a function—and passing an input parameter in parentheses. When I use the DeleteMail method, however, I don't use parentheses because it's not returning a value. Because it doesn't return a value, I don't assign it equal to anything, and I don't use parentheses. How do you know the difference when working with a real object? You'll need to read the object's documentation to be sure.

Collections

Sometimes, programmers create objects that represent a hierarchy of real-world data. One common hierarchy that you're probably familiar with is the file system on a computer: It's a tree of folders and files. If you wanted to manipulate the file system in a script, you'd need an object that represented that hierarchy of folders and files.

COM provides a means for objects to represent hierarchies through *collections*. A collection is simply a special property that represents several other objects. Sound complicated? It's not! Consider a folder named Test, which contains two files: File1 and File2. Test also contains two subfolders, named Test1 and Test2. Test1 contains a file named FileA.

Now, suppose you've created a theoretical file management object and assigned it to variable oFiles. oFiles might have the following useful properties:

▶ A Files property that returns a collection of file objects

▶ A Subfolders property that returns a collection of folder objects

▶ Folder objects that have their own Folders and Files collections

▶ File objects that have properties for FileSize, FileName, and so forth

How would you find the size of the first file under Test? oFile.Files(0).FileSize. That starts with your oFile object reference, grabs the first file object in the Files collection (most collections start numbering at zero, not one), and then gets that file's FileSize property. Notice the periods separating each portion of the object reference.

How would you get the size for FileA? oFile.Subfolders(0).Files(0).FileSize. You would start with your oFile object reference, move onto the first subfolder, grab the first file in that subfolder, and then get the file size.

> **NOTE**
>
> This file management object isn't actually fictional—Windows includes one, called the FileSystemObject library. I'll cover it in Chapter 12.

If all of this seems like a bit much—stick with it. You're getting the "crash course" introduction to objects, right now; we'll be looking at them together in more detail, with a lot more examples.

A Sample Object

It might be easier to see what all of this object stuff is about with a nontechnical example. Here, I'll break my usual policy of only including useful administrative examples in favor of clarity.

Suppose you're a biology major in college, and you're working with trees. You want to create a computer model of a tree so that you can simulate how it lives in various environmental conditions. You write the computer model to the COM specification, creating a Tree object. The object has the following properties:

▸ Species—This read/write property sets or retrieves the species of the simulated tree.

▸ Age—This read/write property sets or retrieves the age of the tree in years.

▸ Environment—This read/write property sets or retrieves the environment of the tree.

▸ Disease—This read-only property retrieves a True or False value, which indicates if the tree has a disease.

In addition, the Tree object has one method:

▸ Grow—This method accepts a parameter indicating how many months the tree should grow in the simulated environment.

To keep it interesting, the Tree object also has a collection:

▸ Leaves—This is a collection of Leaf objects, each of which has its own properties (such as Color and Size) and methods (such as FallOff).

Listing 5.4 shows a simulated script that uses the Tree object.

LISTING 5.4   TreeObject model script. Working with the fictional Tree object.

```
' Assumes the Tree object is referenced by
' variable oTree.

' set initial parameters
oTree.Species = "Oak"
oTree.Age = 12
oTree.Environment = "City"

' grow the tree
oTree.Grow(36)

' retrieve values
MsgBox "Tree is " & oTree.Species & ", " & _
 oTree.Age & " years old, in " & oTree.Environment
MsgBox "Tree is diseased: " & oTree.Disease
```

5

After running this script (if you could, which you can't), you'd get a message box saying "Tree is Oak, 15 years old, in City." A second message box would indicate whether the tree was healthy.

As you can see, the properties, collections, and methods of objects provide a straightforward way to access powerful features. Getting just a bit ahead of myself, here's some additional code that would make each leaf on the tree fall to the ground:

```
For Each objLeaf in objTree.Leaves
  objLeaf.FallOff
Next
```

The special `For Each…Next` loop (which I'll cover in much greater detail in Chapters 10 and 12, "Controlling the Flow of Execution" and "Working with the File System," respectively) is running through each object in the `Leaves` collection. For each object it finds, it executes the object's `FallOff` method, making the leaves fall from the tree. This might be a fictional COM object, but it's a useful programming pattern you'll use again and again when working with many different types of objects.

Scripting with Objects

You've already seen a small version of how to work with objects in script, so it's time for a full example. This is actually a preview of Chapter 12 and uses the `FileSystemObject` I mentioned earlier.

Listing Files   Listing 5.5 shows a brief sample script that displays the name of each file in the root of the C: drive.

LISTING 5.5   `RootFiles`. Filenames will be displayed in message boxes.

```
Dim oFSO, oFile, oFolder
Set oFSO = CreateObject("Scripting.FileSystemObject")
Set oFolder = oFSO.GetFolder("C:\")
For Each oFile in oFolder.Files
 MsgBox oFile.Name
Next
```

Listing Files—Explained   This script starts with a variable declaration. This might be a new type of declaration for you because it declares three variables on one line. This functionally is the same as three separate `Dim` statements, just a bit shorter.

```
Dim oFSO, oFile, oFolder
' Same as:
' Dim oFSO
' Dim oFile
' Dim oFolder
```

Next, the script uses the `Set` statement and `CreateObject` function to create a reference to the `FileSystemObject`. `CreateObject` requires the class name of the object you want; you'll usually get that class name from the documentation for the object. Note that the `Set` command is required whenever you're assigning an object reference to a variable.

```
Set oFSO = CreateObject("Scripting.FileSystemObject")
Set oFolder = oFSO.GetFolder("C:\")
```

That second line of code uses the `FileSystemObject`'s `GetFolder` method, which is actually a function. It accepts the name of a folder and returns a folder object that represents that folder. In this case, the object is assigned to the variable `oFolder`.

The next three lines of text loop through the folder's `Files` collection, one at a time. For each one, it displays the file's name in a message box.

```
For Each oFile in oFolder.Files
 MsgBox oFile.Name
Next
```

If you want to jump ahead and see what `For Each` is all about, you can find it in Chapter 10.

Summary

You've started learning how VBScript works in this chapter. In fact, you've learned about the three main parts of any script: functions and subroutines (which you now know aren't really that different from one another), objects, and variables.

Variables act as temporary storage areas for your data and allow your scripts to change their behavior and manipulate data. VBScript's built-in functions and statements provide the actual functionality of the language, whereas your own functions and subroutines extend VBScript's power to perform custom tasks.

Finally, objects represent the functionality of the Windows operating system and its many features and capabilities. Objects have properties, which govern their behavior, and methods, which perform actions. Administrative scripting is all about using VBScript functions and statements to tie together operating system objects. For example, you might use a file system object to manipulate files and folders or use the Windows Management Instrumentation (WMI) objects to manipulate the Registry.

The next chapter shows you how VBScript accepts input and displays messages, enabling you to create interactive scripts. Chapters 7 through 9 show you how to manipulate the data that your scripts work with. If you're anxious to start working with objects, jump to Chapter 11, which introduces some of VBScript's own built-in objects.

It's rare to need a script that doesn't involve some form of user interaction. At the very least, you might need to display some kind of completion message as an indication that your script has finished running. Sometimes, you'll need more complex interaction, such as the ability to ask Yes or No questions, get server names and other information, and so forth.

VBScript has very limited interactive capabilities. If you're expecting to create even simple dialog boxes like you've seen Visual Basic programmers do, forget about it: VBScript doesn't provide a dialog builder and doesn't provide any means for programmatically creating dialog boxes. If you need a custom user interface, you need to upgrade to a full-fledged programming environment such as Visual Studio. VBScript's capabilities for interaction are limited to basic choices, simple messages, and one-line text input. However, in an administrative script, that's often all you'll need.

> **NOTE**
>
> The script examples in this chapter aren't full administrative scripts. Instead, I provide snippets that you can easily cut and paste into your own scripts whenever you need to display a message, ask for user input, and so forth.

Displaying Messages

VBScript displays messages using the Windows standard message box, which is a short dialog box that has a few display options to customize its behavior and appearance. VBScript exposes this functionality through the `MsgBox` statement and the `MsgBox()` function.

The MsgBox **Statement and Function**

MsgBox is one of the few VBScript elements that can act as both a statement and a function. As a statement, MsgBox just displays a message box to your specifications. As a function, however, MsgBox can act as a form of user input, allowing simple Yes/No choices that can affect the behavior of your scripts.

The basic MsgBox statement accepts up to three parameters: a message, a numeric value designating which system icons or buttons should be displayed, and a message box title. It looks something like this:

```
MsgBox "The script has finished running.", _
 1, "Notice"
```

This command displays a message box that contains the text "The script has finished running." The message box includes an OK button and a Cancel button, and the title of the box contains "Notice." If you don't care about the title of the message box or the buttons it displays, you can take a shortcut and just include your message, such as the following:

```
MsgBox "The script has finished running." & _
 " Please check the server for the new user accounts."
```

The default message box title is displayed, and the default button configuration—an OK button and a Cancel button with no icon—is displayed.

Your scripts will look cooler, though, if you customize them a bit. For example, you might display an information icon on the message box, which helps cue the user that the message isn't an error or a question, but a simple, informative message. You might also display just an OK button; a Cancel button doesn't really make sense because when the script is done, there's nothing left to cancel.

```
MsgBox "The script has finished running.", _
 64, "Thank you."
```

TIP

When you include a system icon, Windows will play any associated event sounds when your message box is displayed. This feature makes your script seem much more professional and integrated with the operating system.

That middle parameter—the number 64, in this case—controls the icons and buttons that display on the dialog box. Table 6.1 shows the options you have available, along with their corresponding values. You can choose from four classes of options:

TABLE 6.1   MsgBox Display Options

Display	Value	Constant
OK button	0	vbOKOnly
OK and Cancel buttons	1	vbOKCancel
Abort, Retry, Ignore buttons	2	vbAbortRetryIgnore
Yes, No, and Cancel buttons	3	vbYesNoCancel
Yes and No buttons	4	vbYesNo
Retry and Cancel buttons	5	vbRetryCancel
Critical error icon	16	vbCritical
Question mark icon	32	vbQuestion
Exclamation mark icon	48	vbExclamation
Information ("i") icon	64	vbInformation
Make the first button the default	0	vbDefaultButton1
Make the second button the default	256	vbDefaultButton2
Make the third button the default	512	vbDefaultButton3
Make the fourth button the default	768	vbDefaultButton4
Application modal	0	vbApplicationModal
System modal	4096	vbSystemModal

▶ **Buttons**—Composed of values 0 through 5, these control which buttons are displayed on the dialog box. You can only select one from this set.

▶ **Icons**—Values 16 through 64 control the icon that displays. An icon value of 0 displays no icon. You can choose only one of these icon options.

▶ **Defaults**—Consisting of values 0, 256, 512, and 768, these options control which of the displayed buttons will be selected if the user presses Enter, rather than clicking on a button. You can choose only one of these options.

▶ **Modality**—Values 0 or 4096 control how your message box affects the rest of Windows. The default, application modal, means your script stops executing until the user clicks a button on the message box. Choosing system modal displays the message box on top of all other applications, requiring the user to respond before doing anything else on Windows (note that not all versions of Windows support this functionality).

To come up with the appropriate value for the second MsgBox parameter, you just need to add up the values for each class of option that you want to display. For example, to display a message box that has a Yes and No button, a question mark icon, and the No button as the default, you add the values 4, 32, and 256, for a total of 292: MsgBox "Are you sure?", 292, "Delete file" is the VBScript code. Note that the message box is application modal because option value 4096 isn't added in.

You're unlikely to remember all of these numeric values. I certainly never can. Fortunately, VBScript defines several *constants* to represent each value. Just use the constant in place of the value. For example, you can display that same "Are you sure?" dialog box using constants, as follows:

```
MsgBox "Are you sure?", _
 vbYesNo + vbQuestion + vbDefaultButton2 + vbApplicationModal, _
 "Delete file"
```

That's *much* easier to remember with a little practice. My script editor even color-codes these constants a different color, which helps me verify that I've typed them correctly. If I type a constant name and it doesn't color-code into the nice teal color I'm used to, then I know I've typed the name wrong, or used a name that VBScript doesn't recognize.

There's still a problem with this MsgBox statement, though. Remember from Chapter 5, "Functions, Objects, Variables, and More," that statements cannot return a value—only functions can do that. So, how does this script know if the user clicked the Yes or No button? As written, it doesn't. Instead, write the MsgBox as a function and assign the return value to a variable.

```
Dim vResult
vResult = MsgBox("Are you sure?", _
vbYesNo + vbQuestion + vbDefaultButton2 + vbApplicationModal, _
 "Delete file")

If vResult = 7 Then
 'put code here to handle
 'the user saying NO
End If
```

Notice that this example places the MsgBox parameters inside parentheses, like any other function. The result is stored in variable vResult. An If/Then construct examines the contents of vResult and ends the script if the variable contains a 7. The value 7 happens to be what MsgBox() returns if the user clicks the No button.

Fortunately, you don't have to remember that 7, either. VBScript also defines constants for the return values, as shown in Table 6.2.

TABLE 6.2   MsgBox Return Values

User Clicked	Value	Constant
OK	1	vbOK
Cancel	2	vbCancel
Abort	3	vbAbort
Retry	4	vbRetry
Ignore	5	vbIgnore
Yes	6	vbYes
No	7	vbNo

To rewrite the example using the constants:

```
Dim vResult
vResult = MsgBox("Are you sure?", _
vbYesNo + vbQuestion + vbDefaultButton2 + vbApplicationModal, _
 "Delete file")

If vResult = vbNo Then
 'put code here to handle
 'the user saying NO
End If
```

NOTE

If your dialog box displays a Cancel button, you can press the Esc (Escape) key on your keyboard. Doing so is the same as clicking the Cancel button and VBScript will return vbCancel.

You can take one more shortcut. You don't have to first assign the MsgBox() return value to a variable; you can use MsgBox() as part of the If/Then construct's logical evaluation.

```
If MsgBox("Are you sure?", _
vbYesNo + vbQuestion + vbDefaultButton2 + vbApplicationModal, _
 "Delete file") = vbNo Then
End If
```

This is a much more compact piece of script, keeps your script nice and easy to read, and performs the same as the previous, longer example. Note that using constants, rather than values, makes your script a lot easier to read: You can look at this script and see that it'll display a question mark icon and Yes/No buttons and that the script will test to see if the No button was clicked. If you used numeric values, none of that information is readily apparent. However, in sample scripts you find on the Internet and elsewhere, be prepared to look at numeric values because most scripters don't realize that the constants are available to them.

More Complex Messages

MsgBox doesn't limit you to a line or two of text. Try running the following script snippet:

```
MsgBox "This is a warning message. " & _
 vbCrLf & vbCrLf & _
 "You have chosen to delete this user or group " & _
 "from the domain:" & vbCrLf & vbCrLf & _
 vbTab & "JohnDoe" & vbCrLf & vbCrLf & _
 "Are you sure this is what you want to do?", _
 vbYesNo + vbExclamation + vbDefaultButton2, _
 "Delete user"
```

TIP

I'm using a lot of underscore characters in this example to make a very long statement spread across several lines of text. This is a requirement when printing scripts in
a book like this, but you should consider using this technique even in a script editor
such as Notepad or PrimalScript. You'll find that you don't have to do as much horizon-
tal scrolling, making your scripts easier to edit.

You should see something similar to the dialog box shown in Figure 6.1.

FIGURE 6.1   Complex message box.

I've used two powerful VBScript constants in this example: vbCrLf and vbTab. vbCrLf
inserts a carriage return and linefeed character, forcing MsgBox to begin a new line of text.
Putting two vbCrLfs in a row puts a blank line in between, helping to emphasize the
message. vbTab inserts a tab character, indenting the first line of a paragraph. I used it in
this example to make the user account name stand out a bit from the rest of the message.
Using these constants, you can create simply formatted messages that have more impact
and convey more information than a simple line or two of text can.

MsgBox **Best Practices**

You should get into the habit of following Windows user interface conventions when
using MsgBox. To begin, select the appropriate icons for your message boxes, as described
in the following list:

▶ Use the information icon to display nonerror, nonwarning messages that don't
   require a choice, such as a message that the script has finished running.

▶ Use the question mark icon when you're asking for a decision that doesn't have
   potentially devastating consequences. For example, you might use this icon when
   you're asking if the user wants to create a new user home directory in addition to
   the user's domain account.

▶ Use the exclamation mark icon to warn the user of a condition that has occurred
   when the condition won't stop the script from running. For example, if a script tries
   to connect to a server to create a home directory but is unsuccessful, an exclamation
   mark is appropriate if the script continues to create the user's domain account and

perform other tasks. Also, use the exclamation mark when asking the user to make a potentially dangerous choice, such as confirming a user account deletion.

▶ Use the critical icon when the script will stop running because of some condition it encountered.

You should also select buttons that are appropriate to the task. For example, don't ask a Yes/No question and then display Abort, Retry, and Ignore buttons. The buttons don't provide answers that correspond to the question you asked.

Finally, always set the default button to be the least dangerous choice. If you're asking whether to delete a user account, set the No button as the default. That way, if the user accidentally presses Enter without thoroughly reading your warning, nothing bad will occur.

Go Generic with `WScript.Echo`

In Chapter 2, "Running Scripts," I introduced you to WScript and CScript, the Windows and command-line scripting hosts. MsgBox works from within either one, although it always pops up with a graphical message box, even when running under CScript.

If you're writing scripts intended entirely for the command line and CScript, you can use another technique to produce output: WScript.Echo. Despite its name, this command can be used within either graphical WScript or command-line CScript scripts. When used in a WScript script, WScript.Echo displays a graphical message box. When used under CScript, it outputs text to the command line.

> **NOTE**
>
> Echo is actually a method of the built-in WScript object. For more information on objects and methods, you can read Chapter 5. I'll cover more of the built-in scripting objects in Chapter 11, "Built-In Scripting Objects."

WScript.Echo is easy enough to use:

```
WScript.Echo "Hello, world! " & _
"It's nice to see you."
```

Under WScript, you'll see a message box like the one shown in Figure 6.2. Notice that you cannot control the icons, buttons, or title of this message box as you can with the MsgBox statement or function; WScript.Echo is much more simplistic.

Execute the exact same script in CScript and you'll see something similar to Figure 6.3. WScript.Echo doesn't provide any means for collecting input, as the MsgBox() function does; its entire purpose is to display messages. Because it functions in both a graphical and command-line environment, it's ideal for scripts that need to run in either environment. It's also the only easy way to create command-line output for CScript scripts.

FIGURE 6.2   WScript.Echo executed within WScript.exe.

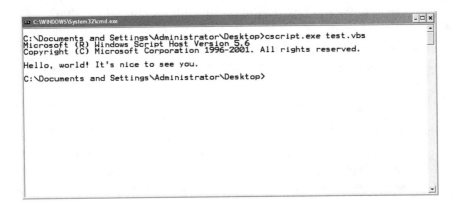

FIGURE 6.3   WScript.Echo executed within CScript.exe.

> **NOTE**
>
> I hate clicking OK buttons so much that I create all of my script output by using
> WScript.Echo. I set CScript.exe to be my default script host, too, by opening a
> command-line window and running CScript //H:CScript. That way, whenever I run a
> script, its WScript.Echo output shows up at the command line, and I don't have any
> OK buttons to click.

Asking for Input

Although the MsgBox() function provides a way to collect simple Yes/No style input, you
might need to collect more complex input, such as server names, usernames, or other
data. VBScript provides a way for users to input this type of string information.

Graphical Input

The InputBox() function displays a graphical input box with a title, a short message, a
one-line text input box, and an OK and Cancel button. Whatever the user types is
returned as the result of the function; if the user clicks Cancel or presses Esc on his
keyboard, the function returns -1. Figure 6.4 shows what this quick sample looks like.

```
Dim vInput
vInput = InputBox("Enter a server name","Server")
MsgBox "You entered " & vInput
```

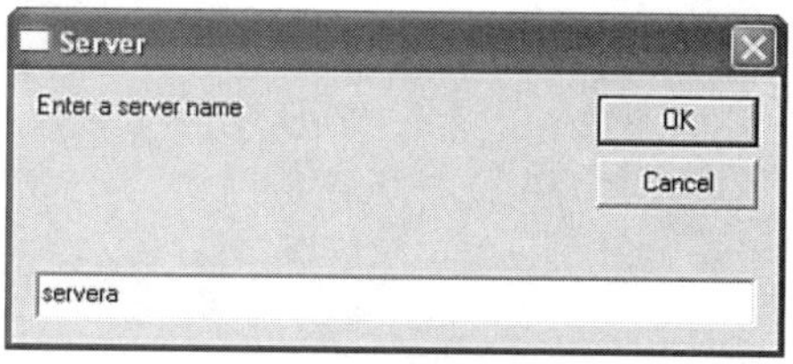

FIGURE 6.4   Collecting text input by using `InputBox()`.

You should always test to see if the user clicked Cancel or pressed Esc:

```
Dim vInput
vInput = InputBox("Enter a server name","Server")
If vInput = -1 Or vInput = "" Then
 MsgBox "You canceled."
Else
 MsgBox "You entered " & vInput
End If
```

This type of check prevents your script from trying, for example, to connect to a server named \\-1 when the user cancels the input box.

You can expand `InputBox()` slightly to provide a default entry. Users can accept your default by simply clicking OK or pressing Enter when the input box is displayed, or they can type their own input instead of your default. Here's how:

```
Dim vInput, vDefault
vDefault = "\\ServerA"
vInput = InputBox("Enter a server name","Server",vDefault)
If vInput = -1 Then
 MsgBox "You canceled."
ElseIf vInput = vDefault Then
 MsgBox "You selected the default, ServerA."
Else
 MsgBox "You entered " & vInput
End If
```

Your default entry simply becomes the third parameter of the `InputBox()` function. It is shown in the input box and selected, allowing users to simply start typing if they want to enter their own input rather than accept your default.

Command-Line Input

Asking for input from a command-line script is a bit more complex. Unfortunately, there's no command-line version of the `InputBox()` function to make things simple. Instead, you have to deal with something called `StdIn`, which is the system's standard input stream, representing text typed by the user. For example:

```
WScript.Echo "Type something, and then press Enter, to continue."
Dim vInput
vInput = ""
Do While Not WScript.StdIn.AtEndOfLine
 Input = Input & WScript.StdIn.Read(1)
Loop
WScript.Echo "You typed " & Input
```

This script collects one character at a time from StdIn until the user presses Enter. At that point, StdIn's AtEndOfLine property is set to True, and the loop terminates. Note that this script *only* works under CScript; WScript doesn't supply access to StdIn when you're running a graphical environment script. Figure 6.5 shows what this example looks like from the command line. If you try to run this script from within WScript, you'll receive an error message on the fourth line of code saying, "The handle is invalid."

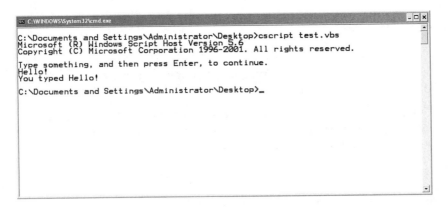

FIGURE 6.5   Collecting text input from the command line.

If you want to learn more about StdIn and command-line text input, refer to the Windows Script Host documentation at http://msdn.microsoft.com/scripting.

Command-Line Parameters as Input

Many of the administrative utilities you use every day are command-line utilities, such as ipconfig, ping, and tracert. These utilities can all perform different tasks, or different variations of a task, through the use of command-line parameters. For example, ipconfig /all displays IP configuration settings, whereas ipconfig /renew refreshes your computer's DHCP address. You also can write scripts that accept command-line parameters, giving you the ability to create flexible command-line utilities of your own.

> **NOTE**
>
> Command-line scripts usually execute under CScript.exe, giving them the capability to produce command-line output. Keep in mind that you'll need to use WScript.Echo rather than MsgBox to produce the command-line output.

Running Command-Line Scripts

Because none of the script file extensions—.vbs, .vb, .scr, and so forth—are recognized as executable by the Windows command-line processor, you'll need to execute CScript.exe directly. Tell CScript which script file you want to execute, and then tack on any of the script's command-line parameters, followed by any CScript parameters. For example:

```
Cscript.exe MyScript.vbs /option:yes /value:4 //B
```

This executes the VBScript MyScript.vbs, passing it a parameter named option and one named value, and telling CScript to suppress any script error messages (see the sidebar, "Power CScript.exe," later in this chapter for more on CScript parameters).

Parsing Parameters

The scripting engine includes a built-in parameter-parsing object named WshNamed, which is designed to help your script accept named command-line parameters. Note that this object is also available to graphical scripts executing under WScript, although it's less common to see those scripts using command-line parameters. WshNamed is part of the WshArguments object, which provides top-level access to all command-line arguments passed to the script. I introduced you to objects in VBScript in Chapter 5.

Suppose you're writing a script that will display basic information about a remote computer. You want the script to accept a command-line parameter named Computer that will provide the computer name to check. You'll execute the script with something like the following:

```
Cscript.exe GetInfo.vbs /computer:server1
```

You want the script to run from the command line, so you'll display the output by using WScript.Echo instead of the MsgBox statement.

Getting Remote Machine Information   Listing 6.1 shows what your script might look like.

LISTING 6.1   *GetInfo.vbs*. This script will retrieve basic information about a remote computer.

```
'Create an arguments object
Dim oArgs
Set oArgs = WScript.Arguments

'Get the named arguments
Dim oNamed
Set oNamed = oArgs.Named

'Get the computer name argument
Dim sComputer
```

LISTING 6.1   Continued

```
sComputer = oNamed("computer")

'Connect to the remote computer by using WMI
Dim oSystem
Set oSystem = GetObject("winmgmts:{impersonationLevel=" & _
  "impersonate}!//" & sComputer & "/root/cimv2:" & _
  "Win32_ComputerSystem='" & sComputer & "'")

'Display information
WScript.Echo oSystem.Caption
WScript.Echo oSystem.PrimaryOwnerName
WScript.Echo oSystem.Domain
WScript.Echo oSystem.SystemType
```

Because this script uses a command-line parameter, or argument, to figure out which computer to connect to, you shouldn't have to make any changes to use it in your environment.

Getting Remote Machine Information—Explained   The script starts by getting a reference to the built-in Arguments object. Notice that you don't need to use CreateObject for this because the object is always loaded when the scripting engine is running.

```
'Create an arguments object
Dim oArgs
Set oArgs = WScript.Arguments
```

Next, the script gets the Named object, which is an array of named command-line parameters.

```
'Get the named arguments
Dim oNamed
Set oNamed = oArgs.Named
```

With access to the Named object, the script can retrieve the value assigned to the "Computer" named argument. This value is stored in a variable named sComputer.

```
'Get the computer named argument
Dim sComputer
sComputer = oNamed("computer")
```

Now, the script uses Windows Management Instrumentation (WMI) to connect to the designated computer.

```
'Connect to the remote computer by using WMI
Dim oSystem
Set oSystem = GetObject("winmgmts:{impersonationLevel=" & _
```

```
"impersonate}!//" & sComputer & "/root/cimv2:" & _
"Win32_ComputerSystem='" & sComputer & "'")
```

To find more information on scripting with WMI, start with Chapter 17, "Understanding WMI." You'll notice a lot of string concatenation here, which can be tricky to read; I cover this in more detail in Chapter 8, "Manipulating Strings." Here, I need a string that reads `Win32_ComputerSystem='computername'`, and that's what the string concatenation is doing for me.

Finally, the script uses the retrieved WMI object to display some information about the computer:

```
'Display information
WScript.Echo oSystem.Caption
WScript.Echo oSystem.PrimaryOwnerName
WScript.Echo oSystem.Domain
WScript.Echo oSystem.SystemType
```

Figure 6.6 shows the type of output you should expect at the command line.

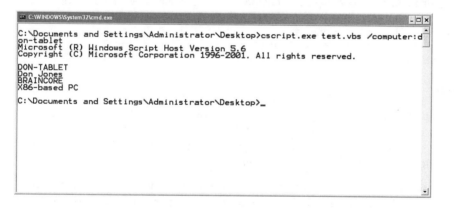

FIGURE 6.6   Running a script with command-line parameters.

Note that I could have chosen not to use the Named object to retrieve the command-line argument in this script. After all, there's only one argument; I could have just as easily used WScript.Arguments(0) to retrieve the first argument. However, I prefer to always use the Named object to access command-line parameters. There are a number of reasons for doing so:

► If an unexpected parameter is included, your script doesn't accidentally mistake it for a legitimate parameter.

► If your script has multiple parameters, accessing them through Named allows the user to include them in any order, as they can with most Windows command-line utilities.

▶ Named parameters are easier to work with when maintaining your script. For example, it's easier to tell what Wscript.Arguments.Named("computer") is doing than to try to figure out what WScript.Arguments(0) stands for.

Power CScript.exe

CScript.exe accepts a number of command-line parameters of its own. To distinguish these from your script's own parameters, CScript's parameters start with two slashes (//) instead of the usual one. You can see a list of available parameters by running CScript from a command line with no parameters or script name; some of the most useful parameters are as follows:

//B—This suppresses script errors and prompts, making your scripts more suitable for use within a batch file or as Task Scheduler jobs.

//H:CScript—This changes the default scripting engine to CScript, so that when you double-click a .vbs file, a command-line window opens and CScript executes the file instead of WScript. //H:WScript puts things back to the default.

//S—This saves your command-line options as the defaults for the current user account.

You can use these and other commands to customize your scripting environment. For example, if you find that most of your scripts are of the command-line variety, set CScript to be the default scripting engine.

Summary

Scripts can be made more general-purpose when they're capable of collecting input and customizing their behavior based upon that input. You can have scripts connect to different servers, create user accounts, delete files, and perform hundreds of other actions when you're able to collect and evaluate user input when the script is run.

Using MsgBox allows you to display messages, even those with some basic formatting. You can also ask for simple Yes/No decisions from the user by using MsgBox() as a function. WScript.Echo provides text-output capabilities that work within a graphical WScript or command-line CScript environment.

InputBox() allows you to collect text input from a graphical script, and you can use WScript.StdIn to collect text input within a command-line script. You can also use script command-line parameters to create scripts that work just like Windows' built-in command-line tools, complete with named parameters that customize the script's behavior.

CHAPTER 7

Manipulating Numbers

Incredibly, I almost became a professional software developer. It's what I wanted to do in high school, and my school even offered a two-year vocational course for programmers. I never pursued it, though, because I'm horrible with higher math. In school, everyone tells you that programmers have to really know their math. That's not true, of course. With VBScript in particular, you'll find that manipulating numeric data and performing even complex calculations is easy. Even better, you probably won't need more than basic math skills for administrative scripting. You won't, for example, run across a lot of trigonometry in administrative scripting, even though VBScript has several functions devoted to cosines and tangents and stuff.

Numbers in VBScript

VBScript considers any unquoted, nondate value to be a number. Issuing the statement MyVariable = 5, for example, assigns the numeric value 5 to the variable MyVariable. The one catch in VBScript is that there are actually different types of numbers.

▶ Any whole number—that is, a number with no decimal portion—is called an *integer*. The numbers 5, -6, 43,233, and -42 are all integers. VBScript integers can be anything from -32,768 to 32,767.

▶ VBScript also supports *long integers,* which are just big integers. They can be anything from -2,147,483,648 to 2,147,483,647.

▶ Numbers with a fractional value can be either *singles* or *doubles*. The only difference between them is how large they can be. A single can be any numeric value from -3.4028235E+38 to -1.401298E-45, or from 3.4028235E+38 to 1.3401298E-45 (in other words, a really big number). Sometimes, however, you might need an even larger number, which is where doubles come in. A double can be truly huge—as big as 1.79769313486231570E+308. I have no idea what you'd call a number like that other than humongous, and I've certainly never used one in a script.

▶ VBScript also supports a *currency* number type. This has a maximum precision of four decimal places and has the added capability to properly recognize and format currencies based on the system's locale settings. That means you can properly display thousandths separators and decimal places according to the system configuration.

Now, as I mentioned in Chapter 5, "Functions, Objects, Variables, and More," you don't usually have to worry much about these different types of numbers because VBScript does it for you. Variables in VBScript can hold any kind of data; if you try to put the number 64,555 into a variable, VBScript will just invisibly make the variable into a long integer. If you add .3 to it, VBScript will convert it into a single. The only time you'll need to worry about data types is if you want to perform some specialized function, such as a currency operation, and then you'll need to explicitly convert the variable into the appropriate type—something I'll cover later in this chapter.

Basic Arithmetic

You use VBScript's mathematical *operators* for most basic math. VBScript's operators should look pretty familiar and self-explanatory:

▶ Addition—+

▶ Subtraction—-

▶ Multiplication—*

▶ Division—/

▶ Order of evaluation—( )

▶ Exponentiation—^ (usually located on the six key on your keyboard)

Normally, you just assign the results of such an operation to a variable or a statement like MsgBox, as in the following examples:

```
myVar = 1 + 2
MsgBox myVar
myVar = myVar + (myVar * .03)
MsgBox myVar
myVar = myVar^2
MsgBox myVar
```

VBScript evaluates expressions from left to right, performing exponentiation first, then multiplication and division, then addition and subtraction. Anything in parentheses is evaluated first, starting at the innermost level of nested parentheses. To put that in context, consider these similar-looking expressions, which all generate a different result because of the order of evaluation.

```
myVar = 1 * 2 + 1
MsgBox myVar
myVar = 1 + 1 * 2
MsgBox myVar
myVar = (1 + 1) * 2
MsgBox myVar
myVar = (1 + (1 * 2))
MsgBox myVar
```

You might be wondering why all this math stuff should be important to you. After all, you're trying to administer services, not launch space shuttles. You might not use *lots* of math in your scripts, but you're likely to use some. For example, you might need to convert bytes to megabytes to make an output message more meaningful, or you might want to write a quick function that generates unique passwords for users. You could use a password-generating function when creating new user accounts or when resetting user accounts. Listing 7.1 shows what the function might look like.

Making Up a Password   You can include this function in another script, and then call it. This function takes a username or another unique string and generates a unique password to go with it. The password generated is based partially upon the current system time, so it'll be different even for the same user if you use it multiple times.

LISTING 7.1   *MakePW.vbs.* This script is intended to be included within another script.

```
Function MakePW(sUserName)
 Dim vTemp, vPasswd, vLetter, vValue
For vTemp = 1 To Len(sUserName)
  vLetter = Mid(sUserName, vTemp, 1)
  vValue = Asc(vLetter) * vTemp
  vValue = vValue - DatePart("n",Now)
  vPasswd = vPasswd & CStr(vValue)
 Next
 MakePW = Right(vPasswd, 8)
End Function
```

The script can be used as is within your other scripts. You might call it by using a statement like sNewPassword = MakePW("JohnD").

Making Up a Password—Explained   In Chapter 4, "Designing a Script," I introduced the concept of functions and subroutines as a means of modularizing your code. I explained them further in Chapter 5. MakePW is a custom function that encapsulates a certain piece of functionality. It's declared with the initial `Function` statement, and I've followed the function declaration with some variable declarations:

```
Function MakePW(sUserName)
 Dim vTemp, vPasswd, vLetter, vValue
```

Next, I use a `For/Next` loop. It will execute the loop contents once for each letter in the username.

For more details on `For/Next`, skip ahead to Chapter 10, "Controlling the Flow of Execution."

```
For vTemp = 1 To Len(sUserName)

Next
```

Within the loop, several functions are used, including some mathematical operations. First, I use the `Mid()` function to extract the current letter of the user's name. Then, I use the `Asc()` function to convert that letter to its ASCII value (65 for A, 66 for B, and so forth). I multiply the ASCII value by the value of `vTemp`, which helps to obfuscate the password-generation scheme and make more random-looking passwords.

Next, I get the minutes from the system clock by using the `DatePart()` function and contract that from the value. This provides a pseudorandomness to the password. Finally, I convert the value to a string and append it to a variable named `vPasswd`.

```
 vLetter = Mid(sUserName, vTemp, 1)
 vValue = Asc(vLetter) * vTemp
 vValue = vValue - DatePart("n",Now)
 vPasswd = vPasswd & CStr(vValue)
```

Finally, I assign the rightmost eight characters of `vPasswd` to the function's name. This returns the rightmost characters to whatever called the function, completing the function's task.

```
 MakePW = Right(vPasswd, 8)
End Function
```

This isn't the most amazing password ever created, and it's all numbers with no letters or symbols, but it provides a useful example of how math functions can be used within an administrative script.

Advanced Arithmetic

If you're getting heavy-duty with the math in a script, you might need to take advantage of some of VBScript's advanced math functions, such as the following:

▶ `Atn()`—Arctangent

▶ `Cos()`—Cosine

- ▶ Sin()—Sine

- ▶ Tan()—Tangent

- ▶ Log()—Logarithm

- ▶ Sqr()—Square root

- ▶ Exp()—Returns *e* (the base of natural logarithm) raised to a power

- ▶ Randomize—Randomizes the system's random number generator

- ▶ Rnd()—Generates a random number

This random number business in particular deserves some explanation because you might think that'd be a much better way to come up with values for a password. It can be, provided you thoroughly understand how randomness works inside a computer.

First, never forget that computers are giant calculating devices. There's nothing remotely random about anything that goes on inside a computer. As a result, no computer can generate a truly random number without special hardware that's designed to do so (one technique involves a piece of hardware that generates numbers based on radio-frequency noise—so when I say *special hardware*, I really mean it).

The Rnd() function returns a value less than 1, but greater than or equal to zero. You can pass a parameter to Rnd() to control its behavior.

- ▶ A number less than zero, such as Rnd(-2), will return the exact same number every time, using the number you supply as the seed. This isn't random at all.

- ▶ A number greater than zero, such as Rnd(2), will return the next "random" number in the computer's sequence. That's right, *sequence*. The computer uses a fixed algorithm for producing random numbers, and using this technique it'll return the same sequence of "random" numbers every time.

- ▶ Zero, or Rnd(0), will return the most recently generated random number again and again.

VBScript's random number generator uses a *seed* as its initial value, and then calculates pseudorandom numbers from there. Given the same seed, VBScript will always calculate the same sequence of random numbers every time because they're not random: They're derived from a mathematical formula.

That's where Randomize comes in. This statement seeds the random-number generator, either with a number you supply—guaranteeing a repeatable sequence of "random" numbers—or with a value from the system's timer. Because the system timer has a millisecond resolution, the odds are good that you'll get a unique "random number" sequence every time.

For example, try the following short script:

```
Randomize 5
For t = 1 to 10
 MsgBox Int((6 * Rnd()) + 1)
Next
```

Run this script on a couple of different computers a couple of different times, and you'll likely get the exact same results every time. Not exactly random, is it? Now, try this modified script:

```
Randomize Timer
For t = 1 to 10
 MsgBox Int((6 * Rnd()) + 1)
Next
```

The difference here is that the generator is seeded from the system timer, which virtually guarantees unique—if not necessarily random—results. Using the timer generally creates "random enough" sequences of numbers.

Making a Better Password   Listing 7.2 revises the password-generating function to generate random sequences of uppercase letters.

LISTING 7.2   *MakePW.vbs*. Revised example uses `Rnd()` and `Randomize` for better-looking passwords.

```
Function MakePW()
 Dim vPasswd, vTemp, vValue
 Randomize
 For vTemp = 1 to 8
  vValue = Int((26 * Rnd()) + 65)
  vPasswd = vPasswd & Chr(vValue)
 Next
 MakePW = vPasswd
End Function
```

This example generates a pseudorandom, eight-character password composed of uppercase letters.

Making a Better Password—Explained   This example begins much like the previous one, with function and variable declarations:

```
Function MakePW()
 Dim vPasswd, vTemp, vValue
```

The `Randomize` statement seeds the generator from the system timer, and then begins a `For/Next` loop that will run eight times.

```
Randomize
For vTemp = 1 to 8
```

First, I calculate a random value from 65 to 91. These are the ASCII values for uppercase A through Z. Remember that the Rnd() function returns a fractional number from zero to less than one; I'm multiplying that by 26, which will give me a result between 0 and 25. I'm adding 65 to the result to get the result in the 65 to 91 range. Finally, I'm using the Int() function to convert the result to a whole number by truncating the decimal portion.

Last, I convert the numeric value to the appropriate ASCII character and append it to the password I'm building.

```
vValue = Int((26 * Rnd()) + 65)
vPasswd = vPasswd & Chr(vValue)
```

Finally, I wrap up the loop and end the function:

```
Next
 MakePW = vPasswd
End Function
```

There you have it: a "random enough" password.

Boolean Math

Boolean math is a special kind of logical math. If you know how to subnet TCP/IP addresses, you already know Boolean math, although you might not realize it. First, here are the basic Boolean operators that VBScript supports:

▶ NOT—Reverses a value from 0 to 1 (or False to True) or vice versa

▶ AND—Returns a True if both values are True

▶ OR—Returns a True if either value is True

▶ XOR—Returns a True if one, but not both, values are True

In VBScript, the value zero represents False; all other values represent True. Internally, VBScript generally uses -1 to represent True. To demonstrate Boolean math, try the following examples:

```
'Not
MsgBox NOT True
MsgBox NOT False

'And
MsgBox True AND False
MsgBox True AND True
```

```
'Or
MsgBox True OR False
MsgBox True OR True

'Xor
MsgBox True XOR False
MsgBox True XOR True
```

You should get the following results in message boxes:

- `False` (the opposite of `True`)

- `True` (the opposite of `False`)

- `False` (both values aren't `True`)

- `True` (both values are `True`)

- `True` (at least one value is `True`)

- `True` (at least one value is `True`)

- `True` (only one value is `True`)

- `False` (both values are `True`)

You'll primarily deal with Boolean math like this in the form of setting flags. For example, Windows domains (Active Directory and NT) store a user flags value, which controls several things, like whether the user account is locked out, expired, disabled, and so forth. The flags are stored as a single byte of information, and each bit in the flag has a different meaning. For example:

- Bit 1, with a value of 1, indicates if the account is locked out.

- Bit 2, with a value of 2, indicates if the account has expired.

- Bit 3, with a value of 4, indicates if the account is disabled.

- Bit 4, with a value of 8, indicates if the password needs to be changed.

- Bit 5, with a value of 16, indicates if the user can change his password.

All bytes have 8 bits, and all bits have a value. In the number 5, for example, bits 1 and 3 are turned on. Their combined values (1 + 4) create the value of 5. To figure that out, here are the values for the 8 bits in a byte:

- Bit 1, value 1

- Bit 2, value 2

- Bit 3, value 4

- Bit 4, value 8

- ► Bit 5, value 16

- ► Bit 6, value 32

- ► Bit 7, value 64

- ► Bit 8, value 128

Thus, a single byte can have a maximum value of 255 because that's the value of all the bits, added up. To make a byte equal to the value 5, you set bits 1 and 3 to be "on"; their values add up to 5. The others bits' values don't add in because they're set to "off." In binary, the value 5 is written as 00000101: That's 8 bits, with the first and third set to "on," or "1," and the other bits set to "off," or "0." You noticed, of course, that the bits are "read" from right to left: The first bit is last, and you work backward from there. Windows Calculator, in Scientific mode, can actually convert from our familiar decimal numbers to binary: Punch in 5 and convert to binary and you'll get 101, because Calculator only displays enough bits to come up with the specified value; the other five bits are assumed to be zero because they aren't displayed.

To test to see if a bit is on or not, you can use the AND operator:

```
'Assume variable vFlag has a flag byte in it
If vFlag AND 1 Then
 MsgBox "Account locked out"
End If

If vFlag AND 2 Then
 MsgBox "Account expired"
End If

If vFlag AND 4 Then
 MsgBox "Account disabled"
End If

If vFlag AND 8 Then
 MsgBox "User must change pw"
End If

If vFlag AND 16 Then
 MsgBox "User cannot change pw"
End If
```

To set these values yourself, you would use the OR operator:

```
'Assume variable vFlag already has a flag byte in it
```

```
'Turn on account disabled
vFlag = vFlag OR 4

'Force password change
vFlag = vFlag OR 8
```

You'll use this type of math a lot when dealing with ADSI. I introduce ADSI in Chapter 14, "Working with ADSI Providers," and start working with user accounts in Chapter 16, "Manipulating Users and Groups." If this business of using Boolean operators to set values seems confusing, you're right; it is. Consider the OR operator, which is the one you'll use the most to set values.

Imagine that vFlag in the preceding example starts out with a value of 0. If you were to expand that out into binary, you'd get 8 bits, all set to zero.

```
00000000
```

Using the code vFlag = vFlag OR 4 tries to combine whatever is in vFlag and the number 4. The number 4, written in binary, looks like this:

```
00000100
```

The first zero in that chain represents the value 128, the second represents 64, then 32, then 16, then 8, then 4, then 2, and then 1. So, the bit representing 4 is set to one, making the total value of the byte 4.

The OR operator compares all the bits in vFlag with all the bits in 4.

```
00000000
00000100
```

OR always accepts two values and returns a 1 whenever either value contains a 1. So OR's output in this case would be

```
00000100
```

which means it simply returned a bit set to 1 whenever it encountered a 1 in either of the input values. Translating that to decimal, the result of 0 OR 4 is 4.

TIP

You can use Windows Calculator in Scientific mode to convert decimal numbers to binary—definitely a quicker way to do the conversion than doing it manually!

Following the example along, vFlag will now contain 4. The second operation is vFlag = vFlag OR 8. Let's convert both vFlag and 8 to binary to see how the OR operator will handle them.

```
00000100
00001000
```

That's vFlag—which currently contains 4—on the top, and 8 on the bottom. OR will return a 1 whenever it encounters a 1 in *either* input, so the output will be

```
00001100
```

Windows Calculator tells me that that converts to 12 in decimal, so vFlag will now contain the value 12. But it's not really the number 12 that's important. In this case, vFlag is being used to represent user account settings, so each bit is really a little switch. The first switch, when turned on, disables the account. The second requires the user to change his password. By using the OR operator, you can flip each switch independently.

What if you want to turn a switch off, reenabling a user account? Use the AND operator. Suppose that vFlag contains 12.

```
00001100
```

You want to flip off the switch that's represented by the value 4. You can't use OR because OR can only turn bits on. Instead, you use AND: vFlag = vFlag AND 8. That's because AND will return a 1 only when both inputs are set to 1. If either input is set to 0, AND will return 0. Breaking down 8 into binary reveals the following:

```
11111011
```

Notice that the bit representing the value 4 is set to 0. So when AND compares vFlag and 251, you get the following:

```
00001100
11111011
```

Only one bit has a mismatch between the two, so the output will be

```
00001000
```

thus turning off the switch representing account disabled.

> **NOTE**
>
> These Boolean operators also play a role in logical comparisons. For example, If v = 1 OR v = 2 is a comparison that will result in True if variable v contains either 1 or 2. Similarly, the comparison If v=1 And v = 2 would never be true, because v cannot contain both 1 and 2 at the same time.

Now that I've walked you through that little exercise, you should know that in *most cases* you'll never have to be able to figure this stuff out yourself. You'll be able to rely on existing examples to determine if a particular bit means that a user's account is disabled.

However, it's useful to be *able* to do this Boolean math if you need to troubleshoot something, so you can always refer back to this section for a brief refresher.

Converting Numeric Data Types

As I mentioned earlier, VBScript happily converts data types for you when necessary. This process is called *coercion,* and it happens entirely behind the scenes as needed. There are times, however, when you want VBScript to handle data in a particular fashion. In those cases, you'll need to explicitly convert the data type.

For example, in Listing 7.2, you saw how I used the Rnd() function to generate a pseudo-random number. This number is a fraction, but I wanted a whole number, and so I used the Int() function to convert it to an integer. Other numeric conversion functions include the following:

▶ Abs(): Returns the absolute value of a number, removing the positive or negative

▶ CBool(): Converts a value to either True or False

▶ CCur(): Converts a value to Currency

▶ CDbl(): Converts a value to a Double

▶ CSng(): Converts a value to a Single

▶ CInt() and Int(): Converts a value to an integer

▶ CLng(): Converts a value to a long integer

You'll often use these functions to convert user input to a specific data type. For example, if you have an input box that accepts the number of servers to shut down, you want to make sure that's a whole number, and not some fractional number because a fraction wouldn't make sense. You might use something like this:

```
Dim vInput
vInput = InputBox("Shut down how many servers?")
If CInt(vInput) = vInput Then
 'Shut them down
Else
 MsgBox "You didn't type a whole number."
End If
```

In this case, I used CInt() to force vInput to be an integer, and then compared the result to the original value in vInput. If the two are the same, the original input is an integer and the script continues. If not, the script displays an error message and ends.

> **TIP**
>
> *Never* assume that some piece of data is a particular type. If the operation you are performing demands a specific type of data, you should explicitly convert your data to the proper type first. Doing so will help prevent runtime errors when unexpected conditions occur.

Converting Other Data Types to Numeric Data

You can also convert some nonnumeric data into numeric data. For example, suppose you have the following in a script:

```
Dim vValue
vValue = InputBox("Enter a number of servers")
```

At this point, you've no idea what vValue contains. You can try to convert it to a number, though. Consider the following examples:

▶ If vValue contains "5 servers," CInt(vValue) would return 5 because the character 5 can be interpreted as an integer.

▶ If vValue contains "five," CInt(vValue) would return 0 because there are no numbers that can be converted to an integer.

▶ If vValue contains "5.2 servers," CInt(vValue) would return 5 because 5.2 can be interpreted as a number and the integer portion of that number is 5.

You can use any of the numeric conversion functions I've already covered to convert nonnumeric data into numeric data. If vValue contains "five or 6 servers," CInt(vValue) would return 0 because the first characters cannot be interpreted as a number.

Summary

VBScript's numeric and mathematical functions can be useful in a variety of situations. You can use basic math operators to perform simple math, and more advanced functions are available for complex geometric and algebraic operations. Boolean math plays a key role in logical comparisons, and VBScript provides a number of functions to convert numeric data into specific forms. You can also convert nonnumeric data, such as strings, to numeric data to work with it.

CHAPTER **8**

Manipulating Strings

Computer names, group names, usernames, queries—strings are all around us in the world of administrative scripting. Learning to manipulate those strings is a key skill. You'll find yourself building file paths, working with server *names*, creating Windows Management Instrumentation (WMI) queries, and much more. In fact, string manipulation is such a fundamental VBScript skill that you'll need to master it to some degree before you can start writing effective scripts.

Strings in VBScript

As you learned in Chapter 5, "Functions, Objects, Variables, and More," VBScript can store any type of data in a variable. *String data* is anything VBScript cannot interpret as another data type, such as a number or a date. Strings are simply any combination of letters, numbers, spaces, symbols, punctuation, and so forth. Often, VBScript might interpret data as different types. For example, 5/7/2003 could be treated as a date or as a string because it qualifies as both. In those instances, VBScript will *coerce* the data into one type or the other, depending on what you're trying to do with the data. Coercion is an important concept, especially when dealing with strings. For more information, refer to Chapter 5.

In your scripts, you'll always include strings within double quotation marks, which is how you let VBScript know to treat data as a string. For example, all of the following are acceptable ways to assign string data to a variable:

```
Var = "Hello"
Var = """Hello"""
Var = "Hello, there"
Var = vSomeOtherStringVariable
```

The second example is worth special attention. Notice that *three* sets of double quotes were used: This method will cause the variable Var to contain a seven-character string that begins and ends with quotes. Use this technique of doubling-up on quote marks whenever you need to assign the quote character itself as a part of the string. Here's how it works: At the beginning, a single double-quotation mark indicates the beginning of a string. Normally, the next double-quotation mark would indicate the *end* of a string. However, because VBScript sees *two* double-quotation marks together, it knows I'm not trying to end a string, but rather include a literal double-quotation mark character. The reverse applies at the end of the string: VBScript knows we're "in" a string, still, and so two double-quotation marks are interpreted as a single literal character. The remaining "leftover" double-quotation actually closes the string.

An easier way, perhaps, to remember this rule is that whenever you want to open or close a string, you type *one* double-quotation mark. When you actually need to include a double-quotation mark character inside a string, type two of them.

VBScript refers to any portion of a string as a *substring*. Given the string Hello, one possible substring would be ell and another would be ello. The substring ello has its own substrings, including llo and ell. VBScript provides a number of functions for working with substrings. For example, you might write a script that accepts a computer name. The user might type just the name, such as Server1, or he might include a UNC-style name, such as \\Server1. Using VBScript's substring functions, you can get just the substring you want.

A large number of VBScript's intrinsic functions are devoted to string manipulation, and I'll cover most of them in this chapter. As a quick reference, here's each one, in alphabetical order, along with a quick description of what each does:

- ▶ Asc()—Returns the ASCII code for any single character.

- ▶ Chr()—Given an ASCII code, returns the corresponding character.

- ▶ CStr()—Converts a variable to a string.

- ▶ Escape()—Encodes a string for proper transmission as part of an Internet uniform resource locator (URL), so that strings such as "Hello world" become "Hello%20world."

- ▶ FormatCurrency()—Accepts a currency value and returns a properly formatted string. For example, formats 45.67 as $45.67.

- ▶ FormatDateTime()—Returns a properly formatted date or time string. For example, formats 4/5/2003 as April 5, 2003.

- ▶ FormatNumber()—Returns a formatted number. For example, formats 1055774 as 1,055,774.00.

- ▶ FormatPercent()—Returns a formatted percentage. For example, formats .67 as 67%.

- ▶ InStr()—Returns the position at which a specified substring can be found within a specified string.

- ▶ InStrRev()—Same as InStr(), but starts its search at the end of the specified string rather than at the beginning.

- ▶ LCase()—Returns a string converted to lowercase.

- ▶ Left()—Returns the specified leftmost characters of a specified string.

- ▶ Len()—Returns the length of a string.

- ▶ LTrim()—Trims spaces from the left end of a string.

- ▶ Mid()—Returns a substring from a specified string, starting with the specified beginning character and continuing for the specified length.

- ▶ Replace()—Replaces all instances of the specified substring with the specified replacement substring.

- ▶ Right()—Returns the specified rightmost characters of a specified string.

- ▶ RTrim()—Trims spaces from the right end of a string.

- ▶ Space()—Returns a string containing the specified number of spaces.

- ▶ StrComp()—Compares two strings and returns an appropriate value.

- ▶ StrReverse()—Reverses the specified string's characters, so that "Hello" becomes "olleH."

- ▶ Trim()—Trims spaces from both ends of a string.

- ▶ UCase()—Returns a string with all characters converted to uppercase.

- ▶ Unescape()—Decodes a string encoded with the Escape() function.

You should realize that none of these functions change the contents of a string variable. For example, Var1 = Trim(Var2) does not change the contents of Var2. Instead, it trims all spaces from the left and right ends of Var2's contents, and assigns the result to Var1. If you want to change the contents of a variable, you can use something like Var1 = Trim(Var1). Internally, VBScript creates a new string to hold the result of the Trim() function, and then assigns that result back to the Var1 variable. This behind-the-scenes assignment is what actually changes the contents of Var1, not the Trim() function.

Working with Substrings

String manipulation is often valuable when dealing with user input. For example, suppose you have a script that will work with a server, and you want the user to enter the server name in an input box. You might start with something like this:

```
Function GetServer()
 Dim sServer
```

8

```
sServer = InputBox("Work with what server?")
GetServer = sServer
End Function
```

> **NOTE**
>
> There doesn't seem much point in making this a special function at present, but bear with me. By the way, don't bother typing in these scriptlets yet—I'll be building on this example throughout the chapter. For now, just read along.

The problem is that the user could type nearly anything. If this is a script that only you will be using, you can probably be sloppy and leave it as is, knowing that you'll always type the right thing. However, if a junior administrator or technician will use the script, you should program some intelligence into it.

As an example, suppose the administrator typed a UNC-style name, such as \\Server1. If your script is expecting a simple name like Server1, the extra characters could cause problems. You can build your function to manipulate the string.

```
Function GetServer()
 Dim sServer
 sServer = InputBox("Work with what server?")

 'trim backslashes
 Do While Left(sServer,1) = "\"
  sServer = Right(sServer, Len(sServer) - 1)
 Loop

 'return result
 GetServer = sServer
End Function
```

In this new example, a Do/Loop construct is used to examine the leftmost character of sServer. As long as the leftmost character is a backslash, the loop will set sServer equal to sServer's rightmost characters. This is done with the Right() function, which accepts sServer as its input string, and then accepts the current length of sServer (via the Len() function), minus one, as the number of characters to pull. The result is that all but the leftmost character—which is known to be a backslash at this point—is saved. The loop repeats until the leftmost character is no longer a backslash.

I haven't covered Do/Loop yet, but if you want to read up on it quickly, skip ahead to Chapter 10, "Controlling the Flow of Execution."

Suppose your company's server-naming convention always starts with a few letters, then a hyphen, and then finishes up with numbers. Perhaps the letters indicate which office the server is located in, and you want to pull that information out so that a user account (or something else) can be created in the appropriate Active Directory organizational unit (OU). No problem.

```
Function GetOffice(sServerName)

 'find the hyphen
 Dim iHyphen
 iHyphen = InStr(1, sServerName, "-")

 'get just the part before the hyphen
 Dim sOffice
 sOffice = Left(sServerName, iHyphen - 1)

 'return result
 GetOffice = sOffice
End Function
```

In this function, I've used the InStr() function to locate the first occurrence of a hyphen within sServerName. Suppose the server name in this case is PHL-77432; the hyphen is at location 4, so variable iHyphen will now contain a 4.

Next, I used Left() to grab the leftmost characters before the hyphen. In this case, I only want the leftmost three characters, so the Left() function is asked to return iHyphen - 1, which in this example evaluates to the leftmost three characters.

Notice the 1, the first input parameter to InStr(). That tells InStr() to start searching at the first character of sServerName. Suppose your server names look something like WIN-7745-PHL and you want to get the office code (PHL). In that case, you need to find the first hyphen, and then start looking *after* it for the second hyphen.

```
Function GetOffice(sServerName)

 'find the first hyphen
 Dim iHyphen1
 iHyphen1 = InStr(1, sServerName, "-")

 'find the second hyphen
 Dim iHyphen2
 iHyphen2 = InStr(iHyphen1, sServerName, "-")

 'get just the part after the 2nd hyphen
 Dim sOffice
 sOffice = Right(sServerName, Len(sServerName) - iHyphen2)

 'return result
 GetOffice = sOffice
End Function
```

First, this script locates the first hyphen by having InStr() start at the beginning of sServerName. Then, the script locates the second hyphen by having InStr() start at the *location after the first hyphen*. Finally, the script uses the Right() function to get everything after the second hyphen. This is done by taking the length of sServerName (which is 12 in this example) and subtracting the character location of the second hyphen (which is 9), giving us the rightmost three characters we want.

You could do this same task with a bit less code by using InStrRev().

```
Function GetOffice(sServerName)

'find the second hyphen
 Dim iHyphen2
 iHyphen2 = InStrRev(sServerName, "-")

 'get just the part after the 2nd hyphen
 Dim sOffice
 sOffice = Right(sServerName, Len(sServerName) - iHyphen2)submit.x:
 41submit.y: 8

 'return result
 GetOffice = sOffice
End Function
```

In this example, InStrRev() would return 4 because the second hyphen is four characters from the end of WIN-7745-PHL. The Right() function is told to subtract one from that value, giving us the rightmost three characters we want.

> **TIP**
>
> Playing with substrings and the associated calculations can be a bit of fun, like working out a puzzle. I find it's often easier to think of a sample string and write it down on paper in large letters. I then number each letter with its character position. Doing so makes it easier to work out the math of the Left(), Right(), InStr(), and InStrRev() functions.

But wait, there's one more substring function! Mid() makes it possible to pull substrings from the middle of other strings. For example, suppose you need to pull the second three characters from a string such as "492NYCFILES." You could use Left() to get the leftmost three characters, and then use Right() to get the rightmost three characters from that. Or, you could just use Mid("492NYCFILES",4,3) to start at the fourth character and pull three characters. If all of your server names were formatted that way, you might rewrite the GetOffice() function as follows:

```
Function GetOffice(sServerName)
 Dim sOffice
 sOffice = Mid(sServerName, 4, 3)
```

```
 GetOffice = sOffice
End Function
```

Concatenating Strings

You've already learned about string concatenation, but let's look at it again. It's a *very* important technique that you'll use repeatedly in your scripts.

For example, suppose you need to display a long, complicated message inside a message box. You could write a single MsgBox statement on a *very* long line of code, but that's harder to do and will make it tougher to maintain the script in the future. Instead, it's often easier to use string concatenation and line-continuation characters.

```
Dim sMessage
sMessage = "The server name you typed is invalid." & _
 vbCrLf & _
 vbCrLf & "Remember that all server names must " & _
 " be seven characters " & _
 "long. The first three characters " & _
 "must be the server's internal " & _
 "serial number. The second three characters " & _
 "must be the three-" & _
 "character code for the office in which the " & _
 "server is located. " & _
 "Finally, the last four characters indicate " & _
 "the server's function:" & _
 vbCrLf & vbCrLf & "FILE = File Server" & _
 vbCrLf & vbCrLf & _
 "DOMC = Domain Controller" & vbCrLf & vbCrLf & _
 "SQLS = SQL Server" & vbCrLf & vbCrLf & _
 "Please try again."
MsgBox sMessage
```

I can't even show you the alternative in this book—there's no way for me to spread a single line of code across multiple pages!

String concatenation is also useful when you're working with variables. For example, suppose you need to generate some kind of unique password for new users. The following function might be used in a script that creates new user accounts:

```
Function MakePassword(sUserName)
 Dim sPassword
 sPassword = Left(sUserName,1)
 sPassword = sPassword & UCase(Right(sUserName,1))
 sPassword = sPassword & DatePart("n",Now)
 sPassword = sPassword & UCase(Mid(sUserName, 3, 2)
 MakePassword = sPassword
End Function
```

This function uses concatenation—and several other functions—to make up a reasonably complex password that can be assigned to new user accounts. String concatenation is used to append the results from each function to the gradually growing password, with a final password that's about seven characters long. I'll cover the `DatePart()` function in the next chapter, and I'll cover the `UCase()` function in the next section of this chapter.

> **NOTE**
>
> Remember that in Chapter 5 I explained how you could use both & and + for string concatenation. I mention it because you might see sample scripts on the web that use +; because + can also be used for addition, you should never use it for string concatenation. Always use &, which VBScript knows can only be used for concatenation.

I can't stress how important string concatenation is, nor how difficult it can be to read in code. For example, let's assume you need to construct the following string:

```
SELECT * FROM Object WHERE Prop = 'Value'
```

This line of text contains two single quotation marks around a string value. This isn't a line of VBScript code; rather, it's an example of what a database or Windows Management Instrumentation query might look like. These queries use single quotes instead of double quotes around strings. As you'll learn later, you'll usually execute these queries by first placing the query itself into a VBScript string variable, and then passing the variable to a special method that takes care of running the query and obtaining its results. The first step, then, is to get this query inside a string variable.

Simply placing this literal query inside a string variable isn't difficult:

```
var = "SELECT * FROM Object WHERE Prop = 'Value'"
```

By simply enclosing the query inside double quotation marks, the query can be assigned to a VBScript variable. However, in the real world, you'd never pass a query exactly like this. Instead, you'd build the query dynamically. For example, perhaps the object name isn't `Object` at all, but is rather contained in a variable named `strObject`. So you'll need to concatenate that into the query, in place of the literal string "Object." Your VBScript code might now look like this:

```
strObject = "MyObject"
var = "SELECT * FROM " & strObject & " WHERE " & _
  "Prop = 'Value'"
```

Notice that I've maintained the spacing after the `FROM` keyword and before the `WHERE` keyword, and concatenated the `strObject` variable. The variable `var` would now contain this text:

```
SELECT * FROM MyObject WHERE Prop = 'Value'
```

When the assignment to var is made, VBScript looks at the entire line of code. First, "SELECT * FROM " is placed into var because that text is contained inside double quotation marks, meaning it's a literal string. Next, VBScript sees that strObject is being concatenated. strObject is not inside double quotes, so VBScript evaluates it, concatenating not the variable's name, but its contents. Contrast that technique with this incorrect example:

```
strObject = "MyObject"
var = "SELECT * FROM  & strObject &  WHERE " & _
 "Prop = 'Value'"
```

Notice that I've maintained the spacing after the FROM keyword and before the WHERE keyword, and concatenated the strObject variable. The variable var would now contain this text:

```
SELECT * FROM & strObject & WHERE Prop = 'Value'
```

Do you see the difference? This time, strObject was included inside the double quotation marks. That means VBScript didn't treat it—or the concatenation operators—as code; instead, it treated them simply as part of a literal string, and placed them into var accordingly.

Where all of this becomes tricky is when you start needing to work with single and double quotes at the same time. For example, suppose I don't want to use the literal string "Value" in my query, but rather want to use the contents of a variable named strValue. I'd need to modify my query as follows:

```
strObject = "MyObject"
strValue = "MyValue"
var = "SELECT * FROM " & strObject & " WHERE " & _
 "Prop = '" & strValue & "'"
```

Notice that I've maintained the spacing after the FROM keyword and before the WHERE keyword, and concatenated the strObject variable. The variable var would now contain this text:

```
SELECT * FROM MyObject WHERE Prop = 'MyValue'
```

Look closely to see what's going on: When VBScript gets to "Prop = '", it concatenates that into var because it's all contained within double quotes. So the single quotation mark required by my query language is included within VBScript's literal string. Then, I close VBScript's string using a double quotation mark, and concatenate the contents of strValue. Finally, I open a new literal string containing only the closing single quotation mark required by my query language.

Just for fun—or horror, depending on how you feel about all this—let's do one last quick exercise. Imagine I want to build a query that looks like this:

```
SELECT * FROM Object WHERE Prop = "Value"
```

This is the same as before, except I'm using double quotation marks instead of single quotation marks. This isn't something you'd typically do with most query languages, but it'll serve as a useful example of an important technique. Suppose that, as before, my object name is in strObject, and my value string is in strValue. My VBScript code would look like this:

```
strObject = "MyObject"
strValue = "MyValue"
var = "SELECT * FROM " & strObject & " WHERE " & _
  "Prop = """ & strValue & """"
```

That's a lot to look at! The difficulty comes after `"Prop ="`. Here, I'm inside a VBScript string, so the first two double-quotation marks are interpreted as a single literal character. The "leftover" quotation mark indicates the close of a literal string, and I then concatenate the strValue variable. Next, VBScript sees four double-quotation marks. What to do? Because we're not already inside a literal string, the first double-quotation mark is taken as the opening of a literal string. Now we're inside a string, so VBScript sees the next two marks as a single literal character, and the "leftover" mark and the end closes the literal string. Honestly, I couldn't type this sort of thing freehand: My script editor, PrimalScript, color-codes literal strings in a dark red. That color-coding makes it easy for me to see when I'm getting all the double-quotation marks together correctly.

If you take one thing away from this chapter, make it concatenation. In fact, this is such an important and often-misunderstood category, that I'm going to give you three exercises to complete. For each of them, start with this code in VBScript:

```
strObject = "Name"
strValue = "Value"
var =
WScript.Echo var
```

You need to complete the third line, assigning something to the variable var, so that VBScript can then display its contents. Your goal is to get the script to produce these three strings (meaning you'll need to run through this exercise three times, once for each string):

1. SET Name = Value

2. SET Name = 'Value'

3. SET "Name" = "Value"

Of course, I don't want you literally typing "Name" and "Value" into your exercise script; instead, concatenate strObject and strValue. Work on this now; I'll provide answers at the end of this chapter.

Changing Strings

VBScript includes a wide array of functions designed to change strings. I'll start with LCase() and UCase(), which change a variable to lower- or uppercase letters, respectively. Try running the following scriptlet to see how these functions work:

```
Dim sInput
sInput = InputBox("Enter a string to try.")

MsgBox "All upper: " & UCase(sInput)
MsgBox "All lower: " & LCase(sInput)
```

TIP

When you're experimenting with a new function, it's often useful to write a short script like this that allows you to see the function's output. Seeing it in action is much more informative than simply reading about it or looking at someone else's example.

These functions can be very useful when dealing with case-sensitive strings, such as passwords, WMI queries, and so forth. Using these functions, you can ensure that the case of the strings is exactly what you need for whatever you're doing.

Combining these functions with the substring functions lets you perform some very powerful tricks. For example, the following function will accept a full username, such as "john doe," and convert it to the proper name case, where the first letters of each name are capitalized, no matter how you capitalize the input.

```
Dim sUserName

'get the username
sUserName = InputBox("Enter username")

'does it contain a space?
If InStr(1, sUserName, " ") = 0 Then

 'no - error message!
 MsgBox "Name must contain a space."

Else
```

8

```
'display the name case version
MsgBox "Proper case is " & NameCase(sUserName)

End If

Function NameCase(sName)

  'lowercase everything
  sName = LCase(sName)

  'locate the space position
  Dim iPos
  iPos = InStr(1, sName, " ")

  'build the output
  sName = UCase(Left(sName,1)) & _
    Mid(sName, 2, iPos-1) & _
    UCase(Mid(sName, iPos + 1, 1)) & _
    Right(sName, Len(sName)-iPos-1)

  NameCase = sName

End Function
```

Try walking through the NameCase() function to see if you can figure out how it works. It's just using substring functions to pull out the first character of the first name, then the rest of the first name, then the first character of the last name, and then the rest of the last name. The first character of each name is run through UCase() to ensure it's upper-cased properly. Of course, this routine only works for two-part names like Don Jones; a three-part name like Rip Van Winkle would require some modifications. That's something you have to watch out for when you design any script: Make sure you know the full range of possible circumstances under which your script might be used, and plan accordingly.

Another very cool string-changing function is Replace(). With it, you can replace any occurrence of one substring with another substring, all without affecting the other contents of the main string. Sound complicated? It's not! Just check out this example:

```
Dim sMsg
sMsg = "Hello, %1%. Today is %2%."

Dim sName
sName = InputBox("What is your name?")

sMsg = Replace(sMsg, "%1%", sName)
sMsg = Replace(sMsg, "%2%", Date)

MsgBox sMsg
```

`Replace()` can be incredibly useful in administrative scripts. For now, concentrate on learning how it works—you'll see plenty of examples of its usefulness throughout this book.

Formatting Strings

VBScript provides several functions designed to format strings—and other data types—into specially formatted strings. For example, suppose you have a function that calculates the total uptime for a server, and you want to display that information as a percentage. The following script is an example of how VBScript lets you format the output:

```
Dim iUpHours, iDownHours
iUpHours = InputBox("How many hours has the server " & _
 "been up?" & _
 " Fractional numbers are OK.")
iDownHours = InputBox("How many hours has the server " & _
 "been down?" & _
 " Fractional numbers are OK.")


Dim sResult
sResult = CalcDownPerc(iUpHours, iDownHours)
MsgBox "The server has been down for " & _
 sResult & " of the " & _
 "time it has been up."


Function CalcDownPerc(iUpHours, iDownHours)
 Dim iPerc
 iPerc = iDownHours / iUpHours

 Dim sDisplay
 sDisplay = FormatPercent(iPerc, 4)


 CalcDownPerc = sDisplay
End Function
```

In this example, `FormatPercent()` is used to format the contents of variable `iPerc` so that the result has four digits after the decimal place, and the result may have a leading zero before the decimal depending upon the computer's locale settings.

Another popular formatting function is `FormatDateTime()`. In the next example, suppose that variable `dLastLogon` contains a user's last logon date:

```
Dim sDate
sDate = FormatDateTime(dLastLogon, vbShortDate)
```

This example will display the date in the computer's short date format (that is, however the computer's regional settings are configured to display short dates), which in the United States looks like 5/26/2003. Other formats include

▶ vbGeneralDate—This can display a date, a time, or both. Dates are formatted using the short date format, and times are displayed as a long time. If both parts are included, both parts are displayed.

▶ vbLongDate—This displays a date using the computer's long date format, such as "Monday, May 26, 2003."

▶ vbShortDate—This displays a date using the computer's short date format, such as "5/26/2003."

▶ vbLongTime—This displays a time using the computer's long time format, such as "8:53 A.M."

▶ vbShortTime—This displays a time using the computer's short time format. This is generally a 24-hour format, such as "13:26" rather than "1:26 P.M."

> **NOTE**
>
> As you'll learn in the next chapter, VBScript stores date and time information in an internal serial number format, so that a date and time together might look something like 857387.5784893. A date by itself might be stored as 859340.0, whereas a time might look like 0.589738. *All* date and time variables contain both a date and time component, so it's best to use FormatDateTime() to display just the portion you want.

VBScript also includes FormatNumber() and FormatCurrency() functions. You can learn more about these in the VBScript documentation if you need them; I find that they have pretty limited application in common administrative scripts.

Converting Other Data Types to String Data

First, keep in mind that the formatting functions I introduced you to in the previous section will return a string value. So, if you use something like this:

```
Dim iNumber, sString
iNumber = 5
sString = FormatPercent(iNumber, 2)
MsgBox sString
```

variable sString will contain a string value because that's what FormatPercent() returns. Technically, the formatting functions are a sort of specialized string conversion function, too.

VBScript does provide a general string conversion function: CStr(). This function simply takes any type of data—numeric, date/time, currency, or whatever—and converts it to a string. The function works by taking each character of the input data and appending it to an output string. So, the number 5 will become "5," the number -2 will become "-2," and so forth. Dates and times are converted to their short display format. For example, try running this:

```
Dim dDate, sString
dDate = Date()
sString = CStr(dDate)
MsgBox sString
```

The result should be a short formatted date, such as "5/26/2003."

> **NOTE**
>
> If your computer is displaying short dates with a two-digit year, you probably have an outdated version of the Windows Script Host or an incredibly old operating system. All newer versions of Windows and the Windows Script Host display four-digit years to help eliminate future recurrences of the infamous "Y2K bug."

Summary

Believe it or not, you've probably covered half of VBScript's functions in this chapter. That alone should help you realize how important string manipulation is, and might explain the spinning feeling in your head right now! Don't worry—string manipulation, like everything else involved in scripting, becomes easier with practice.

For now, keep in mind the basic functions for working with substrings, such as Right(), Left(), Mid(), and InStr(). String concatenation using the & operator is also important, as is the ability to change strings with functions like Replace(). Finally, string conversion functions—especially CStr()—can help make your scripts less error-prone, while enabling you to work with a broad variety of data.

Your string manipulation skills will serve you well in other areas of VBScript, such as date and time manipulation, Active Directory querying, Windows Management Instrumentation, and more.

And at this point, I owe you some answers to the string concatenation exercise I gave you earlier. The first solution is:

```
strObject = "Name"
strValue = "Value"
var = "SET " & strObject & _
 " = " & strValue
WScript.Echo var
```

Here's the second:

```
strObject = "Name"
strValue = "Value"
var = "SET " & strObject & _
 " = '" & strValue & "'"
WScript.Echo var
```

And finally, the third:

```
strObject = "Name"
strValue = "Value"
var = "SET """ & strObject & _
 """ = """ & strValue & """"
WScript.Echo var
```

Trust me, if you didn't get these exact results, go back and play with your code until you do. You'll thank me later because this is one skill that you *must* master before you can work with Windows Management Instrumentation and other more complex scripting technologies.

CHAPTER 9

Manipulating Other Types of Data

In the prior two chapters, you learned a lot of about string and numeric data. In this chapter, I'll cover everything else—the lesser-used data types that are nonetheless so important to VBScript. You'll find yourself using these data types most frequently in complex scripts. For example, I'll begin with date and time data, which you'll use frequently in many Windows Management Instrumentation (WMI) scripts. I'll also cover byte data, which is a lot less common in administrative scripts, but worth knowing about in case you need it. Finally, I'll cover arrays, which aren't really a data type at all. They're a special type of variable capable of holding multiple values, and you'll use them in many of the scripts you write.

Working with Dates and Times

Dates and times allow your scripts to interact more precisely with the real world. You can copy or move files based on their "last changed" date, delete users based on the last time they logged on, and so forth. Next to strings and numbers, dates and times are the third most common data type that you'll use in your scripts.

Dates and Times in VBScript

VBScript stores dates and times in a serial number format that looks like a large decimal number. The serial number counts the number of milliseconds that have elapsed since January 1, 100 C.E., and can represent dates and times up to December 31, 9999. The integer portion of a date serial number—the portion before the decimal point—is used to represent days (and, thus, months and years), whereas the fractional portion—the part after the decimal point— represents milliseconds (and seconds, minutes, and hours).

VBScript includes a number of functions for working with dates and times. For example, the DatePart() function analyzes a date and returns just the specified part of it. DatePart("yyyy", Date()), for example, returns the year portion of the current date. DatePart() accepts a number of different strings, which tell it which portion of the date you're interested in.

▶ yyyy returns the year.

▶ q returns the quarter of the year.

▶ m returns the month.

▶ y returns the Julian date, which is the number of days that have elapsed since the beginning of the year.

▶ d returns the day as a number.

▶ w returns the weekday, such as "Monday".

▶ ww returns the week of the year.

▶ h returns the hour.

▶ n returns the minute. Don't confuse this with m, which actually returns the month.

▶ s returns the second.

The second parameter of DatePart() can be anything VBScript recognizes as a date or time, including string variables that contain date or time information, such as "1/1/2004" or "10:26 P.M."

Getting the Date or Time

VBScript has a number of functions that return the current date or time, or portions thereof:

▶ Date() returns the current date.

▶ Day() returns the current day, numbered 1 to 31.

▶ Now() returns the current date and time.

▶ Month() returns the current month, numbered 1 to 12.

▶ Year() returns the current year.

▶ Weekday() returns the current day of the week, numbered 1 to 7.

▶ Time() returns the current system clock time.

▶ Hour() returns the current hour, numbered 0 to 23.

▶ Minute() returns the current minute of the system clock.

▶ Second() returns the current second of the system clock.

There are a couple of additional functions used to turn numeric date data, such as month or day numbers, into strings:

▶ MonthName() returns the name of the month. For example, MonthName(1) returns January. MonthName(1,True) returns Jan, the abbreviated form of the month name.

▶ WeekdayName() returns the name of a day of the week. WeekdayName(2) returns Monday, whereas WeekdayName(2,True) returns the abbreviated Mon. Sunday is the default first day of the week.

Converting Date and Time Data

You can convert data to a date or time by using the CDate() function. For example, CDate("1/1/2004") will convert the string value "1/1/2004", which looks like a date, into the corresponding date serial number. It's difficult to get VBScript to display the internal serial number, and an example such as the following simply displays something that looks like a normal date:

```
dDate = CDate("1/1/2004")
MsgBox dDate
MsgBox Date()
```

When VBScript executes the MsgBox statements, it redisplays the dates in whatever format your computer is configured to use based on its region settings.

You can also generate date or time data from individual date or time components, by using the DateSerial() and TimeSerial() functions. For example, DateSerial(2004, 5, 12) will return the date 5/12/2004. Similarly, TimeSerial(5, 23) will return 5:23 A.M.

Working with Past and Future Dates

VBScript provides the DateAdd() function, which allows you to perform math with dates and times. DateAdd() requires three parameters: an *interval,* a number, and a starting date or time. Intervals can be the following:

▶ yyyy for the year

▶ q for the quarter of the year

▶ m for the month

▶ y for the Julian date, which is the number of days that have elapsed since the beginning of the year

▶ d for the day as a number

▶ w for the weekday, such as "Monday"

▶ ww for the week of the year

▶ h for the hour

6

▶ n for the minute

▶ s for the second

For example, DateAdd("yyyy", 1, "1/1/2004") will return 1/1/2005, which is the starting date plus one year. You can use DateAdd() to subtract by specifying a negative number: DateAdd("m", -1, "1/1/2004") will return 12/1/2003, removing one month from the starting date. The function is leap-year-aware, meaning that DateAdd("yyyy", 1, "2/29/2000") will *not* return 2/29/2001, because 2001 is not a leap year. The function will instead return 3/1/2001, which is 365 days after the starting date.

DateDiff() is a similar function that returns the difference between two dates. It accepts the same interval parameters as DateAdd(), and accepts two dates for comparison. DateDiff("d", "12/31/2002", "12/31/2003") will return 365 because that's the number of days between the two dates. If the first date specified is later than the second, the number returned will be negative.

Working with Arrays

An *array* is a collection of values assigned to a single variable. Normal variables can hold just one value. For example:

```
Dim sMonths
sMonths = "January"
```

In this example, sMonths could be changed to contain "February", but doing so would eliminate "January" from the variable's contents. With an array, however, a single variable can contain multiple values. For example:

```
Dim sMonths(12)
sMonths(1) = "January"
sMonths(2) = "February"
sMonths(3) = "March"
sMonths(4) = "April"
sMonths(5) = "May"
sMonths(6) = "June"
sMonths(7) = "July"
sMonths(8) = "August"
sMonths(9) = "September"
sMonths(10) = "October"
sMonths(11) = "November"
sMonths(12) = "December"
```

This capability to assign multiple values to a single variable can come in handy in a number of scripting situations.

Arrays in VBScript

VBScript supports *multidimensional arrays*. For example, suppose you declare a variable using `Dim sData(5,4)`. This creates a two-dimensional variable. The first dimension can hold six data *elements,* whereas the second dimension can hold five. Note that elements always begin numbering at zero. I sometimes find it easier to imagine a two-dimensional array as a table of elements. The columns represent one dimension, whereas the rows represent another dimension. Table 9.1 illustrates this sample array.

TABLE 9.1   Sample Array

sData	0	1	2	3	4
0	Harold	Todd	Lura	Ben	Mary
1	Cyndi	David	Deb	Amy	Barb
2	Liza	Judy	Tina	Bette	Will
3	Martha	Doug	Peter	Derek	Jeremy
4	Don	Chris	Joe	Hector	Maria
5	Tom	Mary	Jill	Ruth	Bill

I might decide that the first dimension (the columns) represents different job positions at my company, such as Sales, Marketing, Human Resources, MIS, and Operations. I might decide that the second dimension represents individuals within each role. Therefore, `sData(2,4)` would contain "Joe," the fourth person in the MIS department; `sData(0,1)` would contain "Cyndi," the second person in the Marketing department; and so forth.

Three-dimensional arrays can be pictured as a cube, with each dimension of the cube (X, Y, and Z) representing a dimension of the array. Four-dimensional and larger arrays are a bit more difficult to imagine, but you get the idea; and fortunately, arrays larger than two dimensions are rare in administrative scripts.

Arrays are not actually a data type in and of themselves; they can, in fact, be any type of data I've shown you in this book: strings, numbers, bytes, dates and times, and so forth.

Creating and Manipulating Arrays

You can declare *static* arrays by using the `Dim` keyword, as I've already done in a couple of examples. You can declare a *dynamic* array by using the `Dim` keyword and by leaving one dimension of the array unspecified. For example, to declare a dynamic, single-dimension array, simply use `Dim sVariable()`. Notice that you still need to include the parentheses; these tell VBScript that you're declaring an array, but declining to specifically size it for now.

When you decide to size the array, you do so by using the `ReDim` statement. For example:

```
Dim sArray()
ReDim sArray(4)
```

This example will create a new array, and then size it to have five elements numbered zero to four. Note that ReDim() will *remove* any data in the array when resizing it. If you already have data in an array and want to keep it, add the Preserve keyword, as follows:

```
Dim sArray()
ReDim sArray(2)
sArray(0) = "One"
sArray(1) = "Two"
sArray(2) = "Three"
ReDim Preserve sArray(3)
sArray(3) = "Four"
```

The result of this example is an array of four elements, each containing string data. ReDim is pretty powerful.

▶ You can use it to change the number of dimensions. For example, a one-dimensional array named sArray with four elements can be resized using ReDim sArray(4,2). Doing so adds a new dimension of three elements. However, you cannot use the Preserve keyword when changing the number of dimensions.

▶ When you use the Preserve keyword, you can only resize the *last* dimension. For example, if you have a two-dimensional array named sArray, and already have four elements in each dimension, using ReDim Preserve sArray(8,4) would generate an error because you're trying to resize the *first* dimension in conjunction with the Preserve keyword.

▶ You can resize an array to make it smaller. When you do, any data contained in the truncated portion of the array is lost.

You can also create arrays from an existing value. For example, suppose you have a script that's reading an Internet Information Services (IIS) log file. Normally, those files are comma-delimited values. You might read an entire line of data into a variable named sLog, and that variable might contain something like, 12-12-2003,12:43,index.html,400 or something similar. If you want to get just the name of the web page from that line of the log, you *could* use some heavy-duty string manipulation to find the third comma, pull out the web page name, and so forth. However, because there's a comma delimiting each piece of data, it might be easier to convert the data to an array.

```
'sLog contains log file line
Dim sLogData
sLogData = Split(sLog, ",")

MsgBox "Web page is " & sLogData(2)
```

The magic lies in the Split() function. This function accepts a variable, such as sLog, and a delimiter character, such as the comma. Split() returns an array, with one element for each piece of data separated by a comma. In my example, sLogData would contain four elements, numbered from zero to three. The third element, number two, contains "index.html," which is what I was after in the first place.

The opposite of Split() is Join(). This function accepts a one-dimensional array and a delimiter character, and returns a single delimited string. For example, using my sMonths array from the first part of this section:

```
Dim sMonths(12)
sMonths(1) = "January"
sMonths(2) = "February"
sMonths(3) = "March"
sMonths(4) = "April"
sMonths(5) = "May"
sMonths(6) = "June"
sMonths(7) = "July"
sMonths(8) = "August"
sMonths(9) = "September"
sMonths(10) = "October"
sMonths(11) = "November"
sMonths(12) = "December"

Dim sMonthList
sMonthList = Join(sMonths, ",")
```

sMonthList will contain ",January,February,March,April,May,June,July,August,September, October,November,December". Notice that there are no spaces inserted between the month names; only the specified delimiter—in this example, a comma—is inserted between the list elements.

Also, did you notice that the *first character* is a comma? Here's why: All arrays have a starting element of zero by default. So when I declared sMonths(12), I was creating a 13-element array numbered zero through 12. The Join() function combined all 13 elements, separating each with a comma. So the first element—zero—contained nothing, and it was followed by a comma, which is why the first character in my output is a comma.

Working with Array Data

You can use numeric variables to represent array elements when accessing arrays. For example, the following example works fine:

```
Dim sMonths(12)
sMonths(1) = "January"
sMonths(2) = "February"
sMonths(3) = "March"
sMonths(4) = "April"
sMonths(5) = "May"
sMonths(6) = "June"
sMonths(7) = "July"
```

```
sMonths(8) = "August"
sMonths(9) = "September"
sMonths(10) = "October"
sMonths(11) = "November"
sMonths(12) = "December"

iMonth = InputBox("Enter a number from 1-12")
MsgBox "You selected " & sMonths(iMonth)
```

The last line of this example uses the variable `iMonth` to dynamically access a given element in the array `sMonths`.

> **NOTE**
>
> You'll see a number of examples of arrays in administrative scripts later in this book. For now, just know what an array looks like, and remember that it's a collection of values assigned to a single variable name. It will all come together for you later on; so if you don't see a clear use for arrays yet, don't worry. You will!

One last trick is the `IsArray()` function. This function accepts a variable, and returns `True` or `False` depending on whether the variable is an array.

Working with Bytes

A *byte* variable can contain a single byte of data—that is, a number from 0 to 255. Doesn't sound very useful, does it? Bytes aren't often used alone, though; they're often used in arrays, where a single byte array can represent a stream of binary data. For example, files on a computer's hard drive are a simple one-dimensional array of bytes. A file that's 1KB in length has 1,024 elements in its array, and can be contained with a byte array in an administrative script.

Bytes in VBScript

Your most frequent use for byte variables will be to pass data to WMI functions that require a byte array. You'll usually work with bytes in the form of an array, where the data inside the array represents a file or some other binary data. Still, bytes are reasonably rare in administrative scripts, which is why I won't bore you with a long example. You'll see one or two examples elsewhere in this book that use bytes; I'll call your attention to them and explain them in a bit more detail at that time.

Converting Byte Data

The `CByte()` function converts data to a byte. Generally, only numeric data in the range of 0 to 255 can be successfully converted to a byte.

```
Dim iDouble, bByte
iDouble = 104.76
bByte = CByte(iDouble)
```

In this example, bByte now contains the value 105, which is the closest whole number to what iDouble contains.

Summary

Dates, times, bytes, and arrays are used less often, but are important types of data in VBScript. Although you might not have an immediate need for them in your administrative scripts, keep them in mind. When you do run into them in the future, or when you see them in the sample scripts I'll present throughout this book, you can refer back to this chapter to learn more about them or to refresh your memory.

Bytes, dates, and times use conversion and manipulation functions very similar to those you've learned to use with string and numeric data. Date and time data can also be used with the unique calculation functions DateAdd() and DateDiff(). Arrays, however, aren't really a data type at all; they're a way to collect multiple values into a single variable. Arrays can be strings, numbers, dates, times, or bytes. You can create and manipulate arrays with functions like Join(), Split(), and ReDim.

CHAPTER 10

Controlling the Flow of Execution

At this point, you should know enough VBScript to write some useful administrative scripts. In fact, the previous few chapters contained some great sample scripts that you should be able to put right to use, in addition to using them as reference examples.

What you lack at this point, and what I'll cover in this chapter, is a way to make your scripts automatically respond to certain conditions, and execute different lines of script accordingly. For example, suppose you need to write a script that tells you which user has a particular file open on a file server. Your script must be able to iterate through all of the open resources on a server to find the one you're interested in, and then iterate through the list of users who have the resource open, displaying that information to you. Such a script would require certain lines of code to be repeated over and over, while requiring other lines of code to be executed only if certain conditions are true (such as if the current server resource is the one you're interested in).

VBScript includes *control-of-flow* statements that give your scripts the necessary logical-evaluation capabilities. In this chapter, you'll learn how they work, and see some examples of how to use them in your scripts.

Conditional Execution

Many administrative scripts that you write will execute some simple, straightforward task that doesn't require any decisions. Other scripts, however, will be more complex, and will require your scripts to evaluate conditions and values and make a decision about what to do. VBScript conditional execution statements make this possible, giving your scripts a form of intelligence and decision-making capabilities.

If/Then

The most common conditional execution statement is the If/Then construct. It's referred to as a *construct* because it involves more than a single statement or more than even a single line of code. Here's a very simple example:

```
Dim iMyNumber
iMyNumber = InputBox("Enter a number from 1-100")

If iMyNumber < 1 Or iMyNumber > 100 Then
 MsgBox "I said 1 to 100!"
Else
 MsgBox "Thank you!"
End If
```

The script declares a variable named iMyNumber, and then uses InputBox() to retrieve user input. Next, the script uses an If/Then construct to evaluate the input. Here's how it works:

▶ First, VBScript evaluates the two logical expressions in the If statement. Does iMyNumber contain a number that is less than 1? Does it contain a number that is greater than 100? If *either* of these two conditions is True, VBScript will execute the code following the Then statement. VBScript will accept either of these two conditions because they're connected with an Or statement, which means either one of them being True is acceptable.

▶ If neither of the If conditions are True, VBScript looks for an alternate execution path, which it finds after the Else statement. VBScript executes that code instead of the code following Then.

▶ Conditional execution stops whenever another portion of the If/Then construct is reached.

Boolean Operators

And and Or are examples of *Boolean* operators. These operators are similar to mathematical operators, except that instead of resolving a value, these resolve a logical condition and return a True or False value.

For example, suppose you have a variable named iNumber, which contains the value 4. The logical condition iNumber > 1 And iNumber < 100 would evaluate to True because both subconditions evaluate to True. Similarly, the logical condition iNumber > 1 Or iNumber < 0 would also evaluate to True, because one of the two subconditions evaluates to True.

On the other hand, iNumber > 1 And iNumber > 100 would evaluate to False because only one of the two subconditions evaluates to True. The rules regarding And and Or are pretty simple: With And, both conditions must be True for the overall evaluation to be True. With Or, either or both conditions must be True for the overall expression to be evaluated as True.

You can get complex with Boolean operators, and you can group them with parentheses to control the order of evaluation. Consider this monster example: (iNumber > 10 Or iNumber < 5) And (iNumber <> 5 And iNumber <> 10). How will this evaluate?

First, VBScript looks at the deepest level of parentheses and evaluates them left to right for True or False. The first expression is iNumber > 10 Or iNumber < 5. Because iNumber is less than five, this expression evaluates as True. VBScript now looks at iNumber <>5 And iNumber <> 10. This expression is also True because iNumber is neither 5 nor 10. Now, VBScript evaluates the last expression, which comes down to True And True. The result of this is True, so the overall expression's result is True.

What would this evaluate to if iNumber contained 10? It would be False. The first expression in parentheses is False because iNumber is neither greater than 10 nor less than 5. The second expression is also False because iNumber does equal 10. The final result becomes False And False, which is False.

Let's walk through what happens if you run this script and enter the number 2 in the input box.

1. VBScript evaluates the If conditions and discovers that iMyNumber is neither less than 1 nor greater than 100. VBScript looks for an alternative, which it finds in the Else statement.

2. VBScript executes all code following the Else statement, displaying a message box reading "Thank you!"

3. VBScript encounters the End If statement, meaning the If/Then construct is complete. VBScript begins executing any code that follows End If.

Now, let's look at what happens if you enter 101 in the input box instead.

1. VBScript evaluates the If conditions. The first condition isn't True, but the second one is. Because the conditions are connected by an Or statement (as opposed to an And statement, which would require them both to be True), VBScript resolves the overall If statement as True, and begins executing everything that follows Then.

2. VBScript displays a message box that reads, "I said 1 to 100!"

3. VBScript encounters the Else statement. This tells VBScript that the current block of code is complete, and it looks for the End If statement.

4. VBScript locates End If and begins executing any code that follows it.

10

> **TIP**
>
> In the next example, I slightly indented the lines of code within each section of the If/Then construct. This indenting makes it easier to visually spot which code will execute in either condition.

I want to stress that the If/Then construct only cares about a True or False value. In fact, another way to write the construct's syntax is like this:

```
If {True ¦ False} Then
```

In other words, whatever logical expression you put into the construct needs to evaluate to either True or False. If it's True, the construct executes whatever's inside. If it's False, the construct doesn't. This is a subtle, yet incredibly important concept. For example, consider this:

```
bolValue = True
If bolValue = True Then
  'do something
End If
```

This construct contains a valid comparison because bolValue either equals True (in which case the comparison is True), or it doesn't (in which case the comparison is False). To more clearly illustrate this, I'll take the variable out of the picture, substituting its value instead:

```
If True = True Then
  'do something
End If
```

Of course, True always equals True, just as 1 always equals 1 and "A" always equals "A." So really, this could be written more simply:

```
If True Then
  'do something
End If
```

See, the construct doesn't actually *need a comparison*. It just needs a True or a False value. Most of the time, you're getting a True or False by means of a logical comparison of some kind, but you could simply provide the value True or False directly. Here's the exact same thing, back to using a variable:

```
bolValue = True
If bolValue Then
  'do something
End If
```

Because bolValue *already contains True*, it doesn't need to be compared to True. It *is* True, and the construct simply needs to see True or False. Here's a more real-world application, using the FileSystemObject which I've mentioned before (but have yet to formally introduce you to):

```
Dim objFSO
Set objFSO = CreateObject("Scripting.FileSystemObject")
If objFSO.FolderExists("C:\Test") Then
  'do something
End If
```

Here, the FileSystemObject's FolderExists method returns a True or a False value depending on whether the specified folder exists. Because the method is directly returning a True or False value, it doesn't need to be *compared* to anything; the construct can handle that value directly. I spent all this time pointing this out to you because it's a *very* common technique that you'll run across, but it can be a bit confusing to see an If/Then construct that doesn't include a comparison operator of some kind. Now you'll know what you're looking at!

Nesting If/Then

If/Then constructs can be nested as well, meaning you can place them one within the other. Let's extend the sample script to be a bit more complex.

```
Dim iMyNumber
iMyNumber = InputBox("Enter a number from 1-100")

If iMyNumber < 1 Or iMyNumber > 100 Then
 If iMyNumber > 10000 Then
  MsgBox "You're not being serious!"
 End If
 MsgBox "I said 1 to 100!"
Else
 MsgBox "Thank you!"
End If
```

I didn't change anything after the Else statement, but I did add another If/Then construct after the Then statement. Here's what will happen if you run this script and enter 20,000 in the input box:

1. VBScript will evaluate the If conditions and find that iMyNumber is indeed greater than 100, forcing execution of the code following Then.

2. VBScript will evaluate the second If/Then construct. Because it's True, VBScript will display a message box that reads, "You're not being serious!"

3. VBScript will continue to execute the original Then code, displaying a message box that reads, "I said 1 to 100!"

4. Finally, VBScript will hit the Else statement, telling it to jump right to End If.

> **TIP**
>
> Note the indenting in the following sample. All of the code within each construct is indented. When you start nesting constructs, indenting can help make sure you're matching up `If` and `End If` statements correctly.

Also, notice that the second `If/Then` construct doesn't include an `Else` statement. `Else` is always optional, and you don't have to include it. The only required statements are `If`, `Then`, and `End If`.

If/Then Else/ElseIf

What if you want to evaluate multiple, different, possible values in a single `If/Then` construct? You can, using `ElseIf`. I'll revise the last sample to show you how it works.

```
Dim iMyNumber
iMyNumber = InputBox("Enter a number from 1-100")

If iMyNumber < 1 Then
 MsgBox "That isn't more than 1"
ElseIf iMyNumber > 100 Then
 MsgBox "That isn't less than 100"
Else
 MsgBox "Thank you!"
End If
```

Here's how VBScripts treats that code:

1. The first `If` expression is evaluated. If it's `True`, VBScript executes everything following `Then`.

2. If the first `If` expression is `False`, VBScript evaluates the `ElseIf` expression. If that's `True`, it executes whatever follows `Then`.

3. If the `ElseIf` expression is `False`, VBScript executes whatever is after `Else`.

You can stack up any number of `ElseIf` statements to evaluate various conditions. Listing 10.1 is an over-the-top example to give you the idea.

LISTING 10.1 *ElseIf.vbs*. Using `ElseIf`.

```
Dim iMyNumber
iMyNumber = InputBox("Enter a number from 1-100")

If iMyNumber = 1 Then
 MsgBox "1 is a good number."
ElseIf iMyNumber > 1 And iMyNumber < 50 Then
 MsgBox "2 to 49: Numbers of indecision"
```

LISTING 10.1   Continued

```
ElseIf iMyNumber = 50 Then
 MsgBox "Heading right for the middle, huh?"
ElseIf iMyNumber > 50 And iMyNumber < 99 Then
 MsgBox "51 to 99: You like the upper half"
ElseIf iMyNumber = 99 Then
 MsgBox "99 is just short of 100"
ElseIf iMyNumber = 100 Then
 MsgBox "You went all the way!"
Else
 MsgBox "You didn't enter 1 to 100!"
End If
```

Perhaps not an overly exciting example, but this definitely shows how `ElseIf` can allow your scripts to react to very specific conditions and execute different lines of code for each.

Select/Case

If you've mastered the use of `ElseIf`, you'll really appreciate the `Select/Case` construct. Listing 10.2 shows how it works.

LISTING 10.2   *SelectCase.vbs.* Using `Select/Case`.

```
Dim iMyNumber
iMyNumber = InputBox("Enter a number from 1-5")

Select Case iMyNumber
 Case 1
  MsgBox "1 is a good number."
 Case 2, 3, 4
  MsgBox "2 to 4: Numbers of indecision"
 Case 5
  MsgBox "Heading for the end, huh?"
 Case Else
  MsgBox "What part of 1-5 did you not understand?"
End Select
```

Notice that this script isn't exactly the same as Listing 10.1. Although `If/ElseIf/End If` constructs can evaluate ranges (`iMyNumber > 1 And iMyNumber < 50`), VBScript's `Select/Case` can't. What follows the `Case` statement must be a single value or a list of values, as shown in Listing 10.2, without any operators.

If none of the `Case` expressions evaluate to `True`, VBScript executes whatever it finds with `Case Else`. As with the `Else` statement in an `If/Then` construct, `Case Else` is optional. If

10

you omit it and none of your Case expressions are True, VBScript will just start executing whatever code follows End Select.

Loops

There will be times when you want VBScript to repeat the same task over and over. Perhaps you're having it evaluate a number of different files, or perhaps you simply want to make the computer beep a lot and annoy the person in the cube next to yours! Regardless of your motives, VBScript provides statements that make repetitive execution easy, and gives you full control over how many repetitions VBScript performs.

Do While/Loop **and** Do/Loop While

The Do While/Loop construct is used to execute a given section of code so long as a specified logical condition is True. Here's one way in which Do While/Loop can be used:

```
Dim iNumber
Do
 iNumber = InputBox("Please enter a number.")
Loop While Not IsNumeric(iNumber)
MsgBox "Thank you!"
```

This short script is an excellent example of collecting and validating user input. It starts by declaring a variable, iNumber. Next, VBScript enters the Do loop. Notice that there are no logical conditions specified with Do; it's on a line by itself, meaning VBScript will always execute the code within the loop.

Within the loop, VBScript uses an input box to collect user input, and assigns that input to the variable iNumber. The Loop statement contains the logic of the Do While/Loop construct: Not IsNumeric(iNumber). IsNumeric() is a function that evaluates a variable and returns True if the contents are numeric, and False otherwise. The Not Boolean operator tells VBScript to reverse the output of IsNumeric. So, if iNumber contains a number, the result of Not IsNumeric(iNumber) will be False, the opposite of what IsNumeric(iNumber) would return.

The Loop While statement tells VBScript to return to the Do statement whenever the logical expression is True. In this case, the logical expression will be True only if iNumber doesn't contain a numeric value. In other words, VBScript will continue asking for input repeatedly until that input is numeric.

When the input is finally numeric, VBScript stops executing the loop and responds with a message box reading, "Thank you!" and the script ends.

When you include a logical expression with Loop, VBScript always executes the code within the loop at least once. That's because VBScript executes code in the order in which it finds it, so it doesn't get to the Loop until it has already executed the code within the loop at least once. There might, however, be times when you don't want the script in the loop executed at all, unless a certain condition is True to begin with. For example, suppose you've written a script that opens a text file of unknown length. The file itself is represented by an object name oFile, and that object has an EndOfFile property that will be True when the end of the file is reached. You can use the Read method of the oFile object to read data from the file. In that case, you might use a section of script like this one to read through the entire file:

```
' assumes oFile is some kind of file object
' that is opened for reading
Dim sData
Do While Not oFile.EndOfFile
 sData = oFile.Read
 MsgBox sData
Loop
```

In this chunk of script, the logical condition is included with Do. Again, the Boolean Not operator is used to flip the output of the EndOfFile property. Therefore, the loop will continue to execute so long as EndOfFile is False.

> **NOTE**
>
> Another way to enter this logic would be Do While oFile.EndOfFile = False.

This loop does not necessarily execute at all. If oFile represents an empty file, EndOfFile will be True at the beginning of the loop. VBScript will evaluate this and skip the Do While/Loop construct completely, executing whatever code follows the Loop statement.

> **NOTE**
>
> You can include While and a logical expression with either Do or Loop, but not both. For example, you can have a Do While/Loop, or a Do/Loop While, but you can't use Do While/Loop While. If you try, you'll get an error.

Do Until/Loop **and** Do/Loop Until

The While statement in a Do/Loop construct tells VBScript to continue executing the loop so long as the specified condition is True. Until does exactly the opposite, executing the loop only until the specified condition becomes True. For example, you could rewrite the file reading sample as follows:

```
' assumes oFile is some kind of file object
' that is opened for reading
Dim sData
Do Until oFile.EndOfFile
 sData = oFile.Read
 MsgBox sData
Loop
```

In this case, the script will execute the same. VBScript simply performs the script until oFile.EndOfFile is True.

Like While, Until can be included with either the Do or Loop statement. When you add it to the Loop, VBScript always executes the loop at least once, and then evaluates your Until expression to see if the loop should be executed again. When you include Until with Do, the loop only executes if the Until expression is False to begin with.

For/Next

Sometimes, you just need to execute a script a fixed number of times. For example, suppose you just want to make the computer beep eight times. Using a Do/Loop construct, you could write code like this:

```
Dim iCount
iCount = 1
Do Until iCount = 9
 Beep
 iCount = iCount + 1
Loop
```

This loop executes exactly eight times. However, it's quite a bit of code just to count from 1 to 8, and VBScript offers an easier way: For/Next. You can rewrite the preceding script as follows:

```
Dim iCount
For iCount = 1 To 8
 Beep
Next
```

When VBScript hits the For statement, it sets the specified variable (iCount) to the first specified value (1). Then, VBScript executes the loop's contents. When it reaches Next, VBScript increments the variable (iCount) by one and returns to the For statement for another go-round. When the value of iCount exceeds the specified range (greater than 8 in this example), the loop stops executing and VBScript continues with whatever code follows Next.

Next increments the variable value by one by default, but you can control that. The following sample makes VBScript display the even numbers from 2 to 10.

```
Dim iCount
For iCount = 2 To 10 Step 2
 MsgBox iCount
Next
```

The Step statement tells VBScript to increment iCount by two, rather than one, each time it hits Next. You can specify a negative number to make Step go backward.

```
Dim iCount
For iCount = 10 to 1 Step -1
 MsgBox iCount
Next
MsgBox "Blast off!"
```

This sample will count down from 10 to 1 and then display "Blast off!"

For Each/Next

I've already introduced you to some objects that include collections, such as the FileSystemObject (which I'll discuss in full detail in Chapter 12, "Working with the File System"). The tricky part about a collection of objects is that you might not know how many objects to expect in the collection. For Each/Next provides a useful way to work with each object in the collection, one at a time, without knowing exactly how many objects there are in the collection. Here's an example:

```
' Assume oRoot represents the root folder of C:\
' and has a Subfolders property that is a
' collection of folder objects that represent
' the subfolders of C:\
Dim oSubfolder
For Each oSubfolder In oRoot.Subfolders
 If oFolder.Name = "WINDOWS" Then
  MsgBox "Found the Windows folder!"
 End If
Next
```

VBScript goes through each object in the Subfolders collection, one at a time. For each object in the collection, VBScript assigns the object to the object reference variable oFolder and then executes the contents of the loop. WhenVBScript reaches Next, it sets oFolder to refer to the next object in the collection and executes the loop again. When VBScript finally reaches the end of the collection, it stops executing the loop and starts executing whatever code follows Next.

You'll see a lot more of For Each/Next in Chapter 12, which deals more fully with the FileSystemObject.

10

If you'd like a nontechnical example, consider that `Tree` object I introduced in Chapter 5, "Functions, Objects, Variables, and More." Suppose the `Tree` object has a `Leaves` collection. Each object in the `Leaves` collection is a `Leaf`, and each `Leaf` object includes a `Color` property that retrieves that leaf's current color. You could use `For Each/Next` to count the number of yellow leaves.

```
Dim iYellowLeaves, oLeaf
' assumes oTree is a reference to the
' Tree object
For Each oLeaf in oTree.Leaves
 If oLeaf.Color = "Yellow" Then
  iYellowLeaves = iYellowLeaves + 1
 End If
Next

MsgBox "There are " & iYellowLeaves & _
 " yellow leaves on the tree."
```

Without knowing how many `Leaf` objects there are, `For Each/Next` efficiently steps through the collection one leaf at a time.

Exiting Loops

Suppose you don't always want a loop to finish executing. For example, take that file-reading script that I used in the `Do While/Loop` section earlier in this chapter. Suppose that what I really want to do is read through the file either until I reach the end of the file or until some calculation made on the file's contents is `True`. For example, suppose that the file contains a series of numbers, and I don't want to read any more data if the sum of those numbers exceeds 1,000. Here's how I could do it:

```
' assumes oFile is some kind of file object
' that is opened for reading
Dim iData, iSum
Do Until oFile.EndOfFile
 iData = oFile.Read
 iSum = iSum + iData
 If iSum > 1000 Then
  Exit Do
 End If
Loop
```

The key here is `Exit Do`. If the value of `iSum` ever exceeds 1,000, VBScript immediately exits the loop regardless of whether the `Until` condition was ever `True`. You can do the same thing in a `For/Next` loop.

```
Dim iCount, sInput
For iCount = 1 To 100
```

```
 sInput = InputBox("What's the password?")
 If sInput = "Sesame" Then
  Exit For
 End If
Next
```

In this example, VBScript will continue to ask "What's the password?" until you either type "Sesame" or until you've made 100 wrong guesses. The `Exit For` statement forces VBScript to exit the loop and begin executing whatever code it finds after the `Next` statement.

Putting It All Together

With all of these loops and conditional execution constructs under your belt, you're probably ready to see them in action!

Who Has a File?   Listing 10.3 is a sample script that shows you which user or users has a particular file open on a file server.

LISTING 10.3   *WhoHasFile.vbs*. Shows who has a particular file open.

```
' first, get the server name we want to work with
varServer = InputBox ("Server name to check")

' get the local path of the file to check
varFile= InputBox ("Full path and filename of the file" & _
 " on the server (use the local path as if you were" & _
 " at the server console)")

' bind to the server's file service
set objFS = GetObject("WinNT://" & varServer & _ "/lanmanserver,fileservice")

' scan through the open resources until we
' locate the file we want
varFoundNone = True

' use a FOR...EACH loop to walk through the
' open resources
For Each objRes in objFS.Resources

    ' does this resource match the one we're looking for?
    If objRes.Path = varFile then
        ' we found the file - show who's got it
        varFoundNone = False
        WScript.Echo objRes.Path & " is opened by " & objRes.User
    End If
```

LISTING 10.3   Continued

```
Next

' if we didn't find the file open, display a msg
if varFoundNone = True then
    WScript.Echo "Didn't find that file opened by anyone."
end if
```

Because this script uses an input box to get the server name, you can run it without modification in your environment. Of course, you need to be a Domain Admin or a member of the server's Server Operators group for the script to run; those groups have the permissions necessary to retrieve the information the script requires.

> **NOTE**
>
> Modern Windows operating systems have a ton of configuration parameters, and some of them will make this script not work as intended. Please take this script as an *example*, and don't be disappointed if the file servers in your environment aren't configured in a way that allows the script to function reliably.

Who Has a File—Explained   The first lines of code simply get the file server's name, and the complete path and filename of the file that you want to check. This file path must start with a drive letter, and cannot be a Universal Naming Convention (UNC) path.

```
' first, get the server name we want to work with
varServer = InputBox ("Server name to check")

' get the local path of the file to check
varFile= InputBox ("Full path and filename of the file" & _
    " on the server (use the local path as if you were" & _
    " at the server console)")
```

The next line of code uses Active Directory Services Interface (ADSI) to connect to the server's file server service. Note that ADSI will work fine even against NT file servers, because it's using the WinNT provider.

```
' bind to the server's file service
set objFS = GetObject("WinNT://" & varServer & _ "/lanmanserver,fileservice")
```

If you want to jump ahead and read more about ADSI, head for Chapters 14, 15, and 16 ("Working with ADSI Providers," "Manipulating Domains," and "Manipulating Users and Groups," respectively).

Next, the script sets a variable to False, meaning it hasn't yet found the file that you're interested in.

```
' scan through the open resources until we
' locate the file we want
varFoundNone = True
```

The script uses a For/Next loop to look at each resource opened by the file server service. This is kind of an important concept: When users connect to a file server, the users themselves don't open files. Instead, the file server service (called the Server service in Windows) opens the files on behalf of the user. The file service maintains a collection named Resources that lists each opened file.

```
' use a FOR...EACH loop to walk through the
' open resources
For Each objRes in objFS.Resources

    ' does this resource match the one we're looking for?
    If objRes.Path = varFile then
        ' we found the file - show who's got it
        varFoundNone = False
        WScript.Echo objRes.Path & " is opened by " & objRes.User
    End If
Next
```

Within the For/Next construct, an If/Then construct determines if the current file resource is the one you're interested in.

```
' use a FOR...EACH loop to walk through the
' open resources
For Each objRes in objFS.Resources

    ' does this resource match the one we're looking for?
    If objRes.Path = varFile then
        ' we found the file - show who's got it
        varFoundNone = False
        WScript.Echo objRes.Path & " is opened by " & objRes.User
    End If
Next
```

In other words, does the Path property of the current resource equal the value you provided for the file path and name? If so, the code within the If/Then construct is executed. The variable is set to False, indicating that the script did locate the file you were interested in. The script also displays a message box indicating the username that has opened the resource. If more than one user has the file open, VBScript continues scanning and displays each username as it goes through this loop.

```
' use a FOR...EACH loop to walk through the
' open resources
```

```
For Each objRes in objFS.Resources

        ' does this resource match the one we're looking for?
        If objRes.Path = varFile then
            ' we found the file - show who's got it
            varFoundNone = False
            WScript.Echo objRes.Path & " is opened by " & objRes.User
        End If
Next
```

Finally, the script winds up with a brief message if the file wasn't found. This is only polite; if you don't include this last bit, the script might not appear to be doing anything if the file wasn't found.

```
' if we didn't find the file open, display a msg
if varFoundNone = True then
    WScript.Echo "Didn't find that file opened by anyone."
end if
```

NOTE

You might notice the use of WScript.Echo to display messages. This is functionally the same as the MsgBox statement, and you'll learn more about the WScript object in Chapter 11, "Built-In Scripting Objects."

As you can see, For/Next and If/Then are powerful tools in this complex and highly useful administrative script.

Summary

In this chapter, you've learned to write scripts that can evaluate various criteria and change the execution of the script accordingly. You can use the If/Then construct to evaluate logical conditions and execute different sections of script depending on those conditions. Select/Case is a sort of super If/Then construct, allowing your script to evaluate a number of possible conditions and execute script code accordingly.

You also learned how to write loops, such as Do/Loop and For/Next. These constructs allow your script to execute specific lines of code over and over, while evaluating logical criteria to determine when the repetitive execution should stop. Finally, you learned how to use For Each/Next to iterate through a collection of objects, making it easier to work with collections.

That's about all there is to VBScript! You've already learned about functions, statements, objects, and variables (in Chapter 5), which provide the basis of VBScript's operations. You also learned how to collect user input and display messages (in Chapter 6, "Input and Output"), which provides your script with interactivity. Chapters 7, 8, and 9

("Manipulating Numbers," "Manipulating Strings," and "Manipulating Other Types of Data," respectively) covered how to manipulate various types of data within your script. With all of that under your belt, you're ready to start "gluing together" various operating system objects and writing truly functional administrative scripts.

Incredibly, you have finished learning VBScript. Now, you can start learning about the various objects that provide access to key operating system features. You'll begin with the built-in scripting objects in the next chapter, and move on to the `FileSystemObject` in Chapter 12, "Working with the File System."

10

Built-In Scripting Objects

I've already described how VBScript's real value is as a sort of electronic "glue," which you can use to piece together the many objects of the Windows operating system. Windows Management Instrumentation (WMI) and Active Directory Services Interface (ADSI) are good examples of operating system functionality that you can access by using VBScript. The Windows Script Host (WSH) even has its own built-in object library, and these objects allow you to perform some powerful tasks.

In this chapter, you'll learn to use the WSH Network object, which provides access to the computer's network environment; the Shell object, which allows you to manipulate Windows Explorer and other shell-related information; and the Shortcut object, which allows you to work with Explorer shortcuts and Internet links.

All of these objects can be used in a wide variety of situations, but I think you'll find them more useful in logon scripts. The Network object, for example, allows you to map network drives and printers, which is perhaps the most common job of a logon script.

Chapter 27, "Logon and Logoff Scripts," contains additional logon script examples for both NT and Active Directory domains, and includes some suggestions for using logoff scripts.

The WScript **Object**

All of these objects are accessed through the top-level WScript object. You've already seen WScript in use in

Chapter 6, "Input and Output," where I showed you how `WScript.Echo` can be used to produce both command-line output and message boxes, depending on whether you are using `CScript.exe` or `WScript.exe` to execute your script. The `WScript` object is the only one your scripts get free, meaning you don't have to explicitly create a reference to it. WScript is always available when you're running a script in WSH.

In addition to `Echo`, the `WScript` object has new methods and properties that can be useful to you in your scripts. For example, you can execute the `WScript.Sleep` method, passing a specific number of milliseconds, to have your script pause its execution.

```
'Pause for 5 minutes
WScript.Sleep 300000
```

You can have your scripts immediately stop execution and exit, if you want.

```
If varInput = "" Then
 WScript.Quit
End If
```

In this example, the script will immediately exit if variable `varInput` is empty. You can also ensure that your scripts have a timeout. By default, WSH will continue executing your scripts forever; you might, however, want to automatically have your scripts end if they don't complete within, for example, 30 seconds. That way, a script that has the chance of entering some endless loop, or trying to connect to a remote computer that isn't available, will eventually stop running. To do so, simply set a timeout value.

```
'Specify a timeout in seconds
WScript.Timeout = 30
```

Most important, the `WScript` top-level object provides access to important child objects that you'll need to use in many of your scripts.

The `Network` **Object**

The `WScript.Network` object provides access to drive and printer mapping functions, as well as access to network information, such as the current user and domain names. You must explicitly create an instance of the `Network` object to use it.

```
'Create reference
Dim oNetwork
Set oNetwork = CreateObject("WScript.Network")
```

When created, you can use the object in your scripts.

The `Network` object is designed primarily for use in logon scripts, where you'll need to map both drives and printers. Obviously, it has uses elsewhere, but logon scripts demonstrate its usefulness. The `Network` object provides three functions:

▶ Working with network drives, including mapping and unmapping them, as well as enumerating them

▶ Working with network printers, including mapping and unmapping them, as well as enumerating them

▶ Providing access to the network environment's information, such as the current user and domain names

> **NOTE**
>
> All of the examples in this section assume that you've created a variable named oNetwork and set it to be a reference to the WScript.Network object.

By the way, if you're in a rush to get to WMI, you should know that it's not the be-all and end-all of scripting. In fact, most of the functionality offered by the Network object, particularly mapping network drives, isn't possible through WMI.

Methods and Properties

The MapNetworkDrive object has several different methods for working with drives and printers, and three properties for obtaining network environment information.

MapNetworkDrive
You'll most often see drives mapped using a simplified version of the MapNetworkDrive method.

```
'map a drive
oNetwork.MapNetworkDrive "Z:", "\\Server1\public"
```

However, the method offers other parameters that give you more flexibility and functionality:

▶ **Local name**—This is a required parameter (such as "Z:") and allows you to specify the local drive name for the new mapping.

▶ **Remote name**—This is a required parameter (such as "\\server1\public") and allows you to specify the Universal Naming Convention (UNC) path of the shared folder you want to map to.

▶ **Update profile**—This is an optional parameter and can be either True or False. If True, the user's profile is updated with the new drive mapping. The default is False.

▶ **Username**—This is an optional parameter and allows you to specify an alternate username for authenticating to the remote server.

▶ **Password**—This is another optional parameter, allowing you to specify an alternate password for authenticating to the remote server.

An example of the full method might look like this:

```
oNetwork.MapNetworkDrive "Z:", "\\Server1\public", _
 False, "DonJ", "Pa55word!"
```

> **NOTE**
>
> It's a very poor security practice to include passwords in a script because the pass-
> words can be easily read by almost anyone. Only use the parameters for alternate
> credentials if you plan to use the script for only your own purposes, and if the script is
> secured so that only you have *any* access to it.

RemoveNetworkDrive

As its name implies, the `RemoveNetworkDrive` method disconnects a network drive. You
must pass one parameter, which is the drive letter, to disconnect. Two optional parameters allow you to specify if the drive should be disconnected even if files are in use, and
whether the user's profile should be updated to indicate that the drive is no longer
mapped. If you set that last parameter to `False` (which is the default if you omit the parameter), and the user's profile contains the drive mapping, the drive mapping will be
restored the next time the user logs on.

Here's what the method looks like in action:

```
oNetwork.RemoveNetworkDrive "Z:", _
 False, True
```

This method can generate errors if the drive you try to remove isn't a network drive (if,
for example, you try to unmap the C: drive), or if there are files on the network drive
opened by the client and you don't specify `True` for the second parameter.

EnumNetworkDrives

This method allows your script to list information about connected network drives. Here's
an example:

```
Set oDrives = oNetwork.EnumNetworkDrives
For x = 0 to oDrives.Count - 1 Step 2
 WScript.Echo oDrives.Item(x) & ": " & oDrives.Item(x+1)
Next
```

The `EnumNetworkDrives` method returns a collection, and the items in the collection are
paired. The first item (displayed with `WScript.Echo oDrives.Item(x)` in the example) is
the drive's name, such as `"Z:"`. The second item (`oDrives.Item(x+1)`) is the drive's UNC,
which is the network location that the drive is connected to.

AddWindowsPrinterConnection

Windows-based printers do not require the use of a printer port; the printers simply show up as icons in the Printers (or Printers & Faxes) folder, and Windows applications can then print to them. Adding a connection to a network printer is as easy as using the `AddWindowsPrinterConnection` method.

```
oNetwork.AddWindowsPrinterConnection _
 "\\Server1\LaserJet"
```

The parameter you provide specifies the UNC for the network printer. For NT-based operating systems, including Windows 2000 and Windows XP, that's all you need to provide. In Windows 9x operating systems, however, you also need to specify the name of the printer driver that supports the printer, and that printer driver must already be installed on the client.

```
oNetwork.AddWindowsPrinterConnection _
 "\\Server1\LaserJet", "HP LaserJet 5n"
```

Printer connections made using this method cannot be used by older MS-DOS applications (if you still have any) because MS-DOS applications are designed to print to a local printer port.

AddPrinterConnection

This method is similar to `AddWindowsPrinterConnection`, except that it captures a local printer port (generally LPT1 or LPT2) and makes the printer available to MS-DOS applications. The syntax is also similar.

```
oNetwork.AddPrinterConnection _
 "LPT1:", "\\Server1\LaserJet"
```

It's rare to see this method in use because so few companies have any old MS-DOS applications that they're using to print. Still, if you need it, it's available.

EnumPrinterConnections

This method works very similarly to the `EnumNetworkDrives` method described earlier. Here's an example of it in use:

```
Set oPrinters = oNetwork.EnumPrinterConnections
For x = 0 to oPrinters.Count - 1
 WScript.Echo oPrinters.Item(x) & ": " & oPrinters.Item(x+1)
Next
```

For MS-DOS printer connections, you'll see the printer's captured port (`oPrinters.Item(x)`) and the printer's name (`oPrinters.Item(x+1)`). However, for Windows printer connections, you'll see the printer's local name, which might look like "HP083828288867," instead of a port name. You'll see the printer's UNC for the second item.

SetDefaultPrinter
You can force any connected printer to be the default by using the `SetDefaultPrinter`
method. Simply specify the printer's UNC to make it the default.

```
oNetwork.SetDefaultPrinter( _
 "\\Server1\LaserJet")
```

There's no way, however, to discern the *current* default printer. Therefore, if you change
the user's default printer, you won't easily be able to set it back to whatever the user had
previously selected as the default.

RemovePrinterConnection
Like removing a network drive, you can remove printer connections. You must specify the
printer name to disconnect, and you can specify options to force the disconnect and to
update the user's profile. If you don't force a disconnect and the printer is being used by
the client, you'll receive an error. Here's how to use the `RemovePrinterConnection`
method:

```
oNetwork.RemovePrinterConnection _
 "\\server1\LaserJet", True, True
```

ComputerName, UserDomain, **and** UserName
These properties expose information about the current network environment.

```
Dim sComputer, sDomain, sUser
sComputer = oNetwork.ComputerName
sDomain = oNetwork.UserDomain
sUser = oNetwork.UserName
```

There are some caveats. First, as I'll discuss in more detail in Chapter 27, the `UserName`
and `UserDomain` properties aren't populated on Windows 9x machines until after the
logon process is complete, and scripts can begin executing before that occurs. Also, there's
no way (using this object) to retrieve the domain name of the *computer,* and if your environment contains multiple domains with trusts, you cannot assume that the user's logon
domain is the same as the computer's.

Practical Application

Obviously, the most practical application for the `Network` object is in logon scripts. Listing
11.1 shows a short logon script example that uses the `Network` object.

LISTING 11.1   *Logon.vbs.* Using the `Network` object in a logon script.

```
dim objNetwork
set objNetwork = WScript.CreateObject("WScript.Network")

' let's display a welcome message
```

LISTING 11.1   Continued

```
dim strDomain, strUser
strDomain = objNetwork.UserDomain
strUser = objNetwork.UserName
msgbox "Welcome to the " & strDomain & ", " & strUser & "!"

'we'll map the Z: drive to a network location
objNetwork.MapNetworkDrive "Z:", "\\Server\Share"

'let's connect to a network printer - we'll capture LPT2:
objNetwork.AddPrinterConnection "LPT2", "\\Server\Print1"

'connect a second printer without capturing a printer port
objNetwork.AddWindowsPrinterConnection "\\server\print2", _
 "Lexmark Optra S 1650"

'let's make that the default printer
objNetwork.SetDefaultPrinter "\\Server\Print2"
```

You should be able to easily follow what the script is doing by referring to the method and property descriptions I've provided. This script simply displays a personalized welcome message, maps a network drive, captures a printer port to a network printer, and adds a Windows printer connection as the default printer.

The ADSystemInfo **Object**

Because the WshNetwork object is a bit long in the tooth (having been introduced in 1996), Microsoft has since released a sort of update, called ADSystemInfo. This object doesn't provide drive mapping and similar functions; WshNetwork is still perfectly good for that. What ADSystemInfo does is provide better information about the domain environment and user identity. Getting started with the object is simple:

```
Dim objInfo
Set objInfo = CreateObject("ADSystemInfo")
```

From there, you have a whole raft of properties that provide information about the logged-on user and computer. Fortunately, most of the property names are even self-explanatory:

- ► ComputerName

- ► DomainDNSName

- ► DomainShortName

- ► ForestDNSName

- ► IsNativeMode

- ▶ PDCRoleOwner

- ▶ SchemaRoleOwner

- ▶ SiteName

- ▶ UserName

There are even a couple of user methods:

- ▶ GetAnyDCName()

- ▶ GetDCSiteName()

- ▶ GetTrees()

This object makes it easy, for example, to detect the logged-on computer's Active Directory site, and take specific actions—such as mapping a printer—based upon that site.

The Shell Object

The Shell object must be explicitly created and assigned to a variable, just like the Network object. In this section, I'll assume that your scripts already contain the following code.

```
'Create shell object
Set oShell = CreateObject("WScript.Shell")
```

You can use the Shell object to execute external applications, work with special folders and shortcuts, manipulate environment variables, write to the event log, read and write to the Registry, create timed dialog boxes, and even send keystrokes to another application. Shell is sort of the catchall of the WSH, containing a number of useful functions.

Methods and Properties

The Shell object's methods and properties provide access to its functionality. Many of these methods and properties are complementary, so I'll discuss them together in the following sections.

Run and Exec

Scripting can't do it all. That's an important thing to remember. I always set myself a research time limit: If I can't figure out how to do something in script within 30 minutes of searching on the web, I'll do it whatever way I already know how. If that means launching an external command line, so be it. A good example is setting NTFS permissions on files and folders. You can absolutely do that from within WMI, but it's a thankless, complicated task. I've taken the pain to figure it out a few times, but it's almost always easier to just launch Cacls.exe with the appropriate parameters, so that's what I usually do, using Run and Exec.

Both methods launch new applications in separate processes. With Run, that process is completely detached from your script, and your script will have no access to it. Most of the time, that's fine. With Exec, your script has access to the new process' input and output streams, meaning you can read the output of command-line utilities or other applications into your script, and then do something else based on what happened.

Here's how you can use Run to launch the DIR command:

```
Call oShell.Run("cmd /c dir " & _
 "/a")
```

Notice that you have to launch the command-line processor, CMD, first; you can tell it to run DIR for you. This is an interesting technique, but not useful, as your script has no way to get at the DIR results. You could have DIR redirect its output to a text file, and then read in the text file—but what a pain. There's an easier way.

```
Dim oExecObject, sDir
Set oShell = CreateObject("WScript.Shell")
Set oExecObject = oShell.Exec("cmd /c dir /a")
Do While Not oExecObject.StdOut.AtEndOfStream
 sDir = sDir & oExecObject.StdOut.Readline() & _
  vbCrLf
Loop
WScript.Echo sDir
```

In this example, the Exec method is used, which returns an execution object. That object actually represents the process space of the command window that's running DIR for you. That process has a standard input (StdIn) and standard output (StdOut) property, which you can utilize. In this example, the script is reading the StdOut property line-by-line until there are no more lines to read. Then, the script displays the results. You could, of course, read the results into an array and allow the user to select a specified folder, or whatever you want to do with the output.

You might be wondering why Run is even included if Exec is so useful. Here's why: With Run, you can control the type of window the new process occupies. Simply include a second parameter to Run with one of the following numbers:

- ► 0: Hidden window
- ► 1: Normal window with focus
- ► 2: Minimized window with focus
- ► 3: Maximized window with focus
- ► 4: Display window in its default size, without focus
- ► 5: Activate the window
- ► 6: Minimize the window and give focus to the next window up in the Z-order

- ▶ 7: Minimized window without focus

- ▶ 8: Default size without focus

- ▶ 9: Display the window with focus

The *focus*, of course, refers to the active window. Specifying 7, for example, launches the new application in a minimized window while leaving the current window active. This is nice for running background processes that you don't necessarily want the script's user to see.

Run accepts a third optional parameter, True or False, that decides whether your script will pause and wait for the launched application to finish and quit or launch the application and then continue execution right away. Try this:

```
Call oShell.Run("notepad.exe",,True)
MsgBox "Wow, that took a long time"
```

You'll notice the two serial commas in the Run statement. That's because I didn't want to specify a window style, which is the second parameter. This script executes Notepad, and then continues by displaying a message only after you close Notepad.

SpecialFolders

There might be times when you want to create a shortcut in, or copy a file to, one of Windows' "special" folders, such as My Documents or the Desktop. The SpecialFolders method allows you to figure out the actual path of these special folders so that you can utilize them. Here's how:

```
Dim sPath
sPath = oShell.SpecialFolders("name")
```

Simply replace name with one of the following:

- ▶ AllUsersDesktop

- ▶ AllUsersStartMenu

- ▶ AllUsersPrograms

- ▶ AllUsersStartup

- ▶ Desktop

- ▶ Favorites

- ▶ Fonts

- ▶ MyDocuments

- ▶ NetHood

- ▶ PrintHood

▶ Recent

▶ SendTo

▶ StartMenu

▶ Startup

▶ Templates

NOTE

Even though some of these folders—such as My Documents—don't necessarily use that name in newer versions of Windows (such as Windows Vista), the SpecialFolders method still works. That's because, under the hood, it's using a Windows application programming interface (API) call to determine the folder path, and that Windows API is still implemented the same way even on new versions of Windows.

CreateShortcut

The CreateShortcut method is a quick-and-dirty way to create shortcuts; the CreateShortcut method returns a Shortcut object, which I'll discuss later in this chapter. The basic syntax looks like this:

```
Dim oShortcut
Set oShortcut = oShell.CreateShortcut(path)
```

After the shortcut is created, you use the properties of the Shortcut object to set its target, shortcut keys, and so forth.

Environment

Environment variables are a useful way to access critical system information, such as the path of the Windows folder. The Environment object provides access to this information and allows you to manipulate it. There are actually different categories of environment variables: Computer-specific variables and user-specific variables are the two main ones you'll work with. The user-specific variables are stored in a space named "User," whereas computer-specific variables are stored in "System."

Some variables exist in both locations. For example, "PATH" exists both in the User and System spaces. Why should you care? Because you can also *modify* these variables. If you modify the System space, you're changing the entire computer, even after the current user logs off. If you just want to change an environment variable for your script, use the special "Process" space, which only exists until your script stops running.

Here's how you can retrieve an environment variable:

```
'get the system space
Dim oEnv
```

```
Set oEnv = oShell.Environment("System")

'get the PATH
WScript.Echo oEnv("PATH")
```

You can modify them using a similar technique.

```
'get the system space
Dim oEnv
Set oEnv = oShell.Environment("System")

'set the PATH
oEnv("PATH") = "new path"
```

ExpandEnvironmentStrings

Environment variables can sometimes contain expandable strings, such as "%system-root%." You can use ExpandEnvironmentStrings to expand these into their full values.

```
Dim oEnv
Set oEnv = oShell.Environment("System")
WScript.Echo oShell.ExpandEnvironmentStrings("%TEMP%")
```

LogEvent

Need to log an event to the Windows Event log? No problem.

```
oShell.LogEvent 0, "Success!"
oShell.LogEvent 2, "Warning!"
```

The second parameter is a simple string and will be logged in the event itself. All events are logged to the Application log. The first parameter specifies the type of event:

- ▶ 0: Success

- ▶ 1: Error

- ▶ 2: Warning

- ▶ 3: Informational

- ▶ 8: Audit Success

- ▶ 16: Audit Failure

RegRead, RegWrite, **and** RegDelete

Working with the Registry is easy using the Shell object. Obviously, the usual caveats and warnings about editing the Registry apply: You're messing with the heart and soul of Windows here, so exercise caution.

To read information from the Registry:

```
sVariable = oShell.RegRead( _
 "HKLM\SOFTWARE\Microsoft\Windows NT\" & _
 "CurrentVersion\CurrentVersion")
```

You must provide the complete path to the value you're interested in. Shortcut HKEY_LOCAL_MACHINE by using HKLM; HKEY_ CURRENT_ USER becomes HKCU, and so forth. To create or modify a value, you'll need to know the path, the data for the value, and the data type.

```
oShell.RegWrite( _
 "HKLM\SOFTWARE\Company\Key\Value", "Data", "REG_SZ")
```

Data types are

- ▶ REG_SZ for strings
- ▶ REG_DWORD for numbers
- ▶ REG_BINARY for byte data
- ▶ REG_EXPAND_SZ for expandable strings

If you try to modify a value that doesn't exist, Windows will create it for you. Deleting a key simply requires you to know its name.

```
oShell.RegDelete( _
 "HKCU\SOFTWARE\Test")
```

AppActivate

Your scripts not only can launch external applications using Run and Exec, but can also activate already running applications. You just need to know the window title, or a portion of it.

```
oShell.AppActivate _
 "Notepad"
```

After the application is active and has the system focus, you can send keystrokes to it using SendKeys.

SendKeys

Try this script:

```
oShell.Run "Notepad.exe"
Wscript.Sleep 5000
oShell.AppActivate "Notepad"
oShell.SendKeys "Ghost writing is fun."
```

> **TIP**
>
> Notice the `Sleep` command. This gives Notepad time to launch before the script activates it and starts sending keystrokes to it.

SendKeys allows you to send keystrokes to other applications. This is a wonderful way to control applications that don't provide any other means of doing so; effectively, you're writing your own old-style macros to control the application's functions. You can even send special keys by using the following strings along with `SendKeys`:

▶ {BS}—Backspace

▶ {BREAK}—Break

▶ {CAPSLOCK}—Caps lock

▶ {DEL}—Delete

▶ {DOWN}—Down arrow

▶ {END}—End

▶ {ENTER}—Enter

▶ {ESC}—Escape

▶ {HELP}—Help

▶ {HOME}—Home

▶ {INS}—Insert

▶ {LEFT}—Left arrow

▶ {NUMLOCK}—Num lock

▶ {PGDN}—Page down

▶ {PGUP}—Page up

▶ {PRTSC}—Print screen

▶ {RIGHT}—Right arrow

▶ {SCROLLLOCK}—Scroll lock

▶ {TAB}—Tab

▶ {UP}—Up arrow

▶ +—Shift key, as in +P for Shift+P

▶ ^—Control key, as in ^P for Ctrl+P

▶ %—ALT key, as in %P for Alt+P

Notice that the special keys must be enclosed in curly brackets (braces) as shown, except for Shift, Alt, and Control key combinations.

Popup

You've already seen the MsgBox statement and used it to display dialog boxes; the Popup method displays similar boxes, but puts a time limit and a default response on them. To display a five-second notification:

```
oShell.Popup _
 "Everything is complete", 5
```

You can use the same values as the MsgBox statement, which I covered in Chapter 6, to display icons and buttons. For example, to display a critical error with Yes and No buttons, and to make it time out and accept the default:

```
oShell.Popup _
 "Severe error. Continue?", 5, 16 + 4
```

The Shortcut **Object**

Shortcut objects are created by using the Shell object's CreateShortcut method. This method only specifies the final location for the shortcut; it doesn't allow you to specify the shortcut's own properties. To do that, you modify the properties of the Shortcut object, and then call the Shortcut object's Save method to save your changes.

Methods and Properties

The Shortcut object offers the following properties.

- ▶ Arguments—Any command-line arguments that should be passed when the shortcut is launched.

- ▶ Description—A description of the shortcut.

- ▶ FullName—A read-only property that returns the full name of the target application.

- ▶ HotKey—The hot key that can be used to launch the shortcut from the keyboard. You can use any letter, number, or function key (F1 to F12). You can also specify Control, Alt, or Shift keys, such as Alt+F9.

- ▶ IconLocation—The name of an icon file, along with an index to a specific icon, that should be used for the shortcut.

- ▶ TargetPath—The complete path and filename to the target application. UNCs are acceptable.

- ▶ WindowStyle—The starting window style for the shortcut when launched.

- ▶ WorkingDirectory—The working directory for the application launched by the shortcut.

You can create two types of shortcuts:

▶ *Standard* shortcuts have an .LNK filename extension and generally point to applications on the local computer or network.

▶ *Internet* shortcuts have a .URL filename extension and point to websites.

You'll see examples of both in Listing 11.2.

Practical Application

Listing 11.2 shows a sample script that creates both a normal application shortcut and a URL shortcut.

LISTING 11.2   *Shortcuts.vbs.* Creates shortcuts on the user's desktop.

```
' this sample creates two shortcuts on the current user's desktop
' shows how to use the Shell interface from within Script.

'first, we need to create an instance of the shell object
dim objShell
set objShell = WScript.CreateObject("WScript.Shell")

'next, we need to get the path to the special Desktop folder
dim strDesktop
strDesktop = objShell.SpecialFolders("Desktop")

'now, we can create shortcuts on the desktop

'let's do Internet Explorer
dim objShortcut
set objShortcut= objShell.CreateShortcut(strDesktop & "\IE.lnk")
with objShortcut
     .TargetPath = "iexplore.exe"
     .WindowStyle = 1
     .Hotkey = "CTRL+SHIFT+I"
     .Description = "Launch Internet Explorer"
     .WorkingDirectory = strDesktop
     .Save
end with

'let's create a link to my home page
dim objURL
set objURL = objShell.CreateShortcut(strDesktop & _
  "\SAPIEN Website.url")
objURL.TargetPath = "http://www.sapien.com"
objURL.Save
```

I briefly introduced you to the With/End With construct earlier. Here, it's used so that I don't have to keep retyping objShortcut over and over. Each of the lines following the With statement begins with a period, and so VBScript assumes I'm talking about objShortcut, the object mentioned in the With statement.

Objects in Detail

Okay, it's time for me to come clean about something, because I haven't been entirely honest with you. I've been using the word *object* just a bit loosely. For the most part, it's fine, and in fact if I hadn't decided to provide you with this little full disclosure, you wouldn't be worse off. However, I feel it's important that you understand the little details of working with COM, even if, most of the time, you can be casual and carefree with words like *object*.

I'm going to cover these details using the help of a TLB, or Type Library, Browser. I'll be using the one built into PrimalScript, but if you have another one, feel free to follow along (I actually like the one in PrimalScript primarily because it doesn't try to hide anything; you get the whole gory mess of details about each COM object). A type library is a special file, with a .tlb filename extension, that describes what's inside a COM object. They're a sort of self-documenting feature, although you do have to be trained to read this special type of "documentation." A TLB Browser is simply a tool that opens TLBs and attempts to translate them into something more English-like. Figure 11.1 shows the PrimalScript TLB Browser, opened to the Microsoft Scripting Runtime component—the component that contains the FileSystemObject that I've mentioned before, and which I'm finally covering in detail in the next chapter.

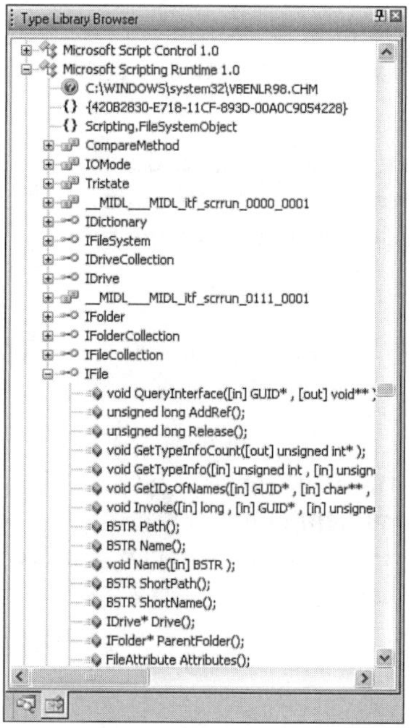

FIGURE 11.1   The TLB Browser in SAPIEN PrimalScript.

The Scripting Runtime is implemented in a single, physical dynamic link library (DLL) file. In fact, each component or type library shown in the TLB Browser represents a single individual DLL file. Within the component, you'll notice several items. First is a reference to the component's actual documentation, in this case C:\Windows\System32\ VBENLR98.CHM, a compiled HTML help file. Next is the component's globally unique identifier, or GUID, followed by its ProgID: Scripting.FileSystemObject.

Next are four *enumerations*. These work a bit like constants, in that they're names for predefined values. Expanding the IOMode enumeration, for example, I see that it has ForReading=1, ForWriting=2, and ForAppending=8. That's good information: If I later see anything that uses IOMode as an input value, I now know that the valid choices are 1, 2, and 8, for Reading, Writing, and Appending.

Next are several *interfaces*, which I've loosely been calling *objects* up to now. You can make out an IDictionary interface, an interface called IFileSystem, one called IDriveCollection, and so forth. Interface names almost always begin with a capital letter *I*, following a standard set down by Microsoft. I'm going to crack open the IFile interface.

Inside an interface are its *members*, which we've been referring to as properties and methods. In the world of COM, there's really no difference between properties and methods—properties are more or less methods that just accept and return values, but don't take any action. For example, about halfway down I see a member named Path(). The TLB Browser tells me that its data type is BSTR, which is COM jargon for string. You'll notice that some of the other members, such as Name, actually have two versions: One is listed as BSTR Name(); and the other as void Name([in] BSTR);. What you're seeing there is a property:

▶ BSTR Name(); is the *read* version of the property. When called, it'll return a string (BSTR).

▶ void Name([in] BSTR); is the *write* half of the property. When called, it doesn't return anything (hence the "void" for its data type). However, it accepts an input value of the type string, which is how you pass the value that you want the property set to.

A bit further down, I see IDrive* Drive(); which is a member named Drive that returns an object of the IDrive type. I could scroll up to the IDrive interface to explore it, if I wanted to see its members.

Knowing this jargon—members, interfaces, types, and so forth—can be useful when you're trying to learn how to use a COM object that isn't documented in a VBScript-friendly fashion. By using a TLB Browser, such as the one in PrimalScript, you can explore the COM objects available on your computer and take a stab at figuring out how they work.

Summary

In this chapter, you've seen how the built-in `WScript`, `Network`, `Shell`, and `Shortcut` objects work. With these, you'll be able to write effective logon scripts, utility scripts, and much more. Perhaps more important, you've seen examples of how VBScript can be used to call on objects that are provided by the Windows operating system. Throughout the rest of this book, you'll be building on that skill to utilize more complex and powerful objects, including ADSI and WMI, to accomplish even the most difficult administrative tasks.

CHAPTER 12

Working with the File System

Y ou'd be surprised how often you might need to access a computer's file system from within an administrative script. For example, a script that adds new users to the domain might need to read those names from a script, or might need to write out new passwords into a file. A script designed to query TCP/IP addresses from workstation computers will need to write that information some-where—why not a text file? File system access is almost a prerequisite for any number of useful scripts, even ones that don't have a basic goal of manipulating files or folders. Fortunately, the Windows scripting library includes the FileSystemObject, or FSO, which provides easy access to the drives, files, and folders on your computer.

The FileSystemObject Library

The FSO is actually an *object library,* which simply means that it's made up of bunches of other objects (or, as I said in the previous chapter, *interfaces*). These other objects represent things like files and folders on your computer. As with any other object—or library—you start working with the FSO in a script by declaring a variable and creating an instance of the object.

```
Dim oFSO
Set oFSO = WScript.CreateObject
("Scripting.FileSystemObject")
```

One look at the FSO's documentation and you might wonder what you've gotten yourself into. The FSO contains an almost bewildering number of properties, objects, and methods for you to work with. Don't let this bounty of options overwhelm you! The FSO only has four basic objects that you'll work with:

- A `Drive` object represents a drive on your system. Drives can include removable drives, fixed drives, mapped network drives, and so forth.

- A `Folder` object represents a folder in the file system.

- A `File` object represents—you guessed it—a file.

- A `TextStream` object represents a stream of text, which is a fancy way of describing a text file. More precisely, a `TextStream` allows you to pull (or stream) text in and out of a file, providing a handy way to work with the contents of text files.

All of the FSO's other methods, properties, and objects are designed for working with these four basic objects. I'll cover each of these objects in their own section, along with their associated properties and methods.

Working with Drives

`Drive` objects represent the logical drives attached to your system, including network drives, CD-ROM drives, and so forth. Drives also provide an entry point into each drive's file system, starting with the root folder of the file system hierarchy. Because the `Drive` object represents one of the simplest aspects of the file system, it's one of the simplest objects in the FSO.

The method you'll use most with drives is GetDrive, which returns a Drive object given a specific drive letter. For example, to obtain a Drive object that represents your C: drive:

```
Dim oDriveC, oFSO
Set oFSO = WScript.CreateObject("Scripting.FileSystemObject")
Set oDriveC = oFSO.GetDrive("C:")
```

You can also use the FSO's root-level Drives collection to iterate through all of the drives attached to your system. Try this without a disc inserted into a CD or DVD drive and see what happens!

```
Dim oFSO, oDrive
Set oFSO = WScript.CreateObject("Scripting.FileSystemObject")
For Each oDrive In oFSO.Drives
 MsgBox "Drive " & oDrive.DriveLetter & _
   " has a capacity of " & oDrive.TotalSize & " bytes " & _
   " and is drive type " & oDrive.DriveType
Next
```

Working with Drive Objects

The previous example illustrates the use of some of the Drive object's properties. The full list includes the following:

▶ AvailableSpace and FreeSpace return the number of bytes available on the disk. FreeSpace returns the amount of free space on the drive; AvailableSpace returns the amount available to the user running the script. File quotas and other concerns can result in a difference between these two properties.

▶ DriveLetter returns the drive's logical letter. Note that not all drives must have a drive letter, especially in Windows 2000 or later, although most of the time they will.

▶ DriveType tells you what kind of drive you're looking at. This property returns a number corresponding to a specific drive type.

▶ FileSystem tells you what kind of file system the drive uses. This is a string, such as FAT, NTFS, or CDFS (used for optical media like CDs and DVDs).

▶ IsReady returns a True or False. This is mainly useful for network and removable drives, and allows you to see if they're ready (connected or with a disk inserted) before trying to use them.

▶ Path returns the drive letter and the root folder; for example, "C:\".

▶ RootFolder returns a Folder object representing the root folder of the file system.

▶ SerialNumber returns the drive's volume serial number.

▶ ShareName gives you the share name (UNC) for network drives, such as \\Server1\Share. For nonnetwork drives, this property returns an empty string.

▶ `TotalSize` is the total size of the drive in bytes. To figure the size in kilobytes, divide by one thousand; to find megabytes, divide by one million; for gigabytes, divide by one billion.

▶ `VolumeName` gives you the name of the drive's logical volume.

> **NOTE**
>
> The term *drive* can be confusing. In Windows, and, therefore, in the FSO, a *drive* is a logical entity. More than one drive can live on a *disk*, with the disk being the physical device. The terms *drive* and *volume* are more or less interchangeable as far as the FSO is concerned.

When working with the `DriveType` property, the following values correspond to specific drive types.

▶ **0: Unknown**—This is rare, although some devices like tape backup drives hooked into a parallel port can show up this way.

▶ **1: Removable**—This applies to any removable media drive, such as a floppy or Zip disk, but not to optical media drives.

▶ **2: Fixed**—This is used for all hard drives, and for some devices that aren't recognized as removable, like older FireWire drives.

▶ **3: Network**—This is used for all mapped network drives.

▶ **4: CD-ROM**—This is used for all optical media drives, including DVD-ROMs.

▶ **5: RAM Disk**—This is rare, as most of us don't use RAM disks anymore. Note that USB "pen" drives show up as either type 1 or 2, not as RAM disks.

The base FSO object has a couple of other interesting methods for working with drives, including `DriveExists`, which accepts a drive letter and returns a `True` or `False` indicating whether the drive exists. This is useful for checking to see if a drive exists before trying to work with it. Note that `GetDrive` returns an error if the drive you specify doesn't exist, so using `DriveExists` first is always a good idea.

Listing 12.1 shows an example of how the FSO's `Drive` object can be used to iterate through available drives and set the volume name for all fixed drives to "Fixed."

LISTING 12.1   *NameDrives.vbs.* Changes the volume name for fixed drives to "Fixed."

```
Dim oFSO, oDrive
Set oFSO = WScript.CreateObject("Scripting.FileSystemObject")
For Each oDrive In oFSO.Drives
 If oDrive.DriveType = 2 Then
  If oDrive.VolumeName <> "Fixed" Then
   oDrive.VolumeName = "Fixed"
```

LISTING 12.1   Continued

```
  End If
  End If
Next
MsgBox "Finished!"
```

This script illustrates an important concept, which is that some `Drive` properties are writable and others aren't. For example, you can change the `VolumeName` property, which changes the actual name of a drive. However, you cannot change the `TotalSize` property. Although it might be nice to have a script expand the size of your drives, it just isn't possible!

Another important concept is the `RootFolder` property. Unlike the other properties, which return a value of some kind, `RootFolder` returns a completely new `Folder` object, which represents the root folder of the drive.

Working with Folders

Folders offer up a bit more complexity. First, the FSO itself offers more methods for manipulating specific folders.

- ▶ `CopyFolder` copies a folder.

- ▶ `CreateFolder` creates a new folder.

- ▶ `DeleteFolder` removes a folder permanently. Note that the deleted folder doesn't ever make it to the Recycle Bin, and there's no "Are you sure?" prompt.

- ▶ `FolderExists`, like `DriveExists`, returns a `True` or `False` indicating whether the specified folder exists.

- ▶ `GetFolder` accepts a complete folder path and, if the folder exists, returns a `Folder` object that represents the folder.

- ▶ `GetParentFolderName` accepts a complete folder path and returns the name of its parent folder. For example, `GetParentFolderName("C:\Windows\System32")` would return `"C:\Windows"`.

- ▶ `GetSpecialFolder` returns the complete path to special operating system folders. For example, `GetSpecialFolder(0)` returns the path for the Windows folder. Use 1 for the System32 folder, and use 2 for the system's temporary files folder.

- ▶ `MoveFolder` moves a file a folder.

The following example illustrates a few of these base functions:

```
Dim oFSO
Set oFSO = WScript.CreateObject("Scripting.FileSystemObject")
```

```
Dim oFolder
If oFSO.FolderExists("C:\MyFolder") Then
 Set oFolder = oFSO.GetFolder("C:\MyFolder")
Else
 oFSO.CreateFolder "C:\MyFolder"
 Set oFolder = oFSO.GetFolder("C:\MyFolder")
End If

MsgBox oFSO.GetParentFolderName(oFolder.Path)
```

This example creates a folder named `C:\MyFolder`, and then displays its parent folder, which, of course, is just `C:\`.

Working with Folder Objects

Although the FSO's base methods are useful for manipulating folders, folders themselves have a number of useful methods and properties that allow a more granular level of control. For example, `Folder` objects have four methods:

▶ Copy copies the folder. You just specify the destination for the copy. This method provides the same functionality as the FSO's `CopyFolder` method.

▶ Delete mimics the FSO's `DeleteFolder` method. However, because you're using the folder's method directly, you don't have to specify which folder to delete.

▶ Move mimics the FSO's `MoveFolder` method.

▶ CreateTextFile returns a `TextStream` object and creates a new text file in the folder. I'll cover this functionality in the next section.

To illustrate these methods, I'll expand on the last example.

```
Dim oFSO
Set oFSO = WScript.CreateObject("Scripting.FileSystemObject")

Dim oFolder
If oFSO.FolderExists("C:\MyFolder") Then
 Set oFolder = oFSO.GetFolder("C:\MyFolder")
Else
 oFSO.CreateFolder "C:\MyFolder"
 Set oFolder = oFSO.GetFolder("C:\MyFolder")
End If

oFolder.Copy "C:\MyOtherFolder"
oFolder.Delete
```

The result is a single folder named `C:\MyOtherFolder`. The operations of creating the new `C:\MyFolder` folder, copying it, and deleting it all occur almost instantly.

Folder objects support a number of useful properties, as well:

- ▶ Attributes
- ▶ DateCreated
- ▶ DateLastAccessed
- ▶ DateLastModified
- ▶ Drive
- ▶ Files
- ▶ IsRootFolder
- ▶ Name
- ▶ ParentFolder
- ▶ Path
- ▶ ShortName
- ▶ ShortPath
- ▶ Size
- ▶ SubFolders
- ▶ Type

Some of these properties are straightforward. For example, you can probably figure out what type of information the `DateLastModified` property will return, and you can guess what the `Path` property will display. A few of these properties, however, deserve further explanation.

The `Type` property in particular is interesting. To see what it returns, try the example in Listing 12.2 (which will work for files and folders, both of which have a `Type` property). Try specifying the Recycle Bin or other special folders to see what you get.

LISTING 12.2   *Types.vbs.* Shows the type of a file or folder.

```
Dim oFSO, oF
Set oFSO = WScript.CreateObject("Scripting.FileSystemObject")

Dim sPath
sPath = InputBox("Enter the path to a file or folder.")

If oFSO.FolderExists(sPath) Then
 Set oF = oFSO.GetFolder(sPath)
ElseIf oFSO.FileExists(sPath) Then
 Set oF = oFSO.GetFile(sPath)
Else
```

LISTING 12.2   Continued

```
MsgBox "Can't find what you typed."
WScript.Quit
End If


MsgBox oF.Type
```

Folder Attributes

The `Attributes` property returns specific attributes of the folder, such as whether it is read-only or compressed. These attributes are numeric, and because a folder can have many different attributes at once—such as both compressed and hidden—you have to manipulate the `Attributes` property a bit to figure out what's what.

The possible values are

- ▶ Normal: 0
- ▶ Read-only: 1
- ▶ Hidden: 2
- ▶ System: 4
- ▶ Volume: 8
- ▶ Directory: 16
- ▶ Archive: 32
- ▶ Alias: 1024
- ▶ Compressed: 2048

To figure out which attributes are turned on, you have to perform some Boolean math. Because you're a systems administrator, I'm going to assume that you don't really care for a detailed explanation of what Boolean math is or does, but that you probably just prefer to see an example of it in action. Listing 12.3 is just that.

LISTING 12.3   *CheckFolder.vbs.* Checks the attributes of a specified folder.

```
Dim oFSO, sFolder, oFolder
Set oFSO = WScript.CreateObject("Scripting.FileSystemObject")
sFolder = InputBox("Full path of folder to check?")

Set oFolder = oFSO.GetFolder(sFolder)
```

LISTING 12.3   Continued

```
Dim sMsg

If oFolder.Attributes AND 0 Then
 sMsg = sMsg & "Folder is normal" & vbCrLf
End If

If oFolder.Attributes AND 1 Then
 sMsg = sMsg & "Folder is Read only" & vbCrLf
End If

If oFolder.Attributes AND 2 Then
 sMsg = sMsg & "Folder is Hidden" & vbCrLf
End If

If oFolder.Attributes AND 4 Then
 sMsg = sMsg & "Folder is a system folder" & vbCrLf
End If

If oFolder.Attributes AND 8 Then
 sMsg = sMsg & "Folder is really a volume" & vbCrLf
End If

If oFolder.Attributes AND 16 Then
 sMsg = sMsg & "Folder is a directory" & vbCrLf
End If

If oFolder.Attributes AND 32 Then
 sMsg = sMsg & "Folder has changed since the last backup" & vbCrLf
End If

If oFolder.Attributes AND 1024 Then
 sMsg = sMsg & "Folder is a shortcut" & vbCrLf
End If

If oFolder.Attributes AND 2048 Then
 sMsg = sMsg & "Folder is compressed" & vbCrLf
End If

MsgBox sMsg
```

12

By using the Boolean AND operator to compare the Attributes property to the predefined values, you can figure out which attributes are turned on and which ones aren't. This script builds up a message in variable sMsg, which contains the status of the various attribute flags.

Some of these attributes can be changed. You can use the Attributes property to alter the read-only status, the hidden status, the system status, and the archive status. You cannot change any of the other attributes. To set an attribute, use the OR operator again.

```
'Set the Read-Only status to be true
oFolder.Attributes = oFolder.Attributes OR 1

'Now try turning on compression:
oFolder.Attributes = oFolder.Attributes OR 2048
```

The last line of code causes an error because the compression attribute is read-only within scripting, and cannot be changed by the FSO. You *can* do it with Windows Management Instrumentation (WMI), though, which I'll cover later.

Properties That Are Objects

Some of a Folder object's properties are actually references to other objects.

▶ The Drive property returns a Drive object that represents the drive that contains the folder.

▶ The Files property returns a collection of File objects, representing the files within the folder. I'll cover File objects in the next section.

▶ The ParentFolder property returns a Folder object that represents the folder's parent folder. If the folder is the root folder, you cannot use ParentFolder because the root doesn't have a parent. Use the IsRootFolder property, which returns True or False, to figure out whether the folder is the root.

▶ The SubFolders property returns a collection of Folder objects, representing the folders contained within the folder.

The SubFolders property provides access to an object hierarchy that represents the folder hierarchy of the file system. Figure 12.1 illustrates the relationship between a Drive object (in this case, a network drive), its RootFolder property (which returns a Folder object), and that folder's SubFolders property (which returns a collection of Folder objects).

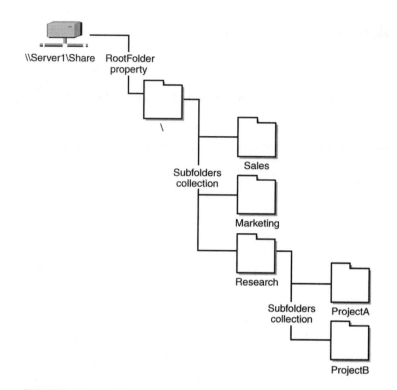

FIGURE 12.1   The hierarchy of `Drive` and `Folder` objects in the FSO.

Working with Files

Files, of course, are the most granular object you can work with inside the FSO, and they're relatively uncomplicated. As with `Drive` and `Folder` objects, the FSO itself has some useful methods for working with files:

▶ `CopyFile`

▶ `DeleteFile`

▶ `FileExists`

▶ `GetFile`

▶ `MoveFile`

These all work similarly to their `Folder` object counterparts, allowing you to obtain a reference to a file (`GetFile`), check for a file's existence (`FileExists`), and copy, delete, and move files. You can also create files, which is a process I'll cover a bit later in this chapter.

Working with `File` **Objects**

`File` objects themselves have a few methods:

- ▶ `Copy` copies a file.

- ▶ `Delete` removes a file without warning and without using the Recycle Bin.

- ▶ `Move` moves a file.

- ▶ `OpenAsTextStream` opens a file for reading (which I'll cover in the next section).

Properties of the `File` object include

- ▶ `Attributes`

- ▶ `DateCreated`

- ▶ `DateLastAccessed`

- ▶ `DateLastModified`

- ▶ `Drive`

- ▶ `Name`

- ▶ `ParentFolder`

- ▶ `Path`

- ▶ `ShortName`

- ▶ `Size`

- ▶ `Type`

These all work identically to their `Folder` object property counterparts, which I covered in the previous section. The `Type` property can return different values for a file; use Listing 12.2 with different files to see what you get back. For example, for a file with a `.txt` file-name extension, you should get something like "Text Document" from the `Type` property.

File Properties and Methods   Listing 12.4 shows an example of the `File` object's properties and methods in use.

LISTING 12.4   *FileProperties.vbs*. This script uses both `File` and `Folder` objects to demonstrate various properties and methods.

```
Dim oFSO, oFolder, oFile, oNewFolder
Set oFSO = WScript.CreateObject("Scripting.FileSystemObject")

Dim sPath
sPath = InputBox("Provide starting folder path")
Set oFolder = oFSO.GetFolder(sPath)
```

LISTING 12.4   Continued

```
If oFSO.FolderExists(sPath) Then

For Each oFile in oFolder.Files
  MsgBox "File " & oFile.Name & " last changed on " & _
    oFile.DateLastModified & " and of type " & _
    oFile.Type & ". It is contained in folder " & _
    oFile.ParentFolder.Path & " and uses the short " & _
    " filename " & oFile.ShortName & "."
 Next
End If


MsgBox "All Done!"
```

This script is ready to execute as is on any system.

File Properties and Methods—Explained   This is a straightforward script. It starts by setting up some variables and creating an FSO.

```
Dim oFSO, oFolder, oFile, oNewFolder
Set oFSO = WScript.CreateObject("Scripting.FileSystemObject")
```

Next, the script asks you to provide a starting path, and it retrieves that folder. An If/Then construct is used to perform the rest of the script's work only if the folder you provide actually exists.

```
Dim sPath
sPath = InputBox("Provide starting folder path")
Set oFolder = oFSO.GetFolder(sPath)

If oFSO.FolderExists(sPath) Then
```

Next, the script uses a For Each/Next construct to loop through each file in the folder that you specified. For each one, it uses several of the File object's properties to display information about the file.

```
For Each oFile in oFolder.Files
  MsgBox "File " & oFile.Name & " last changed on " & _
    oFile.DateLastModified & " and of type " & _
    oFile.Type & ". It is contained in folder " & _
    oFile.ParentFolder.Path & " and uses the short " & _
    " filename " & oFile.ShortName & "."
```

Notice in particular the use of the `ParentFolder` property. This property actually represents a `Folder` object, with all of the properties and methods—including the `Path` property—of any `Folder` object. `oFile.ParentFolder.Path` is using the `Path` property of a `Folder` object—specifically, the folder that contains the file referenced by `oFile`.

The script finishes up by closing loops and constructs and displaying a message.

```
 Next
End If

MsgBox "All Done!"
```

This example should help you see how various properties and methods of the `File` object can be used, particularly those properties that are actually object references, such as `ParentFolder`.

Reading and Writing Text Files

The FSO provides basic functionality for reading from, and writing to, text files. If you think of a text file as one long string of characters, you'll have an idea of how the FSO views text files. In fact, that long string of characters is what the FSO calls a *TextStream*. `TextStream` objects are how you get text into and out of text files.

The FSO has two basic methods for creating a `TextStream`: `CreateTextFile` and `OpenTextFile`. Both methods require you to provide a filename, and allow you to specify optional parameters, such as whether to overwrite any existing file when creating a new one. Here's an example:

```
Dim oFSO, oTS
Set oFSO = WScript.CreateObject("Scripting.FileSystemObject")
Set oTS = oFSO.CreateTextFile("c:\test.txt")
oTS.WriteLine "Hello, World!"
MsgBox "All Done!"
oTS.Close
```

As you can see, the result of the `CreateTextFile` method is a `TextStream`, which is assigned via the `Set` command to variable `oTS`. `TextStream` objects have some properties and methods all their own. First, the methods:

- ▶ `Write` writes one or more characters to the file.

- ▶ `WriteLine` writes one or more characters and follows them with a carriage return/linefeed combination, thus ending the line as you would in Notepad when you press Enter.

- ▶ `Close` closes the `TextStream`.

- ▶ `Read` reads a specified number of characters from a `TextStream`.

▶ ReadLine reads an entire line of characters—up to a carriage return/linefeed.

▶ ReadAll reads the entire TextStream.

One useful property of a TextStream is AtEndOfStream, which is set to True when you've read all the way through a text file and reached its end.

Files must be opened either for reading, writing, or appending. When a file is opened for reading, you can only use the Read, ReadLine, and ReadAll methods; similarly, when the file is opened for writing or appending, you can only use Write or WriteLine. Of course, you can always use Close.

> **NOTE**
>
> Appending a file simply opens it and begins writing to the end of the file, while leaving the previous contents intact. This can be useful for writing messages to an ongoing log file.

Another way to open a file is to use the OpenAsTextStream method of a File object that represents the file. This technique also returns a TextStream object. The OpenAsTextStream method allows you to specify how you want the file opened—for reading, writing, or appending.

Reading and Writing Files   Listing 12.5 is a robust sample script that demonstrates how to read and write text files from within a script. I'll use these same techniques at the end of the chapter, when I'll show you how to create a script that scans Internet Information Services (IIS) log files for Active Server Pages errors.

LISTING 12.5   *FileWork.vbs.* This script creates a file, writes text to it, and then reads the text back in again.

```
Dim sFileName, oFSO, oTS, sText
Set oFSO = WScript.CreateObject("Scripting.FileSystemObject")

sFileName = InputBox("Enter the full path and " & _
 "name of a file to be created.")

If oFSO.FileExists(sFileName) Then
 If MsgBox("This file exists. OK to overwrite?", & _
  "Are you sure?", 4 + 32) <> 6 Then
  MsgBox "Script aborted."
  WScript.Quit
 Else
  Set oTS = oFSO.CreateTextFile(sFileName,True)
 End If
End If
```

LISTING 12.5   Continued

```
oTS.WriteLine "Script log file:"
oTS.WriteLine "Started " & Now()
oTS.WriteLine "Finished" & Now()
oTS.Close

MsgBox "Finished making file. Feel free to edit it," & _
 " and click OK to continue."

Set oTS = oFSO.OpenTextFile(sFileName)
sText = oTS.ReadAll
oTS.Close

MsgBox "Your file contains: " & vbCrLf & vbCrLf & _
 sText
```

This script is ready to run on any system.

Reading and Writing Files—Explained   This is a straightforward script, and it's a good review of VBScript in general because it combines some important elements that you've already learned. It starts by declaring some variables and creating a new FSO.

```
Dim sFileName, oFSO, oTS, sText
Set oFSO = WScript.CreateObject("Scripting.FileSystemObject")
```

Next, it uses an input box to get a filename.

```
sFileName = InputBox("Enter the full " & _
 "path and name of a file " & _
 "to be created.")
```

Next, the script checks to see if the file exists. If it does, it uses a message box to ask permission to overwrite the file. Notice that this is a more complete version of MsgBox() than I usually use in examples. This version provides a title for the message box and specifies that it should contain a question mark icon and Yes and No buttons (4 is the question mark, 32 is Yes/No). I had to look those values up in the VBScript documentation. Finally, MsgBox is being used as a function—if the user clicks Yes, the function will return a 6 (also from the documentation), so this code checks to see if a 6 was returned.

```
If oFSO.FileExists(sFileName) Then
 If MsgBox("This file exists. OK to overwrite?" & _
  "Are you sure?", 4 + 32) <> 6 Then
  MsgBox "Script aborted."
  WScript.Quit
```

If the user clicks Yes, the script creates a new text file. Notice the `True`, which tells `CreateTextFile` to overwrite any existing file, if there is one.

```
 Else
   Set oTS = oFSO.CreateTextFile(sFileName,True)
 End If
End If
```

The script uses the `WriteLine` method to add some text to the file before closing it.

```
oTS.WriteLine "Script log file:"
oTS.WriteLine "Started " & Now()
oTS.WriteLine "Finished" & Now()
oTS.Close
```

Finally, the script displays a message. If you want, open the text file and edit it—that'll prove that the script is reading back the text file in the next step.

```
MsgBox "Finished making file. Feel free to edit it," & _
  " and click OK to continue."
```

In the next step, I reuse the same variable to reference a new `TextStream`, this time reopening the same file by using `OpenTextFile`. I use `ReadAll` to load the entire file into a variable, and then close the `TextStream`. I finish by displaying the contents of the file in a message box.

```
Set oTS = oFSO.OpenTextFile(sFileName)
sText = oTS.ReadAll
oTS.Close

MsgBox "Your file contains: " & vbCrLf & vbCrLf & _
  sText
```

This example is a good reference for you to use when you start working with text files in your own scripts.

Other FSO Methods and Properties

The base FSO object offers a few other useful methods and properties that you might need from time to time.

The first is the `BuildPath` function. It accepts components of a file or folder path and appends them together. Normally, you could do that with the simple & concatenation operator, but `BuildPath` actually worries about getting backslashes in the right place. So, consider this example:

```
Dim sFolder, sFile
sFolder = "C:\Windows"
```

```
sFile = "MyFile.exe"

Dim oFSO
Set oFSO = CreateObject("Scripting.FileSystemObject")
MsgBox sFolder & sFile
MsgBox oFSO.BuildPath(sFolder,sFile)
```

The first message box displays "C:\WindowsMyFile.exe", which isn't right—it is missing the backslash in the middle. The second message box, which uses BuildPath, displays the correct "C:\Windows\MyFile.exe" because the BuildPath function figured out that a backslash was necessary.

While working with paths, you might also have a need to get the absolute or base path name, and the FSO's GetAbsolutePathName and GetBaseName methods will do it for you. Here's an example:

```
Dim oFSO, sPath1, sPath2
Set oFSO = CreateObject("Scripting.FileSystemObject")
sPath1 = "C:\Windows\System32\Scrrun.dll"
sPath2 = "..\My Documents\Files"

MsgBox oFSO.GetAbsolutePathName(sPath1)
MsgBox oFSO.GetAbsolutePathName(sPath2)

MsgBox oFSO.GetBaseName(sPath1)
MsgBox oFSO.GetBaseName(sPath2)
```

The result of this is four message boxes:

▶ "C:\Windows\System32\Scrrun.dll"—There's no difference between the input and output because the input in this case is already a complete, unambiguous path.

▶ "C:\Documents and Settings\Administrator\My Documents\Files"—This is a sample output you might see. The difference is that the path has been resolved into a complete, final path starting at the root of the drive.

▶ "Scrrun"—This is the base name of the last component in the input, without any file extension.

▶ "Files"—Again, this is the base name of the last component, although in this case it's a folder instead of a file.

Finally, there's GetTempName. If you need to create a temporary file or folder, especially within the system's temporary files folder, it's important that you use a filename that other applications won't already be using. GetTempName simply makes up a filename that is unique, allowing you to create your temp file with confidence.

Creating a Log File Scanner

Bringing everything together into a script can make it easier to see how the FSO works. I've decided to create a script that scans through log files from IIS; because these log files are simple text files, the FSO and VBScript's own string-handling functions are sufficient to examine a log file and locate any Web application errors that an administrator or developer might need to pay attention to.

The Log File Scanner   Listing 12.6 shows the complete log file scanner.

LISTING 12.6   *ScanLog.vbs.* Scans for "500" errors in an IIS log file.

```
' Scan a log file from a web server for
' occurrences of " - 500" which indicates an
' internal server error

' get the log file
Dim varLogFile
varLogFile = InputBox ("Enter the complete " & _
 "path and filename " & _
 "of log file to scan.")

' create filesystemobject
Dim oFSO
Set oFSO = WScript.CreateObject("Scripting.FileSystemObject")

' open file into a TextStream object
Dim oTS
Set oTS = oFSO.OpenTextFile (varLogFile)

Dim oTSOut
Set oTSOut = oFSO.CreateTextFile ("c:\errors.htm")

' begin reading each line in the textstream
dim varLine, varFoundNone
varFoundNone = true
Do Until oTS.AtEndOfStream
 varLine = oTS.ReadLine

 ' contains a 500 error?
 If instr(1, varLine, " - 500 ") <> 0 Then
  WScript.Echo varLine
  oTSOut.WriteLine "<b>" & varline & "</b>"
  varFoundNone = False
 End If
Loop
```

LISTING 12.6   Continued

```
' close the textstream
oTS.Close
oTSOut.Close

' found any?
If varFoundNone = True Then
 WScript.Echo "Didn't find any errors."
Else
 WScript.Echo "Found Errors. You need to fix them."
End If
```

Before you can start using this script, you simply need to figure out where IIS stores its log files. Normally, it's in %systemroot%\LogFiles with a subfolder (such as W3Svc) for each virtual web server that you've created.

The Log File Scanner—Explained   The script starts simply enough, by using an input box to ask for the complete path and filename of the log file to scan. This actually is a limitation of the script in its current form; in the next section, I'll enhance it to scan through every log file in a given folder, further automating the error-checking process.

```
' Scan a log file from a web server for
' occurrences of " - 500" which indicates an
' internal server error

' get the log file
Dim varLogFile
varLogFile = InputBox ("Enter the complete path and filename " & _
 "of log file to scan.")
```

Next, the script creates an FSO to work with.

```
' create filesystemobject
Dim oFSO
Set oFSO = WScript.CreateObject("Scripting.FileSystemObject")
```

Because the script has to read a text file, it needs to create a TextStream object. As you've already seen, the way to do this is to simply declare a variable, and then use one of the FSO methods that returns a TextStream. In this case, because the script just needs to read an existing file, it's using the OpenTextFile method.

```
' open file into a TextStream object
Dim oTS
Set oTS = oFSO.OpenTextFile (varLogFile)
```

The script is going to need to log any errors it finds, so it creates a second `TextStream` object. This one represents a new file, and the `TextStream` is obtained from the FSO's `CreateTextFile` method.

```
Dim oTSOut
Set oTSOut = oFSO.CreateTextFile ("c:\errors.htm")
```

Now the script needs to loop through the contents of the log file, which is opened for reading. I've created a variable, `varFoundNone`, and set it to the Boolean value of `True`. I'm using that variable to figure out if I've found any errors so that I can give an appropriate message at the end of the script. To loop through the log file, the script utilizes the `AtEndOfStream` property of the `TextStream` object. This property is automatically set to `True` when the script reaches the end of the file.

```
' begin reading each line in the textstream
dim varLine, varFoundNone
varFoundNone = true
Do Until oTS.AtEndOfStream
```

Next, the script reads a line of text from the file. The `ReadLine` method actually pulls an entire string of text and stores it in `varLine`. At the same time, `ReadLine` moves a pointer in the file to the next line, which is where the next `ReadLine` operation begins. This internal pointer is used to set the `AtEndOfStream` property to `True` when the end of the file is reached.

After reading the line of text, the script needs to see if it contains an ASP application error. Remember, each line of an IIS log file represents one logged message. If that line contains " - 500", it's an application error. To check, the script uses the `InStr()` function, telling the function to start looking for " - 500" at the first character of the line. `InStr()` returns a number indicating the character position where " - 500" was found. I don't really care about that; what's important is that `InStr()` returns a zero if it doesn't find " - 500" within the string.

```
 varLine = oTS.ReadLine

 ' contains a 500 error?
 If instr(1, varLine, " - 500 ") <> 0 Then
```

If there's no error in the line, the script skips down to the `Loop` and goes back to read the next line from the file. However, if `InStr()` finds the string, the script outputs the line of text using the `WScript.Echo` command. It also writes the line of text to the output file, prefixing it with `<b>` and suffixing it with `</b>`, which are the HTML tags for boldfacing.

```
 WScript.Echo varLine
 oTSOut.WriteLine "<b>" & varline & "</b>"
 varFoundNone = False
 End If
Loop
```

Also notice that my tracking variable gets set to `False` when an error is found. At the end of the script, this lets me know that I did, in fact, find an error.

After the script reaches the end of the file, it can start wrapping up. The first step is to close both of the `TextStreams` that are open.

```
' close the textstream
oTS.Close
oTSOut.Close
```

Finally, the script needs to display an appropriate ending message. This is especially important because otherwise there's no clear indication that the script finished running, especially if no errors were found.

```
' found any?
If varFoundNone = True Then
 WScript.Echo "Didn't find any errors."
Else
 WScript.Echo "Found Errors. You need to fix them."
End If
```

As I've already mentioned, the script is lacking in one significant way, which I'll fix in the next section.

The Enhanced Log File Scanner   As you know, IIS stores multiple log files in its log file folder. The odds that you're going to find the time to scan each new log file every day are slim, so it'd be nice if this script just asked for a folder and then scanned automatically through each log file it found there. Listing 12.7 does exactly that. The changes from the original log file scanner are shown in boldface.

LISTING 12.7   *ScanLog2.vbs.* Scans for "500" errors in an IIS log file.

```
' Scan a log file from a web server for
' occurrences of " - 500" which indicates an
' internal server error

' get the log file
Dim varLogPath
varLogPath = InputBox ("Enter the " & _
 "complete path of the logs folder.")

' create filesystemobject
Dim oFSO
Set oFSO = WScript.CreateObject("Scripting.FileSystemObject")

Dim oTSOut
Set oTSOut = oFSO.CreateTextFile ("c:\errors.htm")

' Loop through each file in the folder
Dim oFile, varFoundNone
varFoundNone = true
For Each oFile In oFSO.GetFolder(varLogPath).Files

 'Is this a log file?
 If Lcase(Right(oFile.Name,3)) = "log" Then

  'Open the log file
  Dim oTS
  oTS = oFSO.OpenTextFile(oFile.Path)
' begin reading each line in the textstream
  dim varLine
  Do Until oTS.AtEndOfStream
   varLine = oTS.ReadLine

   ' contains a 500 error?
   If instr(1, varLine, " - 500 ") <> 0 Then
    WScript.Echo varLine
    oTSOut.WriteLine "<b>" & varline & "</b>"
    varFoundNone = False
   End If
  Loop

  ' close the input textstream
  oTS.Close
```

LISTING 12.7   Continued

```
End If

Next

' close the output textstream
oTSOut.Close

' found any?
If varFoundNone = True Then
 WScript.Echo "Didn't find any errors."
Else
 WScript.Echo "Found Errors. You need to fix them."
End If
```

This new script will run as is on just about any system, provided you've given it the path to a folder that contains log files.

The Enhanced Log File Scanner—Explained   This enhanced script starts much like the previous one, but asks only for a folder name. The beauty of the way the FSO treats folder names is that it doesn't matter whether the user includes a trailing backslash; the script works fine either way.

```
' Scan a log file from a web server for
' occurrences of " - 500" which indicates an
' internal server error

' get the log file
Dim varLogPath
varLogPath = InputBox ("Enter the complete path of the logs folder.")
```

Another minor change is that only the output TextStream is opened at this point. Because the script is working with multiple files, it needs to open each one, one at a time, as it encounters them.

```
' create filesystemobject
Dim oFSO
Set oFSO = WScript.CreateObject("Scripting.FileSystemObject")

Dim oTSOut
Set oTSOut = oFSO.CreateTextFile ("c:\errors.htm")
```

Finally, the first big change. I've declared a variable to represent a file object, and I'm using a For Each/Next construct to loop through a collection of objects. Here's how it works: The FSO's GetFolder method returns a Folder object; specifically, it's returning the folder specified by the user from the earlier InputBox() function. The Folder object has a property called `Files`, which is a collection of `File` objects. The construct loops through each file in the collection. Each time through the loop, variable `oFile` will be set to a different file.

```
' Loop through each file in the folder
Dim oFile, varFoundNone
varFoundNone = true
For Each oFile In oFSO.GetFolder(varLogPath).Files
```

I cannot be assured that every file in the specified folder will be a log file, so I've used an `If/Then` construct. If the rightmost three characters of the filename are "log", I'll allow the script to work with the file and scan for errors. Otherwise, I'll skip the file. Notice the use of the `Lcase()` function to force the filename into lowercase characters. This ensures that files with a `.log` or `.LOG` filename extension will be scanned.

```
'Is this a log file?
 If Lcase(Right(oFile.Name,3)) = "log" Then
```

Now I'm ready to open the log file—the current one, that is—into a `TextStream`. I'm still using the `OpenTextFile` method, along with the `Path` property of the `File` object. The `Path` property provides a complete path, including the filename, for the file.

```
  'Open the log file
  Dim oTS
  oTS = oFSO.OpenTextFile(oFile.Path)
```

Most of the rest of the script is the same: Read each line of the file, scan for the error text, and output a message if an error is found.

```
dim varLine
' begin reading each line in the textstream
  Do Until oTS.AtEndOfStream
   varLine = oTS.ReadLine

   ' contains a 500 error?
   If instr(1, varLine, " - 500 ") <> 0 Then
    WScript.Echo varLine
    oTSOut.WriteLine "<b>" & varline & "</b>"
    varFoundNone = False
   End If
  Loop
```

Notice that I've had to rearrange the file closing statements. In this case, I'm finished reading the current input file, so I can close it before looping back up—via the `Next` statement—to open the next file in the folder.

```
' close the input textstream
oTS.Close

End If

Next
```

Finally, I can close the output text file and finish up as I did before.

```
' close the output textstream
oTSOut.Close

' found any?
If varFoundNone = True Then
 WScript.Echo "Didn't find any errors."
Else
 WScript.Echo "Found Errors. You need to fix them."
End If
```

The new script is a much more efficient administrative tool because it can be run whenever you want and always scans through every log file you have.

TIP

You could enhance this script to scan for other types of errors, such as the common errors that occur when a user tries to access a file that doesn't exist, or when users try to access a file that they're not authorized for.

Summary

In this chapter, you learned about the scripting `FileSystemObject`, which can be used to manipulate the files and folders on a computer. You learned about the object's flexible object hierarchy, which emulates the hierarchy of files and folders on your computer. You saw a sample script of how the `FileSystemObject` can be used to move and copy files, delete them, and even open and read through existing text files. The `FileSystemObject` is flexible enough to earn a place in many of your scripts, and you'll see it in many of the sample scripts in upcoming chapters.

CHAPTER 13

Putting It All Together: Creating Your First Script from Scratch

You've already learned just about all the VBScript commands, statements, and functions that you'll need to write administrative scripts. You've learned about some of the built-in scripting objects, and you've had a chance to work with the Windows `FileSystemObject`. Altogether, that's plenty of information and experience to start writing useful administrative scripts!

In this chapter, you'll design and write a tool that rotates Internet Information Services (IIS) log files. As you probably know, IIS can create a log file for each website it operates, and by default, it starts a new log file each day. Your rotation tool will move the previous day's completed log file to an archival folder for long-term storage. At the same time, the script will delete the oldest log file, keeping a rolling 30 days worth of log files in the archival folder.

> **NOTE**
>
> To keep things interesting, I'm going to introduce a couple of *logic errors* into the scripts in this chapter. These scripts should run more or less without error, but they'll have unexpected results because of the way they're written. If you spot the logic errors as you read, great! If not, don't worry—that's what the debugging section of this chapter is for!

Designing the Script

Before you fire up Notepad or your favorite script editor, you need to sit down and figure out exactly what your script will do. This is the best way to answer the question "Where do I start?" which is the most common question you'll have when you start writing your own administrative scripts. By following a specific script design process like the one I'm about to show you, you'll always know exactly where to start, and the script itself will come much easier when you start programming.

Whenever I design a script, I use a three-step process.

1. Gather facts.

   This step lets me document what I know about my environment that will affect the script. I'm simply writing down the various things that my script will need to know, or that I'll need to consider as I write the script. This might include details about how Windows works, specific business requirements, and so forth.

2. Define tasks.

   This step lets me define the specific tasks my script will accomplish. I get detailed here, focusing on each tiny step I'd have to perform if I were manually performing what I want my script to do.

3. Outline the script.

   This step rolls up what I know and what I want to do into a sort of plain-English version of the script. I list each step I think the script will need to take, along with any related information. This becomes the basis for the script I'll write, and scripting itself becomes a simple matter of translating English into VBScript.

> **NOTE**
>
> It might seem silly to walk through this entire design process, but I promise, it isn't. The number one question you'll have when you start writing scripts on your own is "Where do I start?" and this process *answers* that question for you. If you walk through this and participate in the exercises that will follow, you'll have a foolproof procedure for creating your own scripts from scratch.

In the next three sections, I'll go through this design process with the IIS log rotation tool that you'll be helping me develop in this chapter. If you'd like to practice, take a few moments and walk through the process yourself before reading my results in the following sections.

Gathering Facts

What do you know about IIS and log files? You need to capture the information that your script will need to operate, such as log file locations, names, and so forth. After giving it some thought, I come up with the following list:

- ▶ IIS log files use a file-naming format that's based upon the date. Each log filename starts with the letters *ex*, followed by a two-digit year, a two-digit month, and a two-digit day. The log file uses the filename extension `.log`.

- ▶ Files are stored in `C:\Winnt\System32\LogFiles` by default, at least on a Windows 2000 system. Windows Server 2003 uses `C:\Windows\System32\LogFiles`.

- ▶ I can store my archived files anywhere I want, so I'll create a folder named `C:\Winnt\LogArchive`. I'm assuming a Windows 2000 Server computer; for Windows Server 2003, I'd probably use `C:\Windows\LogArchive` instead.

- ▶ IIS closes each log file at the end of the day and opens a new one. I probably shouldn't try to move the log file that's currently opened by IIS; I should just go for *yesterday's* log file, instead.

- ▶ Under the main `LogFiles` folder, IIS creates a subfolder for each website. The first one is named `W3Svc`, the second is `W3Svc2`, and so forth. For now, I'll concentrate on the first website, which uses `W3Svc`.

That seems to be all the facts I can think of about log files, so now it's time to figure out exactly what the script needs to do.

Defining Tasks

Scripts can't use a graphical user interface, so when I start defining the tasks I need to complete I try to think about how I'd do the task from the Windows command line, instead of through the user interface. For example, when I think about how to perform the log rotation task myself, I come up with the following steps.

1. Locate the folder that contains the log files.

2. Locate the folder that contains the archived files.

3. Figure out the name of yesterday's log file.

4. Move yesterday's log file into the archive folder.

5. Figure out the name of the log file from 30 days ago.

6. Delete the 30-day-old log file.

It's a simple list of steps, because it's not a complicated task. Note that working from the command line forces me to consider steps like figuring out the filename, which I wouldn't have to do if I was using Explorer. In Explorer, I could just look at the filenames because they would be listed for me. Because scripts cannot "look" at things, the command line more closely represents the way the script itself will need to function.

With the basic steps out of the way, I can start outlining my script.

> **NOTE**
>
> Have I covered every possible task or situation? No. I haven't dealt with the fact that I might run out of disk space, or that I might forget to run the script one day and wind up with two older files to move. That's okay for this example, and in your projects you can decide how much additional work you need to do to make your script meet your exact needs.

Outlining the Script

The script outline should be a detailed, English explanation of what the script will do, in a systematic fashion. Use your task list as a starting point for the outline. For the log rotation tool, I come up with the following outline. Note that some of these tasks actually get broken down into subtasks.

1. Define the location of the log files.

2. Define the location of the archived files.

3. Figure out yesterday's date.**

4. Figure out the name of yesterday's log file.*

5. Move yesterday's log file into the archive folder.

6. Figure out the date from 30 days ago.**

7. Figure out the name of the log file from 30 days ago.*

8. Delete the 30-day-old log file.

Notice the two steps with an asterisk (*). These are pretty much the same thing: Given a date, give out a matching file log name. This subtask can be broken down as follows.

1. Start with "ex" as the filename.

2. Append the last two digits of the year.

3. Append a two-digit month.

4. Append a two-digit day.

5. Append ".log".

The steps in the main outline with two asterisks also seem to be related because they're both somehow calculating a date in the past. I don't readily know how to do a few of these steps in VBScript, such as how to figure out the exact date from 30 days ago. But I'm sure there's a way, so I'll worry about that later. If VBScript doesn't provide an easy way to do it, I can always break it down into a subtask.

Writing Functions and Subroutines

Generally, any kind of subtask you've identified is a great candidate for a function or subroutine, because subtasks get used more than once. You'll need to carefully examine your subtasks and decide which ones should be written as functions or subroutines. I have a general rule that I use: If a subtask involves more than one line of VBScript to accomplish, I write it as a function or subroutine. If I can do it in one line of VBScript code, I don't bother with a separate function or subroutine.

If you need a quick refresher of functions and subroutines, flip back to Chapter 5, "Functions, Objects, Variables, and More."

Identifying Candidate Modules

In this log rotation tool, I've already identified two potential modules (functions or subroutines): the date calculation and the log filename bit. A quick read through the VBScript documentation leads me to the DateAdd function, which can be used to calculate past or future dates. That seems to cover the date calculation subtask, so I don't think I'll need to write a function for that. I do see several Format commands that will help format a log filename, but none of them seem to do everything that I need in one line of code (at least, not one reasonably short line of code); I'll write the filename formatter as its own module.

Writing the Filename Formatting Function

Before writing a function, I need to consider a couple of facts. One fact is that the function is designed to encapsulate some subtask. Therefore, the function is going to need some kind of input to work on, and it's going to give me back some result that my script needs. Defining that input and output is critical. I want the function to be generic enough to be reusable, but specific enough to be useful.

Defining Function Input

In the case of the filename formatter, I know that the filename is always going to start with "ex," so I don't need that information in the input. The filename will always end in .log, so I don't need that in the input, either. What changes from filename to filename is the date information, so that seems like a logical piece of information for the function's input.

Defining Function Output

I want this function to take a date—its input—and create a fully formatted log filename. The output is obvious: a fully formatted log filename.

Writing the Function

Writing the actual function code requires a bit more task definition. You need to really break the task of formatting a filename down into small pieces. This can be a tough process because the human brain does so many things for you without conscious thought. Think about what a three-year-old would have to do to accomplish this task: Remember, all they have to work with at the beginning is a date.

You might come up with a task list like this:

1. Start with a blank piece of paper.

2. Write "ex" on the piece of paper.

3. On a separate piece of paper, write down the date you were given.

4. Erase everything but the year.

5. From the year, erase everything but the last two digits.

6. Write those last two digits after the "ex" on the first piece of paper.

7. On a new piece of paper, write down the date again.

8. Erase everything but the month.

9. If the month is only one digit long, add a zero to the front of it.

10. Copy the two-digit month to the first sheet of paper, after the two-digit year.

11. On a new piece of paper, write down the date one more time.

12. Erase everything but the day.

13. If the day is only one digit long, add a zero to the front of it.

14. Copy the two-digit day to the first sheet of paper, after the two-digit month.

15. On the first sheet of paper, add ".log" to what's already there.

16. Return the contents of the first sheet of paper.

Now, that's a lot of detail! All you need to do is translate that into VBScript. First, figure out which VBScript functions seem to line up with each step in the task, and eliminate any redundant tasks.

1. Declare a variable.

2. Place "ex" into the variable.

3. Declare a new variable to hold the year portion of the date.

4. Use the DatePart command to extract the year.

5. Use the Right command to take the last two digits of the year.

6. Append the two-digit year to the variable.

7. Declare a new variable to hold the month portion of the date.

8. Use the DatePart command to extract the month.

9. Use the `Len` command to figure out if the month is one digit; if it is, add a zero to the front.

10. Append the month to the variable.

11. Declare a new variable to hold the day portion of the date.

12. Use the `DatePart` command to extract the day.

13. Use the `Len` command to figure out if the day is one digit; if it is, add a zero to the front.

14. Append the day to the variable.

15. Append "`.log`" to the variable.

16. Return the variable.

Now you're ready to put the translated task list into an actual script.

The FormatLogFileName Function   Listing 13.1 shows the function in VBScript.

LISTING 13.1   *FormatLogFileName Function.* Accepts a date and returns an appropriate log filename.

```
Function FormatLogFileName(dDate)

Dim sFileName
sFileName = "ex"

Dim sYear
sYear = DatePart("yyyy",dDate)
sYear = Right(sYear,2)
sFileName = sFileName & sYear

Dim sMonth
sMonth = DatePart("m",dDate)
If Len(sMonth) = 1 Then
 sMonth = "0" & sMonth
End If
sFileName = sFileName & sMonth

Dim sDay
sDay = DatePart("d",dDate)
If Len(sDay) = 1 Then
 sDay = "0" & sDay
End If
sFileName = sFileName & sDay
```

LISTING 13.1   Continued

```
sFileName = ".log" & sFileName

FormatLogFileName = sFileName
```

End Function

Now, that's the complete script for the function, and it's ready to be plugged into the main script.

The FormatLogFileName Function—Explained   This function simply extracts various parts of a specific date, appends them together, and returns the results. I start with a function declaration, which gives the function its name and defines its input. This function will receive a date, which will be stored in a variable named dDate.

```
Function FormatLogFileName(dDate)
End Function
```

Next, I declare a variable to store the filename, and put "ex" in that variable.

```
Dim sFileName
sFileName = "ex"
```

Then, I declare a new variable for the year. The DatePart function extracts the four-digit year from dDate, which was passed as input to the function. Then, the Right function grabs just the last two digits of that four-digit year. Finally, I tack those two digits onto the filename using the ampersand (&) operator.

```
Dim sYear
sYear = DatePart("yyyy",dDate)
sYear = Right(sYear,2)
sFileName = sFileName & sYear
```

I use a similar set of steps for the month. Obviously, the DatePart command gets a slightly different parameter, so that it pulls the month out. This time, I'm not guaranteed a two-character result.

```
Dim sMonth
sMonth = DatePart("m",dDate)
```

I compensate by using the Len function to see if sMonth is only one character long. If it is, I use the ampersand operator again to prepend a zero to the month, and then add the result to the filename I'm building.

```
If Len(sMonth) = 1 Then
  sMonth = "0" & sMonth
```

```
End If
sFileName = sFileName & sMonth
```

I perform the exact same set of steps again for the day portion of the date. Notice the difference in the DatePart command to pull the day, rather than the month or year. You can check out DatePart's other possibilities in the VBScript documentation.

```
Dim sDay
sDay = DatePart("d",dDate)
If Len(sDay) = 1 Then
  sDay = "0" & sDay
End If
sFileName = sFileName & sDay
```

Finally, I add the last part of the filename, ".log", to the variable I'm building. As the last step, I set the name of the function itself equal to the variable that contains the filename. This tells VBScript to pass back the completed filename as the result of the function.

```
sFileName = ".log" & sFileName

FormatLogFileName = sFileName
```

That's all there is to it. Now I have a completed function that rolls up an otherwise reasonably complicated task into a single command. Effectively, I have my own custom FormatLogFileName command, which I can use in the main part of my script.

Variable Names

This isn't the first time you've seen me name variables with a prefix letter like s or d. There's a good reason for this.

First, keep in mind that VBScript doesn't really care what type of data I put into a variable. Data types are all pretty much the same to VBScript. However, VBScript will get upset if I try to perform certain operations with certain data types. For example, if I store "Hello" into variable Var1, and store "Mom" in variable Var2, and then ask VBScript to calculate Var1 * Var2, I'll get an error because VBScript can't multiply two strings.

One purpose of my variable names, then, is to remind me what I've put into them. I use d when the variable contains data I intend to treat as a date, s for strings, i for integers, and so forth.

Another purpose is to avoid overlapping with VBScript reserved words. VBScript doesn't allow variable names to duplicate any of VBScript's built-in names or functions. For example, the VBScript Date() function returns the current system date. Because that's a built-in function, I'm not allowed to name a variable Date, because VBScript wouldn't be able to tell the difference between the built-in function and my variable. By using a name prefix like d, however, I can create a meaningful variable name like dDate without conflicting with VBScript's reserved words.

13

Writing the Main Script

Now you're ready to fire up your script editor and write the main portion of the script. Any functions or subroutines you've written—including the `FormatLogFileName` function—will need to be copied and pasted into the first part of the script.

> **NOTE**
>
> You can add the function to the script at the end, if you want. It's strictly a matter of personal preference.

Log Rotation Script   With the supporting functions out of the way, you can start concentrating on the main script. Refer back to your original task list and translate it to VBScript; you might come up with something like Listing 13.2.

LISTING 13.2   *Log Rotation.vbs.* This is the first-pass script and contains all the important program logic.

```
' Sample log rotation tool
'
' We'll take yesterday's log and move it to
' an archive folder. We'll delete the log file
' that's 30 days old from the archive


' -----------------------------------------------------------
'declare variables
Dim sLogPath, sService, sArchive, sLogFile
Dim oFSO
Dim d30Days, dYesterday


' -----------------------------------------------------------
' set up variables for folder locations
sLogPath = "c:\winnt\system32\logfiles\"
sService = "w3svc2\"
sArchive = "c:\winnt\LogArchive\"


' -----------------------------------------------------------
' get yesterday's date
dYesterday = DateAdd( "d", -1, Date() )


' -----------------------------------------------------------
' create a formatted log filename
' for yesterday's log file
sLogFile = FormatLogFileName(dYesterday)


' -----------------------------------------------------------
```

LISTING 13.2   Continued

```
' Create a file system object
Set oFSO = WScript.CreateObject("Scripting.FileSystemObject")


' ------------------------------------------------------------
' Move the file to the archive path
oFSO.MoveFile sLogPath & sService & sLogFile, _
  sArchive & sLogFile


' ------------------------------------------------------------
' get date for 30 days ago
d30Days = DateAdd( "d", -30, Date() )


' ------------------------------------------------------------
' create a formatted log filename
' for 30-day-ago log file
sLogFile = FormatLogFileName(d30Days)


' ------------------------------------------------------------
' Delete the file from the archive path
oFSO.DeleteFile sArchive & sLogFile
```

Obviously, this didn't include the FormatLogFileName function. Be sure to copy that into the first part of the file before you try to do anything with it. Before you can use this script, you'll need to check a few things.

▶ Make sure the folders specified all exist. For example, if you're on Windows Server 2003, you'll need to change "Winnt" to "Windows" in many cases.

▶ Make sure you add the FormatLogFileName function to the beginning of the script, or you'll get an error message.

Log Rotation Script—Explained   One thing you'll notice about my scripts is that I like to use lots of comment lines. These allow me to document what the script is doing; if I have to make changes or figure out what the script is up to a year later, the comment lines help me remember what I was thinking when I originally wrote the script. I even use comment lines with lots of hyphens to create little separators, breaking the script into logical sections.

The first few lines in any script should explain what it does.

```
' Sample log rotation tool
'
' We'll take yesterday's log and move it to
' an archive folder. We'll delete the log file
' that's 30 days old from the archive
```

Next, I usually declare the variables I intend to use in the script.

```
' -----------------------------------------------------------
'declare variables
Dim sLogPath, sService, sArchive, sLogFile
Dim oFSO
Dim d30Days, dYesterday
```

The first thing in my task list is to define folder locations, and so that's what I do next. Notice that I've actually defined the log file folder path in two parts: the main path and the service. This will make it easier to modify the script to accommodate other websites later, if I want.

```
' -----------------------------------------------------------
' set up variables for folder locations
sLogPath = "c:\winnt\system32\logfiles\"
sService = "w3svc\"
sArchive = "c:\winnt\LogArchive\"
```

Now, I use VBScript's Date() and DateAdd() functions to figure out yesterday's date. VBScript doesn't have a DateSubtract function; instead, just add a negative number. Adding a negative is the same as subtracting.

```
' -----------------------------------------------------------
' get yesterday's date
dYesterday = DateAdd( "d", -1, Date() )
```

Now, I'll use that handy FormatLogFileName function to figure out the filename of yesterday's log file.

```
' -----------------------------------------------------------
' create a formatted log filename
' for yesterday's log file
sLogFile = FormatLogFileName(dYesterday)
```

Next, I create a reference to the FileSystemObject, which will let me manipulate the log files. I'm storing the reference in a variable named oFSO; the "o" prefix tells me that this variable contains an object reference, and not some kind of data. I also have to remember to use the Set command because I'm assigning an object reference to the variable, and not just data.

```
' -----------------------------------------------------------
' Create a file system object
Set oFSO = WScript.CreateObject("Scripting.FileSystemObject")
```

One of the `FileSystemObject`'s handy methods is `MoveFile`. It accepts two parameters: the file to move and where to move it. This accomplishes the task of moving the log file into the archive folder.

```
' ----------------------------------------------------------
' Move the file to the archive path
oFSO.MoveFile sLogPath & sService & sLogFile, _
    sArchive & sLogFile
```

Having accomplished the first major task, I'm ready to delete the oldest log file. I'll need to figure out what date it was 30 days ago, which means using `DateAdd()` to add a negative 30 days to today's date.

```
' ----------------------------------------------------------
' get date for 30 days ago
d30Days = DateAdd( "d", -30, Date() )
```

Now I can use `FormatLogFileName` again to get the filename from 30 days ago.

```
' ----------------------------------------------------------
' create a formatted log filename
' for 30-day-ago log file
sLogFile = FormatLogFileName(d30Days)
```

Finally, use the `FileSystemObject`'s `DeleteFile` command to delete the old log file.

```
' ----------------------------------------------------------
' Delete the file from the archive path
oFSO.DeleteFile sArchive & sLogFile
```

If everything's working well, this script should be ready to run.

Identifying Potential Errors

Rereading the script, I can think of a few things that might go wrong. For starters, the archive folder might not exist. Also, the log file I'm trying to move might not exist if something was wrong with IIS. In addition, it's possible that someone already deleted the old log file, meaning it won't exist when I try to delete it in the script. Any of these obvious conditions could cause an error that would make my script quit running.

How can I avoid these errors?

▶ Make sure the archive folder exists and, if it doesn't, create it.

▶ Make sure files exist before moving or deleting them.

Anticipating what can go wrong allows you to add code to your script to handle potential errors gracefully.

Modified Log Rotation Script   Listing 13.3 presents a modified log rotation script with some error-handling built in.

LISTING 13.3   *LogRotation2.vbs.* This version of the script checks for files and folders rather than assuming they exist.

```
' Sample log rotation tool
'
' We'll take yesterday's log and move it to
' an archive folder. We'll delete the log file
' that's 30 days old from the archive


' -----------------------------------------------------------
'declare variables
Dim sLogPath, sService, sArchive, sLogFile
Dim oFSO
Dim d30Days, dYesterday


' -----------------------------------------------------------
' set up variables for folder locations
sLogPath = "c:\winnt\system32\logfiles\"
sService = "w3svc2\"
sArchive = "c:\winnt\LogArchive\"


' -----------------------------------------------------------
' get yesterday's date
dYesterday = DateAdd( "d", -1, Date() )


' -----------------------------------------------------------
' create a formatted log filename
' for yesterday's log file
sLogFile = FormatLogFileName(dYesterday)


' -----------------------------------------------------------
' Create a file system object
Set oFSO = WScript.CreateObject("Scripting.FileSystemObject")


' -----------------------------------------------------------
' make sure files and folders exist
' first the archive folder
If Not oFSO.FolderExists(sArchive) Then
 oFSO.CreateFolder(sArchvie)
End If


' -----------------------------------------------------------
```

LISTING 13.3   Continued

```
' Move the file to the archive path
If oFSO.FileExists(sLogPath & sService & sLogFile) Then
 oFSO.MoveFile sLogPath & sService & sLogFile, _
   sArchive & sLogFile
End If


' ------------------------------------------------------------
' get date for 30 days ago
d30Days = DateAdd( "d", -30, Date() )


' ------------------------------------------------------------
' create a formatted log filename
' for 30-day-ago log file
sLogFile = FormatLogFileName(d30Days)


' ------------------------------------------------------------
' Delete the file from the archive path
If oFSO.FileExists(sArchive & sLogFile) Then
     oFSO.DeleteFile sArchive & sLogFile
End If
```

Can you spot what's changed in the script?

Modified Log Rotation Script—Explained   There are just three major changes to the script. First, I'm using the FileSystemObject's FolderExists() method to ensure that the archive folder exists. If it doesn't, I use the CreateFolder() method to create the folder, automatically handling the problem before it becomes a problem.

```
' ------------------------------------------------------------
' make sure files and folders exist
' first the archive folder
If Not oFSO.FolderExists(sArchive) Then
 oFSO.CreateFolder(sArchvie)
End If
```

I also modified the code that moves the log file. Now, it's in an If/Then construct that uses the FileSystemObject's FileExists() method to only perform the move if the file exists to begin with.

```
' ------------------------------------------------------------
' Move the file to the archive path
If oFSO.FileExists(sLogPath & sService & sLogFile) Then
 oFSO.MoveFile sLogPath & sService & sLogFile, _
   sArchive & sLogFile
End If
```

Similarly, I modified the line of code that deletes the old log file to only do so if that file already exists.

```
' -------------------------------------------------------
' Delete the file from the archive path
If oFSO.FileExists(sArchive & sLogFile) Then
     oFSO.DeleteFile sArchive & sLogFile
End If
```

Now, the script is prepared to handle these anticipated potential problems. Again, be sure to paste in the `FormatLogFileName` function before attempting to execute this script!

Testing the Script

You're ready to test your script. Just to make sure you're on the same page, Listing 13.4 lists the entire log rotation script, including the `FormatLogFileName` function.

LISTING 13.4   *LogRotation3.vbs.* Here's the entire script, ready to run.

```
' Sample log rotation tool
'
' We'll take yesterday's log and move it to
' an archive folder. We'll delete the log file
' that's 30 days old from the archive

Function FormatLogFileName(dDate)

 Dim sFileName
 sFileName = "ex"

 Dim sYear
 sYear = DatePart("yyyy",dDate)
 sYear = Right(sYear,2)
 sFileName = sFileName & sYear

 Dim sMonth
 sMonth = DatePart("m",dDate)
 If Len(sMonth) = 1 Then
  sMonth = "0" & sMonth
 End If
 sFileName = sFileName & sMonth

 Dim sDay
 sDay = DatePart("d",dDate)
 If Len(sDay) = 1 Then
  sDay = "0" & sDay
```

LISTING 13.4   Continued

```
  End If
  sFileName = sFileName & sDay

  sFileName = ".log" & sFileName

  FormatLogFileName = sFileName

End Function

' ............................................................
'declare variables
Dim sLogPath, sService, sArchive, sLogFile
Dim oFSO
Dim d30Days, dYesterday

' ............................................................
' set up variables for folder locations
sLogPath = "c:\winnt\system32\logfiles\"
sService = "w3svc2\"
sArchive = "c:\winnt\LogArchive\"

' ............................................................
' get yesterday's date
dYesterday = DateAdd( "d", -1, Date() )

' ............................................................
' create a formatted log filename
' for yesterday's log file
sLogFile = FormatLogFileName(dYesterday)

' ............................................................
' Create a file system object
Set oFSO = WScript.CreateObject("Scripting.FileSystemObject")

' ............................................................
' make sure files and folders exist
' first the archive folder
If Not oFSO.FolderExists(sArchive) Then
 oFSO.CreateFolder(sArchvie)
End If

' ............................................................
```

LISTING 13.4   Continued

```
' Move the file to the archive path
If oFSO.FileExists(sLogPath & sService & sLogFile) Then
 oFSO.MoveFile sLogPath & sService & sLogFile, _
   sArchive & sLogFile
End If


' ----------------------------------------------------------
' get date for 30 days ago
d30Days = DateAdd( "d", -30, Date() )


' ----------------------------------------------------------
' create a formatted log filename
' for 30-day-ago log file
sLogFile = FormatLogFileName(d30Days)


' ----------------------------------------------------------
' Delete the file from the archive path
If oFSO.FileExists(sArchive & sLogFile) Then
     oFSO.DeleteFile sArchive & sLogFile
End If
```

Save the script to a .vbs file and double-click to execute it. To make sure it has something to do, make sure you have a log file in the appropriate folder with yesterday's date.

Analyzing the Results

What happens when you run the script? If you type it carefully, either it doesn't do anything or it gives you an error. That's because the code contains two logic errors.

Logic errors are especially difficult to track down because VBScript doesn't usually complain about them. As far as VBScript is concerned, everything is just fine. You're the one with the problem because your script runs, but doesn't do what you want it to do.

There are a couple of ways to catch these errors. Because the errors aren't ones that VBScript cares about, you can't rely on the Script Debugger or other fancy tools. The easiest way to track down the problem is to add debug code.

Adding Debug Code

Debug code is usually as straightforward as a bunch of MsgBox statements that tell you what your script is doing. For example:

```
sLogFile = FormatLogFileName(d30Days)
MsgBox sLogFile
```

The boldfaced line of code tells you what the `FormatLogFileName` function did, by displaying its results. You can use that to double-check what's going on in your code, and find out where things are going wrong.

Log Rotation Script with Debug Code   Listing 13.5 shows the complete log rotation script with debug code added. I've highlighted the debug code in bold so that you can spot it more easily.

LISTING 13.5   *LogRotation4.vbs.* I've added `MsgBox` statements as a debugging aid.

```
' Sample log rotation tool
'
' We'll take yesterday's log and move it to
' an archive folder. We'll delete the log file
' that's 30 days old from the archive

Function FormatLogFileName(dDate)

 Dim sFileName
 sFileName = "ex"

 Dim sYear
 sYear = DatePart("yyyy",dDate)
 sYear = Right(sYear,2)
 sFileName = sFileName & sYear

 Dim sMonth
 sMonth = DatePart("m",dDate)
 If Len(sMonth) = 1 Then
  sMonth = "0" & sMonth
 End If
 sFileName = sFileName & sMonth

 Dim sDay
 sDay = DatePart("d",dDate)
 If Len(sDay) = 1 Then
  sDay = "0" & sDay
 End If
 sFileName = sFileName & sDay

 sFileName = ".log" & sFileName

 FormatLogFileName = sFileName

End Function
```

LISTING 13.5   Continued

```
' -----------------------------------------------------------
'declare variables
Dim sLogPath, sService, sArchive, sLogFile
Dim oFSO
Dim d30Days, dYesterday


' -----------------------------------------------------------
' set up variables for folder locations
sLogPath = "c:\winnt\system32\logfiles\"
sService = "w3svc2\"
sArchive = "c:\winnt\LogArchive\"


' -----------------------------------------------------------
' get yesterday's date
dYesterday = DateAdd( "d", -1, Date() )
MsgBox "Yesterday was " & dYesterday


' -----------------------------------------------------------
' create a formatted log filename
' for yesterday's log file
sLogFile = FormatLogFileName(dYesterday)
MsgBox "Yesterday's log filename is " & sLogFile


' -----------------------------------------------------------
' Create a file system object
Set oFSO = WScript.CreateObject("Scripting.FileSystemObject")


' -----------------------------------------------------------
' make sure files and folders exist
' first the archive folder
If Not oFSO.FolderExists(sArchive) Then
 oFSO.CreateFolder(sArchvie)
 MsgBox "Created Folder"
Else
 MsgBox "Didn't Create Folder"
End If


' -----------------------------------------------------------
' Move the file to the archive path
If oFSO.FileExists(sLogPath & sService & sLogFile) Then
 oFSO.MoveFile sLogPath & sService & sLogFile, _
   sArchive & sLogFile
 MsgBox "Moved File"
Else
```

LISTING 13.5   Continued

```
 MsgBox "Didn't Move File"
End If


' -----------------------------------------------------------
' get date for 30 days ago
d30Days = DateAdd( "d", -30, Date() )
MsgBox "30 days ago was " & d30Days


' -----------------------------------------------------------
' create a formatted log filename
' for 30-day-ago log file
sLogFile = FormatLogFileName(d30Days)
MsgBox "Log file from 30 days ago was " & sLogFile


' -----------------------------------------------------------
' Delete the file from the archive path
If oFSO.FileExists(sArchive & sLogFile) Then
     oFSO.DeleteFile sArchive & sLogFile
 MsgBox "Deleted file."
Else
 MsgBox "Didn't delete file."
End If
```

Run the script again and see what happens. Are you surprised by the results?

Log Rotation Script with Debug Code—Explained   Some of the code I added displays the results of operations by tacking a variable onto the MsgBox statement, like this one.

```
' -----------------------------------------------------------
' create a formatted log filename
' for 30-day-ago log file
sLogFile = FormatLogFileName(d30Days)
MsgBox "Log file from 30 days ago was " & sLogFile
```

Other sections of code added an If/Then construct. This ensures some kind of feedback on the script's progress, no matter how the If/Then condition turned out.

```
' -----------------------------------------------------------
' Delete the file from the archive path
If oFSO.FileExists(sArchive & sLogFile) Then
     oFSO.DeleteFile sArchive & sLogFile
 MsgBox "Deleted file."
Else
 MsgBox "Didn't delete file."
End If
```

Modifying the Script

If you're getting the same results I am, you've probably spotted the logic errors. Here's the first one, in the `FormatLogFileName` function.

```
Dim sDay
 sDay = DatePart("d",dDate)
 If Len(sDay) = 1 Then
  sDay = "0" & sDay
 End If
 sFileName = sFileName & sDay

 sFileName = ".log" & sFileName

 FormatLogFileName = sFileName


End Function
```

The problem is in boldface, and the code is actually backward. It's prepending `".log"` to the filename that's been built, rather than appending it. The result is that every filename coming out of the function is wrong. You would have noticed this with the debug version of the script because the messages, "Didn't move file" and "Didn't delete file" were displayed. You saw those messages because no file with the incorrect filename existed. Correct this line of code to read

```
sFileName = sFileName & sDay

 sFileName = sFileName & ".log"

 FormatLogFileName = sFileName
```

The next error is a simple typo.

```
' -----------------------------------------------------------
' make sure files and folders exist
' first the archive folder
If Not oFSO.FolderExists(sArchive) Then
 oFSO.CreateFolder(sArchvie)
 MsgBox "Created Folder"
Else
 MsgBox "Didn't Create Folder"
End If
```

The result of this code is to see if the archive folder exists, If it doesn't, VBScript attempts to create the folder—except that the wrong variable name is listed. The variable given, sArchvie, is empty, and so VBScript tries to create an empty folder. Depending upon how your system is configured, you might have received an error message on this line of code. Correct it to read

```
' ----------------------------------------------------------
' make sure files and folders exist
' first the archive folder
If Not oFSO.FolderExists(sArchive) Then
 oFSO.CreateFolder(sArchive)
 MsgBox "Created Folder"
Else
 MsgBox "Didn't Create Folder"
End If
```

By the way, this problem could have been caught earlier if you'd included Option Explicit as the first line of your script. With that option, VBScript requires you to declare all variables; when it spotted the undeclared sArchvie variable, it would have given an immediate error.

You can refresh your memory on Option Explicit by referring to Chapter 5.

Completing the Script

Listing 13.6 shows the completed, corrected script, with debug code removed. It's ready to use! Note that I've added the Option Explicit statement to help catch any other variable name typos.

LISTING 13.6   *LogRotation5.vbs.* Here's the entire script, ready to run.

```
Option Explicit
' Sample log rotation tool
'
' We'll take yesterday's log and move it to
' an archive folder. We'll delete the log file
' that's 30 days old from the archive

Function FormatLogFileName(dDate)

 Dim sFileName
 sFileName = "ex"

 Dim sYear
 sYear = DatePart("yyyy",dDate)
 sYear = Right(sYear,2)
 sFileName = sFileName & sYear

 Dim sMonth
 sMonth = DatePart("m",dDate)
```

LISTING 13.6   Continued

```
If Len(sMonth) = 1 Then
 sMonth = "0" & sMonth
End If
sFileName = sFileName & sMonth

Dim sDay
sDay = DatePart("d",dDate)
If Len(sDay) = 1 Then
 sDay = "0" & sDay
End If
sFileName = sFileName & sDay

sFileName = sFileName & ".log"

FormatLogFileName = sFileName

End Function

' ------------------------------------------------------------
'declare variables
Dim sLogPath, sService, sArchive, sLogFile
Dim oFSO
Dim d30Days, dYesterday

' ------------------------------------------------------------
' set up variables for folder locations
sLogPath = "c:\winnt\system32\logfiles\"
sService = "w3svc2\"
sArchive = "c:\winnt\LogArchive\"

' ------------------------------------------------------------
' get yesterday's date
dYesterday = DateAdd( "d", -1, Date() )

' ------------------------------------------------------------
' create a formatted log filename
' for yesterday's log file
sLogFile = FormatLogFileName(dYesterday)

' ------------------------------------------------------------
' Create a file system object
Set oFSO = WScript.CreateObject("Scripting.FileSystemObject")

' ------------------------------------------------------------
```

LISTING 13.6   Continued

```
' make sure files and folders exist
' first the archive folder
If Not oFSO.FolderExists(sArchive) Then
 oFSO.CreateFolder(sArchive)
End If



' ------------------------------------------------------------
' Move the file to the archive path
If oFSO.FileExists(sLogPath & sService & sLogFile) Then
 oFSO.MoveFile sLogPath & sService & sLogFile, _
   sArchive & sLogFile
End If


' ------------------------------------------------------------
' get date for 30 days ago
d30Days = DateAdd( "d", -30, Date() )


' ------------------------------------------------------------
' create a formatted log filename
' for 30-day-ago log file
sLogFile = FormatLogFileName(d30Days)


' ------------------------------------------------------------
' Delete the file from the archive path
If oFSO.FileExists(sArchive & sLogFile) Then
     oFSO.DeleteFile sArchive & sLogFile
End If
```

Polishing Your Script

You can make this script more effective with a little work. For example, as written, the script only works with the first website on the server, which uses the W3CSvc folder. You could modify the script to work with multiple folders by including a For/Next construct or some other kind of loop.

Also, the script requires that you remember to run it each day for the best effect. However, you could use the Windows Task Scheduler to automatically run the script each morning at 1 a.m. or some other convenient time. You simply tell Task Scheduler to run WScript.exe *scriptname*, where *scriptname* is the complete path and filename to your log rotation script.

You could even write the script to run against multiple web servers. That way, it could execute from a single central server and rotate the log files for an entire web farm. The beauty of scripting is that you're in complete control, so you can have the script do anything you want to suit your environment and meet your particular administrative needs.

13

Summary

In this chapter, you combined what you've learned about script design, VBScript basics, and the Windows `FileSystemObject` to create a completely functional tool for rotating IIS log files. I deliberately designed some errors into the first revision of the script to walk you through the debugging process, and I showed you some great tips for easily debugging scripts even without the Microsoft Script Debugger or other fancy tools.

You practiced a couple of key tasks in this chapter. The design process is very important, as it helps you gather facts about what your script needs to accomplish and figure out how to break those tasks down into scriptable steps. The debugging process is also very important, and you'll find that the techniques you practiced in this chapter will come in handy as you start developing your own administrative scripts.

PART III

Windows Management Instrumentation and Active Directory Services Interface

IN THIS PART

Working with ADSI Providers

Active Directory, as well as the local "directory" contained in local computers' Security Accounts Manager (SAM), is a major part of any Windows environment. Many directory-related tasks are some of the most time-consuming and repetitive ones a Windows administrator must perform, and so scripting becomes an obvious solution to make those tasks not only less time-consuming, but simply less boring.

Using ADSI Objects

ADSI, the Active Directory Services Interface, is an object library very similar in nature to the `FileSystemObject` and WScript objects I covered in Chapters 11 and 12, "Built-In Scripting Objects" and "Working with the File System," respectively. ADSI is a bit more complicated than the objects you've worked with so far, mainly because the information ADSI deals with is inherently more complicated.

For example, with the `FileSystemObject`, you learned to use `CreateObject` to have VBScript load the object's dynamic link library (DLL) into memory and provide a reference to your script. For example:

```
Dim oFSO
Set oFSO = CreateObject("Scripting.FileSystemObject")
```

That's not quite how you'll use ADSI, though. For example, to have ADSI change password policy in a domain named SAPIEN, you'd use the following code:

```
Set objDomain = GetObject("WinNT://SAPIEN")

objDomain.Put "MinPasswordLength", 8
objDomain.Put "MinPasswordAge", 10
objDomain.Put "MaxPasswordAge", 45
objDomain.Put "MaxBadPasswordsAllowed", 3
objDomain.Put "PasswordHistoryLength", 8
objDomain.Put "AutoUnlockInterval", 30000
objDomain.Put "LockoutObservationInterval", 30000
objDomain.SetInfo
```

Notice that the `GetObject` statement is used, rather than `CreateObject`. I like to remember the difference by telling myself that I'm not trying to *create* a domain, just *get* to an existing one. Another important part of that statement is `WinNT://`, which tells ADSI which *provider* to use. The two main providers you'll work with are WinNT: and LDAP.

> **NOTE**
>
> ADSI provider names are case sensitive, so be sure you're using WinNT and not winnt or some other derivation.

The WinNT provider can connect to any NT-compatible domain, including Active Directory (AD). Obviously, the provider cannot work with advanced AD functionality like organizational units (OUs), which don't exist in NT domains. The WinNT provider can also connect to the local SAM and other services on member and standalone computers. The LDAP provider can connect to any LDAP-compatible directory, such as the Exchange 5.5 directory or Active Directory. Both providers can be used to obtain a reference to an entire domain, an OU (in AD), users, groups, and much, much more. You'll even find areas of functionality that overlap with Windows Management Instrumentation (WMI); that's because ADSI is a bit older, and when WMI came on the scene, it started taking over. In fact, it's possible (although not, I think, likely) that someday ADSI will fade away entirely and that WMI will become the single means of accessing management information. For now, though, there's plenty that ADSI can do that WMI cannot.

Another important part of the `GetObject` statement is the `ADsPath`, which tells the provider what to connect to. In this example, the path was a simple domain name; it could also be a path like `"//SAPIEN/DonJ,user"`, which would connect to a user object named DonJ in the domain named SAPIEN.

The object reference created by `GetObject`—in this case, the variable `objDomain`—has several basic methods:

▶ `Create`—Creates a new object, provided the reference object is a container of some kind, like a domain or OU

▶ `Get`—Retrieves a specified attribute

▶ `Put`—Writes a specified attribute

▶ SetInfo—Saves changes made by Put

▶ Delete—Deletes an object, provided the reference object is a container of some kind

These methods usually accept one or more parameters. In the example, the Put method requires the name of an attribute to change, along with a new value for the attribute. Obviously, the available attribute names depend on what type of directory you're working with; ADSI itself doesn't care because it's designed to access *any* directory service. In the remainder of this chapter, I'll introduce you to what each of the two main providers can help you accomplish.

Using the WinNT Provider

With Active Directory several years old, why would you bother using the WinNT provider? *Ease of use.* Although the WinNT provider is definitely less functional than the LDAP provider is, it's easier to use, and there are certain functions that you cannot easily do with the LDAP provider, such as connecting to a file server service. You can do some of those things with WMI, but again—ease of use. There are just some things, as you'll see, that the WinNT provider makes easy. For example, in Chapter 10, "Controlling the Flow of Execution," I showed you how the WinNT provider can be used to connect to a file server and find out which users have a particular file open.

Here's an example of how the WinNT provider can be used to connect to a file server and list its available shares:

```
ServerName = InputBox("Enter name of server " & _
 "to list shares for.")

set fs = GetObject("WinNT://" & ServerName & _
 "/LanmanServer,FileService")
For Each sh In fs
    'do something with the share
Next
```

You can do the same thing in WMI:

```
'get server name
strComputer = InputBox("Server name?")

'connect to WMI
Set objWMIService = GetObject("winmgmts:" & _
 "\\" & strComputer & "\root\cimv2")

'retrieve the list of shares
Set colShares = objWMIService.ExecQuery _
```

```
("SELECT * FROM Win32_Share WHERE " & _
 "Type = 0")

'for each share returned...
For Each objShare In colShares
 'do something with the share
Next
```

The ADSI method is obviously easier. Notice something about how the ADSI call is written:

```
set fs = GetObject("WinNT://" & ServerName & _
 "/LanmanServer,FileService")
```

The first part, as I noted earlier, is the provider: WinNT. Next is the server name, which, in this case, is provided in a string variable. Next is the name of the object you want to connect to, a comma, and the type of object that is. The comma and type are optional. For example, the following would usually work fine:

```
set fs = GetObject("WinNT://" & ServerName & _
 "/LanmanServer")
```

This method lets ADSI pick the object based solely on its name. If you have a user or group named LanmanServer, ADSI might pick one of those, which is why I usually specify the object type. Doing so restricts ADSI's options to the type of object I'm expecting. Connecting to a user object would be similar:

```
set fs = GetObject("WinNT://" & ServerName & _
 "/DonJ,user")
```

Or a group:

```
set fs = GetObject("WinNT://" & ServerName & _
 "/Guests,group")
```

What do you specify for the server name? If you want a domain user or group, specify either the domain name or the name of a domain controller. If you want a local user or group, or a service, specify a server name. Keep in mind that all of these techniques will work perfectly with NT, 2000, XP, and 2003 computers in either an NT domain or an AD domain.

WinNT Examples

Here's an example of how to start a service by using the WinNT provider:

```
Set objService = GetObject("WinNT://Server1/browser")
objService.Start
Set objService = Nothing
```

> **NOTE**
>
> Why Nothing? Notice on the last line of the previous example that objService was set to Nothing. In VBScript, this releases the object, freeing up any memory it was using. It isn't strictly necessary: VBScript does this automatically when the script ends. I wanted to include it here so that you could see it, and I could explain it, because you're likely to run across it if you're using sample scripts others have written. As a rule, I tend not to set variables to Nothing simply because it really isn't necessary.

Obviously, you can change the service name to anything valid on the computer. You can stop the service by using the Stop method instead of Start.

Here's an example of how to output all members of a group to a text file. This example uses the FileSystemObject to create the text file and the WinNT provider to access the group membership list:

```
Dim oGroup
Dim sGroupName
Dim sGroupDomain
Dim oMember
Dim oTS
Dim oFSO

const ForReading = 1
const ForWriting = 2
const ForAppending = 8
Const TristateFalse = 0

sGroupDomain = "DomainName"
sGroupName = InputBox ("Group name?")

Set oFSO = CreateObject ("Scripting.FileSystemObject")
Set oTS = oFSO.CreateTextFile ("C:\Scripts\" & _
 sGroupName & " members.txt")

Set oGroup = GetObject("WinNT://" & sGroupDomain & "/" & _
 sGroupName & ",group")

For Each oMember in oGroup.Members
 oTS.WriteLine oMember.Name
Next

WScript.Echo "Complete"
```

14

The following script connects to a domain, iterates through each object, and for the user objects it finds, outputs the total size of the user's home directory:

```
Dim oDomain, oFolder
Dim oFSO, oTS, oUser

Set oFSO = CreateObject("Scripting.FileSystemObject")
Set oTS = oFSO.CreateTextFile("c:\homedirs.txt")
Set oDomain = GetObject("WinNT://DOMAIN")

For Each oUser in oDomain
 If oUser.Class = "User" Then
  Set oFolder = oFSO.GetFolder(oUser.HomeDirectory)
  oTS.WriteLine( _
   oFolder.Name & "," & oUser.HomeDirectory & "," & _
    oFolder.Size)
 End IF
 Set oFolder = Nothing
Next
```

You can see in each of these examples how the WinNT provider makes the task a bit easier by providing ready access to the necessary information. The WinNT provider can do this because it's *specific to Windows*; other providers—such as LDAP, which I'll cover next—are dealing with a more generic technology, and provide less Windows-specific functionality.

Using the LDAP Provider

The ADSI LDAP provider looks superficially similar to the WinNT provider, but uses LDAP-style naming conventions to name specific objects. A typical LDAP connection might look like this:

```
Dim objDomain
Set objDomain = GetObject("LDAP://dc=sapien,dc=com")
```

NOTE

What is LDAP? It stands for Lightweight Directory Access Protocol, and it's an industry-standard means of accessing directories. The LDAP provider can work with any LDAP-compatible directory, not just Active Directory.

Notice that the LDAP provider is specified, and then an LDAP naming path is listed. In this case, objDomain will become a reference to the sapien.com domain. Perhaps the most confusing part of these LDAP paths is figuring out which components to use.

▶ Use DC when specifying any portion of a domain name. Always list the domain name components in their regular order. For example, a domain named east. sapien.com would have an LDAP path of "dc=east,dc=sapien,dc=com". DC stands for *domain component,* not domain controller; this type of LDAP path will force ADSI to find a domain controller following Windows' normal rules for doing so.

▶ Use OU when specifying an organizational unit. For example, to connect to the Sales OU in the sapien.com domain, specify "ou=sales,dc=sapien,dc=com". Notice that the domain name components are still required, so that ADSI can locate the domain that contains the OU.

▶ Use CN when specifying a *common name,* such as a user, group, or *any of the built-in AD containers.* Remember that the Users, Computers, and Built-in containers aren't technically OUs, and so they can't be accessed with the OU component. To connect to the Users container, use "cn=Users,dc=sapien,dc=com". To connect to a specific user, you can just specify the user and domain name: "cn=DonJ,dc=sapien,dc=com".

14

NOTE

Most LDAP directories require you to specify the fully qualified domain name of an object, including their containing OUs, if appropriate. Get into the habit of using these names, such as "cn=DonJ,ou=Sales,dc=sapien,dc=com".

After you've bound to an object, you can work with its properties. For example, suppose I want to modify the description of a particular user group. The following code will do it:

```
Dim objGroup
Set objGroup = GetObject( _
 "cn=Sales,ou=EastSales,dc=domain,dc=com")
objGroup.Put "description", "Eastern Sales representatives"
objGroup.SetInfo
```

The Put method allows me to specify a property to modify (in this case, the description of the group), and a new value. I have to call SetInfo to actually save the change. This is a straightforward technique with single-value properties like description; many AD properties, however, are *multivalued.* For example, the otherTelephone property can contain multiple telephone numbers. Here's how you might modify them:

```
Dim objUser
Set objUser = GetObject("cn=DonJ,ou=Sales,dc=sapien,dc=com")
objUser.PutEx 3, "otherTelephone", Array("555-1212")
objUser.SetInfo
```

The PutEx method accepts three parameters. The last two should look familiar: They're the property name and the value you're adding. The first parameter tells PutEx what you're doing.

- ▶ 1: Clear all values

- ▶ 2: Update all entries

- ▶ 3: Append an entry

- ▶ 4: Delete an entry

You can make these a bit easier to work with by specifying constants. For example:

```
Const MVP_CLEAR = 1
Const MVP_UPDATE = 2
Const MVP_APPEND = 3
Const MVP_DELETE = 4


Dim objUser
Set objUser = GetObject("cn=DonJ,ou=Sales,dc=sapien,dc=com")
objUser.PutEx MVP_APPEND, "otherTelephone", Array("555-1212")
objUser.SetInfo
```

Whenever you're modifying a multivalued property more than once in a script, be sure to call `SetInfo` after each modification. Otherwise, ADSI will lose track of what you're doing, and only the last change will be saved back to the directory.

> **NOTE**
>
> Most of the examples in Chapters 15 and 16, "Manipulating Domains" and "Manipulating Users and Groups," respectively, will use ADSI's LDAP provider.

Other Providers

ADSI doesn't stop with LDAP and WinNT. Here are some of the other providers that you can work with:

- ▶ **GC**—This provider allows you to work with the Global Catalog on AD domain controllers that host a replica of the Global Catalog. It works similarly to the LDAP provider, but uses the TCP ports assigned to access the Global Catalog.

- ▶ **OLE DB**—This provider allows you to perform search operations on AD by using Microsoft's OLE DB database interface.

- ▶ **IIS**—This provides access to the IIS metabase, which contains all of IIS' configuration information.

- ▶ **NDS**—This connects to Novell NetWare Directory Services. Note that later versions of NDS also support LDAP queries, meaning you can use the more generic LDAP provider for some operations.

- ▶ **NWCOMPAT**—This connects to Novell NetWare Bindery directories, found in NetWare 3.x and later.

Because most of your administrative tasks will involve the LDAP and WinNT providers, I'm not going to provide coverage or examples of how to use these other ADSI providers. However, you can access the ADSI documentation online at http://msdn.microsoft.com/ library to learn more about them, if necessary.

Summary

With this brief introduction to ADSI out of the way, you're ready to start managing domains, users, and groups by writing scripts that incorporate ADSI. You've learned how to write ADSI scripts that utilize both the WinNT and LDAP ADSI providers, and you've learned a bit about how the two providers function. Remember that the WinNT provider is *not* limited just to NT domains; it works fine in AD domains, and also provides a way to work with the local SAM and services on standalone and member computers, including NT-based client computers.

14

Manipulating Domains

W orking with domains via Active Directory Services Interface (ADSI) is often easier if you start at the top level. In the last chapter, you learned how to use both the WinNT and LDAP ADSI providers to get an object reference to the domain.

```
Dim objNTDomain, objADDomain
Set objNTDomain = GetObject("WinNT://DOMAIN")
Set objADDomain = GetObject("LDAP://dc=domain,dc=com")
```

After you have a reference to the domain, you can start working with its properties. That is the focus of the first part of this chapter; toward the end of this chapter, I'll show you how to work with the main domain-level objects, organizational units (OUs), by using the LDAP provider.

Obviously, you need to make sure you have ADSI running on your computer in order to use it. ADSI comes with Windows 2000 and Windows XP, as well as Windows Server 2003, Windows Vista, and later versions of Windows. It's available for, but not included with, Windows NT, Windows 95, Windows 98, and Windows Me. To install ADSI, simply install the Microsoft Directory Services client on these older operating systems. You can also visit the ADSI link located at www.microsoft.com/windows/reskits/webresources.

Querying Domain Information

Querying domain information by using the LDAP provider is easy. Connect to the domain and simply use the Get method, along with the desired attribute name.

```
Dim objDomain
Set objDomain = GetObject("LDAP://dc=domain,dc=com")
WScript.Echo objDomain.Get("minPwdAge")
```

Of course, you need to know the attribute names that you want to query. Some of the interesting domain LDAP attributes include the following:

▶ pwdHistoryLength—The number of old passwords the domain remembers for each user

▶ minPwdLength—The minimum number of characters per user password

▶ minPwdAge—The minimum number of days a user must keep his password

▶ maxPwdAge—The maximum number of days a user may keep his password

▶ lockoutThreshold—The number of tries you have to guess a password before the account is locked out

▶ lockoutDuration—The length of time that a password is left locked out

▶ lockOutObservationWindow—The time window during which the lockoutThreshold number of wrong password attempts will cause an account lockout

▶ forceLogoff—Forces account logoff when account restriction time expires

You can explore more of the domain's attributes by examining the domain and domainPolicy classes in the Active Directory (AD) schema; I'll describe how to view the attributes associated with a class later in this chapter.

Querying this information by using the WinNT provider is remarkably similar, although the attributes' names do change somewhat. Here's an example:

```
Dim objDomain
objDomain = GetObject("WinNT://DOMAIN")
WScript.Echo objDomain.Get("MinPasswordAge")
```

As you can see, the syntax is virtually identical, with the ADSI connection string and the attribute name being the only differences.

If you're an advanced AD user, you can also work directly with the domain's root object, configuration partition, and schema partition. To do so, simply connect directly to the appropriate object.

```
Dim objRoot, objConfig, objSchema, objRootDomain

'get the forest root domain:
Set objRoot = GetObject("LDAP://rootDSE")
Set objRootDomain = GetObject("LDAP://" & _
 objRoot.Get("rootDomainNamingContext"))

'get the configuration partition
Set objConfig = GetObject("LDAP://" & _
 objRoot.Get("configurationNamingContext"))
```

```
'get the schema partition
Set objSchema = GetObject("LDAP://" & _
 objRoot.Get("schemaNamingContext"))
```

I'm not going to cover scripting operations that modify the configuration or schema partitions; doing so is pretty dangerous stuff, and it's not the sort of thing you do so frequently that you're likely to need to automate it.

Changing Domain Settings

In the last chapter, I showed you an example of how you can use the WinNT provider to modify a domain's password and lockout policies. Here it is again:

```
' first bind to the domain
set objDomain = GetObject("WinNT://MyDomain")

objDomain.Put "MinPasswordLength", 8
objDomain.Put "MinPasswordAge", 10
objDomain.Put "MaxPasswordAge", 45
objDomain.Put "PasswordHistoryLength", 8
objDomain.Put "LockoutObservationInterval", 30000
objDomain.SetInfo
```

This same syntax works pretty well for LDAP connections to a domain, although as I noted in the previous section the attribute names are different. Here's an LDAP version of the same example:

```
' first bind to the domain
set objDomain = GetObject("LDAP://dc=domain,dc=com")

objDomain.Put "minPwdLength", 8
objDomain.Put "minPwdAge", 10
objDomain.Put "maxPwdAge", 45
objDomain.Put "pwdHistoryLength", 8
objDomain.Put "lockoutObservationWindow", 30000
objDomain.SetInfo
```

As you can see, the basic syntax is to use the Put method, the appropriate attribute name, and the new value, and then to call the SetInfo method when you're finished. SetInfo copies the changes back to the directory, committing the changes.

More important, because you're probably using an Active Directory domain, you should understand that *either of these examples will have the same effect*. Active Directory is backward compatible with older Windows NT-style domains, meaning *both* of these examples *will work with an Active Directory domain*.

Working with OUs

You'll likely do four basic things with an OU. By the way, some of these operations also apply to the built-in, OU-like containers: Users, Computers, and Built-In. Keep in mind that these are *not* OUs; they're containers, and cannot be accessed in quite the same way as I described in the previous chapter. In the next four sections, I'll demonstrate how to use ADSI to create, modify, query, and delete an OU.

> **NOTE**
>
> Because OUs don't exist in NT domains, all of these examples will only use the LDAP provider that works with Active Directory in its native mode.

Creating an OU

Creating an OU is simple enough. First, you need to obtain a reference to the parent of the new OU, and then use that object's `Create` method to create a new OU. To create a new top-level OU named Sales:

```
Dim objDomain, objNewOU
Set objDomain = GetObject("LDAP://dc=domain,dc=com")
Set objNewOU = objDomain.Create("organizationalUnit", "ou=Sales")
objNewOU.SetInfo
```

> **Classes and Attributes**
>
> As you're working with AD, it's important to understand the system of classes and attributes that the AD schema uses for its organization. An *attribute* is some discrete piece of information, such as a name or description. A *class* is simply a collection of attributes that describes some real-world object. For example, a user is a class that includes attributes such as name, description, address, and so forth. A group is another class, which includes such attributes as name, description, and members.
>
> AD does not allow multiple attributes to use the same name. So, when you see two classes with the same attributes (such as description), both classes are actually using the same attribute definition from the AD schema. This sort of reuse makes AD very efficient.
>
> An *instance* is a copy of a class with its attributes' values filled in. For example, DonJ might be the name of a particular user. The user object you see in the AD graphical user interface (GUI) is an instance of the user class.

Notice that the `Create` method returns a reference to the newly created object, and I still have to call that object's `SetInfo` method to save the changes into the directory. I could also modify properties of the new OU prior to calling `SetInfo`. Let me extend this example and create both a top-level Sales OU and a child OU named West under that.

```
Dim objDomain, objNewOU
Set objDomain = GetObject("LDAP://dc=domain,dc=com")
Set objNewOU = objDomain.Create("organizationalUnit", _
 "ou=Sales")
objNewOU.SetInfo
```

```
Dim objChildOU
Set objChildOU = objNewOU.Create("organizationalUnit, "ou=West")
objChildOU.SetInfo
```

The child OU is created by using the Create method of its parent. If you want to create a
child OU under an existing OU, you must obtain a reference to that existing OU first, not
the domain. This is a common pattern for creating new objects: Retrieve a reference to
the new object's parent (such as an OU), and ask the parent to create the new object,
using the parent's Create() method.

```
Dim objParent, objNewOU
Set objParent = GetObject("LDAP://ou=Sales,dc=domain,dc=com")
Set objNewOU = objParent.Create("organizationalUnit", "ou=East")
objNewOU.SetInfo
```

Notice that the GetObject call is now focusing on a specific OU, meaning the new OU
will be created under that specific OU.

Modifying an OU

Need to modify the attributes of an OU? No problem. Simply obtain a reference to it, use
its Put method to change one or more attributes, and use SetInfo to save your changes.

```
Dim objOU
Set objOU = GetObject("LDAP://ou=Sales,dc=domain,dc=com")
objOU.Put "description", "Sales"
objOU.SetInfo
```

The trick to working with the Put method is that you have to know the name of the
attributes that are available to you. One way to see them all is to look right in AD's
schema. To do so:

1. You need to register the AD Schema console the first time you do this. Open a
   command-line window and run regsvr32 schmmgmt.dll.

2. Run MMC from the Start, Run option, or the command-line window, to open a
   blank Microsoft Management Console window.

3. Select Add/Remove Snap-ins from the File menu.

4. Click Add.

5. Double-click Active Directory Schema.

15

6. Click Close, and then click OK.

7. You might want to save this new console for future use.

8. Expand the schema tree in the console, and open the Classes folder.

9. Locate organizationalUnit in the list, and select it. All of the associated attributes will be displayed in the pane on the right of the window, as shown in Figure 15.1.

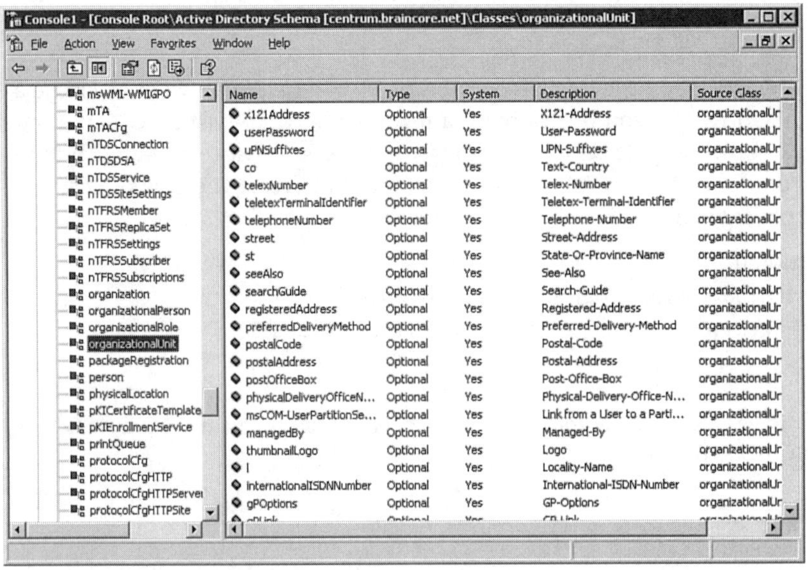

FIGURE 15.1   Exploring classes and attributes in the Schema console.

Many of the optional attributes—the ones shown in the console with Optional as their type—might not make sense. For example, why would an OU need an associated PO box? Some of these attributes aren't even shown in the AD tools' user interface. Others, however, such as description, are definitely useful.

TIP

You can use the console to find the correct attribute names for other classes, too, such as users and groups. You'll want to remember that as you read the next chapter.

Using Put requires you to know the correct attribute name, including the correct capitalization, and the value that you want to put into that attribute.

> **NOTE**
>
> Most OU attributes, such as `description`, only accept a single value. There are AD attributes, however, that are designed to hold an array of values. For more information on working with multivalued attributes, refer to Chapter 14, "Working with ADSI Providers."

Querying an OU

If you just want to read the attributes of an OU, you can use the `Get` method. Just get a reference to the OU, and then use `Get` to retrieve the attributes you're interested in.

```
Dim objOU
Set objOU = GetObject("LDAP://ou=Sales,dc=domain,dc=com")
WScript.Echo objOU.Get("description")
```

As with `Put`, you need to know the name of the attribute you're after. You should also understand about how ADSI works under the hood. When you call either `Get` or `GetEx`, both methods actually call a behind-the-scenes method called `GetInfo`. This method's job is to go out to AD and physically load the attributes and their values into a cache on the client. You can also call `GetInfo` directly, forcing ADSI to load attributes and their values from AD into your client's local attribute cache. Your scripts actually work with this cache. For example, if you suspect that someone else will be modifying AD information while your script is running, `GetInfo` will help ensure that your script's local cache has the latest AD data. Here's how:

```
Dim objOU
Set objOU = GetObject("LDAP://ou=Sales,dc=domain,dc=com")
objOU.GetInfo
```

Note that the `Put` method also works with the local cache; `SetInfo` writes the local cache back to AD. If you use `Put` to change an attribute, and then call `GetInfo`, your changes will be lost when the cache is refreshed. Always make sure you call `SetInfo` first to save the cache back to AD.

Deleting an OU

Deleting an object is perhaps the easiest operation: Connect to the object's parent and call its `Delete` method. Note that there's no "Are you sure?" confirmation, no possibility of undoing the deletion, and unless you have a backup, no way to reverse the operation. Here's how to do it:

```
Dim objOU
Set objOU = GetObject("LDAP:// dc=domain,dc=com")
objOU.Delete "organizationalUnit", "ou=HR"
```

15

In the case of an OU, *every object in the OU will also be deleted,* including users, groups, and child OUs. So, use this capability with extreme caution! Note that you do have to connect to the object's parent, just as if you were creating a new object; you cannot connect to the object itself and call Delete with no parameters.

Putting It All Together

One potential use for domain- and OU-manipulation scripts is to configure a test or pilot domain that resembles your production domain. By using a script, you can install a domain controller in a lab, and then quickly re-create aspects of your production environment, such as OU structure and user accounts.

Preload Domain   Listing 15.1 shows a script that preloads a domain with a specific OU structure. Just for fun, I've thrown in a couple of new methods that copy and move OUs around within the domain. See if you can figure out how they work before you read the line-by-line explanation.

LISTING 15.1   *PreLoad.vbs.* Preloads a specific OU configuration into a domain via LDAP.

```
'bind to domain
Dim oDomain
Set oDomain = GetObject("LDAP://dc=domain,dc=com")

'Create top-level OUs
Dim oSales, oHR, oMIS
Set oSales = oDomain.Create("organizationalUnit", "Sales")
Set oHR = oDomain.Create("organizationalUnit", "HR")
Set oMIS = oDomain.Create("organizationalUnit", "MIS")
oDomain.SetInfo

'set descriptions
oSales.Put "description", "Sales OU"
oHR.Put "description", "HR OU"
oMIS.Put "description", "MIS OU"
'save
oSales.SetInfo
oHR.SetInfo
oMIS.SetInfo

'create child OUs for Sales
Dim oChild
Set oChild = oSales.Create("organizationalUnit", "Widgets")
oChild.SetInfo
Set oChild = oSales.Create("organizationalUnit", "Wodgets")
oChild.SetInfo
Set oChild = oSales.Create("organizationalUnit", "Worm Gears")
```

LISTING 15.1   Continued

```
oChild.SetInfo

'create child OUs for HR
Set oChild = oSales.Create("organizationalUnit", "Recruiting")
oChild.SetInfo
Set oChild = oSales.Create("organizationalUnit", "Counseling")
oChild.SetInfo

'create child OUs for MIS
Set oChild = oSales.Create("organizationalUnit", "Engineering")
oChild.SetInfo
Set oChild = oSales.Create("organizationalUnit", "Desktop")
oChild.SetInfo
Set oChild = oSales.Create("organizationalUnit", _
 "Configuration")
oChild.SetInfo

'set domain-wide password policy
oDomain.Put "minPwdLength", 10
oDomain.Put "maxPwdAge", 30
oDomain.Put "minPwdAge", 2
oDomain.SetInfo

'display contents of Users
Dim sContents, oUsers, oObject
Set oUsers = GetObject("LDAP://cn=Users,dc=domain,dc=com")
For Each oObject In oUsers
 sContents = sContents & oObject.Name & ", "
Next
WScript.Echo "Users contains: " & sContents

'create another top-level OU
Dim oOU
Set oOU = oDomain.Create("organizationalUnit", "Management")
oDomain.SetInfo

'move the top-level OU into Sales
oSales.MoveHere "LDAP://ou=Management,dc=domain,dc=com"

'create a management OU in HR, too
Dim oCopy
oCopy = oHR.Create("organizationalUnit", "Management")
oCopy.SetInfo
```

LISTING 15.1   Continued

```
'now we're going to copy the Sales Management OU
'attributes to the HR Management OU
Dim oTemplate, aAttributes, sAttribute, sValue

'use the Sales OU as a reference
Set oTemplate = GetObject( _
  "LDAP://ou=Management,ou=Sales,dc=domain,dc=com")
aAttributes = Array("description", "location")

'copy each attribute from the source to the target
For Each sAttribute In aAttributes
  sValue = oTemplate.Get(sAttribute)
  oCopy.Put sAttribute, sValue
Next

'save the information
oCopy.SetInfo
```

Before you run this script, you obviously need to modify the LDAP connection strings to point to a domain in your environment. Of course, I highly recommend the use of a test domain, not your production domain!

Preload Domain—Explained   This script begins by binding to the domain itself.

```
'bind to domain
Dim oDomain
Set oDomain = GetObject("LDAP://dc=domain,dc=com")
```

Then, the script creates three top-level OUs: Sales, HR, and MIS. These are each referenced by their own object variables.

```
'Create top-level OUs
Dim oSales, oHR, oMIS
Set oSales = oDomain.Create("organizationalUnit", "Sales")
Set oHR = oDomain.Create("organizationalUnit", "HR")
Set oMIS = oDomain.Create("organizationalUnit", "MIS")
oDomain.SetInfo
```

The script then sets a description for each new OU.

```
'set descriptions
oSales.Put "description", "Sales OU"
oHR.Put "description", "HR OU"
oMIS.Put "description", "MIS OU"
```

Next, I save the information using the `SetInfo` method of each new OU.

```
'save
oSales.SetInfo
oHR.SetInfo
oMIS.SetInfo
```

Now, I create three child OUs under the Sales OU. After creating each, I save it, so that I can reuse the oChild object.

```
'create child OUs for Sales
Dim oChild
Set oChild = oSales.Create("organizationalUnit", "Widgets")
oChild.SetInfo
Set oChild = oSales.Create("organizationalUnit", "Wodgets")
oChild.SetInfo
Set oChild = oSales.Create("organizationalUnit", "Worm Gears")
oChild.SetInfo
```

Now the script creates two child OUs for HR, and three more under MIS. Again, notice the use of `SetInfo` after each call to `Create`.

```
'create child OUs for HR
Set oChild = oSales.Create("organizationalUnit", "Recruiting")
oChild.SetInfo
Set oChild = oSales.Create("organizationalUnit", "Counseling")
oChild.SetInfo

'create child OUs for MIS
Set oChild = oSales.Create("organizationalUnit", "Engineering")
oChild.SetInfo
Set oChild = oSales.Create("organizationalUnit", "Desktop")
oChild.SetInfo
Set oChild = oSales.Create("organizationalUnit", _
  "Configuration")
oChild.SetInfo
```

Now I return to the top-level domain object to set a few domainwide password policy attributes. I've used `Put` to set each one, and then called `SetInfo` to save the new configuration.

```
'set domainwide password policy
oDomain.Put "minPwdLength", 10
oDomain.Put "maxPwdAge", 30
oDomain.Put "minPwdAge", 2
oDomain.SetInfo
```

Just for fun, I have the script iterate through each object in the built-in Users container. Remember: Although it looks like an OU, it isn't one, so it has to be accessed by using the CN component, not the OU component. The result should be a comma-separated list of the object names in the container.

```
'display contents of Users
Dim sContents, oUsers, oObject
Set oUsers = GetObject("LDAP://cn=Users,dc=domain,dc=com")
For Each oObject In oUsers
  sContents = sContents & oObject.Name & ", "
Next
WScript.Echo "Users contains: " & sContents
```

Next, I create another top-level OU.

```
'create another top-level OU
Dim oOU
Set oOU = oDomain.Create("organizationalUnit", "Management")
oDomain.SetInfo
```

The script now moves the new OU to be a child OU of Sales. I could have created the OU directly under Sales, but that wouldn't have shown off the MoveHere method. Notice how this works: I use the MoveHere method of the *parent object*, specifying the LDAP string of the object to be moved. There's no need to call SetInfo in this case.

```
'move the top-level OU into Sales
oSales.MoveHere "LDAP://ou=Management,dc=domain,dc=com"
```

Now I want to copy the Sales/Management OU into HR, so that there will also be an HR/Management OU. I want the attributes of both OUs to be the same. I have to start by creating the new child OU under HR.

```
'create a management OU in HR, too
Dim oCopy
oCopy = oHR.Create("organizationalUnit", "Management")
oCopy.SetInfo
```

I need a reference to my template object, which is the Management OU that already exists under the Sales OU.

```
'now we're going to copy the Sales Management OU
'attributes to the HR Management OU
Dim oTemplate, aAttributes, sAttribute, sValue

'use the Sales OU as a reference
Set oTemplate = GetObject( _
  "LDAP://ou=Management,ou=Sales,dc=domain,dc=com")
aAttributes = Array("description", "location")
```

Next, I can use a For Each/Next loop to copy each attribute from Sales/Management to HR/Management.

```
'copy each attribute from the source to the target
For Each sAttribute In aAttributes
 sValue = oTemplate.Get(sAttribute)
 oCopy.Put sAttribute, sValue
Next
```

When the attributes are copied, a call to SetInfo saves the changes.

```
'save the information
oCopy.SetInfo
```

Using this type of script to quickly load a domain is a valuable trick, and can save you many hours in the test lab. Unlike a backup, which always restores the same thing, this script can be easily tweaked to set up different test environments, or to reflect changes in your production domain.

Summary

ADSI makes it easy to connect to and manipulate domains. You've seen how to query and modify domain-level attributes, and how to create, modify, query, and delete domain-level objects, such as OUs. These techniques can be applied not only to OUs, but also to users and groups, as you'll see in the next chapter. Having the ability to easily manipulate domain and OU information from script can allow you to restructure domains, automate bulk domain configuration tasks, and much more.

CHAPTER 16

Manipulating Users and Groups

User and group maintenance is probably one of the top administrative tasks that you wanted to automate when you picked up this book. You might be interested primarily in domain user and group management, or local computer user and group management, or possibly both. Remember that the WinNT ADSI provider can be used both in NT domains and, for limited operations, in Active Directory (AD) domains. The WinNT provider also gives you access to the Security Accounts Manager (SAM) on standalone and member servers and NT-based client computers, such as Windows XP machines. The LDAP provider is AD's native provider, and gives you the best access to AD's capabilities, including the ability to work with organizational units (OUs).

In an AD domain, the WinNT provider gives you a flat view of the domain: All users are in a single space, not separated into containers and OUs. With the LDAP provider, however, you need to remain aware of your domain's OU structure, and you need to become accustomed to fully qualified domain names (FQDNs) that describe users and groups not only by their name, but also by their position within the domain's OU hierarchy.

Creating Users and Groups

Creating users and groups is probably one of the most frequently automated tasks for administrators, or at least the task they'd most *like* to automate. Scripting makes it easy, whether you're using the WinNT provider or the LDAP provider.

The WinNT Way

With the WinNT provider, you start by obtaining a connection to the domain itself. Because all users and groups exist at the top level of the domain, you don't need to connect to a specific OU. Note that you can also use this technique to create local user and group accounts, by simply connecting directly to a non–domain controller instead of connecting to a domain.

After you are connected, simply use the Create method—much as I did with OUs in the previous chapter—to create the user account. Here's an example:

```
Dim oDomain, oUser
Set oDomain = GetObject("WinNT://DOMAIN")
Set oUser = oDomain.Create("user","DonJ")
```

Not much to it. You need to call SetInfo to save the new user, but first you probably want to set some of the user's attributes. Here's an extended example:

```
Dim oDomain, oUser
Set oDomain = GetObject("WinNT://DOMAIN")
Set oUser = oDomain.Create("user","DonJ")

oUser.SetPassword "pa55w0rd!"
oUser.FullName = "Don Jones"
oUser.Description = "Author"
oUser.HomeDirectory = "\\server1\donj"
oUser.RasPermissions = 9
oUser.SetInfo
```

The WinNT provider helpfully exposes these attributes as properties of the user object, meaning you don't have to use raw attribute names like you do with the LDAP provider (which I'll cover next). However, note that some directories—such as Active Directory—do have some minimum required properties that you have to set to successfully create a new object; sAMAccountName is a good example, and you'll see me use it in an example in just a bit.

Creating a group requires a similar process:

```
Dim oDomain, oGroup
Set oDomain = GetObject("WinNT://DOMAIN")
Set oGroup = oDomain.Create("group","HelpDesk")
oGroup.SetInfo
```

Again, not much to it. Later in this chapter, I'll show you how to manipulate the group's membership list.

The LDAP Way

Creating groups and users with the LDAP provider is very similar, although because the LDAP provider is a bit more generic than the WinNT provider is, you have to provide a bit more detail in the way of attribute names. Also, because LDAP recognizes AD OUs, you need to connect to the parent object—either an OU or a container—that you want the new user or group to live in. If you just connect to the domain, the new object will be created in the domain's default container, which is generally the Users container. Here's an example:

```
Dim oUser, oGroup, oDomain

'Connect to the MIS OU
Set oDomain = GetObject("LDAP://ou=MIS,dc=domain,dc=com")

'Create a user
Set oUser = oDomain.Create("user", "cn=DonJ")
oUser.Put "sAMAccountName", "donj"
oUser.SetInfo

'create a group
Set oGroup = oDomain.Create("group", "cn=HelpDesk")
oGroup.Put "sAMAccountName", "HelpDesk"
oGroup.SetInfo
```

The overall layout is very similar to the WinNT way of doing things. However, when you create a new object, you must specify its canonical name (CN), such as cn=DonJ. You must also provide a value for one of the user class' mandatory attributes, sAMAccountName. Generally, that should be the same as the CN, without the cn= part. Finally, you call SetInfo to save everything. Keep in mind, however, that I haven't set a password or done anything else that you typically do when creating an account manually—right now, this is just a bare-bones example, and it does leave the account vulnerable from a security standpoint.

Querying User Information

Reading user information (or group information, for that matter) requires the use of the Get method, as well as the name of the attribute you want to read. In the previous chapter, I showed you how to use the AD Schema console to browse a class for its available attributes; you can use the same technique on the user and group classes to see what attributes they support. To query information, simply connect to the object in question and use Get to retrieve the attribute values that you need.

```
Dim oUser
Set oUser = GetObject("LDAP://cn=DonJ,ou=MIS,dc=domain,dc=com")
WScript.Echo oUser.Get("name")
WScript.Echo oUser.Get("description")
WScript.Echo oUser.Get("sAMAccountName")
```

That's easy enough. Using the WinNT provider, you can directly access many attributes that are exposed as regular properties.

```
Dim oUser
Set oUser = GetObject("WinNT://DOMAIN/DonJ")
WScript.Echo oUser.Name
WScript.Echo oUser.Description
```

One thing to be careful of with the WinNT provider is that it grabs the first object it finds matching your query. For example, if I have a user *and* a group named DonJ, the preceding example might bind to the user or the group. You can force the object type by specifying it.

```
Dim oUser
Set oUser = GetObject("WinNT://DOMAIN/DonJ,user")
WScript.Echo oUser.Name
WScript.Echo oUser.Description
```

You can also use Get with the WinNT provider, making its syntax parallel to the LDAP provider. Keep in mind that user objects have a number of multivalued attributes, as I mentioned in Chapter 14, "Working with ADSI Providers." Reading those requires a slightly different technique.

```
Dim oUser
Set oUser = GetObject("LDAP://cn=DonJ,ou=MIS,dc=domain,dc=com")

Dim sURL
For Each sURL in objUser.GetEX("url")
 WScript.Echo sURL
Next
```

In this case, I'm working with the "url" attribute of a user object, which can actually contain multiple uniform resource locators (URLs). The GetEx method retrieves them all into a collection, which I iterate through by using a For Each/Next collection.

Changing User Settings

Using the LDAP provider, you can use Put to change user and group attributes.

```
Dim oUser
Set oUser = GetObject("LDAP://cn=DonJ,ou=MIS,dc=domain,dc=com")
oUser.Put "description", "Author"
oUser.SetInfo
```

Keep in mind that users in particular offer a number of multivalued attributes. I discussed how to work with those in Chapter 14. Here's a quick refresher:

```
Const MVP_CLEAR = 1
Const MVP_UPDATE = 2
Const MVP_APPEND = 3
Const MVP_DELETE = 4


Dim objUser
Set objUser = GetObject("cn=DonJ,ou=Sales,dc=sapien,dc=com")
objUser.PutEx MVP_APPEND, "otherTelephone", Array("555-1212")
objUser.SetInfo
```

This example appends another telephone number to a user's otherTelephone multivalued attribute. You can also clear the attribute completely, delete entries, or change a particular entry. The following example adds a new telephone number, and then deletes it:

```
Const MVP_CLEAR = 1
Const MVP_UPDATE = 2
Const MVP_APPEND = 3
Const MVP_DELETE = 4


Dim objUser
Set objUser = GetObject("cn=DonJ,ou=Sales,dc=sapien,dc=com")
objUser.PutEx MVP_APPEND, "otherTelephone", Array("555-1212")
objUser.SetInfo


objUser.PutEx MVP_DELETE, "otherTelephone", Array("555-1212")
objUser.SetInfo
```

The PutEx method accepts the operation type (clear, update, append, or delete), the attribute you want to change, and the value you want to update, append, or delete. In the case of a clear operation, you don't need to provide a new value; the attribute is simply cleared out completely.

If you're using the WinNT provider, either you can set properties directly or you can use Put, just like the LDAP provider.

Working with Groups

You'll want to do two primary things with groups: Modify their membership and check their membership. The former can be useful in scripts that bulk-add new users to the domain; the latter is invaluable in logon scripts. Let's take checking group membership first. The basic trick is to get a reference to a group, and then scan through its members until you find a particular user (or not). This is best implemented as a function, which can be easily reused in different scripts. The function is in Listing 16.1.

LISTING 16.1   *CheckGroupMembership.vbs.* This function checks to see if a specified user belongs to a specified group.

```
Function IsMember(sUser, sGroup)
 Dim oGroup, bIsMember, oMember
 bIsMember = False
 Set oGroup = GetObject("LDAP://" & sGroup)
 For Each sMember in oGroup.GetEx("member")
  If sMember = sUser Then
   bIsMember = True
   Exit For
  End If
 Next
 IsMember = bIsMember
End Function
```

You need to pass FQDNs to this function. For example, to see if user DonJ, located in the MIS OU, is a member of the HelpDesk group, also located in the MIS OU, you'd do something like this:

```
If IsMember( _
 "cn=DonJ,ou=MIS,dc=domain,dc=com", _
 "cn=HelpDesk,ou=MIS,dc=domain,dc=com") Then
 WScript.Echo "He's a member!"
Else
 WScript.Echo "He's not a member!"
End If
```

Notice that the function uses the GetEx method to retrieve the group object's member attribute, which is a multivalued attribute. Each entry in the attribute is the FQDN of a user who belongs to the group. The benefit of a function like this is that it can check for users from different domains belonging to, for example, a Universal security group, because you're using the FQDN of the user, which includes his home domain.

Given this example on how to *read* the group's membership list, you probably have a good idea of how to *modify* that list. Suppose you have a group named HelpDesk in the MIS OU. You want to add a user named DonJ, also from the MIS OU, and delete a user named GregM from the Sales OU. Here's how:

```
Dim oGroup
Set oGroup = GetObject("LDAP://cn=HelpDesk,ou=MIS,dc=" & _
 "domain,dc=com")

'PutEx constants
Const MVP_CLEAR = 1
Const MVP_UPDATE = 2
```

```
Const MVP_APPEND = 3
Const MVP_DELETE = 4

'add user
oGroup.PutEx MVP_APPEND, "member", "cn=DonJ,ou=MIS,dc=" & _
 "domain,dc=com"
oGroup.SetInfo

'delete user
oGroup.PutEx MVP_DELETE, "member", "cn-GregM,ou=Sales,dc=" & _
 "domain,dc=com"
oGroup.SetInfo
```

What if you want to do this with an NT domain or a local SAM? Using the WinNT provider is slightly different. First, you need to connect to the user account to obtain its security identifier (SID), and then you can add that to the group.

```
Dim oUser, oGroup
Set oUser = GetObject("WinNT://DOMAIN/DonJ,user")
Set oGroup = GetObject("WinNT://DOMAIN/HelpDesk,group")

oGroup.Add oUser.ADsPath
```

Here again, you see how the WinNT provider can make things a tiny bit easier because it's designed specifically for dealing with users, groups, and other stuff like that. The LDAP provider, on the other hand, provides more flexibility because it's designed as a generic LDAP provider. That means future changes to AD won't require a new LDAP provider.

Putting It All Together

In the previous chapter, I demonstrated a script that sets up a domain with some OUs, designed to model a production environment in a test lab. But what's a domain without users?

Preload Domain II Listing 16.2 shows a script that utilizes everything I've covered in this chapter. It's designed to be added to the end of Listing 16.1 for a complete domain preloading script. This script creates ten thousand user accounts, some groups, and distributes users into the groups. Note that ten thousand users will take a while to create, so be patient (they'll also increase the size of the domain database significantly, so make sure you're prepared for that).

LISTING 16.2   *PreloadDomain2.vbs.* Creating dummy user and group accounts for a domain in a test environment.

```vbscript
'create 10,000 user accounts
'seriously - don't run this in a
'production domain!

'connect to the root
Dim oRoot
Set oRoot = GetObject("LDAP://rootDSE")

'connect to the Users container
Dim oContainer
Set oContainer = GetObject("LDAP://cn=Users," & _
 oRoot.Get("defaultNamingContext")

'create 10,000 users (or change
'the number to create fewer)
Dim iUser, oUser
For iUser = 1 To 10000
 Set oUser = oContainer.Create("user", _
  "DummyUser" & CStr(iUser))
 oUser.Put "sAMAccountName", CStr(iUser)
 oUser.SetInfo
Next

'create 1,000 groups
Dim iGroup, oGroup
For iGroup = 1 To 1000
 Set oGroup = oContainer.Create("group", _
  "DummyGroup" & CStr(iGroup))
 oGroup.SetInfo
Next

'go through the users and place
'1,000 of them in each group
Dim iLastUser
iLastUser = 1
For iGroup = 1 To 1000

 'get the group
 Set oGroup = GetObject("LDAP://cn=DummyGroup" & _
  CStr(iGroup) & ",dc=domain,dc=com")

 'go through users
 For iUser = iLastUser To iLastUser + 999
```

LISTING 16.2   Continued

```
 oGroup.PutEx 3, "member", _
   "cn=DummyUser" & CStr(iUser) & _
     ",dc=domain,dc=com"
 Next


 iLastUser = iUser


Next
```

CAUTION

Please, please, please note: Don't run this in a production domain. It's intended only for use in a test lab, and it will create 10,000 users and 1,000 groups—definitely a rough burden to place on a production domain that isn't expecting it!

Preload Domain II—Explained   This script starts by connecting to the root domain.

```
'create 10,000 user accounts
'seriously - don't run this in a
'production domain!

'connect to the root
Dim oRoot
Set oRoot = GetObject("LDAP://rootDSE")
```

Next, it gets a reference to the Users container, which is where the new users and groups will be placed.

```
'connect to the Users container
Dim oContainer
Set oContainer = GetObject("LDAP://cn=Users," & _
 oRoot.Get("defaultNamingContext"))
```

Now the script creates 10,000 users, named DummyUser1, DummyUser2, and so forth. Note that they'll all have empty passwords, meaning your domain policies will need to be set to allow a minimum password length of zero. That's *not* the default in Windows Server 2003 domains. You could also modify the script to create a password, but make sure the script writes that password into a file, so that you know what the password is!

```
'create 10,000 users
Dim iUser, oUser
For iUser = 1 To 10000
 Set oUser = oContainer.Create("user", _
   "DummyUser" & CStr(iUser))
```

```
oUser.Put "sAMAccountName", CStr(iUser)
oUser.SetInfo
Next
```

Next, the script creates 1,000 user groups, named DummyGroup1, DummyGroup2, and so forth.

```
'create 1,000 groups
Dim iGroup, oGroup
For iGroup = 1 To 1000
  Set oGroup = oContainer.Create("group", _
    "DummyGroup" & CStr(iGroup))
  oGroup.SetInfo
Next
```

The script next runs through each of the 1,000 groups. I'm using a variable named iLastUser to keep track of the last user I worked with.

```
'go through the users and place
'1,000 of them in each group
Dim iLastUser
iLastUser = 1
For iGroup = 1 To 1000
```

For each group, I get an LDAP reference to the group itself.

```
'get the group
Set oGroup = GetObject("LDAP://cn=DummyGroup" & _
  CStr(iGroup) & ",dc=domain,dc=com")
```

Then, I go through 1,000 users. I preloaded iLastUser with 1, so the first pass will be 1 to 999. After the last Next, iUser will equal 1,000, so the second loop will be 1,000 to 1,999. I add each user's FQDN to the member property of the group.

```
'go through users
For iUser = iLastUser To iLastUser + 999
  oGroup.PutEx 3, "member", _
    "cn=DummyUser" & CStr(iUser) & _
    ",dc=domain,dc=com"
Next

iLastUser = iUser

Next
```

That's a neat way to quickly load a bunch of data into a domain, so that you can do load testing, application testing, backup and restore testing, or whatever else you need to do. You've seen examples of how to use both the LDAP and WinNT providers to work with users and groups, and you'll continue to see more examples throughout this book. In fact, Chapter 30, "WMI and ADSI Scripts," contains additional ready-to-run sample scripts that focus entirely on Windows and domain administration, and Chapter 20, "Putting It All Together: Your First WMI/ADSI Script," allows you to combine your knowledge of ADSI and WMI—which is coming up next—to design, write, test, and debug a complete Windows and domain management script.

Summary

Working with users and groups is relatively easy from within ADSI. Remember that you can use the WinNT provider to access not only Windows NT domains, but also Active Directory domains, standalone computers, domain member computers, and so forth. Native Active Directory access is provided through the LDAP provider, which also provides access to other LDAP-based directories, such as Exchange 5.x. Some of the most useful scripts you'll develop will use ADSI to manage local user accounts, such as service accounts and built-in accounts like Administrator.

16

Understanding WMI

W henever I speak at conferences, I'm nearly always asked about Windows Management Instrumentation, or WMI. WMI first caught on in Windows 2000 (although it's partially supported in Windows NT 4.0), and administrators have been hearing about how wonderful a tool it is for managing systems, especially through scripting. Unfortunately, WMI is also one of the most complex-looking technologies to have come out of Redmond in a long time, and many administrators are justifiably concerned about having to spend the rest of their lives understanding it. In this chapter and the two that follow, however, I'm going to show you that WMI isn't as complicated as it looks. In fact, I'll even provide you with some code templates that you can modify to query or set almost any kind of management information from a Windows computer.

The WMI Hierarchy

One of the most complicated parts of WMI is the sheer number of acronyms that come with it: DMTF, CIM, Win32, and so forth. First, bear in mind that you don't really need to remember any of them to use WMI effectively. However, it can be helpful to understand what they all mean because they help WMI make more sense.

The DMTF is the Desktop Management Task Force. It's an industry group primarily concerned with making desktop computers (they do care about servers, too) easier to manage. Microsoft pays close attention to the DMTF and is a contributing member. One of the things that the DMTF realized is that every hardware, software, and operating system vendor has different names for the same things. Windows, for example, has logical disks, partitions, volumes, and so forth; Novell NetWare uses these terms for slightly different things. To clear up the confusion, the DMTF created the Common Information Model, or CIM.

The CIM is essentially a generic way of describing everything associated with a computer, at both a hardware and a software level. The CIM defines many base *classes* to represent things like disks, processors, motherboards, and so forth. The CIM classes only include properties that are universal. For example, the `CIM_DiskDrive` class includes a property for `Name` because all disk drives can be assigned a descriptive name. It also includes a property for `MaxBlockSize` because all disk drives manufactured today have an associated maximum block size. The class doesn't include a property that indicates the file system used to format the disk, nor does it show whether a disk is basic or dynamic. Those are operating system–specific features not addressed by the CIM.

The CIM is, however, extensible. When Microsoft created WMI, it created its own series of Win32 classes that are Windows-specific. The Win32 classes are based on, or *inherited* from, CIM classes. For example, there's a `Win32_DiskDrive` class. It includes all of the properties associated with the `CIM_DiskDrive` class, and includes additional properties— such as `PNPDeviceID`—that are specific to the Windows operating system.

TIP

You might want to explore the WMI reference information online, just to see how the Win32 classes build upon their CIM counterparts. Go to http://msdn.microsoft.com/library to start. In the navigation tree on the left, open Win32 and COM Development, Administration and Management, Windows Management Instrumentation, WMI Reference, and WMI Classes. You'll see sections for CIM classes and Win32 classes.

The main part of WMI is understanding that it's composed of these *classes,* which represent the hardware and software in a computer. My laptop, for example, has one *instance* of the `Win32_DiskDrive` class, which simply means that the machine contains one disk drive. My desktop machine has two instances of `Win32_DiskDrive`, which means it contains two hard disks. Absolutely everything in WMI is set up to handle multiple instances of classes. Sometimes, that doesn't seem to make any sense. After all, how many computers do you know of that contain multiple instances of a class like `Win32_MotherboardDevice`? Not many! But WMI is designed to be forward looking. Who knows; we might someday be working with computers that *do* have multiple motherboards, and so WMI is set up to deal with it.

Multiple instances can make querying WMI information seem complex. For example, suppose you want to query the IP address of a workstation's network adapter. Unfortunately, you cannot just ask for the IP address from the first adapter WMI knows about. Windows computers all contain multiple network adapters, if you stop to consider virtual private network (VPN) adapters, the virtual loopback adapter, and so forth. So, when you write WMI queries, you have to take into account the fact that the computer probably contains multiple instances of whatever you're after, and write your script accordingly. As a quick example, try the script in Listing 17.1.

LISTING 17.1   *ShowNIC.vbs.* Shows the IP address and MAC address of each network adapter you have.

```
Dim strComputer
Dim objWMIService
Dim colItems

strComputer = "."
Set objWMIService = GetObject("winmgmts:\\" & _
 strComputer & "\root\cimv2")

Set colItems = objWMIService.ExecQuery( _
 "Select * from Win32_NetworkAdapterConfiguration",,48)

For Each objItem in colItems
    WScript.Echo "IPAddress: " & objItem.IPAddress
    WScript.Echo "MACAddress: " & objItem.MACAddress
    WScript.Echo "MTU: " & objItem.MTU
Next
```

NOTE

Because it's possible for one network adapter to have more than one IP address bound to it, this script might not work on your system. Modifying `objItem.IPAddress` to be `objItem.IPAddress(0)` should show the first bound IP address.

Also, that 48 in the `ExecQuery()` method is a parameter that isn't strictly necessary; it specifies a connection option that is the default. I've included it to help ensure backward compatibility, but in most cases you'll be able to eliminate the 48 and the script will work the same.

Unbelievably, WMI isn't any more complicated than that. Don't worry for now about how this script works; you'll be seeing many more like it in this and the next two chapters, along with complete explanations.

Providers and Consumers

One pair of terms you'll run across in the WMI documentation is *providers* and *consumers.* A *consumer* is simply an application that utilizes WMI to retrieve or change system management information. Your WMI scripts, for example, are WMI consumers. A *provider* is a piece of software that makes WMI information available. Windows comes with a number of providers that make system hardware, software, and performance information available through WMI. Third-party applications can include WMI providers, which make those applications manageable through WMI.

17

The fact that these providers are buried within Windows disguises some of the power and flexibility of WMI. WMI isn't what I'd call an integral part of the Windows operating system; it's really an additional set of services that runs on Windows. You can even see the service on Windows 2000 and newer computers if you look in the Services control panel. I'm not suggesting that WMI isn't fully integrated with Windows, but simply that Windows can run without WMI, and that WMI extends Windows' inherent capabilities. Why is this an important distinction?

First, Microsoft isn't really doing anything with WMI that you can't do in other ways. You already know how to set IP addresses, for example—you didn't need WMI to come along and give you that capability. WMI simply makes these administrative tasks available through scripts, meaning you can better automate administrative tasks than you could before. Second, Microsoft isn't doing anything with WMI that other companies can't do. WMI is completely open and extensible, and anyone can write a provider that opens up his application to your scripts.

WMI Versions

WMI has been available in the NT and 9x product lines since Windows NT 4.0, although WMI wasn't full-featured until Windows 2000. Windows XP and Windows Server 2003 have gradually added WMI features, making more and more of the operating system accessible through WMI.

WMI is installed by default in Windows 2000, Windows XP, Windows 2003, and Windows Me. You can install WMI on Windows 95 OSR2, all editions of Windows 98, and Windows NT 4.0. I'll discuss installation requirements later in this chapter.

Exploring WMI's Capabilities

Perhaps the easiest way to understand WMI is to simply start playing with it. Windows XP and Windows Server 2003 include Wbemtest.exe, a tool that can be used to test WMI functionality and explore its capabilities.

> **NOTE**
>
> Another acronym! WBEM stands for Web-Based Enterprise Management, Microsoft's implementation of several key DMTF technologies that includes WMI. You don't see the WBEM name as much as you used to, but it still pops up in tool names and the like.

To run Wbemtest, simply select Run from the Start menu, type **wbemtest**, and click OK. You'll see the main Wbemtest panel, shown in Figure 17.1.

The first thing you need to do is connect to a WMI provider. Generally, that means connecting to the Windows Management Instrumentation service on your local machine or on another computer. I like to connect to the one on another computer because it demonstrates WMI's real power as a remote administration tool. To connect, click the Connect button. You'll see the Connect dialog box, shown in Figure 17.2

To connect to a remote computer, type **computername****root****cimv2**. This instructs WMI to look for the specified computer name, connect to its root WMI namespace, and then switch to the cimv2 namespace. Cimv2 is simply the section that contains all of the Win32 classes, which are the ones you'll work with most often. Be sure to specify a user and password that has administrative privileges on the remote computer, because by default only administrators are allowed to work with WMI. Click Connect to make the connection.

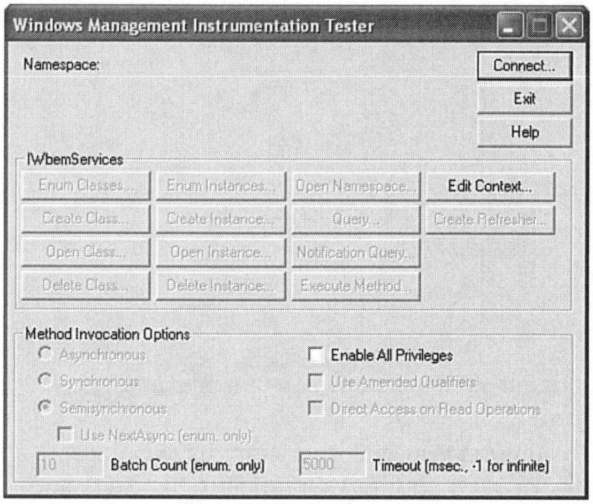

FIGURE 17.1   The WMI Tester's main window.

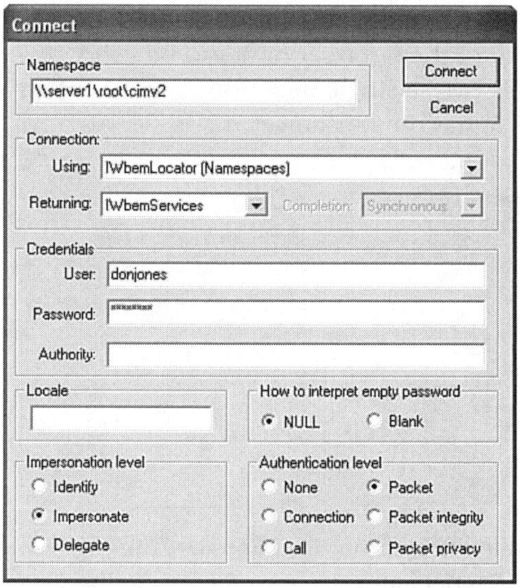

FIGURE 17.2   Connecting to a remote machine's WMI namespace.

After you're connected, click Enum Classes to force WMI to enumerate all available classes in the namespace. You'll be prompted for a superclass name; just leave it blank and click OK. You should see a dialog box similar to the one shown in Figure 17.3, listing all of the classes—both CIM and Win32 classes—that WMI found.

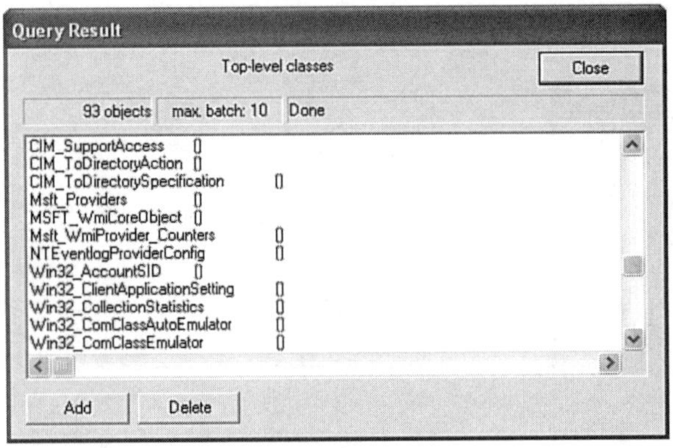

FIGURE 17.3   Enumerating the classes in the remote computer's `cimv2` namespace.

The next fun thing is to try querying. WMI supports a special query language called, appropriately enough, WMI Query Language, or WQL. It looks remarkably like SQL, and if you're familiar with writing SQL queries, WQL will look like an old friend. Start by clicking the Query button, and you'll see a dialog box similar to the one shown in Figure 17.4. Enter a query, such as **SELECT * FROM Win32_NetworkAdapterConfiguration**. Be sure that WQL is selected for the query type, and click Apply. You'll see another dialog box, like the one in Figure 17.5. This dialog box lists all of the *instances* retrieved by your query. Remember, each instance represents, in this case, a single network adapter configuration. My computer, as you can see in Figure 17.5, has nine instances.

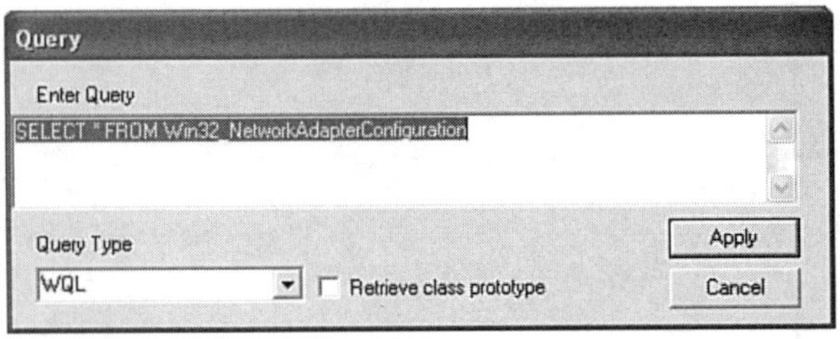

FIGURE 17.4   Writing a WMI query.

You can double-click any of the instances to display its information, as shown in Figure 17.6. This particular instance, as shown, has DHCP enabled.

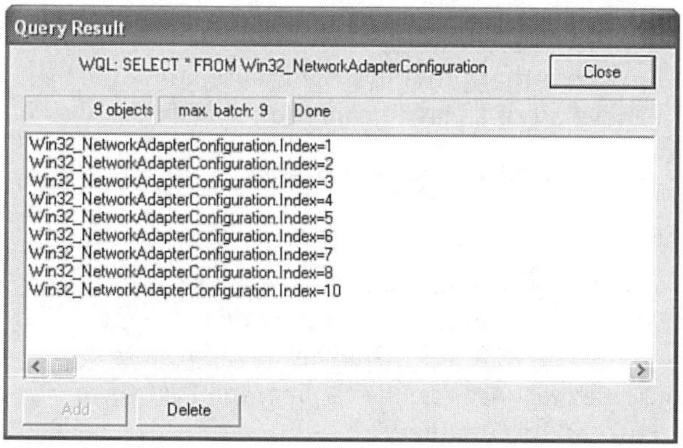

FIGURE 17.5   Instances returned by the query.

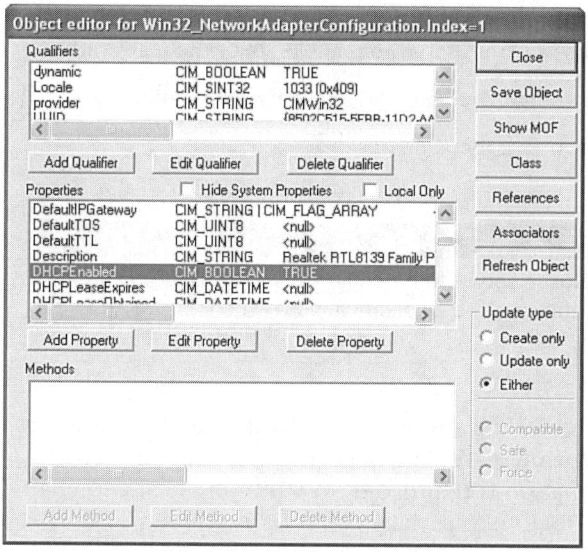

FIGURE 17.6   Examining an instance's properties.

Hey, you've written your first WMI query! You might not even have noticed!

WQL Queries

Wbemtest is a great way to test WQL queries before including them in your scripts. You'll be able to immediately see what the query does, what information it returns, and so forth, which helps prevent errors in your scripts later on down the line.

WQL queries themselves are simple enough, and have five basic parts, one of which is optional. These parts are as follows:

17

- ▶ SELECT, which must start each WQL query.

- ▶ The properties you want to query. You can either provide a comma-separated list of property names, or if you want to retrieve all of a class' properties, specify *.

- ▶ FROM, which must follow the list of properties that you want to query.

- ▶ The name of the class you're querying.

- ▶ Optionally, you can include WHERE and a conditional statement. A WHERE clause limits the instances returned by your query. For example, if I include WHERE DHCPEnabled=TRUE in my earlier query, I receive fewer instances in the results because only those instances of Win32_NetworkAdapterConfiguration that have DHCPEnabled set to True would be returned by the query.

Here are some sample WQL queries. If you want, try them in Wbemtest to see what they do!

- ▶ SELECT * FROM Win32_NetworkAdapterConfiguration WHERE DHCPEnabled=TRUE

- ▶ SELECT Description FROM Win32_Account WHERE Name='Administrator'

- ▶ SELECT Freespace,DeviceID FROM Win32_LogicalDisk

> **NOTE**
>
> Notice that the string value "Administrator" needed to be enclosed within single quotation marks in the WMI query. However, numeric and Boolean values—such as the TRUE in the first example—don't need quotes.

Honestly, the best advice I can offer for quickly learning WMI is to explore the WMI class reference and start writing queries in Wbemtest. You'll quickly become familiar with WQL, and you'll see what type of information is returned by WMI. In the next two chapters, I'll focus on dealing with that information, especially complex information like IP addresses. Most important, *do not be afraid to break something in Wbemtest.* Even if you write the worst, malformed query known to mankind, the worst that can happen is Wbemtest will crash and you'll have to reopen it. No big deal, so experiment away!

Installing WMI

As I mentioned earlier, WMI is preinstalled on Windows 2000 and all later Windows operating systems, including Windows Me. However, if you're using anything earlier, you might need to install WMI before you can start deploying WMI scripts. WMI must be installed on every computer that you intend to query, regardless of where your scripts will actually run; WMI must also be installed on any computer that will run WMI scripts. To obtain the WMI installer, go to the Microsoft home page and select Downloads. From the menu on the left, select the System Management Tools category. Look for the Windows Management Instrumentation (WMI) CORE download for WMI version 1.5. Downloads are available for Windows 9x and NT 4.0. If you cannot spot the downloads in the list, simply type **WMI** into the keyword search at the bottom of the page.

The installer is an executable, not an MSI package. Unfortunately, because these older operating systems don't support Group Policy software deployment, you'll have to manually install the package, or deploy it through alternative means such as Microsoft Systems Management Server (SMS).

I also recommend that you download and install the WMI Administrative Tools. Because Microsoft rearranges their downloads frequently, just visit their main Downloads page and search for "WMI Tools" to locate the download. I'll discuss the administrative tools in the next section.

Using the WMI Tools

I've already introduced you to Wbemtest, which is a great way to experiment with WMI and get a feel for what it can do. The WMI Administrative Tools, however, includes the WMI Object Browser, which is an exceptionally cool tool. After downloading and installing the tools, launch the Object Browser from the Start menu. Have it connect to the root/CIMV2 namespace, and provide logon credentials if necessary. You'll see the main screen, shown in Figure 17.7.

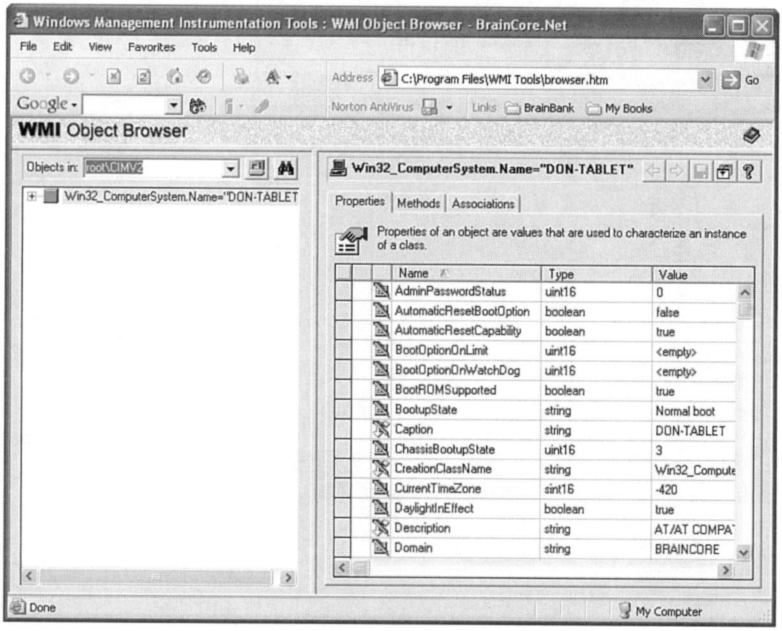

FIGURE 17.7   The main Object Browser screen.

The Browser lets you see all the properties associated with each class. For example, it starts connected to the `Win32_ComputerSystem` class that represents your entire computer; you can see the properties of the class—such as `AutomaticResetBootOption`—that govern many aspects of your computer's behavior.

On the Object Browser's Methods tab, shown in Figure 17.8, you can see the actions that the class can perform. The `Win32_ComputerSystem` class, for example, offers a `JoinDomainOrWorkgroup` method, a `Rename` method, a `SetPowerState` method, and an `UnjoinDomainOrWorkgroup` method. These methods can be programmatically called from within your scripts (which I'll explore in the next two chapters), allowing you to change the computer's configuration.

How can the Object Browser help you write WMI scripts? The Object Browser provides an easy way to see what's lurking under the hood of WMI. I've always said that the toughest part about using WMI lies in figuring out what the heck you're going to query or change; Object Browser makes it a bit easier to figure out what classes, properties, and methods you want to work with.

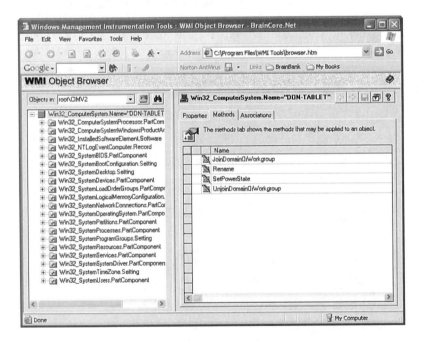

FIGURE 17.8   Examining the methods of a WMI class.

Scriptomatic

There's one more WMI tool that I want to introduce: the WMI Scriptomatic. This handy tool was written by Microsoft's "Scripting Guys," who write a regular scripting column on the Microsoft TechNet website. You can download the Scriptomatic from Microsoft: Just go to the Microsoft home page, click Downloads, and search the downloads to find the Scriptomatic.

The Scriptomatic performs a function very similar to the WMI Query Wizard in PrimalScript, the script editor I use (available from www.sapien.com). You just pick a WMI class—like `Win32_ComputerSystem`—and the tool produces a template script that queries the class and displays all of its properties. It's a handy way to quickly see the appropriate syntax for a WMI query, but if you look at a couple of different classes you'll realize something very important: All of the scripts produced by the Scriptomatic (and the WMI Query Wizard in PrimalScript) look nearly identical. All that changes is the class name being queried, and the property names being displayed. That's because querying WMI isn't complicated! One simple, generic script—like the one I showed you in Listing 17.1—can be easily modified to query almost anything from WMI.

The Easy Way to Write WMI Scripts

In my conference lectures on scripting, I always try to prove how easy WMI scripting really is. I usually ask students to call out some piece of computer information that they'd like to be able to query. Believe me, I haven't memorized the hundreds of WMI classes that are available, so it's unlikely that I'll already know how to query whatever they ask for. It's a great way to show how a little documentation and a couple of tools can quickly result in a powerful WMI script. For example, suppose you need to query a server to see if any persistent routes have been added by using the `route -p add` command. No problem. Here are the four steps to writing almost any WMI script.

Find the Class

First, I have to figure out what to query. This is easily the toughest part of the entire process. I usually start in the WMI Reference documentation, looking at the five categories of Win32 classes:

1. Computer System Hardware

2. Operating System

3. Installed Applications

4. WMI Service Management

5. Performance Counter

Of these five, Operating System seems to be the most likely choice for routing information, so I'll expand that topic. Unfortunately, that leaves me with a whole bunch of classes still to work through. Fortunately, they're alphabetical, so I can scroll right down to the R section and look for something like `Win32_Route`. Nope, nothing. In fact, `Win32_Registry` is the only thing under R, and that clearly isn't it.

Idly scrolling back up, I do see `Win32_IP4RouteTable`. Aha! That makes sense; Windows XP and Server 2003 both support IPv4 and IPv6; WMI clearly needs some way to distinguish between the two. Looking more closely, I also see `Win32_IP4PersistedRouteTable`, which looks exactly like what I want.

Here's what the Microsoft MSDN Library has to say about `Win32_IP4PersistedRouteTable`.

> The `Win32_IP4PersistedRouteTable` WMI class represents persisted IP routes. By default, the routes added to the routing table are not permanent. Rebooting the computer clears the routes from the table. However, the following Windows NT command makes the route persist after the computer is restarted:
>
> `route -p add`
>
> Persistent entries are automatically reinserted in the route table each time the route table is rebuilt. Windows NT stores persistent routes in the registry. This class is only applicable to IP4 and does not address IPX or IP6. An entry can be removed through the method call `SWbemServices.Delete` (in the Scripting API for WMI) or `IWbemServices::DeleteInstance` (in the COM API for WMI). This class was added for Windows Server 2003 family.

That last sentence gives me some pause: "This class was added for Windows Server 2003 family." Scrolling to the bottom of the page reveals that the class is present in Windows XP and Windows Server 2003, meaning I cannot use this on Windows 2000. That's not unusual; as WMI becomes more popular, Microsoft expands it to include more and more aspects of the operating system. By checking this ahead of time in the documentation, though, you can save yourself an incredible amount of time and effort.

For the sake of argument, let's say I'm working entirely with Windows Server 2003 servers, which means I'll have access to this class. The documentation does imply that I can use this class to delete entries, but I'm just interested in seeing if any exist to begin with right now.

Write the Query, Test the Query

I have to write a WQL query that will retrieve all instances of this class. Something like `SELECT * FROM Win32_IP4PersistedRouteTable` should do the trick. Time to fire up Wbemtest and try the query. After running it on my Windows XP machine, just to try it out, I get a results dialog box like the one in Figure 17.9. Sure enough, I have a persistent route on my laptop! According to the properties shown, the route's destination is for 63.171.9.180.

What if my laptop is more typical and doesn't have any persistent routes? My query would return nothing, and there's a valuable lesson: When testing your queries, always make sure there's something for them to return. In this case, *create* a persistent route, if necessary; that way, you'll be able to tell if your query is working properly.

Double-clicking the instance reveals all the properties of the class, with the values for this instance, as shown in Figure 17.10.

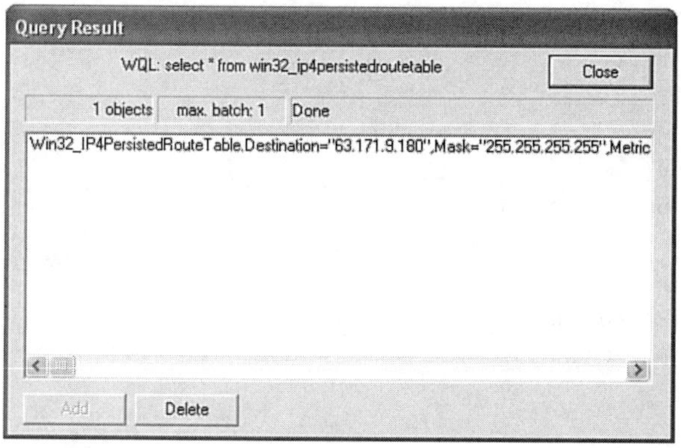

FIGURE 17.9   Examining returned instances of `Win32_IP4PersistedRouteTable`.

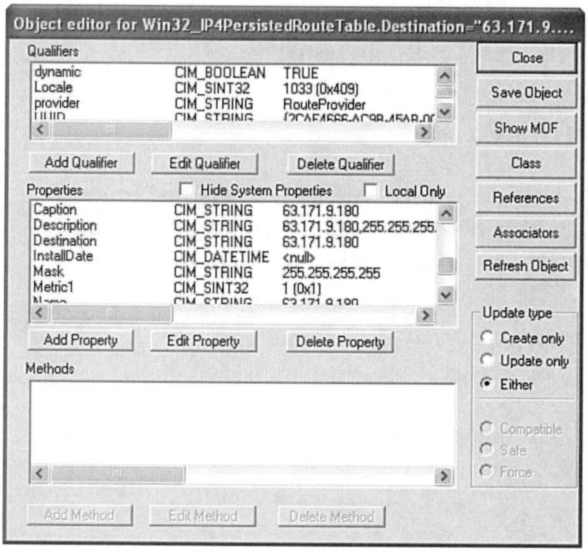

FIGURE 17.10   Properties of my persisted route.

Write the Script

Remember that WMI query script I showed you in Listing 17.1? Here it is again just as a reference.

```
Dim strComputer
Dim objWMIService
Dim colItems
```

```
strComputer = "."
Set objWMIService = GetObject("winmgmts:\\" & _
 strComputer & "\root\cimv2")

Set colItems = objWMIService.ExecQuery( _
 "Select * from Win32_NetworkAdapterConfiguration",,48)

For Each objItem in colItems
 WScript.Echo "IPAddress: " & objItem.IPAddress
 WScript.Echo "MACAddress: " & objItem.MACAddress
 WScript.Echo "MTU: " & objItem.MTU
Next
```

This is a generic WMI query script, and I just need to adapt it to my current needs. I've provided you with several other template scripts in Chapter 30, "WMI and ADSI Scripts," which will help you get just about anything you want out of WMI. For this example, I first need to replace the query with the one I just wrote and tested.

```
Set colItems = objWMIService.ExecQuery( _
 "Select * from Win32_IP4PersistedRouteTable",,48)
```

Next, I need to modify the properties that are being used. After all, a persisted route doesn't have a MAC address or an MTU, which were both used in the original script. I want the script to display the route's caption, which tells me its destination address.

```
For Each objItem in colItems
 WScript.Echo "Route to: " & objItem.Caption
Next
```

I'd also like the script to count the persisted routes and tell me the total of how many it finds. I can add that information easily.

```
Dim iCounter
For Each objItem in colItems
 iCounter = iCounter + 1
 WScript.Echo "Route to: " & objItem.Caption
Next
WScript.Echo iCounter & " routes were found."
```

Finally, I'd like the script to connect to a specified server, not just my local machine. Again, this is a relatively simple change in VBScript.

```
strComputer = InputBox("Enter server name to check")
Set objWMIService = GetObject("winmgmts:\\" & _
 strComputer & "\root\cimv2")
```

That's it. Listing 17.2 shows the final, completed script that should do what I need.

LISTING 17.2   *CheckRoutes.vbs.* Checks for persisted IPv4 routes on a specified 2003 or XP machine.

```
Dim strComputer
Dim objWMIService
Dim colItems

strComputer = InputBox("Enter server name to check")
Set objWMIService = GetObject("winmgmts:\\" & _
 strComputer & "\root\cimv2")

Set colItems = objWMIService.ExecQuery( _
 "Select * from Win32_IP4PersistedRouteTable",,48)

Dim iCounter
For Each objItem in colItems
 iCounter = iCounter + 1
 WScript.Echo "Route to: " & objItem.Caption
Next
WScript.Echo iCounter & " routes were found."
```

You should be able to type this in (or download it from http://www.ScriptingAnswers. com/books.asp) and run it as is.

Test the Script

The last step, of course, is to test it. This example should work perfectly; if your future scripts don't work so well, just debug them one error at a time. Following these four simple steps, you've accomplished quite a bit: You located an appropriate WMI class, you created and tested a WQL query, you modified a template script to meet your needs, and you tested the script. That's all there is to it!

Summary

WMI *looks* complex, but that's primarily because there's so darn much of it. Boiled down, WMI isn't difficult at all, and can really be a lot of fun when you get used to it. In this chapter, you've learned how WMI works, how you can access it from your scripts, and how to methodically create WMI scripts to perform almost any task. You also learned about some of the tools that make WMI easier to work with, such as Wbemtest and the WMI Object Browser. I also introduced you to the WMI Scriptomatic from Microsoft, which makes creating new WMI scripts a real breeze.

17

Querying Basic WMI Information

In the previous chapter, I showed you a standard template-style WMI query that you can modify to query almost anything from Windows Management Instrumentation (WMI). What I didn't do is show you exactly how that query works, how you can easily incorporate it into other scripts, and how to utilize the information you retrieve. If you start using WMI examples from the web, you might even notice that different script authors write their WMI queries in completely different ways. There's nothing wrong with that because WMI is flexible enough to work in different ways and still achieve the results you need.

The WMI Query Language (WQL)

The WMI Query Language, or WQL, is a subset of the industry-standard Structured Query Language (SQL) defined by the American National Standards Institute (ANSI). Although there are other ways to retrieve information from WMI, writing a WQL query is probably the easiest because WQL closely resembles normal English syntax and grammar.

In the previous chapter, you saw examples of some basic WQL queries.

▶ SELECT * FROM Win32_NetworkAdapterConfiguration WHERE DHCPEnabled= TRUE

▶ SELECT Description FROM Win32_Account WHERE Name= 'Administrator'

▶ SELECT Freespace,DeviceID FROM Win32_LogicalDisk

Queries like these will likely be the ones you use most; however, it's useful to understand what else you can do with WQL, especially when working with complex information.

Regular SQL has literally hundreds of keywords and clauses; WQL, on the other hand, has 19. That's a much more manageable number, and it means you'll be able to master WQL without rivaling your company's database administrators in SQL prowess. Of course, if you already know SQL, WQL is going to be a snap.

Complex WMI Information

I've used the phrase *complex information* a couple of times in this and the previous chapter; the next chapter, in fact, has *complex information* right in the title. What does it mean?

I divide WMI information into two categories: simple and complex. Simple information is the kind that typically only has one instance on a computer. For example, if I want to query a computer's serial number, there's only going to be one of those. More complex information, like TCP/IP addresses, require more effort as a programmer because each computer can have multiple network adapters, and each network adapter can have multiple addresses.

Security information can be even more complex. For example, WMI provides a way to access NTFS file permissions. Each file on the hard drive is an instance of a WMI class, and each user or group in the computer or domain is represented by a different class. In between those two classes are *access control entries*, or ACEs, which grant a specific permission on a specific file to a specific user or group. So, to access NTFS file permissions, you're dealing with at least three interrelated classes. Complex enough for you?

Properly written WQL queries can reduce this complexity by allowing you to query for specific sets of data, rather than having to wade through all the interrelated classes.

NOTE

I'm not going to cover all 19 keywords. Several of them are intended for querying WMI events, which are special notifications generated by WMI when specific things occur, such as a file being modified. Dealing with WMI events is a bit beyond the scope of this book, and is better suited to traditional programming than scripting.

WMI Query Basics

You've already met the primary players in a WQL query:

▶ SELECT, which must start each WQL query.

▶ The properties you want to query. You can either provide a comma-separated list of property names, or if you want to retrieve all of a class' properties, specify *.

▶ FROM, which must follow the list of properties that you want to query.

▶ The name of the class you're querying.

▶ Optionally, you can include WHERE and a conditional statement. A WHERE clause limits the instances returned by your query. For example, if I include WHERE DHCPEnabled=TRUE in my earlier query, I receive fewer instances in the results, because only those instances of Win32_NetworkAdapterConfiguration that have DHCPEnabled set to True would be returned by the query.

SELECT, a property list (or *), FROM, and a class name are the minimum required elements for any WQL query. Everything else is optional and is used to restrict the amount of information returned by WMI. For example, SELECT * FROM Win32_ComputerSystem WHERE Name = 'Server1' returns all instances of the Win32_ComputerSystem class with the appropriate server name.

> **NOTE**
>
> It might seem odd to specify the computer name in a query, when you have to connect to that computer—in this example, Server1—to begin with. What other computer systems could exist on Server1, after all? However, consider so-called blade systems, where a single chassis might contain multiple independent computers. WMI is designed so that a WMI-compliant chassis could be queried for information about any of the computers it contains, although in practice I'm not aware of any chassis that can do so yet.

Boolean Operators

Whenever you specify a WHERE clause in a WQL query, you have to provide some sort of logical expression. WMI returns all instances that meet your logical condition. For example, WHERE Name = "Server1" is a logical condition because it includes the logical = operator.

You can specify more than one logical condition and combine them with Boolean operators. For example, WHERE Name = "Server1" AND Domain = "MYCOMPANY" provides two conditions that must both be matched. AND serves in this case as a Boolean operator.

WQL supports two primary Boolean operators:

▶ AND—Combines two conditions, both of which must evaluate to True for an instance to be returned in the query results. For example, WHERE Name = "Server1" AND Domain = "MYCOMPANY".

▶ OR—Combines two conditions, either of which may evaluate to True for an instance to be returned in the query results. For example, WHERE Name = "Server1" OR Domain = "MYCOMPANY".

18

Logical expressions can be grouped in parentheses. For example, suppose you're querying the Win32_LogicalDisk class. You might write an expression like the following:

```
SELECT * FROM Win32_LogicalDisk
 WHERE (DriveType = 2) OR
 (DriveType = 3 AND FreeSpace < 1000000)
```

This query would return all instances of Win32_LogicalDisk that are either removable drives (DriveType = 2) or fixed drives (DriveType = 3) with less than 1MB free.

Comparison Operators

Sometimes, you might need to query for instances that have a particular property set to NULL. For example, if you query Win32_NetworkAdapterConfiguration for a configuration that isn't set to use Dynamic Host Configuration Protocol (DHCP), the DHCPLeaseExpires property will be NULL. NULL is a special value, and you cannot use a query like SELECT * FROM Win32_NetworkAdapterConfiguration WHERE DHCPLeaseExpires = NULL. Instead, you have to use the special IS operator, as in SELECT * FROM Win32_NetworkAdapterConfiguration WHERE DHCPLeaseExpires IS NULL. To query for the opposite condition, you could use SELECT * FROM Win32_NetworkAdapterConfiguration WHERE DHCPLeaseExpires IS NOT NULL. Here they are again:

▶ SELECT * FROM Win32_NetworkAdapterConfiguration WHERE DHCPLeaseExpires = NULL—This doesn't work because you cannot use normal comparison operators like = or <> in combination with NULL.

▶ SELECT * FROM Win32_NetworkAdapterConfiguration WHERE DHCPLeaseExpires IS NULL—This selects all instances where the property is set to a null value.

▶ SELECT * FROM Win32_NetworkAdapterConfiguration WHERE DHCPLeaseExpires IS NOT NULL—This selects all instances where the property is not set to a null value.

You cannot use IS or IS NOT in place of the normal comparison operators; IS and IS NOT are designed to be used only in conjunction with NULL. The normal comparison operators are

▶ =—Equal to

▶ >—Greater than

▶ <—Less than

▶ <=—Less than or equal to

▶ >=—Greater than or equal to

▶ <> or != —Not equal to

There's one more comparison operator, LIKE, which is worth looking at. LIKE is sort of a "soft" equality operator, and allows you to use wildcards to match string data. Suppose, for example, that you want to query all network connections that have the word *Office* in their caption, such as "Office Dial-Up" or "Office VPN." You could use the following query:

```
SELECT * FROM Win32_NetworkConnection
 WHERE Caption LIKE '%Office%'
```

> **NOTE**
>
> The LIKE operator is available for WMI queries executed on Windows XP or later.

The LIKE operator supports several wildcard characters:

▶ Use % to represent zero or more characters that you don't care about. For example, %Office% returns "My Offices," "Office VPN," and "Office." On the other hand, Office% returns "Offices" and "Office VPN," but it does not return "My Offices" because there's no percent sign preceding "Office."

▶ Use square brackets ([ ]) to return a specific range of characters. For example, [A-Z]ars returns "Mars," "Wars," and "Tars," but not "Stars."

▶ Use a caret (^) to negate a character range. For example, [^A-M]ars returns "Wars" and "Tars," but does not return "Mars" because "M" is in the excluded range.

▶ Use an underscore (_) to return any single character. M_rs returns "Mars," "M3rs," or any other string beginning with "M," ending in "rs," and having one character in between.

Finally, you'll notice that many WMI class properties can be set to either True or False, such as the DHCPEnabled property of the Win32_NetworkAdapterConfiguration class. WQL allows you to use the keywords TRUE and FALSE to query these properties, such as:

```
SELECT * FROM Win32_NetworkAdapterConfiguration
 WHERE DHCPEnabled = TRUE
```

Don't be tempted to write the query with DHCPEnabled IS TRUE, because it won't work; remember that IS and IS NOT only work in conjunction with NULL.

Associators, References, and Keys

If you're looking through the WMI documentation at the WQL reference, you'll notice some additional keywords: REFERENCES OF, KEYS, and ASSOCIATORS OF. These are all used to query more complex WMI information, and I'll cover them in the next chapter.

Determining What to Query

I mentioned in the previous chapter that actually figuring out which WMI class to query is the truly tough part about working with WMI, and it's true. The Microsoft MSDN Library reference to the WMI classes, particularly Microsoft's Win32 classes, is the most comprehensive and useful place to start looking. The documentation can be found online at http://msdn.microsoft.com/library. Because the organization of the online library changes, I suggest using the search function to locate a common WMI class, such as Win32_Service. The search function will locate the class documentation, and you can browse the table of contents from there for the remainder of the WMI documentation.

Microsoft currently divides the classes into five categories, although that will almost certainly change over time as the classes are expanded. The current categories are

▶ Computer System Hardware, which includes everything you can physically touch and see. This includes network adapters, the motherboard, ports, and so forth.

▶ Operating System, which includes everything associated with Windows itself: users and groups, file quotas, security settings, COM settings, and more.

▶ Installed Applications, which covers the Windows Installer subsystem and all managed applications.

▶ WMI Service Management, which covers the configuration and management of WMI itself.

▶ Performance Counter, which provides access to performance monitoring data through WMI.

After you've narrowed down the proper category, my best advice is to dive into the documentation and scroll through the class names until you find one that looks like it will do what you want. Need to force a hard drive to run CHKDSK? Hard drives are hardware, but CHKDSK is Windows-specific. After all, you don't really run CHKDSK on a hard drive, do you? You run it on a *volume,* which is a Windows thing. So, start with the Operating System category. There's the Win32_LogicalDisk category, which represents a volume like C: or D:. Lo and behold, it has a ChkDsk method and a ScheduleAutoChk method, one of which is sure to do the trick. The documentation also helpfully notes that the method is included only in Windows XP and Windows Server 2003, meaning that you'll have to find another way to handle earlier clients.

Microsoft's categorization of the WMI classes is far from consistent. For example, Win32_NetworkAdapterConfiguration is included in the Computer System Hardware category. Although I agree that a network adapter is definitely hardware, surely its actual configuration is part of the operating system, right? In other words, be prepared to do a little browsing to find the right classes, especially until you become accustomed to them.

TIP

The Appendix of this book is a Quick Script Reference I put together to help you locate the right WMI classes more quickly. For example, if you need to write a WMI query to retrieve Windows Product Activation information, just look up "Activation" in the Quick Script Reference. You'll see a reference to WMI, an indication that it's covered in Chapters 17 through 19, and the specific classes involved: `Win32_WindowsProductActivation`, for example.

No matter what, *don't get discouraged.* Keep browsing through the list until you find what you want. Just so you know, WMI isn't complete, yet. Microsoft hasn't provided a WMI "hook" for each thing Windows can do. In fact, the coverage for Windows XP and Windows Server 2003 is light-years better than what's in Windows 2000, and that's better still than NT. But even Windows Server 2003's implementation of WMI doesn't let you query or control the DHCP service, modify IPv6 in any way, modify DNS server records (although you can do that through ADSI in Active Directory–integrated DNS zones), or a hundred other tasks. Eventually, you'll probably be able to do all of those things with WMI, but not today.

Which Versions Include What?

The WMI documentation in MSDN Library is the most authoritative source for which WMI classes are included in which versions of WMI. Keep in mind that some classes gained new properties in newer versions of Windows. Near the end of each class' documentation page, you'll see something like the following:

Client: Included in Windows XP, Windows 2000 Professional, Windows NT Workstation 4.0 SP4, and later.

Server: Included in Windows Server 2003, Windows 2000 Server, Windows NT Server 4.0 SP4, and later.

Note that I'm obviously using a pre-Vista version of the documentation; you can take it as a given that later versions of Windows support the same things as earlier versions in almost all cases. Anyway, those lines in the documentation are your official indications that the class (`Win32_SystemTimeZone`, in this example) is included in the listed versions of Windows. Take `Win32_NetworkAdapter` as a second example. The documentation indicates that it's available in Windows NT 4.0 SP4 and later, but check out the `InterfaceIndex` property. That property includes a note:

Windows XP and earlier: The `InterfaceIndex` property is not available.

This means, of course, that the property was introduced in Windows Server 2003. This particular property had to be added to `Win32_NetworkAdapter` when Microsoft added the `Win32_IP4RouteTable` class, because the route table class needed some unique number with which it could refer to network adapters. As WMI continues to grow with new classes, supporting properties will be added to existing classes to make the package complete.

Suppose you want to work with disk quotas on your Windows 2000 file servers. You find a great-looking class, `Win32_DiskQuota`, but your scripts don't seem to have any effect on your Windows 2000 machines. That's because, as the documentation notes, the class was introduced in Windows XP. How can you retrofit it to 2000? You can't. Unfair, but that's progress.

Testing the Query

In the previous chapter, I showed you how to write and test a query using the Wbemtest tool. I recommend that you test every query you plan to write, by running Wbemtest on the target operating system. That way, you'll know your queries are returning the correct results before you spend a lot of time writing an actual script.

For specific instructions on testing a query, see Chapter 17, "Understanding WMI."

If your script will run on multiple operating systems (as in a logon script or a script being used to manage multiple remote servers), be sure to test the query on each potential operating system. That way, you'll quickly spot any WMI version incompatibilities, and you can take the appropriate steps. Don't forget that you can also test your query by using a generic WMI query script, such as the kind generated by the WMI Scriptomatic or by PrimalScript's WMI Query Wizard.

For example, suppose I want to test the Win32_QuotaSetting query. By using PrimalScript, I just run the wizard, select Win32_QuotaSetting from the class list, and click Insert. The wizard creates the following script:

```
On Error Resume Next
Dim strComputer
Dim objWMIService
Dim colItems

strComputer = "."
Set objWMIService = GetObject( _
 "winmgmts:\\" & strComputer & "\root\cimv2")
Set colItems = objWMIService.ExecQuery( _
 "Select * from Win32_QuotaSetting",,48)
For Each objItem in colItems
 WScript.Echo "Caption: " & objItem.Caption
 WScript.Echo "DefaultLimit: " & objItem.DefaultLimit
 WScript.Echo "DefaultWarningLimit: " & _
  objItem.DefaultWarningLimit
 WScript.Echo "Description: " & objItem.Description
 WScript.Echo "ExceededNotification: " & _
  objItem.ExceededNotification
 WScript.Echo "SettingID: " & objItem.SettingID
 WScript.Echo "State: " & objItem.State
 WScript.Echo "VolumePath: " & objItem.VolumePath
WScript.Echo "WarningExceededNotification: " & objItem.WarningExceededNotification
Next
```

If I want to make a more complex query, I can just modify the template before testing the script. For example, I might change the query to something like this:

```
Set colItems = objWMIService.ExecQuery( _
 "Select * from Win32_QuotaSetting WHERE " & _
 "VolumePath = "C:\\",,48)
```

Did you notice the double backslashes in that query? Normally, backslashes are a special *escape* character in WMI queries; when you need to use an actual backslash—as in a file path—you have to type *two* backslashes, or WMI won't interpret the file path correctly.

This revised query would return all quota settings affecting the C: volume, as opposed to all quota settings on the entire server. Then, I can save the query, copy it to whatever servers I plan to run the final script on, and run the query. The template scripts generated by Scriptomatic and the Query Wizard are noninvasive, meaning they only display information rather than try to change it. That makes them perfect for generating harmless test scripts that allow you to make sure your queries run without error.

Perhaps one of the most annoying aspects of troubleshooting WMI queries is that they don't often return error messages. Consider this example:

```
On Error Resume Next
Dim strComputer
Dim objWMIService
Dim colItems

strComputer = "."
Set objWMIService = GetObject("winmgmts:\\" & _
 strComputer & "\root\cimv2")
Set colItems = objWMIService.ExecQuery( _
 "Select * from Win32_Service WHERE Nmae = 'spooler'",,48)
For Each objItem in colItems
 WScript.Echo "Caption: " & objItem.Caption
Next
```

This example began life as a PrimalScript WMI Query Wizard–generated template, but I modified the WQL query. If you look closely, you'll see that I did it wrong: Name is spelled Nmae. Nonetheless, running this script as is produces no error of any kind, from either VBScript or WMI. That's because WMI looks for all instances of Win32_Service that have a Nmae property set to "spooler." It doesn't find any, of course, because *no* instance of Win32_Service has a Nmae property. So, the script completes cleanly without returning any information.

If your queries aren't returning instances, and you think they should, double- and triple-check the spelling of your class names and service names.

Writing the Query in VBScript

If you're like me, you like your final scripts to be clean, consistent, and easy to read. Using the Wizard- or Scriptomatic-generated scripts isn't the best way to achieve consistency. For example, the PrimalScript Wizard always includes the following code:

```
On Error Resume Next
Dim strComputer
Dim objWMIService
Dim colItems


strComputer = "."
Set objWMIService = GetObject("winmgmts:\\" & strComputer & "\root\cimv2")
```

First, you might not want error-checking turned off, which is what On Error Resume Next does. You might use a different variable-naming convention (I often do, mainly because I'm a bit too lazy to type **str** instead of just **s** for string variables and the like), or you might have already defined a variable name that the wizard is using. Understand that you can always revise and modify the template scripts to fit better within your overall scripts. Not only *can* you change them, you probably *should* change them.

Suppose you want to write a script that restarts a remote server. You've done your browsing, and Win32_OperatingSystem has a method named Shutdown that looks like it'll do the trick. Using Scriptomatic or the WMI Query Wizard, you generate code similar to the following:

```
On Error Resume Next
Dim strComputer
Dim objWMIService
Dim colItems
strComputer = "."
Set objWMIService = GetObject("winmgmts:\\" & _
  strComputer & "\root\cimv2")
Set colItems = objWMIService.ExecQuery( _
  "Select * from Win32_OperatingSystem",,48)
For Each objItem in colItems
  WScript.Echo "BootDevice: " & objItem.BootDevice
  WScript.Echo "BuildNumber: " & objItem.BuildNumber
  WScript.Echo "BuildType: " & objItem.BuildType
  WScript.Echo "Caption: " & objItem.Caption
  WScript.Echo "CodeSet: " & objItem.CodeSet
  WScript.Echo "CountryCode: " & objItem.CountryCode
  WScript.Echo "CreationClassName: " & objItem.CreationClassName
  WScript.Echo "CSCreationClassName: " & _
```

```
     objItem.CSCreationClassName
WScript.Echo "CSDVersion: " & objItem.CSDVersion
WScript.Echo "CSName: " & objItem.CSName
WScript.Echo "CurrentTimeZone: " & objItem.CurrentTimeZone
WScript.Echo "Debug: " & objItem.Debug
WScript.Echo "Description: " & objItem.Description
WScript.Echo "Distributed: " & objItem.Distributed
WScript.Echo "EncryptionLevel: " & _
 objItem.EncryptionLevel
WScript.Echo "ForegroundApplicationBoost: " & _
 objItem.ForegroundApplicationBoost
WScript.Echo "FreePhysicalMemory: " & _
 objItem.FreePhysicalMemory
WScript.Echo "FreeSpaceInPagingFiles: " & _
 objItem.FreeSpaceInPagingFiles
WScript.Echo "FreeVirtualMemory: " & objItem.FreeVirtualMemory
WScript.Echo "InstallDate: " & objItem.InstallDate
WScript.Echo "LargeSystemCache: " & objItem.LargeSystemCache
WScript.Echo "LastBootUpTime: " & objItem.LastBootUpTime
WScript.Echo "LocalDateTime: " & objItem.LocalDateTime
WScript.Echo "Locale: " & objItem.Locale
WScript.Echo "Manufacturer: " & objItem.Manufacturer
WScript.Echo "MaxNumberOfProcesses: " & _
 objItem.MaxNumberOfProcesses
WScript.Echo "MaxProcessMemorySize: " & objItem.MaxProcessMemorySize
WScript.Echo "Name: " & objItem.Name
WScript.Echo "NumberOfLicensedUsers: " & _
 objItem.NumberOfLicensedUsers
WScript.Echo "NumberOfProcesses: " & objItem.NumberOfProcesses
WScript.Echo "NumberOfUsers: " & objItem.NumberOfUsers
WScript.Echo "Organization: " & objItem.Organization
WScript.Echo "OSLanguage: " & objItem.OSLanguage
WScript.Echo "OSProductSuite: " & objItem.OSProductSuite
WScript.Echo "OSType: " & objItem.OSType
WScript.Echo "OtherTypeDescription: " & _
 objItem.OtherTypeDescription
WScript.Echo "PlusProductID: " & objItem.PlusProductID
WScript.Echo "PlusVersionNumber: " & objItem.PlusVersionNumber
WScript.Echo "Primary: " & objItem.Primary
WScript.Echo "ProductType: " & objItem.ProductType
WScript.Echo "QuantumLength: " & objItem.QuantumLength
WScript.Echo "QuantumType: " & objItem.QuantumType
WScript.Echo "RegisteredUser: " & objItem.RegisteredUser
WScript.Echo "SerialNumber: " & objItem.SerialNumber
WScript.Echo "ServicePackMajorVersion: " & _
```

```
 objItem.ServicePackMajorVersion
WScript.Echo "ServicePackMinorVersion: " & _
 objItem.ServicePackMinorVersion
WScript.Echo "SizeStoredInPagingFiles: " & _
 objItem.SizeStoredInPagingFiles
WScript.Echo "Status: " & objItem.Status
WScript.Echo "SuiteMask: " & objItem.SuiteMask
WScript.Echo "SystemDevice: " & objItem.SystemDevice
WScript.Echo "SystemDirectory: " & objItem.SystemDirectory
WScript.Echo "SystemDrive: " & objItem.SystemDrive
WScript.Echo "TotalSwapSpaceSize: " & _
 objItem.TotalSwapSpaceSize
WScript.Echo "TotalVirtualMemorySize: " & _
 objItem.TotalVirtualMemorySize
WScript.Echo "TotalVisibleMemorySize: " & _
 objItem.TotalVisibleMemorySize
WScript.Echo "Version: " & objItem.Version
WScript.Echo "WindowsDirectory: " & objItem.WindowsDirectory
Next
```

First, you weren't interested in querying and displaying *any* information, so you can start by wiping out all of the WScript.Echo lines, leaving you with the following:

```
On Error Resume Next
Dim strComputer
Dim objWMIService
Dim colItems
strComputer = "."
Set objWMIService = GetObject("winmgmts:\\" & _
 strComputer & "\root\cimv2")
Set colItems = objWMIService.ExecQuery( _
  "Select * from Win32_OperatingSystem",,48)
For Each objItem in colItems
Next
```

Regardless of how many operating systems the computer thinks it has, the one that's running is the one you want to shut down, and that'll be the primary one. You can modify the WQL query to just retrieve that instance of the class.

```
On Error Resume Next
Dim strComputer
Dim objWMIService
Dim colItems

strComputer = "."
Set objWMIService = GetObject("winmgmts:\\" & _
```

```
 strComputer & "\root\cimv2")
Set colItems = objWMIService.ExecQuery( _
 "Select * from Win32_OperatingSystem WHERE " & _
 "Primary = TRUE",,48)
For Each objItem in colItems
Next
```

You probably don't want to shut down just the local computer, so you'll want to add some kind of prompt that collects the appropriate computer name.

```
On Error Resume Next
Dim strComputer
Dim objWMIService
Dim colItems

strComputer = InputBox("Shut down what computer?")
Set objWMIService = GetObject("winmgmts:\\" & _
 strComputer & "\root\cimv2")
Set colItems = objWMIService.ExecQuery( _
 "Select * from Win32_OperatingSystem WHERE " & _
 "Primary = TRUE",,48)
For Each objItem in colItems
Next
```

Now, suppose you want to use different variable names, and you don't want to turn off error checking. No problem—just be sure you change the variable names every time they appear in the script. A search and replace function is the most reliable way to do so, and you'll wind up with something like this:

```
Dim sComputer
Dim oWMIService
Dim oItems, oItem

sComputer = InputBox("Shut down what computer?")
Set oWMIService = GetObject("winmgmts:\\" & _
 sComputer & "\root\cimv2")
Set oItems = oWMIService.ExecQuery( _
 "Select * from Win32_OperatingSystem WHERE " & _
 "Primary = TRUE",,48)
For Each oItem in oItems
Next
```

Now, you need to add the actual Shutdown method.

```
Dim sComputer
Dim oWMIService
```

```
Dim oItems, oItem

sComputer = InputBox("Shut down what computer?")
Set oWMIService = GetObject("winmgmts:\\" & _
 sComputer & "\root\cimv2")
Set oItems = oWMIService.ExecQuery( _
 "Select * from Win32_OperatingSystem WHERE " & _
 "Primary = TRUE",,48)
For Each oItem in oItems
 oItem.ShutDown()
Next
```

There, you've customized the template script to meet your exact needs. Really, you're not using much of the original wizard-generated code: You kept the variable declarations, the basic WQL query, and the For Each/Next construct. That's about it.

> **NOTE**
>
> It might seem odd to use a For Each/Next construct when you know your modified query will only return one instance. Why bother? Because the ExecQuery method will *always* return a collection, even if the query only returns one instance into the collection. You could have eliminated the For Each/Next construct and used oItems(0).Shutdown() instead, using the oItems(0) syntax to reference the first (and to your knowledge, the only) instance in the collection. Either way works fine.

Using the Query Results

Let's look at a real-world use for WMI, and walk through the process of building the script. Suppose you want to modify a remote computer's network configuration so that all network adapters have DHCP enabled. Actually, you'll probably want to check multiple machines at once, so you'll need the script to read computer names from a text file that you'll create, using one computer name per line within the file. If the script finds that DHCP is already enabled, you want it to tell you so.

> **NOTE**
>
> A slightly more real-world task might be to modify the configuration only for a specific network adapter, like the one named Local Area Network, in each machine. That requires working with WMI associator classes, which I'll cover in the next chapter.

The first part I like to handle is the WMI bit. I've found the Win32_ NetworkAdapterConfiguration class, which has an EnableDHCP method that should do the job. I used the PrimalScript WMI Query Wizard to generate a template script for the class, and then trimmed it down to look like this:

```
On Error Resume Next
Dim strComputer
Dim objWMIService
Dim colItems

strComputer = "."
Set objWMIService = GetObject("winmgmts:\\" & _
 strComputer & "\root\cimv2")
Set colItems = objWMIService.ExecQuery( _
 "Select * from Win32_NetworkAdapterConfiguration",,48)
For Each objItem in colItems
 WScript.Echo "DHCPEnabled: " & objItem.DHCPEnabled
 WScript.Echo "Caption: " & objItem.Caption
Next
```

I need to have the script run through a text file, so I'll add the appropriate code. I showed you how to work with files and folders in Chapter 12, "Working with the File System."

```
Dim strComputer
Dim objWMIService
Dim colItems
Dim objFSO, objTS

Set objFSO = CreateObject("Scripting.FileSystemObject")
Set objTS = objFSO.OpenTextFile("c:\input.txt")

Do Until objTS.AtEndOfStream

 strComputer = objTS.ReadLine
 Set objWMIService = GetObject("winmgmts:\\" & _
  strComputer & "\root\cimv2")
 Set colItems = objWMIService.ExecQuery( _
  "Select * from Win32_NetworkAdapterConfiguration",,48)
 For Each objItem in colItems
  WScript.Echo "DHCPEnabled: " & objItem.DHCPEnabled
  WScript.Echo "Caption: " & objItem.Caption
 Next

Loop
```

So far, this script is just displaying the caption and current DHCP status for each network adapter configuration. I need to add some logic to enable DHCP if it isn't already enabled.

```
Dim strComputer
Dim objWMIService
```

18

```
Dim colItems
Dim objFSO, objTS

Set objFSO = CreateObject("Scripting.FileSystemObject")
Set objTS = objFSO.OpenTextFile("c:\input.txt")

Do Until objTS.AtEndOfStream

 strComputer = objTS.ReadLine
 Set objWMIService = GetObject("winmgmts:\\" & _
  strComputer & "\root\cimv2")
Set colItems = objWMIService.ExecQuery( _
  "Select * from Win32_NetworkAdapterConfiguration",,48)
 For Each objItem in colItems
  If objItem.DHCPEnabled = True Then
   WScript.Echo "DHCP Enabled for: " & objItem.Caption
  Else
   WScript.Echo "Enabling DHCP for: " & objItem.Caption
   objItem.EnableDHCP
  End If
 Next

Loop
```

This modification has an If/Then construct examining the DHCPEnabled property, rather than simply displaying the property. If the property isn't True, the script executes the EnableDHCP method to turn on DHCP for the network adapter configuration. In either event, an appropriate message is displayed to let me know what's happening.

Alternative Methods

As I mentioned earlier in this chapter, you're likely to run across other ways of performing WMI queries. For example, here's a short script that returns some information about a remote machine named Server1:

```
Set System = GetObject("winmgmts:{impersonationLevel=" & _
 "impersonate}!//server1/root/cimv2:" & _
 "Win32_ComputerSystem=""SERVER1""")

WScript.Echo System.Caption
WScript.Echo System.PrimaryOwnerName
WScript.Echo System.Domain
WScript.Echo System.SystemType
```

> **NOTE**
>
> Did you notice the "impersonate" directive in that query? When you use WMI, your credentials are passed to the WMI service that you're querying, and the service uses those credentials to execute your query. When WMI was first introduced, the default settings didn't permit it to *impersonate* you in this fashion, so WMI connections had to explicitly allow impersonation. Now, impersonation is enabled by default, so including it in your connections isn't strictly necessary—but you'll still run into a lot of VBScript that includes it anyway.

This doesn't follow the template-style query I've been using so far; in fact, it doesn't even use WQL. However, this example is functionally the same as the following one:

```
On Error Resume Next
Dim strComputer
Dim objWMIService
Dim colItems

strComputer = "server1"
Set objWMIService = GetObject("winmgmts:\\" & _
 strComputer & "\root\cimv2")
Set colItems = objWMIService.ExecQuery( _
 "Select * from Win32_ComputerSystem WHERE " & _
 "Name = 'SERVER1'",,48)
For Each objItem in colItems
 WScript.Echo "Caption: " & objItem.Caption
 WScript.Echo "Domain: " & objItem.Domain
 WScript.Echo "PrimaryOwnerName: " & objItem.PrimaryOwnerName
 WScript.Echo "SystemType: " & objItem.SystemType
Next
```

There is practically no difference between the two. The first example uses `GetObject` to connect directly to a specified server's WMI service and retrieve a particular class (`Win32_ComputerSystem`) where the system's name is "SERVER1." The retrieved object is a WMI object, and can be used to display whatever information you want.

The second example uses the template I've used throughout this chapter (and the previous one) to fire off a WQL query, return an object collection, and then display the information. Which one is better? Technically, they're both identical. The second one has the benefit of being consistent with my other examples, and it lends itself easily to modification so that you can write more complex WQL queries to meet your specific needs. You're welcome to use either style, or even both if that's what you want to do.

18

Summary

You've seen several examples of how to query basic WMI information in this chapter. I showed you how to look for the proper WMI classes, write more complex WQL queries, and test your queries. I also showed you how to start with a wizard-created template script and modify it to suit your needs, even if those needs involve changing something or performing an action, rather than simply displaying or retrieving WMI information. I've shown you examples of how WMI can be queried in different ways that will help you work with the many different examples you'll find on the web and in other publications.

All of this will help you work with most of the simpler WMI classes. Some classes, however, represent more complex bodies of information, and have to be handled a bit differently. I'll cover those in the next chapter.

CHAPTER 19

Querying Complex WMI Information

In the previous chapter, I briefly described how some Windows Management Instrumentation (WMI) classes have complex interrelationships with other classes, and promised to show you—in this chapter—how to deal with the information contained in those relationships. I even mentioned specific WMI Query Language (WQL) keywords, including REFERENCES OF and ASSOCIATORS OF—that are used to query these complex classes. Now it's time to dive in and put them to work.

Understanding WMI Relationships

Probably the best way to understand the more complex WMI classes is with an example. Take Win32_NetworkAdapter. This class represents a physical network adapter inside a computer, whether it's an Ethernet adapter, an IEEE 1394 (FireWire) adapter, or whatever. If you examine the class properties in the WMI documentation, you'll see that it only includes properties that deal with the physical hardware, such as its MAC address, whether it supports media sense (which tells Windows that a cable is unplugged), its maximum speed, and so forth.

WMI also defines a class named Win32_NetworkAdapterConfiguration, which includes the software aspects of a network adapter, including its IP address, IPX settings, and so forth. In theory, a single hardware adapter can have multiple possible configurations, which is why these properties are split into two classes. In fact, it's theoretically possible for one configuration to be shared by two different physical adapters. WMI needs some way to relate the two classes to one another, and that way is called an *associator class.* In this case, the associator class is Win32_NetworkAdapterSetting, which associates a network adapter and its configuration settings.

An examination of Win32_NetworkAdapterSetting's documentation reveals that it has only two properties: Win32_NetworkAdapter and Win32_ NetworkAdapterConfiguration. In other words, the two properties refer back to the associated classes. The associator, then, represents a single combination of adapter and configuration, as illustrated in Figure 19.1.

First, run Wbemtest and connect to your local computer's root\cimv2 namespace. Then, click Open Class and open the Win32_NetworkAdapterSetting class. You should see a dialog box similar to the one shown in Figure 19.2. Of particular interest are the two main properties: Element and Setting. According to the WMI documentation, this class' Element represents a Win32_NetworkAdapter, and the Setting represents an associated Win32_NetworkAdapterConfiguration.

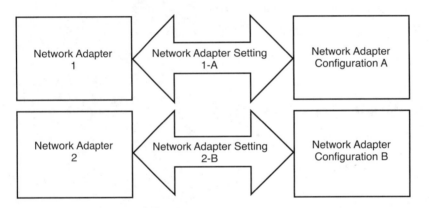

FIGURE 19.1   Associating two classes.

Click Instances to retrieve all instances of this class. The dialog box that opens lists one line for each combination of adapter and configuration. You'll notice that the Element property is listed as something like \\\\computername\\root\\cimv2:Win32_ NetworkAdapter.DeviceID=\"1\". The Setting property will look something like \\\\computername\\root\\cimv2:Win32_NetworkAdapterConfiguration.Index=1. Here's how to interpret that:

▶ First, understand that both backslashes and double quotes are illegal characters for WMI. The backslash is actually an *escape* character, meaning it's used to prefix illegal characters. So \\ should be interpreted as a single backslash, and \" should be interpreted as a double quotation mark.

▶ The first part of each property value is the namespace: *computername*\root\cimv2. The property's value derives from this namespace.

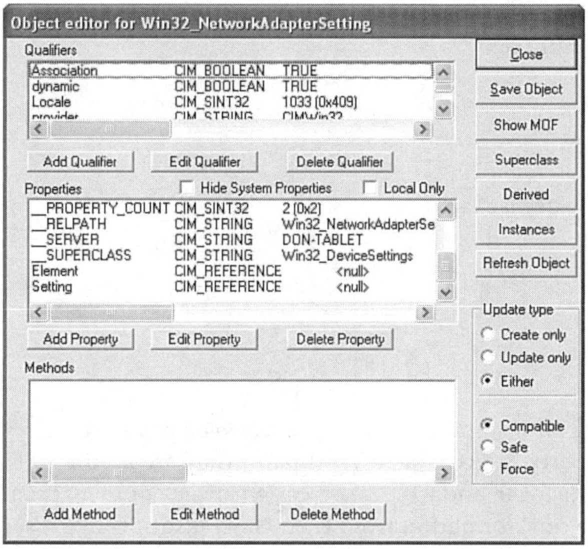

FIGURE 19.2   Examining the `Win32_NetworkAdapterSetting` class.

▶ The next part of each property value is the class name, followed by a period and the property name.

▶ The property name is followed by an equal sign, and then the associated property value.

In this example, the `Element` represents the instance of `Win32_NetworkAdapter` with the `DeviceID` of 1, and the `Setting` represents the instance of `Win32_NetworkAdapterConfiguration` with the `Index` of 1.

A quick-and-dirty way to query this information would be something like the following:

```
Dim oWMI, oSettings, oSetting
Dim oAdapter, oConfig

'connect to WMI
Set oWMI = GetObject("winmgmts:\\.\root\cimv2")

'retrieve all settings
Set oSettings = oWMI.ExecQuery( _
 "SELECT * FROM Win32_NetworkAdapterSetting")

'go through all settings
For Each oSetting in oSettings

 'get the element
 Set oAdapter = GetObject("winmgmts:" & _
```

```
    oSetting.Element)
WScript.Echo "Adapter: " & oAdapter.Caption

  'get the setting
  Set oConfig = GetObject("winmgmts:" & _
  oSetting.Setting)
  WScript.Echo "  DHCP: " & oConfig.DHCPEnabled

  'print a divider
  WScript.Echo String(20,"-")

Next
```

This script uses a WQL query to retrieve all instances of Win32_NetworkAdapterSetting. Because each Element and Setting property is a complete WMI path, they are used to retrieve the appropriate Win32_NetworkAdapter and Win32_NetworkAdapterConfiguration classes. The script then prints one piece of information from each class, just to prove it's doing something. This is a standardized way that you can work with associator classes.

▶ Retrieve the associator class.

▶ Use its properties, such as Element and Setting in this example, to retrieve the associated classes.

▶ Work with the associated classes however you want.

Not all associator classes use Element and Setting. For example, Win32_PrinterShare associates a local printer and a network share, from Win32_Printer and Win32_Share. Win32_PrinterShare uses Antecedent to refer to a Win32_Printer instance, and Dependent to refer to a Win32_Share class, instead of Element and Setting. However, you can query the associator class and its associations in exactly the same way.

```
Dim oWMI, oPShares, oPShare
Dim oPrinter, oShare

'connect to WMI
Set oWMI = GetObject("winmgmts:\\.\root\cimv2")

'retrieve all settings
Set oPShares = oWMI.ExecQuery( _
  "SELECT * FROM Win32_PrinterShare")

'go through all settings
For Each oPShare in oPShares

  'get the element
  Set oPrinter = GetObject("winmgmts:" & _
```

```
 oPShare.Antecedent)
WScript.Echo "Printer: " & oPrinter.Name

'get the setting
Set oShare = GetObject("winmgmts:" & _
 oPShare.Dependent)
WScript.Echo "  Share: " & oShare.Name

'print a divider
WScript.Echo String(20,"-")

Next
```

Note that all I've done in this case is change the variable names and property names. The structure of this example is identical to the first.

Associating WMI Instances

Hopefully, my previous two examples make it easier for you to understand WMI associations. However, they're bad examples for truly working with associated classes. Why? Because you aren't ever going to begin knowing which instance of the associator class you want; you're going to begin with one of the associated classes instead. Using the preceding technique, suppose you want to find the shares for a particular printer. You'd have to

▶ Get the correct `Win32_Printer` class first to get its `DeviceID`.

▶ Query `Win32_PrinterShares` for all instances where the `Antecedent` property references the `DeviceID` you're looking for.

▶ Take the results of that query and retrieve all referenced instances of `Win32_Share`.

ASSOCIATORS OF

The aforementioned technique is an awkward way to get the information, and that's why WQL offers the `ASSOCIATORS OF` command. Suppose you have a printer with a device ID of "LaserJet 5." You've created three or four shares of the printer, each with different permissions. You want to use WMI to retrieve the name of each share, and list the maximum concurrent number of users allowed to use each share. You could write a WQL query like this: `ASSOCIATORS OF {Win32_Printer.DeviceID = "LaserJet 5"}`. Note that `ASSOCIATORS OF` replaces the `SELECT`, property list, `FROM`, and class name elements of a more traditional WQL query. Also note that the class must be listed in curly braces {}—not parentheses. That messes me up every time. Figure 19.3 shows the results of this query in Wbemtest (assuming you have a printer named LaserJet 5, that is; for this example, I used a different printer name).

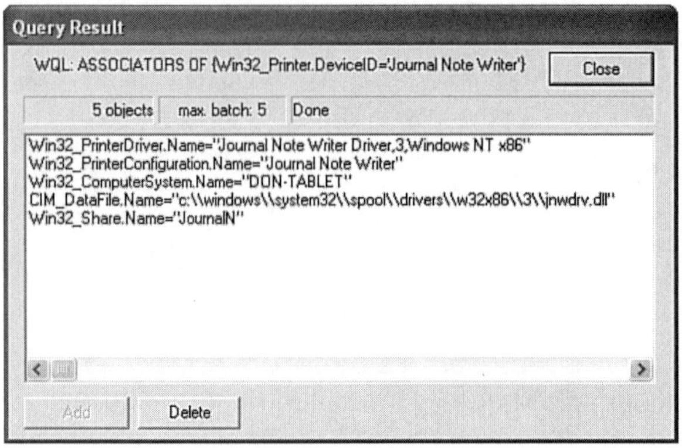

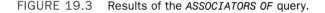

FIGURE 19.3   Results of the *ASSOCIATORS OF* query.

It turns out there are several associated classes:

- ▶ Win32_PrinterDriver
- ▶ Win32_PrinterConfiguration
- ▶ Win32_ComputerSystem
- ▶ CIM_DataFile
- ▶ Win32_Share

You can restrict the list just to the Win32_Share class by modifying the query a bit.

```
ASSOCIATORS OF {Win32_Printer.DeviceID = "LaserJet 5"}
 WHERE AssocClass = Win32_PrinterShare
```

This modified query just returns an instance of Win32_Share for each share that exists for the printer. Note that the query does *not* return Win32_PrinterShare instances; WMI is smart enough to know that although Win32_PrinterShare is the associator class, you're really after the other side of the relationship, which is Win32_Share.

The following script displays each share name for the specified printer, and the number of connections each accepts:

```
Dim oWMI, oPShares, oPShare
Dim oShare

'connect to WMI
Set oWMI = GetObject("winmgmts:\\.\root\cimv2")

'retrieve all settings
Set oPShares = oWMI.ExecQuery("ASSOCIATORS OF {Win32_Printer.DeviceID='LaserJet 5'}
WHERE AssocClass = Win32_PrinterShare")
```

```
For Each oShare in oPShares

 'display share info
 If oShare.AllowMaximum = False Then
  WScript.Echo "Share " & oShare.Name & _

   " allows " & oShare.MaximumAllowed & _
   " concurrent connections."
 Else
  WScript.Echo "Share " & oShare.Name & _
   " allows max connections."
 End If

Next
```

REFERENCES OF

The WQL REFERENCES OF query works similarly to ASSOCIATORS OF. It's designed to return all association instances that refer to a specified source instance. However, whereas ASSOCIATORS OF attempts to retrieve the endpoint instances (such as mapping Win32_ Printer all the way through to Win32_Share), REFERENCES OF only attempts to find the associator classes (such as Win32_PrinterShare).

For example, use Wbemtest to execute the following query:

```
REFERENCES OF
 {Win32_Printer.DeviceID = 'printername'}
```

Of course, replace *printername* with a valid printer on your computer.

> **NOTE**
>
> Remember, to execute a query in Wbemtest, first connect to the \default\cimv2 namespace. Then, click the Query button and type the query into the text box.

The query returns several classes:

- ▶ Win32_DriverForDevice
- ▶ Win32_PrinterSetting
- ▶ Win32_SystemDevices
- ▶ Win32_PrinterShare (if the printer is shared)
- ▶ Win32_PrinterDriverDll

19

These are all of the associator classes that refer to the specified `Win32_Printer` instance. If you want to get the endpoint of the association—in other words, the actual driver, printer setting, device, share, or driver dynamic link library (DLL)—you'd use `ASSOCIATORS OF` instead. I don't find much need for `REFERENCES OF` in my administrative scripts because I'm usually looking for the other end of the association, not the middle point.

Using WHERE with ASSOCIATIONS OF and REFERENCES OF

Both the `ASSOCIATIONS OF` and `REFERENCES OF` queries support a `WHERE` clause; I showed you an example using the `AssocClass` keyword earlier. `REFERENCES OF` accepts the following keywords in its optional `WHERE` clause:

▶ `ClassDefsOnly`—This causes the query to return the class definition, rather than instances of the class being queried.

▶ `RequiredQualifier`—This allows you to specify a qualifier that all returned classes must meet. For example, `RequiredQualifier = Dependent` restricts query results to those association classes that have a property named `Dependent`.

▶ `ResultClass`—This allows you to restrict the query results to a particular class, such as `ResultClass = Win32_PrinterShare`. This cannot be used in conjunction with `ClassDefsOnly`.

`ASSOCIATORS OF` supports different `WHERE` options:

▶ `AssocClass`—This allows you to specify the associator class that will be used. Use this, as I did in my earlier example, to restrict your results to those from a particular class. For example, `AssocClass = Win32_PrinterShare`.

▶ `ClassDefsOnly`—This forces the query to return the definition for the result classes, rather than the actual instances of the class. This cannot be used with `ResultClass`.

▶ `RequiredAssocQualifier`—This tells the query to only return instances that are related by means of an associator class that includes the specified qualifier. Sound complex? Here's an example: `RequiredAssocQualifier = Dependent`. With this specified, the query only returns endpoint instances whose relationship to the queried class is through an associator class that has a property named `Dependent`.

▶ `RequiredQualifier`—This specifies a property that must be present in the endpoint classes returned by the query. For example, `RequiredQualifier = AllowMaximum` restricts the associated classes returned by the query to those with an `AllowMaximum` property.

▶ `ResultClass`—This specifies that the query only return specified classes. For example, `ResultClass = Win32_Share` ensures that only instances of `Win32_Share` are returned.

All of these `WHERE` clause keywords can be combined (except as I've noted here), and do not require commas or any other separation. For example:

```
ASSOCIATORS OF {Win32_Printer.DeviceID = 'LaserJet5'}
  WHERE
```

```
ResultClass = Win32_Share
RequiredQualifier = AllowMaximum
```

Don't be tempted to include an AND keyword like you would in a traditional WHERE clause, because WMI will return an error.

Writing the Query

You've seen the whole associated class thing in action, but I want to start fresh with a new example and walk you through the entire query- and script-creation process. In the last chapter, I showed you how to set all the network adapters on a computer to use Dynamic Host Configuration Protocol (DHCP). In this chapter, I want to be more specific, and only modify the properties of a specific network adapter within the computer. More specifically, I want to

- ▶ Read a list of computer names from a text file.

- ▶ Connect to WMI on each computer and locate the network adapter named "Local Area Connection."

- ▶ Ensure that each configuration for that adapter is set to use DHCP.

It seems like the following query should do what I want:

```
ASSOCIATORS OF
{Win32_NetworkAdapter.NetConnectionID="Local Area Connection"}
WHERE
RESULTCLASS = Win32_NetworkAdapterConfiguration
```

That should pull all Win32_NetworkAdapter instances where the NetConnectionID is "Local Area Connection," and then retrieve the associated Win32_NetworkAdapterConfiguration instances.

Testing the Query

Wbemtest is the place to test my new query. Unfortunately, executing it yields an error: "Invalid object path." Uh-oh.

I'm guessing the problem is that Win32_NetworkAdapter and Win32_NetworkAdapterConfiguration are associated through Win32_NetworkAdapterSetting, which uses Win32_NetworkAdapter.DeviceID and Win32_NetworkAdapterConfiguration.Index to perform the association. In other words, the associator class has no clue about Win32_NetworkAdapter.NetConnectionID.

Just to confirm that, I'll retest the query using this.

```
ASSOCIATORS OF {Win32_NetworkAdapter.DeviceID="1"} WHERE
RESULTCLASS = Win32_NetworkAdapterConfiguration
```

Sure enough, this query returns the expected instance of Win32_
NetworkAdapterConfiguration. Here's what I'm going to have to do:

▶ Read a list of computer names from a text file.

▶ Connect to WMI on each computer and locate the network adapter named "Local
Area Connection."

▶ Get the DeviceID from the Win32_NetworkAdapter instances returned.

▶ For each instance, query the associated Win32_NetworkAdapterConfiguration
instances.

▶ For each of *those* instances, ensure that each configuration for that adapter is set to
use DHCP.

I just need to code these actions into a script.

Writing the Query in VBScript

Now it's time to incorporate the query into a script. This time, I'll start with the shell of
the script, which will read the computer names from the text file.

```
Dim oFSO, oTS, sComputer

Set oFSO = CreateObject("Scripting.FileSystemObject")
Set oTS = oFSO.OpenTextFile("c:\input.txt")

Do Until oTS.AtEndOfStream

  sComputer = oTS.ReadLine

Loop
```

That is easy enough. Now, for each, I need to retrieve a specified instance of Win32_
NetworkAdapter. The caption I'm looking for—"Local Area Connection"—is stored in a
property named NetConnectionID.

TIP

How did I know which property to use? Simple: Wbemtest. I clicked EnumInstances
and typed Win32_NetworkAdapter as the superclass name. Then, I double-clicked on
the first instance that was returned to display its properties. I scrolled down, looking
for "Local Area Connection" in the values column, and I found it in a property named
NetConnectionID. If I hadn't found "Local Area Connection" at all, I would have tried
the next instance in the list, and kept browsing until I found it.

Actually, I don't want to retrieve the Win32_NetworkAdapter instance at all. Instead, I need to retrieve all associated Win32_NetworkAdapterConfiguration instances. However, as I discovered earlier, I need to retrieve the DeviceID on my own, based on a simpler WQL query. Here's the modified script:

```
Dim oFSO, oTS, sComputer
Dim oWMI, oConfigs, oConfig, oAdapters, oAdapter

Set oFSO = CreateObject("Scripting.FileSystemObject")
Set oTS = oFSO.OpenTextFile("c:\input.txt")

Do Until oTS.AtEndOfStream

 sComputer = oTS.ReadLine

 Set oWMI = GetObject("winmgmts:\\" & _
  sComputer & "\root\cimv2")

 Set oAdapters = oWMI.ExecQuery( _
  "SELECT DeviceID FROM Win32_NetworkAdapter " & _
  "WHERE NetConnectionID = 'Local Area Connection')

 For Each oAdapter in oAdapters

  Set oConfigs = oWMI.ExecQuery( _
   "ASSOCIATORS OF {Win32_NetworkAdapter.DeviceID='" & _
   oAdapter.DeviceID & "'} " & _
   "WHERE RESULTCLASS = Win32_NetworkAdapterConfiguration")

 Next

Loop
```

Of course, simply retrieving the class doesn't do anything. Keep in mind that oConfigs will contain a collection of Win32_NetworkAdapterConfiguration instances, although in almost all cases the collection will only contain one instance. I'll need to loop through the instances and check each one to see if DHCP is enabled. Here's how:

```
Dim oFSO, oTS, sComputer
Dim oWMI, oConfigs, oConfig

Set oFSO = CreateObject("Scripting.FileSystemObject")
Set oTS = oFSO.OpenTextFile("c:\input.txt")

Do Until oTS.AtEndOfStream
```

19

```
    sComputer = oTS.ReadLine

  Set oWMI = GetObject("winmgmts:\\" & _
   sComputer & "\root\cimv2")


  Set oAdapters = oWMI.ExecQuery( _
   "SELECT DeviceID FROM Win32_NetworkAdapter " & _
   "WHERE NetConnectionID = 'Local Area Connection')

  For Each oAdapter in oAdapters

   Set oConfigs = oWMI.ExecQuery( _
    "ASSOCIATORS OF {Win32_NetworkAdapter.DeviceID='" & _
    oAdapter.DeviceID & "'} " & _
    "WHERE RESULTCLASS = Win32_NetworkAdapterConfiguration")

   For Each oConfig In oConfigs

    If oConfig.DHCPEnabled Then
     WScript.Echo "DHCP Enabled on " & sComputer
    Else

     WScript.Echo "Enabling DHCP on " & sComputer
     oConfig.EnableDHCP
    End If

   Next

  Next

Loop
```

That's it! The script will read the text file and set each computer's Local Area Connection to use DHCP. If you want to test it, Listing 19.1 shows the complete listing, along with inline comments.

LISTING 19.1   *SetDHCP.vbs.* This script sets the Local Area Connection adapter to use DHCP for each computer named in the text file.

```
Dim oFSO, oTS, sComputer
Dim oWMI, oConfigs, oConfig

'get a filesystemobject and open the input file
Set oFSO = CreateObject("Scripting.FileSystemObject")
Set oTS = oFSO.OpenTextFile("c:\input.txt")
```

LISTING 19.1   Continued

```vbscript
'for each line of the input file...
Do Until oTS.AtEndOfStream

 'read the computer name from the file
 sComputer = oTS.ReadLine

 'connect to WMI on the remote computer
 Set oWMI = GetObject("winmgmts:\\" & _
  sComputer & "\root\cimv2")

 'query a collection of Win32_NetworkAdapter
 'instances that have a NetConnectionID of
 ' Local Area Connection
 Set oAdapters = oWMI.ExecQuery( _
  "SELECT DeviceID FROM Win32_NetworkAdapter " & _
  "WHERE NetConnectionID = 'Local Area Connection')

 'for each of those adapters...
 For Each oAdapter in oAdapters

  'query the associated network adapter configurations
  Set oConfigs = oWMI.ExecQuery( _
   "ASSOCIATORS OF {Win32_NetworkAdapter.DeviceID='" & _
   oAdapter.DeviceID & "'} " & _
   "WHERE RESULTCLASS = Win32_NetworkAdapterConfiguration'")

  'for each of those configurations...
  For Each oConfig In oConfigs

  'is DHCP enabled?
  If oConfig.DHCPEnabled Then

   'yes - display a message
   WScript.Echo "DHCP Enabled on " & sComputer

  Else

   'no - display a message and enable it
   WScript.Echo "Enabling DHCP on " & sComputer
   oConfig.EnableDHCP

  End If
```

19

LISTING 19.1   Continued

```
  Next

Next

Loop
```

You'll need to provide the appropriate input file, c:\input.txt, to use this script.

Another Example

This business of using associator classes is complicated, so I'm including an additional example of how they work. For this example, suppose you want to list all of the shared folders on a particular file server, along with the physical file path that each share represents. For each of those physical folders (or *directories*), you want to enable NTFS file compression. Here's what you need to do:

▶ Connect to WMI on a specified server.

▶ Retrieve a list of Win32_Share class instances that represent file shares (as opposed to printer or other shares).

▶ For each instance, retrieve the physical folder as a Win32_Directory class.

▶ For each physical folder, use the Compress method.

Compressing All Shared Folders   Listing 19.2 shows the entire script you'll need to use.

LISTING 19.2   *CompressAll.vbs.* This script compresses all shared folders on a specified file server.

```
'get server name
strComputer = InputBox("Server name?")

'connect to WMI
Set objWMIService = GetObject("winmgmts:" & _
 "\\" & strComputer & "\root\cimv2")

'retrieve the list of shares
Set colShares = objWMIService.ExecQuery _
 ("SELECT * FROM Win32_Share WHERE " & _
 "Type = 0")

'for each share returned...
For Each objShare In colShares

  'retrieve the associated folders
```

LISTING 19.2   Continued

```
Set colFolders = objWMIService.ExecQuery _
 ("ASSOCIATORS OF {Win32_Share.Name='" & _
 objShare.Name & "'} WHERE " & _
 "AssocClass=Win32_ShareToDirectory")

'for each folder returned...
For Each objFolder in colFolders

 'is it already compressed?
 If objFolder.Compressed Then

  'yes - message
  Wscript.Echo objFolder.Name & " is already compressed."

 Else

  'no - message & compress it
  WScript.Echo "Compressing " & objFolder.Name
  objFolder.Compress

 End If

Next

Next
```

You shouldn't need to make any modifications to this script to run it, and it should work with NT 4.0 and later servers.

Compressing All Shared Folders—Explained   The script starts by simply asking for the server name. Provide the name of any NT 4.0 or later file server that's already running WMI.

```
'get server name
strComputer = InputBox("Server name?")
```

Next, the script connects to the WMI service on the remote computer.

```
'connect to WMI
Set objWMIService = GetObject("winmgmts:" & _
 "\\" & strComputer & "\root\cimv2")
```

The script now executes a simple WMI query to return all shares of type 0, which are shared folders. The WMI documentation for the Win32_Share class lists other types, including printers (1), devices (2), IPC shares (3), and administrative shares.

```
'retrieve the list of shares
Set colShares = objWMIService.ExecQuery _
 ("SELECT * FROM Win32_Share WHERE " & _
 "Type = 0")
```

A For Each/Next loop iterates through each file share.

```
'for each share returned...
For Each objShare In colShares
```

An ASSOCIATORS OF query is used to retrieve the associated folder (Win32_Directory) instances for the current Win32_Share instance. Notice that the associator class, Win32_ShareToDirectory, is specified.

```
'retrieve the associated folders
Set colFolders = objWMIService.ExecQuery _
 ("ASSOCIATORS OF {Win32_Share.Name='" & _
 objShare.Name & "'} WHERE " & _
 "AssocClass=Win32_ShareToDirectory")
```

A For Each/Next loop iterates through each folder returned. Under current Windows operating systems, this will be only one folder per share (although you might theorize that some future version would allow multiple, load-balanced physical folders per share, which is why WMI requires you to write the script this way).

```
'for each folder returned...
For Each objFolder in colFolders
```

The script checks to see if the folder is already compressed, and behaves accordingly.

```
'is it already compressed?
If objFolder.Compressed Then

  'yes - message
  Wscript.Echo objFolder.Name & " is already compressed."

Else

  'no - message & compress it
  WScript.Echo "Compressing " & objFolder.Name
  objFolder.Compress

End If
```

Finally, the script closes the two open `For Each`/`Next` loops.

```
 Next
```

```
Next
```

The powerful and easy `ASSOCIATORS OF` query makes scripts like this easier to write. Without it, you'd be stuck with many more `For`/`Next` loops and a much-harder-to-maintain script.

Summary

In this chapter, I've shown you how different WMI classes can be related to one another through associator classes. I've also introduced you to the WQL `ASSOCIATORS OF` query, which allows you to query those relationships. You've learned how to use Wbemtest to test your queries, incorporate your queries into a script, and then utilize the query results to perform administrative tasks.

By now, you should have a solid understanding of how WMI works from within a script, and how you can use it to both query and modify configuration settings within your computers. You should feel comfortable working with the simpler queries that Scriptomatic or the PrimalScript WMI Query Wizard can generate for you, and you should be comfortable writing more complex queries that utilize WMI associations and class relationships. As always, of course, the toughest part about WMI is figuring out which classes to query, but hopefully by now you're becoming comfortable with the WMI class reference in the MSDN Library, and you're able to browse through the class list and select the appropriate classes.

19

CHAPTER 20

Putting It All Together: Your First WMI/ADSI Script

By now, you should have a good idea of what WMI and ADSI can do for you. In this chapter, I'll walk you through the complete design process for an entirely new script. This time, I'll use both WMI and ADSI in the same script. The script's job will be to check in on every computer in an Active Directory or NT domain and query some information about its operating systems. I want the script to output this information to a text file on a file server. The information I want to collect includes operating system version, service pack level, number of processors in the machine, maximum physical memory in the machine, and so forth. This is a useful way to quickly inventory a network and see what machines might need to be upgraded before deploying a new application, or to see what machines don't have the latest service pack applied.

Designing the Script

My script is a reasonably complex undertaking, so it helps to break it down into manageable tasks. I need the script to do three things:

1. Query a list of computers from the domain.

2. Query information from each computer.

3. Write information out to a text file.

The last bit is probably the easiest. I can use the FileSystemObject to open a text file, write information to it, and then close the text file. Something like the following would work:

```
Dim oFSO, oFile
Set oFSO = CreateObject("Scripting.FileSystemObject")
Set oFile = oFSO.CreateTextFile("output.txt")
oFile.Write "Information"
oFile.Close
```

For more information on using the FileSystemObject, refer to Chapter 12, "Working with the File System."

Querying a list of computers from the domain shouldn't be too hard, either. If I want the script to work with both NT and Active Directory domains, I need to use the WinNT ADSI provider because only that provider works with both domains. I can query all of the objects in the domain, and then use an If/Then construct to work with only the computer objects. Code such as the following should do the trick:

```
Dim oDomain
Set oDomain = GetObject("WinNT://" & sDomain)
Dim oObject, sComputerName, sDetails
For Each oObject In oDomain

 'is this object a computer?
 If oObject.Class = "Computer" Then

  'yes - do something with it

 End If
Next
```

For more information on querying domains by using ADSI, see Chapter 14, "Working with ADSI Providers," and Chapter 15, "Manipulating Domains."

Pulling the operating system (OS) information is tougher. WMI seems like the way to go, but WMI has about three gazillion classes. Which one do I need? Fortunately, I have a way to cheat. My script editor includes a WMI Script Wizard.

Running the wizard displays the dialog box shown in Figure 20.1. The left side of the dialog box shows a list of every WMI class that my computer knows about. Scrolling through the list, I find that there's a class named Win32_OperatingSystem. That seems like a good place to start.

Clicking the Win32_OperatingSystem class changes the dialog box to look like the one shown in Figure 20.2. Here, the wizard has filled in a sample script capable of querying information from the selected class. I see things like service pack level and operating system version, so this is probably the class I want. The wizard offers an Insert button to immediately insert this code into my script, and a Copy button to copy the code to the clipboard. Listing 20.1 shows the complete wizard code.

> **NOTE**
>
> I've added line breaks and line continuation characters (_) to Listing 20.1 so that it will fit in this book.

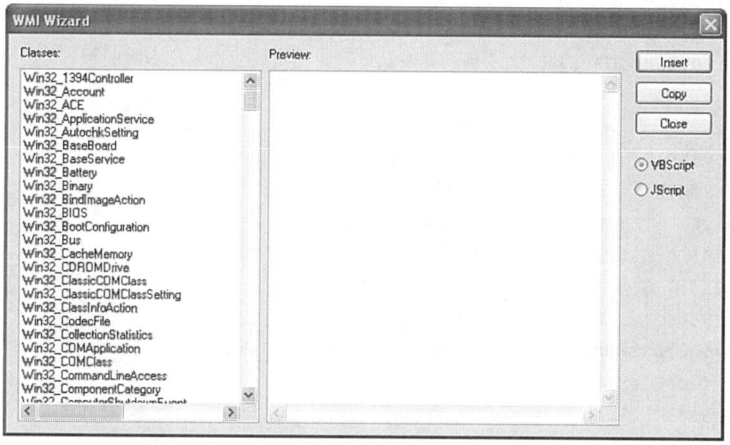

FIGURE 20.1   The WMI Wizard starts with a list of all available WMI classes.

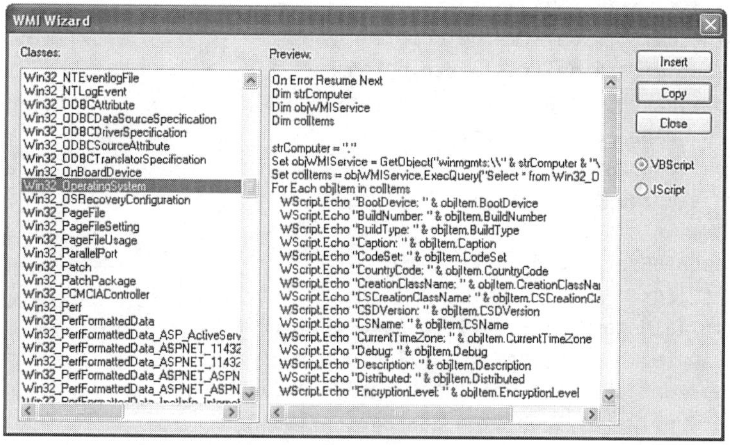

FIGURE 20.2   The wizard generates sample code to query the selected class.

LISTING 20.1   *WizardCode.vbs*. This code queries the `Win32_OperatingSystem` class and outputs all of the classes' attributes and their values.

```
On Error Resume Next
Dim strComputer
Dim objWMIService
```

LISTING 20.1   Continued

```
Dim colItems

strComputer = "."
Set objWMIService = GetObject("winmgmts:\\" & _
 strComputer & "\root\cimv2")
Set colItems = objWMIService.ExecQuery( _
 "Select * from Win32_OperatingSystem",,48)
For Each objItem in colItems
     WScript.Echo "BootDevice: " & objItem.BootDevice
     WScript.Echo "BuildNumber: " & objItem.BuildNumber
     WScript.Echo "BuildType: " & objItem.BuildType
     WScript.Echo "Caption: " & objItem.Caption
     WScript.Echo "CodeSet: " & objItem.CodeSet
     WScript.Echo "CountryCode: " & objItem.CountryCode
     WScript.Echo "CreationClassName: " & objItem.CreationClassName
     WScript.Echo "CSCreationClassName: " & _
  objItem.CSCreationClassName
     WScript.Echo "CSDVersion: " & objItem.CSDVersion
     WScript.Echo "CSName: " & objItem.CSName
     WScript.Echo "CurrentTimeZone: " & objItem.CurrentTimeZone
     WScript.Echo "Debug: " & objItem.Debug
     WScript.Echo "Description: " & objItem.Description
     WScript.Echo "Distributed: " & objItem.Distributed
     WScript.Echo "EncryptionLevel: " & objItem.EncryptionLevel
     WScript.Echo "ForegroundApplicationBoost: " & _
  objItem.ForegroundApplicationBoost
     WScript.Echo "FreePhysicalMemory: " & _
  objItem.FreePhysicalMemory
     WScript.Echo "FreeSpaceInPagingFiles: " & _
  objItem.FreeSpaceInPagingFiles
     WScript.Echo "FreeVirtualMemory: " & objItem.FreeVirtualMemory
     WScript.Echo "InstallDate: " & objItem.InstallDate
     WScript.Echo "LargeSystemCache: " & objItem.LargeSystemCache
     WScript.Echo "LastBootUpTime: " & objItem.LastBootUpTime
     WScript.Echo "LocalDateTime: " & objItem.LocalDateTime
     WScript.Echo "Locale: " & objItem.Locale
     WScript.Echo "Manufacturer: " & objItem.Manufacturer
     WScript.Echo "MaxNumberOfProcesses: " & objItem.MaxNumberOfProcesses
     WScript.Echo "MaxProcessMemorySize: " & objItem.MaxProcessMemorySize
     WScript.Echo "Name: " & objItem.Name
     WScript.Echo "NumberOfLicensedUsers: " & objItem.NumberOfLicensedUsers
     WScript.Echo "NumberOfProcesses: " & objItem.NumberOfProcesses
     WScript.Echo "NumberOfUsers: " & objItem.NumberOfUsers
     WScript.Echo "Organization: " & objItem.Organization
```

LISTING 20.1   Continued

```
        WScript.Echo "OSLanguage: " & objItem.OSLanguage
        WScript.Echo "OSProductSuite: " & objItem.OSProductSuite
        WScript.Echo "OSType: " & objItem.OSType
        WScript.Echo "OtherTypeDescription: " & objItem.OtherTypeDescription
        WScript.Echo "PlusProductID: " & objItem.PlusProductID
        WScript.Echo "PlusVersionNumber: " & objItem.PlusVersionNumber
        WScript.Echo "Primary: " & objItem.Primary
        WScript.Echo "ProductType: " & objItem.ProductType
        WScript.Echo "QuantumLength: " & objItem.QuantumLength
        WScript.Echo "QuantumType: " & objItem.QuantumType
        WScript.Echo "RegisteredUser: " & objItem.RegisteredUser
        WScript.Echo "SerialNumber: " & objItem.SerialNumber
        WScript.Echo "ServicePackMajorVersion: " & _
objItem.ServicePackMajorVersion
        WScript.Echo "ServicePackMinorVersion: " & _
  objItem.ServicePackMinorVersion
        WScript.Echo "SizeStoredInPagingFiles: " & _
  objItem.SizeStoredInPagingFiles
        WScript.Echo "Status: " & objItem.Status
        WScript.Echo "SuiteMask: " & objItem.SuiteMask
        WScript.Echo "SystemDevice: " & objItem.SystemDevice
        WScript.Echo "SystemDirectory: " & objItem.SystemDirectory
        WScript.Echo "SystemDrive: " & objItem.SystemDrive
        WScript.Echo "TotalSwapSpaceSize: " & _
  objItem.TotalSwapSpaceSize
        WScript.Echo "TotalVirtualMemorySize: " & _
  objItem.TotalVirtualMemorySize
        WScript.Echo "TotalVisibleMemorySize: " & _
  objItem.TotalVisibleMemorySize
        WScript.Echo "Version: " & objItem.Version
        WScript.Echo "WindowsDirectory: " & objItem.WindowsDirectory
Next
```

The wizard's code pulls more information than I want, and it's displaying the information in message boxes, rather than writing them to a file, but the code makes a great place to start. I can easily modify it to meet my needs.

The script is designed! I identified the three major tasks that the script needs to be able to complete, and I've created some prototype code that can be adapted to the script's exact requirements. In short, I now know how to do everything I need; I just need to rearrange it and customize it.

20

What, No Wizard?

If you're not using PrimalScript, there are some other tools you can use to make WMI scripting easier. In Chapter 18, "Querying Basic WMI Information," for example, I introduced Microsoft's Scriptomatic tool, which performs a similar function to the PrimalScript WMI Wizard. You can also dive into the WMI documentation in the MSDN Library (http://msdn.microsoft.com/library), which documents each WMI class and includes some scripting examples. Newer versions of PrimalScript do include an ADSI Wizard, but it doesn't produce boilerplate code like the WMI Wizard does.

Writing Functions and Subroutines

The one bit of functionality that seems to be standalone is the code generated by the wizard, which will do my WMI querying for me. I might need to use that code in another script someday, and I'll definitely be using it over and over in the script I'm writing now, so it makes sense to write it as a function.

I want the function to accept a computer name, query that computer for specific operating system information, and then compile all that information into a neatly formatted string. The function should return the string to the main script, which can then write it to a file or whatever.

Adapting the wizard's code isn't too difficult. Listing 20.2 shows my new GetOSInfo() function. Note that this isn't intended to be run as a standalone script; as a function, it must be called by another script, which must provide the name of the computer to connect to as the function's input parameter.

LISTING 20.2   *GetOSInfo.vbs.* This function queries a computer's operating system information and returns the results in a string.

```
Function GetOSInfo(sComputer)

    'declare variables
    Dim objWMIService
    Dim colItems
    Dim strOutput

    'get WMI service
    Set objWMIService = GetObject("winmgmts:\\" & _
      strComputer & "\root\cimv2")

    'get item collection
    Set colItems = objWMIService.ExecQuery( _
      "Select * from Win32_OperatingSystem",,48)

    'init output string
    sOutput = String(70,"-") & vbCrLf
```

LISTING 20.2   Continued

```
        sOutput = sOutput & sComputer & vbCrLf

        'append info to output string
        For Each objItem in colItems
strOutput = strOutput & "BuildNumber: " & _
            objItem.BuildNumber & vbCrLf
            strOutput = strOutput & "BuildType: " & _
            objItem.BuildType & vbCrLf
            strOutput = strOutput & "Caption: " & _
            objItem.Caption & vbCrLf
            strOutput = strOutput & "EncryptionLevel: " & _
            objItem.EncryptionLevel & vbCrLf
            strOutput = strOutput & "InstallDate: " & _
            objItem.InstallDate & vbCrLf
            strOutput = strOutput & "Manufacturer: " & _
            objItem.Manufacturer & vbCrLf
            strOutput = strOutput & "MaxNumberOfProcesses: " & _
            objItem.MaxNumberOfProcesses & vbCrLf
        strOutput = strOutput & "MaxProcessMemorySize: " & _
            objItem.MaxProcessMemorySize & vbCrLf
      strOutput = strOutput & "Name: " & _
            objItem.Name & vbCrLf
            strOutput = strOutput & _
            "NumberOfLicensedUsers: " & _
            objItem.NumberOfLicensedUsers & vbCrLf
            strOutput = strOutput & "NumberOfProcesses: " & _
            objItem.NumberOfProcesses & vbCrLf
            strOutput = strOutput & "NumberOfUsers: " & _
            objItem.NumberOfUsers & vbCrLf
            strOutput = strOutput & "OSProductSuite: " & _
            objItem.OSProductSuite & vbCrLf
            strOutput = strOutput & "OSType: " & _
            objItem.OSType & vbCrLf
            strOutput = strOutput & "OtherTypeDescription: " & _
            objItem.OtherTypeDescription & vbCrLf
            strOutput = strOutput & "Primary: " & _
            objItem.Primary & vbCrLf
            strOutput = strOutput & "ProductType: " & _
            objItem.ProductType & vbCrLf
            strOutput = strOutput & "RegisteredUser: " & _
            objItem.RegisteredUser & vbCrLf
            strOutput = strOutput & "SerialNumber: " & _
            objItem.SerialNumber & vbCrLf
            strOutput = strOutput & _
```

20

LISTING 20.2   Continued

```
                "ServicePackMajorVersion: " & _
                objItem.ServicePackMajorVersion & vbCrLf
            strOutput = strOutput & _
                "ServicePackMinorVersion: " & _
                objItem.ServicePackMinorVersion & vbCrLf
            strOutput = strOutput & "Version: " & _
                objItem.Version & vbCrLf
            strOutput = strOutput & "WindowsDirectory: " & _
                objItem.WindowsDirectory & vbCrLf
    Next

'return results
    GetOSInfo = sOutput


End Function
```

I didn't have to do much to adapt the script. First, I deleted all the lines that I didn't want in my script. I changed all the WScript.Echo commands to strOutput = strOutput &, which appends the information into a string rather than displays it in a message box. I also added & vbCrLf to the end of each line, which adds a carriage return and linefeed character. Those help keep the final output file looking nice.

I also dressed up the code at the beginning of the function.

```
        'declare variables
        Dim objWMIService
        Dim colItems
        Dim strOutput

        'get WMI service
        Set objWMIService = GetObject("winmgmts:\\" & _
         strComputer & "\root\cimv2")

        'get item collection
        Set colItems = objWMIService.ExecQuery( _
         "Select * from Win32_OperatingSystem",,48)

        'init output string
        sOutput = String(70,"-") & vbCrLf
        sOutput = sOutput & sComputer & vbCrLf
```

I added some comments to document the code—PrimalScript isn't so good about that—and I initialized my sOutput variable. I also started sOutput off to contain a line of 70 hyphens, and the name of the computer I'm querying. These extra touches help make the final output file easier to read and more useful.

Writing the Main Script

The function was probably the toughest part to write; with that out of the way, I can adapt my prototype code to create the main script, shown in Listing 20.3.

LISTING 20.3 *MainScript.vbs.* Queries the domain, creates the output file, and calls the custom function I already wrote.

```
Dim sDomain
sDomain = InputBox("Enter domain to inventory")

'connect to domain and retrieve
'a list of member objects
Dim oDomain
Set oDomain = GetObject("WinNT://" & sDomain)

'get the filesystemobject
Dim oFSO
Set oFSO = CreateObject("Scripting.FileSystemObject")

'open an output file
Dim oOutput
Set oOutput = oFSO.CreateTextFile("\\server1\public\output.txt")

'run through the objects
Dim oObject, sComputerName, sDetails
For Each oObject In oDomain

 'is this object a computer?
 If oObject.Class = "Computer" Then

  'yes - get computer name
  sComputerName = oObject.Name

  'get OS info
  sDetails = GetOSInfo(sComputerName)

  'write info to the file
  oOutput.Write sDetails

 End If
Next

'close the output file
oOutput.Close
```

20

LISTING 20.3   Continued

```
'release objects
Set oOutput = Nothing
Set oFSO = Nothing
Set oObject = nothing
Set oDomain = Nothing

'display completion message
WScript.Echo "Output saved to \\server1\public\output.txt"
```

I'll provide my usual walk-through of this script in a bit; for now, try to pick out the adapted pieces of prototype code. Notice where I'm querying the domain, opening and writing to the text file, closing the text file, and calling the GetOSInfo() function.

Inventorying the Domain   Listing 20.4 shows the complete, ready-to-run script. Get this ready to run, but don't execute it just yet. In the next section, I'll cover testing and troubleshooting this script.

LISTING 20.4   *InventoryDomain.vbs.* The complete domain inventory script.

```
'get domain name
Dim sDomain
sDomain = InputBox("Enter domain to inventory")

'connect to domain and retrieve
'a list of member objects
Dim oDomain
Set oDomain = GetObject("WinNT://" & sDomain

'get the filesystemobject
Dim oFSO
Set oFSO = CreateObject("Scripting.FileSystemObject")

'open an output file
Dim oOutput
oOutput = oFSO.CreateTextFile("\\server1\public\output.txt")

'run through the objects
Dim oObject, sComputerName, sDetails
For Each oObject In oDomain

  'is this object a computer?
  If oObject.Class = "Computer" Then

    'yes - get computer name
```

LISTING 20.4   Continued

```
    sComputerName = oObject.Name

     'get OS info
    sDetails = GetOSInfo(sComputerName)

     'write info to the file
    oOutput.Write sDetails

  End If
Next

'close the output file
oOutput.Close

'release objects
Set oOutput = Nothing
Set oFSO = Nothing
Set oObject = Nothing
Set oDomain = Nothing

'display completion message
WScript.Echo "Output saved to \\server1\public\output.txt"

Function GetOSInfo(sComputer)

        'declare variables
        Dim objWMIService
        Dim colItems
        Dim strOutput

        'get WMI service
        Set objWMIService = GetObject("winmgmts:\\" & _
         strComputer & "\root\cimv2")

        'get item collection
        Set colItems = objWMIService.ExecQuery( _
         "Select * from Win32_OperatingSystem",,48)

        'init output string
        sOutput = String(70,"-") & vbcrlf
        sOutput = sOutput & sComputer & vbcrlf

        'append info to output string
        For Each objItem in colItems
```

20

LISTING 20.4   Continued

```
            strOutput = strOutput & "BuildNumber: " & _
             objItem.BuildNumber & vbCrLf
            strOutput = strOutput & "BuildType: " & _
             objItem.BuildType & vbCrLf
            strOutput = strOutput & "Caption: " & _
             objItem.Caption & vbCrLf
            strOutput = strOutput & "EncryptionLevel: " & _
             objItem.EncryptionLevel & vbCrLf
            strOutput = strOutput & "InstallDate: " & _
             objItem.InstallDate & vbCrLf
            strOutput = strOutput & "Manufacturer: " & _
             objItem.Manufacturer & vbCrLf
            strOutput = strOutput & "MaxNumberOfProcesses: " & _
             objItem.MaxNumberOfProcesses & vbCrLf
        strOutput = strOutput & "MaxProcessMemorySize: " & _
             objItem.MaxProcessMemorySize & vbCrLf
      strOutput = strOutput & "Name: " & _
             objItem.Name & vbCrLf
            strOutput = strOutput & _
             "NumberOfLicensedUsers: " & _
             objItem.NumberOfLicensedUsers & vbCrLf
            strOutput = strOutput & "NumberOfProcesses: " & _
             objItem.NumberOfProcesses & vbCrLf
            strOutput = strOutput & "NumberOfUsers: " & _
             objItem.NumberOfUsers & vbCrLf
            strOutput = strOutput & "OSProductSuite: " & _
             objItem.OSProductSuite & vbCrLf
            strOutput = strOutput & "OSType: " & _
             objItem.OSType & vbCrLf
     strOutput = strOutput & "OtherTypeDescription: " & _
             objItem.OtherTypeDescription & vbCrLf
            strOutput = strOutput & "Primary: " & _
             objItem.Primary & vbCrLf
            strOutput = strOutput & "ProductType: " & _
             objItem.ProductType & vbCrLf
            strOutput = strOutput & "RegisteredUser: " & _
             objItem.RegisteredUser & vbCrLf
            strOutput = strOutput & "SerialNumber: " & _
             objItem.SerialNumber & vbCrLf
            strOutput = strOutput & _
             "ServicePackMajorVersion: " & _
             objItem.ServicePackMajorVersion & vbCrLf
            strOutput = strOutput & _
             "ServicePackMinorVersion: " & _
```

LISTING 20.4   Continued

```
                objItem.ServicePackMinorVersion & vbCrLf
            strOutput = strOutput & "Version: " & _
             objItem.Version & vbCrLf
            strOutput = strOutput & "WindowsDirectory: " & _
        objItem.WindowsDirectory & vbCrLf
Next


 'return results
     GetOSInfo = sOutput


End Function
```

You need to change where this script puts its output file before using it in your environment. The script prompts for the domain name, so you won't have to make any changes there.

Inventorying the Domain—Explained   The script starts by prompting for the domain name. This allows the script to be used in a multidomain environment. The domain name is stored in a string variable.

```
'get domain name
Dim sDomain
sDomain = InputBox("Enter domain to inventory")
```

Next, the script uses ADSI to connect to the domain and retrieve a list of all domain objects. This might be a lengthy operation in a large domain because computer, user, and all other objects are included in the results.

```
'connect to domain and retrieve
'a list of member objects
Dim oDomain
Set oDomain = GetObject("WinNT://" & sDomain)
```

The script creates a new FileSystemObject and assigns it to a variable.

```
'get the filesystemobject
Dim oFSO
Set oFSO = CreateObject("Scripting.FileSystemObject")
```

The script now creates a new text file by using the FileSystemObject's CreateTextFile method. The method returns a TextStream object, which is assigned to the variable oOutput.

```
'open an output file
Dim oOutput
oOutput = oFSO.CreateTextFile("\\server1\public\output.txt")
```

20

oDomain now represents all of the objects in the domain; I'll use a For Each/Next loop to iterate through each object in turn. Within the loop, oObject will represent the current object.

```
'run through the objects
Dim oObject, sComputerName, sDetails
For Each oObject In oDomain
```

Because oDomain contains more than just computers, I need to check each object to see if its Class property equals "Computer." That way, I can just work with the computer objects and skip the rest.

```
'is this object a computer?
If oObject.Class = "Computer" Then
```

For objects that are a computer, I pull the computer name into a variable. Then, I assign the results of GetOSInfo() to variable sDetails. Finally, I write sDetails to the output text file using the TextStream object's Write method. I then close up the loop with Next to move on to the next object in the domain.

```
'yes - get computer name
sComputerName = oObject.Name

'get OS info
sDetails = GetOSInfo(sComputerName)

'write info to the file
oOutput.Write sDetails

End If
Next
```

When I'm done with all the objects, I close the output file, release all the objects I created by setting them equal to Nothing, and then display a simple completion message.

```
'close the output file
oOutput.Close

'release objects
Set oOutput = Nothing
Set oFSO = Nothing
Set oObject = Nothing
Set oDomain = Nothing

'display completion message
WScript.Echo "Output saved to \\server1\public\output.txt"
```

Here's that function I wrote earlier. It starts with a basic variable declaration.

```
Function GetOSInfo(sComputer)

        'declare variables
        Dim objWMIService
        Dim colItems
        Dim strOutput
```

Next is pure wizard code, which uses `GetObject` to connect to the specified computer's WMI service.

```
        'get WMI service
        Set objWMIService = GetObject("winmgmts:\\" & _
          strComputer & "\root\cimv2")
```

After I am connected, I execute a query to retrieve the `Win32_OperatingSystem` class.

```
        'get item collection
        Set colItems = objWMIService.ExecQuery( _
          "Select * from Win32_OperatingSystem",,48)
```

I set up my output string to include a line of hyphens and the current computer name.

```
        'init output string
        sOutput = String(70,"-") & vbcrlf
        sOutput = sOutput & sComputer & vbcrlf
```

Finally, I append the WMI information to the output string.

```
        'append info to output string
        For Each objItem in colItems
              strOutput = strOutput & "BuildNumber: " & _
               objItem.BuildNumber & vbCrLf
              strOutput = strOutput & "BuildType: " & _
               objItem.BuildType & vbCrLf
              strOutput = strOutput & "Caption: " & _
               objItem.Caption & vbCrLf
              strOutput = strOutput & "EncryptionLevel: " & _
               objItem.EncryptionLevel & vbCrLf
              strOutput = strOutput & "InstallDate: " & _
               objItem.InstallDate & vbCrLf
              strOutput = strOutput & "Manufacturer: " & _
               objItem.Manufacturer & vbCrLf
              strOutput = strOutput & "MaxNumberOfProcesses: " & _
               objItem.MaxNumberOfProcesses & vbCrLf
        strOutput = strOutput & "MaxProcessMemorySize: " & _
              objItem.MaxProcessMemorySize & vbCrLf
```

20

```
strOutput = strOutput & "Name: " & _
            objItem.Name & vbCrLf
          strOutput = strOutput & _
           "NumberOfLicensedUsers: " & _
           objItem.NumberOfLicensedUsers & vbCrLf
          strOutput = strOutput & "NumberOfProcesses: " & _
           objItem.NumberOfProcesses & vbCrLf
          strOutput = strOutput & "NumberOfUsers: " & _
           objItem.NumberOfUsers & vbCrLf
          strOutput = strOutput & "OSProductSuite: " & _
           objItem.OSProductSuite & vbCrLf
          strOutput = strOutput & "OSType: " & _
           objItem.OSType & vbCrLf
          strOutput = strOutput & "OtherTypeDescription: " & _
           objItem.OtherTypeDescription & vbCrLf
          strOutput = strOutput & "Primary: " & _
           objItem.Primary & vbCrLf
          strOutput = strOutput & "ProductType: " & _
           objItem.ProductType & vbCrLf
          strOutput = strOutput & "RegisteredUser: " & _
           objItem.RegisteredUser & vbCrLf
          strOutput = strOutput & "SerialNumber: " & _
           objItem.SerialNumber & vbCrLf
          strOutput = strOutput & _
           "ServicePackMajorVersion: " & _
           objItem.ServicePackMajorVersion & vbCrLf
          strOutput = strOutput & _
           "ServicePackMinorVersion: " & _
           objItem.ServicePackMinorVersion & vbCrLf
          strOutput = strOutput & "Version: " & _
           objItem.Version & vbCrLf
          strOutput = strOutput & "WindowsDirectory: " & _
           objItem.WindowsDirectory & vbCrLf
      Next
```

With the main script finished, I return the output string as the function's result.

```
'return results
    GetOSInfo = sOutput


End Function
```

There you have it—a nice, easy-to-use administrative script that uses both WMI and ADSI to accomplish a useful task.

Testing the Script

If you jumped ahead and already tried to execute the final script, you realize that it's flawed. If you haven't, go ahead and give it a whirl now. Take a few minutes to see if you can track down the problem. There are actually three errors, and here are some hints:

▶ One is a simple typo.

▶ One is a sort of logic error, where something isn't being used properly for the situation.

▶ The last one is a typo, and could have been avoided if I had followed my own advice from earlier in the book.

Can you find them all? The first one is an easy mistake: I simply forgot a closing parenthesis.

```
'connect to domain and retrieve
'a list of member objects
Dim oDomain
Set oDomain = GetObject("WinNT://" & sDomain
```

The correct code should be `Set oDomain = GetObject("WinNT://" & sDomain)`. The next one's a bit trickier.

```
'open an output file
Dim oOutput
oOutput = oFSO.CreateTextFile("\\server1\public\output.txt")
```

Can you see it? I'm using oOutput to represent an object, but I forgot to use the Set keyword when making the assignment. VBScript requires Set whenever you're assigning an object to a variable. The corrected code looks like this:

```
'open an output file
Dim oOutput
Set oOutput = oFSO.CreateTextFile("\\server1\public\output.txt")
```

The last error is tricky, too. It's in the GetOSInfo() function.

```
Function GetOSInfo(sComputer)

    'declare variables
    Dim objWMIService
    Dim colItems
    Dim strOutput

    'get WMI service
    Set objWMIService = GetObject("winmgmts:\\" & _
     strComputer & "\root\cimv2")
```

20

Did you find it? The problem is that I used the wizard-generated code, which uses "str" as a prefix for string variables. I'm in the habit of using the shorter prefix "s" for string variables, and that's where my problem lies. In the function definition, I declared sComputer, but in the line of code that connects to the WMI service, I used strComputer. I continued using sComputer elsewhere, so strComputer is wrong. Here's the corrected code snippet:

```
Function GetOSInfo(sComputer)

        'declare variables
        Dim objWMIService
        Dim colItems
        Dim strOutput

        'get WMI service
        Set objWMIService = GetObject("winmgmts:\\" & _
          sComputer & "\root\cimv2")
```

The problem with this error is that it doesn't cause a problem for the script; the script will execute just fine. You just won't get any results because the script would try to connect to a computer named "". I mentioned that I could have avoided this problem by following my own advice. Had I included Option Explicit, VBScript would have produced an error on the offending line of code because strComputer wasn't declared. sComputer, on the other hand, is implicitly declared because it's part of a function declaration. You'll notice that I did the same thing with strOutput and sOutput, meaning they'll have to be corrected, too.

Just to make sure you've got it all, Listing 20.5 includes the complete, corrected script. Remember that this script is also available in the book's downloads at http://www.ScriptingAnswers.com/books.asp.

LISTING 20.5   *InventoryDomain2.vbs.* This corrected script produces the expected results.

```
'get domain name
Dim sDomain
sDomain = InputBox("Enter domain to inventory")

'connect to domain and retrieve
'a list of member objects
Dim oDomain
Set oDomain = GetObject("WinNT://" & sDomain)

'get the filesystemobject
Dim oFSO
Set oFSO = CreateObject("Scripting.FileSystemObject")

'open an output file
Dim oOutput
```

LISTING 20.5   Continued

```
Set oOutput = oFSO.CreateTextFile("\\server1\public\output.txt")

'run through the objects
Dim oObject, sComputerName, sDetails
For Each oObject In oDomain

  'is this object a computer?
  If oObject.Class = "Computer" Then

    'yes - get computer name
    sComputerName = oObject.Name

    'get OS info
    sDetails = GetOSInfo(sComputerName)

    'write info to the file
    oOutput.Write sDetails

  End If
Next
'close the output file
oOutput.Close

'release objects
Set oOutput = Nothing
Set oFSO = Nothing
Set oObject = nothing
Set oDomain = Nothing

'display completion message
WScript.Echo "Output saved to \\server1\public\output.txt"

Function GetOSInfo(sComputer)

    'declare variables
    Dim objWMIService
    Dim colItems
    Dim strOutput

    'get WMI service
    Set objWMIService = GetObject("winmgmts:\\" & _
     sComputer & "\root\cimv2")

    'get item collection
```

20

LISTING 20.5   Continued

```
Set colItems = objWMIService.ExecQuery( _
 "Select * from Win32_OperatingSystem",,48)

'init output string
strOutput = String(70,"-") & vbcrlf
strOutput = strOutput & sComputer & vbcrlf

'append info to output string
For Each objItem in colItems
        strOutput = strOutput & "BuildNumber: " & _
         objItem.BuildNumber & vbCrLf
        strOutput = strOutput & "BuildType: " & _
         objItem.BuildType & vbCrLf
        strOutput = strOutput & "Caption: " & _
         objItem.Caption & vbCrLf
        strOutput = strOutput & "EncryptionLevel: " & _
         objItem.EncryptionLevel & vbCrLf
        strOutput = strOutput & "InstallDate: " & _
         objItem.InstallDate & vbCrLf
        strOutput = strOutput & "Manufacturer: " & _
         objItem.Manufacturer & vbCrLf
        strOutput = strOutput & "MaxNumberOfProcesses: " & _
         objItem.MaxNumberOfProcesses & vbCrLf
    strOutput = strOutput & "MaxProcessMemorySize: " & _
         objItem.MaxProcessMemorySize & vbCrLf
  strOutput = strOutput & "Name: " & _
         objItem.Name & vbCrLf
        strOutput = strOutput & _
         "NumberOfLicensedUsers: " & _
         objItem.NumberOfLicensedUsers & vbCrLf
        strOutput = strOutput & "NumberOfProcesses: " & _
         objItem.NumberOfProcesses & vbCrLf
        strOutput = strOutput & "NumberOfUsers: " & _
         objItem.NumberOfUsers & vbCrLf
        strOutput = strOutput & "OSProductSuite: " & _
         objItem.OSProductSuite & vbCrLf
        strOutput = strOutput & "OSType: " & _
         objItem.OSType & vbCrLf
        strOutput = strOutput & "OtherTypeDescription: " & _
         objItem.OtherTypeDescription & vbCrLf
        strOutput = strOutput & "Primary: " & _
         objItem.Primary & vbCrLf
        strOutput = strOutput & "ProductType: " & _
         objItem.ProductType & vbCrLf
```

LISTING 20.5   Continued

```
            strOutput = strOutput & "RegisteredUser: " & _
             objItem.RegisteredUser & vbCrLf
            strOutput = strOutput & "SerialNumber: " & _
             objItem.SerialNumber & vbCrLf
            strOutput = strOutput & _
             "ServicePackMajorVersion: " & _
             objItem.ServicePackMajorVersion & vbCrLf
            strOutput = strOutput & _
             "ServicePackMinorVersion: " & _
             objItem.ServicePackMinorVersion & vbCrLf
            strOutput = strOutput & "Version: " & _
             objItem.Version & vbCrLf
            strOutput = strOutput & "WindowsDirectory: " & _
             objItem.WindowsDirectory & vbCrLf
        Next

    'return results
        GetOSInfo = strOutput

End Function
```

Testing a large script like this is much easier with the Script Debugger. You can spot lines that are causing trouble just by following the execution path.

For more information on the Script Debugger, see Chapter 13, "Putting It All Together: Creating Your First Script from Scratch." You can also read up on the Script Debugger in the VBScript documentation at http://msdn.microsoft.com/scripting.

Summary

Pulling together ADSI and WMI into a single script offers some powerful functionality. More important, though, the example in this chapter should make you feel more comfortable with the sometimes-daunting task of creating a script from scratch. Just break down the tasks that need to be completed, and then develop some prototype code for each task. Use wizards, examples from the web, or samples from this book to help create prototype code. After all, there's no sense reinventing the wheel when there's a large library of samples on the web and in this book to work with!

With your task list and prototype out of the way, you can start assembling the script. Write functions and subs to perform repetitive tasks, or tasks that you might want to reuse in future scripts. Write the main script, and then start testing. With this methodology in mind, most scripts can be whipped together quickly!

20

Testing and Debugging WMI and ADSI Queries

I think that one of the most frustrating parts about scripting is debugging Windows Management Instrumentation (WMI) and Active Directory Services Interface (ADSI) scripts that look like they should work perfectly—but which don't do what I expect them to. In other words, the script code itself looks perfect, but for some reason the script just doesn't do anything. Take this as a quick example of what I'm talking about:

```
sName = "server2"
Dim cPingResults, oPingResult
Set cPingResults = _
 GetObject("winmgmts://./root/" & _
   "cimv2").ExecQuery("SELECT " & _
   "* FROM Win32_Ping WHERE " & _
   "Address = '" & sName & "'")
On Error Resume Next
For Each oPingResult In cPingResults
    If Not IsObject(cPingResults) Then
        Ping = False
    ElseIf oPingResult.StatusCode = 0 Then
        Ping = True
    Else
        Ping = False
    End If
Next
WScript.Echo Ping
```

You might recognize this from the previous chapter, and you might spot what's changed. If you do, don't let on! There's something specific about this script that I want to walk you through. If you just type this in and try to run it, you'll find that it doesn't work properly: No matter what computer name you provide, it always outputs "True," or -1. So what's the problem? I'll save you some reading and just come right out and tell you: There's nothing wrong with the VBScript code at all.

Debugging Outside the Script

WMI and ADSI are both external technologies that VBScript is able to tap into. However, like any relationship, the one between VBScript and external technologies sometimes suffers from communications issues. In other words, when things go wrong in the external technology, it doesn't always give VBScript a clear idea of what the problem is—or even that there *is* a problem! So VBScript often just plows ahead and does the best job it can.

That's why, whenever a WMI or ADSI script isn't working correctly, *the very first thing* you have to do is stop using VBScript to troubleshoot the problem. Accept the fact that VBScript isn't the best troubleshooting environment; instead, you need to use external tools that are native to whatever technology you're working with.

Debugging WMI Queries

The tool for "getting out of the script" in the case of WMI is Wbemtest.exe, which I've looked at in previous chapters. It's built in to Windows XP and later: Just select Run from the Start menu, type Wbemtest, and click OK to start it up.

The trick with using Wbemtest is to compare apples to apples: In other words, make sure Wbemtest is being told to do *exactly* what your script is being told to do. I'll walk you through what I mean: Start by running Wbemtest. Figure 21.1 shows the initial dialog box for the tool.

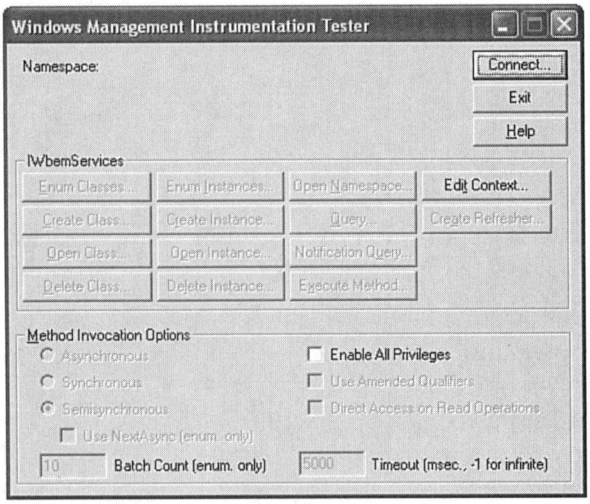

FIGURE 21.1   The initial Wbemtest screen.

It's pretty obvious that you'll be clicking the Connect button because that's just about the only one that's not disabled! When you do so, a new dialog box opens, which is shown in Figure 21.2.

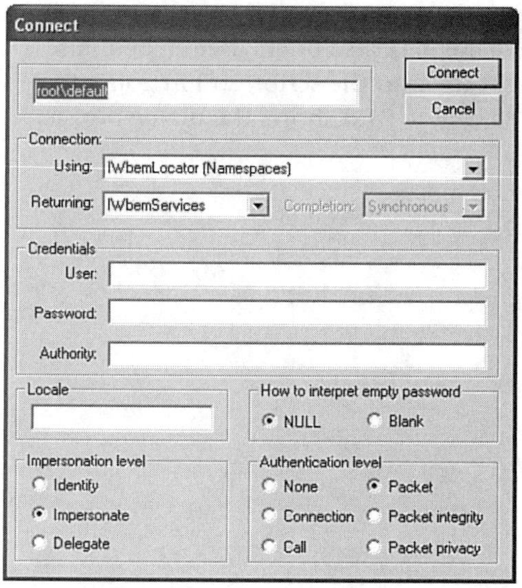

FIGURE 21.2   Connecting Wbemtest to WMI.

This is where your first set of decisions comes in. What do you enter on this screen? For the answers, *look to your script*. What information is your script using to make a WMI connection? For accurate debugging, don't enter any information that isn't in your script, or you won't be accurately testing what your script is trying to do. Let's look at the script again:

```
sName = "localhost"
Dim cPingResults, oPingResult
Set cPingResults = _
 GetObject("winmgmts://./root/" & _
   "cimv2").ExecQuery("SELECT " & _
   "* FROM Win32_Ping WHERE " & _
   "Address = '" & sName & "'")
On Error Resume Next
For Each oPingResult In cPingResults
    If Not IsObject(cPingResults) Then
        Ping = False
    ElseIf oPingResult.StatusCode = 0 Then
        Ping = True
    Else
        Ping = False
```

```
    End If
Next
WScript.Echo Ping
```

I can see that the connection directive is winmgmts://./root/cimv2. So that's exactly what goes into the dialog box in Wbemtest. The dialog box also offers user credentials and other options; I don't see any other options specified in the script, so I'm going to leave everything in the dialog box at their defaults. Figure 21.3 shows the dialog box as I've configured it.

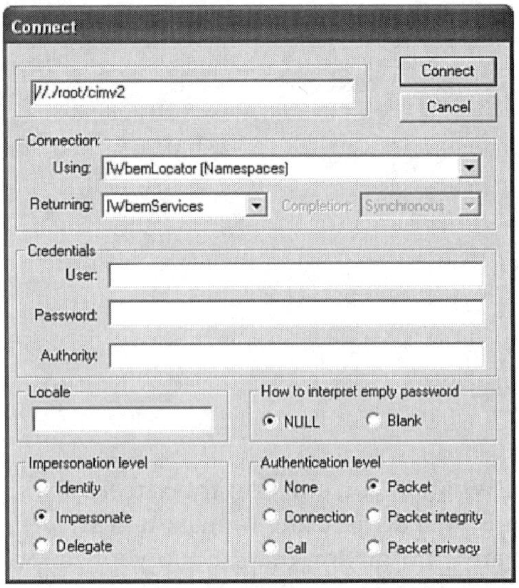

FIGURE 21.3   Configuring the WMI connection.

What does my script do next? It looks like it's executing a query, and I do see a Query button in Wbemtest, so I'm going to click it. As before, I'm simply going to copy the query out of my script and paste it into Wbemtest, as shown in Figure 21.4. But this is where I run into a bit of a snag: Wbemtest isn't VBScript, so I can't just run a query that's full of VBScript stuff like concatenation operators. I need to edit my query down to *just* the actual WMI query, eliminating the VBScript syntax. That's shown in Figure 21.5. And that leaves just one more snag: I don't want to ping a computer named sName; sName was a VBScript variable. My script had assigned the value "localhost" to sName, so I'm going to put "localhost" into my WMI query. Figure 21.6 shows the final query; I can now click Apply to enter the query.

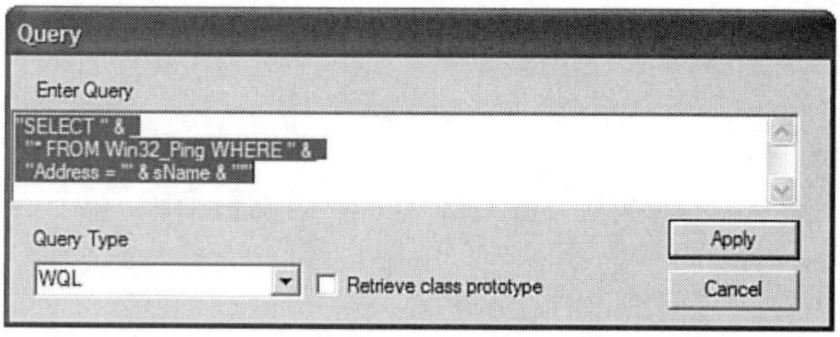

FIGURE 21.4   Setting up the WMI query.

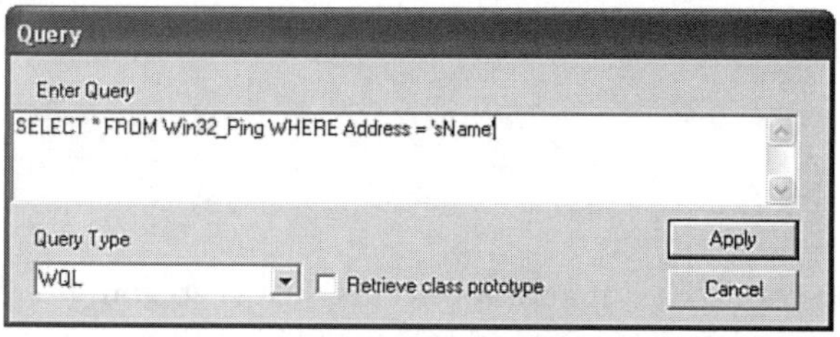

FIGURE 21.5   Tweaking the WMI query.

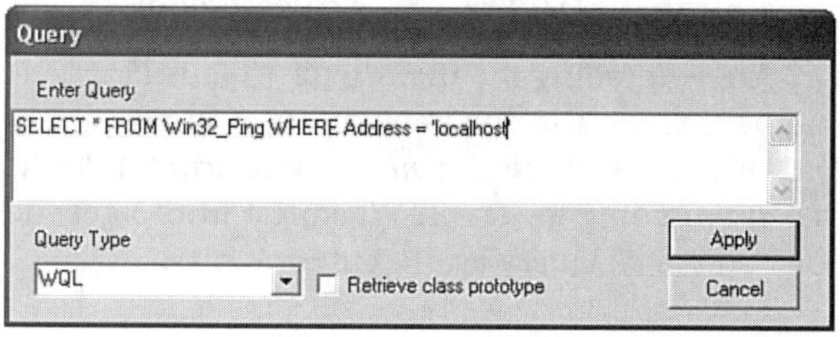

FIGURE 21.6   Filling in values for VBScript variables.

Kaboom! As shown in Figure 21.7, I immediately got an error: Invalid class. Now why didn't VBScript ever give me that error? Well, for one thing, VBScript isn't always the best when it comes to WMI errors. For another thing... well, see for yourself: I'll highlight the culprit in boldface.

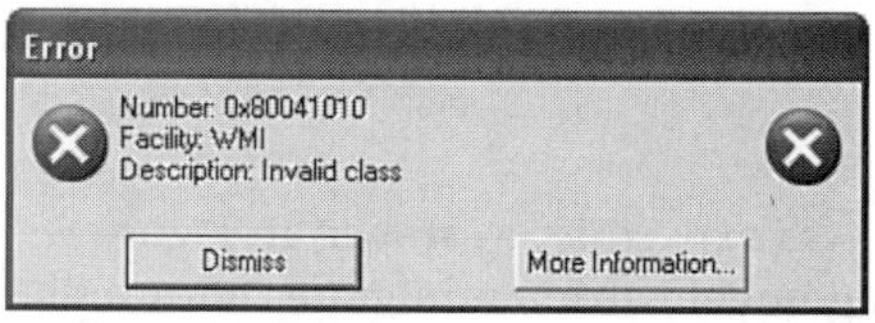

FIGURE 21.7   Wbemtest will warn you if you try to select an invalid class.

```
sName = "server2"
Dim cPingResults, oPingResult
Set cPingResults = _
```

```
GetObject("winmgmts://./root/" & _
  "cimv2").ExecQuery("SELECT " & _
  "* FROM Win32_Ping WHERE " & _
  "Address = '" & sName & "'")
On Error Resume Next
For Each oPingResult In cPingResults
    If Not IsObject(cPingResults) Then
        Ping = False
    ElseIf oPingResult.StatusCode = 0 Then
        Ping = True
    Else
        Ping = False
    End If
Next
WScript.Echo Ping
```

On Error Resume Next basically tells VBScript, "Hey, if an error occurs, just keep going—don't worry about it." You'll find it in a lot of scripts for good reasons (which I'll cover in Chapter 26, "Debugging Tips, Tools, and Techniques"), but when you're trying to troubleshoot it actually suppresses the errors that might tell you what the problem is. In this case, it was suppressing the "Invalid class" error that WMI was trying to pass along.

And what about that "Invalid class" error? Are you telling me that Win32_Ping isn't a valid class? Oh... oops. The actual class name, I see in the documentation, is Win32_ Ping**Status**. Okay: A major debugging trick is to *resist the urge to modify your script.* I don't *know* that this is the only problem I have, so I'm going to stay in Wbemtest until I get the results I want. I'll dismiss the error message and click Query again, entering my new query, shown in Figure 21.8.

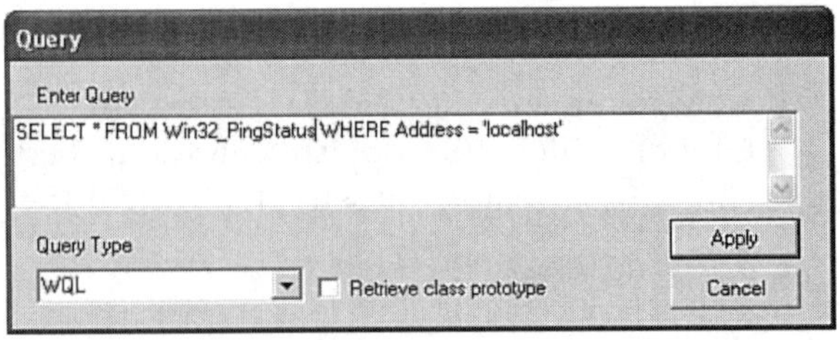

FIGURE 21.8   Revised WMI query.

This time, when I click Apply, I get back the result I was expecting, as shown in Figure 21.9. This confirms that my only issue was the class name; I can then migrate that modification into my script:

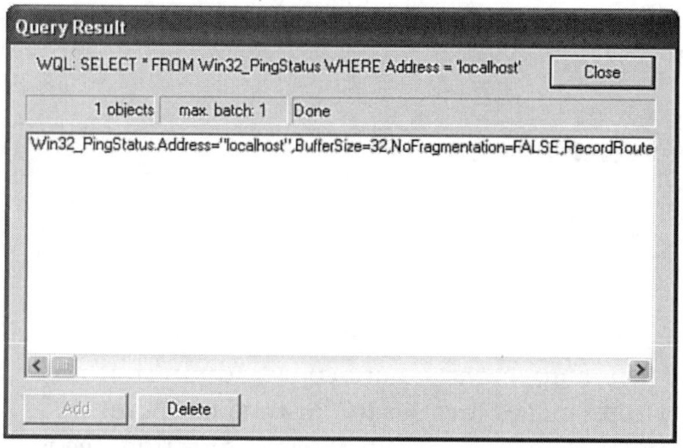

FIGURE 21.9   WMI query results.

```
sName = "server2"
Dim cPingResults, oPingResult
Set cPingResults = _
 GetObject("winmgmts://./root/" & _
   "cimv2").ExecQuery("SELECT " & _
   "* FROM Win32_PingStatus WHERE " & _
   "Address = '" & sName & "'")
On Error Resume Next
For Each oPingResult In cPingResults
    If Not IsObject(cPingResults) Then
        Ping = False
    ElseIf oPingResult.StatusCode = 0 Then
        Ping = True
    Else
        Ping = False
    End If
Next
WScript.Echo Ping
```

Now my script works. I can't stress enough, however, that the idea of an exact script-to-tool comparison is absolutely critical. For example, if your script is being run as a logon script, then it's running under the user context of a plain old user, now an administrator; to perform a fair and accurate test, you need to run Wbemtest under that same security context, using Runas, if necessary to get Wbemtest running under the proper credentials. That way, Wbemtest will be doing *exactly* what your script is doing, under the same circumstances.

Alternate credentials are something to watch out for, as well. Consider this snippet:

```
strComputer = "testbed"
Dim objLocator, objWMI
Set objLocator = CreateObject("WbemScripting.SWbemLocator")
Set objWMI = objLocator.ConnectServer( _
 strComputer, "root\cimv2", _
 "Administrator", "Password!")
```

This code is using an alternate means of connecting to WMI, which allows the use of alternate user credentials. For the record, this snippet has a hard-coded Administrator password, which is a very bad idea, but which makes it easier to illustrate my point. Because this connection is using alternate credentials, your Wbemtest connection needs to do the same thing. Run Wbemtest under whatever user credentials the script itself would run under; then, configure the Wbemtest connection dialog box, as shown in Figure 21.10. That way, your script and Wbemtest will be doing the exact same thing.

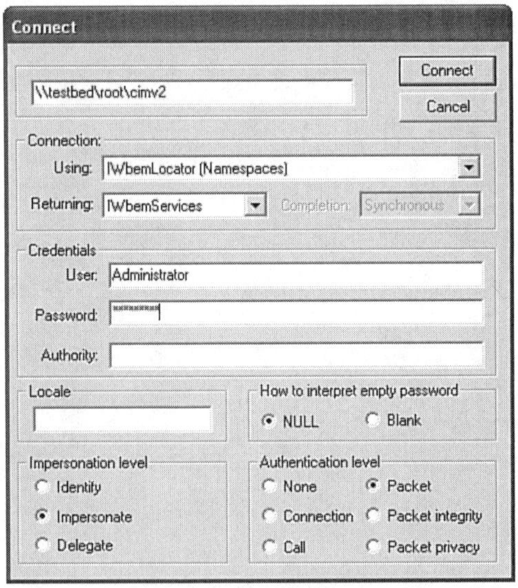

FIGURE 21.10   WMI connection with alternate credentials.

Use Wbemtest to completely verify everything your script is doing. Here's another sample script that doesn't work:

```
strComputer = "."
Dim objWMI
Set objWMI = GetObject("winmgmts:\\" & strComputer & "\root\cimv2")
Dim colResults, objResult, strWMIQuery
strWMIQuery = "SELECT * FROM Win32_OperatingSystem"
Set colResults = objWMI.ExecQuery(strWMIQuery)
```

```
For Each objResult In colResults
        WScript.Echo objResult.ServicePackVersion
Next
```

When I run this script, I get an error message: `"Microsoft VBScript runtime error:`
`Object doesn't support this property or method: 'ServicePackVersion'."` Okay,
that's helpful—but what property does it support? I know service pack version information is in this WMI class because I've heard about other folks using it. I *could* go to the
documentation—and I'd never discourage someone from doing so—but Wbemtest can
help, too. Let's walk through it:

I'll start by connecting and querying, just as in the previous example. In Figure 21.11,
you'll see my query results: one instance of the `Win32_OperatingSystem` class. By double-
clicking that instance, I can see its properties, shown in Figure 21.12. Notice that I've
selected the check box to hide system properties, so I can just focus on the actual properties of the class.

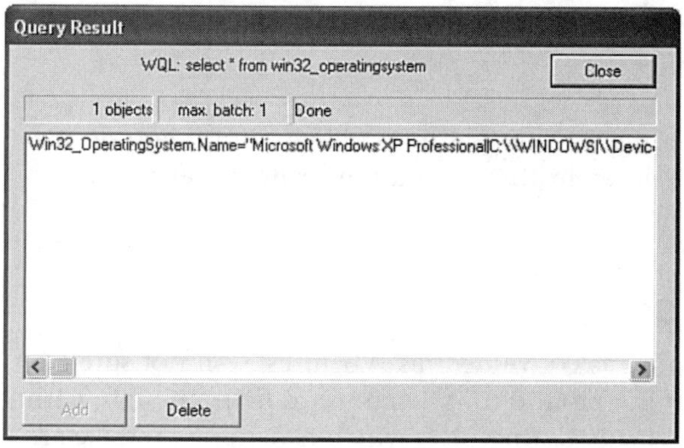

FIGURE 21.11   WMI query results.

I notice that there are really *two* properties for the service pack information:
`ServicePackMajorVersion` and `ServicePackMinorVersion`. Wbemtest conveniently shows
data from these, as well: `ServicePackMajorVersion` is 2, which is the information I was
after. So now I can modify my script to use the correct property:

```
strComputer = "."
Dim objWMI
Set objWMI = GetObject("winmgmts:\\" & strComputer & "\root\cimv2")
Dim colResults, objResult, strWMIQuery
strWMIQuery = "SELECT * FROM Win32_OperatingSystem"
Set colResults = objWMI.ExecQuery(strWMIQuery)
For Each objResult In colResults
        WScript.Echo objResult.ServicePackMajorVersion
Next
```

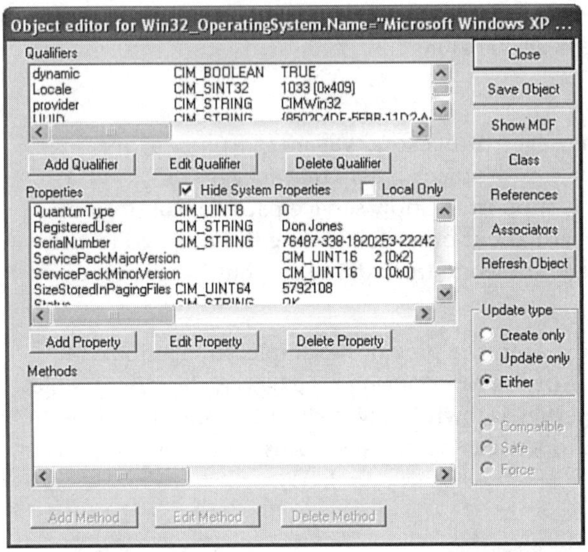

FIGURE 21.12   WMI instance properties.

Using Wbemtest in this fashion makes it *much* easier to find problems and fine-tune the script without stumbling around, trying different things, and not really understanding what's going on under the hood.

Debugging ADSI Queries

Unfortunately, ADSI doesn't offer anything as convenient as Wbemtest. I'm not sure why; perhaps the folks at Microsoft just never got around to it. I can try to help, though, with a couple of test scripts I've written. The first is Listing 21.1, which is designed to take an ADSI query, retrieve the specified directory object, and display all of that object's properties. It does assume that the query is valid, so you'll want to get it *working* first.

LISTING 21.1   ShowProperties.vbs Displays the properties of an ADSI object.

```
'change the WinNT path below
' to whatever directory object
'you want to check
Set objUser = GetObject("WinNT://PC/donjones,user")

Dim objUser, intCount
objUser.GetInfo
intCount = objUser.propertyCount
WScript.Echo objUser.Class & " " & objuser.Name & _
  " has " & intCount & " properties:"
WScript.Echo
```

LISTING 21.1   Continued

```
Dim t, prop, strOutput, strType
For t = 0 To intCount - 1
    Set prop = objUser.Item(t)
    strOutput = "   " & prop.Name & " ("

    Select Case prop.AdsType
        Case 1
            strType = "DN string"
        Case 2
            strType = "Case-sensitive string"
        Case 3
            strType = "Case-insensitive string"
        Case 4
            strType = "Printable string"
        Case 5
            strType = "Numeric string"
        Case 6
            strType = "Boolean"
        Case 7
            strType = "Integer"
        Case 8
            strType = "Octet"
        Case 9
            strType = "Time"
        Case 10
            strType = "Large integer"
        Case 11
            strType = "Provider-specific"
        Case 12
            strType = "Object class"
        Case 13
            strType = "Case-insensitive list"
        Case 14
            strType = "Octet list"
        Case 15
            strType = "Path"
        Case 16
            strType = "Address"
        Case 17
            strType = "Timestamp"
        Case 18
            strType = "Backlink"
        Case 19
            strType = "Typed name"
```

LISTING 21.1   Continued

```
        Case 20
            strType = "Hold"
        Case 21
            strType = "Net addr"
        Case 22
            strType = "Replication ptr"
        Case 23
            strType = "Fax"
        Case 24
            strType = "Email"
        Case 25
            strType = "SID"
        Case 26
            strType = "?"
        Case 27
            strType = "DN binary"
        Case 28
            strType = "DN string"
        Case Else
            strType = "Undefined type"
    End Select

    strOutput = strOutput & strType & ") Value: "
    If not IsArray(objUser.Get(prop.Name)) Then
        strOutput = strOutput & _
            objUser.Get(prop.Name)
    Else
        strOutput = strOutput & "(is an array)"
    End If
    WScript.Echo strOutput
Next
```

Testing queries is trickier. Listing 21.2 is essentially a query-testing script that traps all possible errors, and tries to translate some of the more common (and obscurely worded) errors into plain English.

LISTING 21.2   ADSIDebug.vbs Allows you to test an ADSI query.

```
Dim sQuery
sQuery = InputBox("Enter ADSI query to test:")
If sQuery = "" Or sQuery = -1 Then
    WScript.Quit
End If
```

LISTING 21.2   Continued

```
On Error Resume Next
Dim oObject
Set oObject = GetObject(sQuery)
If Err <> 0 Then
    WScript.Echo Err.Number & " " & Err.Description
    WScript.Echo "An error occurred - couldn't " & _
     "connect using the provider specified, or " & _
     "object doesn't exist"
    Select Case Err.Number
        Case -2147027843
            WScript.Echo "Couldn't connect to " & _
             "server."
        Case -2147467259
            WScript.Echo "Unknown provider."
        Case -2147022676, -2147023520
            WScript.Echo "Server says object " & _
             "doesn't exist."
        Case -2147463168
            WScript.Echo "Illegal query - " & _
             "did you use backslahes by mistake?"
    End Select
    WScript.Quit
End If


WScript.Echo "Object returned: "

If Not IsObject(oObject)  Then
    WScript.Echo "No object was returned"
Else
    WScript.Echo " Name: " & oObject.Name
    If Err <> 0 Then
        WScript.Echo " does not have a Name " & _
         "property"
    End If

    WScript.Echo " Class: " & oObject.Class
    If Err <> 0 Then
        WScript.Echo " does not have a Class " & _
         "property"
    End If
End If
```

When you run this script, it will pop up a graphical dialog box where you can type or paste an ADSI query; it'll then attempt to run the query. If the query is successful, it will display the name and type of the object that was returned; otherwise, it'll try to display some useful error information to help you figure out what went wrong. It's not as good as Wbemtest, but it's better than nothing!

The same rules apply to ADSI query debugging as for WMI query debugging: Apples to apples. Try to copy a query out of your script to paste into these two tools, so that these tools are testing exactly what your scripts are attempting to do.

Summary

Debugging WMI and ADSI queries can be frustrating, and doing so from within a complex script can be much more time-consuming than it needs to be. With tools like the ADSI scripts I've provided, and the Wbemtest tool, you can get outside (to some degree) the context of a VBScript, and instead work with tools that better understand the errors that WMI and ADSI can come up with. By getting your WMI and ADSI queries working on their own, you'll save time and avoid headaches as you develop WMI- and ADSI-related scripts.

PART IV

Advanced Scripting Techniques

IN THIS PART

Modular Script Programming

Throughout this book, I advocate the use of functions and subs to encapsulate useful script routines. This type of encapsulation makes it easy to cut and paste functions and subs into future scripts, allowing you to easily reuse script code that may have taken you a while to write and debug. I'll start this chapter with a methodical look at modularization.

Looking for Modules

Modularization can sometimes seem like a lot of extra work. It's really a matter of training yourself, though: I generally find that writing my code in modules doesn't take any extra time if I do so to begin with (obviously, *converting* code to modules takes a bit of extra time). Modularization is entirely worth it, too, because it *will* save you time in the future. For example, consider the following code, which attempts to ping a computer named Server1 to see whether it's available (note that this only runs on Windows XP and later):

```
sName = "server1"
Dim cPingResults, oPingResult
Set cPingResults = _
  GetObject("winmgmts://./root/" & _
  "cimv2").ExecQuery("SELECT " & _
  "* FROM Win32_PingStatus WHERE " & _
  "Address = '" & sName & "'")
On Error Resume Next
For Each oPingResult In cPingResults
        If Not IsObject(cPingResults) Then
                bTestPing = False
        ElseIf oPingResult.StatusCode = 0 Then
```

```
                bTestPing = True
        Else
                bTestPing = False
        End If
Next
WScript.Echo bTestPing
```

This example works great, and it would be easy enough to copy and paste it into other scripts. One problem with that technique, though, is that this script is pretty specific in the way it works: I have the server name hard-coded into a variable, for example, and the result is simply displayed on the screen. Other scripts that might use this technique might need to ping a different machine, or do something different with the result. That's one good reason for making this into a standalone module; another reason is testing purposes. If I were to paste this code right into another script, I'd basically be inserting "moving parts" into that script. In other words, by adding code to a script, I'm adding complexity. This code isn't entirely self-contained, which means it might have some kind of effect on whatever script I added it into, which would increase my debugging time. No matter what I do, I *never* want to increase my debugging time!

By modularizing this code, I can make it entirely self-contained. That makes it easy to copy and paste, but reduces any negative impact to any scripts I paste it into. The first step in modularizing is to look for all the input that the code requires. In this case, that's easy: It simply requires a computer name or IP address, which is currently in the variable sName. I also want to identify the output, which is also easy: This script is storing a value in the variable bTestPing, and that's the final output.

Because this code takes input *and* returns some kind of output, I know I need to build a function. If it didn't return any output, a VBScript sub (or subroutine) would be appropriate. I start by coming up with a name for the function:

```
Function Ping()
    sName = "server1"
    Dim cPingResults, oPingResult
    Set cPingResults = _
     GetObject("winmgmts://./root/" & _
       "cimv2").ExecQuery("SELECT " & _
       "* FROM Win32_PingStatus WHERE " & _
       "Address = '" & sName & "'")
    On Error Resume Next
    For Each oPingResult In cPingResults
        If Not IsObject(cPingResults) Then
            bTestPing = False
        ElseIf oPingResult.StatusCode = 0 Then
            bTestPing = True
        Else
            bTestPing = False
        End If
    Next
```

```
    WScript.Echo bTestPing
End Function
```

Now I need to remove my hard-coded input value, and move the input into the function declaration, so that the input becomes an input argument.

```
Function Ping(sName)
    Dim cPingResults, oPingResult
    Set cPingResults = _
     GetObject("winmgmts://./root/" & _
      "cimv2").ExecQuery("SELECT " & _
      "* FROM Win32_PingStatus WHERE " & _
      "Address = '" & sName & "'")
    On Error Resume Next
    For Each oPingResult In cPingResults
        If Not IsObject(cPingResults) Then
            bTestPing = False
        ElseIf oPingResult.StatusCode = 0 Then
            bTestPing = True
        Else
            bTestPing = False
        End If
    Next
    WScript.Echo bTestPing
End Function
```

Now, I need to remove my output code, and instead return my output as the result of the function. To do that, I simply assign my output value to the name of the function itself.

```
Function Ping(sName)
    Dim cPingResults, oPingResult
    Set cPingResults = _
     GetObject("winmgmts://./root/" & _
      "cimv2").ExecQuery("SELECT " & _
      "* FROM Win32_PingStatus WHERE " & _
      "Address = '" & sName & "'")
    On Error Resume Next
    For Each oPingResult In cPingResults
        If Not IsObject(cPingResults) Then
            Ping = False
        ElseIf oPingResult.StatusCode = 0 Then
            Ping = True
        Else
            Ping = False
        End If
    Next
End Function
```

Now my code is modularized. As a quick check, I want to make sure that the code inside my function isn't relying on anything from outside the function. In other words, all of the function's variables and values should be entirely contained within the function. That keeps the function self-contained, or *encapsulated*, and makes it more standalone—which makes it easier to share between scripts.

I also want to test my new function. To do so, I'll just add a line of code in the main body of the script that calls the function:

```
WScript.Echo Ping("localhost")
```

```
Function Ping(sName)
    Dim cPingResults, oPingResult
    Set cPingResults = _
     GetObject("winmgmts://./root/" & _
      "cimv2").ExecQuery("SELECT " & _
      "* FROM Win32_PingStatus WHERE " & _
      "Address = '" & sName & "'")
    On Error Resume Next
    For Each oPingResult In cPingResults
        If Not IsObject(cPingResults) Then
            Ping = False
        ElseIf oPingResult.StatusCode = 0 Then
            Ping = True
        Else
            Ping = False
        End If
    Next
End Function
```

By running the script, I can ensure that the function is working as expected. I made sure to run this with `localhost`, which should always produce a `True` (or `-1`) output, and I also ran it with a computer name that I know isn't on my network, to make sure I got the expected `False` (or `0`) output.

This little module is now easy to reuse in other scripts. For example:

```
If Ping("Server1") Then
    'connect to server using WMI
Else
    WScript.Echo "Couldn't connect"
End If
```

Copying and pasting this function is easy enough, but if you're using SAPIEN PrimalScript, it's even easier to reuse modules. Highlight the entire function, and right-click the highlighted block of code. From the context menu, select Save As Snippet and provide a name for your new Snippet—I used the name `TestPing`. From then on, you can reuse this module very easily: Just type the name of your Snippet into the code editor on a new line, and press Ctrl+J. Your Snippet magically appears. You can also drag the Snippet from the Snippets Browser (one of the many "Nexus" windows), but I'm a big fan of the keyboard shortcut because it lets me immediately continue typing something else into my script.

When Do You Modularize?

There are really two reasons to modularize: The first is to make it easier to reuse your code. From that perspective, then, you would modularize any bit of code that you think you might use more than once—and which can be encapsulated within a sub or function (to be fair, PrimalScript Snippets can just be one or two lines of code—they don't need to be self-contained—but Snippets in and of themselves are really modularization; they're just a more convenient way of copying and pasting). As an example, I've created functions that ping computers, display debug windows, query data from databases, and so forth.

> **NOTE**
>
> You can find many of my modules and nonencapsulated Snippets at http://www. ScriptingOutpost.com; click on the Add-Ons category once you're there.

The other reason to modularize is to make debugging easier. Think of a script as a complex machine, full of moving parts, not unlike an automobile. When a complex machine breaks, the best way to find the problem is to try to isolate various subsystems and test them independently. For example, if you think you have a radiator leak, you pressure-test the radiator independently because that reduces the number of parts your test affects. Modules help accomplish that kind of isolation in a script. For example, if I have a huge script that contains all kinds of different functionality, it's very difficult to trace problems down to one particular line of code. On the other hand, if the script primarily consists of various modules, then it's easy to pull each module out into a stand-alone script, one at a time, and test each module, one at a time. If each module provides the correct output, it passes the test and you move on to the next one; if a module fails, you've significantly narrowed down the code that you need to troubleshoot.

The Downside of Copy-and-Paste

Cutting and pasting is great, as are Snippets, but it has some fundamental flaws. For example, if you decide to improve a particular function, you have to improve every copy of it that you've ever made—one copy at a time. Fortunately, VBScript provides a way to centralize and reuse the functions and subs you write: Windows Script Components (WSC).

Introduction to Windows Script Components

To properly introduce WSC, I need to dive a bit deeper into developer-speak than I'm accustomed to doing; so bear with me. First, you should realize that you're already using programming objects in your scripts. Specifically, you're using objects—or *components*—written to Microsoft's Component Object Model, or COM. I briefly touched on COM in Chapter 5, "Functions, Objects, Variables, and More," but here's a quick refresher on what it does for you.

When you create, or *instantiate*, a COM class in a script, you do so by using the `CreateObject` statement. For example, `CreateObject("Scripting.FileSystemObject")` creates a new `FileSystemObject`. When VBScript executes that command, it asks COM to load `Scripting.FileSystemObject` into memory and make it available to VBScript. COM looks up the class `Scripting.FileSystemObject` in the Registry. You can open the Registry yourself, using Regedit or another editor, and search for `Scripting.FileSystemObject`. You'll find that it has a globally unique identifier (GUID) of `{0D43FE01-F093-11CF-8940-00A0C9054228}` and that its *in-process server* (`InprocServer32`) is `C:\Windows\System32\scrrun.dll`, which is the Microsoft Scripting Runtime dynamic link library (DLL). COM loads that DLL into memory when you ask for a `FileSystemObject`.

All COM components must have an in-process server. When you create a new WSC, you're essentially creating a script that *pretends* to be a COM component. That pretense is helped by `Scrobj.dll`, which is the WSC in-process server. You can create instances of WSCs within scripts, and when you do so, COM loads `Scrobj.dll`, which, in turn, loads the actual WSC script and executes it. So, a WSC is a regular VBScript masquerading as a DLL! In fact, any programming language that uses DLLs—including Visual Basic, Delphi, VBScript, C++, and more—can use a WSC because WSCs meet all of the requirements for regular COM components.

Okay, that's enough developer-*ese* for one chapter. It's time to start looking at how you create these things.

Scripting and XML

WSCs are regular text files, but they require a special Extensible Markup Language (XML) formatting to contain the script. The XML helps describe what the WSC does, and how it is activated and used. Probably the easiest way to see how it works is to see an example, so take a look at Listing 22.1. This is a sample WSC that performs several Windows Management Instrumentation (WMI) functions. I adapted the script from one first provided on http://www.wshscripting.com, an unfortunately now-defunct website (please don't visit it—it's now one of those annoying "cybersquatter" sites that launches pop-up windows in your web browser) that offered scripting examples.

LISTING 22.1   WMIFunctions.wsc. Example WSC.

```xml
<?xml version="1.0"?>
<package>
 <comment>
 WMI Management Library
 </comment>
 <component id="WMILIB">
  <?component error="true" debug="true" ?>
  <registration progid="WMILIB.WSC"
  classid="{61E6E0DC-4554-4D12-A9F4-D8E70DBCF318}"
  description="WMI Library" remotable="no" version="1.00">
  </registration>
  <public>
   <method name="Shutdown">
    <parameter name="Host"/>
   </method>
   <method name="Reboot">
    <parameter name="Host"/>
   </method>
   <method name="StartProcess">
    <parameter name="Host"/>
    <parameter name="CommandLine"/>
    <parameter name="StartDirectory"/>
   </method>
   <method name="Processes">
    <parameter name="Host"/>
   </method>
   <method name="EndProcess">
    <parameter name="Host"/>
    <parameter name="ProcessID"/>
   </method>
  </public>
  <implements id="ASP" type="ASP"/>
  <reference guid="{00000205-0000-0010-8000-00AA006D2EA4}"
  version="2.0"/>
  <object id="Recordset" progid="ADODB.Recordset"/>
  <script id="Implementation" language="JScript">
<![CDATA[
var description = new WMILIB;

function WMILIB()
{
 this.Processes = Processes;
 this.StartProcess = StartProcess;
 this.EndProcess = EndProcess;
```

22

LISTING 22.1   Continued

```javascript
 this.Reboot = Reboot;
 this.Shutdown = Shutdown;
}

function Shutdown(Host)
{
 try
 {
  var wql = "SELECT * FROM Win32_OperatingSystem WHERE
  Primary=True";
  var os = GetObject("winmgmts://" + Host +
  "/root/cimv2").ExecQuery(wql);
  for(var en = new Enumerator(os); !en.atEnd();
  en.moveNext())
   en.item().ShutDown();
  return true;
 }
 catch(e)
 {
  return false;
 }
}

function Reboot(Host)
{
 try
 {
  var wql = "SELECT * FROM Win32_OperatingSystem WHERE
  Primary=True";
  var os = GetObject("winmgmts://" + Host +
  "/root/cimv2").ExecQuery(wql);
  for (var en = new Enumerator(os); !en.atEnd();
  en.moveNext())
   en.item().Reboot();
  return true;
 }
 catch(e)
 {
  return true;
 }
}

function StartProcess(Host, CommandLine, StartDirectory)
```

LISTING 22.1   Continued

```
{
 try
 {
  var ProcID;
  var Proc = GetObject("WinMgmts://" + Host +
  "/root/cimv2").Get("Win32_Process");
  Proc.Create(CommandLine, StartDirectory, ProcID);
  return true;
 }
 catch(e)
 {
  return false;
 }
}

function EndProcess(Host, ProcessID)
{
 try
 {
  var wql = "SELECT * FROM Win32_Process WHERE ProcessId="
  + ProcessID;
  var procs = GetObject("WinMgmts://" + Host +
  "/root/cimv2").ExecQuery(wql);
  for(var en = new Enumerator(procs); !en.atEnd();
  en.moveNext())
   en.item().Terminate;
  return true;
 }
 catch(e)
 {
  return false;
 }
}

function Processes(Host)
{
 try
 {
  var wql = "SELECT * FROM Win32_Process";
  var procs = GetObject("WinMgmts://" + Host +
  "/root/cimv2").ExecQuery(wql);
  var values = new ActiveXObject("Scripting.Dictionary");
  for(var en = new Enumerator(procs); !en.atEnd();
```

LISTING 22.1   Continued

```
en.moveNext())
 values.Add(en.item().ProcessId, en.item().Description);
 return values;
}
catch(e)
{
 return new Array(e.description);
 }
}
]]>
  </script>
 </component>
</package>
```

This particular WSC is actually written in JScript (Microsoft's implementation of
ECMAScript, which is an industry-standard language evolved from JavaScript), not
VBScript. That's an important thing to note because it doesn't matter what language the
WSC is in. You can still use it in your own VBScript files. For this example, I ignore the
actual script code and focus just on the XML packaging that makes this a WSC.

> **NOTE**
>
> Let me stress my point: *I'm not worried about the JScript code*. I just wanted to provide
> you with a usable WSC, and the code inside it is absolutely not important. What I want
> to highlight is the WSC XML formatting; if the JScript looks foreign to you, good! You'll
> be more inclined to ignore it at this point and just look at the WSC formatting.

All WSCs need to start with a basic XML declaration, and a <package> tag. This tag marks
the beginning of the WSC package.

```
<?xml version="1.0"?>
<package>
```

Next, the script includes a comment contained in <comment> tags. The comment provides
a helpful description of what the WSC does. Notice the closing </comment> tag; all XML
tags must come in pairs. Therefore, <comment> is paired with </comment>. Tags must also
be nested, which means the </comment> tag *must* appear before a </package> tag, thus
fully enclosing the comment within the package.

```
<comment>
WMI Management Library
</comment>
```

Next, the script creates an actual component. Note that each WSC file can contain multiple components within a single package, but a single file can only contain a single package. This component also contains a special tag that specifies how errors will be handled. Setting error equal to true forces errors that occur within the WSC to be displayed; setting debug to true allows the component to be debugged using the Windows Script Debugger.

```
<component id="WMILIB">
  <?component error="true" debug="true" ?>
```

Next is an important piece of the WSC: the registration. Just as the FileSystemObject has a class ID and GUID, so must your WSCs. Most important, these must be unique. There are a number of parameters required:

- ▶ Progid is optional, but provides other programmers with a friendly way of referencing your WSC. Scripting.FileSystemObject is an example of a progid.

- ▶ Classid is required, and must be a unique GUID. Microsoft provides utilities such as Uuidgen.exe to produce unique GUIDs that you can use. Editors like PrimalScript can also make one up for you.

- ▶ Description is optional, and provides a brief description of the component. This description appears in certain visual development tools when your component is loaded.

- ▶ Version is also optional, and should be a numeric version number, as shown here.

- ▶ Remotable is optional, and indicates whether the script can be running remotely using Distributed COM. I won't be covering remote WSCs in this book, although you can read more about them at http://msdn.microsoft.com/scripting.

```
<registration progid="WMILIB.WSC"
classid="{61E6E0DC-4554-4D12-A9F4-D8E70DBCF318}"
description="WMI Library" remotable="no" version="1.00">
</registration>
```

Next, your WSC needs to advertise the functions and subs it offers. These are referred to using the COM term, *method*. As you can see here, each method has its own name and list of parameters, which correspond to the input parameters of the appropriate functions or subs. These are all contained with a <public> section, indicating that these methods can be used by other scripts.

```
<public>
 <method name="Shutdown">
  <parameter name="Host"/>
 </method>
 <method name="Reboot">
```

```
    <parameter name="Host"/>
  </method>
  <method name="StartProcess">
    <parameter name="Host"/>
    <parameter name="CommandLine"/>
    <parameter name="StartDirectory"/>
  </method>
  <method name="Processes">
    <parameter name="Host"/>
  </method>
  <method name="EndProcess">
    <parameter name="Host"/>
    <parameter name="ProcessID"/>
  </method>
</public>
```

This WSC specifies an `<implements>` tag, which in this case grants it access to the Active Server Pages (ASP) object model. This isn't necessary, unless you want the WSC to be accessible from ASP pages. The `<reference>` tag specifies an external type library used by the script; this is also optional. In this case, the external type library is Microsoft's ActiveX Data Objects (ADO), so an `<object>` tag is used to reference it.

```
<implements id="ASP" type="ASP"/>
<reference guid="{00000205-0000-0010-8000-00AA006D2EA4}"
version="2.0"/>
<object id="Recordset" progid="ADODB.Recordset"/>
```

Next comes the actual script, enclosed by a `<script>` tag that includes the language. Following that are the actual functions and subs that make up the script—in this case, all JScript, but they could be VBScript just as easily. Notice that the parameters of each correspond to the parameters specified for the `<method>` tags earlier.

```
  <script id="Implementation" language="JScript">
<![CDATA[
var description = new WMILIB;

function WMILIB()
{
  this.Processes = Processes;
  this.StartProcess = StartProcess;
  this.EndProcess = EndProcess;
  this.Reboot = Reboot;
  this.Shutdown = Shutdown;
}
```

```
function Shutdown(Host)
{
 try
 {
  var wql = "SELECT * FROM Win32_OperatingSystem WHERE
  Primary=True";
  var os = GetObject("winmgmts://" + Host +
  "/root/cimv2").ExecQuery(wql);
  for(var en = new Enumerator(os); !en.atEnd();
  en.moveNext())
   en.item().ShutDown();
  return true;
 }
 catch(e)
 {
  return false;
 }
}

function Reboot(Host)
{
 try
 {
  var wql = "SELECT * FROM Win32_OperatingSystem WHERE
  Primary=True";
  var os = GetObject("winmgmts://" + Host +
  "/root/cimv2").ExecQuery(wql);
  for (var en = new Enumerator(os); !en.atEnd();
  en.moveNext())
   en.item().Reboot();
  return true;
 }
 catch(e)
 {
  return true;
 }
}

function StartProcess(Host, CommandLine, StartDirectory)
{
 try
 {
  var ProcID;
```

```
  var Proc = GetObject("WinMgmts://" + Host +
  "/root/cimv2").Get("Win32_Process");
  Proc.Create(CommandLine, StartDirectory, ProcID);
  return true;
 }
 catch(e)
 {
  return false;
 }
}

function EndProcess(Host, ProcessID)
{
 try
 {
  var wql = "SELECT * FROM Win32_Process WHERE ProcessId="
  + ProcessID;
  var procs = GetObject("WinMgmts://" + Host +
  "/root/cimv2").ExecQuery(wql);
  for(var en = new Enumerator(procs); !en.atEnd();
  en.moveNext())
   en.item().Terminate;
  return true;
 }
 catch(e)
 {
  return false;
 }
}

function Processes(Host)
{
 try
 {
  var wql = "SELECT * FROM Win32_Process";
  var procs = GetObject("WinMgmts://" + Host +
  "/root/cimv2").ExecQuery(wql);
  var values = new ActiveXObject("Scripting.Dictionary");
  for(var en = new Enumerator(procs); !en.atEnd();
  en.moveNext())
   values.Add(en.item().ProcessId, en.item().Description);
  return values;
 }
```

```
 catch(e)
 {
  return new Array(e.description);
 }
}
]]>
```

The script winds up by closing the open <script>, <component>, and <package> tags. That's it!

```
  </script>
 </component>
</package>
```

To make the WSC usable on your computer, there are two additional steps you need to take. First, you should generate a type library. This enables editors like PrimalScript to display pop-up help when using the WSC in another script; you can use tools like PrimalScript to generate the type library file, which is saved in a file with a .tlb filename extension. Generally, you can also right-click the WSC file itself and select Generate Type Library from the context menu.

You also need to register the library. This adds it to the system Registry by using Regsvr32, in much the same way that new DLLs are registered with the system. Again, right-clicking the WSC file usually displays a Register Component option on the context menu, and tools like PrimalScript also offer registration menu options. Note that the component needs to be registered on *each computer* where it will be used. You can also manually register the component from the command line:

```
Regsvr32 scrobj.dll /n /i:\path\filename.wsc
```

After the WSC is properly registered, you can start using it within your scripts. For the example in this chapter, you would use something like this:

```
Dim oWMILib
Set oWMILib = CreateObject("WMILIB.WSC")
```

If a WSC isn't registered, you can still get to it. You just have to use a slightly different method. If the WSC file is named WMILib.wsc, and stored in C:\My Documents, you could use the following:

```
Dim oWMILib
Set oWMILib = GetObject("script:c:\My Documents\WMILib.wsc")
```

This technique locates and loads the script, without having the WSC actually listed in the system Registry. However, you do have to know the exact location of the WSC file.

Summary

Modularization is a great way to make your code easier to reuse. All you need to do is become accustomed to clearly defining the input and output required of a piece of code, and then you can easily make that piece into a reusable module, such as a function or sub. Of course, copying and pasting code doesn't make long-term maintenance any easier, but that's where Windows Script Components come into play. Windows Script Components, or WSCs, are special scripts that can be executed like COM components. They make it easy to package, redistribute, and reuse scripts and routines that have taken you a long time to perfect, thus making your scripting efforts faster and more efficient. WSCs are written much like normal scripts, but have a special XML layout that allows them to be executed by `Scrobj.dll`.

CHAPTER 23

Scripts Packaging and Protection

Do you ever worry about your users seeing your script source code and somehow learning more than they should? Or, perhaps you just want to ensure that your scripts aren't modified and run by someone who shouldn't be doing so. Encrypted or encoded scripts offer a solution to these problems, and Microsoft offers a Script Encoder tool to use with your administrative scripts. The Encoder can take a script and turn it into something like this:

```
//**Start Encode**#@~^QwIAAA==@#@&0;mDkWP7nDb0zZKD.n1YAMGhk+Dvb`@#@&P,kW`UC7kLlDG
Dcl22gl:n~{'~Jtr1DGkW6YP&xDnD+OPA62sKD+ME#@#@&P,~~k6PvxC\rLmYGDcCwa.n.k
kWUbx[+X66Pcr*cJ#,@*{~!*P~P,P~. YEMU`DDE bIP,P,+s/n@#@&P~P,~PM+O;Mx`WC^
/n#pN6EU1YbWx,o Obaw.WaDrCD+nmL+v#@#@&~P7lMPdY.q,'~J_CN,Y4rkP4nnPCx,C1Y
;mV,+(PkrY~~l,wCL PmKhwmYk(snPSkDt~JI@#@&P~\m.PkY.+,'PE8MWA/ .kPGDt D
PDtmUPri@#@&,P-CMP/D.&,'Pr\rmMWkWWY~(YnDnY,2a2^WDn.,*!,Ep@#@&,P7lD,/D.
c,'~JSW;s9Ptm-+,4+ U~VK19+[REI,Pr0,c\ DrWHZW.. mOAMGS/nM`*#@#@&P,
~P9W^Es+UOchDbO+v/YMq~_,/DDfPQ~kY.c*IP,+sd @#@&~~,P[W1;s+UDRSDkD+vdYMF
~_,/O.yP_,dYM&P3~dYMc*iNz&R @*^#~@
```

Although it looks like gibberish, it still runs perfectly. You can be assured that nobody will change the script because changing a single character of the encoded script will render it useless.

Installing the Script Encoder

Microsoft's Script Encoder can be downloaded from the Scripting website at http://msdn.microsoft.com/scripting. Just click the Download link and look for the Script Encoder. You can find complete documentation online at http://msdn.microsoft.com/library/default.asp?url=/library/en-us/script56/html/seconscriptencoderoverview.asp.

The Script Encoder is a command-line tool, and is designed to run against an already written and debugged script. After you encode the script, you cannot change it; if you do need to make changes, you have to work with the original unencoded version and then re-encode the changed script.

Encoded Versus Encrypted

The Script Encoder *looks* like a form of encryption. In a way, in fact, it is a form of encryption: Clear-test script code is run through a mathematical algorithm and the result is illegible (at least to humans). The Windows Script Host (WSH) understands how to decode the script, though, allowing it to retrieve the original script code and execute it. Therefore, the Encoder can be said to use a form of encryption.

However, the Encoder isn't designed to foil all attempts at accessing your source code. *All* scripts are encoded using the same algorithm, so that any copy of the Windows Script Host can decode and execute the script. That means it isn't impossible—or even necessarily difficult—for a clever person to figure out the encoding algorithm used and create his own decoder.

You can rely on the Encoder to stop casual access to your source code, and to stop casual users from attempting to modify your scripts. However, you cannot rely on the Encoder to provide absolute protection for your scripts.

Writing Encoded Scripts

You write encoded scripts the same way you would almost any script, at least to start. Listing 23.1 shows an example.

LISTING 23.1   *ResetPW.vbs.* An unencoded administrative script written in VBScript.

```
'get user account
varUserID = inputbox ("Reset password for what user ID?")

'bind to domain user
set objUser = GetObject("WinNT://MyDomain/" & varUserID & _
  ",user")

'make up a random password
varPass = DatePart( "y", Date() )
varPass = varPass & left(varUserID, 2)

'set password
objUser.SetPassword varPass

'show password
WScript.echo "New password is " & varPass
```

You don't need to add anything special to the file; the Script Encoder recognizes the .vbs filename extension and deals with the file appropriately. To encode the file, simply run SCRENC /f resetpw.vbs. The Encoder produces a file named ResetPW.vbe, which is an encoded VBScript file. Here's what it will look like:

```
#@~^pAEAAA==@#@&BL Y,E/ D,Cm1W;xD@#@&-
mDjknD&fP{~rxaED4G6~crIn/ OPalddSWD[~6W.PS4mY~!/ DP&fQE#@#@&@#@&E4rU9PY
K~NK:1bU~Ek+M@#@&/nO,W8L`d+MPx~V+Y68N+^YvEqkUgK=zztXGG:mkUzrP'~71D`d+Mq
f,'~JBEk+.Jb@#@&@#@&BsC3 P;2,1P.C
      NG:,2m/dSWMN@#@&\m.nm/dP{P9CD+nm.YvPJHESPG1D+c#~b@#@&-
1MK1k/~x,\1.Km/dPL~^+WD`71D`/ .qG~~ *@#@&@#@&B/ OPal/kAGD9@#@&W8Lid D
? Onm/dAKDN~-mDK1kd@#@&@#@&BktWSPaC/khGD9@#@&
      UmDb2Yc+m4G~Jg+SP21ddSW.N,r/,J~',\1.Km/d@#@&@#@&2HoAAA==^#~@
```

You can also run the Script Encoder with the following syntax: SCRENC inputfile outputfile, in which case you can specify an output filename. The Script Encoder also supports the following command-line parameters:

▶ /s—Silent operation, with no feedback to the screen

▶ /f—Instructs the Encoder to overwrite the input file with the output file

▶ /l language—Specifies a new default language, either JScript or VBScript

▶ /e defaultExtension—Overrides the filename extension .vbs or .js

If you're writing scriptlets, you need to add some extra code to your scripts. Scriptlets contain <SCRIPT> and </SCRIPT> tags, as shown here:

```
<SCRIPT>
'get user account
varUserID = inputbox ("Reset password for what user ID?")

'bind to domain user
set objUser = GetObject("WinNT://MyDomain/" & varUserID & _
 ",user")

'make up a random password
varPass = DatePart( "y", Date() )
varPass = varPass & left(varUserID, 2)

'set password
objUser.SetPassword varPass

'show password
WScript.echo "New password is " & varPass
</SCRIPT>
```

You need to provide the Encoder with some cue as to how to process the file:

```
<SCRIPT LANGUAGE="VBSCRIPT">
'**Start Encode**
'get user account
varUserID = inputbox ("Reset password for what user ID?")

'bind to domain user
set objUser = GetObject("WinNT://MyDomain/" & varUserID & _
 ",user")

'make up a random password
varPass = DatePart( "y", Date() )
varPass = varPass & left(varUserID, 2)

'set password
objUser.SetPassword varPass

'show password
WScript.echo "New password is " & varPass
</SCRIPT>
```

These additions, shown in boldface, tell the Encoder which language to use and where to begin the encoding process. Anything before the **Start Encode** comment line won't be encoded, allowing you to preserve copyright statements and other comments. For example:

```
<SCRIPT LANGUAGE="VBSCRIPT">
'copyright (c)2007 Don Jones
'**Start Encode**
'get user account
varUserID = inputbox ("Reset password for what user ID?")

'bind to domain user
set objUser = GetObject("WinNT://MyDomain/" & varUserID & _
  ",user")

'make up a random password
varPass = DatePart( "y", Date() )
varPass = varPass & left(varUserID, 2)

'set password
objUser.SetPassword varPass

'show password
WScript.echo "New password is " & varPass
</SCRIPT>
```

The Encoder can also bulk-encode scripts. Simply provide a wildcard as the input file and a folder name as the output: SCRENC *.vbs c:\encoded. The Encoder encodes each script and places the encoded version in the specified folder.

Running Encoded Scripts

Encoded scripts can normally be executed just like any other script, using WScript.exe or CScript.exe, with a couple of caveats. First, if your scripts don't include <SCRIPT> tags, the filename extensions must be either .vbe (for VBScript) or .jse (for JScript). The different filename extension tells Windows Script Host (WSH) that it needs to decode the script before executing it; if you change the filename extension to .vbs (or .js), you receive a runtime error when executing the script.

When the Encoder goes to work on a file that does use <SCRIPT> tags, it changes the LANGUAGE attribute. <SCRIPT LANGUAGE="VBScript"> becomes <SCRIPT LANGUAGE= "VBScript.Encode">, for example, giving WSH the cue it needs to decode the script before trying to execute it.

Encoding: The Downside

Before you get too excited about encoding, let me stress that it can only stop a very casual user. Here's the problem with encoding: Obviously, WSH itself has to be able to *decode* your scripts to run them. If any copy of WSH, running on any computer, can decode an encoded script, then it follows that all scripts are encoded in exactly the same way. That means the encoding algorithm is static, and probably easy for a clever programmer to reverse-engineer. In fact, a web search for "Windows Script Decoder" will turn up several free tools designed to quickly decode an encoded script. In other words, while you can rely on encoding to protect your script's source code against a very casual observer, anyone with a little time on their hands can decode your script and look at the source.

That unfortunately means you can't safely include any kind of sensitive information in your script, such as administrative passwords. Yes, it might be tempting to write a script that does something under administrative credentials because you could distribute that script to users and allow those users to accomplish some task they wouldn't ordinarily have permission to do. But you can't—because those same users could decode your script, obtain the administrative password, and then proceed to do whatever they wanted.

You can't use NTFS permissions to help out, here, either: To run a script, a user must be able to read it (in other words, have Read NTFS permission to it). If they can read it to execute it, they can also read it to decode it or open it in Notepad. So it would seem that there's no real way to fully protect your scripts, or, more to the point, create a script that can do something which the person running the script wouldn't ordinarily be able to do.

Script Packaging

Script *packaging* is a better solution than encoding, especially if you need to protect the contents of your script, have your script run under security credentials other than those of the user actually running the script, and even bundle multiple files along with your script. A script *packager* is an application or utility that takes your script (sometimes more than one script, if you desire), accompanying data files, and required COM components and bundles them into a standalone executable (EXE) file. This isn't exactly "compiling," even though it produces an EXE file; your script isn't translated into native binary code, which is what usually happens when a developer compiles their source code. Instead, your script is "wrapped" in an EXE shell. When the EXE is run, it extracts your script and any associated files, and executes them. The EXE may be able to launch your script using alternate user credentials, which were specified when you created the package.

One packager you can try is the Evolved Script Packager (ESP) included in SAPIEN PrimalScript Professional and PrimalScript Enterprise (versions 4.0 and later). The ESP is available as a shortcut in the PrimalScript environment: Selecting Check/Compile Script from the Script menu, or clicking the equivalent toolbar button, will package the currently displayed script into an EXE file. However, you can gain much better control over your finished result by selecting Script Packager from the Script menu. When you do so, the Script Packager dialog box displays, as shown in Figure 23.1.

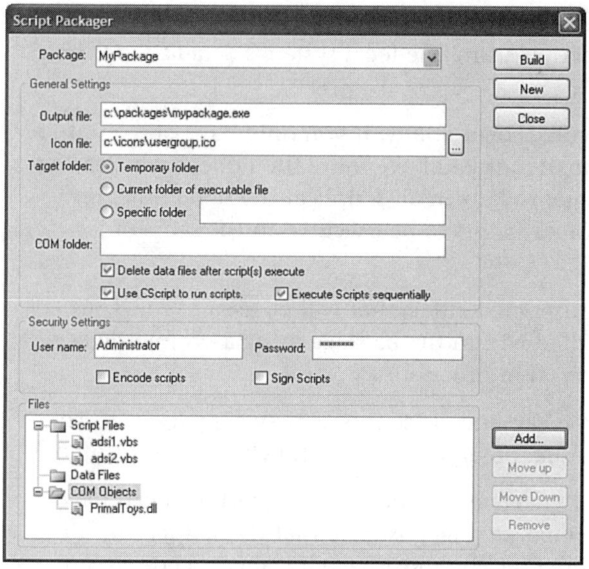

FIGURE 23.1   Script Packager dialog box.

Here's what you can do with the ESP:

▶ Specify a name for your package. This first entry field in the dialog box is actually a combo box, meaning you can type the name of a new package, or select an existing package using the drop-down list.

▶ Specify the package's output file and location. This must be a file with a .exe file-name extension.

▶ Specify a custom icon to use for the package. The icon file must be in the .ico file format; if you don't specify an icon, a default one is used.

▶ Specify the target folder. This is the folder where the packaged script will write temporary files when the package is executed. By default, it uses the system's default Temp folder. However, you can also have files written to the same folder that the EXE itself is in, or to a specific folder. What's important is that the user running the EXE must have Read-Write permissions to whatever folder you specify. Note that the temporary files *can* be read by the person running the script, if they're quick enough to open the temp file while the script is still running. Be aware of that if you decide to include any sensitive information, such as passwords, in the script.

▶ Specify a COM folder. This is the folder that will be used to store any COM objects you include in the package.

▶ You can specify that any data files included with the package be deleted as soon as the package's scripts have finished running.

▶ You can specify that CScript be used to run all scripts. If you don't select this check box, the packager will launch the scripts using the local system's default script host, which will usually be WScript.

▶ You can specify that scripts be executed sequentially. If you only have one script in your package, this option doesn't matter; if you have more than one, then clearing this check box will cause the packager to launch all scripts at the same time, in parallel. Selecting this check box forces scripts to be executed in the same order they're listed within the package.

▶ If desired, you can provide a set of user credentials that will be used to run your scripts. These credentials are encrypted within the package using a symmetric key and Windows' own CryptoAPI encryption functions.

▶ As an added measure of security, you can encode scripts as they are packaged. This will help protect the scripts from casual observation while they're being executed.

▶ If you've implemented WSH security (covered in the next chapter), you can have the packager sign your scripts before packaging, ensuring that the scripts will run under your security restrictions. Note that you must have installed a code-signing certificate and configured PrimalScript to use it for this option to work.

▶ Finally, you can add scripts, data files, and any COM objects your scripts need that wouldn't already be present on whatever computers you'll deploy the package to. You can move scripts up and down in the list, which determines their order of execution when you've selected the Execute Scripts Sequentially check box.

After the package is configured, click the Build button to create the EXE file. You can then distribute the file. When someone tries to run the file, here's what happens:

1. The package writes any included COM components to the COM folder and registers them on the local computer, so that they're available for your script to use.

2. The package writes any included data files to the target folder.

3. The package extracts your scripts and writes them to the target folder.

4. The package executes your scripts, launching them under alternate credentials if configured to do so.

5. After all scripts have finished running, the packager deletes the script files from the target folder.

6. If configured to do so, the packager deletes any included data files that were written to the target folder.

It's worth noting that all of the files bundled into the final EXE are encrypted, using a symmetric encryption key. That's not to say the files can't ever be extracted from the EXE by a hacker; after all, *nothing* is 100% secure (for example, the packager might write temp files that could be reviewed while the script is running). However, the encryption is quite strong, and decrypting the scripts would be fairly time-consuming and take quite a bit of technical knowledge; the encryption should be more than sufficient to stop users on your own network, for example, from seeing what's inside of your scripts. Certainly, the encryption provides a somewhat higher level of security than script encoding.

Summary

Script encoding offers a way to protect the source code of your scripts from prying eyes, and a way to ensure that your scripts aren't modified. Encoding doesn't provide any kind of runtime security; in other words, by default, Windows Script Host will execute *any* encoded script it's asked to execute. Packaging provides a somewhat higher level of protection for your scripts, and also provides more options for deploying your scripts, including carrying along COM components, running scripts under alternate credentials, and so forth. And PrimalScript's ESP is compatible with WSH's own security subsystem; in the next chapter, I'll show you how to use that security subsystem to lock down WSH so that only your authorized scripts execute in your environment.

23

Scripting Security

Scripting has two primary security issues associated with it. First, the Windows Script Host (WSH) is included with just about every version of Windows since Windows 98. Second, WSH associates itself with a number of filename extensions, making it very easy for users to click an email file attachment and launch unauthorized scripts. The knee-jerk reaction of many administrators is to simply disable scripting altogether, which also removes a beneficial administrative tool from the environment. In this chapter, I'll focus on ways to address the two primary security issues associated with scripting, helping you to configure a safer scripting environment.

Why Scripting Can Be Dangerous

"Why can scripting be dangerous?" isn't a question many administrators have to ask. A noticeable percentage of all new viruses, according to some authorities, are script based; certainly some of the most devastating viruses, including Nimda, Melissa, and others, propagate at least partially through scripts sent via email. Even internally produced scripts can be dangerous, as scripts can delete users, create files, and perform any number—in fact, an almost unlimited number—of tasks. There's little question about the damage scripts can do, making it vitally important that your environment be secured to allow *only* those authorized, tested scripts that you or your fellow administrators authorize.

Perhaps the most dangerous aspect of administrative scripting is the easy accessibility scripts have to the system. Users can launch scripts without even realizing that they're doing so; a large number of file extensions are registered to the Windows Script Host, and double-clicking any file with one of those extensions launches the script. In Windows XP, the default script extensions are

▶ .js for JScript files

▶ .jscript for JScript files

- ▶ .jse for JScript encoded files

- ▶ .vbe for VBScript encoded files

- ▶ .vbs for VBScript files

- ▶ .wsc for Windows Script Components

- ▶ .wsf for Windows Script Files

Note that older computers might also register .vb for VBScript files, .scr for script files, and other extensions; Windows XP cleaned up the filename extension list a bit. Don't forget, of course, static Hypertext Markup Language (HTML) files—with .html or .htm filename extensions—which can contain embedded client-side script.

> **NOTE**
>
> Other types of scripts exist, such as the Visual Basic for Applications (VBA) embedded into Microsoft Office documents. However, I'm going to focus this discussion on scripts associated with or executed by the Windows Script Host.

The goal of any security program should be to allow beneficial, authorized scripts to run, while preventing unauthorized scripts from running.

Security Improvements in Windows XP and Windows Server 2003

Windows XP and Windows Server 2003 introduced a new concept called *software restriction policies*; later versions of Windows, including Vista, also include this new feature. These policies, which are part of the computer's local security settings and can be configured centrally through Group Policy, define the software that may and may not run on a computer. By default, Windows defines two possible categories that software can fall into: *disallowed,* meaning the software won't run, and *unrestricted,* meaning the software will run without restriction. Unrestricted is the default system security level, meaning that by default all software is allowed to run without restriction.

Windows also defines *rules,* which help to categorize software into either the disallowed or unrestricted categories. By default, Windows comes with four rules, defining all system software—Windows itself, in other words—as unrestricted. This way, even if you set the default security level to disallowed, Windows will continue to be categorized as unrestricted.

You can define your own rules, as well:

- ▶ Certificate rules identify software based on the digital certificate used to sign the software.

- ▶ Hash rules identify software based on a unique checksum, which is different for any given executable file.

▶ Path rules identify software based on its file path. You can also specify an entire folder, allowing all software in that folder to run or to be disallowed.

▶ Internet Zone rules identify software based on its Internet zone location.

Therefore, you create rules that allow Windows to identify software. The rules indicate if the identified software belongs to the unrestricted or disallowed categories. Software not specifically identified in a rule belongs to whichever category is set to be the system default.

Suppose, for example, that you set the system default level to disallowed. From then on, no software will run unless it is specifically identified in a rule and categorized as unrestricted. Although it takes a lot of configuration effort to make sure everything is listed as allowed, you can effectively prevent any unauthorized software—such as scripts—from running on your users' computers.

Software restriction policies also define a list of filename extensions that are considered by Windows to be executable, and the list includes (by default) many standard WSH scripting filename extensions. The dynamic link library (DLL) filename extension is notably absent from the list. That's because DLLs never execute by themselves; they must be called by another piece of software. By allowing DLLs to run unrestricted, you avoid much of the configuration hassle you might otherwise expect. For example, you can simply authorize `Excel.exe` to run, and not have to worry about the dozens of DLLs it uses, because they aren't restricted. The default filename extension list does *not* include `.js`, `.jscript`, `.jse`, `.vbe`, `.vbs`, or `.wsf`, and I heartily recommend that you add them. For example, Figure 24.1 shows that I've added `.vbs` to the list of restricted filenames, forcing scripts to fall under software restriction policies.

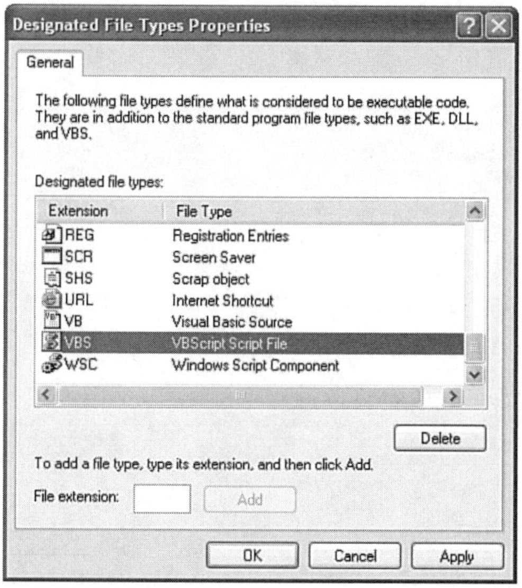

FIGURE 24.1   Placing VBS files under software restriction policy control.

With effective use of software restriction policies, you can gain immediate and effective control over which scripts run in your environment, as well as control other types of executable software. One of the most effective ways to ensure that only *your* scripts run is to sign them, and then create a software restriction policy rule that identifies your scripts by their digital signature.

Digitally Signing Scripts

A signed script includes a digital signature as a block comment within the file. You need to be using the WSH 5.6 or later Extensible Markup Language (XML) format because it contains a specific element for storing the certificate. Take Listing 24.1 as an example.

Script Signer   This script signs another script for you. Just run it with the appropriate command-line parameters shown, or run it with no parameters to receive help on the correct usage.

LISTING 24.1   *Signer.wsf.* This script signs another one.

```
<job>
 <runtime>
  <named name="file" helpstring="The script file to sign"
   required="true" type="string" />
  <named name="cert" helpstring="The certificate name"
   Required="true" type="string" />
  <named name="store" helpstring="The certificate store"
   Required="false" type="string" />
 </runtime>
 <script language="vbscript">

 Dim Signer, File, Cert, Store
 If Not WScript.Arguments.Named.Exists("cert") Or _
  Not WScript.Arguments.Named.Exists("file") Then

  WScript.Arguments.ShowUsage()
  WScript.Quit

 End If

 Set Signer = CreateObject("Scripting.Signer")
 File = WScript.Arguments.Named("file")
 Cert = WScript.Arguments.Named("cert")

 If WScript.Arguments.Named.Exists("store") Then
  Store = WScript.Arguments.Named("store")
 Else
  Store =" "
```

LISTING 24.1   Continued

```
End If

Signer.SignFile File, Cert, Store

</script>
</job>
```

Script Signer—Explained   This script is stored in an XML format, which describes its
command-line parameters. That's what the first block of XML does.

```
<job>
 <runtime>
  <named name="file" helpstring="The script file to sign"
   required="true" type="string" />
  <named name="cert" helpstring="The certificate name"
   Required="true" type="string" />
  <named name="store" helpstring="The certificate store"
   Required="false" type="string" />
 </runtime>
```

Then, the actual script begins. It checks first to see that both the "cert" and "file"
command-line arguments were provided; if they weren't, the script displays the help
information and exits.

```
<script language="vbscript">

 Dim Signer, File, Cert, Store
 If Not WScript.Arguments.Named.Exists("cert") Or _
  Not WScript.Arguments.Named.Exists("file") Then

  WScript.Arguments.ShowUsage()
  WScript.Quit

 End If
```

Assuming everything was provided, the script creates a new Scripting.Signer object and
passes it the "file" and "cert" command-line arguments.

```
 Set Signer = CreateObject("Scripting.Signer")
 File = WScript.Arguments.Named("file")
 Cert = WScript.Arguments.Named("cert")
```

If a specific certificate store is specified, that's passed to the `Signer` objects, too.

```
If WScript.Arguments.Named.Exists("store") Then
  Store = WScript.Arguments.Named("store")
Else
  Store =" "
End If
```

Finally, the `Signer`'s `SignFile` method is called to actually sign the target script file. The file is opened, and its signature is written to a comment block.

```
Signer.SignFile File, Cert, Store
```

```
</script>
</job>
```

Note that anyone can get into the file and modify its signature. However, the signature no longer matches the script, and it cannot pass the trust test conducted by WSH. Similarly, any changes to the script's code, after it is signed, fail the trust test.

Running Only Signed Scripts

If you don't want to mess around with software restriction policies, you can also rely on WSH's own built-in form of security policy. This policy allows you to specify that only signed scripts will be run; unsigned scripts won't be. This is probably the easiest and most effective way to prevent most unauthorized scripts.

To set the policy, open the Registry key HKEY_CURRENT_USER\SOFTWARE\Microsoft\Windows Script Host\Settings\TrustPolicy. Set the value to 0 to run all scripts, 1 to prompt the user if the script is untrusted, and 2 to only run trusted scripts. What's a *trusted* script? Any script that has been digitally signed by a certificate that the user's computer is config- ured to trust. For example, if you purchase a certificate from VeriSign (which all Windows computers trust by default), and use that certificate to sign your scripts, they'll run. Unfortunately, a hacker could do the same thing—but you could easily investigate the source of the certificate because it's a way to uniquely identify the signer.

WSH trust policy actually gets even more complex than that. For example, you can also set this Registry key in HKEY_LOCAL_MACHINE; the setting there will apply to all users who don't have their own setting in HKEY_CURRENT_USER. There's also a machinewide key that forces the machinewide setting to override any user-specific settings. There are other settings, as well, which govern whether the trust policy is overridden by software restric- tion policies (on Windows XP and later, software restriction policies take precedence by default) and so forth. I'll explain how to access these additional settings in a moment.

Using this built-in trust policy allows you to run only signed scripts no matter what version of Windows your users have, provided you've deployed WSH 5.6 or later to all computers. Note that this technique, because it relies on WSH and not the operating system, works on all Windows versions capable of running WSH. Many of the other techniques in this chapter—such as Software Restriction Policies—run only on Windows XP, Windows Server 2003, and later.

Ways to Implement Safe Scripting

Although Software Restriction Policies offer a promising way to control what runs on your users' computers, it's only available on XP and 2003 (and later, of course), and does require some pretty significant planning before you can roll it out. Are there any alternatives to safe scripting? Absolutely.

The Filename Extension Game

One of the easiest ways is to configure your users' computers to no longer associate `.vbs`, `.scr`, `.wsf`, and other filename extensions with the `WScript.exe` executable. Removing these file associations prevents users from double-clicking any script files and having them automatically run. To keep your own scripts running, simply associate a new filename extension—such as `.corpscript`—with `WScript.exe`. Name trusted scripts appropriately, and they'll run. It's unlikely a hacker can guess your private filename extension, making this a simple, reasonably effective means of establishing a safer scripting environment. Of course, keep in mind that WSH itself doesn't care about filename extensions. In other words, by changing filename extensions, you're simply deciding what files can be double-clicked to have WSH execute them. An attacker could still contrive a way to run something like `WScript.Exe MyVirus.txt` and, if `MyVirus.txt` contained valid script code, WSH would run it. So changing filename extensions is only marginally useful as a security measure.

Deleting the Files

You might think that simply deleting `WScript.exe` and `CScript.exe` would prevent scripts from running. Not really. To begin with, both files are under Windows File Protection (on Windows 2000 and later), meaning Windows will put the files right back in a few seconds. And, although you can tweak Windows File Protection to not include those two files, they *are* a part of the core Windows operating system, which means they're included in service packs, some hotfixes, and so forth; if deleting these files is your answer to the scripting security problem, prepare to spend a *lot* of time *keeping* them deleted. In addition, deleting them means you're *disabling* scripting, including the beneficial scripts you write yourself.

Script Signing

As I described earlier in this chapter, signing your scripts is a simple and effective way to guarantee their identity. By globally setting the WSH trust policy, you can prevent your computers from running untrusted scripts. There doesn't have to be much expense associated with this technique: You can establish your own Certification Authority (CA) root, use Group Policy to configure all client computers to trust that root, and then use the root to issue yourself a code-signing certificate.

Implementing TrustPolicy

If there's a downside to the WSH trust policy, it's that the policy has to be set on a per-machine basis. Fortunately, the policy is a Registry setting, and Group Policy can be used to modify *any* Registry setting. In the downloads for this book, at http://www.ScriptingAnswers.com/books.asp, you'll find `Wsh.adm`, a Group Policy administrative template, or add-in. Using it, you can configure *all* of the WSH trust policy settings centrally, in Active Directory.

> **NOTE**
>
> The WSH trust policy settings aren't normal Group Policy settings because they permanently change, or *tattoo*, the Registry. For that reason, the Group Policy object (GPO) Editor console won't normally show the WSH settings—the "Windows Script Host" section added by the .adm file I provide will appear empty. You need to configure the console's advanced view by right-clicking Administrative Templates, and in the dialog box, selecting the option to display unmanaged settings.

Antivirus Software

Most modern antivirus software watches for script launches and displays some kind of warning message. I don't consider this an effective means of protecting your enterprise from unauthorized scripts; it's difficult to communicate to your users which scripts are "good" and which are "bad,"' putting them into just as much trouble as before the antivirus solution stepped in to help. However, such software can provide an easy-to-deploy means of protecting against scripts, especially if you aren't planning to use your own scripts on users' machines (as in logon scripts).

Defunct Techniques

Some popular techniques have been used in the past to control scripting that I want to discuss very briefly. I don't consider these methods reliable, secure, or desirable:

▶ Removing `WScript.exe` and `CScript.exe`—As I've already described, under Windows 2000 and later, these two files are under Windows File Protection and are not easily removed to begin with. Plus, doing so completely disables scripting, which probably isn't a goal if you're reading this book.

▶ Disassociating the `.vbs`, `.wsf`, and other filename extensions—Scripts can still be executed by running `WScript.exe` *scriptname* because that doesn't require a filename extension. In other words, it doesn't require much effort for hackers to email shortcuts that do precisely that, thus defeating this technique as a safety measure.

▶ Renaming `WScript.exe` to something else—This is ineffective. Although it prevents the existing file extensions (`.vbs`, etc.) from launching `WScript.exe`, it doesn't necessarily prevent scripts from running. In addition, because `WScript.exe` is under Windows File Protection on Windows 2000 and later, the file might eventually wind up being replaced under your nose.

Summary

Scripting *can* be made safe in almost any environment. The capability of WSH to spot signed scripts and execute them, combined with your ability as an administrator to customize the filename extensions on client and server computers, can provide an effective barrier against unauthorized scripts, still allowing your own scripts to run.

24

CHAPTER **25**

Introduction to HTML Applications

Html Applications, or HTAs, have been around for a long time—since about the time that Microsoft Internet Explorer 4.0 was released, in fact. It's only fairly recently, though, that Windows administrators have started looking at them as an easy way to produce graphical utilities using nothing more than the VBScript they already know, plus some simple HTML markup code.

> **NOTE**
>
> I consider HTAs to be a fairly advanced topic, and, in fact, cover them in some detail in *Advanced VBScript for Windows Administrators* (Microsoft Press), a book I coauthored with Jeffery Hicks. In this book, I'm keeping the topic at a very introductory level, just to get you started, but do be aware that there's a lot more you can do with HTAs than what I'll cover here.

What's the allure of HTAs? After you start becoming more proficient with VBScript, you might find yourself wanting to develop script-based tools for other administrators, or even for users in your environment, who aren't very script-savvy themselves. HTAs offer a way to do that, by wrapping a simple graphical user interface, or GUI, around your VBScript. Generally speaking, an HTA can do anything a normal VBScript can do, only with some sort of simple GUI attached.

There's one caveat about HTAs, which also applies to any VBScript: An HTA runs under the security context of whatever user is running the HTA. That means the HTA can only do things that the user running the HTA has permission to do. In other words, you can't write an HTA capable of performing domain administration tasks and then give that HTA to a nonadministrator and expect it to work. Yes, for certain things you *could* code the HTA to use alternate credentials; however, there's absolutely no reliable means of preventing the person running the HTA from *seeing* those credentials. HTAs are *not* a means of bypassing Windows' security: If you want a user to be able to do something, you *have* to give them permission to do so.

Also keep in mind that HTAs are, by definition, *graphical*. That means they're no good as scheduled tasks because scheduled tasks usually run in the background where there's no way for a user to interact with the application. A normal VBScript is a much better choice for a scheduled task.

With all that out of the way, let's look at how HTAs work.

Event-Driven Scripting

Regular VBScripts are called *procedural* programs because when you run the script it immediately starts executing the first line of code, and continues executing each subsequent line of code, in order, until it reaches the end. HTAs, on the other hand, are *event-driven* programs. That is, when you run the HTA, no code actually executes by default. Instead, the HTA basically just sits and waits for the user to do something. Users' actions trigger *events*, and you can provide script code that runs in response to these events. For example, when a user clicks on a button, that generates an onClick event for that button; you can have a script that runs in response to that event.

Certain system events are also available for you to hook your scripts into. For example, whenever an HTA loads, an onLoad event is automatically triggered, and you can have a script run in response to that event, as well. Getting used to this event-driven model takes a little bit of time, because it's so different from how a normal VBScript works. After you do start to get a feel for how it works, though, you'll find that it's a pretty powerful model: You let Windows itself tell you when the user is doing something.

How an HTA Is Built

An HTA starts as a simple HTML page. Not an Active Server Pages (ASP) or other dynamic page, mind you, but a simple, static HTML page. In fact, you can start your HTA creation in any HTML editor you like, including Windows Notepad (although I prefer a What-You-See-Is-What-You-Get editor such as Microsoft FrontPage, Adobe Dreamweaver, Microsoft Expression, and so forth). Within the HTA, you usually add HTML form controls, like text boxes and buttons. Then, in a <SCRIPT> block within the HTML, you add your VBScript code. You can add subs and functions, just as you would to a normal VBScript; you also add specially named subs that are executed in response to events. These specially named subs are called *event handlers*. You can put almost any VBScript code you want within an event handler; typically, I put the majority of my HTA's functionality into standalone subs and functions, and then call those subs and functions from my event handlers.

HTA Differences

When you run an HTA, it's executed by `Mshta.exe`, a built-in component of Windows. Most notably, your HTA is *not* run by the Windows Script Host. That means your HTA script code can't use the intrinsic WScript object, for example, because that object *isn't* intrinsic to `Mshta.exe`. `Mshta.exe` also uses the installed version of Internet Explorer to actually render the HTML—that is, to turn the HTML markup tags into a visual web page. Internet Explorer, of course, is not without its quirks when it comes to things like security, so you're limited in your ability to insert things like ActiveX controls. You might also need to configure Internet Explorer's security to allow HTAs to run at all, depending on which version of Internet Explorer you have and how it's configured in the first place.

Steps for Writing an HTA

I can't stress enough that you start writing your HTA by *writing the functional VBScript code first.* Do this in completely standalone VBScript files, not an HTA; HTAs are a more complex development task, and fewer good tools are available for working with script code inside an HTA than there are for making a good VBScript. I like to write all of my functionality as subs and functions, test them in a standalone script, and *then* move them—fully debugged and working—into an HTA.

Writing the Functional Code First

For example, let's say I want to write an HTA that allows a user to type a computer name, and then see the service pack version installed on that computer. I know I'll have one piece of input: the computer name. I'll have some output, too: the service pack version number. This is a simple enough task that I can probably roll it up into a single function.

I'll start by just writing a standalone script that does what I want—no sense in complicating things until I get the basic functionality working!

```
strComputer = "."

Dim objWMI
Set objWMI = GetObject("winmgmts:\\" & _
 strComputer & "\root\cimv2")
Dim colResults, objResult, strWMIQuery
strWMIQuery = "SELECT * FROM Win32_OperatingSystem"
Set colResults = objWMI.ExecQuery(strWMIQuery)
For Each objResult In colResults
  WScript.Echo objResult.ServicePackMajorVersion
Next
```

Testing this, I can see that it works, so now I want to make it self-contained by wrapping it into a function. The first thing I need to be aware of is that call to `WScript.Echo`: That's not supported in an HTA, to begin with, and it's actually outputting what I want for my function's return value. In the interest of changing as few things as possible at a time—because changes are how bugs occur—I'm going to make just one minor change, and then test again.

```
strComputer = "."

Dim objWMI
Set objWMI = GetObject("winmgmts:\\" & _
 strComputer & "\root\cimv2")
Dim colResults, objResult, strWMIQuery
strWMIQuery = "SELECT * FROM Win32_OperatingSystem"
Set colResults = objWMI.ExecQuery(strWMIQuery)
For Each objResult In colResults
  strVer = objResult.ServicePackMajorVersion
Next

WScript.Echo strVer
```

This still uses `WScript.Echo`, but only as a way to test and make sure `strVar` contains the value I expected. Aside from the first and last line, then, this is pretty self-contained, so I'll make it into a function.

```
WScript.Echo GetSPVer(".")

Function GetSPVer(strComputer)
 Dim objWMI
 Set objWMI = GetObject("winmgmts:\\" & _
  strComputer & "\root\cimv2")
 Dim colResults, objResult, strWMIQuery
 strWMIQuery = "SELECT * FROM Win32_OperatingSystem"
 Set colResults = objWMI.ExecQuery(strWMIQuery)
 For Each objResult In colResults
   strVer = objResult.ServicePackMajorVersion
 Next
 GetSPVer = strVer
End Function
```

My function is totally self-contained: The only data going *into* the function is through an input argument; the only data coming *out* of the function is in its return value. I'm still using `WScript.Echo`, but only to *test* the function. Because it's still producing the results I expected, it's ready to be moved into an HTA.

Designing the User Interface

My function needs one piece of input and produces one piece of output, so I know that my user interface—which I'll build in HTML—needs a text box where a computer name can be typed, a button that can be clicked to run my script code, and a place for the function's output to be displayed. A complete discussion of HTML is beyond the scope of this book, but I'm going to start by simply building something in an HTML editor. Figure 25.1 shows good old Microsoft FrontPage, with a very simple web page.

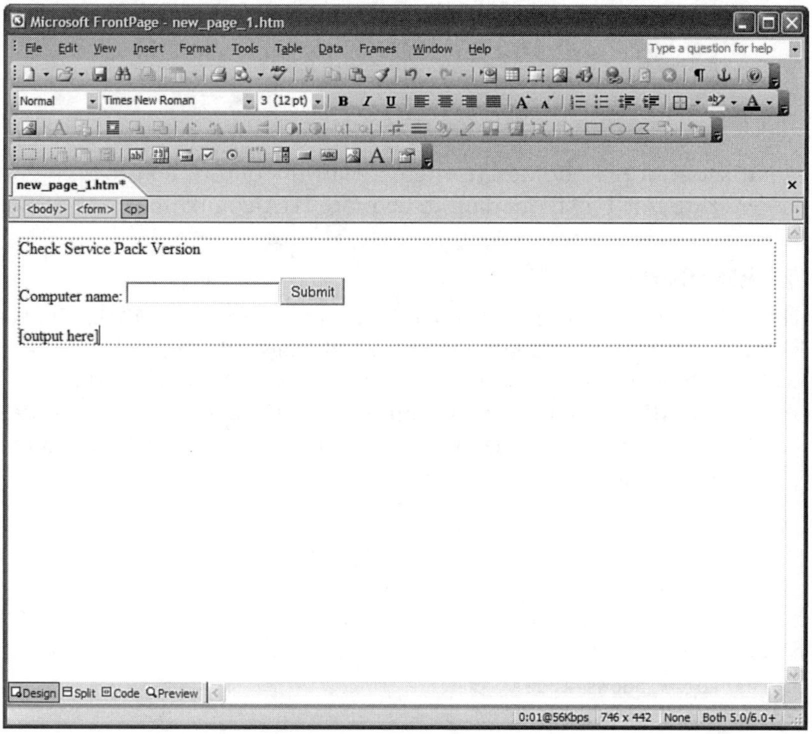

FIGURE 25.1   Building the user interface in FrontPage.

And here's the HTML that was produced:

```
<html>
<head>
<meta http-equiv="Content-Language"
 content="en-us">
<meta http-equiv="Content-Type"
 content="text/html; charset=windows-1252">
<title>New Page 1</title>
</head>

<body>

<form method="POST">
    <p>Check Service Pack Version</p>
```

```
    <p>Computer name: <input type="text"
     name="T1" size="20"><input type="submit"
      value="Submit" name="B1"></p>
    <p>[output here]</p>
</form>

</body>

</html>
```

You'll notice that I've put a sort of placeholder in where I want my output text to go. Next, I need to start converting this HTML markup to be more HTA-compatible.

Converting the HTML Code

HTAs use standard HTML, but for your scripts to properly interact with that HTML, you'll need to make some changes. First, I need to remove the <FORM> tags, which aren't necessary in an HTA and which will create some complications for my script. I also need to give an ID attribute to each HTML element I intend to interact with. Right now, that's the text box—which I need to get a computer name out of—and the button—which I need to be able to respond to a click event for. Here are my changes:

```
<html>
<head>
<meta http-equiv="Content-Language"
 content="en-us">
<meta http-equiv="Content-Type"
 content="text/html; charset=windows-1252">
<title>New Page 1</title>
</head>

<body>

<p>Check Service Pack Version</p>
<p>Computer name: <input type="text"
 name="txtComputer" id="txtComputer"
  size="20"><input id="btnSubmit"
  type="submit"
  value="Submit" name="btnSubmit"></p>
<p>[output here]</p>

</body>

</html>
```

You'll notice that, in addition to adding the ID attribute to the two `<INPUT>` tags, I also changed their existing `Name` attribute to match the ID I'd selected. This isn't strictly necessary, but it does help prevent confusion over what to call each tag. Next, I need to provide a place where my script can place the output from my function. This is done by using a `<DIV>` tag or a `<SPAN>` tag. These tags don't have any visual appearance, but they provide a "container" that a script can insert text into.

```
<html>
<head>
<meta http-equiv="Content-Language"
 content="en-us">
<meta http-equiv="Content-Type"
 content="text/html; charset=windows-1252">
<title>New Page 1</title>
</head>

<body>

<p>Check Service Pack Version</p>
<p>Computer name: <input type="text"
 name="txtComputer" id="txtComputer"
  size="20"><input id="btnSubmit"
  type="submit"
  value="Submit" name="btnSubmit"></p>
<p><span id="lblOutput"></span></p>

</body>

</html>
```

This HTML is almost ready to go. The last step is to save it in a file with an HTA filename extension, and to add the special `<HTA>` tag. This tag allows you to control aspects of the HTA like its window size, window border, icon, and so forth. You'll find a complete reference to this tag at http://msdn2.microsoft.com/en-us/library/ms536471.aspx. I'll just add a basic `<HTA>` tag to get things started.

```
<html>
<head>
<meta http-equiv="Content-Language"
 content="en-us">
<meta http-equiv="Content-Type"
 content="text/html; charset=windows-1252">
<title>New Page 1</title>
<hta:application
        applicationname="MyHTA"
        border="dialog"
```

25

```
            borderstyle="normal"
            caption="My HTML Application"
            contextmenu="no"
            icon="myicon.ico"
            maximizebutton="no"
            minimizebutton="yes"
            navigable="no"
            scroll="no"
            selection="no"
            showintaskbar="yes"
            singleinstance="yes"
            sysmenu="yes"
            version="1.0"
            windowstate="normal"
>
</head>

<body>

<p>Check Service Pack Version</p>
<p>Computer name: <input type="text"
 name="txtComputer" id="txtComputer"
  size="20"><input id="btnSubmit"
  type="submit"
  value="Submit" name="btnSubmit"></p>
<p><span id="lblOutput"></span></p>

</body>

</html>
```

Note that the <HTA> tag goes into the <HEAD> section of the HTML, which is also where your script code will go.

Adding Code

The next step is to add your script code to the HTA. Code is added into a <SCRIPT> block, and you can basically just copy and paste any subs or functions.

```
<html>
<head>
<meta http-equiv="Content-Language"
 content="en-us">
<meta http-equiv="Content-Type"
 content="text/html; charset=windows-1252">
<title>New Page 1</title>
<hta:application
```

```
        applicationname="MyHTA"
        border="dialog"
        borderstyle="normal"
        caption="My HTML Application"
        contextmenu="no"
        icon="myicon.ico"
        maximizebutton="no"
        minimizebutton="yes"
        navigable="no"
        scroll="no"
        selection="no"
        showintaskbar="yes"
        singleinstance="yes"
        sysmenu="yes"
        version="1.0"
        windowstate="normal"
>
<script language="vbscript">
Function GetSPVer(strComputer)
 Dim objWMI
 Set objWMI = GetObject("winmgmts:\\" & _
  strComputer & "\root\cimv2")
 Dim colResults, objResult, strWMIQuery
 strWMIQuery = "SELECT * FROM Win32_OperatingSystem"
 Set colResults = objWMI.ExecQuery(strWMIQuery)
 For Each objResult In colResults
   strVer = objResult.ServicePackMajorVersion
 Next
 GetSPVer = strVer
End Function
</script>
</head>

<body>

<p>Check Service Pack Version</p>
<p>Computer name: <input type="text"
 name="txtComputer" id="txtComputer"
  size="20"><input id="btnSubmit"
  type="submit"
  value="Submit" name="btnSubmit"></p>
<p><span id="lblOutput"></span></p>

</body>

</html>
```

25

Here, I've just added a VBScript <SCRIPT> tag into the <HEAD> section of my HTA, and pasted in the already tested function from earlier. The last step is to wire up an event handler, so that my code executes when the user clicks the button.

Wiring Up Events

There are two ways to wire up event handlers. The first, and for me the easiest, is to create a specially named subroutine in the <SCRIPT> section of the HTA:

```
Sub btnSubmit_onClick()
End Sub
```

This sub's name isn't case sensitive, but it does have a special syntax: first, the ID of the HTML control that I want to handle an event for, then an underscore, and then the name of the event I want to handle. You can visit http://msdn2.microsoft.com/en-us/library/ms533054.aspx for a complete list of HTML tags and the events that each one supports.

The second way to wire up an event is to create a sub with an arbitrary name:

```
Sub Go()
End Sub
```

And then add a special event handler attribute to the HTML tag:

```
<input id="btnSubmit"
  type="submit" onclick="Go"
  value="Submit" name="btnSubmit">
```

Here, I've set up an onClick event, telling it to run the Go subroutine when that event occurs to the tag—that is, to the button. This method is useful if you want multiple controls to call a single subroutine or function when an event occurs. For the remainder of this example, though, I'll continue to use the first method of wiring up the event.

Whichever method you use, you need to put some code into your event handler. This code needs to get the computer name that was typed, call the GetSPVer() function, and put the function's output into the <SPAN> tag I created earlier. I'll do this in three lines of VBScript:

```
Sub btnSubmit_onClick()
 strComputer = txtComputer.value
 strResult = GetSPVer(strComputer)
 lblOutput.innerHTML = strResult
End Sub
```

Here, I've gotten the value—that is, the contents—of the txtComputer text box, and stored it in the strComputer variable. Next, I run the GetSPVer() function, passing it the computer name, and saving the function's output in the strResult variable. I then put the contents of strResult into the <SPAN> tag's innerHTML property—the property that controls what appears *between* the <SPAN> and </SPAN> tags. The result is Listing 25.1.

LISTING 25.1   SampleHTA.hta Queries the service pack version from a remote computer

```
<html>
<head>
<meta http-equiv="Content-Language"
 content="en-us">
<meta http-equiv="Content-Type"
 content="text/html; charset=windows-1252">
<title>New Page 1</title>
<hta:application
        applicationname="MyHTA"
        border="dialog"
        borderstyle="normal"
        caption="My HTML Application"
        contextmenu="no"
        icon="myicon.ico"
        maximizebutton="no"
        minimizebutton="yes"
        navigable="no"
        scroll="no"
        selection="no"
        showintaskbar="yes"
        singleinstance="yes"
        sysmenu="yes"
        version="1.0"
        windowstate="normal"
>
<script language="vbscript">
Function GetSPVer(strComputer)
 Dim objWMI
 Set objWMI = GetObject("winmgmts:\\" & _
  strComputer & "\root\cimv2")
 Dim colResults, objResult, strWMIQuery
 strWMIQuery = "SELECT * FROM Win32_OperatingSystem"
 Set colResults = objWMI.ExecQuery(strWMIQuery)
 For Each objResult In colResults
   strVer = objResult.ServicePackMajorVersion
 Next
 GetSPVer = strVer
End Function
Sub btnSubmit_onClick()
 strComputer = txtComputer.value
```

25

LISTING 25.1   Continued

```
 strResult = GetSPVer(strComputer)
 lblOutput.innerHTML = strResult
End Sub
</script>
</head>

<body>

<p>Check Service Pack Version</p>
<p>Computer name: <input type="text"
 name="txtComputer" id="txtComputer"
  size="20"><input id="btnSubmit"
  type="submit"
  value="Submit" name="btnSubmit"></p>
<p><span id="lblOutput"></span></p>

</body>

</html>
```

Give this HTA a try!

Summary

This has been a very quick look at HTAs, what they can do, and how to build them. As I mentioned before, this is a fairly advanced topic, but it's becoming so popular that I wanted to at least introduce you to HTAs. If you decide to explore them further, there are several places you can go to for more information:

▶ The Forums on http://www.ScriptingAnswers.com include a special forum specifically for HTA scripting.

▶ As I mentioned, my book *Advanced VBScript for Windows Administrators* (Microsoft Press) covers HTAs in more detail.

▶ Microsoft's MSDN Library, a free online reference, includes reference information for both HTML tags and for HTAs themselves. Start exploring at http://msdn2. microsoft.com/en-us/library/aa155093.aspx.

Obviously, the more you play with HTAs, the more you'll want to customize them, and you can make HTAs that look almost like a "real" Windows application. Most of that work is just in formatting your HTA to look the way you want, and a good HTML editor can help you do that pretty easily.

CHAPTER 26

Debugging Tips, Tools, and Techniques

Face it: Bugs happen. Even the best scripter in the world manages to squeeze a bug or two into a script every now and then. Obviously, one goal while writing a script should be to prevent the bugs you can, and I'll share some tips for doing so. However, bugs are pernicious, and you're going to have to spend time hunting them down and eliminating them. What I want to do, then, is show you some ways to make debugging more efficient and effective, so that you don't have to spend any more time doing it than is absolutely necessary.

Types of Bugs

There are really only two types of bugs, or errors, in the world: *syntax errors* and *logic errors*. A syntax error is often just as simple as a typo, and VBScript will often give you an error message indicating exactly what the problem is and where it's located. Syntax errors can also be prevented as you're writing the script, if you're using the right techniques. In fact, I'd guess that you can prevent perhaps 90% or more of your syntax errors just by being careful and using the right scripting technique.

Logic errors, on the other hand, are more painful. They're not "errors" in the classic sense, in that VBScript doesn't necessarily stop running your script and display an error message. Instead, a logic error causes your script to behave unexpectedly. Perhaps VBScript is producing an error that doesn't make any sense, or perhaps your script just isn't producing any output where you expect it to. These errors are the most frustrating, and they can take the most time to track down. I can't promise to help you prevent these types of bugs, but I *can* show you some ways to track them down and fix them a lot faster. However, let's start with the easy bugs, first: syntax errors.

Preventing Syntax Errors

Preventing syntax errors is easy enough: Just don't ever make a mistake. That would be nice, wouldn't it? Unfortunately, as mere humans, we're all too likely to make mistakes. Heck, this book undoubtedly has a few typos, and that's after several editors have had a look at it—these things just happen! Fortunately, there are some things you can do to help keep typos and other syntax errors from sneaking into your scripts.

Use a VBScript Editor—and Pay Attention!

The first thing to do is to use a script editor. And not just any editor—especially not Notepad—but rather an editor specifically designed for VBScript. I use SAPIEN PrimalScript, as I've mentioned before; however, most of the features I'm going to show you right now are available in nearly any commercial script editor, so take your pick. The first is syntax color-coding. That's where the editor automatically colors VBScript keywords one color, string literals another color, comments a third color, and so forth. The feature is often billed as making your code easier to read—which it certainly does— but if you're paying attention as you're typing, then it'll also help prevent typos. For example, in my editor, VBScript keywords are colored blue. So, if I type a keyword like Dim, it turns blue right after I type the *m*. However, if I've misspelled the keyword— perhaps "Dom"—it won't turn blue. Because I'm watching the screen as I type, the color-change I expect never occurs, and that alerts me visually to a problem. Right away, I backspace and fix my typo—*before* it becomes a bug.

Newer versions of PrimalScript offer an enhancement to this feature called Live Syntax Checking (I'm not aware of any other VBScript editors that provide this, although it's also a feature in Microsoft Visual Studio). This basically works like automatic spell-checking in Microsoft Word: After you finish typing a line of VBScript code, the editor passes it off to the VBScript language engine. Many different types of errors—such as failing to close an If with an End If—can be detected at this point, and any errors are underlined with a special red underline (just like in Word!) to draw your attention. Again, this is just a matter of paying attention to what the editor is showing you: These visual cues like color-coding and underlining can help prevent bugs.

Most script editors that understand VBScript also provide some kind of code-completion feature. These are those little pop-up menus, shown in Figure 26.1, that help to complete language keywords, COM ProgIDs, and so forth. You've probably thought of these features—often referred to by brand names such as IntelliSense (a Microsoft brand), PrimalSense, and so forth—as a convenience, or as a way to write scripts a bit faster. They're certainly a convenience, but they also help prevent bugs: If you're letting your editor do more of the typing, you're less likely to make a typing mistake yourself. You're also less likely to use an improper property or method name. For example, I get used to WMI's ExecQuery() method. When I start using ActiveX Data Objects (ADO) to do database scripting, I'll forget and try to use ExecQuery() with my database connection.

Unfortunately, ADO uses `Execute()`. When I'm using code completion, though, I never make that mistake because I just type `Exec`—the first part of the method name—and press Enter, letting my editor complete the method name based on the ones it knows are valid for that situation.

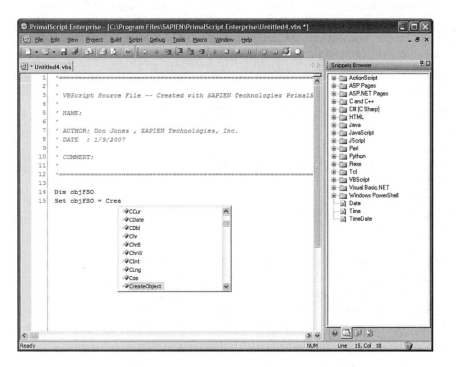

FIGURE 26.1   Code-completion in a VBScript editor.

A well-built editor can help prevent bugs in any number of ways, after you've trained yourself to use its features and pay attention to the visual cues it's giving you.

Use Option Explicit

I think the number-one cause of syntax errors—and more than a few logic errors, actually—is variable declaration. This is easier to illustrate than to just talk about, so take a look at this short script snippet:

```
Dim objFSO, objTS
Set objFSO = CreateObject("Scripting.FileSystemObject")
Set objTA = objFSO.OpenTextFile("c:\file.txt")
Do Until objTS.AtEndOfStream
  WScript.Echo objTS.ReadLine
Loop
```

Can you spot the error? It's just a single character. VBScript will actually produce an error message with this script, but it'll tell me that the error is on line 4 (that's the Do Until statement). That's misleading because there's not a thing in the world wrong with line 4. Line 4 uses the variable objTS, which I clearly defined on the first line of this script. The problem is actually just above it, on line 3: See where I misspelled variable objTS, instead typing objTA? Because VBScript allows implicit variable declaration, it just created variable objTA on the fly and made that my text stream. Variable objTS—the one I intended to use—never got set to anything, so it wasn't available when line 4 came around.

This is especially hard to trace down in a larger script, and VBScript is no help at all because it just keeps pointing you to "errors" on lines where there's not really a problem. The trick is to make VBScript stop allowing implicit variable declaration:

```
Option Explicit
Dim objFSO, objTS
Set objFSO = CreateObject("Scripting.FileSystemObject")
Set objTA = objFSO.OpenTextFile("c:\file.txt")
Do Until objTS.AtEndOfStream
  WScript.Echo objTS.ReadLine
Loop
```

I've added just one line of code to my script: Option Explicit. Now, VBScript will produce an error on the actual line where the error is, which is now line 4. Because I declared objTS and not objTA, any use of objTA will result in an error, and VBScript will tell me that I have an undeclared variable. That's a sensible, understandable error message, and it'll point to the proper line of the script, helping me fix the problem faster.

Now, I'll admit that I didn't declare every variable in this book's scripts, and I didn't use Option Explicit most of the time. I'm allowed: The scripts in the book are meant as examples, after all, and I wanted to eliminate anything that wasn't pertinent to help keep things clear and focused. However, when I'm writing scripts for actual use in my production environment, or for customers, I *always* use Option Explicit. In fact, I've modified the template .vbs file that my script editor uses when I start a new VBScript file, so that the template itself contains the Option Explicit statement. That way, I can't forget to use it, and it's always there helping to make sure I don't mistype a variable name.

Reuse Your Code

Another really easy to way to prevent bugs is to reuse script code that you've already debugged. Some script editors have a "snippet" function—I've mentioned PrimalScript's before—that lets you browse a library of code snippets and drag them right into your script. So, anytime I write a little piece of code that I think might be useful again in the future, I make a snippet out of it. Then, whenever I need to use that code again, I just insert the snippet into my script. At this point, I have close to 300 of these snippets, and perhaps 50 or so that I use regularly enough that I actually remember the filenames I've assigned them. I just type the filename and press a hotkey in my editor, and I'm done. This not only makes scripting faster, but it helps prevent bugs because I'm not actually *typing* any script code—there's no opportunity for me to make a mistake!

For example, when working with WMI, I'll start in my script by typing `WMIConnection` and pressing Ctrl+J, and then typing `WMIQuery` and pressing Ctrl+J. Those are the names of two snippets I've saved that connect to WMI and issue a WMI query. It's about a dozen lines of code, which are completely debugged already.

In the end, it doesn't matter *how* you choose to reuse your code—either by using something like snippets or just keeping a big text file full of chunks of script code—so long as you realize that reusing code not only saves time, it helps to prevent bugs.

Debugging Logic Errors

Now it's time for the toughest bugs of all: the logic errors. The ones that defy your every attempt to squash them, produce no actual error messages, and just frustrate the heck out of you. You *can* solve these types of errors using a very basic methodology, which I'm about to share. However, I'll warn you: You have to actually *follow these steps*. There are no shortcuts—in fact, you'll find over time that shortcuts do nothing but make the debugging process take even longer.

Do Not Spaghetti-Debug!

I've started using the phrase *spaghetti debugging* to describe the way I see a lot of administrators trying to debug their scripts. It's a lot like trying to see if spaghetti is cooked or not by throwing pieces at the wall: Nope, that didn't stick. Nope, that didn't stick, either. They just keep staring at their script until they *think* they see something that *might* be a problem. When they do, they cry, "Eureka!" and make a change to their script As often as not, this doesn't fix the problem, so they start over. Before long, there's spaghetti all over the floor and they're frustrated as heck. So the first thing I try to teach them is to *never make a change unless you can prove it's necessary*. This is that Scientific Method you might have learned in school: If you have a theory about why your script isn't working, try to gather some evidence to prove or disprove that theory. *Then* make a change to your script, based on the evidence you found, to fix it. This is a lot faster and more accurate than just making random changes here and there. It's definitely less frustrating! Another good technique is to only make one change at a time. If it doesn't fix the problem, undo it and make the next change. That way, you're not introducing all-new bugs with your changes and making the process even more complicated as you go.

To illustrate this debugging process, I'm going to start with the following script, *which definitely has bugs in it*. I'm pointing that out so you don't try to just type it in and run it—please don't. And feel free to scan it now and see if you can find any bugs—but remember, until you can *prove* that something in particular is causing a problem, with hard evidence, you're not allowed to shout "Eureka!" or anything.

```
'computers are a comma-delimited list
Dim strComputers
strComputers = "Don-laptop,localhost," & _
  "server1,server2"
```

```
'break the list into an array
Dim arrComputers
arrComputers = Split(strComputers,".")

'go through the array and ping
Dim strComputer
For Each strComputer In arrComputers
    If TestPing(strComputer) Then
        WScript.Echo strComputer & _
          ": Reachable"
    Else
        WScript.Echo strComputer & _
          ": Not reachable"
    End If
Next

Function TestPing(sName)
    On Error Resume Next
    Dim cPingResults, oPingResult
    Set cPingResults = _
     GetObject("winmgmts://./" & _
     "root/cimv2").ExecQuery("SELECT * " & _
     "FROM Win32_PingStatus WHERE Name = '" & _
     sName & "'")
    For Each oPingResult In cPingResults
        If oPingResult Is Null Then
            TestPing = False
        ElseIf oPingResult.StatusCode = 0 Then
            TestPing = True
        Else
            TestPing = False
        End If
    Next
End Function
```

The theoretical purpose of this script is to take a comma-delimited list of server names and ping them. I know that at least the "localhost" server should be reachable, so I expect to get some output from my script. When I run it, however, I get unexpected output:

```
Microsoft (R) Windows Script Host Version 5.6
Copyright (C) Microsoft Corporation 1996-2001. All rights reserved.

Don-laptop,localhost,server1,server2: Not reachable
Exit code: 0 , 0000h
```

Time to start debugging.

Break It Down

This isn't a supercomplicated script, but it does have a few separate sections. What I want to do first is start breaking these down and testing them individually. Face it, it's always easier to find a problem when you've got fewer "moving parts," so to speak, so my goal right now is to just reduce the number of moving parts I have to test at the same time. I'm going to start by moving just this code into its own script for testing:

```
'computers are a comma-delimited list
Dim strComputers
strComputers = "Don-laptop,localhost," & _
 "server1,server2"

'break the list into an array
Dim arrComputers
arrComputers = Split(strComputers,".")
```

On its own, this isn't going to do anything visible that I can test, so I need to add a few more lines of code just to produce some test results.

```
'computers are a comma-delimited list
Dim strComputers
strComputers = "Don-laptop,localhost," & _
 "server1,server2"

'break the list into an array
Dim arrComputers
arrComputers = Split(strComputers,".")

For Each strComputer In arrComputers
  WScript.Echo strComputer
Next
```

My expectation is that my four computer names will each appear on a line by themselves. When I run the script, I get the following.

```
Microsoft (R) Windows Script Host Version 5.6
Copyright (C) Microsoft Corporation 1996-2001. All rights reserved.

Don-laptop,localhost,server1,server2
Exit code: 0 , 0000h
```

Not quite what I was expecting. It printed all of the computers on one line, with the commas, almost as if they hadn't been split into an array at all. That makes me suspect line 8, which is where I use the `Split()` function. With my attention drawn to the right area, I spot the problem: I'm feeding the function a comma-delimited list, but asking it to split the list on the period character—and there aren't any periods in the string. That's an easy typo to overlook in an editor because the difference between a period and a comma is just a couple of pixels on the screen. However, I *do not* go back to my original script at this point: I've got some evidence of a problem, but I'm going to test this independently until I get it working. I change the period to a comma on line 8, and try again.

```
Microsoft (R) Windows Script Host Version 5.6
Copyright (C) Microsoft Corporation 1996-2001. All rights reserved.


Don-laptop
localhost
server1
server2
Exit code: 0 , 0000h
```

That's what I was expecting. So I'll make this same change in my original script, and run it again.

```
Microsoft (R) Windows Script Host Version 5.6
Copyright (C) Microsoft Corporation 1996-2001. All rights reserved.


Don-laptop: Not reachable
localhost: Not reachable
server1: Not reachable
server2: Not reachable
Exit code: 0 , 0000h
```

Better, but I'm pretty sure `localhost` should be reachable, and I can manually ping Server2 on my network, so that one doesn't make any sense, either. Time for more debugging.

Get Inside the Script

At this point, I need to get inside my script and see what's actually going on. I need to see what data is in each variable, and what each operation is producing. To begin with, I'm going to add a *very* useful little snippet I wrote to the end of my script. Here it is:

```
Dim oIE
Sub Debug(strText)

        'HOW TO USE:
        ' --> Debug("This is the text")
        ' This will display "this is the text" in a debug window

        'uncomment the next line to turn off debugging
        'Exit Sub

    If Not IsObject(oIE) Then
```

```
    Set oIE = CreateObject("InternetExplorer.Application")
    oIE.Navigate "about:blank"
    oIE.Visible = True
    oIE.ToolBar = False
    oIE.Width = 200
    oIE.Height = 300
    oIE.Left = 10
    oIE.Top = 10
    Do While oIE.Busy
     WScript.Sleep 100
    Loop
    oIE.Document.Body.InnerHTML = "<b>" & Now & _
     "</b><br>"
  End If
  oIE.Document.Body.InnerHTML = _
    oIE.Document.Body.InnerHTML & strText & _
      "<br>" & VbCrLf
  End Sub
```

Whenever I call this subroutine, and pass it a line of text or something, it'll display that text in a Microsoft Internet Explorer window, which it opens the first time I call the subroutine. I call this a "debug window" or a "trace window," and you'll see how I use it in a moment. I like this technique because it keeps my "debug output" separate from any legitimate output of my script, and because I can easily turn off "debugging mode" just by uncommenting the Exit Sub line within the subroutine. With this sub added to the end of my script, I'm going to modify my script as follows:

```
'computers are a comma-delimited list
Dim strComputers
strComputers = "Don-laptop,localhost," & _
 "server1,server2"

'break the list into an array
Dim arrComputers
arrComputers = Split(strComputers,",")

'go through the array and ping
Dim strComputer
For Each strComputer In arrComputers
        Debug "strComputer: " & strComputer
    If TestPing(strComputer) Then
        Debug "TestPing True"
        WScript.Echo strComputer & _
          ": Reachable"
    Else
        Debug "TestPing False"
```

```
        WScript.Echo strComputer & _
          ": Not reachable"
    End If
Next

Function TestPing(sName)
    On Error Resume Next
    Debug "TestPing: sName: " & sName
    Dim cPingResults, oPingResult
    strQuery = "SELECT * " & _
     "FROM Win32_PingStatus WHERE Name = '" & _
     sName & "'"
    Debug "TestPing: strQuery: " & strQuery
    Set cPingResults = _
     GetObject("winmgmts://./" & _
     "root/cimv2").ExecQuery(strQuery)
    For Each oPingResult In cPingResults
        Debug "TestPing: Enumerating Results"
        If oPingResult Is Null Then
            TestPing = False
        ElseIf oPingResult.StatusCode = 0 Then
            TestPing = True
        Else
            TestPing = False
        End If
    Next
End Function

Dim oIE
Sub Debug(strText)

        'HOW TO USE:
        ' --> Debug("This is the text")
        ' This will display "this is the text" in a debug window

        'uncomment the next line to turn off debugging
        'Exit Sub

    If Not IsObject(oIE) Then
     Set oIE = CreateObject("InternetExplorer.Application")
     oIE.Navigate "about:blank"
     oIE.Visible = True
     oIE.ToolBar = False
     oIE.Width = 200
     oIE.Height = 300
```

```
        oIE.Left = 10
        oIE.Top = 10
        Do While oIE.Busy
         WScript.Sleep 100
        Loop
        oIE.Document.Body.InnerHTML = "<b>" & Now & _
         "</b><br>"
    End If
    oIE.Document.Body.InnerHTML = _
      oIE.Document.Body.InnerHTML & strText & _
        "<br>" & VbCrLf
End Sub
```

I boldfaced the lines I changed so that you can see them. Essentially, I've called Debug each time I change the contents of a variable, writing the variable's new contents into my window. This ensures that I know exactly what data my script is working with. I've also modified my TestPing() function so that the WMI query is going into a string variable. This change allows me to write the query itself to my debug window, so that I can make sure it's what I wanted it to be—and for another debugging trick I'll show you in a moment.

When I run the script this time, an Internet Explorer window pops up containing the following:

```
1/9/2007 8:21:27 AM
strComputer: Don-laptop
TestPing: sName: Don-laptop
TestPing: strQuery: SELECT * FROM Win32_PingStatus WHERE Name = 'Don-laptop'
TestPing: Enumerating Results
TestPing False
strComputer: localhost
TestPing: sName: localhost
TestPing: strQuery: SELECT * FROM Win32_PingStatus WHERE Name = 'localhost'
TestPing: Enumerating Results
TestPing False
strComputer: server1
TestPing: sName: server1
TestPing: strQuery: SELECT * FROM Win32_PingStatus WHERE Name = 'server1'
TestPing: Enumerating Results
TestPing False
strComputer: server2
TestPing: sName: server2
TestPing: strQuery: SELECT * FROM Win32_PingStatus WHERE Name = 'server2'
TestPing: Enumerating Results
TestPing False
```

Another advantage of that debug window is that it's easier to copy and paste the output—allowing me to paste it into this book, for example. As you can see, my variables—strComputer, sName, and strQuery—do contain data, and it's more or less what I expect. I mean, the WMI queries look valid and all that, but the TestPing() function is still producing False when it shouldn't be. Next step: Stop scripting.

Get Out of the Script

Whenever you're getting into an inexplicable error, it helps to stop using a script to test things. Instead, try to use some external tool. In this case, because I'm working with WMI, I'm going to turn to Wbemtest.exe, an external graphical tool that I've covered several times throughout this book. Fortunately, I have my exact WMI query helpfully displayed in my debug window, so after opening Wbemtest and connecting to the root\cimv2 namespace (the same namespace my script is using), I can just copy and paste my query into Wbemtest. So I grab my first query, SELECT * FROM Win32_PingStatus WHERE Name = 'localhost', from the debug window and paste it into Wbemtest, which promptly informs me that this is an "Invalid Query." Aha—maybe that has something to do with why my script isn't working!

But wait a minute, why isn't VBScript itself giving me this error? Because I've enabled error handling on line 26 with On Error Resume Next. That suppresses any errors VBScript might want to complain about, even though I'm not explicitly checking for errors on my own. So my first change is going to be to comment out the On Error Resume Next, so that I can *see* any errors that occur. However, I still have this invalid WMI query to fix. The query *looks* okay to me, but what do I know? So I hop onto the WMI documentation for the Win32_PingStatus class, available at http://msdn2. microsoft.com/en-us/library/aa394350.aspx. Take a look and see if you can spot the problem.

Did you see it? The Win32_PingStatus class doesn't define a Name property—it has an Address property instead. Oops! That's possible evidence of a problem in my query. However, I'm *not* going to rush into my script and make a change until I've *proven* that this is the problem: Back to Wbemtest, where I'll execute a modified query, SELECT * FROM Win32_PingStatus WHERE Address = 'localhost'. Eureka! My query worked this time, so it's back to my script to make that same, single change.

Running my script takes longer this time—because it's actually doing something—but I still get the same old output. Rats. Okay, I'm going to add more detailed debugging output; here's the revised portion of my script:

```
For Each oPingResult In cPingResults
    Debug "TestPing: Enumerating Results"
    If oPingResult Is Null Then
            Debug "Result was Null"
        TestPing = False
    ElseIf oPingResult.StatusCode = 0 Then
            Debug "StatusCode was 0"
        TestPing = True
```

```
    Else
            Debug "Else - StatusCode " & _
            oPingResult.StatusCode
        TestPing = False
    End If
Next
```

Once again, I've boldfaced the changed lines. You can see that all I'm doing is outputting something to my debug window no matter which path the script takes through that If/ElseIf/Else/End If construct, so that I can get a better idea of what's going on inside the script. Running again, I get the following debug output (this is just a portion of it so that you can see what's happening):

```
TestPing: sName: localhost
TestPing: strQuery: SELECT * FROM Win32_PingStatus WHERE Address = 'localhost'
TestPing: Enumerating Results
Result was Null
TestPing False
```

Interesting. It's telling me that my ping results were Null each time. Well, I know that's not true because I tested this query in Wbemtest and it returned something other than Null. I don't know why that's going on; I'd added the check for Null because I'd read that, if you try to use Win32_PingStatus with an unreachable address, it didn't return anything. Just for kicks, let's take that out of my script—perhaps I misunderstood. Here's the revision:

```
For Each oPingResult In cPingResults
    Debug "TestPing: Enumerating Results"
    'If oPingResult Is Null Then
    '       Debug "Result was Null"
    '    TestPing = False
    If oPingResult.StatusCode = 0 Then
            Debug "StatusCode was 0"
        TestPing = True
    Else
            Debug "Else - StatusCode " & _
            oPingResult.StatusCode
        TestPing = False
    End If
Next
```

Running this, I see that it works! Double Eureka! It turns out that even the unreachable addresses produce the correct output, so there was no reason for me to have included that Null business in the first place—I just misunderstood what I'd read. However, it was the clue in the debug window—the fact that it kept *always* going to that section of my code—that made me suspect it, and decide to try taking it out as a test.

26

But I wanted to do some further research. It turns out that Null is a special value in VBScript. It doesn't mean *nothing*, it means Null. And anything, compared to Null, *is* Null, so that's why my initial If statement was always being executed. In fact, if you use Win32_PingStatus to ping an address that isn't reachable, you get back *nothing*, which isn't the same as Null. If you ping a reachable address, you get back a collection, which is an object; VBScript can test to see if something is an object or not by using the IsObject() function. So, I decided to modify my script slightly to test for that: If my results are an object, then I *got* a result; if the results aren't an object, then the address wasn't reachable. Here's the modified—functional—code:

```
For Each oPingResult In cPingResults
    Debug "TestPing: Enumerating Results"
    If Not IsObject(oPingResult) Then
            Debug "Result was Null"
        TestPing = False
    ElseIf oPingResult.StatusCode = 0 Then
            Debug "StatusCode was 0"
        TestPing = True
    Else
            Debug "Else - StatusCode " & _
            oPingResult.StatusCode
        TestPing = False
    End If
Next
```

All I have to do now is uncomment that Exit Sub line in the Debug subroutine, and my script will run normally. However, I'm going to go one step further: I'm going to manually remove the calls to Debug from my TestPing() function, and save the entire function as a snippet on my computer. It took a while to debug this, and I can see the value in having this function in other scripts; by making it into a snippet I can reuse it easily and won't ever have to debug it again.

What About a Debugger?

In theory, a debugger would make a lot of sense for VBScript. A debugger should let you pause your script as it runs, execute a single line of script code at a time, and review all of your variables' values as you go. This would almost eliminate the need for a "debug window" like the one I used in this chapter, and would give you a lot of insight into what your script is doing. Microsoft does offer a free Microsoft Script Debugger that does *some* of these things, and is unfortunately worth about what you pay for it: I have a terrible time getting it to work on some computers, and it's nearly impossible for me to get it running reliably on Windows Vista. Almost all script editors have a built-in debugger, but unfortunately many of them are simply integrating the Microsoft Script Debugger, which doesn't solve the problem. I'm aware of two commercial script editors which *do* have an internal debugger that isn't just the Windows Script Debugger, and which *do* provide all the features a debugger should have. The first one is called PrimalScope (www. primalscope.com; it's also included in PrimalScript Professional and higher editions), and the second one is built into VBSEdit (www.vbsedit.com). Feel free to try these out and decide which one's right for you; the actual step-by-step procedures to use these products are a bit beyond this book's scope, though.

Summary

Hopefully, this chapter has given you a better idea of how to prevent and eliminate bugs in your scripts. The idea is to use a scripting environment—such as a VBScript editor—that provides you with visual cues and syntax checking to help prevent simpler bugs, and to use a simple, step-by-step methodology for eliminating logic errors. Always start by methodically *proving* the reason for a bug, rather than just flinging possible fixes at the problem and possibly making things worse. Get inside your script to see what data your script is actually using, and get *outside* your script to test things, when possible, so that the complexity of the script itself isn't contributing to the problem. If you take the time to actually follow these steps, you'll find that debugging winds up going a lot faster than you might have thought was possible.

Next up is four chapters full of administrative scripts, each with line-by-line explanations. The idea is to not only give you some working scripts that you can use with relatively little modification, but to also give you some longer, more complex scripts so that you can see how they work.

26

PART V

Ready-to-Run Examples

IN THIS PART

Logon and Logoff Scripts

Perhaps one of the most common uses for scripting is the creation of logon (and, for Active Directory [AD] domains, logoff) scripts. A number of scripting languages have been created almost exclusively for use in these scripts, including Microsoft's unsupported Kixtart, the more general-purpose WinBatch, and many others. Dozens of command-line utilities exist that allow batch files to stand in as logon scripts. Although VBScript has a steeper learning curve than these other products, it also offers unmatched power and flexibility. VBScript's capability to use Component Object Model (COM) objects and directly access many operating system features allows it to immediately take advantage of new technologies and techniques.

Because every environment requires a unique logon script, it's impossible to offer examples that you can truly use without modification. Instead, I've tried to create examples that are modular, allowing you to pick and choose the various tasks you need for your own logon scripts. As a result, some of the tasks my examples perform are slightly less than real world. For example, you'll see examples where I'm using a script to execute a relatively useless command-line utility. The point of the example isn't the utility itself, but rather the ability to execute external commands. You should be able to quickly modify the pieces of these examples to assemble your own highly useful scripts.

> **NOTE**
>
> I'm assuming that you know how to designate logon (and logoff) scripts for whatever domain environment you're working in. If you don't, consult the operating system's documentation for more information.

NT and Active Directory Logon Scripts

The first sample script works in either an Active Directory (AD) or NT domain environment. It includes a number of common logon script tasks.

> **NOTE**
>
> One thing to be careful of: Windows 9x scripts actually execute before the operating system finishes the user logon process. As a result, the technique I use to retrieve the current user's name won't always work properly. There's no pretty workaround for this; I'll show you one example of how to make your script essentially sit and wait until Windows finishes and the username becomes available. I always hope that nobody's still using these older versions of Windows, but I'm almost always surprised to find that some folks still are.

Logon Script One   Listing 27.1 shows the script code. I've included comments to help identify each task, so that you can easily break this apart and reuse various bits in your own scripts.

LISTING 27.1   *Logon1.vbs.* This script includes most common logon script tasks.

```
' sample logon script

' first let's create the objects we'll be using
dim objShell, objNetwork
set objShell = WScript.CreateObject("WScript.Shell")
set objNetwork = WScript.CreateObject("WScript.Network")

' let's display a welcome message
dim strDomain, strUser
strDomain = objNetwork.UserDomain
strUser = objNetwork.UserName
msgbox "Welcome to the " & strDomain & ", " & strUser & "!"

'we'll map the Z: drive to a network location
objNetwork.MapNetworkDrive "Z:", "\\Server\Share"

'let's connect to a network printer and make it
' the default - we'll capture LPT2:
objNetwork.AddPrinterConnection "LPT2", "\\Server\Print1"

'connect a second printer without capturing a printer port
objNetwork.AddWindowsPrinterConnection _
"\\server\print2", "Lexmark Optra S 1650"

'let's make that the default printer
```

LISTING 27.1   Continued

```
objNetwork.SetDefaultPrinter "\\Server\Print2"


'now let's see if this fellow is a Domain Admin
dim objAdmins, user, IsMember
IsMember = False
set objAdmins = GetObject("WinNT://Domain1/Domain Admins")
for each user in objAdmins.members
 if user.name = strUser then
  IsMember = True
 end if
next


'if user is Domain Admin map the Y: drive
if IsMember = true then
 objNetwork.MapNetworkDrive "Y:", "\\Server\C$"
end if
```

You obviously need to adjust server names, domain names, and so forth to make this run in your environment. However, rather than getting *this* script to run in your environment, I recommend pulling out the pieces you like and building your own script from scratch.

Logon Script One—Explained   I begin by creating the various objects I need to use and assigning them to variables. If you break apart this script, be sure to pull out the appropriate object creation statements.

```
' sample logon script


' first let's create the objects we'll be using
dim objShell, objNetwork
set objShell = WScript.CreateObject("WScript.Shell")
set objNetwork = WScript.CreateObject("WScript.Network")
```

I use `MsgBox()` to display a friendly welcome message that includes the domain name and username.

```
' let's display a welcome message
dim strDomain, strUser
strDomain = objNetwork.UserDomain
strUser = objNetwork.UserName
msgbox "Welcome to the " & strDomain & ", " & strUser & "!"
```

I mentioned earlier that this doesn't work so well on Windows 9x computers, because UserName isn't available right away. If you need to ensure that this will work properly on 9x machines, try adding the following modification.

```
' let's display a welcome message
dim strDomain, strUser
Do Until objNetwork.UserName <> ""
 WScript.Sleep(5000)
Loop
strDomain = objNetwork.UserDomain
strUser = objNetwork.UserName
msgbox "Welcome to the " & strDomain & ", " & strUser & "!"
```

This modification (shown in boldface) has the script sleep in 5-second increments, and then check to see if Windows has finished logging on and populated the UserName property of the Network objects.

Moving on, I next map a drive to a network location. Easily the single most common logon script task, this is accomplished in just one line of code.

```
'we'll map the Z: drive to a network location
objNetwork.MapNetworkDrive "Z:", "\\Server\Share"
```

Next, I capture the LPT2 port to a network printer. This is less common nowadays, because so few of us are running old DOS applications that require captured printer ports, but here it is in case you need it.

```
'let's connect to a network printer - we'll capture LPT2:
objNetwork.AddPrinterConnection "LPT2", "\\Server\Print1"
```

Far more common is the need to map a network printer. Note that this only works if Windows "Point and Print" is enabled. In other words, if you run this command and the print server doesn't have the appropriate printer drivers for your client, the command fails. Generally, NT-based clients printing to same-generation NT-based servers (such as XP printing to Windows 2000 or 2003) use the server's printer drivers, and this command works fine.

The second parameter defines the name of the printer driver; this can take some experimentation to find the right string.

```
'connect a second printer without capturing a printer port
objNetwork.AddWindowsPrinterConnection "\\server\print2", _
 "Lexmark Optra S 1650"
```

You can make a mapped printer the default, as shown here. Just specify the Universal Naming Convention (UNC) path. Note that the printer should already be mapped for this to work best.

```
'let's make that the default printer
objNetwork.SetDefaultPrinter "\\Server\Print2"
```

Checking for group membership is the roughest thing a logon script has to do. I start by
defining a variable, IsMember, and setting it to False. Then, I use the Active Directory
Services Interface (ADSI) to query for the domain's Domain Admins group. Note that I'm
using the WinNT provider: This will work *just fine* with Active Directory, but the data
returned by the WinNT provider is a bit more flexible, so it's easier to check for group
membership.

```
'now let's see if this fellow is a Domain Admin
dim objAdmins, user, IsMember
IsMember = False
set objAdmins = GetObject("WinNT://Domain1/Domain Admins")
```

Next, I run through each member of the group to see if the current user is a member of
the group. If I find the current user in the group, I set IsMember to True. This technique
will *not* check for *nested* group membership, however—keep that in mind.

```
for each user in objAdmins.members
 if user.name = strUser then
  IsMember = True
 end if
next
```

The preceding routine is just a tad inefficient; after I locate the current user in the group,
there's no need to continue checking other members. The routine can be made just a bit
more efficient by adding one line, shown here in boldface.

```
for each user in objAdmins.members
 if user.name = strUser then
  IsMember = True
  Exit For
 end if
next
```

My last action is to map a drive to a server's administrative share if the user is, in fact, a
domain administrator. Checking for membership first ensures that this command runs
without error because only domain admins (by default) have permission to server administrative shares.

```
'if user is Domain Admin map the Y: drive
if IsMember = true then
     objNetwork.MapNetworkDrive "Y:", "\\Server\C$"
end if
```

27

One thing this script doesn't accommodate is nested group membership. For example, if the user is a member of a group, and the group is a member of Domain Admins, this script doesn't pick up on that. Checking for nested group membership is a bit more complex. For scripts like this, I usually don't worry about it because for security reasons, I try to avoid including other groups in Domain Admins.

Logon Script Two   Listing 27.2 shows another logon script that runs in any domain environment. This one performs a few more advanced tasks, such as writing to the Registry and running a command-line utility. This script also checks to see if it was run from CScript.exe (rather than WScript.exe), and exits if it wasn't.

LISTING 27.2   *Logon2.vbs.* This logon script performs more advanced logon tasks.

```
Dim oShell
Dim oNetwork

Set oShell   = WScript.CreateObject ("WScript.shell")
Set oNetwork = WScript.CreateObject("WScript.Network")

'ensure this was run by using Cscript
Dim oRegExp, bIsCScript
Set oRegExp = New RegExp
oRegExp.IgnoreCase  = true
oRegExp.Pattern = "cscript\.exe$"
bIsCScript = oRegExp.Test(WScript.ScriptFullName)
Set oRegExp = Nothing
If Not bIsCScript() Then
  Wscript.echo WScript.FullName & _
    " must be run with CScript."
  Wscript.Quit
End If

'run command line
oShell.Exec "NET TIME /RTSDOMAIN:SAPIEN /SET"

'write registry key
oShell.RegWrite "HKLM\Software\Company" & _
  "\Software\Key\Value", 1, "REG_DWORD"
```

Logon Script Two—Explained   As usual, I start by declaring variables and creating the objects I'll use in the script.

```
Dim oShell
Dim oNetwork

Set oShell   = WScript.CreateObject ("WScript.shell")
Set oNetwork = WScript.CreateObject("WScript.Network")
```

The next bit of code uses a regular expression to see if the script was executed via
CScript.exe. I start by creating the regular expression object.

```
'ensure this was run by using  Cscript
Dim oRegExp, bIsCScript
Set oRegExp = New RegExp
```

Next, I tell it to ignore upper- and lowercase differences in the comparison I'll have it
make, and I tell it that I'm looking for a string that ends with "cscript.exe".

```
oRegExp.IgnoreCase  = true
oRegExp.Pattern = "cscript\.exe$"
```

I test the comparison pattern against the full name of the currently running script. If the
result comes back empty (Nothing), I know the script wasn't run with CScript.exe, so I
display a message and quit. This is a useful technique if you want to ensure command-
line output formatting or some other feature unique to CScript.exe.

```
bIsCScript = oRegExp.Test(WScript.FullName)
Set oRegExp = Nothing
If Not bIsCScript() Then
  Wscript.echo WScript.ScriptFullName & _
    " must be run with CScript."
  Wscript.Quit
End If
```

Next, I have the script execute a command-line utility. In this case, it's the NET TIME
command, used to set the local computer's clock. This demonstrates how to run external
command-line utilities from within a script. This is also a good reason to run the script
from CScript, so that a new command-line window doesn't pop open just to execute this
command, which is what would happen if you used WScript.

```
'run command line
oShell.Exec "NET TIME /RTSDOMAIN:SAPIEN /SET"
```

Finally, I write a Registry value. You could also write operating system values to force
Server Message Blocks (SMB) signing or other features.

```
'write registry key
oShell.RegWrite "HKLM\Software\Company" & _
 "\Software\Key\Value", 1, "REG_DWORD"
```

This script is another example of the flexibility VBScript can bring to your logon scripts.

27

Calling VBScript Logon Scripts in NT Domains

NT wasn't built to understand VBScript, and its ability to define logon scripts is pretty much limited to executable (.exe) and batch (.bat) files. Fortunately, those are enough to get VBScript scripts up and running.

One option is to define the logon script for your users as WScript.exe scriptname.vbs, calling WScript.exe directly and passing the name of the script to run. That technique has problems with some clients, however, because they aren't expecting a space in the logon script name.

Another technique is to create a simple batch file that launches WScript.exe and the appropriate logon script. You can then define that batch file as the users' actual logon script, and it'll get your code up and running appropriately.

Keep in mind that all users expected to run your script must have the Windows Script Host (WSH) installed, and that the latest version (5.6 as of this writing) is preferred.

Active Directory–Specific Logon Scripts

If you're in an AD domain, you can take advantage of AD's newer technologies and built-in scripting interfaces, such as ADSI, to perform more powerful and flexible tricks in your logon scripts.

AD Logon Script   Listing 27.3 shows a sample logon script designed to run within an AD environment.

LISTING 27.3   *ADLogon1.vbs.* This script requires Active Directory to run.

```
Const G_SALES = "cn=sales"
Const G_MARKETING = "cn=marketing"
Const G_EXECS = "cn=executives"

Set oNetwork = CreateObject("WScript.Network")
oNetwork.MapNetworkDrive "h:", "\\FileServer\Users\" & _
 oNetwork.UserName
Set oADSystemInfo = CreateObject("ADSystemInfo")
Set oUser = GetObject("LDAP://" & oADSystemInfo.UserName)
sGroups = LCase(Join(oUser.MemberOf))

If InStr(sGroups, G_SALES) Then
 oNetwork.MapNetworkDrive "S:", "\\FileServer\SalesDocs\"
 oNetwork.AddWindowsPrinterConnection "\\PrintServer\Quotes"
 oNetwork.SetDefaultPrinter "\\PrintServer\Quotes"
End If

If InStr(sGroups, G_MARKETING) Then
 oNetwork.MapNetworkDrive "M:", "\\FileServer\MarketingDocs\"
 oNetwork.AddWindowsPrinterConnection "\\PrintServer\ColorLaser"
```

LISTING 27.3   Continued

```
oNetwork.AddWindowsPrinterConnection "\\PrintServer\BWLaser"
oNetwork.SetDefaultPrinter "\\PrintServer\BWLaser"
End If

If InStr(sGroups, G_EXECS) Then
oNetwork.MapNetworkDrive "X:", "\\FileServer\ExecDocs\"
oNetwork.AddWindowsPrinterConnection "\\PrintServer\Execs"
oNetwork.SetDefaultPrinter "\\PrintServer\Execs"
End If
```

As with the other scripts in this chapter, you need to rename the server and share names appropriately.

AD Logon Script—Explained   I start by creating constants for each user group I want to check the membership of. These constants make it easier to read the rest of the script. Notice that I'm using AD-style naming, specifying the *cn*, or common name, of each group.

```
Const G_SALES = "cn=sales"
Const G_MARKETING = "cn=marketing"
Const G_EXECS = "cn=executives"
```

The next bit of code creates a WScript.Network object, and maps a single drive to the user's home directory. The earlier caveat about Win9x machines applies: UserName isn't populated right away so you need to add some wait time into the code.

```
Set oNetwork = CreateObject("WScript.Network")
oNetwork.MapNetworkDrive "h:", "\\FileServer\Users\" & _
 oNetwork.UserName
```

Next, I use ADSI to retrieve the current domain information and logged-on username. Then, I connect to ADSI via LDAP to retrieve the list of groups the user belongs to. This information is returned in a string, which I've stored in sGroups.

```
Set oADSystemInfo = CreateObject("ADSystemInfo")
Set oUser = GetObject("LDAP://" & oADSystemInfo.UserName)
sGroups = LCase(Join(oUser.MemberOf))
```

Checking for group membership is now as easy as seeing if sGroups contains the group name, which I can do by using the InStr() function. For each group the user belongs to, I map the appropriate network drives and printers. Because users might belong to more than one group (an executive could also be in sales or marketing, for example), each group is handled individually.

27

> **NOTE**
>
> This technique isn't foolproof. For example, because of the way InStr works, I might be checking to see if someone belongs to the Sales group, and I'd get a false positive if they belonged to the WholesaleSupport group—because "WholesaleSupport" does contain the string "sales."

```
If InStr(sGroups, G_SALES) Then
 oNetwork.MapNetworkDrive "S:", "\\FileServer\SalesDocs\"
 oNetwork.AddWindowsPrinterConnection "\\PrintServer\Quotes"
 oNetwork.SetDefaultPrinter "\\PrintServer\Quotes"
End If


If InStr(sGroups, G_MARKETING) Then
 oNetwork.MapNetworkDrive "M:", "\\FileServer\MarketingDocs\"
 oNetwork.AddWindowsPrinterConnection "\\PrintServer\ColorLaser"
 oNetwork.AddWindowsPrinterConnection "\\PrintServer\BWLaser"
 oNetwork.SetDefaultPrinter "\\PrintServer\BWLaser"
End If


If InStr(sGroups, G_EXECS) Then
 oNetwork.MapNetworkDrive "X:", "\\FileServer\ExecDocs\"
 oNetwork.AddWindowsPrinterConnection "\\PrintServer\Execs"
 oNetwork.SetDefaultPrinter "\\PrintServer\Execs"
End If
```

That's easy enough! This is a great way to build a logon script that maps several different drives. Note that this same technique doesn't work as well in an NT domain because NT domains don't provide an easy way to retrieve all of a user's groups into a single, convenient string variable.

AD Logon Script Two   You can also create site-aware logon scripts. This is especially useful for mapping printers, as it allows you to map a *local* printer for the user. Roaming users who travel between sites appreciate always having a nearby printer to print to. Listing 27.4 shows a script that does just this, as well as maps a drive to the logon server's Utilities share. This might be a means of providing users with local access to a set of companywide utilities or document templates, for example.

LISTING 27.4   *ADLogon2.vbs.* This script is site and logon server–aware.

```
Dim oSystemInfo
Dim oShell
Dim sLogonServer, sSiteName

'get logon server
```

LISTING 27.4   Continued

```
Set oShell = Wscript.CreateObject("Wscript.Shell")
sLogonServer = oShell.ExpandEnvironmentStrings("%LOGONSERVER%")

'get AD site name
Set oSystemInfo = CreateObject("ADSystemInfo")
sSiteName = oSystemInfo.SiteName

'map printer based on site
Select Case sSiteName
 Case "Boston"
  oNetwork.AddWindowsPrinterConnection "\\BOS01\Laser1"
  oNetwork.SetDefaultPrinter "\\BOS01\Laser1"
 Case "New York"
  oNetwork.AddWindowsPrinterConnection "\\NYC02\LaserJet"
  oNetwork.SetDefaultPrinter "\\NYC02\LaserJet"
 Case "LA"
  oNetwork.AddWindowsPrinterConnection "\\LASrv\HP2"
  oNetwork.SetDefaultPrinter "\\LASrv\HP2"
 Case "Las Vegas"
  oNetwork.AddWindowsPrinterConnection "\\VEG4\LaserJet"
  oNetwork.SetDefaultPrinter "\\VEG4\LaserJet"
 Case "Houston"
  oNetwork.AddWindowsPrinterConnection "\\TX2\HP03"
  oNetwork.SetDefaultPrinter "\\TX2\HP03"
End Select

'show message
MsgBox "Your default printer has been " & _
 "set to a printer at the local office."

'map L: drive to logon server's
'UTILITIES share
oNetwork.MapNetworkDrive "L:", sLogonServer & _
 "\Utilities\"
```

Again, to pull bits of this script into your own, you need to modify the UNCs to suit your environment.

AD Logon Script Two—Explained   I start by declaring variables.

```
Dim oSystemInfo
Dim oShell
Dim sLogonServer, sSiteName
```

Next, I create a WshShell object to retrieve the logon server name. This information is stored in an environment string; note that this technique can be used to retrieve any environment string, such as the system temp folder.

```
'get logon server
Set oShell = Wscript.CreateObject("Wscript.Shell")
sLogonServer = oShell.ExpandEnvironmentStrings("%LOGONSERVER%")
```

I use the AD SystemInfo object to retrieve the current site name. This is only available on AD clients, including downlevel (9x and NT) clients running the Directory Services client.

```
'get AD site name
Set oSystemInfo = CreateObject("ADSystemInfo")
sSiteName = oSystemInfo.SiteName
```

Next, the script uses a Select/Case construct to map a printer based on the current site location. The printer is made the default, making it easier for users to just click Print in their applications.

```
'map printer based on site
Select Case sSiteName
 Case "Boston"
  oNetwork.AddWindowsPrinterConnection "\\BOS01\Laser1"
  oNetwork.SetDefaultPrinter "\\BOS01\Laser1"
 Case "New York"
  oNetwork.AddWindowsPrinterConnection "\\NYC02\LaserJet"
oNetwork.SetDefaultPrinter "\\NYC02\LaserJet"
 Case "LA"
  oNetwork.AddWindowsPrinterConnection "\\LASrv\HP2"
  oNetwork.SetDefaultPrinter "\\LASrv\HP2"
 Case "Las Vegas"
  oNetwork.AddWindowsPrinterConnection "\\VEG4\LaserJet"
  oNetwork.SetDefaultPrinter "\\VEG4\LaserJet"
 Case "Houston"
  oNetwork.AddWindowsPrinterConnection "\\TX2\HP03"
  oNetwork.SetDefaultPrinter "\\TX2\HP03"
End Select
```

I also notify the users that this printer assignment has been made. That way, they know what to expect when printing. For large offices, you might want the message to include the printer name and location, so the user knows where to find his hard copy.

```
'show message
MsgBox "Your default printer has been " & _
  "set to a printer at the local office."
```

Finally, I map a drive to the Utilities share of the authenticating domain controller.

```
'map L: drive to logon server's
'UTILITIES share
oNetwork.MapNetworkDrive "L:", sLogonServer & _
 "\Utilities\"
```

You now have another useful script that leverages VBScript's access to domain information like the logon server and site name!

Active Directory Logoff Scripts

Keep in mind that AD actually offers four types of automated scripts: logon, startup, logoff, and shutdown. *Logon* scripts execute when a user logs on, whereas *startup* scripts execute when a computer starts. Startup scripts are a good place to perform configuration changes, such as changing a computer's IP address. Logon scripts, which are what I've shown you so far in this chapter, make changes to the user's environment.

AD also supports *logoff* scripts, which execute when a user logs off, and *shutdown* scripts, which execute when a computer shuts down. It's tougher to find practical applications for these scripts, but there definitely are some. For example, you might copy a custom application's database file to a network server, if the server is available when the user logs off. That would provide a convenient, automated backup for laptop users. If you're mapping drive letters and printers in a logon script, you might unmap those in a logoff script. That way, mobile users won't see those resources if they log on to their machines while they are disconnected from the network.

Logoff Script   Listing 27.5 shows a sample logoff script that unmaps a network printer, which was mapped in a logon script. Note that I use `On Error Resume Next` in this script, so that the script doesn't generate an error if the printer isn't already mapped (which would be the case if the user had manually deleted the mapping already). Note that this is essentially a reverse script of Listing 27.4, and undoes everything that script accomplishes.

LISTING 27.5   *Logoff.vbs.* This script is designed to run when a user logs off his computer.

```
Dim oSystemInfo
Dim oShell
Dim sLogonServer, sSiteName

'get logon server
Set oShell = Wscript.CreateObject("Wscript.Shell")
sLogonServer = oShell.ExpandEnvironmentStrings("%LOGONSERVER%")

'get AD site name
Set oSystemInfo = CreateObject("ADSystemInfo")
sSiteName = oSystemInfo.SiteName
'turn off error checking
```

27

LISTING 27.5   Continued

```
On Error Resume Next

'unmap printer based on site
Select Case sSiteName
 Case "Boston"
  oNetwork.RemovePrinterConnection "\\BOS01\Laser1"
Case "New York"
  oNetwork.RemovePrinterConnection "\\NYC02\LaserJet"
Case "LA"
  oNetwork.RemovePrinterConnection "\\LASrv\HP2"
Case "Las Vegas"
  oNetwork.RemovePrinterConnection "\\VEG4\LaserJet"
Case "Houston"
  oNetwork.RemovePrinterConnection "\\TX2\HP03"
End Select

'unmap L: drive to logon server's
'UTILITIES share
oNetwork.RemoveNetworkDrive "L:", True
```

This script obviously needs to be modified with the correct UNCs and site names before it can be used.

Logoff Script—Explained   I start as usual, by declaring variables. As in the earlier logon script example, I use an environment variable to retrieve the name of the logon server, and use the AD client to discover the current site name.

```
Dim oSystemInfo
Dim oShell
Dim sLogonServer, sSiteName

'get logon server
Set oShell = Wscript.CreateObject("Wscript.Shell")
sLogonServer = oShell.ExpandEnvironmentStrings("%LOGONSERVER%")

'get AD site name
Set oSystemInfo = CreateObject("ADSystemInfo")
sSiteName = oSystemInfo.SiteName
```

Because any of these printer or drive connections could already be gone, I disable error checking. This allows the script to continue even if it encounters an error.

```
'turn off error checking
On Error Resume Next
```

Based on the site name, I remove the printer connection. Note that
`RemovePrinterConnection` undoes mappings created with both `AddPrinterConnection`
and `AddWindowsPrinterConnection`.

```
'unmap printer based on site
Select Case sSiteName
 Case "Boston"
  oNetwork.RemovePrinterConnection "\\BOS01\Laser1"
Case "New York"
  oNetwork.RemovePrinterConnection "\\NYC02\LaserJet"
Case "LA"
  oNetwork.RemovePrinterConnection "\\LASrv\HP2"
Case "Las Vegas"
  oNetwork.RemovePrinterConnection "\\VEG4\LaserJet"
Case "Houston"
  oNetwork.RemovePrinterConnection "\\TX2\HP03"
End Select
```

Finally, I remove the drive L: mapping created in the logon script. Notice the `True` parameter, which forces the drive to be unmapped even if the computer is using resources
located on that drive; we're logging off, so it doesn't matter if there's a file open. It won't
be open for long.

```
'unmap L: drive to logon server's
'UTILITIES share
oNetwork.RemoveNetworkDrive "L:", True
```

Other uses of logoff scripts might include copying instant messenger contact lists to a
central location, for later retrieval by a logon script. Alternatively, you might kick off a
database replication process between a central database and a local copy, causing sales
orders or whatever to be updated. Logoff scripts are most useful in implementing these
kinds of automated business processes, rather than performing the configuration changes
we usually associate with logon scripts.

Summary

You've seen several examples of how logon (and logoff) scripts can be used in both AD
and NT domains to provide automated client computer configuration. Don't forget,
though, that servers are computers, too; using startup and shutdown scripts can be a great
way to start third-party utilities on servers, collect software or hardware inventory information, and so forth. In any case, VBScript provides the flexibility and power you need to
perform just about any task automatically at startup, logon, logoff, and shutdown.

However, let me make an important observation on the topic of startup and shutdown
scripts: You know that logon and logoff scripts are user-related; that is, they run when the
user logs on and off, and they run under that user's security context. Logon and logoff
scripts have an advantage in that the computer itself has already established a trusted

communications channel to the domain, because such a channel is necessary to authenticate the user to begin with. That means a logon and logoff script can basically do anything that the user has permission to do. That is *not* the case with a startup and shutdown script: Those scripts do *not* run under a user's security context. That means those scripts are running under the *computer's* security account, which is LocalSystem. As you might know, LocalSystem has no permissions apart from the local computer, so a shutdown or startup script can't do anything that involves the network—such as connecting a network drive. Furthermore, the LocalSystem account doesn't have a profile on the computer, so even if it could connect a network drive, there would be no profile for that connection to live in. So you can't use a startup script to, for example, create a network drive mapping that will appear to all users. This combined lack of security permissions, local-only context, and no profile severely limits the usefulness of startup and shutdown scripts. Basically, you can only use them to perform tasks that take place entirely on the local machine, and that are designed to run entirely in the background without any user input or interaction.

CHAPTER 28

Windows and Domain Administration Scripts

A number of different tasks exist within a domain that you might want to automate. Some that pop into mind are automating the process of creating new user accounts, finding users who haven't logged on in a long time and disabling their accounts, and collecting information from the computers in your domain. Whatever your needs, scripting is an excellent solution, and the three sample scripts in this chapter should give you a good idea of what you can accomplish.

Automating User Creation

In this example, I'll show you how to use ActiveX Data Objects (ADO) to query information from a Microsoft Excel spreadsheet, put that information into script variables, and use those variables to create and configure new domain user objects.

> **NOTE**
>
> I've not covered ADO, and I find it doesn't come up often in many administrative scripts. I don't provide a comprehensive explanation of it here, but this example should give you a starting point if you have a need for a similar script in the future.

To run this script, you're going to need to create an Excel spreadsheet. Leave the first sheet named Sheet1, which is the default, and enter the following column headers on row 1:

▶ UserID

▶ FullName

- ▶ Description
- ▶ HomeDirectory
- ▶ Groups
- ▶ DialIn

Populate the remaining rows as follows:

- ▶ **UserID**—Enter the unique user ID you want this user to have. Note that the script doesn't do any error checking, and Windows lets you create users with duplicate names in a script. Be careful, though, because user accounts with duplicate names don't behave properly.

- ▶ **FullName**—Enter the full name of the user.

- ▶ **Description**—Optionally, enter a description of the user.

- ▶ **HomeDirectory**—This needs to be a subfolder under a file server's root folder. You'll see how this gets used later.

- ▶ **Groups**—Enter a comma-delimited list of groups the user should be placed in.

- ▶ **DialIn**—Enter a *Y* or *N* (for *Yes* or *No*, and note that these are case sensitive) describing whether the user should have dial-in permissions.

TIP

This script is designed to work in any Windows domain, from Windows NT to Active Directory.

Automating User Creation   Automating the creation of new user accounts is a must-have administrative utility in many environments because it helps reduce administrative time and improve the consistency of the created accounts. Listing 28.1 shows a script that reads user information from an Excel spreadsheet and creates the appropriate domain user accounts.

LISTING 28.1   *AddUsers.vbs.* This script pulls new user information from an Excel spreadsheet and creates the user accounts.

```
' PART 1: Open up the Excel spreadsheet
' using ActiveX Data Objects
Dim oCN
Set oCN = CreateObject("ADODB.Connection")
oCN.Open "Excel"

Dim oRS
```

LISTING 28.1   Continued

```
Set oRS = oCN.Execute("SELECT * FROM [Sheet1$]")

' PART 2: Get a reference to the
' Windows NT domain using ADSI
Dim oDomain
Set oDomain = GetObject("WinNT://DOMAIN")

' PART 3: Open an output text file
' to store users' initial passwords
Dim oFSO, oTS
Set oFSO = CreateObject("Scripting.FileSystemObject")
Set oTS = oFSO.CreateTextFile("c:\passwords.txt",True)

' PART 4: For each record in the recordset,
' add the user, set the correct user
' properties, and add the user to the
' appropriate groups

' create the necessary variables
Dim sUserID, sFullName, sDescription
Dim sHomeDir, sGroups, sDialIn
Dim sPassword, oUserAcct, oFolder
Dim sGroupList, iTemp, oGroup

' define the base path for the home
' directories to be created in
Dim sHomePath
sHomePath = "\\iridis1\c$\users\"
' now go through the recordset one
' row at a time
Do Until oRS.EOF

  ' get the user information from this row
  sUserID = oRS("UserID")
  sFullName = oRS("FullName")
  sDescription = oRS("Description")
  sHomeDir = oRS("HomeDirectory")
  sGroups = oRS("Groups")
  sDialIn = oRS("DialIn")

  ' make up a new password
  sPassword = Left(sUserID,2) & DatePart("n",Time) & _
   DatePart("y",Date) & DatePart("s",Time)
```

28

LISTING 28.1   Continued

```
' create the user account
Set oUserAcct = oDomain.Create("user",sUserID)

' set account properties
oUserAcct.SetPassword sPassword
oUserAcct.FullName = sFullName
oUserAcct.Description = sDescription
oUserAcct.HomeDirectory = sHomeDir

' set RAS permission
If sDialIn = "Y" Then
  oUserAcct.RasPermissions = 9
Else
  oUserAcct.RasPermissions = 1
End If

' save the account
oUserAcct.SetInfo

' get a reference to the new account
' this gets us a valid SID & other info
Set oUserAcct = GetObject("WinNT://NT4PDC/" & _
 sUserID & ",user")

' write password to file
oTS.Write sUserID & "," & sPassword & vbCrLf

' PART 4A: Add user account to groups
' use the Split function to turn the
' comma-separated list into an array
sGroupList = Split(sGroups, ",")

' go through the array and add the user
' to each group
For iTemp = 0 To uBound(sGroupList)

  ' get the group
  Set oGroup = GetObject("WinNT://NT4PDC/" & _
   sGroupList(iTemp) & ",group")

  ' add the user account
  oGroup.Add oUserAcct.ADsPath

  ' release the group
```

LISTING 28.1   Continued

```
    Set oGroup = Nothing

  Next


    ' PART 4B: Create the user's Home Directory
    ' (append UserID to the Home Path variable)
    Set oFolder = oFSO.CreateFolder(sHomePath & sUserID)

    ' PART 5: All done!
    ' release the user account
    Set oUserAcct = Nothing

    ' move to the next row in the recordset
    oRS.MoveNext

Loop

' PART 6: Final clean up, close down
oRS.Close
oTS.Close
WScript.Echo "Passwords have been written to c:\passwords.txt."
```

Before you can run this script, you need to create a System ODBC DSN (Open Database Connectivity Data Source Name) named Excel that points to your Excel spreadsheet. You'll also need to edit the server and domain names in the script to match your environment.

Automating User Creation—Explained   This is a hard-working script that has quite a bit of functionality. It starts by defining an ADO connection, and then opening it. Note that for the script to work, a System ODBC DSN named Excel must exist, and it must point to a spreadsheet matching the description I gave you earlier.

```
' PART 1: Open up the Excel spreadsheet
' using ActiveX Data Objects
Dim oCN
Set oCN = CreateObject("ADODB.Connection")
oCN.Open "Excel"
```

Next, the script creates an ADO recordset—a set of database records—by querying the rows from the Excel spreadsheet. Notice the unusual way in which Excel sheet names must be referenced: ending with a dollar sign and enclosed in square brackets.

```
Dim oRS
Set oRS = oCN.Execute("SELECT * FROM [Sheet1$]")
```

28

Now, the script uses Active Directory Services Interface (ADSI) to get a reference to the Windows domain. In this example, notice that I'm using the WinNT provider. I often do this even when working with Active Directory (AD) simply because that provider is a bit easier to work with than the LDAP provider. It'll connect to the domain's PDC Emulator. The only downside to this technique is that you can't specify an organizational unit (OU) for the new users; they'll be created in the default Users container. For more on using ADSI to connect to a domain, see Chapter 15, "Manipulating Domains."

```
' PART 2: Get a reference to the
' Windows NT domain using ADSI
Dim oDomain
Set oDomain = GetObject("WinNT://DOMAIN")
```

The last preliminary step is to create an output text file, where I store the new users' passwords. For more information on how to create and write to text files, turn to Chapter 12, "Working with the File System."

```
' PART 3: Open an output text file
' to store users' initial passwords
Dim oFSO, oTS
Set oFSO = CreateObject("Scripting.FileSystemObject")
Set oTS = oFSO.CreateTextFile("c:\passwords.txt",True)
```

The script can begin its real work. The first step is to define several variables, which are used to store information about each user as we create each user's account.

```
' PART 4: For each record in the recordset,
' add the user, set the correct user
' properties, and add the user to the
' appropriate groups

' create the necessary variables
Dim sUserID, sFullName, sDescription
Dim sHomeDir, sGroups, sDialIn
Dim sPassword, oUserAcct, oFolder
Dim sGroupList, iTemp, oGroup
```

Next, I define a variable for where I want the users' home directories created. Note that I'm using the C$ administrative share of a particular server. Whatever information is in the HomeDirectory column for each user will be appended to this file path, and the user's user ID will be appended to that. For example, if I want my own home directory to be \\SAPIEN\C$\Users\DonJ, I'd leave the HomeDirectory column blank in the spreadsheet.

```
' define the base path for the home
' directories to be created in
Dim sHomePath
sHomePath = "\\SAPIEN1\C$\Users\"
```

Now, I use a `Do/Loop` to go through each row in the recordset—meaning each row in the Excel spreadsheet—one at a time. The recordset is an `EOF` property that will be set to `True` when I reach the end of the recordset, so having the loop check that keeps everything running smoothly.

```
' now go through the recordset one
' row at a time
Do Until oRS.EOF
```

I pull information from the current row into variables, just to make the information easier to work with. Notice that I simply tell the recordset object which column's information I want, and the information is retrieved. This does depend on the Excel sheet having these column names in the first row—if it doesn't, these lines won't execute properly.

```
' get the user information from this row
sUserID = oRS("UserID")
sFullName = oRS("FullName")
sDescription = oRS("Description")
sHomeDir = oRS("HomeDirectory")
sGroups = oRS("Groups")
sDialIn = oRS("DialIn")
```

I need to make up a new password for the user. I'm using the leftmost two characters of the user ID, and the current minutes, Julian date, and seconds from the system clock. It's not a great password, and might not meet your domain's complexity requirements, but it's reasonably unique, tough to guess, and easy to communicate to the user when he shows up for his first day of work.

```
' make up a new password
sPassword = Left(sUserID,2) & DatePart("n",Time) & _
  DatePart("y",Date) & DatePart("s",Time)
```

Next, I ask ADSI to create a new user account.

```
' create the user account
Set oUserAcct = oDomain.Create("user",sUserID)
```

The account isn't created yet, but I can still set its initial properties, based on the values in the variables.

```
' set account properties
oUserAcct.SetPassword sPassword
oUserAcct.FullName = sFullName
oUserAcct.Description = sDescription
oUserAcct.HomeDirectory = sHomeDir
```

The ADSI documentation tells me that the `RasPermissions` property should be set to 9 if the user should have dial-in permissions, and 1 otherwise—that's how I'll set the property.

```
' set RAS permission
If sDialIn = "Yes" Then
  oUserAcct.RasPermissions = 9
Else
  oUserAcct.RasPermissions = 1
End If
```

I need to tell ADSI to save the information, which creates the user account. This also creates the account's unique security identifier (SID).

```
' save the account
oUserAcct.SetInfo
```

I'm going to need that SID in a minute, so I need to tell ADSI to get the new user account again. I just use an ADSI query to pull the user account by using its user ID, which I already know. I'll use a variable, oUserAcct, to reference the new account.

```
' get a reference to the new account
' this gets us a valid SID & other info
Set oUserAcct = GetObject("WinNT://NT4PDC/" & _
  sUserID & ",user")
```

Before I forget, I should write that new password out to a file, so that I can tell the user what it is.

```
' write password to file
oTS.Write sUserID & "," & sPassword & vbCrLf
```

Now comes the fun part: adding the user to groups. First, I'm going to use the `Split` function to change that comma-delimited list into a string array. Each element in the array holds one group name.

```
' PART 4A: Add user account to groups
' use the Split function to turn the
' comma-separated list into an array
sGroupList = Split(sGroups, ",")
```

I use a `For/Next` loop to go through the array of group names. Notice that the array starts at zero. I can use the `Ubound()` function to find out how big the array is.

```
' go through the array and add the user
' to each group
For iTemp = 0 To Ubound(sGroupList)
```

Now, I have one specific group name to work with, so I can ask ADSI to get a reference to that group.

```
' get the group
Set oGroup = GetObject("WinNT://NT4PDC/" & _
  sGroupList(iTemp) & ",group")
```

Then, I can use the group's Add method to add the user's SID to the group. This is why I needed the user's SID; groups are nothing but lists of SIDs.

```
' add the user account
oGroup.Add oUserAcct.AdsPath
```

Just to be tidy, I can release the group object when I'm finished with it.

```
' release the group
Set oGroup = Nothing
```

```
Next
```

To create the user's home directory, I use the FileSystemObject (FSO) to create the appropriate folder. I might also need to set NTFS permissions; I could use Windows Management Instrumentation (WMI) to do that, but it's beyond the scope of this example.

```
' PART 4B: Create the user's Home Directory
' (append UserID to the Home Path variable)
Set oFolder = oFSO.CreateFolder(sHomePath & sUserID)
```

I'm finished! I can release the user account and move on to the next record.

```
' PART 5: All done!
' release the user account
Set oUserAcct = Nothing

' move to the next row in the recordset
oRS.MoveNext
```

```
Loop
```

When I've made it through all of the records, I can shut down the recordset and the output file, and display an informative message.

```
' PART 6: Final clean up, close down
oRS.Close
oTS.Close
WScript.Echo "Passwords have been written to c:\passwords.txt."
```

That's it! You have a fully functional script to add users to your domain automatically.

28

Finding Inactive Users

This is a script I like to run from time to time, just to find out how many user accounts haven't logged on for a while. Often, they're accounts of employees who have left, but another administrator (certainly not me!) forgot to remove the accounts. Because the accounts represent a potential security threat, I like to disable them until I can figure out if they're still needed for something.

NOTE

This script works reliably only in Active Directory domains that use Windows Server 2003 domain controllers running in native mode. Unfortunately, the attribute in Active Directory that stores the last logon date is not reliably updated and replicated in NT or Windows 2000 domains. The only way to use this script in older domains is to run it independently against each domain controller and then compare the results because each domain controller maintains an independent list of last logon times.

Finding Inactive Users   Listing 28.2 demonstrates how to use ADSI to locate users who haven't logged on in a while.

LISTING 28.2   *FindOldUsers.vbs.* This script checks the `LastLogonTimestamp` date to see when users last logged on to the domain.

```
Dim dDate
Dim oUser
Dim oObject
Dim oGroup
Dim iFlags
Dim iDiff
Dim iResult
Const UF_ACCOUNTDISABLE = &H0002

'Set this to TRUE to enable Logging only mode -
'no changes will be made
CONST LogOnly = TRUE

'Point to oObject containing users to check
Set oGroup = _
 GetObject("WinNT://MYDOMAIN/TestUsers")
On error resume next
For each oObject in oGroup.Members

  'Find all User Objects Within Domain Users group
  '(ignore machine accounts)
  If (oObject.Class = "user") And _
   (InStr(oObject.Name, "$") = 0) Then
```

LISTING 28.2   Continued

```
  Set oUser = GetObject(oObject.ADsPath)

 Set oLogon = oUser.get("LastLogonTimestamp")
 iLastTime = oLogon.HighPart * (2^32) + oLogon.LowPart
 iLastTime = iLastTime / (60 * 10000000)
 iLastTime = iLastTime / 1440
 dDate = iLastTime + CDate("1/1/1601")

'find difference in weeks between then and now
 iDiff = DateDiff("ww", dDate, Now)

 'if 6 weeks or more then disable the account
 If iDiff >= 6 Then
  iFlags = oUser.Get("UserFlags")

 If (iFlags AND UF_ACCOUNTDISABLE) = 0 Then

  ' Only disable accounts if LogOnly set to FALSE
  If LogOnly = False Then
   oUser.Put "UserFlags", iFlags OR UF_ACCOUNTDISABLE
   oUser.SetInfo
  End if

  sName = oUser.Name
  iResult = Log(sName,iDiff)
 End If
End If
End If
Next

Set oGroup = Nothing
MsgBox "All Done!"

Function Log(sUser,sDate)

 'Constant for Log file path
 CONST StrLogFile = "C:\UserMgr1.txt"

 Set oFS = CreateObject("Scripting.FileSystemObject")
 Set oTS = oFS.OpenTextFile(strLogFile, 8, True)
 oTS.WriteLine("Account:" & vbTab & sUser & vbTab & _
  "Inactive for:" & vbTab & sDate & vbTab & "Weeks" & _
  vbTab & "Disabled on:" & vbTab & Date & vbTab & "at:" & _
  vbTab & Time)
```

28

LISTING 28.2   Continued

```
oTS.Close
Set oFS = Nothing
Set oTS = Nothing

End Function
```

You need to set the domain controller name to one that's within your environment. You can also customize the script to specify the number of weeks that can go by before you consider a user inactive. Finally, as is, the script only tells you which accounts it would like to disable; you need to make one minor modification, which I discuss in the next section, to have it make the change.

Finding Inactive Users—Explained   I start the script by defining a bunch of variables and a couple of constants. *Constants*, you might recall, are simply friendly names for difficult-to-remember values. In this case, I define one constant to be the value that a user account's flags take on when the account is disabled. I use another constant to tell the script whether to simply log its recommendations or disable old accounts; edit the script and change the constant to `False` if you want the script to disable accounts for you. See Chapter 5, "Functions, Objects, Variables, and More," for more coverage of variables and constants.

```
Dim dDate
Dim oUser
Dim oObject
Dim oGroup
Dim iFlags
Dim iDiff
Dim iResult
Const UF_ACCOUNTDISABLE = &H0002

'Set this to TRUE to enable Logging only mode -
'no changes will be made
CONST LogOnly = TRUE
```

The script now needs to connect to the domain using ADSI and retrieve the `TestUsers` group (which contains the users I want to check). Look to Chapter 15 for more on connecting to domains. Once again, I'm choosing to use the WinNT provider for this—however, you could easily change this to use the LDAP provider, too. The `GetObject()` string would be something like `"cn=Domain Admins,cn=Users,dc=mydomain,dc=com"` modified, of course, to suit your domain's actual name.

```
'Point to oObject containing users to check
Set oGroup = GetObject("WinNT://MYDOMAIN/TestUsers")
```

Now, I use a `For Each`/`Next` loop to go through each user in the domain, one at a time.

```
On error resume next
For Each oObject in oGroup.Members
```

Even in NT, groups can technically contain computers as well as users. To make sure I'm only dealing with users, I add an `If`/`Then` to test the current account's object class.

```
'Find all User Objects Within Domain Users group
'(ignore machine accounts)
If (oObject.Class = "user") And _
 (InStr(oObject.Name, "$") = 0) Then
 Set oUser = GetObject(oObject.ADsPath)
```

I want the script to pull in the `LastLogonTimestamp` date. Now, unfortunately, this attribute isn't actually a date. Instead, it's the number of time units that have elapsed since a specific date. So, I'm going to have to do some math to convert that to an actual date.

```
Set oLogon = oUser.get("LastLogonTimestamp")
 iLastTime = oLogon.HighPart * (2^32) + oLogon.LowPart
 iLastTime = iLastTime / (60 * 10000000)
 iLastTime = iLastTime / 1440
 dDate = iLastTime + CDate("1/1/1601")
```

I use the `DateDiff()` function to find the difference between the last logon date and today. The `"ww"` tells `DateDiff()` that I want the difference expressed in weeks, instead of days or some other interval.

```
'find difference in weeks between then and now
 iDiff = DateDiff("ww", dDate, Now)
```

If the difference is 6 weeks or more, I retrieve the user's existing `UserFlags` property, which includes whether the account is disabled.

```
'if 6 weeks or more then disable the account
 If iDiff >= 6 Then
 iFlags = oUser.Get("UserFlags")
```

If the user account isn't already disabled, I disable it—*if* that constant is set to `False`.

```
 If (iFlags AND UF_ACCOUNTDISABLE) = 0 Then

 ' Only disable accounts if LogOnly set to FALSE
 If LogOnly = False Then
 oUser.Put "UserFlags", iFlags OR UF_ACCOUNTDISABLE
 oUser.SetInfo
End If
```

28

Regardless of whether I disable the account, I use a function named `Log` to add this user account to the log file.

```
  sName = oUser.Name
  iResult = Log(sName,iDiff)
 End If
 End If
 End If
Next
```

At this point, I've run through all of the accounts and I can display a message indicating that the script is finished.

```
Set oGroup = Nothing
MsgBox "All Done!"
```

The last thing in the script is the `Log` function. It accepts two parameters: the user's name and a date. This information is saved to a text file, and the name of that file is defined in a constant. Chapter 5 covers custom functions and subroutines.

```
Function Log(sUser,sDate)

 'Constant for Log file path
 CONST StrLogFile = "C:\UserMgr1.txt"
```

You might notice that the function opens the text file each time the function is called. That's because I also close the file each time the function is finished. It might seem inefficient, but this ensures that the file is safely closed if the script crashes in the middle for some reason. Note that the 8 used in the `OpenTextFile` method opens the file for appending. See Chapter 12 for more on reading and writing to text files.

```
 Set oFS = CreateObject("Scripting.FileSystemObject")
 Set oTS = oFS.OpenTextFile(strLogFile, 8, True)
```

All that's left now is to write the information into the log file, close the file, and release the objects I've created.

```
 oTS.WriteLine("Account:" & vbTab & sUser & vbTab & _
  "Inactive for:" & vbTab & sDate & vbTab & "Weeks" & _
  vbTab & "Disabled on:" & vbTab & Date & vbTab & "at:" & _
  vbTab & Time)
 oTS.Close
 Set oFS = Nothing
 Set oTS = Nothing

End Function
```

This is a great script to run on a regular basis, and you can even use Task Scheduler to automate it. Just make sure it's running under an administrator's account if you want it to actually disable the inactive user accounts.

Collecting System Information

Software like Microsoft Systems Management Server (SMS) does a great job of collecting information from all of the computers in your environment. However, it's an expensive, complicated product, and sometimes you might just need a quick-and-dirty means of collecting the same information. This script is a great starting point for an inventory collection system that you can make a part of your users' logon scripts.

Collecting System Information   Listing 28.3 shows how a WMI script can be used to inventory information from a computer. For example, you could modify this script to run against multiple machines at once, letting you know which servers are running particular types of hardware.

LISTING 28.3   *CollectSysInfo.vbs.* This script inventories a computer and displays the information.

```
Set oSystemSet = _
GetObject("winmgmts:").InstancesOf("Win32_ComputerSystem")

For Each oSystem in oSystemSet
 system_name = oSystem.Caption
 system_type = oSystem.SystemType
 system_mftr = oSystem.Manufacturer
 system_model = oSystem.Model
Next
Set oProcSet = _
GetObject("winmgmts:").InstancesOf("Win32_Processor")

For Each oSystem in oProcSet
 proc_desc = oSystem.Caption
 proc_mftr = oSystem.Manufacturer
 proc_mhz = oSystem.CurrentClockSpeed
Next

Set oBiosSet = _
 GetObject("winmgmts:").InstancesOf("Win32_BIOS")

For Each oSystem in oBiosSet
      bios_info = oSystem.Version
Next
```

28

LISTING 28.3   Continued

```
Set oZoneSet = _
 GetObject("winmgmts:").InstancesOf("Win32_TimeZone")

For Each oSystem in oZoneSet
       loc_timezone = oSystem.StandardName
Next

Set oOSSet = _
 GetObject("winmgmts:").InstancesOf("Win32_OperatingSystem")

For Each oSystem in oOSSet
 os_name = oSystem.Caption
 os_version = oSystem.Version
 os_mftr = oSystem.Manufacturer
 os_build = oSystem.BuildNumber
 os_dir = oSystem.WindowsDirectory
 os_locale = oSystem.Locale
 os_totalmem = oSystem.TotalVisibleMemorySize
 os_freemem = oSystem.FreePhysicalMemory
 os_totalvirmem = oSystem.TotalVirtualMemorySize
 os_freevirmem = oSystem.FreeVirtualMemory
 os_pagefilesize = oSystem.SizeStoredInPagingFiles
Next

sMsg = ("OS Name:   " & os_name & Chr(10))
sMsg = sMsg & _
 ("Version:   " & os_version & " Build " & os_build & _
 Chr(10))
sMsg = sMsg & _
 ("OS Manufacturer:   " & os_mftr & Chr(10))
sMsg = sMsg & _
 ("oSystem Name:   " & system_name & Chr(10))
sMsg = sMsg & _
 ("oSystem Manufacturer:   " & system_mftr & Chr(10))
sMsg = sMsg & _
 ("oSystem Model:   " & system_model & Chr(10))
sMsg = sMsg & _
 ("oSystem Type:   " & system_type & Chr(10))
sMsg = sMsg & _
 ("Processor:   " & proc_desc & " " & proc_mftr & _
 " ~" & proc_mhz & "Mhz" & Chr(10))
sMsg = sMsg & _
 ("BIOS Version:   " & bios_info & Chr(10))
```

LISTING 28.3   Continued

```
sMsg = sMsg & _
("Windows Directory:   " & os_dir & Chr(10))
sMsg = sMsg & _
 ("Locale:   " & os_locale & Chr(10))
sMsg = sMsg & _
("Time Zone:   " & loc_timezone & Chr(10))
sMsg = sMsg & _
("Total Physical Memory:   " & os_totalmem & "KB" & _
 Chr(10))
sMsg = sMsg & _
 ("Available Physical Memory:   " & os_freemem & "KB" & _
 Chr(10))
sMsg = sMsg & _
("Total Virtual Memory:   " & os_totalvirmem & "KB" & _
 Chr(10))
sMsg = sMsg & _
 ("Available Virtual Memory:   " & _
 os_freevirmem & "KB" & Chr(10))
sMsg = sMsg & _
 ("Page File Space : " & os_pagefilesize & "KB" & _
 Chr(10))

MsgBox sMsg, 0,"System Summary Information"
```

This script is ready to run as is on any system that supports WMI. Right now, the script is programmed to display its information in a message box. However, if you want to collect remote computer information, you could make this script part of a logon script and rewrite it to save its information to a file or database located on a file server. After all of your users log on and run the script, you'll have a complete central inventory of your computers!

Collecting System Information—Explained   To save space, I've left out the variable declarations in this script. That's normally a poor programming practice, but I hope you'll forgive me in light of the length of the script. Rather than declaring variables, this script jumps right in by using WMI to connect to the local management provider. You can learn more about WMI starting in Chapter 17, "Understanding WMI."

```
Set oSystemSet = _
GetObject("winmgmts:").InstancesOf("Win32_ComputerSystem")
```

Next, I loop through each system instance that WMI found and retrieve its caption, system type, manufacturer, and model. Normally, there will only be one of these per computer. However, the WMI specification supports multiple "machines within a machine," so to speak, and that's why I've created a loop.

```
For Each oSystem in oSystemSet
 system_name = oSystem.Caption
 system_type = oSystem.SystemType
 system_mftr = oSystem.Manufacturer
 system_model = oSystem.Model
Next
```

Processors are next, and I save their caption, manufacturer, and clock speed.

```
Set oProcSet = _
GetObject("winmgmts:").InstancesOf("Win32_Processor")

For Each oSystem in oProcSet
 proc_desc = oSystem.Caption
 proc_mftr = oSystem.Manufacturer
 proc_mhz = oSystem.CurrentClockSpeed
Next
```

Now for the BIOS; I just retrieve the version.

```
Set oBiosSet = _
 GetObject("winmgmts:").InstancesOf("Win32_BIOS")

For Each oSystem in oBiosSet
      bios_info = oSystem.Version
Next
```

It might be useful to see which time zone your computers are configured for. Remember that some applications use time stamps for auditing purposes; having all of your computers in one time zone (at least, the ones that really are in the same time zone) makes that auditing information more accurate.

> **NOTE**
>
> Time zones don't affect domain operations, which all use Universal (Greenwich) time.

```
Set oZoneSet = _
 GetObject("winmgmts:").InstancesOf("Win32_TimeZone")

For Each oSystem in oZoneSet
      loc_timezone = oSystem.StandardName
Next
```

Next, I query a bunch of information about the operating system, including its name, version, manufacturer, and build number; location of the Windows folder; language locale; and stats on the system's memory configuration.

```
Set oOSSet = _
 GetObject("winmgmts:").InstancesOf("Win32_OperatingSystem")

For Each oSystem in oOSSet
 os_name = oSystem.Caption
 os_version = oSystem.Version
 os_mftr = oSystem.Manufacturer
 os_build = oSystem.BuildNumber
 os_dir = oSystem.WindowsDirectory
 os_locale = oSystem.Locale
 os_totalmem = oSystem.TotalVisibleMemorySize
 os_freemem = oSystem.FreePhysicalMemory
os_totalvirmem = oSystem.TotalVirtualMemorySize
 os_freevirmem = oSystem.FreeVirtualMemory
 os_pagefilesize = oSystem.SizeStoredInPagingFiles
Next
```

Now, I format all of the information I've collected into a string variable.

```
sMsg = ("OS Name:  " & os_name & Chr(10))
sMsg = sMsg & _
 ("Version:  " & os_version & " Build " & os_build & _
 Chr(10))
sMsg = sMsg & _
 ("OS Manufacturer:  " & os_mftr & Chr(10))
sMsg = sMsg & _
 ("oSystem Name:  " & system_name & Chr(10))
sMsg = sMsg & _
 ("oSystem Manufacturer:  " & system_mftr & Chr(10))
sMsg = sMsg & _
 ("oSystem Model:  " & system_model & Chr(10))
sMsg = sMsg & _
 ("oSystem Type:  " & system_type & Chr(10))
sMsg = sMsg & _
 ("Processor:  " & proc_desc & " " & proc_mftr & _
 " ~" & proc_mhz & "Mhz" & Chr(10))
sMsg = sMsg & _
 ("BIOS Version:  " & bios_info & Chr(10))
sMsg = sMsg & _
("Windows Directory:  " & os_dir & Chr(10))
sMsg = sMsg & _
 ("Locale:  " & os_locale & Chr(10))
sMsg = sMsg & _
("Time Zone:  " & loc_timezone & Chr(10))
sMsg = sMsg & _
("Total Physical Memory:  " & os_totalmem & "KB" & _
```

28

```
 Chr(10))
sMsg = sMsg & _
 ("Available Physical Memory:   " & os_freemem & "KB" & _
 Chr(10))
sMsg = sMsg & _
 ("Total Virtual Memory:   " & os_totalvirmem & "KB" & _
 Chr(10))
sMsg = sMsg & _
 ("Available Virtual Memory:   " & _
 os_freevirmem & "KB" & Chr(10))
sMsg = sMsg & _
 ("Page File Space : " & os_pagefilesize & "KB" & _
 Chr(10))
```

Finally, I finish by using a message box to display the information. As I pointed out earlier, you could modify this to write the information to a central file or database.

```
'display results
MsgBox sMsg, 0,"System Summary Information"
```

This script is a great example of how WMI can save you time and effort when you need to perform enterprisewide operations in a limited amount of time or on a limited budget. It is not SMS, but it's free, easy to write yourself, and can help solve a similar problem.

Templates

My last two scripts for this chapter are both templates. That is, neither of them do anything especially interesting on their own, but they provide a useful framework for you to insert your own code into. First up is Listing 28.4, which is designed to read a list of computer names from a text file (one computer name per line, in the file), and then execute some code against every one of those computers.

Targeting Lists of Computers   Listing 28.4 actually does contain some useful code, merely as a demonstration of the template: It'll query the current service pack version number from each computer in the file you provide.

LISTING 28.4   *TargetingLists.vbs.* A template used to perform an action against a list of computers.

```
Dim strFilename
strFilename = "C:\computers.txt"

Sub DoObject(strName)

  'this is where YOUR code goes: strName will contain
  'the current computer (or whatever) name. In this example,
```

LISTING 28.4   Continued

```
'we'll use it to query the service pack number. Notice
'how the error trapping works.

'first, turn on error trapping
On Error Resume Next

'try to make a WMI connection - note the use of the
'computer name from our strName variable
Dim objWMI, colOS, objOS
Set objWMI = GetObject("winmgmts:\\" & _
 strName & "\root\cimv2")

'did an error occur?
If Err <> 0 Then
  WScript.Echo "Couldn't connect to " & strName
Else

  'execute WMI query
  Set colOS = objWMI.ExecQuery("SELECT " & _
   "ServicePackMajorVersion FROM Win32_OperatingSystem")

  'go through each returned object
  For Each objOS In colOS
     WScript.Echo strName & " is on SP " & _
       objOS.ServicePackMajorVersion
  Next

End If

'turn off error trapping
On Error GoTo 0

End Sub

Dim objFSO, objTS, strName
Set objFSO = CreateObject("Scripting.FileSystemObject")
Set objTS = objFSO.OpenTextFile(strFilename)
Do Until objTS.AtEndOfStream
  strName = objTS.ReadLine
  WScript.Echo "Read " & strName & _
   " from file..."
  DoObject strName
Loop
objTS.Close
```

28

Keep in mind that this isn't intended to run as is; you're meant to modify it with some task of your own, and you'll need to supply the text file (and filename, in the first part of the script) containing the computer names.

Targeting Lists of Computers—Explained   This script starts by defining the filename that contains the computer names.

```
Dim strFilename
strFilename = "C:\computers.txt"
```

Next is the DoObject subroutine. I've filled in an example, but normally you'd delete all the code within this subroutine and provide your own code. You're given a variable, strName, which contains the current computer name. Your code can then work with that to do whatever it needs to do. As you can see in this example, I'm connecting to the specified computer using WMI and retrieving its service pack version number.

```
Sub DoObject(strName)

  'this is where YOUR code goes: strName will contain
  'the current computer (or whatever) name. In this example,
  'we'll use it to query the service pack number. Notice
  'how the error trapping works.

  'first, turn on error trapping
  On Error Resume Next

  'try to make a WMI connection - note the use of the
  'computer name from our strName variable
  Dim objWMI, colOS, objOS
  Set objWMI = GetObject("winmgmts:\\" & _
   strName & "\root\cimv2")

  'did an error occur?
  If Err <> 0 Then
    WScript.Echo "Couldn't connect to " & strName
  Else

    'execute WMI query
    Set colOS = objWMI.ExecQuery("SELECT " & _
     "ServicePackMajorVersion FROM Win32_OperatingSystem")

    'go through each returned object
    For Each objOS In colOS
       WScript.Echo strName & " is on SP " & _
       objOS.ServicePackMajorVersion
    Next
```

```
End If

'turn off error trapping
On Error GoTo 0

End Sub
```

What follows is the actual working code of the template: It reads in the text file one line at a time. For each line, it calls the DoObject subroutine and passes along the name it read in.

```
Dim objFSO, objTS, strName
Set objFSO = CreateObject("Scripting.FileSystemObject")
Set objTS = objFSO.OpenTextFile(strFilename)
Do Until objTS.AtEndOfStream
  strName = objTS.ReadLine
  WScript.Echo "Read " & strName & _
    " from file..."
  DoObject strName
Loop
objTS.Close
```

I've used this script in any number of situations. In fact, I've made it into a Snippet in my script editor (PrimalScript) so that I can bring the entire template into a new script just by typing the script name and pressing Ctrl+J.

Targeting Users and Computers in AD   Next is Listing 28.5, which performs a similar function. Rather than targeting computers listed in a file, however, this grabs every user and computer name out of Active Directory.

LISTING 28.5   *TargetingAD.vbs*. A template used to perform actions against computers in Active Directory.

```
'connect to the root of AD
Dim rootDSE, domainObject
Set rootDSE=GetObject("LDAP://RootDSE")
domainContainer = rootDSE.Get("defaultNamingContext")
Set oDomain = GetObject("LDAP://" & domainContainer)

'start with the domain root
WorkWithObject oDomain

Sub DoObject_User(strName)
        'your code goes here - strName
        'is a username. If you don't care
        'about users, just leave this empty.
```

LISTING 28.5   Continued

```
End Sub

Sub DoObject_Computer(strName)
        'your code goes here - strName
        'is a computer name. If you don't care
        'about computers, just leave this empty.
End Sub

Sub WorkWithObject(oContainer)
 Dim oADObject
 For Each oADObject in oContainer
  Select Case oADObject.Class
   Case "user"
    'oADObject represents a USER object;
    'do something with it
    DoObject_User oADObject.cn
   Case "computer"
    'oADObject represents a COMPUTER object;
    'do something with it
        DoObject_Computer oADObject.cn
   Case "organizationalUnit" , "container"
    'oADObject is an OU or container...
    'go through its objects
    WorkWithObject(oADObject)
  End select
 Next
End Sub
```

This script doesn't have any sample code in it, so it'll run without modification—but it won't do anything.

Targeting Users and Computers in AD—Explained   This script starts by connecting to the root of your AD domain. It does use the LDAP provider, so it's easy enough to modify if you want to target a specific OU, rather than the entire domain.

```
'connect to the root of AD
Dim rootDSE, domainObject
Set rootDSE=GetObject("LDAP://RootDSE")
domainContainer = rootDSE.Get("defaultNamingContext")
Set oDomain = GetObject("LDAP://" & domainContainer)
```

To target a specific OU, simply change the final line to the LDAP string for the OU you're interested in. Keep in mind that the script will automatically recurse sub-OUs. Next, the script executes a subroutine, WorkWithObject, and passes the root of the domain—or, if you've modified it, the OU you specified—into the subroutine. I'll get to that subroutine in a moment.

```
'start with the domain root
WorkWithObject oDomain
```

These next two subroutines are executed for every user *and* computer in the domain. Of course, if you only want to deal with computers, then just don't add any code to the DoObject_User subroutine. As with the previous template, strName will contain the current object's name, so that your code can do whatever it needs to do.

```
Sub DoObject_User(strName)
        'your code goes here - strName
        'is a username. If you don't care
        'about users, just leave this empty.
End Sub

Sub DoObject_Computer(strName)
        'your code goes here - strName
        'is a computer name. If you don't care
        'about computers, just leave this empty.
End Sub
```

And last is that WorkWithObject routine. I'm using a For Each/Next loop to go through each object in whatever container I'm looking at. When the script first calls this, that container would be the entire domain. Anytime I run across an object that's a user or computer, I call the appropriate DoObject subroutine. However, if I find an OU or another container, *I call this same subroutine again.* This is called *recursively* calling a subroutine, meaning the subroutine actually calls itself to deal with the new container. This will occur over and over for however deeply nested your OUs are, ensuring that the script finds every user and computer object in the domain.

```
Sub WorkWithObject(oContainer)
 Dim oADObject
 For Each oADObject in oContainer
  Select Case oADObject.Class
   Case "user"
    'oADObject represents a USER object;
    'do something with it
    DoObject_User oADObject.cn
   Case "computer"
    'oADObject represents a COMPUTER object;
    'do something with it
        DoObject_Computer oADObject.cn
   Case "organizationalUnit" , "container"
    'oADObject is an OU or container...
    'go through its objects
```

28

```
    WorkWithObject(oADObject)
  End select
 Next
End Sub
```

Summary

Managing domains and Windows by using scripts is an effective, efficient use of your VBScript skills. You'll probably find that a good half of the scripts you write, in fact, are designed for Windows or domain management because those tasks are most often in need of automation. The samples in this chapter provide a great jump-start for improving your environment's security, consistency, and maintainability, all with a few lines of script code!

CHAPTER 29

Network Administration Scripts

Administrative scripts can be some of the most useful tools in your administrator's toolbox. Perhaps the scripts automate some repetitive task; perhaps they enable you to remotely accomplish tasks that would otherwise require a visit to a user's desktop; or, perhaps they simply allow you to accomplish something that would otherwise be too difficult. In any case, the examples in this chapter cover a wide range of uses, and should give you a better idea of what scripts can help you accomplish.

Shutting Down Remote Computers

This is always a useful trick to have up your sleeve. After you've figured out how to do it, you can perform a number of other useful tricks with remote computers.

Shutting Down Remote Computers   Listing 29.1 shows the basic script. You are prompted for a computer name, and then that computer is shut down. This script does use Windows Management Instrumentation (WMI), so both your computer and the one you're shutting down must support WMI, and your user credentials must be accepted on the remote machine as an administrator.

LISTING 29.1   *Shutdown.vbs*. Shuts down a remote computer by using WMI.

```
'get machine to shut down
Dim sMachine
sMachine = InputBox("Shut down what computer?")

'create WMI query
Dim sWMI
sWMI = "SELECT * FROM Win32_OperatingSystem WHERE" & _
 "Primary = True"

'Contact specified machine
Dim oOS
Set oOS = GetObject("winmgmts://" & sMachine & _
 "/root/cimv2".ExecQuery(sWMI))

'run through all returned entries
Dim oItem
For Each oItem in oOS
 oItem.Shutdown
Next
```

You don't need to make any changes to this script to get it to run.

Shutting Down Remote Computers—Explained   This script is typical of most WMI scripts you've seen, except that it uses a method of the queried WMI instance instead of simply querying information. The script starts by getting the name of the computer you want to work with.

```
'get machine to shut down
Dim sMachine
sMachine = InputBox("Shut down what computer?")
```

Next, the script creates a basic WMI query to get all instances of Win32_OperatingSystem that are the primary operating system on the remote machine. I'm not aware of any circumstances under which this query could return more than one operating system, but it is theoretically possible.

```
'create WMI query
Dim sWMI
sWMI = "SELECT * FROM Win32_OperatingSystem WHERE" & _
 "Primary = True"
```

Next, the script executes the WMI query to obtain a list of results.

```
'Contact specified machine
Dim oOS
Set oOS = GetObject("winmgmts://" & sMachine & _
 "/root/cimv2".ExecQuery(sWMI)
```

Finally, because it's theoretically possible for a machine to have more than one primary operating system installed, I run through each one and use its Shutdown method to tell it to shut down. This performs a clean shutdown, meaning applications are asked to exit.

```
'run through all returned entries
Dim oItem
For Each oItem in oOS
 oItem.Shutdown
Next
```

That's all there is to it. The WMI documentation says that the Win32_OperatingSystem class exposes three methods associated with rebooting and shutting down. They are

1. Shutdown, which I've used here. This is a basic clean shutdown.

2. Win32Shutdown, which provides more control over the shutdown process. You can pass this method a flag indicating what type of shutdown you want. For example, 0 is a logoff, 1 is a shutdown, 2 is a reboot, and 8 is a power off. Add 4 to any value to force the action, making 6, for example, a forced reboot.

3. Reboot, which is a simple, clean reboot cousin of Shutdown.

You can modify the sample script here to use any one of these. For example, to implement a forced shutdown:

```
'run through all returned entries
Dim oItem
For Each oItem in oOS
 oItem.Win32Shutdown(5,0)
Next
```

I'm often asked if there's a way to automatically log users off their computers at a specific time; many organizations want to use this capability to better manage software deployments as well as keep workstations more secure. There is a way! Just use Win32Shutdown with the appropriate parameter and run the script from Task Scheduler. Provided the script runs under the credentials of a domain administrator, it should be able to force all machines in the domain to remotely log off, if desired. Just provide it with a list of computers, either from a file or from the results of a domain query.

29

Listing Remote Shares

Ever wonder what shares are available on a remote file server? I've often needed a complete list. Yes, you can use NET VIEW or another command-line utility, but what if you want to list several servers at once, or have the list of shares output to a text file or be used by another script? Having a script capable of generating this list can be a handy tool.

Listing Shares   Listing 29.2 shows how to pull a list of shares from any remote computer, using ADSI.

LISTING 29.2   *Shares.vbs.* Listing remote shares.

```
sServerName = _
 InputBox("Enter name of server to list shares for.")

Set oFS = GetObject("WinNT://" & sServerName & _
 "/LanmanServer,FileService")
For Each sSh In oFS
     WScript.Echo sSh.name
Next
```

Not very complicated, is it? That's the power of ADSI. You shouldn't have to make any changes to run this script, and it will run on NT, 2000, XP, and 2003 systems.

Listing Shares—Explained   This script starts out by simply asking for the name of the server that you want to list shares for.

```
sServerName = InputBox("Enter name of server to list shares for.")
```

Next, it queries ADSI. The ADSI query connects to the specified server's LanManServer, which is a file service. Physically, the Server service is present on all Windows NT-based computers, including NT, 2000, XP, and 2003.

```
Set oFS = GetObject("WinNT://" & sServerName & _
 "/LanmanServer,FileService")
```

The file service has a collection of shares, and this next loop simply iterates each of them and displays each in a message box (or outputs to the command line, if you're running through CScript.exe).

```
For Each sSh In oFS
     WScript.Echo sSh.name
Next
```

You can customize this script easily. For example, to output the server's shares to a text file, just modify the latter half of the script as follows:

```
Dim oFSO, oTS
Set oFSO = CreateObject("Scripting.FileSystemObject")
Set oTS = oFSO.CreateTextFile("c:\shares")

oTS.WriteLine "Shares for server " & sServerName
For Each sSh in oFS
 oTS.WriteLine sSh.Name
Next
oTS.Close
```

You can modify the script to read a list of servers and output each of their file share lists. Listing 29.3 shows the complete script.

LISTING 29.3   *ListShares.vbs*. Listing shares for servers from a text file.

```
Dim oFSO, oTSIn, oTSOut
Set oFSO = CreateObject("Scripting.FileSystemObject")

'Create output file
Set oTSOut = oFSO.CreateTextFile("C:\shares.txt")

'Open input file
Set oTSIn = oFSO.OpenTextFile("c:\servers.txt")

'go through servers
Do Until oTSIn.AtEndOfStream

'get server name
Dim sServerName
sServerName = oTSIn.ReadLine

 Dim oFS, sSH
 Set oFS = GetObject("WinNT://" & sServerName & _
  "/LanmanServer,FileService")

 'go through shares
 For Each sSh in oFS
  oTSOut.WriteLine sSh.Name
 Next

 Set oFS = Nothing

Loop

'close files
oTSIn.Close
```

29

LISTING 29.3   Continued

```
oTSOut.Close

'finished!
MsgBox "Finished!"
```

The input file in this example should list one server name per line, with as many servers as you want.

Finding Out Who Has a File Open

It's not uncommon for users to call their organization's help desk when they're having problems accessing a locked file—that is, a file which is opened for exclusive use by another user. This script is designed to scan through the list of open server resources and list all users who have a specified file open.

Who Has a File   This script is a good example of using the WinNT provider. Note, however, that newer versions of Windows—Windows Server 2003 and later—may not run this script correctly, due to some changes in the way they handle open resources. I've experienced inconsistent results on some servers, but this still stands as a good example of how the WinNT provider operates.

Listing 29.4 shows the script.

LISTING 29.4   *WhoHas.vbs*. Shows who has a particular file open.

```
' first, get the server name we want to work with
varServer = InputBox ("Server name to check")

' get the local path of the file to check
varFile= _
 InputBox ("Full path and filename of the file on the" & _
 "server (use the local path as if you were " & _
 "at the server console)")

' bind to the server's file service
set objFS = GetObject("WinNT://" & varServer & _
 "/lanmanserver,fileservice")

' scan through the open resources until we
' locate the file we want
varFoundNone = True

' use a FOR...EACH loop to walk through the
' open resources
```

LISTING 29.4   Continued

```
For Each objRes in objFS.Resources

        ' does this resource match the one we're looking for?
        If objRes.Path = varFile Then

                ' we found the file - show who's got it
                varFoundNone = False
                WScript.Echo objRes.Path & " is opened by " & _
                 objRes.User
        End If
Next

' if we didn't find the file open, display a msg
If varFoundNone = True Then
        WScript.Echo "Didn't find that file opened by anyone."
End If
```

To operate this script, simply type the name of a server and the full path and filename of a file. This path must be the local path on the server; typing a UNC doesn't work. For example, suppose ServerA has a folder named C:\SalesDocs, which contains a file named Sales.doc. The folder is shared as Sales, and you want to find out who has the file \\ServerA\Sales\Sales.doc open. You'd enter ServerA for the server name, and C:\SalesDocs\Sales.doc as the file path and name.

I have to give you a warning, though: Because of the way that Windows Server 2003 and later versions handle file sharing, this script might not work in every circumstance. I've still had good results when using it with Windows XP computers (which are, after all, a sort of miniserver in that they can share files and printers). I still think the script is a good example of how the WinNT ADSI provider is useful for things other than directory management, which is why I've included it here.

Who Has a File—Explained   As with most scripts, this one begins by collecting some basic information: in this case, the name of a server and the complete path and name of a file.

```
' first, get the server name we want to work with
varServer = InputBox ("Server name to check")

' get the local path of the file to check
varFile= _
 InputBox ("Full path and filename of the file on the" & _
 "server (use the local path as if you were " & _
 "at the server console)")
```

29

Next, the script uses ADSI to bind to the specified server's Server service.

```
' bind to the server's file service
set objFS = GetObject("WinNT://" & varServer & _
 "/lanmanserver,fileservice")
```

First, the script sets a variable indicating that the requested file hasn't yet been found.

```
' scan through the open resources until we
' locate the file we want
varFoundNone = True
```

Now the script uses a For Each/Next construct to iterate through the open files.

```
' use a FOR...EACH loop to walk through the
' open resources
For Each objRes in objFS.Resources
```

Each resource is checked to see if its path matches the specified file path and filename.

```
    ' does this resource match the one we're looking for?
    If objRes.Path = varFile Then
```

If there's a match, the variable is set to False, meaning the file was found. The name of the user who has the file open is displayed in a message box. Notice that the script doesn't use Exit For at this point; more than one user can have a file open, so the script needs to continue looking for other open resources matching the specified file path. There is one resource for each user who has the file open.

```
        ' we found the file - show who's got it
        varFoundNone = False
        WScript.Echo objRes.Path & " is opened by " & _
         objRes.User
    End If
Next
```

Finally, the script displays a message if that variable still equals True. This tells you that the script has finished running, but didn't find any open resources matching the file you specified.

```
' if we didn't find the file open, display a msg
If varFoundNone = True Then
    WScript.Echo "Didn't find that file opened by anyone."
End If
```

Because this script uses the WinNT ADSI provider, it works with Windows NT 4.0, 2000, XP, and 2003.

Uninstalling Remote MSI Packages

Using WMI to interact with MSI packages seems tricky, but it's not too complicated. Wouldn't it be nice to have a script that shows you which MSI packages are installed on a remote computer, and lets you selectively uninstall one? You could remotely weed out unapproved applications on users' machines, maintain servers, and a host of other useful tasks.

Remote MSI Uninstall   Listing 29.5 shows the script. It prompts you for a machine name, and then shows you which packages are installed. Note that the one thing this script doesn't do is work against the machine it's running on; that's because WMI doesn't allow you to specify alternate user credentials when accessing the local machine. If you want to uninstall something locally, use Control Panel!

> **NOTE**
>
> This script runs on Windows NT 4.0, Windows XP, and Windows 2000. However, Windows Server 2003 requires the optional Windows Installer provider, which is included on the Windows Server 2003 CD-ROM.

LISTING 29.5   *Uninstall.vbs*. Uninstalls a remote MSI package.

```
'get remote computer name
Dim sMachine
sMachine = InputBox("Computer name?")

'get admin credentials
Dim sAdminUser, sPassword
sAdminUser = InputBox("Enter the admin username.")
sPassword = InputBox("Enter the user's password. ")

'get a WMI Locator
Dim oLocator
Set oLocator = CreateObject("WbemScripting.SWbemLocator")

'connect to remote machine
Dim oService
Set oService = oLocator.ConnectServer(sMachine, "root\cimv2", _
    sAdminUser, sPassword)

'get a list of installed products
Dim sMsg, sName
Set cProducts = oService.ExecQuery("SELECT * " & _
 "FROM Win32_Product")
For Each oProduct in cProducts
```

29

LISTING 29.5   Continued

```
    'is this the product we want?
    sMsg = "Product: " & VbCrLf
    sMsg = sMsg & oProduct.Name
    sMsg = sMsg & vbCrLf & "Uninstall this product?"

    If MsgBox(sMsg, 4) = 6 Then
        sName = oProduct.Name
        Exit For
    End If

Next

'Get the named package
Set cProducts = oService.ExecQuery("SELECT * " & _
"FROM Win32_Product WHERE Name = '" & _
sName & "'")
For Each oProduct in cProducts

    'uninstall it
    oProduct.Uninstall

    'done!
    MsgBox "Uninstalled " & sName

Next
```

This script should run with no alterations in your environment.

Remote MSI Uninstall—Explained   This script begins by collecting the computer name and administrative credentials. Note that your admin password is displayed in clear text on the screen, but that it isn't transmitted in clear text across the network.

```
'get remote computer name
Dim sMachine
sMachine = InputBox("Computer name?")

'get admin credentials
Dim sAdminUser, sPassword
sAdminUser = InputBox("Enter the admin username.")
sPassword = InputBox("Enter the user's password. ")
```

Next, the script fires up WMI and creates a locator. Then, it uses the locator to connect to the specified machine by using the specified credentials. This bit makes the script throw an error if you try to run it against your local machine.

```
'get a WMI Locator
Dim oLocator
Set oLocator = CreateObject("WbemScripting.SWbemLocator")

'connect to remote machine
Dim oService
Set oService = oLocator.ConnectServer(sMachine, "root\cimv2", _
    sAdminUser, sPassword)
```

The script now queries WMI for a list of installed packages, or products.

```
'get a list of installed products
Dim sMsg, sName
Set cProducts = oService.ExecQuery("SELECT * " & _
 "FROM Win32_Product")
For Each oProduct in cProducts
```

The script builds a message that displays the name of the current product.

```
 'is this the product we want?
 sMsg = "Product: " & vbCrLf
 sMsg = sMsg & oProduct.Name
      sMsg = sMsg & vbCrLf & "Uninstall this product?"
```

The script uses MsgBox() to ask if this is the product you want to uninstall. If it is, the script sets the product's name into a variable for later use, and stops going through products.

```
 If MsgBox(sMsg, 4) = 6 Then
  sName = oProduct.Name
  Exit For
 End If

Next
```

Now, the script gets the named package through another WMI query.

```
'Get the named package
Set cProducts = oService.ExecQuery("SELECT * " & _
 "FROM Win32_Product WHERE Name = '" & _
 sName & "'")
For Each oProduct in cProducts
```

29

The script executes the package's Uninstall method, which remotely runs the uninstall. Normally, the user on the remote computer doesn't see a thing, although that can differ from package to package.

```
'uninstall it
    oProduct.Uninstall
```

Finally, the script displays a message to let you know it finished.

```
    'done!
    MsgBox "Uninstalled " & sName

Next
```

Notice that the uninstall routine occurs inside a For Each/Next loop; this uninstalls any packages with the same name as the name you selected. Normally, each package has a unique name, so just one package is uninstalled each time you run this script.

Listing Hot Fixes and Software

Wouldn't it be nice to have a script that you could run on each computer in your enterprise to get an inventory of hot fixes and software applications? It's not hard! Rather than showing you a single sample script, though, I want to walk through this example a bit more modularly. The first thing I need is a routine that determines the local computer's name, and then opens an output text file on a file server somewhere.

```
Dim oNetwork
Set oNetwork = CreateObject("WScript.Network")

Dim sLocal
sLocal = oNetwork.ComputerName

Dim oFSO, oTS
Set oFSO = CreateObject("Scripting.FileSystemObject")
Set oTS = oFSO.CreateTextFile("\\server\share\" & _
 sLocal & ".txt")
```

This results in an object oTS, which is a TextStream object representing an output text file. The file is named after the computer on which it runs, and you can modify the location to be a file server in your environment.

I just need to find a list of hot fixes and applications, and I don't need to turn any further than the Scriptomatic tool, or the WMI Query Wizard in PrimalScript. Hot fixes are formally known as QFEs, or Quick Fix Engineering patches, and there's a WMI class just for them. The following wizard-generated code queries it for me:

```
On Error Resume Next
Dim strComputer
```

```
Dim objWMIService
Dim colItems

strComputer = "."
Set objWMIService = GetObject("winmgmts:\\" & strComputer & "\root\cimv2")
Set colItems = objWMIService.ExecQuery("Select * from
Win32_QuickFixEngineering",,48)
For Each objItem in colItems
 WScript.Echo "Caption: " & objItem.Caption
 WScript.Echo "CSName: " & objItem.CSName
 WScript.Echo "Description: " & objItem.Description
 WScript.Echo "FixComments: " & objItem.FixComments
 WScript.Echo "HotFixID: " & objItem.HotFixID
 WScript.Echo "InstallDate: " & objItem.InstallDate
 WScript.Echo "InstalledBy: " & objItem.InstalledBy
 WScript.Echo "InstalledOn: " & objItem.InstalledOn
 WScript.Echo "Name: " & objItem.Name
 WScript.Echo "ServicePackInEffect: " & _
  objItem.ServicePackInEffect
 WScript.Echo "Status: " & objItem.Status
Next
```

Similarly, I can query for installed products (software packages) with the following code:

```
On Error Resume Next
Dim strComputer
Dim objWMIService
Dim colItems

strComputer = "."
Set objWMIService = GetObject("winmgmts:\\" & strComputer & "\root\cimv2")
Set colItems = objWMIService.ExecQuery("Select * from Win32_Product",,48)
For Each objItem in colItems
 WScript.Echo "Caption: " & objItem.Caption
 WScript.Echo "Description: " & objItem.Description
 WScript.Echo "IdentifyingNumber: " & objItem.IdentifyingNumber
 WScript.Echo "InstallDate: " & objItem.InstallDate
 WScript.Echo "InstallDate2: " & objItem.InstallDate2
 WScript.Echo "InstallLocation: " & objItem.InstallLocation
 WScript.Echo "InstallState: " & objItem.InstallState
 WScript.Echo "Name: " & objItem.Name
 WScript.Echo "PackageCache: " & objItem.PackageCache
 WScript.Echo "SKUNumber: " & objItem.SKUNumber
 WScript.Echo "Vendor: " & objItem.Vendor
 WScript.Echo "Version: " & objItem.Version
Next
```

29

Again, that's straight from the wizard, so there's not much effort involved. Now, PrimalScript's WMI Query Wizard generates code that echoes to the command line or a message box; to write to my output file, I can just replace the Wscript.Echo with oTS.WriteLine. I can eliminate any queried information that I don't care about, and eliminate redundant lines in the two segments of wizard-generated code. Listing 29.6 shows the completed script.

LISTING 29.6   *Inventory.vbs*. Lists all hot fixes and software on the local computer and outputs the list to a text file.

```vbs
Dim oNetwork
Set oNetwork = CreateObject("WScript.Network")

Dim sLocal
sLocal = oNetwork.ComputerName

Dim oFSO, oTS
Set oFSO = CreateObject("Scripting.FileSystemObject")
Set oTS = oFSO.CreateTextFile("\\server\share\" & _
 sLocal & ".txt")

On Error Resume Next
Dim strComputer
Dim objWMIService
Dim colItems

oTS.WriteLine
oTS.WriteLine "INSTALLED HOTFIXES"
oTS.WriteLine

strComputer = "."
Set objWMIService = GetObject("winmgmts:\\" & strComputer & "\root\cimv2")
Set colItems = objWMIService.ExecQuery("Select * from Win32_QuickFixEngineer-
ing",,48)
For Each objItem in colItems
 oTS.WriteLine "HotFixID: " & objItem.HotFixID
 oTS.WriteLine "ServicePackInEffect: " & _
  objItem.ServicePackInEffect
 oTS.WriteLine "Status: " & objItem.Status
 oTS.WriteLine
Next

oTS.WriteLine
oTS.WriteLine "INSTALLED SOFTWARE"
oTS.WriteLine
```

gestion that their culture is not that of their white schoolmates, that they have no share in the mythic America imagined by the Founders and by Emerson and Whitman, the America partially realized by Lincoln and by King.

That mythic America is a great country, and the insecure and divided actual America is a pretty good one. As racist, sexist, and homophobic as the United States is, it is also a two-hundred-year-old functioning democracy—one that has overcome divisions and mitigated inequalities in the past and may still have the capacity to do so. But by proclaiming the myth a fraud, multiculturalism cuts the ground out from under its own feet, quickly devolving into anti-Americanism, into the idea that "the dominant culture" of America, that of the WASPs, is so inherently oppressive that it would be better for its victims to turn their backs on the country than to claim a share in its history and future.

Although multiculturalism, as a political movement, is guilty of certain blunders and excesses, its critics have greatly exaggerated the threat it poses and the influence it wields. In his recent book *Dictatorship of Virtue: Multiculturalism and the Battle for America's Future*, Richard Bernstein, one of the best reporters at the *New York Times*, writes that "ideological multiculturalism" has brought about "a great inversion in American intellectual life," so that

> whereas before the oppressive force came from the political right, and had to do with a particular view of patriotism, standards and traditional values, the threat of intellectual tyranny now comes from the left, and it now has to do with collective guilt, an overweening moralism and multiculturalism. The danger to such things as free speech and genuine diversity of opinion is no longer due to conservatism; it is due to the triumph of a modish, leftist, moralistic, liberalism.

Nothing in reality (or in Bernstein's book) justifies that last, utterly misleading sentence. Although the book does show that there are more shallow-pated, resentful multiculturalists around than one might have thought, and that they have managed to get control of a primary school system here and a university English department there, the well-organized, well-financed, and very energetic religious right is a hundred times more threatening to free speech and diversity of opinion than all the multiculturalists put together.

Allies of the religious right and conservative intellectuals would like to persuade the public that Allan Bloom was right in suggesting that the universities are under the control of a "Nietzscheanized left," and that the life of the mind in America survives only in conservative think tanks. There is, to be sure, such a left; though it has managed to achieve a lot of good, it is remarkably shortsighted and sometimes pretty silly. Still, its members total perhaps 10 percent of university teachers of the humanities and social sciences and perhaps 2 percent of all university teachers.

The right has been astonishingly successful in impugning the integrity of the entire system of higher education by pointing to the frivolity and self-righteousness of this 2 percent. The conservatives have some good points, but their exaggerations and lies are shameless. It is quite true that if you are a recent Ph.D. in the humanities or social sciences, your chances of finding a teaching job are very good if you are a black female and pretty bad if you are a white male. But such preferential hiring has, on balance, been a good thing for our universities. Those black females—few of whom were seen on university campuses during the first two hundred years of U.S. history—include some of our leading intellectuals. It is quite true that an undergraduate occasionally finds herself in a course devoted to leftist political indoctrination, but she can always drop that course—and many do. (There are also, needless to say, courses that consist largely of rightist political indoctrination.) It is also true that the 2 percent continue to write in a barely intelligible jargon. But compared with the ravings of the fundamentalist preachers about God's hatred for gays and lesbians, such prattle is merely quaint.

There is, indeed, a battle for America's future going on—but it is not the one Bernstein describes in his book. It is a battle between those who see the widening gap between rich and poor as a disaster for the country, and those who see it as just what the poor deserve. It is a struggle for the mind of an electorate that is largely coextensive with the suburban white middle class—a middle class terrified by the downsizing of American firms caused by the globalization of the labor market, and by the thought that its children may wind up on the wrong side of the gap. Politicians like the new Speaker of the House, Newt Gingrich, and wowsers like Pat Robertson have capitalized, with the utmost cynicism and with complete disregard for the nation's future, on this terror. One of their strategies is to portray the professoriate as a conspiracy of leftist fools and knaves.

It is greatly to the advantage of Gingrich and Robertson to convince the public that the colleges and universities—the places where blacks and gays, women and recent immigrants are treated best—are eccentric, dissolute, corrupt, and perverse. This enables them to dismiss out of hand the warnings of liberal professors—warnings about creating an underclass without hope and of letting the national agenda be dominated by the fears of the suburbs. Such warnings can be brushed aside by treating the academy as having succumbed to a "modish, leftist, moralistic liberalism." We can expect, in the next few years, to see more and more attempts to discredit the colleges and universities, for the right is well aware that the American academy is now (after the breakdown of the labor movement) the last remaining defender of the poor against the rich and of the weak against the strong.

Liberalism and the Culture:
A Turning of the Tide?[2]

Lately a few youngish journalists like E.J. Dionne of the *Washington Post*, Mickey Kaus of the *New Republic*, and Jacob Weisberg of *New York* magazine have been trying to persuade themselves and the rest of us that liberalism is once again in the ascendant. But everyone else recognizes that the secular decline in its political fortunes over the past 25 years continues apace.

Thus, the central tenet of contemporary American liberalism in the political sphere—that the federal government is the best instrument we have for dealing with our social and economic problems—has fallen into such disrepute with the voters that even the leader of the Democratic party has felt obliged to repudiate it. "The era of big government is over," Bill Clinton announced in his State of the Union address this year, and his own political fortunes have risen steadily as he has followed through on this fundamental concession to the Republicans by coopting one after another of their positions on one issue after another.

This larcenous campaign has culminated in the President's decision to sign a bill whose entire purpose is to transfer the locus of power over the welfare system from Washington to the states. When the great Tory leader Benjamin Disraeli stole the thunder of the opposition by sponsoring the Reform Bill of 1867, he gloated that he had "dished the Whigs," the liberals of his day. Well, Bill Clinton, applying the same technique from the other end of the political spectrum, has now dished the Tories of our day, turning himself in the process into what some unhappy Democrats have described as the most conservative President to sit in the White House since Grover Cleveland.

Nevertheless, and very significantly, no one mounted even a quixotic primary challenge to Clinton from the Left. His two Democratic predecessors, Lyndon Johnson and Jimmy Carter, both had to face such challenges (as, obversely, did Republican Presidents like Richard Nixon and George Bush from the Right), but so weak is liberalism today that Clinton was given a free ride to renomination. Consequently, if he should be elected to a second term, his success would spell not a resurgence of liberalism but a paradoxical confirmation of its moribund state even within the party which has on the whole been its champion for more than 50 years.

Yet just as virtually everyone acknowledges that liberalism is in critical condition in the political arena, most people recognize that it has continued to reign supreme in the cultural realm. While liberal politicians, dependent on their appeal to an increasingly conservative electorate, have been falling on harder and harder times, the culture, in contrast to what Mr. Dooley famously said about the Supreme Court, has not followed the election returns. For the past quarter of a century and more, conservative electoral victories have come and gone without making more than a barely visible dent in the power exercised by liberalism over the main institutions of our culture. The reason is simply that the arts, the universities, the major media of information and entertainment, and the mainstream churches are all, for better or worse, protected in various ways and to various degrees from the pressures of public opinion, whether exercised through the ballot box or through the commercial marketplace.

As any attentive observer can see, and as many surveys (notably those conducted by Stanley Rothman and his colleagues) have confirmed, this is a world inhabited and controlled by people whose attachment to the liberal creed has proved at least as unshakable as the religious faith of the most fervent fundamentalist. Indeed, for all their trumpeted devotion to "pluralism," the culturati could give the Christian Coalition a lesson or two in intolerance of other points of view. A recent instance is the gang-up on Charles Murray and the late Richard J. Herrnstein for the heresy of stressing the heritability of intelligence in *The Bell Curve*—not to mention the bigotry with which the Christian Coalition itself is routinely discussed in liberal circles.

Moreover, not since the Stalinists of the 30's have we seen a political faction so slavish as the liberal culturati have been in following every new twist in their party's line, even if it represents a 180-degree turn—say, from the principle of individual merit to the principle of group entitlements, or from the anathematization of genetic theories where intelligence is concerned to the sanctification of genetic theories in the case of homosexuality.

No wonder, then, that the culturati have responded to the growing power of their conservative adversaries in the political realm by digging in ever more deeply in the territories they continue to occupy, by consolidating their control over those territories, and by using them as staging areas for ideological attacks on the enemy's ideas and attitudes.

It was thus reasonable to expect the culturati to launch a ferocious assault on Clinton for adopting so many of those ideas and attitudes. On the whole, however, they have been as silent as the liberal politicians who so conspicuously failed to mount a primary challenge against him.

This silence among the culturati becomes all the more striking when we consider that it is not only on narrowly political questions that Clinton now sounds more like a conservative than a liberal. He has also worked hard to dish the Tories on the so-called "values issues."

For example, instead of blaming social factors or "root causes" for the spread of violent crime, as liberals have traditionally done, he has in good conservative fashion stressed the need for more police. (Whether he has actually put as many cops on the street as he claims is another matter.) So too, having begun his term by espousing the cause of gays in the military, he is ending it, or rather trying to extend it, by supporting the Defense of Marriage act, which was framed to prevent the legalization of same-sex marriages (the demand for which, ironically, is itself a kind of "conservative" turn by a movement that formerly celebrated the joys of unrestrained promiscuity—but that is another story). And of course the welfare-reform bill, in addition to adopting the devolutionary political philosophy of the conservatives, mandates a shift from the liberal concept of collective responsibility to the conservative focus on individual responsibility, and on the standard conservative themes of work and family as well.

Why then have the *culturati* held their tongues? One reason clearly has to do with their almost pathological fear of the religious Right. They are convinced that the Christian Coalition now dominates the Republican party and that Pat Robertson and Ralph Reed, helped along by Pat Buchanan, would inaugurate a reign of cultural terror in America if Bob Dole should be elected. Hence to weaken Bill Clinton by attacking him is to undermine the only bulwark that presumably stands between us and a return to the repressions of a barbaric puritanical past.

Hence, too, the silence of the *culturati* in the face of Bill Clinton's move to the Right cannot by itself be taken as a sign of the same weakness reflected in the failure of the liberals to challenge him in the primaries. But the question is whether this silence, taken together with a number of other developments, may perhaps suggest that the power of liberalism is beginning to wane even in the circles where it has thus far been all but absolute.

The most visible such development is the ridicule that has come to be heaped on "political correctness"—the sardonic term for knee-jerk obedience to the dogmas of liberal orthodoxy— even among many people who still consider themselves liberals. Another is the extraordinary commercial success over the past decade of assaults on the liberal culture like the late Allan Bloom's *The Closing of the American Mind*, William J. Bennett's *The Book of Virtues*, and Murray and Herrnstein's *The Bell Curve*. These books have all been savaged by liberal critics, but they could never have become such huge best-sellers if liberal readers, who make up a large proportion of the book-buying public, had not rebelled by buying (and possibly even reading) them. And a third such development is the new willingness—again among people who still consider themselves liberals—to defend the idea that the great classics of Western literature and philosophy constitute a "canon" and to argue that college students should be required to read them. David Denby, the long-time film critic of *New York* magazine who is now also a contributing editor of the *New Yorker*, is a telling case in point.

About five years ago, Denby, finding himself increasingly unhappy over the attacks on the canon emanating from what he calls "the cultural Left," hit upon an intriguing way to check them out personally. What he did was arrange to sit once again, at the age of forty-eight, through the two "great-books" courses—Literature Humanities, or Lit Hum, devoted mainly to literature and philosophy, and Contemporary Civilization, or CC, devoted mainly to political theory—which he had been required to take as a freshman at Columbia College in New York exactly 30 years earlier, and which still form the bedrock of Columbia's undergraduate curriculum. He dutifully read the assigned texts, he regularly attended classes along with the current crop of first-year students (who now included women), and he also conducted interviews with them and with their professors. Now, in *Great Books*, which carries the deliberately provocative subtitle "My Adventures with Homer, Rousseau, Woolf, and Other Indestructible Writers of the Western World," he has given us an account of his year as a "second-time student."

Proceeding author by author through the two reading lists, Denby compares his responses as a callow eighteen-year-old with the way these books strike him today as a successful middle-aged man enjoying a settled and prosperous middle-class life with a wife and two young sons. He also describes the responses of today's callow eighteen-year-olds, as well as the techniques employed by the professors teaching the two courses to elicit and direct those responses. And as he goes along, many occasions present themselves for autobiographical musings and critical reflections on our contemporary cultural condition, all of which he seizes upon with eagerness and gusto. Hobbes brings to mind the time he was mugged; King Lear elicits memories of how he treated his mother when she became old and infirm; and so on.

A few of the writers on the two reading lists (especially Aristophanes and Goethe) leave him cold or with nothing much to say, but he has a great deal to say about most of the others. Though his analyses are neither brilliant nor original, they are almost always interesting, they are lucidly presented, and they are enlivened by skillfully chosen quotations, pertinent anecdotes, and sometimes by an infectious excitement.

In general Denby is relieved and reassured to discover that most of the assigned readings turn out to be richer and more compelling than he remembered. These are, after all, great writers and thinkers; there is, after all, good reason for continuing to read and study them; they do, after all, still have much to teach and much pleasure to give us today; they are, after all, a true embodiment of the culture of the West; it is, after all, a glorious civilization, whose glories include a capacity for recognizing its own flaws and failings and crimes; and women and ethnic minorities, after all, have nothing to fear from being exposed to this culture and much to gain.

In affirming these things, Denby is conducting a polemic, sometimes explicit, sometimes implicit, against two different lines of attack on courses like Lit Hum and CC. The first, which originated with the radicals of the 60's, condemned such courses politically as lacking "relevance" to the problems of the contemporary world, and culturally as "elitist" in promoting the kind of works traditionally preferred by the upper reaches of society while contemptuously dismissing anything that appealed to popular taste.

This particular line of attack was so successful that by the end of the 60's, great-books courses were dropped from the curricula of many colleges. But as the influence of the New Left and the counterculture began to fade a bit in the 70's, the banished courses began being brought back here and there. Then, a few years later, the wind shifted once more, and a fresh line of attack was developed and mounted. This time there was less talk about relevance, but the old charge of elitism was revived and broadened into an even more brazen assault on the entire concept of the classics. To cite only one item in a long parade of horribles, an eminent professor of literature at a major university declared that to choose between Shakespeare and Jacqueline Susann was "no different from choosing between a hoagie and a pizza."

Nor was this the only way in which the old charge of elitism was broadened. Having been confined to questions of aesthetic standards and taste, it now came to embrace the newer issue of "representation." The most notorious battleground was Stanford, where a required course in Western culture was reinstated in 1980. Perhaps because this course was proving so popular with a new generation of students, a movement sprang up demanding that it either be dropped altogether or subjected to affirmative action through the inclusion of "works by women, minorities, and persons of color." Why? Because the reading list—which, like the courses Denby took at Columbia, consisted of such authors as Plato, Augustine, Dante, Rousseau, Mill, and Nietzsche—was marked by a "European-Western and male bias" (or to use the tag that would later become so familiar, "Dead White European Males") and by "sexist and racist stereotypes."

But if Denby was put off by these charges, he was equally bothered by the efforts of those who had responded to them by springing to the defense of the Western cultural heritage:

Such complaints, which issued generally from the academic Left, especially from a variety of feminist, Marxist, and African-American scholars, were answered in turn by conservatives with resoundingly grandiose notions of the importance of the Western tradition for American national morale.... The clear implication of their more polemical remarks was that if we ceased to read the right books, we could not keep Communism or relativism—or

"...if we ceased to read the right books, we could not keep Communism or relativism— or whatever threatened the Republic—at the gates."

whatever threatened the Republic—at the gates. There were national, even geopolitical considerations at stake. Literature had become a matter of policy.

It is hard to decide whether Denby is being dishonest here or merely disingenuous. I incline toward the former, because surely he must know that it was the ideologues of the Left, not the conservatives, who beginning back in the 60's first made the great-books courses "a matter of policy." Surely he must know that the leftist attacks on these courses derived not primarily, and in many cases not at all, from aesthetic considerations or even a hunger for "relevance." Surely he must know that these attacks were instead mainly driven by a hatred of "Amerika" (so spelled to suggest an association with Nazi Germany) and by extension the entire civilization of which this country had become the leader and principal defender. And surely he must know that the same hatred lay behind the latter-day demand for "diversity" and "inclusion," as the Stanford demonstrators perhaps inadvertently revealed when they marched around the campus behind Jesse Jackson chanting, "Hey hey, ho ho, Western culture's got to go."

Because he shies away from this entire dimension of the debate over the canon, Denby is unable (unwilling?) to explain why so much passion should have been aroused by what on the surface might seem a question of interest only to professional educators or to faculty committees designing a few introductory courses for college freshmen.

Let me, then, help him out. As it happens, exactly fifteen years before Denby entered Columbia College, I myself sat as a Columbia freshman through Lit Hum (which was then called Humanities A) and CC. To give Denby his due, he does a very good job of describing what it was like to take these courses. I must also admit I was amazed to discover that despite all the upheavals of the ensuing half-century, Humanities and CC have remained pretty much as they were.

To be sure, the reading lists have been tampered with, most egregiously in bowing to the feminists by substituting Virginia Woolf for Dostoevsky, and bumping Rabelais to make room for Simone de Beauvoir—changes over which Denby, in a perhaps ideologically inspired collapse of critical judgment, falls into a veritable swoon of approval. But there has been much less of this kind of thing than I would have expected: most of the books I had to read as a freshman are still on the lists, and there have even been a few worthy additions.

What is unclear from Denby's account is whether taking Humanities and CC will have the same effect on the students of today as it had on those of the pre-60's era. That effect was well described in a report on the Columbia educational system published in the late 50's by the sociologist Daniel Bell, who claimed that the two courses shocked many students into "a new appreciation of the dimensions of thought and feeling."

As one of those students, I can vouch for the accuracy of this claim. Years later, working on a memoir of my youth, I realized what I had sensed less clearly then: that before Columbia I had never truly understood what men were doing when they committed words to paper. Before Columbia I had never truly understood what an idea was or how the mind could play with it. Before Columbia, I had never truly understood that I was the product of a tradition, that past ages had been inhabited by people like myself, and that the things they had done bore a direct relation to me and to the world in which I lived. At Columbia, thanks to those two courses, all this began opening up for me, and it set my brain on fire.

It also left me incapable of believing in the sincerity of the charge that would later be made by the Left that these courses were "irrelevant," though evidently it did not do as much for Denby, who takes the sincerity of that charge at face value even as he registers his disagreement with it.

Again unlike Denby, I was also left, as a Jew, incapable of accepting the good faith of the students who would later complain that because of race or sex they felt ignored and demeaned by the great classic texts of the West. (To my astonishment, Denby even praises one such student for being courageous in voicing this most politically correct of complaints.) The texts in question included very few by Jews, and if they referred to Jews or Judaism at all, it was more often than not in an unfriendly and even hostile spirit. Yet working through the two reading lists as a Columbia student, I felt that an inheritance of indescribable richness which in the past had often been inaccessible to my own people was now mine for the taking. Far from being excluded, I was being invited in, and I looked upon the invitation as a great opportunity and a privilege. For their part, the Columbia authorities looked upon the invitation as a means of transforming the children of immigrants like me, who were being admitted in greater numbers to the college, into properly cultivated American gentlemen.

Contrary to the other major charge the Left would later make, no secret political intent or agenda lurked behind the two courses. It is true, as Denby points out, that CC was originally instituted as a defense of Western civilization, but this was in the 20's, long before Western civilization was turned into the kind of political issue it would become 40 years later. As for Lit Hum, it dates from the 30's, and from the start it reflected the belief that students ought to be introduced to the books that had shaped the world in which they lived. It was further assumed, in the spirit of Matthew Arnold's famous definition of culture, that these books were among the best things that had been thought and said in the entire history of the human race.

No doubt there were some at Columbia who also thought that these works were superior to the products of other civilizations (a judgment I for one would be prepared to defend); but even 50 years ago, long before anyone was demanding "inclusion" and "representation," Columbia set up a parallel course in Oriental civilization in which we sampled the great classics of China, Japan, and India in exactly the same way as we did the classics of the West. So much for the allegation that the great-books courses were an instrument of cultural imperialism aimed at reinforcing the "hegemony" of Dead White European Males.

That said, I must in all honesty add that the radicals in the 60's who tried to abolish Humanities and CC and courses like them in other colleges knew what they were doing (even if Denby still does not). For in addition to being shocked into "a new appreciation of the dimensions of thought and feeling," something else also happened to many students as a result of those courses. Daniel Bell characterizes it as a kind of "conversion experience"—a conversion not to another religion but, "so to speak, to culture." Though he does not say so explicitly, by culture Bell specifically means the heritage of Western civilization, and on this point too I can offer personal testimony that bears him out. There is no doubt that Columbia left me with a reverence for Western civilization that was nothing short of religious in intensity and that has lasted all my life.

It was because they wanted to put a stop to this "conversion experience" that the radicals zeroed in on the courses that were producing it. Beyond that, their object was to clear the way for the opposite conversion experience: one that would leave most students feeling not reverence for Western civilization but hatred and contempt.

In other words, it was not because the great books were "irrelevant" that the radicals of the 60's opposed studying them; it was because they were all too relevant. Similarly, it was not "inclusion" that the "multiculturalists" of a later period wanted, as their liberal apologists soothingly reassured us (and as Denby still seems to imagine). What they wanted was to carry forward the work of destruction begun by their radical predecessors of the 60's, and in this they were egged on and helped along by some of those predecessors who had now become professors themselves.

And where were the liberals in all this? Almost from the first moment of the New Left campaign against the universities—the opening shots were fired at Berkeley in 1964—the liberals responded by mollifying, appeasing, and even joining in. What made this unlovely spectacle even uglier and more bizarre was the fact that it was the liberals themselves who were the main target of the radical movement.

Of course, the New Left hated the Right, but to these young radicals the Right was so self-evidently evil that there was no point wasting energy in fighting it. The real villains were liberalism and the "liberal establishment," on whom the New Left heaped all the blame for everything that in its eyes was wrong with America—for starting and refusing to end the cold war and the "arms race" (and, a little later, the war in Vietnam); for perpetuating a social and economic system that fostered racism and poverty; and for creating colleges and universities whose main purpose was to turn out slavish participants in that system and cannon fodder for its imperialistic aggressions in the third world.

To all this, the liberals almost to a man, and especially those teaching in the colleges and universities, pleaded, in effect, guilty with an explanation, and threw themselves on the mercy of their student judges. Nor did the liberals stand up for themselves against the parallel assault of the counterculture. Indicted for fostering a middle-class culture based on repression (just as their socioeconomic system was founded on oppression), they bowed their heads humbly in acquiescence, and tried to expiate by giving their blessing to the holy trinity of "sex, drugs, and rock and roll."

Only a very small number of intellectuals, whether inside the academy or out, could summon the self-respect, the resources, and the courage to defend the canon and the cultural heritage it embodied. Some were conservatives to the manner born, and some were "neoconservatives" who, precisely out of disgust with this very turn of events, had grown estranged from the liberal or radical communities to which they had up till then comfortably belonged.

Provoked by the leftist "demystification" of the canon as an instrument of Western tyranny, these intellectuals fought back by turning the tables on the radical critique, demystifying it as a cover for an anti-American political agenda, and aggressively reasserting the glories that were being besmirched by that critique. Now, for their pains, Denby accuses them of having introduced politics into the debate. He is scarcely less scurrilous in alleging that they regarded literature as "an ineffably noble but essentially static body of values that could, and should, be inoculated into every generation of American students." I know of no conservative intellectual who ever took, or takes, so silly a view of the nature of literature and its relation to any "body of values."

With the conservative counterattack being met by liberal silence or liberal vilification, there was not enough resistance to check the spreading power of the Left—a coalition of Marxists, Africanists, feminists, gay propagandists, and deconstructionists who were united politically by their hatred of American society and all its works, and intellectually by their rejection of the belief in scholarly or aesthetic standards and objective truth. Nor was the influence of this coalition confined to the universities. Its ideas and attitudes spilled over into the culture at large—the movies, television, popular music, and the critical coverage of these areas in the major newspapers and magazines.

So it was that things went from bad to worse—until finally, a few years ago, they got to be too much even for some liberals who now rushed in where only conservatives had formerly dared to tread. The late social critic Christopher Lasch produced a series of impassioned protests against "the culture of narcissism"; the historian Arthur M. Schlesinger, Jr. went public with his worries about "the disuniting of America" as a result of the radical emphasis on the rights and grievances of ethnic, racial, and sexual groups; the art critic Robert Hughes pronounced himself bothered by the "culture of complaint" that was growing out of the same emphasis; and now David Denby has entered the lists as a champion of the canon and everything it represents.

Each of these cases is different, but in Denby's, the force that seems to have pushed him into speaking up was a growing panic over what was happening to his two young sons. Both in *Great Books* and in a recent article in the *New Yorker* entitled "Buried Alive," he dwells almost obsessively on the malign effects of the popular culture of today over his own children and everyone else's. Television, movies, popular music, and the new medium of video games are more violent, more vulgar, and more sexually explicit than their earlier counterparts, and they are coarsening the tastes and poisoning the minds of the kids while inflicting who knows what other "internal injuries along the way."

"Television, movies, popular music, and the new medium of video games are more violent, more vulgar, and more sexually explicit than their earlier counterparts..."

As a parent, Denby tries to counter this influence. He reads Dickens aloud to his boys when they are on vacation, he plays Toscanini's recording of the Beethoven Seventh on the stereo for them, and he occasionally forbids them to see a certain movie or watch a certain program. But it is a losing battle. Even though they seem to enjoy Dickens and Beethoven, "asserting control over the boys' tastes is no longer possible beyond a certain point. How can you control what they breathe?"

A few parents of his acquaintance, Denby reports, "have turned themselves into authoritarians, banning television, banning many kinds of 'unsuitable' movies." Yet for him and his wife (the novelist Cathleen Schine), "the issue is not so simple." Unlike those inflexible conservative "bullies," he and his wife "are not eager to stand over the children, guiding their progress all day long like missionaries leading the savages to light." Nor are they prepared to devote the amount of energy to their children that such vigilance would require.

Besides, Denby asks plaintively, throwing up his hands in despair, "How can you fight what you enjoy yourself?" And to make matters even more difficult, he realizes that people like him bear a fair share of responsibility for the incredible coarseness of pop culture today:

> We left-wing types popularized rudeness and slangy candor as a style of public discourse 30 years ago—our language, we thought, would discredit the official hypocrisies—and now everyone is going in for it.

Having admitted this much, however, Denby is still unwilling to confront the part played by critics like himself in erasing the distinction between high and low in the arts, or the extent to which this opened the way to the swamping of the high by the low which he now decries as the loss of a precious pocket of resistance. But he does confess to one "minor crime," namely,

> the too-easy use of such loaded words as "subversive" and "transgressive" to praise movies and rock albums that offer a little more sex and violence than other good movies and albums. A few years ago, liberal-minded cultural critics, terrified of standing with the squares, got bullied out of any sort of principled public resistance to pop. They took themselves out of the game, and left the field open for William Bennett's iron moralism.

He then goes on to advocate that liberals get back into the game by working for the break-up of the huge new media conglomerates, and for more regulation of the airwaves.

Placing at least part of the blame on capitalism and looking to Washington for a solution is the only indigenously liberal contribution Denby makes to the discussion—the only idea he comes up with that is not filched from the "squares" and the conservatives he is still "terrified of standing with." Everything else—in an act of intellectual theft fully worthy of Bill Clinton's analogous maneuvers in the political sphere—he lifts without thanks or credit from the conservative position:

> If parents are not to feel defeated by the media and pop culture, they must get over their reluctance to make choices that are based on clear assertions of moral values. They cannot leave to the "virtuecrats" the defense of religion, high culture, the meritocracy, the Western literary classics, or anything else that implies a hierarchy of taste.

And finally, in an implicit plug for his new book, he urges liberals to "join the discourse and make it aesthetically and morally alive."

It would seem, then, that Denby has wound up standing with the squares and the conservatives after all—while (exactly like Robert Hughes before him) pretending that he is not doing so by making snide remarks about them even as he follows in their footsteps. But ungracious and ungrateful though this is, more is at stake here than decent intellectual manners and morals. For throughout both his book and his article, Denby consistently weakens his effort to defend the traditional culture against the Left by paying excessive deference to the latter's ideas and attitudes—the very ideas and attitudes that have brought us to the path out of which he is now struggling to find a negotiable path.

Sometimes this deference takes the small but by no means insignificant form of sycophantic gestures like using "she" as the generic pronoun instead of "he." Sometimes it manifests itself in his endorsement of leftist sentiments like hostility to capitalism and sympathy for anything deemed subversive (notice that when he apologizes above for having praised certain movies as subversive, it is not because he now questions his old assumption that subversive automatically means good, but because those particular movies did not truly deserve such high praise). And for all his new determination to uphold "hierarchies of taste," he can still put quotation marks around the word "high" when writing of the arts, and he can still speak of his favorite movies and television shows as though they belonged in the same universe as the great classics and were fully worthy of inclusion in the canon.

The upshot is that as a champion of high culture and the values it enshrines, and as a fighter against the depredations of the academic Left and its comrades and acolytes in the media and the popular culture, Denby leaves much to be desired. Nevertheless, there can be no doubt that his case provides another sign that liberalism in the cultural sphere, even though it is nowhere near the moribund condition into which it has by now fallen in the world of electoral politics, is no longer quite so powerful as it was even a few short years ago.

Philanthropical Correctness[3]

Tuxedoed waiters glide through the lobby of the San Francisco Museum of Modern Art bearing silver serving trays on whose oval surfaces repose, like the answer to a problem in geometry, dozens of round-mouthed glasses of dry white wine. One by one the glasses are gratefully plucked from the trays by the program officers of America's foundations. They are gathered here on the final, gala night of the Council on Foundations's annual conference, "Philanthropy and the Public Good."

Drinking wine, snacking on a multicultural assortment of canapés from America, Japan, Mexico, China, Italy and France, the staff of America's foundations offer a pleasing testament to the vision of the council and of its departing president, James Joseph. It is a vision that, in Joseph's words, will combine "the civic habits of the Iroquois" admired by Benjamin Franklin, "the Afro-American passion for justice," the "neo-Confucian" respect for benevolence and giving, the brotherhoods for mutual assistance established by Latinos "as early as 1598" and the traditions of "Native Americans, who engaged in giveaways." The staff of America's major foundations are male and female, black and white, Asian and Hispanic, in their 30s and 40s. Among them circulate perhaps 400 foundation trustees, mostly male, ten to fifteen years older, whose erect carriage and well-modulated voices testify, in a genial, unhurried way, to the life-enhancing effects of giving away large sums of money.

In the past twenty-five years, the assets of American foundations have more than tripled, to stand at $189.2 billion. Last year, they gave away approximately $10 billion in grants. The offices in which foundation staff work range from the blandly corporate to the Ford Foundation's modernist masterpiece in Manhattan—two blocks from the U.N.—with its twelve-story atrium and transparent glass walls that, on a sunny day, transform the gray canyons of midtown into glorious, shimmering wallpaper. Most remarkable of all are the terraced indoor gardens, a dense green jungle four stories high, suggesting a dream dreamt by Nebuchadnezzar of Babylon and executed by Mies van der Rohe.

The dream embodied by the Ford Foundation's soaring glass walls and by its 300 employees, who gave away $285 million in grants last year—a mere fraction of the interest on Ford's $6.7 billion endowment—is the dream of an America remade according to the blueprints of the best and the brightest. Foundations embody, in institutional form, the noble dream that has lifted the hearts of American liberals since the days of the young Walter Lippmann, of the nation as a vast laboratory for the reasoned

---

[3] Article by David Samuels, freelance writer for *The New Republic*, from *The New Republic* 213:28-9 + S 18-25 '95. Copyright © 1995 *The New Republic*. Reprinted with permission.

programs of the elite. Charities, churches and synagogues might feed and house the hungry and the homeless. The task of foundations like Ford is different: to launch programs that carry public policy in new and uncharted directions, to benefit the whole of society.

In the decades following the Second World War, foundations served as leading instruments of the liberal consensus, using their position at the intersection of the elite worlds of government, politics, academia and the press to remake America in their own progressive image. Foundations funded, in whole or in part: the early expansion of our system of public libraries, Jonas Salk's discovery of the polio vaccine, the writing of Gunnar Myrdal's *An American Dilemma*, the Public Broadcasting Corporation, the "Grey Areas" project that led to Model Cities, and the Michigan study that yielded Head Start. Other, less successful, foundation efforts—Ford's meddlesome financing of radical black activists in Bedford-Stuvyesant, for example—are best forgotten. What was striking about the foundations of the '50s and '60s, however, was not so much the merit of their ideas as the extent of their influence. John Gardner, president of the Carnegie Corporation from 1955 to 1965, served as Lyndon Johnson's Secretary of Health, Education and Welfare, taught at Harvard and MIT, worked at the FCC and founded Common Cause. McGeorge Bundy, president of Ford from 1966 to 1979, was a former dean of the faculty of arts and sciences at Harvard and national security adviser under Kennedy and Johnson. With years of experience and contacts throughout interlocking worlds of the elite, Gardner and Bundy conveyed their ideas to academics, editors, members of Congress and presidents and, in many cases, saw them enacted into law.

What is most striking about American foundations today, however, is the absence of ambitious—and ultimately successful—undertakings like Head Start, the Salk Vaccine or PBS from the thousands of projects, pilots, reports and commissions they annually sponsor. Asked to name a foundation-sponsored project of the last twenty-five years that has had a significant impact on American society, Council President James Joseph shakes his head. "There are many good programs," he says, "but as for the kind of program you describe, a Head Start or a PBS, I can't think of one."

Of the major players in the foundation world—Ford and Carnegie included—none has proved more influential in standardizing professional practices and in setting a common multiculturalist agenda for foundations big and small than the Council on Foundations. To wander the halls of the council-sponsored conference in San Francisco is to see the cartoon pages of William Bennett and Dinesh D'Souza brought spectacularly to life. When not attending the conference sessions—which range from "Philanthropic Courage: Promoting an Agenda of Genuine

Inclusion" to "The Colors of Desire: A Multimedia, Multicultural Performance"—participants can eat, drink and make new friends at receptions sponsored by any one of the council's influential "affinity groups": "Native Americans in Philanthropy," "Asian Americans in Philanthropy," "Hispanics in Philanthropy," "Women in Philanthropy" and the "Association of Black Foundation Executives." Or they can relax in the Marriott screening room and watch some of the many foundation-sponsored videos, reflecting the great and increasing interest among foundation staff in sponsoring film, performance and other alternative media projects. The screenings include: "Look Who's Laughing" ("Six Comedians with Physical Disabilities Talk About Their Lives"), "Meeting Ancestors" ("An Indian Tribe in the Amazon Shares a Camcorder with a More Remote Tribe") and "Saviors of the Forest" ("Two Hollywood 'Camera Guys' Set Off to Save the Rainforest and Become Involved with Greenpeace and a Host of Environmental Activists and Sustainable Harvest Entrepreneurs").

If Michael Ovitz is unlikely to come calling at the Marriott anytime soon, neither are supporters of more traditional public arts like fiction, poetry, music or ballet. Where the Ford Foundation of the 1950s and '60s spent its money on efforts to promote writing and scholarship at major universities and on symphony orchestras and ballet companies in dozens of American cities, Ford today spends its money on arts projects designed to "promote tolerance and social understanding" and ensure "access and equity." The adoption of such goals has led to what might otherwise seem like a puzzling artistic emphasis on documentary films by little-known filmmakers—and at Ford. "As a video artist," Simone Farkhondeh explains to readers of the 1994 Rockefeller Foundation Report, "I am convinced that it is important to continually critique the media's powerful yet limited images of many in our society.... In my experimental documentary, I illustrate the multifaceted lives of Iranian women." Whatever the worth of such programs, Rockefeller's stated emphasis on "cultural diversity" in funding for the arts is a far cry from the goals set out by the foundation in its annual report of 1968, where it boasts of having "enabled such leading writers as Ralph Ellison, Wright Morris, and Philip Roth to continue and complete novels; poets W.S. Merwin and William Meredith to continue their work; Eudora Welty and Richard Taylor to complete books of short stories; Kenneth Burke and Josephine Herbst to write scholarly works." If Newt Gingrich truly believes, as he has stated, that private philanthropies can and should supplant government in providing for the public good and promoting lasting art, he is in for something of a surprise.

Multiculturalism is one reason that foundations no longer set America's social policy agenda as they did in the 1960s. The other is that they have exempted their recipients from the schol-

"Multiculturalism is one reason that foundations no longer set America's social policy agenda as they did in the 1960s."

arly outside review that used to give them credibility with poli-cymakers. The tens of thousands of grant proposals that pour into foundation offices every year are sorted by program officers. It is they who decide which of these programs their foundation will sponsor. "There is no application form," Ford advises its prospective grantees, who are requested to provide program offi-cers with information about their objectives, programs, budgets and the qualifications of persons engaged in the work. Most pro-gram officers are generalists who often hold degrees from bureaucratic training grounds like the Woodrow Wilson School at Princeton or the Kennedy School at Harvard. Few have any spe-cial expertise or experience in the fields in which they make grants. Says Waldemar Nielsen, author of *The Big Foundations* and a program officer at Ford for almost two decades, "In the end, when there's no real way to determine whether your project has succeeded or not, you write it up for the annual report: 'We have set elementary education on an entirely new course.'"

"Of 240 grants made by the Carnegie Corporation in 1989, totaling $37 million, only 27.5 percent (sixty grants) went to American universities."

One obvious antidote to the lighter-than-air atmosphere that often permeates foundation work is the strict evaluation of pro-grams by outside researchers and academics. Head Start, the last foundation-sponsored project to have resulted in a major public policy initiative, was exhaustively evaluated by researchers, whose conclusions were accepted by politicians and the public. As researchers writing for an audience composed in part of other social scientists, academic recipients of foundation largess were forced to put the pilots and models they devised into falsifiable forms that could be attacked—or accepted—by their peers. What the academy offered foundations was more than a promise of expert knowledge or a reassuring association with Harvard or Yale. It was, above all, the power to convince others that the solutions they advocated might work, that they represented something more than the wishful thinking of those within foun-dation walls.

In the past twenty-five years, however, a startling shift in foun-dation funding has occurred, away from research and toward the support of advocacy groups and the kinds of social service pro-grams best accomplished by government and private charity. Of 240 grants made by the Carnegie Corporation in 1989, totaling $37 million, only 27.5 percent (sixty grants) went to American universities. Most were relatively small, and many went to non-research oriented projects such as an "international negotiations network" at Emory University's Carter Presidential Center, or "Reprinting and Disseminating the Handbook for Achieving Sex Equity Through Education and the Sex Equity Handbook for Schools." Most of the Carnegie grants fell into one of two cate-gories: funding and disseminating a host of high-flown reports by Carnegie-sponsored commissions; and funding advocacy groups including the Organizing Institute, the International Peace Academy, the ACLU Foundation, the National Council of La Raza, the Fund for Peace and the Children's Defense Fund. It is the stuff of which Republican careers will doubtless be made: a multi-billion-dollar tax exemption for the political agenda of liberal elites.

Those who share the broader social concerns of the foundations might wonder as well whether doling out hundreds of millions of dollars to ideologically driven advocates—who lack the time, the training or the inclination to evaluate what they do—is the best prescription for future innovations in public policy. Foundations enjoy their present tax-free moorings because they claim to operate as a nonpartisan force dedicated to the pursuit of innovative solutions to our pressing social ills, sheltered from the shifting partisan winds. The preponderance of foundation grants to advocacy groups, however, suggests that foundations are less devoted to the reasoned pursuit of the public good than to the multiculturalist dogmas propounded by their staff.

To read the foundation reports of the '60s is to enter a very different world. Of 128 grants, $12.2 million in all, made by the Carnegie Corporation in 1965, for example, 53 percent of the total (sixty-eight grants) went to American colleges and universities, from the Bank Street College of Education to Harvard, to pursue research and to set up pilot programs that would influence our practical understanding of the built environment of cities, of teaching, of police work, of the low-wage economy, of state and local government and of other aspects of society for decades to come. (Nearly all of the remaining grants went to universities abroad for similar goals.) In 1968, under Bundy, Ford devoted 17 percent of its $203 million to grants designed to promote research and education. Of the 33 percent of the foundation budget devoted to its international programs, most went to universities. The 31 percent devoted to national affairs included grants of $3 million each to MIT, Chicago and Harvard, and more than $4 million to Columbia to come up with ways of easing tensions between black urban communities and the police, an effort which resulted, in part, in reforms that have become popular under the heading of "community policing."

By contrast, the Ford Foundation Report of 1994 reads more like a guide to the professional advocacy industry, with grantees including the Ms. Foundation, the Women's Legal Defense Fund, the National Women's Law Center, and the Institute for Women, Law and Development as well as the Board of Global Ministries of the United Methodist Church and the National Council of Churches of Christ. Only thirty-eight of 100 grants given under the rubric education and culture went to universities; most went to local community colleges.

No longer subject to academic review, evaluations of foundation programs today are carried out by foundation staff and by grantees themselves. Certainly many of these recipients are worthy and well-intentioned. The trouble is that, under the new system, it's almost impossible to evaluate what actual good they do.

One recipient of major foundation grants, an educator in a Northeastern city who refused to allow his name to be published, described the process with a cynicism that appears to be general: "They think they're being clever by asking you to come up with your own criteria for success—60 percent of children in the eighth grade will be reading at a ninth-grade level in two years, or whatever. And they ask you to select an 'independent evaluator' to report on whatever progress has been made. It's all very numerical: but the goals you select are always goals that you know you can reach. Maybe 60 percent of eighth graders are already reading at a ninth-grade level. Maybe it's 70 percent. The foundations don't know. And the evaluators you select are people with a stake in the project. They're getting a salary—from you, or an organization related to yours; some part of their income comes from that grant. And so the project is evaluated, declared a success, and everyone—the program officer, the trustees and you—can go home happy."

Over the past twenty-five years, the men and women who staff America's major foundations have become a tight-knit world unto themselves. The columns of *The Foundation News* regularly track the progress of foundation staff from one foundation to another. "The Nord Family Foundation in Elyria, Ohio," one recent announcement reads, "has named David R. Ashenhurst executive director. Ashenhurst held positions with the Pew Charitable Trusts, the John D. and Catherine T. MacArthur Foundation and the Rotary Foundation of Rotary International." Nearly 40 percent of foundation CEOs now come from the non-profit sector; according to the Council on Foundations nearly 30 percent are hired from within their own foundations. As hirings from within increase, the quality of leadership has declined. If McGeorge Bundy's name remains familiar to many Americans, the name of his successor at Ford, Franklin Thomas, is little known outside the foundation world. Thomas's successor, Susan Berresford, has spent her entire professional life in the service of Ford. It is possible that, like Mikhail Gorbachev, she has spent decades nurturing secret, sweeping plans for reform. However, with no independent experience in government, industry, academia or the media, she will be hard-pressed to put any bold new plans she might have into practice. Was there a better choice than Susan Berresford? We will never know, since Berresford was selected to head the $6.7 billion Ford Foundation, America's largest and most influential, without even the formality of an outside search. It's hard to imagine any other American institution of comparable size and influence—Harvard, Yale or the Ford Motor Company, for that matter—selecting its leader without at least a polite nod to the world outside its walls.

Because foundations are unique among our major institutions in their freedom from public scrutiny over their finances, programs and decision-making processes, it is impossible to say with certainty how or why they chose to fund certain programs and decline to fund others. A conference "site-visit" to the Tenderloin district of San Francisco, however, offers a glimpse into the minds of the program officers who determine what programs their foundations will pursue. "Long considered the underbelly of downtown," the conference program explains, "the Tenderloin suddenly became a family neighborhood when thousands of immigrants and refugees from Vietnam, Cambodia and Laos arrived after the Vietnam War. Arriving also in the 1970s and 1980s," it adds, "were hundreds of activists and millions of foundation dollars."

We are all eager to escape from the Marriott, from the disorientation and lethargy induced by the glare of artificial lights and the absence of clocks or windows. Not even the presence of the uniformed security guard on the sidewalk alongside us, nor the mumbled offers of "sniff, grass, joint," nor the shouts of "motherf—" from a wandering vagrant in a pink foam-rubber baseball cap can dampen the spirits of the group. What the Tenderloin needs, according to surveys of its residents, is an active police force, more jobs and small business loans. What it gets from foundations and other sources are grants to build housing, parks and community centers, big-ticket items whose sheer physical presence is often enough to convince program officers—and their boards—that they are doing good work. On our way to visit a local housing development corporation we pass Boedekker Park, a handsome facility built by the city of San Francisco at no small expense. It offers sturdy benches along well-paved pathways situated to take maximum advantage of the available space for trees and grass. There is a playground for children, which at noon, in a district whose population includes more than 2,000 children, is empty. The park, however, is occupied by aimless men in their 30s and 40s holding brown paper bags and leaning drunkenly from the benches. As I stand and watch, a man in a tattered plaid shirt leans over, vomits, leans back and closes his eyes.

A small knot of well-groomed children between the ages of 4 and 10 has gathered on the sidewalk outside a building run by the Indo-Chinese Housing Development Corporation (IHDC), the only Indo-Chinese-run nonprofit housing corporation in the Tenderloin. In the building's dark, well-ordered basement, the IHDC's executive director, Bill Ng, a mild-looking man in his 40s, addresses a pitch for funding to the foundation staff. Behind him, like a scene from some long-ago civics class, sit a row of his tenants in their Sunday best. "I want you to think about these people and the wars, the beatings, the tortures, the murders they escaped in order to come here," Ng says, "and then I want you to think about how they are living now and raising their children, with the crime, the drugs, the fear and the violence. Ask yourselves this question: Are they really better off?"

Ng's voice cracks, and he seems a little unnerved. Before him, after all, is a foundation man who could, on the spot, write out a check for thousands of dollars. "Are you better off here?" the foundation man asks one of the tenants, an older Cambodian man who smiles in a friendly, dignified way as he waits for the question to be translated. He hears, nods and replies. The translator shrugs. "He is very happy to be an American."

"But is he better off here than where he came from?" the foundation man asks again. As the question is translated, Ng shifts uneasily from one foot to another, with the expression of a man who, glancing down at his cards, realizes too late that he may have overplayed his hand. "He says he is better off here," the translator says. "He says he has two children in college, one at U.C.-Davis and one at Santa Cruz." As the tenant beams, Ng is plainly beside himself. It's not the old man's fault, but he has just given the worst possible answer. After all the talk of beatings and tortures, calculated to make the foundation people feel that the tenants are victims deserving of aid, the old man has to go on about his children in college. That the old man's children have made it out of the Tenderloin to the safe harbor of college might, in a universe very different from the one that program officers inhabit, be taken as a sign that this poor community is able to make the best of its obviously limited resources, that the dollars invested here would be dollars well spent. But what the foundations really want to hear, as Ng knows, are not tales of success but failure. If only the old man's children were on crack instead of in college! Instead of pursing their lips and exchanging disapproving glances—as they are doing now—the program officers would be moved, to tears perhaps, and the mighty waves of foundation dollars would come rolling in.

Bill Ng's other problem is that all his tenants are Asians. What program officers value most in the projects they sponsor is the appearance of "multiculturalism," that is, the joint participation in housing, recreational and employment projects—not of Laotians, Vietnamese and Cambodians—but of officially sanctioned racial groups: Asians, blacks and Latinos. "The problem for me had to do with the lack of other groups at the table," one program officer, a young white woman with a shoulder-length bob, says later. "Too narrow," says another. "I was left wondering about the indigenous population," says a program officer from Chicago, using a term that in the foundation world is commonly used to refer to blacks, Hispanics and other residents of poor neighborhoods such as the Tenderloin.

Indeed, the ideologically driven pursuit of "diversity" and "inclusiveness" is perhaps the one area in which today's foundations are influencing public policy with anything like the force of their powerful predecessors of the '50s and '60s. To say that foundations influence policy, however, is not to say that the pursuit of "diversity" and "inclusiveness" they advocate is succeeding in our poor, multiracial cities. Exactly what happens when foundation-bred "inclusiveness" schemes are put into practice is disturbingly illustrated by a conference session titled "Realities of Multiculturalism: Barriers and Opportunities for Public Housing Tenants." Moderated by Diane Bermudez of the Evelyn and Walter Haas Jr. Fund, a small San Francisco-based foundation, the session, whose message starkly contrasts with the rest of the conference's, is clearly intended as a reality check for the well-dressed program officers in attendance. The session is devoted to the origins and the progress of a lawsuit brought by the Asian Law Caucus in response to a 1992 San Francisco HUD decision to "integrate" public housing by moving black families into pre-dominantly Asian projects and vice versa. One of today's pan-elists, Don Bonus, is a Vietnamese college student whose family was moved into the predominantly black Sunnyvale project by San Francisco HUD and was forced out by fellow tenants in 1993.

"The first day it was nice and everything," Bonus recalls. "The next day, when we were moving furniture in, people started harassing us, shouting, 'Go home, Chinaman.' We were harassed every day. People shot at our apartment and broke all the win-dows. It would take days to get the windows replaced. When we went outside we'd get robbed. We called the cops, but the cops would not show up to protect us." According to Gen Fujioka, the lawyer who brought the lawsuit against HUD, the incidents were part of a pervasive pattern of racially motivated harassment and violence that first came to the center's attention during Christmastime of 1992, when Asian tenants were beaten up in their apartments in the middle of night in what sounds suspi-ciously like an organized pogrom. "We went to the housing authorities," Fujioka recalls, "and they told us these were not racial incidents. The best we can do, they told us, is get them out."

Panelist Roberta Achtenberg, former assistant secretary of HUD and chief fair-housing enforcement officer during the years this peculiar drama was played out, has only sympathy for its vic-tims. Achtenberg, now a candidate for mayor in San Francisco, blames "local HUD officials" and "a lack of resources" for the disaster. The violence, she says, could have been avoided if HUD officials had instituted "potlucks or sleep-overs for groups that are not familiar with each other.... Those kinds of things are easy to do." And no doubt they are. Yet the belief that HUD's pursuit of "diversity," based on integrationist models developed for blacks and whites in the 1960s South, failed for lack of "potlucks" or "sleep-overs" is a symptom of the same delusion that led HUD to embark upon the scheme in the first place. It is a delusion to which multiculturalist foundations contribute mightily: namely, that "community" and "civil society" refer not to the groups people form of their own volition but, instead, to the carefully integrated groups of well-fed, well-dressed black, white, Hispanic and Asian children who play so happily togeth-er in the pages of major foundation annual reports.

That poverty in America is caused by racism and can be elimi-

"...the incidents were part of a pervasive pattern of racially motivated harassment and violence..."

nated through education is one of the fundamental assumptions of the liberal politics American foundations so effectively promoted in the '50s and '60s. It has become increasingly difficult, however, to see America as a prosperous country, a minority of whose citizens are denied the right to vote or to work on the basis of their race. We are, instead, a prosperous country in which a well-educated, relatively well-integrated, professional elite rules over a poor and angry majority whose anger has made itself felt from the slums of L.A. to the plains of Oklahoma.

That the problems of the poor in America are, most often, the problems of poor whites is a fact not recognized by any speaker at any session at the conference in San Francisco. What is billed as "A Study in Immigration Backlash" in Marin County's Canal Area, however, appears to offer some hope: that hope does not last long. "These are the white homeowners," our tour guide intones. "Notice how wide and clean the streets are and how nice and big the houses are." The residents of these modest tract-homes, with ten-year-old Cutlass Sierras and Toyota hatchbacks parked outside, it turns out, are the enemy.

At the Pickleweed Park Community Center, Tom Peters of the Marin County Department of Health and Human Services explains his opposition to Proposition 187 to an approving audience of foundation staff. An older man from Texas stands up: after stating his own strong opposition to Proposition 187, he wonders whether illegal immigration might pose a real problem for the state of California. "We must oppose the scapegoating of welfare mothers, gays and lesbians," answers a young woman from the audience, in grim, declarative tones. "The rights of our so-called 'illegal immigrants' must be firmly protected." Staffer after staffer agrees.

Despite this show of unanimity, a dissenter—of sorts—can be found in our midst. As we leave the Marriott, our bus driver takes up the microphone. Passing lightly over local landmarks, restaurants, the Fire of 1907, she arrives at the subject that will occupy her, without pausing, for ten minutes at least: the San Francisco earthquake of 1992 and the role played by the media in defaming the city. "It was the media, the reporters, the TV people, who showed those buildings burning, the same three buildings, crawling over the rubble, flying over in helicopters," she says. "Everything was fine. But the media just wouldn't let up. They caused all the problems, all the bad feelings, by showing those pictures, week after week, the fires burning and buildings collapsing."

There is no escape. We slump down in our seats, roll our eyes. If we ignore her, maybe she'll stop. What is she so mad about? Later that day, I meet Beth Smith, president of the Hyams Foundation of Boston, a prim, attractive woman in her late 40s on whom Henry James might have modeled a character much like his sympathetic Dr. Prance in *The Bostonians*. After Smith tells me about the programs she sponsors, I ask her whether the

Hyams Foundation serves poor whites. "It's funny you should say that," she says, "because just last week I was listening to NPR, and I was surprised to hear that two of the poorest Census districts in the country, with average incomes of about $9,000, were in Boston and that both of those districts were white." That's when an explanation for our bus driver's behavior occurs to me: in our suits and ties, polished penny-loafers and leather pumps, with our college degrees and secure, well-paying jobs, we are—in her eyes, at least—the media. We are the elite, and we are to blame.

In her conspiratorial imagination of a malign elite, our angry bus driver is hardly alone. From C. Wright Mills to Barry Goldwater, voices on the left and the right have long protested that America is run by an elite whose members have been said to include the leadership of both major parties, the Rockefeller family, the Ford Foundation, the Joint Chiefs of Staff, bankers, academics and the press. A look backward, to the years when American foundations supported *An American Dilemma*, the civil rights movement, Head Start, even Model Cities, suggests that the conspiracy theorists are at least half right: there was an elite. It succeeded by pursuing strategies designed to ensure the civil rights of all Americans, while assuming the economy would take care of itself.

The new American elite is wealthier, better educated, more diverse. That it has failed so completely to build on the successes of its predecessors is the ruling irony of our national life. Unique among our institutions for their unlimited wealth, ability to bridge professional divisions and freedom from partisan constraints, foundations are more guilty of this failure than most. With the federal government burdened by debt and liberal ideals held in fierce contempt by the governing majority in Congress—and by the public that elected them—the need for fresh solutions to our social problems is more pressing now than at any time since the Great Depression. Blinkered by their self-imposed regime of philanthropical correctness, America's major foundations are unlikely to be of much help.

"The new American elite is wealthier, better educated, more diverse."

Political Correctness at Rutgers[4]

In 1944 when Gunnar Myrdal published his monumental study of U.S. race relations, he named it *An American Dilemma*. After half a century of struggle we are still caught in the same dilemma, but what once was tragedy is becoming farce.

The civil rights movement battled lynch mobs, racial segregation—imposed by law in Southern states, by custom in the North—disenfranchisement in the South, and levels of discrimination everywhere that made it virtually impossible for blacks to succeed in any business or profession outside the ghetto. Today, especially on college campuses, the struggle for freedom and equality has degenerated into the pursuit of (frequently segregated) facilities and privileges in the name of multiculturalism and "diversity." Those who complain or deviate from the unofficial party line can expect reprisals.

The recent effort to remove Rutgers President Francis L. Lawrence from office illustrates why political correctness has been called the enforcement arm of multiculturalism. Most of the well-publicized cases of faculty and students being disciplined for careless remarks in recent years have involved unknown figures. But Lawrence is not only president of a large state university— 47,000 students spread over three campuses—he is also totally committed to affirmative action. In seeking his ouster the politically correct were trying to devour an ally, and thereby revealed more nakedly than before the true nature of their business.

Lawrence's trials began last January 31, when the *Star-Ledger*, New Jersey's largest daily newspaper, ran a front page story reporting that he had told a group of faculty members the "genetic hereditary background" of "disadvantaged" students kept them from scoring well on standardized tests. The occasion was a meeting of some 30 people held at RU's Camden campus on November 11, 1994, to discuss a "post-tenure review" process the university is establishing.

The *Star-Ledger* story triggered volleys of demands for Lawrence's resignation from black leaders around the state, and from the student governments of Rutgers' many undergraduate schools and colleges. Demonstrations began almost at once, with students chanting "Hell no, our genes ain't slow" outside the President's office on the New Brunswick campus. The most conspicuous of these was a student sit-in on February 7 during the half-time of a televised basketball game between Rutgers and the University of Massachusetts, then fourth in the national rankings. When some 150 students refused to leave the floor the game had to be suspended. The media blitz focused on

---

[4] Article by William L. O'Neill, veteran contributor and professor of American history at Rutgers University, from *The New Leader* vol. 78 p.11-14 F 13-27 '95. Copyright © 1995 by the American Labor Conference on International Affairs, Inc. Reprinted with permission.

Lawrence, already intense, went national after that incident, and inspired even more criticism of him and support for the protesting students.

On behalf of the Rainbow Coalition, Jessie Jackson and Angela Davis sent a letter of encouragement. Benjamin Chavis, recently deposed executive director of the NAACP, appeared in person at a campus rally on February 14. So did the rap performer Sista Souljah, a former Rutgers student who is best known locally for her antiwhite sentiments.

Lawrence may have expected the fuss to die down quickly, because he made his slip in the course of defending affirmative action at Rutgers, which, like many universities, routinely admits minority students whose SAT and other scores would otherwise keep them out. Waiving the normal entry requirements is a policy he strongly supports, and has talked of expanding. Once it became clear that the context of his remarks did not make any difference to critics, Lawrence apologized, citing not only his record at Rutgers since he became president in 1990, but also at Tulane University, where as provost he had substantially increased the number of black admissions.

"Rutgers was first in African-American enrollment... and first in the percentage of full-time black faculty."

His achievement at Rutgers has been less striking, mainly because Rutgers committed itself to diversity years ago. Still, it is a commitment Lawrence has enthusiastically honored. Not long after his arrival, he wrote an open letter saying that "Strength Through Diversity," the motto of RU's Livingston College, should extend to the entire institution, and he has been as good as his word. Black enrollment has grown from 9.7 to 9.9 per cent during his presidency, while minority student representation has risen from 26.9 to 31.3 percent. The percentage of faculty who are black has increased from 5.4 to 5.7 per cent. Many women and blacks have been appointed to administrative positions too.

At its February 10 meeting formally supporting Lawrence, the Board of Governors itemized these gains. It noted that compared with other members of the Association of American Universities (AAU)—a group of 58 leading research universities, 29 of them state-assisted—Rutgers was first in African-American enrollment among the public members and first in the percentage of full-time black faculty. The flagship campus in New Brunswick ranks second nationally among predominantly white universities in awarding baccalaureate degrees to African-Americans. Initiatives Lawrence was particularly responsible for include a large increase in minority scholarships and a three-year, $5 million Campaign for Community, Diversity and Educational Excellence. Tides of paper promoting these and other programs flow regularly into faculty mailboxes.

Repeated invocations of his record, and repeated apologies by Lawrence, failed for several weeks to stop the cycle of heavily reported protests and denunciations. Lawrence refused to resign and seems to have ridden out the crisis, though the damage is likely to persist. A calamity for him, these events have been particularly painful for a university that is just coming to be recognized as a first-rate institution. Like most Eastern state universities, Rutgers had long been in the shadow of its more famous Western cousins. But several decades of expansion, and the recruitment of a distinguished faculty, have begun to pay off. The recent admission of Rutgers into the prestigious AAU was one encouraging sign; another has been the lengthening list of awards and prizes given to faculty members—such as the Pulitzer Prize in Biography for 1994 won by historian David Levering Lewis. Now it seems as if Rutgers will be best known for losing football teams and Lawrence's remark.

Lawrence's November gaffe became public thanks to RU's chapter of the American Association of University Professors (AAUP). As the faculty bargaining agent it tries to be as virulently anti-management as the most class-conscious trade union. Its president actually attended and taped the Camden meeting. Along with everyone else who was present, she claimed not to have heard the offending remark. The AAUP contends that it merely distributed copies of the tape to its 119 campus representatives, and has no idea which member, or members, caught Lawrence's slip and notified the *Star Ledger*. Despite the AAUP's denials, it scheduled a press conference to denounce Lawrence's words for the very day the story broke, and that happened to occur as bargaining talks with the administration were about to begin. Even if the apparent coordination was not a calculated move to weaken the university administration at a critical moment, there is no doubt that but for the union no crisis would have developed.

Just as Lawrence's position explains why some wished to get him, his personality has a bearing on the relative lack of support he received at first. To be sure, a few important figures rose to his defense. One was Carlton A. Holstrom, chairman of the Board of Governors; another was Paul Robeson Jr. Rutgers takes great pride in Robeson's father, its most famous graduate, so the son is a frequent visitor and knows Lawrence personally. A few black faculty and administrators also spoke up for Lawrence, and so did a number of students. But to most students and faculty Lawrence is a remote figure, thus he has practically no constituency on campus. That was made painfully clear by the New Brunswick Faculty Council on February 9, when it resolved that "President Lawrence's ability to lead the university effectively has been seriously compromised," and called upon the Board of Governors to "review his stewardship" in that light.

An obvious lesson here is that the president of a large, multiracial university has to watch his tongue. Those parts of Lawrence's talk on November 11 that have been published show it to be rambling and disjointed. It must have been hard to follow, and that is probably why no one present objected to what he said at the time. Or perhaps his audience understood that he meant "environmental" rather than "genetic hereditary" background. A third possibility is that the words were intended to be part of a rhetorical question. The full inflammatory sentence, which came after what could be construed as two rhetorical questions, was: "Or do we deal with a disadvantaged population that doesn't have that genetic hereditary background to have a higher average." Had it begun, "Are we dealing with," the rhetorical nature of the statement, and its implied negative, would have been more apparent.

Lawrence attributed his slip to the controversy surrounding *The Bell Curve*, a book holding that for genetic reasons blacks are inferior to other races. He has said he regards the very idea as so immoral that he refused to read the book, but that the publicity arising from it somehow poisoned his vocabulary, leading him to say the opposite of what he meant. This is entirely plausible to those at Rutgers who have heard him make similar, if less dangerous errors—a proclivity some attribute to the excessive workload he carries.

Mostly, though, the crisis has pointed up how reasoned discourse disappears when race becomes the issue. Few of the black students quoted in newspaper stories displayed any interest in what Lawrence meant to say, or the context of his remarks, or his record, except to disparage it. The chair of one black student organization said, "All the stuff he claims he's responsible for have been the result of student demands." Yet, another student leader stated publicly that the Latino Cultural Center came into being only after Lawrence arrived and threw his weight behind it.

At a February 3 meeting on campus where the President apologized to about 300 students, one called upon him to resign and then walked out, followed by a good share of the audience. A first-year student was quoted as saying, "There is a price that you have to pay. Sorry is just not going to do it. You have to coincide with our rules now." This suggests that while some people were hurt by Lawrence's words, others relished the opportunity for a show of force. The turmoil was certainly spontaneous in origin, but it was exploited by a small group of campus radicals who have been organizing protests—notably against tuition hikes—for years. They resent the President because he has consistently opposed their efforts. One of them wrote to the *Daily Targum*, Rutgers' leading student newspaper, that after Lawrence resigns students should "focus our attention on the whole racist, sexist, classist structure that controls Rutgers (and America), in which the replacing of one part doesn't change the entire corrupt machine."

Such statements display the politically correct mind at work. In addition, like the entire affair, they show that all those academics who have insisted there is no such thing as PC, or that it is only a club invented by conservatives out to hammer progressive measures, are wrong. At Rutgers, and virtually every major university, students and faculty with any reservations about the politically correct line have learned to be very cautious.

"The turmoil... was exploited by a small group of campus radicals who have been organizing protests..."

Lawrence is partly to blame for this. For although he is by no means a Leftist, he has supported various PC measures, among them efforts to ban "hate speech" through restrictive student codes. The irony did not go unnoticed. George Will was one of several commentators who observed that Lawrence helped author his own misfortune by encouraging political correctness.

Much confusion surrounds the question of exactly what kind of speech is punishable at Rutgers. At one rally, the *Targum* reported, several residence hall staff members said they felt that under the current student code of conduct they would have to bring up on charges any dormitory resident who used the words Lawrence uttered on November 11. This appears to be untrue; the Rutgers code exempts constitutionally protected speech, which Lawrence's remark certainly was. Nevertheless, that some students believe they can be disciplined for verbally challenging the PC line, and know for sure they will be labeled racists if they do, discourages open debate and the free exchange of ideas. Perhaps Lawrence's current troubles will lead him to think again about whether speech should be restricted at all. In any event, he should have learned by now that political correctness is about intimidation and has nothing to do with justice.

In addressing the "larger issues" raised by the confrontation, student activists, the New Brunswick Faculty Council and Lawrence himself have called for redoubled efforts to promote affirmative action. The *Targum* seems to do this daily, hardly a surprise since for the past 25 years its editors have been trying to keep the spirit of the '60s alive in the face of overwhelming student apathy. It has printed, and endorsed, a host of demands that Rutgers expand its commitment to African-American and Latino students and faculty, including those of the newly-formed United Student Coalition, an umbrella group consisting of 40 campus organizations. Yet Rutgers already does more than most universities to promote diversity, and, though Lawrence dare not say so, it is running up against certain limits.

Because the supply of highly qualified black scholars and scientists is small in relation to demand, raiding other universities has become the chief means of acquiring them. Consequently, once hired they are hard to keep. That is the case even at the richest schools, as Duke University found out. In 1988 it ordered every department and program to hire at least one new black by 1995 or face penalties. The quota has not been filled, for in the bidding war that political correctness inspires no university can win. Duke attracted some important people, only to have them lured away by better outside offers. Universities could relax their faculty standards, but the most competitive are the most reluctant to do that, hence the game of musical chairs.

To attract black (and Hispanic) students universities employ true affirmative action principles by lowering their admission requirements, but here too the law of diminishing returns applies. Disadvantaged students require financial aid, and are more likely to fail or drop out than other students, so that much of the aid is wasted. In addition, with many white students now taking five years to get a degree, the norm for minority graduation has been set at six. By this measure Rutgers looks pretty good, ranking eighth among the public AAU members. To be exact, 54 per cent of the black members and 56 per cent of Latinos in the class of 1990 had graduated by 1992 (the rate for whites was 76 per cent).

The total, however, includes black and Latino students who got into Rutgers on merit, so the figure for those affirmatively admitted has to be significantly lower. This means that dipping deeper into the minority applicant pool would cost a good deal of money, produce a small increase in the number of minority graduates, and further depress the graduation rate of blacks and Latinos. As a matter of public policy, accepting ever larger numbers of potential dropouts does not make a great deal of sense. Nor does it contribute in any significant way to solving the real problems of minorities—poverty, crime, illegitimacy, and the like—which are invariably lost sight of during campus struggles over diversity.

Given what it already is doing, there is little more Rutgers can do to recruit black faculty and promote affirmative action. At most a little more funding may be made available for race-based programs. In the light of these realities, demonstrators lacked a plausible agenda. Indeed, by week three the crisis seemed about over. Lawrence began to receive support from his fellow academic presidents in New Jersey and from newspapers. A *New York Times* editorial asked that he be given a second chance.

All this had its effect upon student turnouts. A widely advertised demonstration held on February 16 drew only a hundred people, by the *Targum*'s count, and it never errs on the low side. None of the many protest events ever attracted more than 700 people, and then only once, while the next largest drew 300, and it was downhill from there. The small turnouts compared with those of the '60s suggest that the movement to oust Lawrence had little grass-roots backing—even from minority students.

In fact, the protests themselves inspired a backlash. On February 13 the College of Engineering Governing Council, one of several student government bodies that had passed a resolution earlier urging Lawrence to step down, reversed itself. Calling the media frenzy "repulsive," the Council's president explained that the original resolution did not express the views of a majority of engineering students. On February 22 the *Targum* ran a plaintive editorial urging the United Student Coalition to continue going after Lawrence: "When students march down College Avenue and demand Lawrence's resignation, those who disagree ridicule their attempts. Protesters feel abandoned by students who will not join them and faculty members who remain quiet." That there was something ridiculous, not to say malignant, about trying to destroy a person of good will for a slip of the tongue, would never occur to the *Targum*.

Petty and demeaning vendettas are not what was expected after the great victories of the '60s—the Civil Rights Act of 1964, the Voting Rights Act of 1965, and the affirmative actions that followed. Those achievements were supposed to lift up minorities as a whole, not divide them into a crippled underclass and an empowered middle class whose politics are directed at winning marginal benefits and empty symbolic victories. No one seriously believes that Rutgers can become much more diverse than it is. And if it could, what difference would that make to the mass of poor people whose lives are a million light-years removed from the world of higher education?

The reasoning seems to be that while aiding the underclass is a hopeless cause, politically incorrect victims can be sacrificed to inspire fear in others and attract a few extra dollars. How cynical and, alas, how true. The very word "diversity" no longer stands for anything worth embracing. As the late Christopher Lasch pointed out in his *The Revolt of the Elites*, it is a slogan that "has come to mean the opposite of what it appears to mean. In practice 'diversity' turns out to legitimize a new dogmatism in which minorities take shelter behind a set of beliefs impervious to rational discussion." Martin Luther King's dream seems farther away than ever.

Curriculum and Culture: New Round Is Opened in a Scholarly Fistfight[5]

In 1987, Allan Bloom, then an obscure translator of Plato and Rousseau, touched a raw nerve when he argued in his book *The Closing of the American Mind* that the surrender of college and university administrations and faculties to the demands of student, feminist and Black Power movements in the 1960's and 1970's had fatally compromised American higher education.

Writing with zest and hyperbole, the political philosopher compared radical feminism to the Reign of Terror in the French Revolution, dismissed the anthropologist Margaret Mead as a "sexual adventurer," likened the Woodstock gathering to Hitler's Nuremberg rallies and denounced "cultural relativism," which treats all cultures as equals. Professor Bloom called this "the suicide of science." He also argued that efforts to include non-Western cultures in the curriculum were displacing what he regarded as the more valuable teaching of the Western canon.

The book appeared on *The New York Times* best-seller list for 10 weeks, sold more than a million copies and made Professor Bloom, who died in 1992, one of the most widely quoted and criticized authors.

While Professor Bloom has his followers, many liberal-minded scholars are now saying he has finally met his match.

Even before its official publication date on Sept. 3, 1996 *The Opening of the American Mind* (Beacon Press, $20), by Lawrence W. Levine, a longtime professor of cultural history at the University of California at Berkeley, is being both hailed and denounced with unusual fervor.

Professor Levine's book is a defense of all that Professor Bloom held unholy. The debate centers on how open or closed society should be to many cultures. The enemy to Professor Bloom was cultural relativism and the lack of restraint that came with it. Professor Levine, on the other hand, champions multiculturalism, which he sees as the inevitable, and praiseworthy, product of constitutional democracy.

"Multiculturalism," Professor Levine said in an interview, "means that in order to understand the nature and complexities of American culture, it is crucial to study and comprehend the widest possible array of the contributing cultures and their interaction with one another."

Among the major points made in his book are these:

Conservative critics like Professor Bloom, who blame the frag-

---

mentation of American society on the university, do not realize that it has been "endemic in the United States from the outset."

The college curriculum is not immutable, as Professor Bloom said, but has steadily evolved over the last 200 years.

The prospect for the future is "increasing openness, greater inclusiveness, expanded choice, the study of the modern as well as of the ancient, a concentration on American, African and Asian as well as European culture."

Professor Levine is also critical of higher education. He calls for more courses that "build on one another," minimizing jargon, better communication with colleagues in other disciplines and a renewed emphasis on teaching ability.

Throughout the summer, as the book became available, scholars began to take sides.

"The college curriculum is not immutable...but has steadily evolved over the last 200 years."

"This is the book we've been waiting for," said Stanley N. Katz, president of the American Council of Learned Societies. "It should put an end to the 'culture war' talk."

Lynne Cheney, who served as chairwoman of the National Endowment for the Humanities under Presidents Reagan and Bush, and who is criticized in the book, disagreed. "It's the same-old, same-old," she said. "It's the Left deliberately misconstruing the arguments of its opponents while offering no substantive evidence for its own."

A MacArthur fellow, Professor Levine is the former president of the Organization of American Historians. After spending 32 years at Berkeley, he joined the faculty of George Mason University in Fairfax, Va., where he now teaches history.

"What I tried to show in this book," he said, "is that the genius of America has been its ability to renew its essential spirit by admitting a constant infusion of different peoples who demand that the ideals and principles embodied in the Constitution be put into practice."

"The result has been to open America to great diversity, and colleges and universities are beginning to reflect this heterogeneity. It has not led to repression as Bloom argued, but to the very opposite—a flowering of ideas and scholarly innovation unmatched in our history."

Professor Bloom's book, he said was a reaction to this.

"He and the people who agreed with him could not accept the expansion of interests, the less parochial world view, and the more comprehensive view of what was important to teach and to learn."

Over the years, many authors have written intellectual sequels to Professor Bloom's book—including William Bennett, Dinesh D'Souza, Roger Kimball and John Searle. And not a few authors also have attacked Professor Bloom—among them Michael Berube, Henry Louis Gates Jr., Gerald Graff, Francis Oakley, Peter N. Stearns and W. B. Carnochan.

The battle of the books did not originate with Allan Bloom; it can be traced back at least to 1762 when Rousseau argued in "Emile" that it was more important for students to read a commercial novel like *Robinson Crusoe* than to read Aristotle.

Through the centuries, classicists and modernists have clashed over how best to educate the young. Fundamentally, the issue was whether to stuff them or stretch them—stuff them with the classics or stretch them with contemporary issues.

Yet while this current battle of the books has raged, none of Professor Bloom's supporters or detractors have generated anything like the mass appeal of Professor Bloom's initial assault.

Professor Levine's champions, however, remain optimistic. An unremitting attack by conservatives could be the key to maintaining public interest. Dr. Katz called the book "the first to make the case in a serious way for multiculturalism in higher education," and he thinks freshness will inspire debate.

Professor Gates, chairman of the department of Afro-American Studies at Harvard, called the book "highly readable," and Elliott Gorn, a professor of history at Miami University in Ohio, said he thought the positive "something's right with the academy" tone of the book would attract a following.

Beacon Press plans a first printing of 40,000 copies, an unusually large press run for an academic treatise.

Roger Kimball, managing editor of the neoconservative *New Criterion*, another who is criticized in Professor Levine's book, lashed out after reading it. "How can Levine say that nothing's wrong?" he said in an interview. "It is incontrovertible that the academy has been taken over by left-wing radicals. The riches of the humanistic tradition are being perverted by a conjury of ideological assaults. You can't deny that."

Professor Levine said he decided to write *The Opening of the American Mind* when it struck him that Professor Bloom's desire "to rescue education from the virus of democracy" paralleled the way in which a turn-of-the-century elite captured for itself exclusively cultural icons like Shakespeare, art museums and symphony orchestras—a development that inspired Professor Levine's earlier book, "Highbrow/Lowbrow."

"I became increasingly upset at myself and my colleagues for not explaining to students and their parents why we are teaching multiculturalism." he said. "We left ourselves vulnerable. There is a need to explain."

"We weren't turning our backs on Western Civilization. That hadn't even existed as a subject until just after the First World War. Thomas Jefferson never heard of something called Western Civilization."

Professor Levine said he was appalled by the fact that he graduated from the City College of New York in the 1950's "knowing very little about the vast majority of the people in the world."

"We studied Northern and Western Europe," he said. "Nothing on Africa, Asia and Latin America. Even Canada was a great blank." My own father was an immigrant from Lithuania and my grandparents were from Odessa, but we talked only about Northern and Western Europe. There's something wrong with that."

II. Multiculturalism and the Curriculum

Editor's Introduction

As Section I notes, the issue of multiculturalism is heavily steeped in debate. When it is viewed in an academic context, the focus of Section II, the prevalence of debate around the issue of multiculturalism becomes even more pronounced. The canon, being the body of works taught in literature classes, is central to this debate. The question most commonly asked by detractors of multiculturalism is: How can the canon, and the curriculum in general, adhere to the tenets of multiculturalism and include for discussion works by as many diverse cultures as possible? Inevitably, including non-mainstream works in the canon means replacing some of those Western works that are already being taught.

The first article in this section, "All Quiet on the (post) Western Front?," by Clifford Orwin, begins with an illuminating history and definition of multiculturalism. Tracing several of the notions that constitute multiculturalism back to Matthew Arnold, Orwin states that present day multiculturalism is the product of cultural relativism, the civil rights movements, and the "mass influx into North American universities of students of non-Western background." Consequently, multiculturalism strives to create a curriculum in which all cultures are equally recognized. Orwin asserts that academia has strayed from these noble intentions and, owing to politicization and other factors, become fixated on attacking Western civilization rather than supplementing it with information from other cultures.

A three day institute in which 19 educators read literature by ethnically diverse authors, discussed responses, and planned ways to use the works in class is reported in the following article by Stephen Z. Athanases, David Christiano, and Elizabeth Lay. The authors conclude that the particular struggles of those groups outside Western culture can be reflected and taught by taking measures which include the "thoughtful selection of texts," "the consideration of underlying questions and attacks on stereotypes," and "teacher modeling and collaboration with others equally sensitive to these concerns." Regardless of the particular approach, these authors believe that multiculturalist concerns can in fact be instituted and followed, often with great success. The article ends with a list of those works which will most clearly facilitate an understanding of, and empathy with, cultures outside the Western tradition.

Sandra Stotsky, writing in the *Phi Delta Kappan*, takes a dimmer view of a multiculturalist concern in America's secondary school literature programs. Multiculturalism, she maintains, has a marked tendency to dilute American literature and an American national identity because literature from Canada and South America, for example, may be included in a course called "American Literature." What is needed, Stotsky believes, is a curriculum which includes works that will foster "knowledge of and sympathy towards the diverse cultures of the world." This, she feels, would be far more effective than couching works from diverse cultures within a Western framework.

The debunkment of Western literature as a consequence of creating a curriculum which embodies a multicultural concern is the focus William J. Reeves' article—"Will Zealots Spell the Doom of Great Literature?" In a vehement attack upon multiculturalists, Reeves asserts that the Great Books of Western civilization are all students need to read. While many of Reeves' conclusions are debatable, particularly his belief that multiculturalists urge students "to resist reading books by white males," his furious and adamant tone reflects the feelings of many who do not wish to sacrifice certain books to make room for those from non-Western cultures.

In academia multiculturalism has aroused debate that goes beyond concern for the canon or the curriculum. Andrew Delbanco, writing for *The New Yorker*, describes Lee M. Bass' rescinded $20 million donation to Yale University. Bass rescinded the donation because the Yale community would not honor his stipulation that the money be used to create a new Western Civilizations course taught by professors of his choosing. The dispute undoubtedly points to "a conflict that goes far beyond" Bass and Yale University. As Delbanco notes, the already precarious relationship between institution and donor is further threatened when the institution adopts a multicultural concern that is not agreeable to the donor. To insure progress, Delbanco advises removing the "confrontational mood" and "dogmatism" that so often transforms ideological disagreements into hate and "polemical label-mongering."

The last article in this section describes a series of student protests at Columbia University. The protesters called for "an independent ethnic studies department with its own budget and its own power to hire faculty." As Columbia is known for "teaching about non-Western cultures" the protesters were given very little attention by either the media or other students. In many ways such a reaction indicates the ability to applaud the existing institutional effort to espouse multiculturalism. The author also discusses some of the pitfalls of creating ethnic studies departments.

All Quiet on the (post) Western Front?[1]

Class criticized poem for its lack of a woman's perspective. Note the unconscious gender privileging—his terror, his glory, his phallic monuments.

> —A student's notes of a class on Yeats's "Meru,"
> from Philip Roth's *Sabbath's Theater*.

"Multiculturalism" is not an ideal on the North American campus today but an entrenched reality. Those who do not love it bear it, and those who accuse it are few. It defines the core of the moral mission of the contemporary university. The very question of culture as it presents itself in the university today is identical with that of multiculturalism. This is not without implications for the university's role within the broader society.

At the same time, there is more to the university than its moral mission, and imperatives other than moral ones to which it must respond. In what follows, I will consider not only multiculturalism but other factors that collaborate with it to shape the mood on campus. First, however, for the benefit of those who have been paying scant attention, a crash course in multiculturalism. It is only multiculturalism in the university that I will discuss; it may be that in more reasonable milieux, multiculturalism, too, manifests itself more reasonably.

What is Multiculturalism?

The notion of multiculturalism depends on that of culture. More precisely, it depends on the relativistic understanding of "culture" which has dominated the intellectual life of postwar North America.

The history of the notion of culture is complex. For our purposes, it may suffice to refer to the distinction between culture as employed in the still intelligible expression "a cultured person" and culture as it figures in multiculturalism or such other current expressions as "biker culture." For culture as in "biker culture" no more suggests a cultured person than a biker could be described as cultured.

Until not long ago, the transmission of culture in the older sense was taken to define the noblest task of the university. The most eloquent proponent of this view of education was Matthew Arnold (1822-1888), the British man of letters who became naturalized in post-World War II America. In *Culture and Anarchy*, composed in 1867-1868 at a moment of grave political crisis in

---

[1] Article by Clifford Orwin, from *The Public Interest* 123:3-21 Spr '96. Copyright © 1996 National Affairs, Inc. Reprinted with permission.

Britain, Arnold had defended the cause of culture against the strictures of each of the three great parties of the day, the aristocrats (Arnold's "Barbarians"), the middle class (his "Philistines"), and the as yet unenfranchised workers (the "Populace").

For Arnold, "culture" retained its Latin sense of cultivation; it was want of education and a consequent vulgarity with which he taxed all three of his opponents. His project was the education of both sentiment and reason, and his models were Hellenic and Hebraic, the two great fountainheads of the Western tradition. Culture was the (somewhat uneasy) synthesis of these two strands, the Hellenic, which was preeminent in intellect and taste, and the Hebraic, which was preeminent in earnestness. Arnold's claim was that culture was the very opposite of dogmatism and its only effective antidote. It alone could lift us above our petty passions as individuals and those of our party and our time. Culture thus was good not only for the individual but for the polity: It defined the education suitable for free men.

"...the university of the fifties was already actuated...by more utilitarian concerns..."

Arnold was the grandfather of the vision so pervasive in American universities of the fifties and early sixties: the education of all citizens, regardless of race, religion, or class, in "the best that has been done and thought" (Arnold's phrase)—and the residual faith that this best was to be found in the masterworks of the Western tradition originating in the Bible and classical antiquity. Everyone of my generation knew teachers still inspired by this faith.

This vision of higher education had not reigned unchallenged even prior to the tumult of the sixties. On the one hand, the university of the fifties was already actuated (as those in a democracy will be) by more utilitarian concerns, as well as by an ethos of social justice which vied (and sometimes merged) with that of liberal education. On the other, the patronage of distinguished refugees from National Socialism had spurred the dissemination of a newer notion of "culture" incompatible with Arnold's.

This innovation was the work of German philosophy but first entered the American academy early in this century in the garb of anthropology; here the great name was Franz Boas. "Cultural relativism" taught that every people had a "culture" (the totality of its social practices) and that all cultures were equal in the specific sense that there were no neutral principles for the evaluation of cultures, no such principles that were not themselves relative to a particular culture. The ultimate implications of this allegation were murky; Nietzsche, who thought hard about them, concluded that the irreconcilability of cultures implied implacable warfare among them. Be this as it may, in America cultural relativism aroused from the outset enthusiasm in progressive circles for its perceived support of egalitarianism and tolerance of diversity. By 1950, it had become the reigning doctrine of North American liberalism and so of academic life. Those who subscribed to it as often as not embraced neo-Arnoldian notions of liberal education as well; the tension between the two was not yet evident. Today, the dogma of cultural relativism supplies the common denominator of the bewildering variety of usages of "culture" typical of current discourse.

Multiculturalism is a more recent development. It presupposes not only the doctrine of cultural relativism but the civil-rights and other liberation movements, the mass influx into North American universities of students of non-Western background, the influence of the "postmodernist" celebration of "difference," and the anti-Americanism of the 1960s (repackaged as anti-Westernism).

The Politics of Multiculturalism

In approaching the current situation in the universities, it is useful to follow my Toronto colleague H.D. Forbes in distinguishing between multiculturalism as a fact and multiculturalism as a policy. *Multiculturalism as a fact*—a great variety of "cultures" or (more precisely) of racial and ethnic backgrounds among the inhabitants of any one polity—is increasingly as much a feature of life on campus as of the broader North American society. Today, most entering students at my formerly rather homogeneous university arrive from households in which English was not the first language. To many of these, the classics of political philosophy which I teach represent not the "high culture" of the milieu whence they come but at most that of the one which they aspire to enter.

Multiculturalism as a policy is, among other things, a response to multiculturalism as a fact. Universities face the task of integrating large numbers of students of non-Western or Third World background, just as these students face that of adjusting to the university. Much as bilingualism in elementary education is touted by its proponents as easing the integration of Hispanic students into American society, so the promotion of "cultural difference" on campus is said to further the successful integration of "culturally diverse" students. We give the newcomers their own societies, their own residences, their own pride days, their own courses, and even their own academic programs, as well as "representation" in the mainstream curriculum—all in the hopes of making them feel full citizens of the broader academic community.

One may describe the preceding as the liberal defense of multiculturalism, and its attractiveness is obvious. So conceived, multiculturalism may easily appear the natural extension of the tolerance and openness on which liberals have always prided themselves, adapted to the wider diversity of ethnicity, and so of "culture," which now characterizes North American society. Unfortunately, this appearance has proved misleading.

For multiculturalism as a policy is not only, or even primarily, a response to multiculturalism as a fact. It is also and primarily an ideology, one as uniquely Western as the cultural relativism on which it draws. If all cultures must be presumed equal

"...multiculturalism may easily appear the natural extension of the tolerance and openness on which liberals have always prided themselves..."

because all standards for the assessment of cultures are themselves culture-bound, then there seems no reason why a university should transmit one culture (i.e., Western culture) to the
exclusion of others—and every reason why it shouldn't. For so to
"privilege" Western culture—a favorite term of accusation
among multiculturalists—is an affront to those cultures that are
neglected thereby. Inasmuch as liberal thought today both sub-
scribes to cultural relativism and understands itself and liberal
democracy as (merely) Western, the paradoxical conclusion
looms that to "privilege" liberalism is itself illiberal. This paradox has plagued liberals off campus as well as on it.

No matter that to subscribe to cultural relativism is itself to
"privilege" Western culture, since the former is a distinctly
Western conclusion that follows only from distinctly Western
arguments. The appeal of multiculturalism has never depended
upon its theoretical consistency. This appeal is *political*. Once one
frames the situation on campus in terms of neglect and recognition, it is inevitable that student, community, and faculty champions of the different "cultures" on hand will insist on increased
representation in the curriculum as a token of the acknowledgment of a worth fully equal to that of other "cultures." Like all
human constituencies that have not retired to a hermitage, multicultural ones tend to press their clout to the utmost.

Clamoring for Recognition

What multiculturalism demands of the university is not mere tolerance but the equal "recognition" of all cultures. Ultimately, it
is not at all clear what this could mean. Pious professions aside,
no one really believes that all cultures are equal, that all deserve
unconditional recognition, and that there is no rational basis for
discrimination among them. (The multiculturalists believe this
least of all, as witness their lengthy indictment of the sins of
Western culture, with the clear implication—and often the
explicit assertion—that not only is Western culture not better
than other cultures but is actually much worse than they.) Nor
can there be any intellectual vitality to a university in which one
is forbidden to raise the question of the right way of life. This last
point is implicitly granted by multiculturalists themselves, who
promote "diversity" as furthering this very quest—by expanding
the horizons of those engaged in it.

Once one grasps that the equality of all "cultures" or ways of
life is an empty nostrum, cultural recognition on demand
becomes condescending and meaningless. Like the brontosaurus
stamp applied to the hand of each child entering the natural history museum, it signifies not that all are giants (let alone that
they are equally so) but only that all are present. This problem
of how to extend equal recognition to all cultures without by that
very token trivializing it is one with which no less a thinker than
Charles Taylor has struggled without success.

Practically, however, the implications of "recognition" are clear enough. They include increased "representation" of each culture in the general curriculum and a free hand to its champions to construct a playground of their own at university expense: a course, a program, even a residence. Given the proliferation, and therefore fragmentation, of "cultures" clamoring for recognition on campus today, the politics of multicultural recognition tends toward the formation of ever more recondite groups (e.g., "Gays and Lesbians of Color"). It also promotes a general inclination to treat students ascriptively rather than as individuals.

Even without the adoption of multiculturalism as the official doctrine of the university, one can presume that the newer groups on the academic block would press for some representation of their respective legacies in the university curriculum. It is only natural that they would wish for their offspring the opportunity to devote part of their higher education to the study of their own past; and their pride would suggest to them that their legacy was worthy of the consideration of other students also. Such has been the pattern with the Jews, Italians, Slavs, and Balts, all of whom have as both individuals and communities initiated programs and endowed chairs. So too one must applaud the farsightedness of those universities that have taken it upon themselves to establish new departments of this kind even in the absence of an immigrant constituency—one thinks of the first departments of Russian and of East Asian studies in North America, founded around the turn of the century. Such initiatives are in every way to be welcomed, and have enriched the university curriculum to the benefit of all.

If this were the model for multiculturalism, if the chief concern of its proponents were greater opportunity for students of whatever background to study pre-Western or non-Western ways of life under the guidance of competent and unprejudiced scholars, no sane person could object. Unfortunately, while multiculturalism sometimes fosters expansion of opportunities of this sort, this is not really what it is about.

These earlier expansions of the university curriculum were just that, expansions. They were not offered as a repudiation of existing practice. There was no attempt to compel the attention of the indifferent, whether by transforming the core curriculum or otherwise revolutionizing the manner in which other subjects were taught on campus. Doubtless it was deemed good for the Jews that Jewish Studies be taught at Harvard. But it would not have been deemed good for them that Gentiles should have their noses rubbed in it by a revision of the Harvard curriculum to feature Gentile oppression of the Jews, as if that oppression were the central fact of Western culture, for which Dante, Shakespeare, and Goethe must eternally be called to account. Yet just this would define the program of a hypothetical Jewish "multiculturalism."

Sameness and Difference

As I have already suggested, multiculturalism is an ideology, an expression of our current Western, North American culture. The fuel of highest octane to be found in its tank is "post-Modernism," with its theoretical celebration of "difference." Postmodernism is itself the progeny of the Western philosophy of the past century. Whatever else may be said for or against it, there is not a non-Western trick in its bag. African-American postmodernists—as well as "people of color" (including that inevitable subset "women of color") from the Third World who cultivate a "postcolonialist" and/or "feminist" critique of Western "cultural hegemonism"—inhabit a single world of intellectual discourse with their white Western counterparts. That world of discourse is Western. I haven't surveyed the whole vast postmodernist literature, and would expect to find occasional exceptions to the rule that I am stating. Still, one will rarely encounter a more efficient engine of intellectual sameness than this ideology which celebrates difference.

"...the multicultur-alists' presentation of non-Western cultures tends to be in the service of their critique of the West."

From which it follows that so-called multiculturalism has less to do with exposing Western students to the serious study of other cultures than with persuading them of a certain interpretation of our own. It differs from the New Left of the sixties not so much in the sins of which it accuses North America (although it accords a new emphasis to those of "sexism" and "heterosexism") as in its ascription of those sins not to big business or the military but to North American or, better still, Western culture.

Accordingly, the multiculturalists' presentation of non-Western cultures tends to be in the service of their critique of the West. The very multiculturalist understanding of "culture" proves to be political rather than anthropological. Women, African Americans, homosexuals are all counted as "cultures," and to many multiculturalists these are the ones that matter most. Since "cultures" are exalted in opposition to the dominant "culture," the badge of a culture is the degree of neglect or oppression that it has suffered. As for serious examination of actual non-Western ways of life the greatness of which is not in doubt—such as ancient India or Confucian China or medieval Islam—multiculturalists tend to show little interest in it. For these rich civilizations possess neither the charm of marginality nor that of primitivism—the characteristics best adapted to flaying Western oppressiveness and rationalism, respectively.

To be sure, multiculturalists must cope with the problem that no non-Western culture has ever been "multicultural" in the desired sense. Other civilizations have much to teach us; but not that. One way of evading this difficulty is by casting non-Western societies as players in current Western melodrama. An ancient European matriarchy shimmers, one which allegedly worshipped "the Goddess." Great civilizations rise in Africa, along with Hellenic larcenies from them. The American Indian replaces

Smokey the Bear as protector of the environment. It is these half-truths, cardboard cutouts, and figments of ideological imagination that cast the gravest shadow on the alleged scholarly benefits of multiculturalism.

If it is bad for students to contract misguided notions of other ways of life, it is worse for them to acquire distorted views of their own. The greatest harm that multiculturalism does is to the teaching of Western "culture" itself. There is first the tendency to exaggerate the relative sinfulness of the West, as if all-too-human vices (racism, imperialism, etc.) were distinctively Western vices. It is, of course, appropriate to a university setting that we study our own society as much as possible in a critical spirit rather than a celebratory one. Indeed, one of the strongest arguments for a liberal education has always been that it provides one with that distance from one's own time which is necessary for grasping its shortcomings. It serves, in other words, as an antidote to unreflecting partisanship.

Multiculturalism, on the other hand, endorses partisanship (in the form of intransigent group self-assertion)—so long as it is directed against "the West." In order to do so, it must dismiss all productions of Western culture, including (and especially) those previously most admired, as themselves mere expressions of partisanship—racist, sexist, classist, "Eurocentric."

"The term 'canon' is used much more by people who attack its supposed existence than by those who defend Great Books programs."

Multiculturalism and "The Canon"

We can now grasp the significance of those attacks on "the canon" which comprise the cutting edge of multiculturalism. The denizens of Arnold's lofty precinct are deemed to comprise not an aristocracy but an oligarchy, which has oppressed the rest of us for far too long. Accordingly, the "expansion" of "the canon" is not for the sake of rectifying unwarranted omissions in the membership of Arnold's circle of "the best that has been thought and done" (by admitting Al-Farabi or the Buddha or George Eliot or Proust, for instance). (Indeed, today's multicultural warriors speak not of the expansion of the canon but of "canon-busting.") At issue is rather the achievement of that distribution of group representation currently deemed equitable. No one really claims enduring greatness for Frantz Fanon or Toni Morrison or Rigoberta Menchú—their presence in the core curriculum attests to the dethronement of that standard. (That they belong somewhere else in the curriculum I do not mean to deny.)

Debate over what few books are most worth reading has always occurred and is both necessary and revivifying. (I bracket "canon" because, as Christopher Kelly has noted in the *Gallatin Review*, it is misleading and prejudicial when applied to works other than the sacred texts of religion: "The term 'canon' is used much more by people who attack its supposed existence than by those who defend Great Books programs.") The question is the standard to invoke in this debate: the merits of the candidate, regardless of the group to which he or she belongs, or of that proportional representation by "cultures" which dictates that only three Greeks be admitted (one of whom must be Sappho).

In practice, the preferred solution appears to be a compromise between "the canon" and multiculturalism. However benign in intention, this yields an incoherent mishmash of older works of recognized greatness and newer ones representative of preferred "constituencies." Precisely in the case of these latter, however, the point is not to scrutinize but to "validate" them (and the self-esteem of the constituencies in question). So while one is permitted (or even required) to denounce Yeats, one mustn't criticize Maya Angelou. Even where the rubric under which an older writing is presented is not clearly invidious, it tends to be so anachronistic and trendy, so completely removed from the concerns of the author, as to foreclose serious engagement with the work.

While it is typical of multiculturalists to denounce "the canon" as homogeneous, the homogeneity that they ascribe to it is spurious. Upon examination, "Western culture" proves to owe its millennial vigor precisely to the persistence within it of outlooks in permanent tension with one another. What has saved the West from ossification is a chronic state of spiritual warfare. Hellenic versus Hebraic, Christian versus Jewish versus Muslim (for Islam too has contributed largely to "the West"), premodern versus modern, nature versus history, the contemplative life versus the active one—these and countless other tensions from which the life of the mind has been forged in the West disappear from the purview of the multiculturalists. What remains is the "white," the "male," the "Eurocentric," the "Western"—a lowest common denominator or, more precisely, an ideological construct.

The defining feature of "the canon" reduced to straw man is its alleged function as the public-relations arm of the bourgeois capitalist status quo. However improbable this is as a reading of Sophocles or Augustine or Dante (to say nothing of such more recent additions to the list as Marx and Nietzsche), anything is possible through the magic of "cultural studies." If one begins with the axiom that all works of the mind are nothing but (unwitting) representations of the flaws of the surrounding society, it is but a short step to proving it. In fact, as the late Peter Shaw notes in a recent *Sewanee Review*, "not only do the canonical works not advance the interests of ruling classes at all, but they also do not primarily serve the stability of the social order.... [They] are much more likely to be oppositional than to embody [conservative] values." The fact is that the "canon" has always comprised a highly diverse body of works each of which has evoked the most diverse interpretations. It defies reduction to anyone's caricature of the "Western."

Repressive Tolerance

Lastly, the axiom of cultural relativism that forbids us to pronounce one culture superior to another also forbids us to pronounce one "subculture" superior to another. Again, any such assertion is construed as an oligarchic power play. The result is that so-called popular culture gains in panache, whether interpreted as a conspiracy by which the people is oppressed, and which must therefore be debunked—popular culture as the new opiate of the masses—or as the means by which the people expresses its resistance to oppression. And indeed, if the main aim of criticism is sociological (as is the case with "cultural studies"), yes, the Mickey Mouse Club was more typical of fifties America than was Wallace Stevens, just as the trashy tabloids parodied by Joyce were more typical of twenties Dublin than he was. Sociology (including critical sociology) has its place in the curriculum. The question is whether it ought to shape the core thereof.

In the absence of standards of high culture (and in the presence of so powerful an animus against them), the curriculum risks degenerating into pandering to students in the guise of "raising their consciousness." They may be encouraged to lift their sights as high as making a documentary of a Grateful Dead concert or to spend an entire semester contemplating the significance of black hair in America. Or they may be asked to confront an Aristotelian doctrine with an animistic one (no matter how arbitrary the comparison), so as to be admonished that the former was "logocentric" (a vice from which the latter was thankfully free). These are not hypothetical examples. I owe them to David Sacks and Peter Thiel, whose *The Diversity Myth* chronicles the decline of Stanford University. Others have amply documented such shenanigans elsewhere.

Multiculturalism, then, aspires to a specific transformation of the curriculum and a corresponding one in the minds of the students subjected to it. At its heart is the advocacy not of cultural diversity but of a specific critique of Western culture. Its advocates view the liberation of students from their presumed bondage to Western culture as the highest purpose of higher education. In the decisive respect, then, the program of multiculturalism is not ecumenical but adversarial. Eurocentrism ranks with sexism, racism, and heterosexism as the cardinal sins on campus today, and the latter three are frequently presented as aspects of the former.

It is not surprising, then, that multiculturalism has spawned many encroachments on academic freedom. The valuable task of chronicling these has been ably performed by others, notably Dinesh D'Souza from a conservative perspective (*Illiberal Education*) and Richard Bernstein from a liberal one (*Dictatorship of Virtue*). These abuses warrant grave concern. More often than not, however, multiculturalism can afford to be dismissive of the older learning rather than intolerant of it. For who on campus are defending liberal education, and how many divisions have they got?

Lockean Multiculturalism?

Among the defining decisions of the new Stanford CIV curricu-

lum ("Cultures, Ideas, and Values") was the displacement of
John Locke from it. True, he was the classic exponent of the elements that came to define Western liberalism—representative
and limited government, political, economic, and religious freedom, and an orientation toward economic growth—and the only
such personage who had figured in the old core curriculum.
Once one recognizes, however, that the whole canon consists of
surreptitious legitimators of these odious practices, the presence
of an explicit one is apparently *de trop*.

The Stanford decision was typical of the multiculturalist dis-
paragement of the titans of Western thought. Yet Locke can still
boast a constituency on campus today, even an ever growing
one. As Tocqueville remarked that the Americans of his day were
Cartesians without ever having studied Descartes, so today's typical student is a Lockean without having studied Locke. This I
believe is the solid basis for the claim that students are increasingly "conservative." It has little to do with what they think, and
nothing to do with any attachment of theirs to the old. The so-
called conservatism of today's students is their immersion in
their own narrow concerns. Their orientation (at least within the
university) is toward the useful rather than the exciting, and their
notion of the useful is an acquisitive one. They concur in Locke's
endorsement of *homo economicus*, but they do so almost apolo-
getically—you have to look out for Number One—and without
the slightest curiosity as to what he, or any other thinker, may
have said in its justification.

It would be gratifying (to me, at least) to be able to tout this
development as the revenge of the Lockean nerds. And in fact,
those whose primary aim in attending university is the acquisi-
tion of employment skills are unlikely to be ardent multiculturalists. Ideology doesn't interest them, and neither does culture.
For these same reasons, however, they are unlikely to be very
hostile to multiculturalism. In the first place, it's no skin off their
backs. They view any course in the liberal arts as something to
be endured and passed, preferably with as little trouble as possible. Multiculturalism possesses the charm of the progressive and
often that of the easy too. (This is especially so given the multiculturalist preoccupation with popular culture.) Many such
courses are taught by teachers whose affirmation of "difference"
importantly includes the purveying of sameness—in the form of
high grades for everybody. ("I don't think that I have ever given
any one a C, if that helps with your course selection," warbles a
priestess of popular culture at Stanford. And why should she,
given the multiculturalist critique of academic standards?) As for
the student, he or she will now have more time to devote to
courses that matter. In economics and chemistry, at least,
Stanford is still Stanford.

There are, moreover, positive (which is to say careerist) induce-
ments to take at least certain kinds of multiculturalist courses.
The outlook of ambitious students today is likely to be vaguely

internationalist, that being where the economic opportunities are thought to lie. As "plastics" was the talisman urged upon the hero of *The Graduate*, so "the globalization of the economy" and "the information highway" are the mantras of today. And for the first of these lucrative pursuits, at least, a smattering of the "non-Western" is deemed to offer a useful foundation.

Even on the domestic front, both corporations and public bureaucracies (including, of course, universities) are persuaded of the necessity of "diversity training" not only for moral reasons but as a management and marketing imperative. And diversity training is what multiculturalism is all about. So accounting or computer science as the main course, with a little multiculturalism on the side, would seem to be a far more useful preparation for the "culture" that really matters to many students today—namely corporate-bureaucratic culture—than the study of Homer or the Bible.

Thus students' very indifference to multiculturalism's ideological critique of commercial society, and their single-minded preoccupation with their careers, contributes to their acquiescence in a menu of multiculturalist course electives. Equally indifferent to the older type of liberal education, they will not object to multiculturalism's domination of what has replaced it. It's not as if they know any better.

Multiculturalism and the Decline of Reading

Another factor, which collaborates with multiculturalism, is perhaps in the long run even more consequential for the fate of the North American university. It is the aversion of today's students to reading. This last is an activity for which high schools no longer prepare them. Few have acquired a taste for reading complex texts, and fewer still the skills for it. Only in the last five years has it come to pass that most of the students in my large introductory course in political philosophy duck the readings (all of which are in primary sources) as simply too difficult for them. This majority is silent but sullen; I can't help but suspect that they blame me for assigning these works. This is not just my problem, as many colleagues in many places have corroborated it.

The current vogue in high schools is not for books. For many of today's students, a book is just a data base waiting to be digitalized. While literature is of course still taught, it tends to feature contemporary short stories. As a result, the English of past centuries is a foreign language to today's students. (They would sooner read works in other languages, for these are at least available in translations into *current* English.)

Even in the absence of ideological considerations, the older education was bound to suffer because of its dependence on books and the habits of rumination appropriate to them. While it would be foolish to predict the demise of the book, there is no overlooking its diminishing centrality to education and to the lives of the educated. The trivialization of university courses under the aegis of multiculturalism thus caters to the illiteracy of the students.

Yet ideological considerations are not absent. Multiculturalism is itself complicit in the decline of reading. In the high-school curriculum, it has favored the near total eclipse of Europe. It promotes the replacement of those older authors who are the glory of literature in English—the Swifts and the Dickenses and the Hawthornes—with easier ones deemed "relevant" (and representative of the different strands of multiculturalism). Whether in high school or in university, multiculturalism makes the case not for the serious reading of old books but against it.

If there is one point that all schools of "cultural studies" hold in common, it is the denial that old books (or any books) can serve as permanent beacons for thoughtful human beings. It treats all writers and thinkers as Poe's Montresor treated Fortunato: It immures them and leaves them to suffocate. The walls are the confines of their societies, and above all of its prejudices and iniquities, which God forbid that any one should ever be thought to have transcended. The greatest protagonists of the life of the mind become but relics of a past culture, as dead for the student as that culture is. Hence the fix is in for their displacement by representatives of today's hot cultures, which is to say of multiculturalism.

As Allan Bloom has argued, this approach deprives the student of the requisite incentive to master the skills of reading old books. True, in studying these today, we are encouraged to note their complicity in the great historic offenses of the West (sexism, heterosexism, etc.). Occasionally, we are even encouraged to see them as implying protests against these sins. But in neither of these cases do the books have anything essential to teach us; when it comes to the issues of our own lives, we learn nothing that we did not know already, nothing but what the monotonous celebration of difference permits us to know. Reading old books leads to class discussions of the sort captured by Philip Roth in the lines that I chose as my epigraph—and such discussions reinforce, in their turn, students' indifference to the books.

In all of these crucial respects, "multicultural" courses are simply artifacts of contemporary Western culture and therefore far more accessible to today's students than the great works of past Western centuries. So multiculturalism does not involve the replacement of the familiar by the strange, but the replacement of the strange by the familiar. At the end of the day (and even at the beginning of it), Edmund Spenser is a far stranger and more forbidding figure to today's graduate of Scarsdale High than is Toni Morrison or Rigoberta Menchu—which is to say that he is (as Arthur Melzer has remarked in the *New Republic*) a far more "diverse" one.

If I am right that it is far easier, as well as apparently more useful and obviously more "relevant," to study Morrison or Menchu than Spenser or Shakespeare, then one should not hope to find among students and parents a determined constituency for the defense of the older liberal education. It is always the case in democracy that the basic tastes in education are for the easy, the useful, and the relevant. Increasingly, it will only be students in rebellion from these tastes who will feel the charm of the older education. Some such students there will always be, but they too will feel the pull of multiculturalism. For the novelty, the radical egalitarianism, the Third World chic, and the rebellion against "Western values" preached by multiculturalism are bound to appeal to the young and the restless.

To teach the classics of Western thought has become ever more difficult in the past two decades. I would not, however, ascribe this primarily to the ethnic diversity of today's students. Judging from my experience, most Chinese- or Korean- or Indian-Canadian students do not find the study of Plato or Hobbes or Nietzsche obviously more difficult than do their Anglo-Saxon counterparts. Even apart from the fact that recently many of my best, and most serious, students have been Asian Canadians, we should not exaggerate the handicap under which these labor. Innocent as many of them may be not only of the classics of Western civilization but of the general background required to approach them, their Anglo-Saxon classmates are hardly less so. This common ignorance is then the result not of having been born in Hong Kong but of having been educated in North America. It has less to do with multiculturalism as fact than with multiculturalism as policy, and less to do with either than with the decline of reading (to which, however, multiculturalism contributes). Whatever the ethnic diversity among current students, their common uneasiness in the company of books is an element of uniformity among them, and must be explained as such.

Two Views of Culture, Two Universities

The two views of culture yield two different relationships between the university and society. The newer notion, with its insistence on a variety of cultures coexisting within society, each of which has a quasi-political right to "representation" in the university, implies a university that is political (and politicized) at its core and to its peak. A university so conceived is responsive to society not only inasmuch as it provides it with the advanced vocational training and scientific and economic progress that it seeks, but inasmuch as such "responsiveness" defines its highest intellectual mission. As Jimmy Carter preached a government that was "as good as the American people," multiculturalism seeks a university that is as "diverse" as that people.

In principle, a university so understood leads society by following it. It sees itself as "progressive" to the extent that it is "culturally correct," an accurate reflection of all of the diverse tendencies and constituencies in society which it is willing to legitimate as "cultures." In practice, as I have argued, such a university aspires to lead society by discrediting what it takes to be the dominant "culture," while empowering those previously "marginalized." It is to this end that it forbids critical scrutiny of the claims of the latter, and it is to this end that it casts the giants of Western thought and art as running dogs of some prohibited -ism.

The older notion of culture implies a university that offers a place for reflection upon society precisely because it is not as an institution simply reflective of society. This was Arnold's hope, difficult of attainment in his (as in any) society, and still more so in ours. Such a university seeks to lead society by shouldering the Arnoldian task of making the students whatever their background somewhat more cultured (less conventional, less partisan, less the creatures of that background) than they were when they entered. It requires in those who would undertake this task not only an education hard to come by these days but unremitting modesty and self-criticism. (For it is true that only with the greatest difficulty does liberal education avoid complacency and unwitting complicity in ideology.) At the summit, such a university aspires to foster at least a large handful of students capable of surveying society not through slits in the walls of their class, ethnic, or gender warrens but from a vantage point achieved through the study of figures who rise above such divisions.

This task will always be suspect in the eyes of society. If American universities enjoyed (with many qualifications) a heyday in the fifties and early sixties, it was only because these represented the peak of public acceptance of the notion that liberal education in the broader sense responded to the needs of liberal democracy. The pursuit of a human excellence that transcended democracy, so long as it was open to all, was not deemed incompatible with democracy and was even thought to crown it. (Though Homer and Dante and Jane Austen were not democrats, they were presumed to speak to democrats. The current vogue for Austen, loving and ironic chronicler of a squirearchical way of life, suggests that this broader view of "relevance" remains accessible to us.) The particular challenge facing the advocates of such an education today is to sustain this pursuit in the face of students who are ever more "diverse," on the one hand, and ever more similar in their initial indifference and unpreparedness, on the other.

Such a neo-Arnoldian view might embrace not only a vast expansion of those to whom culture would now be available (of which Arnold himself would certainly have approved) but also lively controversy as to the list of works most worthy of study. (Arnold himself was a revisionist in matters of "the Canon.") All such controversy would grant, however, that the applicable standard was Arnold's: that of enduring pre-eminence in addressing the human situation. It would imply permission to teach that certain thinkers and artists have walked this earth as representatives not of their nation, class, gender, and sexual orientation but of humanity as such.

Fostering Empathy and Finding Common Ground in Multiethnic Classes[2]

Our kids come in balkanized and isolated. The empathy is so important to create a community.

It's at the heart of my objectives...even though they appear to be diverse, students must learn to find connections to one another so they can respect one another, both in the classroom and in the outside world.

We're concocting the glue that is going to help hold our schools together in the coming years.

This is a very important theme for English classes—extremely relevant and immediate, especially with all the outside ethnic and racial conflicts going on. We all need to find common ground quickly.

In a three-day institute sponsored by ACCESS, a partnership between the University of California, Berkeley, and the Oakland Unified School District, 19 educators read literature by ethnically-diverse authors, discussed responses, and planned ways to use the works in class. A theme emerging from this work was the value of empathy, the need for reconciliation among groups divided by differences, biases, and histories of injustice. The teacher remarks above are a sampling from a follow-up workshop that explored empathy in more detail; they illustrate the need we and our colleagues feel to address empathy through literary study and the urgency of helping students, often divided by differences, develop into cooperative communities of learners and citizens.

"...they illustrate the need we and our colleagues feel to address empathy through literary study..."

While we stress in our work the importance of difference and, like Gloria Ladson-Billings (1994), keep issues of race and racism on our multicultural agenda, we also find essential to literature study and to teaching students in multiethnic classes in the 1990s the need to explore points of connection. Margaret A. Gibson (1984) argued that a conceptual failing of multicultural education has been its lack of attention to points of connection, to what is shared across cultures. This failing, she argues, can perpetuate racist notions, a belief that many groups are sufficiently different from us to hold them at a distance as "other."

Such divisions can impede building class community for collaborative language work and can prevent students' deep understanding and appreciation of the complexities of American cultures depicted in literature. Building community and cultivating

---

empathy in any class can be challenging, but in multiethnic inner-city classes often fraught with anger, racial tensions, and histories of "balkanization," these challenges can be daunting. To address these concerns at the workshop on empathy, we shared relevant literature and teaching resources, read and discussed poems, and shared classroom experiences that demonstrated ways we have wrestled with the issues in our work. Drawing on these shared materials (poems, essays, handouts, lesson plans), on tapes and teacher notes from small- and large-group discussions and presentations, and on response forms completed at the end of the workshop, we have distilled a set of principles that members of the group have tested and found fruitful in shaping classroom communities open to the challenges of learning about difference and recognizing and embracing essential points of connection. We illustrate these principles with scenes from our teaching.

The Thoughtful Selection of Texts

Text selection can enhance the potential of literature to foster empathy when guided first by criteria for sensitive representation of diversity (e.g., Bishop 1992; Stotsky 1994; Yokota 1993). The annotated list of literature and films that is with this article includes works we have found particularly useful in sensitizing students to diversity, in fostering empathy, and in helping students find common ground. Some works achieve this goal by embracing diversity. For example, Maya Angelou's "On the Pulse of Morning" (1993) dignifies the diversity of Americans; Langston Hughes' "Daybreak in Alabama" (1969) paints a dream of a racially harmonious world, a fine contrast to the poet's dream-deferred montage.

Other works from our list depict characters stretching to understand and deal with difference. Nadine Gordimer's white South African protagonist in *July's People* (1981) awakens to what it means to live in the back country, as her servant July always has, when she is forced to take cover in his hut after a black revolution. Other works from our list depict characters attempting to repair relationships, providing models for young readers of how people dealing with barriers can reach toward deeper understanding, despite differences. Arturo Islas' *The Rain God* (1984), for instance, features divisions among people based on ethnicity, region, gender, and sexual orientation, but characters in the novel struggle toward reconciliation. Twelfth graders in the classes of some members of our group have found this novel particularly effective in describing how empathy is possible. We have also found that tailoring literary selections to represent the student body of a class can help ensure that all students, if they wish, can emerge as cultural experts. In addition, family themes often tap issues that adolescents share, despite differences.

An Inviting Physical Environment

Seating Arrangements

Even as students enter a class, the physical setting can reveal and shape attitudes. We have found that the physical layout of the room and the use of wall space can help to create a classroom climate that supports community-building. In Elizabeth Lay's class, for example, relevant and controversial literature units demand seating arrangements that help support a developing intimacy needed to effectively grapple with such units. Collaborative group seating, balanced for gender, culture, and heterogeneity, facilitates everyone's active participation, especially when students recognize the clearly-stated classroom goal that everyone's voice counts, not just that of one group, one gender, or one culture. Whole-class circle seating reinforces a desired climate of mutual trust and respect as students face each other and everyone else in active listening and respected discussion. Students more comfortably achieve accountability and individual responsibility in such a climate. U-shaped or half-circle seating for individual or small group oral presentations also fosters shared trust and mutual respect.

"Among the themes in the posters are those of equal access to, and positive images of, success..."

Bulletin Boards and Wall Displays

Visual images and quotations on classroom walls can communicate to students that members of all groups are welcome, supported, and encouraged here. In a recent piece in the newspaper at David Christiano's school, a student wrote of how the walls in the classroom David shares with a colleague boast cultural heroes and role models that richly reflect the diversity of the student body. Posters depict literary and historical figures, pop culture heroes, and musical artists, such as Pablo Neruda, Rosa Parks, and Bob Marley. Among the themes in the posters are those of equal access to and positive images of success, ranging from a calendar of "Black Heroes" to a poster of rap star KRS-One boasting "Read So You Can See." Students of color recognize support through these materials and through the posting of articles such as one entitled "Snapple Fights Rumors that It Supports KKK."

Posting newspaper clippings can serve other purposes, as well. To examine violence in literature and contemporary life, Steven Athanases asked his 10th graders to analyze what caused characters to devolve so far from acts of caring to acts of violence as they read of a lynching in William Faulkner's "Dry September" (1930), of an abusive escaped convict in Flannery O'Connor's "A Good Man Is Hard to Find" (1976), and of other acts in Ron Kovic's *Born on the Fourth of July* (1976), Truman Capote's *In Cold Blood* (1966), or William Golding's *Lord of the Flies* (1962). Published essays on roots of violence, kinds of violence, and non-violence provided frameworks to help students move toward insights and personal stands. Responding to the claim that violence is inevitable, students wrote essays on constructive ways to respond to violent trends through enhanced family communication, education, continued war on poverty, gun control, an improved prison system, and checks on media violence.

Still, some students protested that "Everything we read is so depressing." Just as Barbara Pace (1992) has argued the need for anthologies to include literary selections depicting women and people of color in empowered states to balance stories of subjugation, so too did the violence unit need models of caring to balance the grim picture of societal violence.

Steven then created a bulletin board of "Good News at the Breakfast Table" to display students' newspaper clippings of upbeat news, tales of heroism and good deeds, stories showing superior acts of caring and building common ground. He has kept clippings for class use of people countering prejudice and hate: one entitled "Korean Merchants' Black Street Diplomat" about a group of Chicago shopowners who hired an African-American woman as cultural liaison and as a bridge to the African-American community and another on how an Oakland choir has brought together students of varied ethnicities to perform for the community. Articles such as these, posted and labelled, provide models of caring and reconciliation, a backdrop of hope, particularly in communities torn by violence and despair, and they serve as informative class reading in conjunction with literary works.

Exhibits of Student Work
The messages of equal access to classroom learning and of trust and respect are further enhanced through the frequent placing of all students' work on walls, not just stellar examples, especially for assignments that call for a wide canvas of responses neither right nor wrong, but clearly varied and cohesive. Visitors to Elizabeth's classroom see boards and walls filled with student essays and graphic responses to literature, such as, during one unit, large-group posters with symbolic representations of themes, with titles such as "Mis/Interpreting Culture" and "Emotional Impact of Difference." The posters and writings reinforce the point that student voices are integral to the work of the class.

A Social Climate of Trust and Respect

Just as the physical setting of the classroom can invite, attract, and support students, so too can the social climate invite students to relate to one another in productive ways. We have had good results shaping such climates when we have worked to make classrooms hubs of engaging, learner centered activities in which students have a say in shaping procedures. We have found an increasing need to make the classroom a sanctuary or refuge for students so they can leave outside the classroom, in the hall, their personal troubles and emotional baggage (ranging from a relationship breakup or a fight with a parent, to dealing with the arrest, trauma, or death of a family member).

One strategy for establishing such a climate is the use of activities that validate each student's experiences and identity. To launch their American Literature/U.S. History curriculum, David and his colleague assign an oral history project on "How We Got to California" and for another course an autobiographical story modeled after Sandra Cisneros' story "My Name" from *The House on Mango Street* (1986). These assignments structure opportunities for students to introduce themselves to the class; inviting students to share personal and family experiences around a common theme helps to forge common ground.

Ideally, the learning environment would be filled with the voices of everyone participating. The use of "response journals" or "learning logs" can help a class move toward this ideal. In such written records, students jot down what especially impressed them about a class text, film, or discussion. These responses can help produce more active voices if frequently reviewed and if selected examples are either read aloud (perhaps anonymously) or typed and distributed the next day as the basis for discussion. The teacher can ask for student volunteers to read responses aloud, allowing for class discussion on each. Generally reticent students frequently gain motivation to claim their voices in the class once they hear their words read aloud by classmates and approved by still others, enriching the class environment.

"Students need to feel that they can voice diverse interpretations and opinions without feeling that their ideas will be judged in an intolerant way."

In order to build a classroom community, teachers in our group advocate a climate that combines candor with safety. Students need to feel that they can voice diverse interpretations and opinions without feeling that their ideas will be judged in an intolerant way. The environment supports the students' right to state what their values are, but students are reminded that they are members of larger communities, that they cannot remain insular, that there is a level of decency that we can expect all human beings to live by.

Tackling Stereotypes Head-on

Student expression of stereotypes can disturb a teacher interested in diversifying literature curricula, in promoting social justice, and in creating a safe space for all students; it can prove even more deeply disturbing when the teacher or a student is a member of the group stereotyped. One intern teacher, Asian American, told of a number of students saying, "Asians should 'go home' to Asian nations"; "Asians are less American and will always side with their home country." Against such expressed attitudes, the teacher felt helpless. One of her student teacher colleagues reported pain and frustration when an eighth grader made a series of homophobic remarks, some confrontational, in class. While such comments in some cases merely mirror what students hear at home, among peers, or in the larger society, they reveal stereotype formation. The acceptance of these stereotypes impedes the educational goal of sensitizing students to the diversity of people reflected in U.S. literature and reflected in class-rooms, and sensitizing them to the stories of injustices that those marginalized have suffered. Members of our group tackle such stereotypes head-on.

In David's U.S. literature/history class, students examine impressions of racial and ethnic groups. During study of slavery and Reconstruction, students learn the history of racism regard-ing African Americans through readings about stereotypes and through viewing the film "Ethnic Notions," Marlon Riggs' 1986 documentary on racist imagery of African Americans. In studying Latino culture and experiences, students read an excerpt from Piri Thomas' *Down These Mean Streets* (1967), poetry by Pat Mora (1985), historical texts, essays by Carlos Fuentes and others; and view a slide presentation of California Chicano murals and films such as "Nuestro Pueblo" (a 1991 documentary about Chicanos in Northern California) and the Hollywood feature film *Zoot Suit* (1991). In groups, students explore cultural assimilation and the phenomenon of feeling lost between two worlds.

To culminate this unit, students who identify as Latino answer questions that tap personal responses: How do your views of your ethnic identity differ from what you see as the general, popular impressions? What do you consider to be the most prevalent stereotypes about Latinos and to what extent do they accurately reflect prevailing attitudes, behavior, and values of your culture?

Non-Latino students respond personally to questions such as these: When you hear the term *Mexican, Chicano, Latino* or *Hispanic*, what kind of image comes to mind? What is the source of this image (how did it form in your mind)? While the first question invites students to reveal whatever cultural notions they hold, however stereotypical, about Latinos, the second pushes students to examine how such notions developed. Students also answer questions such as these: What are some stereotypes you've come across having to do with Latinos? To what extent do you believe that these stereotypes have any truth to them?

To examine the transformative power of these units, David and his colleague ask students to report any changes in their percep-tions as a result of exposure to the sources and to their writings, discussions, interviews, and presentations. Students who are not members of the cultural group under study, for example, write about the most influential and least influential source or sources in terms of providing them with new, valuable information that may have changed their previous views about the cultural group.

Despite students' tendencies to remain within their own cul-tural groups and despite some tensions between African Americans and Asians at David's school, African-American stu-dents have repeatedly acknowledged learning that Asians had been oppressed, even treated like slaves at times in American history. Students have cited Maxine Hong Kingston's *China Men* chapter entitled "Grandfather of the Sierra Madre" (1980) as instrumental in showing them the terrible conditions of Chinese men working in the California mountains, including the lower wages these men earned and their being driven out of the area to urban ghettoes after their labor was no longer needed.

The units began to break down barriers between racial groups, generating conversation across racial lines. Students moved from their personal experiences, often reactionary and purely emotional, to a consciousness of the widespread nature of racism in America. This deeper understanding of the larger social and political picture helped students begin to see the value of moving beyond divisiveness to unity among people of color and others interested in combatting racism.

Crosscutting Themes and Questions

Students can better assimilate literary depictions of difference when they have curricular tools to guide their thinking. Some members of our group identify underlying themes and questions that cut across units, recurring over the course of the year, providing a structure students can internalize for handling new challenges. For example, while she resists Eurocentrism, moving toward multiculturalism and a wealth of values, one teacher in our group finds it also essential for her students to critique cultures. Underlying questions in her integrated world literature and history course are these: Which values we read about are universal; which are of western orientation; which are good; which are bad? From their past education, she argues, students believe that everyone's cultural values can be validated because they are theirs; every cultural value is good, and we cannot stand as judges. We can *make* judgments, she argues, and we *can* judge cultures based on how far they've come from relics of barbarism, things students explore in her curriculum. Making reference to readings from her curriculum, she uses women's rights as an example:

> When we hear about police states that strap electrodes to men's genitals and zap them, we say that's against human rights. But when we hear about women, aunties, who mutilate their nieces (in rites of circumcision in parts of Africa), that's a cultural thing. My question is, why is it based on gender superiority of men over women; why is it all right for a society to subjugate women in some cultural rite when it's not all right for the police state to do this to a (male) dissident?

Over the year, as students reflect on readings, their teacher returns to core questions of value: Which are universal, which are of western orientation, which are good, which are bad, why? These questions help structure students' inquiries.

Similarly, Elizabeth provides a set of questions that underlie a 10-week unit for her heterogeneously grouped 12th-grade students entitled "The Politics of Identity," designed not just to investigate differences but to explore remedies to conflicts between groups. The literary works provide ample evidence of injustices done to

"Students moved from their personal experiences...to a consciousness of the widespread nature of racism in America."

groups, but students are not left with merely images of oppression. A core question drives the unit: "If these are the problems (as depicted in the literary works), what are the solutions?"

Students read Islas' *The Rain God* and Jerzy Kosinski's *The Painted Bird* (1965) as core texts and thematic packets of short writings. Kosinski's work invokes the theme of antisemitism and responses to difference based on hate, denial, and ultimately genocide. Many of Elizabeth's students of color have identified with the ways the young protagonist feels as he is ostracized for being a Jew and called "gypsy bastard." As they encounter this and other readings, students engage in a series of structured steps they eventually internalize for application to all reading assignments perceived as challenging, controversial, and relevant. Designed to introduce new material in small, personal increments, the structure then enables students to connect to increasingly complex, critical responses, thus making even bigger stretches.

A set of prompts invites personal, engaged responses: What in this piece surprises you, clarifies, raises questions, answers a question, states a key idea, reveals something you didn't know, pleases you, angers you? Students highlight texts, underline, take notes, write out a response, then meet in groups to share their diverse findings and to discover both differences and similarities in their collective responses, an essential component of literary interpretation (Bleich 1975; Rosenblatt 1976). Students report findings in whole-class discussion where they ask each other questions; agree/disagree, generating evidence from other readings and general knowledge; consider implications (if this is true here, what of other situations, circumstances?); and make connections to other readings, personal experience, general knowledge. From such work, students learn more reasoned responses to difference.

Just as they examined issues of race and ethnicity, religion, and gender, students read texts at the end of the unit addressing "The Politics of Sexual Orientation." Because homosexuality is so charged in U.S. society and because sexuality in general is new and often difficult terrain for adolescents, this final portion of the unit could easily collapse. Instead, when Steven observed Elizabeth's classes during this portion of the unit, he found students' responses and interactions sophisticated.

As they entered class, students moved into group discussion circles to examine their responses to readings, comfortably and candidly reacting through questioning and critical crosstalk. Soon a guest speaker sat on a stool in front of the class. Students clustered around as he spoke of his work as an author and high school English teacher at a neighboring school and the politics of being an African-American gay man. Students asked questions that tapped their knowledge from the unit, demonstrating their understanding of how the speaker's membership in two groups often marginalized in the U.S. would raise particular challenges.

The support provided by the unit enabled students to address here and at other times the unit's underlying questions:

1. How can we understand or come to terms with differences within and between various groups such as those defined by race, culture, gender, or sexual orientation?

2. How can these differences in identity expand rather than restrict the potential for human life and democratic possibilities?

Perspective Taking through Creative Writing and Role Playing

Imaginative writing and drama can support exploration of difference. Writing autobiographical narratives related to literary themes not only aids literary understanding (Smith and White, in press), but, as Sarah Lawrence Lightfoot (1993) argues, such stories "weave the tapestry of human connections," providing resources that link our own and others' experiences, enable us to reveal and reflect on values, and help us think about morality and justice. We have found that students likewise experience perspective taking when they try on others' points of view. Steven has frequently asked students to write narratives and poems from the points of view of people involved in current crises in the news and to role play characters from literary works involved in imaginary scenes. In these ways students voice and embody others' experiences. Dramatic monologues of literary characters (and of people responding to their stories) scripted and performed by students likewise invite perspective taking.

To close a unit examining culture and stereotypes of Asians, Asian Americans, and Pacific Islanders, David and his team-teaching colleague asked students to conduct interviews in Oakland's Chinatown with storekeepers and with people on the streets, learning perceptions of life in Chinatown versus life in the homeland and learning about differences between recent Asian immigrants and those who have been in the U.S. for generations.

In one class, students performed scenes of a job interview where: an Asian applicant is rejected on racist grounds; Asian Americans stereotype immigrant Asians; and a bus ride during which non-Asians react to Asians in bigoted ways. These enactments of the day-to-day realities of the racial stereotyping studied in course materials helped to ground students in the issues, making the themes more engaging and more accessible to examination, and potentially fostering movement toward deeper understanding of difference.

Class or Small Group Projects

Well-structured group projects can enable students to weave together individual initiative and cooperative problem-solving, often involving research, reflection, and multimodal presentation (written, spoken, and visual). In addition, such project work can enable students often divided by group differences to work together and lessen the gaps that often divide. Maxine Greene

(1993) has argued that literary encounters are essential in providing the stuff for deeper understanding across such gaps, and
that experiences of working together can serve similar purposes:
"We need to learn to open ourselves to authentic personal
encounters that help us to move beyond categorizing, distancing,
and allowing ourselves to be made other."

Modeling Empathy through Talk and Action

Teachers in our group repeatedly identified teacher modeling as
an essential lesson in empathy. Students recognize a teacher's
caring, demonstrated through sensitive selection and treatment
of curricular materials, through expressed feeling for people and
literary characters, through sharing of stories relevant to class
study. As teachers share with students beliefs, experiences, and
interpretations of texts, students often similarly share how pieces
of their lives relate to literature under study. In a memorable
scene, David told his class how he had observed a carload of
young white men shouting harassing remarks at an African-
American woman walking by and of how one of the men reached
out and lifted the woman up and dropped her to the ground.
David told of his shock at this scene and of how he chased after
the car and reported the men to the police. Students were
absolutely engaged in David's story, in which various things
were embedded: disgust at racially-charged meanness, an enact-
ment of caring, the importance of actively addressing a wrong.

In a recent conference talk, Maya Angelou (1994, California
Association of Teachers of English Annual Meeting, Oakland,
CA) identified not the random acts of caring and education about
diversity that count most but the consistent effort, the constant
acts of courage that require even asking a guest to leave one's
home if a racial or sexual slur is uttered there. Teachers in our
group believe that when the teacher demonstrates to students
the right course of action in the face of meanness or injustice, or
demonstrates an act of courage, students can see and hear empathy enacted through illustrations we all need.

Warding Off Burnout

A new teacher in our group told how during a unit on Mexican-
American literature she staged a courtroom drama with the
"English Only" proposal on trial. When the class overwhelmingly
supported "English Only," including immigrant students of various Latino and Asian ancestries, an African-American young
woman argued vehemently that with language goes culture. She
later told the teacher through tears, "They don't understand; I can
never have the language or culture of my homeland." The teacher,
herself a Chicana, regretted that with her preoccupation with the
demands of planning and teaching that she had remained
detached, had not mustered empathy to feel what her student felt.

A teacher of many years experience responded by linking act-
ing with teaching, recalling how she learned from a drama direc-

tor that:

> You can't *become* these characters or you will lose your-self. When I identify with my students so much...where can I lead them if I *am* them? If you take it to its extreme, it's a loss of self, of what you have to give. I can remember my first three years of teaching. I lost a marriage through it. Every night, just crying, literally crying. What can I *do*? I care so much and don't know what to *do* about it.... I think empathy is what we have to create, we have to work for that. I think we have to beware that action needs to come out of the empathy, though.

We believe that the good work of teaching comes in small repeated doses through our curriculum, our instruction, our class environments, and our modeling. We need to beware, however, of feeling so burdened by painful stories in our students' lives that we cannot remain fresh for the challenge. We have found help in building supportive relationships with colleagues who demonstrate the interest and skill in fostering empathy and building common ground in classes.

Conclusion

In "Musée des Beaux Arts" (1958), a poem we discussed in our workshop on empathy, W. H. Auden reflects on the fall of Icarus after Icarus refused his father's advice and flew too close to the sun, his wax wings melting and dashing him to a death in the sea. Auden remarks on Brueghel's painting of Icarus: Rather than place Icarus at the heart of the scene, the painter has dwarfed Icarus' drama, placing it at the back of the painting, depicting him as merely a tiny pair of legs entering the water with a small splash. Dominating the scene are a ploughman, oblivious, doing his daily work, and a ship that "sailed calmly on." Auden says this painting reveals that Brueghel understood the nature of human suffering, "how everything turns away/Quite leisurely from the disaster."

At the close of our workshop, reflecting on our work together, one teacher remarked that maybe through the efforts of many teachers addressing the urgent need for community building in classes, that another person's drama might be "not just a splash you can see in the distance, but maybe we can be touched by other people's struggles." Through efforts such as those we have described, from thoughtful selection of texts to creating an appropriate physical and social environment, from the use of projects and role playing, to the consideration of underlying questions and attacks on stereotypes, and through teacher modeling and collaboration with others equally sensitive to these concerns, we believe that the study of literature and language can help students explore essential points of connection with and respect for others, however different. We believe that the times call for attention to these concerns.

"We believe that the good work of teaching comes in small repeated doses through our curriculum, our instruction, our class environments, and our modeling."

LITERARY WORKS AND FILMS THAT ADDRESS
EMPATHY AND COMMON GROUND

Poetry

Angelou, Maya. 1993. "On the Pulse of Morning." New York: Random House.

In this poem delivered at the Clinton presidential inauguration, Angelou embraces the range of people who make up the American population.

Auden, W. H. 1958. "Musée des Beaux Arts." *Selected Poetry of W. H. Auden*. New York: The Modern Library. 49.

Classic poem on human suffering and the problem of empathy; works well with picture of Brueghel's "Icarus," the painting that inspired the poem, available in many library collections.

Berry, Wendell. 1984. "My Great-Grandfather's Slaves." *The Generation of 2000: Contemporary American Poets*. Princeton: Ontario Review Press. 14-15.

Explores how descendants of slaves and slave owners are inextricably linked through a terrible past.

Cochran, Jo Whitehorse. 1991. "Halfbreed Girl in the City School." *Rethinkng Columbus*, Special Edition. *Rethinking Schools*.

Powerful rendering of what I stripped of your culture.

Hughes, Langston. 1969. "Daybreak in Alabama." *The Panther and the Lash*. New York: Knopf. 101.

Good contrast to the poet's "Dream Deferred" montage; in this piece, he holds on to an inspired dream of a racially/ethnically harmonious world.

Jordan, June. 1989. "Poem for Mark." *Naming our Destiny: New and Selected Poems*. New York: Thunder's Mouth Press. 200-201.

African-American woman discovers ground with a British man in "the silly land of Philip and Diana," discovering he is one of "my people."

Levertov, Denise. 1970. "The Gulf (During the Detroit Riots, 1967)." *Relearning the Alphabet*. New York: New Directions Publishing. 15-16.

Using the gulf as metaphor, poet reflects on divisions between groups.

Lorde, Audre. 1994. "For the Record (in Memory of Eleanor Bumpers)." *Every Shut Eye Ain't Asleep*. Eds. Michael S. Harper and Anthony Walton. Boston: Little, Brown & Company. 123.

Reflects on the sisterhood of "colored girls" such as Bumpers and Indira Gandhi, two 67-year-old women killed.

Mora, Pat. 1985. *Chants*. Houston, TX: Arte Publico Press.

Piri, Thomas. 1967. *Down These Mean Streets*. New York: Random House.

Wong, Nellie. 1981. "When I Was Growing Up." *This Bridge Called My Back: Writings by Radical Women of Color*. Eds. Cherrie Moraga and Gloria Anzaldua. New York: Kitchen Table, Women of Color Press.

Moving poem that reveals a young Asian woman's longing to be white.

Stories

Cisneros, Sandra. 1986. *The House on Mango Street*. Houston, TX: Arte Publico Press.

Faulkner, William. 1930. *Collected Stories of William Faulkner*. New York: Random House.

Garza, Daniel. 1963. "Everybody Knows Tobie." *Descant: The Literary Journal of Texas Christian University*, vii (3).

> Explores, from a child's point of view, the levels of prejudice that exist among Anglos, Chicanos, and Mexicans in a Texas border town.

Jimenez, Francisco. 1984. "The Circuit." *Cuentos*. Eds. Rudolfo Anaya and Antonio Marques. Albuquerque: University of New Mexico Press.

> Reveals, from a migrant worker child's point of view, the recurring trauma of being uprooted to find seasonal work.

Kingsolver, Barbara. 1993. "Rose-Johnny." *First Sightings: Contemporary Stories of American Youth*. New York: Persea Books.

> Coming-of-age story in a small Southern town. A young girl's growing empathy for a woman who has been shunned because of her family and personal history contributes to the girl's emotional development.

O'Connor, Flannery. 1976. *A Good Man Is Hard to Find and Other Stories*. San Diego: Harcourt Brace Jovanovich.

Autobiographies

Kovic, Ron. 1976. *Born on the Fourth of July*. New York: McGraw Hill.

Rodriguez, Luis J. *Always Running: La Vida Loca, Gang Days in L.A.* Willimantic, CT: Curbstone Press.

> Revealing account of lives of Mexican immigrants to Southern California.

Novels

Capote, Truman. 1966. *In Cold Blood*. New York: Random House.

Golding, William. 1962. *Lord of the Flies*. New York: Coward-McCann.

Gordimer, Nadine. 1981. *July's People*. New York: Penguin Books.

> A white South African learns for the first time what it means to live in the back country, as her servant July always has, when she is forced to take cover in his hut after a black revolution.

Islas, Arturo. 1984. *The Rain God*. New York: Avon Books.

> Features divisions among people based on ethnicity, region, gender, and sexual orientation, but characters in the novel struggle to ward reconciliation.

Kosinski, Jerzy. 1965. *The Painted Bird*. Boston: Houghton Mifflin.

Mukherjee, B. 1989. *Jasmine*. New York: Fawcett Crest.

> Focuses on a young Indian woman's interior and exterior journey across cultures and her attempt to find a place within American culture without losing her own cultural identity.

Novels (cont'd)

Tan, Amy. 1989. *The Joy Luck Club*. New York: Ivy Books.

> Focuses on conflict and reconciliation—particularly between a group of overseas born Chinese American women and their American born daughters.

Essays

Kingston, Maxine Hong. 1980. *China Men*. New York: Knopf.

Reed, Ishmael. 1988. "America: The Multinational Society." *Graywolf Annual Five: Multicultural Literacy*. Eds. Rick Simonson and Scott Walker. St. Paul: Graywolf Press.

> A short essay emphasizing the diversity of American society. Reed makes the point that "The world has been arriving at these shores for at least ten thousand years from Europe, Africa, and Asia." He sees America as becoming "a place where the cultures of the world crisscross."

Takaki, Ronald. 1993. *A Different Mirror: A History of Multicultural America*. Boston: Little, Brown, and Company.

> A multicultural history of the different cultural groups that contributed to and make up America.

Plays

Smith, Anna Deavere. 1994. *Twilight: Los Angeles*. 1992. 1994. New York: Anchor.

> A series of monologues about the uprising in South Central Los Angeles after the first trial of policemen who assaulted Rodney King. The work extends the theme of developing empathy and finding common ground to larger social and community issues.

Feature Films

Eat a Bowl of Tea. 1989. Wayne Wang, director. American Playhouse Series.

> Combines humor and poignancy to provide rare glimpses into inner workings of a Chinese-American community in New York City during the late 1940s and early 1950s. 100 minutes.

Powwow Highway. 1988. Jonathan Wacks, director.

> Considered a "cult favorite" on contemporary reservations for the open, honest, and thoroughly upbeat look it takes through the eyes of Native Americans struggling against "the system." 91 minutes.

Thunderheart. 1992. Michael Apted, director. Burbank, CA: Columbia TriStar Home Video.

> Explores the tensions of Native American cultural identity and assimilation in the context of a political murder mystery. 118 minutes.

Zoot Suit. 1991. Luis Valdez, director. Universal City, CA: MCA Universal Home Video.

> Explores the persecution of Chicano youth in the Los Angeles area during World War II through the lens of a true-life story known as "The Sleepy Lagoon Case." 104 minutes.

Changes in America's Secondary School Literature Programs[3]

Vast changes have taken place over the past three decades in the content of history textbooks and in the teaching of American and world history. Vast changes have also occurred in the content of reading and literature programs. But in contrast to the professional and public attention that has been focused on changes in history textbooks and curricula, relatively little attention has been paid to reading and literature programs. Several recent studies suggest how much secondary literature curricula have changed, not only in recent decades but over the course of the 20th century.

In a review of relevant studies over the course of this century, using a 1907 report by George Tanner as a base line, I found that a dramatic cultural transformation has taken place in the secondary schools of this country. At the time of Tanner's report, not surprisingly, in 67 high schools in the Midwest only nine of the 40 most frequently assigned works for grades 9 through 12 were written by Americans; the rest were by British writers. Less than 90 years later, two studies by Arthur Applebee and one study by Philip Anderson and me suggest that the situation has reversed, not just for individual works but for secondary school anthologies as well.

After asking English department chairs in 322 representative schools around the country to list for each grade in their school "the book-length works of literature which all students in any English class study," Applebee found that—of the top 43 titles reported for grades 7 through 12—26 are by American authors (Table 1, p. 84). About 20 titles reflect 20th-century life, and all of these, except for George Orwell's *1984* and *Animal Farm* and William Golding's *Lord of the Flies*, are by Americans. Interestingly, only four of Applebee's 43 titles appeared on Tanner's 1907 list.

After asking all secondary school members of the New England Association of Teachers of English (NEATE) to name 10 well-known and 10 less-well-known titles that they would recommend to their colleagues for whole-class instruction, based on their own experience in teaching these works, Anderson and I found that 29 of the top 45 titles recommended for grades 7 through 12 are by American authors (Table 2, p. 85). Only five of the 45 titles also appeared on Tanner's 1907 list. (Our questionnaires were returned by 27% of the secondary school members of NEATE.)

What I think is most informative about these two studies is

[3] Article by Sandra Stotsky, research associate in the Department of Language and Literacy, Graduate School of Education, Harvard University, Cambridge, MA, from *Phi Delta Kappan* 76:605-13 Ap '95. Copyright © 1995 *Phi Delta Kappan*. Reprinted with permission.

that the lists do not look very different, despite differences in methodology, in the question each study asked, and in the limitations of each study. For example, the NEATE study was much smaller in scope than Applebee's, and we did not survey a random sample of English teachers. On the other hand, as Applebee noted in a later report, the department chairs in his study may not have known what each teacher was teaching. Nor, we might add, do teachers necessarily teach what a curriculum guide or course catalogue suggests they are teaching.

In the face of these differences, the similarities between these two lists suggest that the two studies are capturing a reality: the predominance of American works over British works in contemporary secondary school literature programs. And it appears from Applebee's survey of leading secondary school literature anthologies, all copyrighted in 1989, that here too we now have an America-centered curriculum. Applebee found that between 68% and 79% of the works collected for grades 7 through 10 were written by "North American authors." (Grade 11 anthologies focus solely on American literature, and grade 12 anthologies focus on British literature or world literature.) It is surprising that the change from a British-centered curriculum to an America-centered one has received almost no attention from scholars and teachers of literature.

"Applebee found that between 68 percent and 79 percent of the works collected for grades 7 through 10 were written by 'North American authors.'"

Other changes have also begun to show up in our school literature programs. In comparing his results with a survey of literature anthologies conducted in the early 1960s by James Lynch and Bertrand Evans, Applebee noted that, "over the past 30 years, literature anthologies have broadened their selections to include a wider representation of works by women and of works from alternative literary traditions" and that this is "particularly true in the volumes intended for use in Grades 7 through 10." Moreover, Applebee's survey results indicate that, in the anthologies for grades 7 and 8, about 21% of the authors are "nonwhite" (these are the authors who are considered to reflect "alternative literary traditions"), while 30% of the authors are female. Overall, between 26% and 30% of the selections in the anthologies for grades 7 through 10 were written by women.

In sum, in just the past half-century, great changes have occurred in both the specific selections and the cultural content of secondary school literature programs. Just as English teachers over the course of the 20th century have gradually altered the selection of works they have offered their students because they thought it appropriate for American public schools to focus on American authors, so too today's English teachers have begun to alter the content of their programs to reflect the variety of ethnic, religious, racial, and other social groups in this country. The NEATE list in particular, because it is based on what teachers themselves recommend from their own teaching experiences, shows clearly how the major works being taught in the schools today reflect the continuing efforts of English teachers to update and broaden their literature programs—a trend that is now being accelerated and shaped by a curricular philosophy called multiculturalism.

It is commendable that publishers are now including in their anthologies larger numbers of works about social groups in this country and elsewhere that were previously slighted in literature programs. All students should be able to see the multiethnic and multiracial nature of this country (and of the world) in the literature they are asked to read. They should also be able to see members of different ethnic and racial groups as leading characters in what they read, so that as readers they have opportunities to identify with all types of human beings, male and female.

However, my examination of some of the most recently published literature anthologies—as well as of some of the individual works that are considered multicultural and that are frequently taught (or recommended for teaching) in the middle grades or high school—raises a number of concerns. To put it plainly, it seems that the original goals of multiculturalism have been seriously distorted. As Richard Bernstein comments in an insightful analysis of the evolution of multiculturalism in our national culture, "it is a universe of ambitious good intentions that has veered off the high road of respect for difference and plunged into a foggy chasm of dogmatic assertions, wishful thinking, and pseudoscientific pronouncements about race and sex."

My aim here is to note some of the different ways in which multiculturalism seems to have "veered off the high road of respect for difference" in our school literature programs. I do so because I believe that the issues raised require a great deal of professional and public discussion. Although the charge of Eurocentrism continues to be leveled at both the history and the English curricula, other features or tendencies in today's literature programs demand far more of our critical attention than that charge if our school literature programs are to fulfill both their civic purposes and the original goals of multiculturalism. Before I describe some of the problematic features of today's literature programs, however, let me briefly outline what I see as the essential principles and goals of multiculturalism as they pertain to literature programs.

Goals of Multiculturalism in Literature Programs

Literature programs designated as multicultural or multiethnic are intended to reflect two broad principles: inclusiveness and the avoidance of stereotyping. Inclusiveness means that the curriculum acknowledges the existence of all self-identified ethnic/racial/religious groups in this country by assigning literary works by or about members of these groups. When designers of self-described multicultural programs choose to extend the meaning of culture to social groups defined by gender, sexual orientation, or physical or mental disability, then inclusiveness refers to the curricular acknowledgment of these groups as well. As a matter of practice, curricular inclusiveness almost always refers to works by women as well as by members of various ethnic groups.

With respect to preventing stereotyping (or deconstructing existing stereotypes), teachers are urged to make sure that the works they offer in their literature programs do not consistently characterize members of any group of people in a way that can be considered either unflattering, demeaning, or limited. As Robert Fullinwider suggests, the overall civic goal of multiculturalism is to create the grounds for mutual respect among students by teaching them to understand and appreciate their different cultural backgrounds and histories.

Problematic Features of Today's Literature Programs

"One cannot help but be struck by the narrow range of American ethnic groups featured in these anthologies."

Because literature anthologies are used in well over half of our English classrooms, it is reasonable to assume that they influence students' perceptions of this country. Although they should be helping our students understand and appreciate this country's extraordinary ethnic, racial, and religious diversity, one major problem in contemporary secondary school anthologies is the paucity of works about the experiences of European ethnic groups in this country and the misleading implications that result from their absence. One cannot help but be struck by the narrow range of American ethnic groups featured in these anthologies. For the most part, the authors and groups highlighted in publishers' materials describing the collections' "multicultural" content and represented in multiple selections are those in the four affirmative action categories: African Americans, Asian Americans, Hispanic Americans, and Native Americans.

In addition, this designated multicultural content usually includes not only the works by or about members of certain groups within these four affirmative action categories, but also works by or about their ethnic kin in their countries of origin. For example, for its Literature series, Prentice-Hall lists four categories for its multicultural "Authors, Characters, and Themes": African and African American, Hispanic and Hispanic American, Asian and Asian American, and Native American. For its Elements of Literature series, Holt, Rinehart & Winston lists five major groups: one includes African Americans along with Africans, Caribbeans, Haitians, and/or Nigerians; a second includes Mexican Americans, Puerto Ricans, Dominican Americans, Colombians, Chileans, and/or Spaniards; a third is simply labeled Asian; a fourth, Native American; and a fifth, "other." For its Language and Literature series, McDougal, Littell lists under its "Multicultural Authors and Selections" African American, Black African, Caribbean Black, Hispanic, Native American, Asian, and Asian American. Although in the selections themselves or in the authors' biographical sketches members of groups within these broad categories are usually accorded their specific ethnic identities (e.g., Mexican Americans,

Japanese Americans, Chippewa Indians, and so on), the extraordinary ethnic and religious diversity of people of European descent—who make up a larger portion of the U.S. population than all the members of the affirmative action categories combined—is barely acknowledged.

Interestingly, the category of Asian or Asian American is also a limited one in most anthologies for grades 7 through 10. For the most part, it seems to refer to works about Japan, China, or countries in Southeast Asia or to works by authors in this country whose origins may be traced to those countries and who write about the experiences of their ethnic group in America. Only rarely does one find a selection reflecting, for example, Korean, Hindu, or Persian culture, even though there are in this country large numbers of Koreans, Indians, and Iranians, to say nothing of the Lebanese, Copts, Armenians, Sikhs, Chaldeans, Palestinians, Israelis, and other groups that hail from various parts of the vast continent of Asia. While there may not yet be a great many works by members of most of these groups about their experiences in this country, some fine works about the experience of Armenian Americans and Syrian/Lebanese Americans are available and could have been included.

Given the scarcity in the anthology selections of identifiable members of the vast number of European ethnic groups in this country, as well as the almost total absence of selections about the early experiences of these groups in this country (selections which, for the most part, did not appear in earlier anthologies either), it would not be at all surprising if students classified in the four affirmative action categories ended up with a completely erroneous understanding of American history and of who Americans are. These students may end up believing that students who are not members of these four categories—those who supposedly belong to the "mainstream"—are all of Anglo-Saxon stock and are all alike with respect to values, beliefs, and customs. Only works by or about whites from the South seem to portray distinctive cultural or regional characteristics.

Furthermore, both the students in the four affirmative action categories and those considered "mainstream" may easily come to believe that members of affirmative action categories are basically different from other Americans and similar to their ethnic kin in their countries of origin. (Neither conclusion is apt to be true after the first generation in this country.) Indeed, students may believe that members of groups in the four categories constitute "cultures" that are somehow parallel to a so-called "mainstream" culture, rather than that they constitute ethnic groups that are not distinct cultures at all and whose experiences over several generations parallel those of most European ethnic groups in this country.

Finally, if the experiences of the different European ethnic groups in this country are ignored, all students may see the story of prejudice and exploitation in this country's history only in racial terms. And if only a limited number of Asian American groups are portrayed—so that the racial differences among Asians are not apparent—they may even come to see as reasonable a race-based multicultural curriculum, such as the one proposed by James Banks and adopted by the board of directors of the National Council for the Social Studies, in which students are taught according to someone's notion of their race's "learning style." (This concept echoes some utterly discredited 19th-century views of race.)

Yet race is not coterminous with continent or culture; all Asians do not look like the Chinese, Japanese, or Koreans; "white" people come not just from Europe, but from Asia Minor and South America; and each continent contains multiple cultures. A race-based curriculum would only damage all students insofar as it denies the enormous differences within and across individual ethnic groups and plays down the far more important influence of socioeconomic class on literacy learning among members of any ethnic group.

A second problem that is becoming apparent in classroom literature programs and in current academic thinking is the dilution of what constitutes American literature itself. What is being promoted is not a more inclusive, America-centered curriculum, but a less inclusive, less America-centered one that features works by foreign authors who hail from other countries in North, Central, and South America but who are being considered "American" authors by a semantic sleight of hand. The attempt to stretch the meaning of "American" to include works by anyone from the two Americas (and to separate the word "American" from any generally understood reference to the literature created by inhabitants of the United States) can be seen, for example, in the brochure advertising a 1994 summer institute for teachers of literature, sponsored by the college section of the National Council of Teachers of English. The brochure indicated that participants would rethink "American literature" because they will have "recogniz[ed] that American literature has moved beyond the boundaries of the United States and that changing demographics have challenged us to reconceptualize our definition of American literature." The brochure also indicated that, in examining "this 'new' American literature" that "crosses cultural boundaries within and outside of the United States," participants would discuss such essential questions as, "What do we mean by literature of the Americas?" and "In what ways does the literature of North America compare with Caribbean literature?"

This use of "North America" can also be seen in Applebee's table listing the characteristics of the authors included in the seven anthologies that he surveyed. In giving a breakdown by "national additions," the term "North America" is used as if works by Canadian and Mexican writers should be seen as culturally allied with American literary traditions; the same lack of distinction holds true for works within the other categories of "national traditions" listed in that table (those from the United Kingdom, Western Europe, Russia and Eastern Europe, Central and South America, Africa, and Asia). Again we see not a set of culturally meaningful "traditions" but an equation of continent with culture.

Yet another example of the attempt to expand the content of the generally understood meaning of American literature can be seen in a flier for the Assembly on *American Literature*, a special interest group within the National Council of Teachers of English. As part of its appeal for more members, it claims, "We already have Mark Twain, Toni Morrison, Langston Hughes, Eudora Welty, John Steinbeck, Margaret Atwood, Kate Chopin, Gabriel García Márquez, Edgar Allan Poe and Isaac Bashevis Singer." Of these 10 "American" authors, Márquez is from South America, Atwood is a Canadian, and I. B. Singer, despite American citizenship and his long residence in this country, wrote in Yiddish and about an Eastern European culture that disappeared in the Holocaust.

The implications of this change in the definition of American literature are obvious. By making "American" cover so many different groups and countries, we clearly diminish students' sense of their own identity as Americans. An example of this effort to dilute American literature and an American national identity can be seen in the description of a new full-year elective course for juniors titled "American Literature" at Brookline High School in Massachusetts. The course was newly created for the 1994-95 academic year by several English teachers with the help of a grant from the American Council of Learned Societies. (So far, there is only one section of this course; most juniors are enrolled in one of the seven sections of the one-semester traditional American literature course.)

Although it accompanies the study of U.S. history, the new course contains as its "central source materials" (in the description of the course presented to and approved by the Brookline School Committee in the spring of 1994) the following works: *The Adventures of Huckleberry Finn*, by Mark Twain; *Walden*, by Henry Thoreau; *The Scarlet Letter*, by Nathaniel Hawthorne; *Arrowsmith*, by Sinclair Lewis; *Death Comes for the Archbishop*, by Willa Cather; *One Hundred Years of Solitude*, by Gabriel García Márquez; *Cat's Eye*, by Margaret Atwood; *The Apprenticeship of Duddy Kravitz*, by Mordecai Richler; *Woman Warrior*, by Maxine Hong Kingston; *Laughing Boy*, by Oliver LaFarge; *The Bean Trees*, by Barbara Kingsolver; and *Song of Solomon*, by Toni Morrison. These books were supplemented by a number of short works. Three of the 12 major authors suggested for study are Canadian or South American. Although students in American high schools should read Canadian or South American literature somewhere in their studies (particularly in a world literature course), what is at issue is whether they should be doing so in a course labeled "American Literature," especially when they and their parents are unlikely to expect Canadian and South American literature in a course with that label.

One of the stated goals of the course is "to relate the literature of the United States to the broader context of the literature of the rest of the Americas," but there is no explanation of why American literature needs to be so related. Nor is any justification offered for the fact that roughly half of the works are from the past several decades, with only three major works and only two or three short stories from pre-20th-century America. In short, the selection of works for this literature course appears to have been guided by criteria reflecting gender balance, gender orientation, and representation of the four affirmative action categories, despite their lack of relevance in a course that should help students understand this nation's historically significant literary traditions and works.

Clearly, the substitution of contemporary American works for American works of earlier decades diminishes students' understanding of American history, while the tendency to stretch "American literature" to include works from the Americas in effect reduces altogether the number of works by American/U.S. authors that students can read. While parents who were highly educated in this country may be able to make up this deficit in their children's education, students whose parents received little education or little education in this country may learn little about this country's past.

Nowhere is there any indication that this "cultural amnesia" is what most parents want for their children. What most of them do not understand, of course, is that the attempt to "rethink" American literature—i.e., to dilute it by broadening it to include works from national or cultural traditions outside the boundaries of the United States—is an explicit attempt by many at the college level to eliminate what they see as an "oppressive nationalist ideology which is the nightmare side of the 'American dream,'" as one professor, Gregory Jay, has described it. Instead of a "nationalist" American literature, Jay urges a "multicultural and dialogical paradigm for the study of writing in the United States." Thus the goal of multiculturalism that he sees is clearly not to make American literature more inclusive but to eliminate our sense of a national literature altogether and thereby to wipe out what he feels is an offensive civic identity.

Jay is, of course, entitled to his views about the country he lives in. But whether the views he and others advocate should be promoted at the college level and in the lower grades without any sustained public discussion and without any examination of their ultimate civic consequences is another matter. Jay and those of a similar mindset need to be helped to see that, without a civic identity, a diverse group of students is unlikely to develop a sense of social responsibility. The least that can be said is that what Jay and others are advocating does not seem to represent an effort to teach students to respect one another's cultural backgrounds, including our own as Americans.

A third problem—one related to the dilution of American literature with Canadian, Mexican, Central American, and South American literature—is just beginning to be more visible: the scaling back of what has often been called "mainstream" American literature beyond the point of what might be seen as a reasonable balance with American ethnic and non-American literature. Based on my own ongoing examination of leading literature anthologies for the secondary school, it is clear that changes in authors and in cultural content have continued since 1989.

The number of selections in current anthologies for grades 7 through 10 whose authors or content might be seen as reflecting the four affirmative action categories or non-American national traditions altogether ranges from one-third to more than one-half. For four leading anthologies, whose dates of publication range from 1991 to 1994, the percentages of selections whose authors were in some way identifiable as ethnic Americans or who were not American at all range from 29% to 43%. Conversely, the percentages of selections whose authors seem to be simply Americans (generally because they are not identified as ethnic Americans or as foreign born) range from 54% to 35%. These percentages do not reflect the current demographics of this country, even if that were considered a relevant criterion for selection.

For this analysis, I did not count as authors those who retold or translated folk tales, legends, myths, and trickster tales, which constitute about one-fifth of each anthology. However, when the cultural content of these types of selections is accounted for, we see that the percentages of selections whose content is clearly ethnic American or non-American rises steadily from 43% for the series published in 1991 to 59% for the series published in 1994.

The increase in identifiable ethnic and non-American authors and content in the literature anthologies published since 1990 can also be seen when the leading K-8 series for reading instruction published in 1993 is compared to versions published in the 1980s. Even greater increases may take place in the anthologies and readers that will be published in the publishing cycle from 1995 to 1997. To judge by one tentative table of contents I have seen for a grade 6 reader to be published in 1997, the American ethnic and non-American content amounts to almost 70% of those selections with cultural content. (There is a larger number of "white male" and "white female" authors than would be suggested by the amount of ethnic and foreign content, because many of the selections are retellings of tales and legends from foreign countries; this is an interesting way to increase "non-mainstream" content while seeming to maintain a reasonable number of "mainstream" authors.)

It will not be easy for students—whether part of the "mainstream" or not—to understand and appreciate the "mainstream" culture if there is so little of it left by the turn of the century. On the other hand, if literature by members of the four affirmative action categories is to be seen (rightly, I believe) as part of our national literature, then it should not be designated as multiethnic or multicultural in publishers' brochures or in textbooks for teachers or students. Of course, including that literature as part of our national literature would mean eliminating all multicultural categories and quotas.

A fourth problem requiring urgent discussion is the matter of reverse cultural stereotyping. Although it is difficult to tell how prevalent this problem is, school literature programs now seem to feature many works that reveal reverse stereotyping—often to the point of mean-spirited caricature. For example, whites are portrayed as bigoted, violent, or otherwise despicable in such frequently taught works as *Farewell to Manzanar*, an autobiographical story by Jeanne Wakatsuki Houston and James Houston about the internment of Japanese Americans on the West Coast during World War II; in *The Bluest Eye*, a novel by Toni Morrison that highlights the rape of a young black girl by her father; and, with the exception of two characters, in *Dragonwings*, a story by Lawrence Yep about a personable young Chinese boy in San Francisco's Chinatown in the early 20th century.

While Yep's and Morrison's novels have literary merit, some works with reverse cultural stereotyping are little more than crude pieces of anti-Western propaganda. Peter Smagorinsky offers as one example "Chee's Daughter," a short story by Juanita Platero and Siyowin Miller that is frequently anthologized (e.g., in McDougal, Littell's *Language and Literature*, grade 10, and in Prentice-Hall's *Literature*, grade 10). As Smagorinsky describes it, a "potentially compelling story" about a clash between a Navajo "who lives according to the traditional ways of his culture and his in-laws who have attempted to adopt Western capitalistic ways" deteriorates into caricature, "with the in-laws becoming one-dimensional figures embodying the worst of Western ways." Smagorinsky believes that, if such "didactic texts" as "Chee's Daughter" have a place in the classroom, they should be used as "examples of manipulative, propagandistic texts whose message has distorted their medium." I agree with this recommendation.

What we need to be aware of are the rhetorical effects of works that employ reverse cultural stereotyping. Stories about victims of prejudice in this country can easily spark feelings of guilt in those who consider themselves "white." Indeed, Stanley Crouch, former staff writer for *The Village Voice*, has harshly criticized Toni Morrison among other contemporary black women writers for "manipulat[ing] the guilt of whites." In discussing *The Bluest Eye* as an example of what I have termed the literature of "white guilt," I have urged teachers to help their students think through the crucial difference between compassion and guilt. Otherwise, uncritical study of the literature of white guilt is likely to prevent the development of that sense of shared citizenship and mutual empathy that a multiethnic nation requires. Instead, it is likely to make students classified as "white" become hostile to those who've made them feel guilty.

One begins to wonder whether some changes inspired by the desire to avoid stereotypes will give our students a completely mythical picture of contemporary America. Indeed, it's not difficult to see how students may be deprived of any semblance of contemporary reality if the multicultural guidelines for educational publishers recently issued by Macmillan/McGraw-Hill are followed scrupulously. For example, two pages after stating that "[i]n our materials we will take care to portray our pluralistic society, not a mythical, typical U.S. society," a guidepost under "Objectionable Stereotypes" indicates that "[w]e will take care to assure that materials do not perpetuate any of the following stereotypical images of the working class: prejudiced, narrow-minded, poor, lazy, intellectually and culturally inferior, childlike, and prone to violence." Given this injunction, it is not unlikely that the only people who will be depicted with these traits in reading/literature or other educational materials put out by Macmillan/McGraw-Hill will be "white" middle-class Americans.

As another example, in a section on avoiding racial stereotypes in art, the Macmillan/McGraw-Hill guidelines suggest that among the stereotyped images of Asian Americans are pictures of males as "peasants, coolies, waiters, laundry owners, math students." The injunction regarding the last henceforth-to-be-avoided image cannot help but stun, especially when the *New York Times* reports that Asian Americans take more college-preparatory math courses than any other group in the city and do better than any other group. Why should publishers avoid such a positive stereotype? Why shouldn't students labeled white, black, or Hispanic see Asian American students as good math students? Would it damage their self-esteem? One wonders if this injunction means that the only students who may be depicted as successful math students in Macmillan/McGraw-Hill materials will be those who are not Asian Americans.

These two examples suggest the way in which the moral dogmatism that Bernstein describes in his book may unintentionally lead to bizarre forms of reverse stereotyping. Indeed, the reverse cultural stereotyping that already exists in many individual literary texts may be even more damaging to interethnic and interracial relations than the stereotypes they claim to be fighting. Much depends on how many examples of the literature of white guilt students are asked to read and how they are taught to study them. Clearly all such works can't be dismissed as lacking in literary merit. But students should be discussing these works for what they are and what they do. They also need to know that works deemed multicultural or works about such topics as the internment of the Japanese during World War II are not necessarily anti-American or obsessed by racism. For example, Yoshiko Uchida's *Journey to Topaz* and Monica Sone's *Nisei Daughter*, which do not portray all whites as despicable bigots, could easily replace *Farewell to Manzanar*, even though they, too, are based on experiences in an internment camp.

Where Do We Go from Here?

Unless the problems I have discussed here are addressed, our classroom literature programs may well retard rather than advance the integration of new immigrants into the political and economic structures of the country they have chosen as their own. We may also convey the impression that these immigrants, along with African Americans and American Indians, are not "genuine" Americans but members of separate cultures simply inhabiting this continent together.

This separateness does not seem to be what most of the people in these groups desire for their children. For example, in the most extensive effort to date to measure Hispanic attitudes, a survey reported by Roberto Suro in the *New York Times* indicated that "an overwhelming majority of those who call themselves American citizens said the goal [of bilingual education] should be to teach English or both languages rather than to preserve the Spanish language and culture among Hispanic young people."

Literature teachers and literature programs need to live up to the original promise of multiculturalism: to teach our students to understand and appreciate one another's ethnic heritage as well as their common heritage as Americans. As E. D. Hirsch, Jr., put it, all American students deserve a "centrist curriculum" that "encourages knowledge of and sympathy towards the diverse cultures of the world," that "fosters respect for every child's home culture as well as for the cosmopolitan school-based cultures," and that "gives all children competence in the current system of language and allusion that is dominant in the nation's economic and intellectual discourse."

And one of the specific things that publishers and teachers can do is to offer students more works like William Blinn's *Brian's Song*, which focuses on the friendship between two football players, one black and one white. Although many fine pieces of literature labeled multicultural already appear in reading instructional texts and in high school literature anthologies, there are few that include, let alone emphasize, positive interaction between peoples of different racial or ethnic groups in this country. Yet, contrary to what many in the academic world seem to think, these are the works that realistically portray much of American life.

Another specific action that publishers and teachers could undertake is simply to ask students to point out *positive* examples of interethnic and interracial interaction when they are reading literary works that demonstrate racial or ethnic prejudice. In all the literature anthologies, instructional readers, and other curricular materials for teaching literature that I have read in the past decade, I have yet to come across a suggested question for discussion that directs students to reflect on, discuss, or write about positive examples of interethnic and interracial relationships. On the other hand, I have found many questions for discussion or writing assignments that ask students to note examples of prejudice or intolerance that they, their families, or their ancestors have experienced or to discuss those examples that they see highlighted in the media. Perhaps it is time for teachers and the editors of literature anthologies and of readers to demonstrate their social responsibility by including questions that direct student attention to the numerous examples of interethnic and interracial cooperation and harmony that an impartial observer can find in this society. As Bernstein puts it in a long, important chapter titled "The Search for Sin," this country is not mired in racist iniquity.

As educators, parents, and citizens, we need to think carefully about the use of works that demonize "mainstream" Americans, however subtly, and that may increase rather than decrease interracial and interethnic hostility in this country. A racist multicultural curriculum is no more desirable than a racist Eurocentric curriculum. Indeed, a racist multicultural curriculum in the English class and in the social studies class may serve, ultimately, to alienate young Americans from this country's political institutions, procedures, and processes.

"A racist multicultural curriculum is no more desirable than a racist Eurocentric curriculum."

If we want to develop our students' sense of responsibility for one another and for the common good—despite racial, ethnic, and religious differences—then we will want to develop their civic identity. For, as Richard Rorty remarks, without pride in their national identity, they will not care about our country's social problems and will not be willing emotionally and financially to do something about them. This effort means eliminating the use of labels that designate certain groups of people as "cultures" when members of the groups in the four affirmative action categories are in fact members of only one of many dozens of ethnic groups in this country and are all American citizens once a generation has been born here. Above all, it means valuing the America-centered literature that it took our public schools 200 years to develop and preserving the literary heritage that belongs to all our students, regardless of background.

Frances Fitzgerald concluded her examination of U.S. history textbooks in the 20th century by urging textbook writers and curriculum developers not to show a "lack of respect for history" and "deprive American children of their birthright." She wrote these words in the context of deploring both a sanitized view of American history with respect to relations between social groups and the "incessant moralism" and "manipulativeness" of education reform movements.

Going from one extreme to another in the teaching of history or literature does not promote the academic focus that Fitzgerald sought to encourage. To attempt to redress a perceived exclusion of some social groups from our school literature programs in the past by eliminating the literature that belongs to all American children and to attempt to teach tolerance and understanding by manipulating the content of our school literature programs to make racial differences appear as the central experience in the lives of all Americans will only perpetuate a lack of respect for history and deprive every American child of his or her birthright as a citizen.

TABLE 1.

The 43 Books Most Frequently Taught in 5% or More of Public Schools, Grades 7-12

Title	Author	Schools % (n=322)
The Adventures of Huckleberry Finn	Mark Twain	78
The Adventures of Tom Sawyer	Mark Twain	32
Animal Farm	George Orwell	51
Antigone	Sophocles	28
Call of the Wild	Jack London	51
Catcher in the Rye	J. D. Salinger	26
A Christmas Carol	Charles Dickens	20
The Crucible	Arthur Miller	47
A Day No Pigs Would Die	Robert Newton Peck	22
Death of a Salesman	Arthur Miller	36
The Diary of a Young Girl	Anne Frank	56
Fahrenheit 451	Ray Bradbury	20
The Glass Menagerie	Tennessee Williams	24
The Grapes of Wrath	John Steinbeck	28
Great Expectations	Charles Dickens	44
The Great Gatsby	F. Scott Fitzgerald	54
Hamlet	William Shakespeare	56
Johnny Tremain	Esther Forbes	21
Julius Caesar	William Shakespeare	71
The Light in the Forest	Conrad Richter	24
Lord of the Flies	William Golding	56
Macbeth	William Shakespeare	81
The Miracle Worker	William Gibson	32
1984	George Orwell	28
The Odyssey	Homer	29
Oedipus Rex	Sophocles	21
Of Mice and Men	John Steinbeck	60
Othello	William Shakespeare	20
Our Town	Thornton Wilder	44
The Outsiders	S. E. Hinton	39
The Pearl	John Steinbeck	64
The Pigman	Paul Zindel	38
Pygmalion	George Bernard Shaw	21
The Red Badge of Courage	Stephen Crane	47
The Red Pony	John Steinbeck	31
Romeo and Juliet	William Shakespeare	90
The Scarlet Letter	Nathaniel Hawthorne	62
A Separate Peace	John Knowles	48
Shane	Jack Shaefer	28
A Tale of Two Cities	Charles Dickens	41
To Kill a Mockingbird	Harper Lee	74
Where the Red Fern Grows	Wilson Rawls	21
Wuthering Heights	Emily Brontë	26

Source: Arthur Applebee, A Study of Book-Length Works Taught in High School English (Albany: Center for the Learning and Teaching of Literature, State University of New York, Albany, Report Series 1.2, 1989), App. 2.

TABLE 2.

The 45 Books Most Frequently Recommended by NEATE Members, Grades 7-12

Rank	Title	Author	Number of Nominations
3	*The Adventures of Huckleberry Finn*	Mark Twain	32
17	*Animal Farm*	George Orwell	15
32	*Black Boy*	Richard Wright	9
36	*Call of the Wild*	Jack London	8
1	*Catcher in the Rye*	J. D. Salinger	35
15	*The Crucible*	Arthur Miller	16
22	*Cry, the Beloved Country*	Alan Paton	12
19	*A Day No Pigs Would Die*	Robert Newton Peck	13
11	*Death of a Salesman*	Arthur Miller	20
22	*The Diary of a Young Girl*	Anne Frank	12
19	*Ethan Frome*	Edith Wharton	13
30	*Flowers for Algernon*	Daniel Keyes	10
32	*The Glass Menagerie*	Tennessee Williams	9
13	*The Grapes of Wrath*	John Steinbeck	17
22	*Great Expectations*	Charles Dickens	12
3	*The Great Gatsby*	F. Scott Fitzgerald	32
12	*Hamlet*	William Shakespeare	19
32	*Heart of Darkness*	Joseph Conrad	9
36	*I Know Why the Caged Bird Sings*	Maya Angelou	8
19	*Jane Eyre*	Charlotte Brontë	13
36	*Johnny Tremain*	Esther Forbes	8
30	*Julius Caesar*	William Shakespeare	10
9	*Lord of the Flies*	William Golding	24
5	*Macbeth*	William Shakespeare	28
13	*Night*	Elie Wiesel	17
36	*Oedipus Rex*	Sophocles	8
6	*Of Mice and Men*	John Steinbeck	27
26	*The Old Man and the Sea*	Ernest Hemingway	11
36	*One Flew Over the Cuckoo's Nest*	Ken Kesey	8
32	*Our Town*	Thornton Wilder	9
26	*The Outsiders*	S. E. Hinton	11
15	*The Pearl*	John Steinbeck	16
36	*The Pigman*	Paul Zindel	8
26	*A Raisin in the Sun*	Lorraine Hansberry	11
36	*The Red Badge of Courage*	Stephen Crane	8
26	*Roll of Thunder, Hear My Cry*	Mildred Taylor	11
8	*Romeo and Juliet*	William Shakespeare	26
6	*The Scarlet Letter*	Nathaniel Hawthorne	27
9	*A Separate Peace*	John Knowles	24
36	*Silas Marner*	George Eliot	8
36	*A Streetcar Named Desire*	Tennessee Williams	8
18	*A Tale of Two Cities*	Charles Dickens	14
22	*Their Eyes Were Watching God*	Zora Neale Hurston	12
1	*To Kill a Mockingbird*	Harper Lee	35
36	*Wuthering Heights*	Emily Brontë	8

Source: Data gathered by Sandra Stotsky and Philip Anderson for "Variety and Individualism in the English Class: Teacher-Recommended Lists of Reading for Grades 7-12," *The Leaflet*, Fall 1990, pp.1-11.

Will Zealots Spell the Doom of Great Literature?[4]

Political correctness is the McCarthyism of the 1990s. Today, the politically correct storm troopers, operating from their positions as college professors, attack Western civilization, the bedrock values of the U.S., and white males. Their mentor appears to have been Sen. Joseph McCarthy (R.-Wis.), who trampled on individual liberty in his zeal to expose communism.

Like McCarthy, the politically correct crowd are fanatics, and they have assembled a cultural hit list that I call "The Unteachables." I've been a college professor for 20 years, and this list, like the ponderous life chain created by Ebenezer Scrooge, has grown with each passing year. It now includes: the Declaration of Independence and the Constitution, the King James Bible, *Moby Dick*, *The Scarlet Letter*, *The Great Gatsby*, *Hamlet*, *King Lear*, *Othello*, *Macbeth*, *The Sun Also Rises*, *Pride and Prejudice*, *The Maltese Falcon*, and the poems of Rudyard Kipling.

"...in cities like Los Angeles and Washington, D.C., 75 percent of the store owners are Asian."

One of the better known politically correct gurus is Ronald Takaki, whom I observed, to paraphrase former Vice Pres. Spiro Agnew, nattering his negativity at Princeton University. Of course, no PC professor calls himself PC, so Takaki is a self-confessed MC—a multiculturalist.

He warmed up the Ivy League crowd with fond reminiscences of students at his college taking over a campus building in order to correct the curriculum so that it mirrored the diversity which is America. As he detailed this hooliganism, he threw in a few barbs at some professors who challenge his conclusions, such men of distinction as Alan Bloom and Nathan Glazer, who begged to differ with Takaki about the existence of the great books and affirmative action.

After venting his spleen by bashing those who believe in the values of Western civilization, the PC/MC professor spoke on the conflicts between Asian and African Americans, pointing out the tensions caused by the fact that, in cities like Los Angeles and Washington, D.C., 75 percent of the store owners are Asian. His thesis—addressed to an upwardly mobile audience of Asian- and African-American students sitting in absolute isolation from one another—was that white male America was praising Asians as the "ideal minority." He made use of revisionist history by citing examples from the 19th century, when white planters in Mississippi brought in Chinese workers as an exemplum for the black sharecroppers, thereby driving home his propaganda that Asians and blacks are at odds because of whites.

---

[4] Article by William J. Reeves, professor of English at Brooklyn College of The City of New York, from *USA Today* magazine 125:68-9 S '96. Copyright © 1996 by the Society for the Advancement of Education. Reprinted with permission.

Takaki offered a remedy for the mind-set that divides people of color in America, exhorting students to "read about themselves," to "embrace diversity," or, in other words, to resist reading books written by white males since these people function in society as prison wardens. It is the Takakis of America who've turned the great books, the classics, into the Unteachables.

In the 20-plus years I've taught, the great books have declined into the Unteachables. The PC crowd has a propaganda tag for many of the hallmarks of Western civilization, including:

• The Constitution—a sexist, racist document written by the Founding Fathers, all of whom were rich, white, slave-owning swine. At the time the Constitution was written, women and blacks were so marginalized in society that they did not appear in the text. The document should be redone by self-proclaimed civil rights leader Rev. Al Sharpton and feminist Gloria Steinem.

• The King James Bible—a misogynistic mythology. From Genesis onward, the Bible presents women negatively. Eve is blamed for Adam's fall; Lot's daughters are presented as sexual predators; and the supreme creator is referred to as "Father." It is outmoded for the 1990s; New Age is the answer.

• *The Scarlet Letter*—a classic case of the sexual double standard. Hester Prynne gets branded with an A for Adultery while the man is let off easy. Nathaniel Hawthorne was an apologist for harassment.

• *Moby Dick*—blatant whaleism. The entire book celebrates animal abuse. During the 1990s, the PC hordes freed Willy; in the 19th century, white males hunted Moby Dick.

• *The Great Gatsby*—classist claptrap. All of the characters are either bourgeois beauties or capitalist creeps. The novel focuses on the idle rich who feed off the honest labor of the proletariat. Gatsby got what he deserved.

• *Hamlet*—male pattern sexual abuse. Hamlet seduces Ophelia, dumps her, then mind-rapes his mother. He is a demented Dane who denounced women.

• *King Lear*—daughter denial. A tale of a greedy, violence-prone father denying his daughters their just rewards. They should have kicked him out years earlier.

• *Othello*—miscegenation and the Mafia. A family of Italians conspire against a black man. Guess who they don't want to come home for dinner?

• *Macbeth*—witch-bashing. Three sisters who practice an alternative religion are depicted negatively. The play reveals the necessity for separation of church and state.

• *The Sun Also Rises*—Hemingway's homophobic horror show. Jake Barnes' real problem is not his missing sexual apparatus, but his refusal to come out of the closet and be all that he can be. Just like "Poppa" himself, Jake protested too much.

• *Pride and Prejudice*—a marriage manual. Jane Austen, a traitor to her sex, ended all of her books with happy marriages. Shame, shame, shame.

• *The Maltese Falcon*—suicide sexism. Sam Spade sent over Brigid O'Shaughnessy for killing his partner. The truth was that Miles Archer so hated women that he shot himself in the heart in order to frame Brigid.

• Rudyard Kipling—a militaristic maniac who wrote poems about the plight of soldiers in peacetime: "It's Tommy this and Tommy that, and Tommy go away, but it's Thin Red line of Heroes when the band begins to play." Homages to a nation's hired killers.

I've heard, in one form or the other, every one of the above libels against classic works of literature.

The following five works of literature have the seal of approval from the PC/MC thought cavalry:

"The Sky Is Gray" is taught because it was written by a black man and deals with a day in the life of a black woman and her son in America in 1940. It takes considerable misreading not to conclude that the mother is a monster.

Her son has a toothache so severe that she has to take a day off from work in order to get the boy attended to by a dentist. The night before the dentist visit, she forces the seven-year-old to kill his pet chicken for dinner. After refusing, the small boy is struck in the face, directly on the site of his infected tooth. The mother has other, similar, lessons for her child, including a demand that he not turn up his coat collar to protect his aching jaw against a biting winter wind, this done because, she says, "You're not a bum, you're a man."

If a big, white man had slapped his small, sick son for not killing an animal and then told the boy this was done to make him into a man, can anyone honestly say that the writer of such a short story would not be condemned for condoning child abuse? Yet, Ernest Gaines, the author of this vicious tale, is in the PC Hall of Fame.

Equally horrific, and equally politically correct, is *Things Fall Apart*, written by Nigerian Chinua Achebe. The hero is Okonkwo, an African warrior famous because of his wrestling prowess. Possessed of at least four wives, Okonkwo shoots his rifle at one of them, causing her to flee over the garden wall, then he terrorizes the other three into cowering silence. The story's central event centers around the man's beheading, via machete, of his adopted son to satisfy a rule of conduct between two tribes.

If this African tale were the biography of an Irishman from Chicago, satisfying his lust through polygamy, using one of his wives for target practice, and decapitating his son because it was the law of the land, the book not only would be banned by the PC patrols, it would be burned to a crisp.

On a somewhat less violent note, there is Amy Tan's *The Joy Luck Club*, which is just what those like Takaki believe is good for what ails America. The thesis of this novel is the struggle of four immigrant women to maintain their Chinese identity in the midst of American society.

This is fine, but would Takaki be so accepting if the book were entitled *The Weiner Schnitzel Crowd* and featured four young German males in emotional torment as they fight to retain their Teutonic heritage? What is the difference between the 20th-century German past and Chinese life under Mao Tse-tung, wherein the dictator's wife presided over the killing of 10,000,000 people during the Red Guard reign of terror? The answer is that the PC cultural police are selective when it comes to which ethnic identities are worth preserving, praising Asia, the Third World, and Africa while deriding all of Western Europe.

A Doll's House is unique because it is one of the few works of literature accepted by the politically correct that was written by a white male, a 19th-century Norwegian, Henrik Ibsen. The reason? The play is about a woman who frees herself from the prison house of her marriage by leaving her oppressive husband (along with her children) and venturing forth into the world to find herself.

The praise of this play reveals that the PC gendarmes never really read the texts they teach. The crucial question is why did the heroine, Nora Helmer, leave her husband? The answer is that she deserted her family because her husband refused to take the blame for a crime she had committed. She says, "I was so absolutely certain you would come forward and take everything upon yourself and say: I am the guilty one."

Feminist author Betty Friedan would hit the roof if she heard a husband suggest that his wife take the fall for one of his crimes. *A Doll's House* is, in effect, exactly the opposite of what a true feminist should desire since it rests upon complete inequality. When I taught the play and pointed out this fact, the feminists in the class believed me to be "hopelessly insensitive." They probably were right.

Possibly the most popular PC text is Kate Chopin's *The Awakening*, written in 1899. One of this novelette's major themes is the quest by the heroine, Edna Pontellier, for "erotic freedom." This is accomplished when she rejects her husband and relinquishes her role as mother of her sons and allows herself to be pursued, and caught, by a young lover. Unable to be fulfilled completely, Edna swims away into the sea, never to return, drowning, literally, in her sorrow.

The topic of this book is adultery. Would a feminist so readily concede that a middle-aged man could ditch his wife and kids so that he could have a fling with a young, pliable damsel, the reason being that erotic freedom was more important than familial responsibility? Their answer would be an emphatic, vociferous No!

These works have certain things in common: They all glorify men and women much like the PC professors themselves, who are largely privileged white woman and Asian- and African-American would-be revolutionaries; exhibit a disdain for

Western civilization; and engage in white male-bashing. As misguided as some of these books are, they are on the reading lists at the reputedly best colleges in America. They are taught while classic texts are dismissed as Unteachables.

The specter of political correctness, disguised as multiculturalism, is threatening America. Its proponents continue to advance their agenda. Recently, *Change: The Magazine of Higher Education* devoted an entire issue to the college curriculum and multiculturalism, reaching the conclusion that "Multiculturalism today touches, in varying degrees, a majority of the nation's colleges." Thus, the PC/MC virus is on its way to devouring American higher education.

There are some outposts of resistance, organizations such as the National Association of Scholars, whose president contends that the PC battalions have politicized the college curriculum and that their leaders absolutely are opposed to the values contained in the classic texts of Western civilization.

College students should be exposed to—as the 19th-century poet and critic Matthew Arnold said—the best that has been known and thought. The Great Books of Western Civilization fill this need. The best defense is a vigorous offense, which, in my case, as an entrenched professor of English, consists of teaching William Shakespeare, Dante Alighieri, Geoffrey Chaucer, Miguel de Cervantes, Jane Austen, Charles Dickens, Ernest Hemingway, and T.S. Eliot, and rejecting as ideological twaddle the book lists generated by the PC propagandists.

Author F. Scott Fitzgerald said that life consists of beating against the current in order to survive. The current today is the PC tidal wave, and it must be resisted by establishing the Great Books as the centerpiece of higher education.

Contract with Academia[5]

A lamentable record was set last week. At the request of a billionaire alumnus, Lee M. Bass, Yale University returned twenty million dollars that Mr. Bass had donated for the teaching of courses on Western civilization—the largest rescinded donation, apparently, in the history of American education.

To the traditionalists at Yale, the Bass gift had represented a welcome chance to correct what they saw as a drift away from liberal education toward "multiculturalism." To the "politically correct" crowd, Mr. Bass's stipulation that his money be used for a new Western Civ course seemed redundant and retrograde, since much of Yale's humanities curriculum is already devoted to the high culture of the West. In an academic atmosphere where flogging "dead white males" has become standard practice, and soap operas and pornography have entered the curriculum as legitimate "texts" for study, it's hardly surprising that donors like Mr. Bass are trying to intervene. When, however, he requested control not only over the subject matter but also over the choice of "his" course, the Yale community came together in a principled consensus that no amount of money would be worth countenancing Steinbrennerism in the academy.

So Yale's debate about what to do with Mr. Bass's money is history. But the fuss signaled a conflict that goes far beyond New Haven. Universities have always had uneasy relations with their benefactors—the wealthy individuals who support them with gifts and bequests, and the middle-class parents on whose tuition and taxes they depend. On the one hand, universities are deeply "conservative" institutions—financed by private endowments, public funds, and fees collected from parents who hope, at considerable sacrifice, to purchase a prosperous future for their children. Such financial commitments are acts of faith in the culture in which the money was earned, inherited, or borrowed. Until now, private universities have been beneficiaries of this cashable faith because they have been places where the culture in which alumni prospered has been transmitted to their children, and, through the mechanism of financial aid, disseminated to some who were previously excluded from its benefits.

On the other hand, universities are meant to foster suspicion toward every untested piety and to raise doubts about every axiom. They are, properly, places of experiment and irreverence; they will never please those who expect them to be mainly curatorial. The few years that most people spend in the university are *supposed* to be a time of ferment; and especially now, in the national climate of reaction, universities have an obligation to

---

[5] Article by Andrew Delbanco, staffwriter, from the *New Yorker* 71:28 Mr 27 '95. Copyright © 1995 by Andrew Delbanco. Reprinted by agreement with the Virginia Barber Literary Agency. All rights reserved.

keep alive the spirit of blasphemy that has always been part of the true life of the mind.

How well any university holds these two functions in equilibrium is an index of its health. By this measure, things are out of balance at many places besides Yale. As both sides—"politically correct" younger faculty and alarmed older alumni—harden their positions, fund-raisers find it increasingly difficult to obtain endowments for chairs and programs in the humanities. At Yale, the most famous member of the humanities faculty, Harold Bloom, has denounced the takeover of literary studies by what he calls the "resentniks." Harvard last week was the happy recipient of a seventy-million-dollar gift from John L. and Frances Lehman Loeb, but none of it was earmarked for the planned (Your Name Here) Humanities Center: it has yet to find its donor.

The *Wall Street Journal,* which functions as a kind of All Ivy League alumni bulletin, has described the Bass controversy as an "object lesson to alumni who come bearing large gifts." The *Journal* is waging a campaign against multiculturalism, slamming universities as sanctuaries for what William Bennett calls "the radical nihilism of post-modern art; homosexual and lesbian self-celebration; Marxism; Neo-Marxism; radical feminism and multiculturalism; deconstructionism; and various manifestations of political correctness."

Polemical label-mongering of this kind doesn't do much to advance reasoned discussion. But Mr. Bennett as a symptom is more significant than Mr. Bennett as an analyst. He articulates a widespread public sense that universities have become places where the idea of a collective American heritage is no longer safe from derision, and where the writings of the oppressed have replaced time-honored Great Books as the best works through which students are invited to study (now with anger and reproach) what used to be called (with reverence) the "Western mind." A young woman who is an English major at a distinguished liberal-arts college recently wrote in a letter to a friend, "I have already read Langston Hughes, Zora Neale Hurston, Amy Tan, Richard Wright, Malcolm X, Toni Morrison, Gabriel García Márquez, Kate Chopin, Adrienne Rich, and Alice Walker. I have never had to read for school any Hemingway, Faulkner, Thoreau, Steinbeck, James Fenimore Cooper, Blake, Melville, Jack London, Virginia Woolf, Milton, Poe, Donne, Keats, Shelley, Byron, Wordsworth, Wilder, Homer—the list goes on." Her point was not that there is anything wrong with the inclusion of the first list but that there *is* something wrong with the exclusion of the second.

Either/or dogmatism is the problem. All the writers on the first (politically correct) list have been readers of the second; and all the writers on the second ("Western mind") list would have been interested in the first. If the confrontational mood—which afflicts some faculty members and university patrons far than it does real readers and writers continues to harden, more institutions will find themselves in the kind of impasse that Yale came up against in trying to negotiate a compromise with Mr. Bass. This more than a passing instance of the perennial friction between academia and society. It is a standoff that threatens the unstated compact between universities and the middle class which accounts, in large part, for what has been a golden age for American higher education since the Second World War. Under this compact the middle class consented to pay a lot and, especially since the nineteen-sixties to pay even more in order to subsidize those who could not pay; in return, the university agreed to inculcate habits of intellectual discipline in their children, and to justify their faith that America remains a society where what you know and what you can do are more important than who, in some genealogical sense, you are.

This bargain is beginning to come apart. Given the post-Cold War contraction of government support for defense-related research, the exploding cost of fringe benefits for students, faculty, and staff, and the rise of tuition able levels, universities have never been more vulnerable than they are today. The institutions that continue to thrive will be the ones that find a way to encourage daring, experimental thought, unpopular as it may be with their financial supporters, while continuing to honor the traditions that their alumni learned in the schools they remember. The Bass fiasco has made that balance harder than ever to achieve.

The Espresso Uprising[6]

Some man-bites-dog news from the highly politicized field of ethnic studies.

To the wonderment of all, Columbia University did not cave in to student protesters who demanded ethnic-studies departments as antidotes to the school's "hegemonic and white supremacist curriculum." And at the City College of New York, the black-studies department once chaired by the wild Afrocentrist Leonard Jeffries is about to disappear. A year after removing Jeffries as chairman, the college decided to eliminate the department and three other ethnic departments. Courses will continue to be available. In fact, the college said the number of such courses will triple, but as interdisciplinary programs, i.e., integrated into the whole curriculum.

The downgrading of the departments at City College was said to be an effort to save money—the college is in severe financial trouble. Yet the real reason, sources said, was to make sure that politicized ethnic fiefdoms do not arise again at City. The college was profoundly embarrassed by Jeffries's anti-white, antisemitic bombast and doesn't want to go through anything similar ever again.

Fiefdoms were precisely what the Columbia demonstrators demanded. Columbia has a long and outstanding history of research and teaching about non-Western cultures, particularly Asian cultures. It does not seem like a prime candidate for multicultural unrest. It offers 83 courses in African-American studies and more than 30 in Latino and Latin-American studies, and all undergraduates must take two courses in non-Western civilizations.

But the student protesters had something else in mind: an independent ethnic studies department with its own budget and its own power to hire faculty. And they quite clearly wanted an enclave devoted to ethnic self-esteem and psychic uplift. One Latino student complained of sitting in classes "with all these white kids reading Homer and Euripides and feeling that my culture didn't even count," a revealing and fashionably esteem-based approach to the classics.

"Students do not design our curriculum nor enforce our standards," said Columbia President George Rupp, announcing a novel approach to college administration.

Protest tradition. About a hundred demonstrators, representing a coalition of Hispanic, Asian-American, white and black students, blockaded and occupied campus buildings. Some were arrested. Three conducted a 15-day hunger strike. This fit right

6 Article by John Leo, from *U.S. News & World Report* 120:23 My 6 '96. Copyright © 1996 *U.S. News & World Report*. Reprinted with permission.

in with a Columbia tradition—it had a student occupation of buildings in 1985 over disinvestment in South Africa, and one of the more traumatic student uprisings of the 1960s. But those protests were about the real world, not about rearranging academic furniture in the pursuit of group esteem.

So the New York media seemed more bemused than serious in their coverage. When one student demonstrator complained bitterly that Columbia was forcing her to read *Pride and Prejudice*, columnist Terry Golway wrote: "What could those patriarchal oafs at Columbia have been thinking, forcing a woman to read a novel by...a woman?" Even the *New York Times* offered light-hearted coverage, despite the perfect PC credentials of the cause. Its headline proclaimed, "Protests at Columbia signal spring," and reporter Neil MacFarquhar noted that the occupiers avoided "rousing polemics on social justice" and instead "ordered take-out *caffè lattes* from Cooper's Coffee Bar."

As the protests wound down, an editorial in the *New York Observer*, a popular weekly, said of the hunger strikers: "The absurdity is that, if they get their wish, they will exchange physical hunger for mental hunger" and will have "wasted much of their college years splashing around in a media-stoked stew of identity politics, bereft of the core academic background that makes for an independent-minded, truly liberal thinker."

True enough. The attitude of the media and the dominant student reaction to the protests (yawns) were healthy signs. Still, ethnic studies departments are entrenched at some 700 colleges, and for each solid and serious one, there seem to be 10 or 12 organized as what the author Jim Sleeper calls "ethnic playpens."

Columnist Linda Chavez had to endure some playpen abuse last week while visiting the University of Illinois at Urbana-Champaign for a debate on affirmative action (she was opposed; columnist Clarence Page was in favor). Students jeered her as a fake Latino. During the debate, her detractors marched in carrying signs, banners and a Mexican flag. Chavez says she needed a police escort to get to her room. Earlier at a campus book store, according to the *Daily Illini*, an egg and copies of her book *Out of the Barrio* were thrown, and coconuts were placed on a table where she was signing books. This was to indicate that she offends Latinos by being "brown on the outside, white on the inside."

In identity politics, built around the campus power base of ethnic studies, dissent is indeed viewed as betrayal. This is why colleges should have plenty of ethnic study courses and programs but be very wary of setting up enclaves of groupthink and separatism that have nothing to do with actual thinking or learning.

"The attitude of the media and the dominant student reaction to the protests (yawns) were healthy signs."

III. The Presentation of the Past

Editor's Introduction

Section Three of this volume discusses multiculturalism in the context of two very specific incidences. The first is the Smithsonian's Enola Gay exhibit, and the second is the National Standards for History project. The Enola Gay exhibit showcased the August 1945 dropping of atomic bombs on Hiroshima and Nagasaki. Controversy aroused in response to what many believed to be an excessive focus on the inhumanity of the bomb's destructive capabilities in lieu of the American victory achieved as a result of dropping the bombs. In a similar vein, many voiced outrage because of the National Standards project whose National History Standards was understood as overlooking many American accomplishments and concentrating on those of women and minorities. As is common with issues that involve multiculturalism, both the Enola Gay exhibit and the National Standards for History project evoked polarized reactions of condemnation and praise.

The opening article by Stephen Budiansky, writing in *U.S. News & World Report*, discusses the turmoil surrounding the Smithsonian's Enola Gay exhibition. Enormous public pressure and protest was brought upon the exhibit because it was believed that the exhibit represented the dropping of the atom bomb on Hiroshima solely as a horrible act of vengeance. Budiansky also points out that the Enola Gay exhibit is representative of a new museum strategy to provide interpretations of what is being shown, rather than simply showcase the artifacts.

In a related article, reprinted from *The Bulletin of the Atomic Scientists*, Stanley Goldberg condemns the inflammatory editorials written by patriotic groups in response to the Enola Gay exhibit. He wonders if any of these protestors had ever read the offending exhibit script. Goldberg, who was on the advisory board that devised the exhibit, believes the pressure to remove the exhibit, placed by Congress and groups such as the American Legion, amounted to an act of censorship.

In a very intelligent and insightful article, Tom Engelhardt, in "Fifty Years Under a Cloud," asserts that the controversy surrounding the Enola Gay exhibit is owed to the new realization that the dropping of the bomb caused a level of destruction and death so horrific the world would never be the same. Perhaps multiculturalism, as it raises our awareness of other cultures, is responsible for calling our attention to the sobering, painful reality that is the atomic bomb. As Engelhardt notes "To see what happened to tens of thousands of people in that single instant was to experience not the glories of immediate triumph but the horrors of possible future loss."

The National Standards for History project is the focus of the remaining articles in this section. John Wiener, writing in *The New Republic*, remarks that when the National Standards for History volumes were about to be published, Lynne Cheney, former head of the National Endowment for the Humanities, wrote an article in the *Wall Street Journal*, attacking the volumes for skimping on the achievements and contributions of white men. Wiener claims that Cheney and her fellow critics projected a misleading idea of its contents and that their attack may be a bit flawed.

Although the National Standards Project issued a revised version of its National History Standards, the battle over how schools should teach American and Western heritages continued. Walter A. McDougall, writing in *Commentary*, believes such debate should be dropped so that more serious educational issues, including the collapse of authority and the prevalence of drugs, violence, and truancy can be given primacy.

The last article in this section counters the criticism heaped upon the National Standards Project. Eric Alterman asserts that the "conservatives' real enemy is multiculturalism in all its forms." Conservative attacks upon the new history standards are, in Alterman's assessment, based on the fear that relaying America's failings in the curriculum will "corrupt the mind's of America's youth." Yet, Alterman, like McDougall in the previous article, is also quick to note that while debate may rage over an issue such as the National Standards Project, "we are currently in the midst of an educational crisis that threatens the very foundations of young people's future" as soaring dropout rates, violence, and drugs should be understood as the real threat to American education.

A Museum in Crisis[1]

The New York taxi driver, who talked as if he had once been a card-carrying member of the Communist Party, turned to his passenger as the cab pulled up at the Cooper-Hewitt Museum. "Hey, this is part of the Smithsonian, isn't it?" he said. "Have you heard what those bastards are doing to the Enola Gay?"

His passenger had indeed. He was Michael Heyman, the secretary of the Smithsonian Institution. And he had just met yet another World War II veteran furious over the Smithsonian's plans to display the Enola Gay—the plane that dropped the atomic bomb on Hiroshima 50 years ago—in an exhibit that made the Japanese out to be innocent victims of an unnecessary act of vengeance.

The decision last week by the Smithsonian's Board of Regents to cancel the controversial exhibit was inevitable, Heyman says, given "gargantuan" opposition from across the political spectrum. The American Legion complained; so did 20,000 subscribers to *Smithsonian* magazine. Among the many veterans who protested that the atomic bombing saved their lives by averting an invasion of Japan were two of the Smithsonian's own regents—former congressman and World Bank president Barber Conable and Sen. Daniel Patrick Moynihan. Perhaps even more to the point, the opposition included key members of Congress who were threatening to hold investigations and beginning to talk ominously about cutting the $371 million federal contribution to the Smithsonian, which makes up 77 percent of its budget.

Although the cancellation of the exhibit has removed the immediate threat of congressional retaliation, it is by no means the end of the story. The Enola Gay incident has been a severe blow to the reputation of a revered institution at a time when the Smithsonian is trying to woo much-needed corporate sponsors for its planned 150th anniversary celebration in 1996.

And it has, if anything, inflamed a long-festering dispute over how the Smithsonian ought to be telling the story of American history. House Speaker Newt Gingrich heralded the victory on the Enola Gay as the first battle in a new phase of the culture war. "You are seeing a reassertion and a renewal of American civilization," he told the National Governors' Association. "The Enola Gay fight was a fight, in effect, over the reassertion by most Americans that they're sick and tired of being told by some cultural elite that they ought to be ashamed of their country."

And Rep. Sam Johnson of Texas, newly appointed by Gingrich to the Board of Regents, made it clear that more changes are coming: "We've got to get patriotism back into the Smithsonian.

[1] Article by Stephen Budiansky, from *U.S. News & World Report* 118:73-5 F 13 '95.
Copyright © 1995 *U.S. News & World Report*. Reprinted with permission.

We want the Smithsonian to reflect real America and not something that a historian dreamed up."

For now, the Smithsonian is in full retreat. Vietnam veterans' groups will soon receive a letter saying that an exhibit on air power in the Vietnam War, planned for the Air and Space Museum, will be put off for at least five years. Heyman has promised the regents he will review, and rectify where necessary, current exhibits that board members believe reflect "revisionist history." Board sources told *U.S. News* that Air and Space Director Martin Harwit will soon be dismissed for his part in overseeing the planned Enola Gay exhibit.

The incident has also left curators and researchers throughout the Smithsonian shellshocked. The institution has long enjoyed a scholarly independence and a public reputation unique among government institutions. Twenty-five million people visit its 16 museums each year. Its collections, from well-known icons to recondite scientific artifacts—George Washington's false teeth and Dorothy's ruby slippers to 300,000 sorted and labeled water bugs—are universally admired by casual museum-goers and serious researchers alike.

Backlash's impact. "I'm anticipating a sort of political scrutiny we're not used to," says Robert Post, a curator at the American History Museum. A half-dozen other curators contacted last week agreed. While many disapproved of the way the Air and Space Museum had handled the Enola Gay exhibit, they said they feared that the political backlash would virtually end any attempt at providing context or interpretation in exhibits. "Once it's known that Air and Space sat down to a line-by-line review of the script with the American Legion," says Post, referring to the ultimately unsuccessful negotiations that took place over the Enola Gay exhibit, "who's next? The Christian Coalition?"

Like many museums, the Smithsonian has been gradually moving away from a style of exhibit that curators derisively call the "curiosity in a case" approach. Most museum experts agree it was a much needed change, especially for the stodgy Smithsonian. Under Dillon Ripley, secretary from 1964 to 1984, the Smithsonian had struck an unabashedly "celebratory" tone that glossed over subtleties and emphasized the display of "icons" like the Hope diamond, the first ladies' gowns, and the Wright Flyer. "History museums are becoming forums, not temples," says Prof. Edward Linenthal of the University of Wisconsin.

But Heyman and other Smithsonian officials admit that the change to a more interpretive approach has occurred with virtually no oversight by top management and no official guidelines. Heyman acknowledges, too, that critics of "political correctness" in some of the newer and more interpretive exhibits have a point and that the museum has unnecessarily angered many of its supporters. Last week, he met with top officials of the American Physical Society, including two Nobel Prize winners, in an

"Twenty-five million people visit its 16 museums each year."

attempt to smooth over the outrage provoked by one of these exhibits, "Science in American Life." This show infuriated many scientists—including the American Chemical Society, which put up $5.3 million to underwrite the exhibit—with its antitechnology tone, including large displays on the atomic bomb, DDT and the supposed dangers of genetic engineering, the latter illustrated with Frankenstein, scenes from *Jurassic Park* and the Teenage Mutant Ninja Turtles.

"Everyone came in loving the Smithsonian," says Marcel LaFollette, a professor at George Washington University who served on the advisory board for the exhibit. But she says the board became disillusioned by the approach the curators were taking: "There was such a deliberate attempt to be negative rather than laying out the history and letting people make their own judgments."

Another show that has raised hackles is an American History Museum exhibit on life after the Revolution. It offers such insights as, "White Americans won and preserved their freedom from England in large part through the labors of the African-Americans they enslaved." A display of a paneled room in a small Virginia farmer's house is presented with narration that deconstructs the wall decoration as nothing but a reflection of the owner's status-seeking "ambition."

Treading gently. Heyman is trying to finesse the whole situation by suggesting, in effect, that the choice is not simply one of ideological, inflammatory interpretation versus flag-waving mush. He has ordered a review to develop basic guidelines for interpretive exhibits; one possible outcome, he says, may simply be a recommendation to do smaller exhibits. Shows like the one planned for the Enola Gay, he says, which are "half writing and half objects," are in any case "an absolute disconnect" with the visiting public; people are not willing to spend the three to five hours required to go through them and read everything.

Another remedy, he suggests, may be to focus the interpretation and context offered within an exhibit on explaining events as they were understood and experienced by the people living at that time; books or symposiums may be a better way to "raise the questions that have come up since," he says.

Whatever the outcome, the days of the Smithsonian as a genteel, scholarly place soaring above the political fray are clearly gone. Robert McCormick Adams, Heyman's predecessor, who left last September, "saw it more as a university—the [museum] directors are deans and they run their own show," says Heyman. "Clearly that has to change."

Smithsonian Suffers
Legionnaires' Disease[2]

Fifty years ago, I was an 11-year-old paperboy for the afternoon *Cleveland Press*. On the afternoon of August 6, 1945, the bundled papers waiting for me had a banner headline saying: "Atom Bomb Hits Japan." The second line said: "Blast Force Equals 2000 Blockbusters." Amazing. Although the news was momentous, the readers of the *Cleveland Press*—at least the readers on my route—had to wait for it. I read every word of the several articles on this new thing called an atomic bomb before delivering the papers.

In the coming years, I continued to read everything I could on the atomic bomb—as well as on the promise of nuclear energy and the field of nuclear physics. In a way, that was the start of my professional career as a historian of science. And that interest—an obsession, really—eventually led me to play a role in the recent *Enola Gay*-Smithsonian Institution fiasco—a long-running and ultimately dispiriting morality play in three acts.

ACT ONE: An "Impressive Piece of Work"

In the fall of 1984, Roger Kennedy, the director of the Smithsonian's National Museum of American History asked me to meet with him and some of the museum's curators to discuss the fact that nowhere in the museum was there a mention of two of the defining moments of the twentieth century: the obliteration of Hiroshima and Nagasaki by atomic bombs.

There was enthusiasm around the table that day for mounting such an exhibit in time for the fortieth anniversary of the bombing. Kennedy asked me to identify artifacts, produce a "script," and oversee the installation. In museum-speak, a script is the blueprint that specifies how an exhibition will be laid out, and what artifacts, photos, and documents it will present. The script also contains the language that will be in the "labels."

The 1985 exhibit—composed of Hiroshima- and Nagasaki-type bomb casings as well as photos and artifacts in two display cases—sketchily described both the Manhattan Project and the destructive power of the bombs. Because I was worried about the emotional impact the exhibit might have on unprepared visitors, I drained the emotion from the labels. Nevertheless, the guiding principle of the exhibit was simple, even simpleminded. I wanted to make it clear that nuclear devastation was not merely an abstract topic discussed by Cold War theorists. Nuclear weapons—and their effects—were real. Among the artifacts were

---

[2] Article by Stanley Goldberg, historian of science, author of *Understanding Relativity: Origins and Impact of a Science Revolution* and currently completing a biography of Gen. Leslie Groves, from *The Bulletin of the Atomic Scientists* 51:28-33 My/Je '95. Copyright © 1995 by the Educational Foundation for Nuclear Science. Reprinted with permission.

roof tiles that had bubbled from the heat. One of the photos showed a man whose head was badly flash-burned, except where his hat had offered some protection.

The exhibit was well received. Scheduled to be on the floor only during the month of August, it was retained through November. Kennedy asked me to undertake a year-long study as to how a large and permanent exhibit could be handled. I plunged in, but a year later, the museum's administration had lost its enthusiasm. Although the Smithsonian gets public money, many of its activities must be funded privately, and private funding for an atomic bomb exhibit had not been forthcoming. That was no great surprise. When it came to fundraising for not-very-popular projects, curators at the museum sometimes spoke of the museum administration as having "a whim of iron."

To this day, the Smithsonian's National Museum of American History has no separate display on the Manhattan Project or the use of atomic bombs in war. It does, however, have a small and spare atomic display tucked into a larger exhibit on "Science and American Life."

Given the failure of the American History Museum to pursue the project, I was surprised and pleased in 1991 when I learned that the Smithsonian's National Air and Space Museum would install a major exhibit on the end of World War II, which would be in place by May 1995.

The exhibit—called "The Last Act: The Atomic Bomb and the End of World War II"—would feature the front portion of the *Enola Gay* fuselage, and it would explore the role played by the atomic bomb in bringing the war to an end. I was asked, along with nine others, to serve on the Exhibit Advisory Board. The first draft of the exhibit script, put together by the museum's curators and distributed to the advisory board in January 1994, was a heavyweight—upwards of 750 pages of text and illustrative material.

The board met with the curators in February to go over the script. Our role was to review and suggest. The content of the final exhibit, we believed then, would be in the hands of the curators.

Rather than retelling the whole story of the Pacific war, which would not have been possible in the space allotted, the curators linked the atomic bombings to the evolution of the strategic bombing campaign of the XXI Bombing Command of the 20th Air Force, Gen. Curtis LeMay's outfit that was systematically incinerating one Japanese city after another. Rather than having to use hundreds of planes in a raid, the Air Force could now achieve the same effect with one plane. The theme did not originate with the curators; it had been explored widely and thoroughly over the years. See, for instance, Michael S. Sherry's definitive *The Rise of American Air Power*, published in 1987.

The flow of the script was logical. After some unremarkable references to the start of the war and the attack on Pearl Harbor, the exhibit began with V-E Day and concentrated on the battles for Iwo Jima and Okinawa. Together, these two campaigns were almost as costly in American casualties as the first three years of the Pacific war.

The decision to use the bomb—and how to use it—was a complicated one, but the curators had done a fine job of making the subject accessible to a general audience. That was no easy task. The story line then moved to an exploration of the "miracle" of the design and production of the B-29. This was followed by a section on the training of the crews chosen to deliver the bombs—the 509th Composite Group—and the construction of the 509th facilities on the island of Tinian in the Marianas.

After describing—in words, photos, and artifacts—the scene at and near ground zero in Hiroshima and Nagasaki, the exhibit ended with a section on the legacy of the atomic bomb: An abrupt halt to the war, and a fierce and competitive nuclear arms race between the United States and the Soviet Union.

The advisory committee represented a wide range of disciplines and professional expertise. But there was unanimous agreement at the advisory board meeting that the initial approach of the curators was sound. Although the curators' plan was not the only one they could have used, they had done a careful and professional job. The task now at hand was one of fine tuning.

This is not to say that members of the advisory board had no criticisms. Some of us believed the script overemphasized the role that international politics played in the decision to use the bomb—the argument that the bombs represented the first shots in the coming Cold War. In fact, there were at least four other overarching reasons for using the bomb—all important, but some of which had gotten short shrift in the script:

• The momentum of the Manhattan Project itself, the biggest single scientific and industrial enterprise of the war.

• Domestic politics, which guaranteed that the Truman administration would pay a fearful price if the American people ever learned that a superweapon had been developed but not used.

• Personal ambition, particularly Gen. Leslie Groves's conviction that he was playing *the* pivotal role in ending the war, and J. Robert Oppenheimer's obsessive concern with the kind of immortality the bomb would bring him.

• Humanitarian concerns that the war should be ended quickly, not only for the sake of Americans but for the Japanese. Although peace factions within the Japanese government were exploring ways to end the war and they might have prevailed, Japanese militarists were still running the show in the summer of 1945. Meanwhile, the fire-bomb raids continued. General LeMay believed that his men would be able to burn down every Japanese city of consequence by October. Had the war continued that long, the continued fire-bombing would almost surely have produced hundreds of thousands of civilian casualties.

All of these concerns were a matter of emphasis. They could have been addressed by a little refining. There was nothing odd or unexpected or sinister about that. One would never expect that a first-draft script of a complex topic would not raise questions in a peer-review process. Some labels had to be reworded, expanded, shortened. But the consensus of the advisory board was clear: The exhibit would inform, challenge, and commemorate.

As Air Force Historian Richard Hallion, a member of the board, put it in his written remarks: "Overall, this is a most impressive piece of work, comprehensive and dramatic, obviously based upon a great deal of sound research, primary and secondary."

ACT TWO: Everyone's Unhappy

Shortly after the advisory board meeting, the script was leaked to the Air Force Association. When I heard through the grapevine that the association was unhappy with it because of its alleged pro-Japanese and anti-American and anti-nuclear bias, I was neither surprised nor alarmed. The curators had presented a solid script rooted in the latest historical scholarship.

Besides, it was common knowledge that the Air Force Association believed that the Air and Space Museum should be devoted exclusively to celebrating the accomplishments of U.S. air power and space ventures. But when the budding controversy was picked up by the news media, and when the American Legion joined in, I began to realize that the exhibit was in for a tough go.

For starters, there was simply no agreement on the meaning of "history." In writing history, professional historians follow a process analogous to the methods identified with science. They develop ideas about how and why something happened and then they test those ideas against whatever documentary evidence they can locate. Finally, they make their data and conclusions available to other historians to be confirmed and refined—or ripped and shredded.

But journalists sometimes follow a different process. The arcana of scholarly methodology would not only bore readers and viewers, it would drive them away. Readers and viewers love controversy and conflict, and journalists devote great energy and talent to reporting it. Once the Air Force Association and the American Legion got into the act, the ingredients for a fine drama were in place. On one side were some of the vets who actually fought the war, or their spiritual descendants. On the other side were academic curators and historians, often described as "revisionist," and sometimes seen as picky and pedantic.

In late September, Ken Ringle, a *Washington Post* reporter, summed up the controversy admirably, without quite realizing it. In an article in the *Post*, he contrasted the documentary evidence used by historians with the memories of veterans who served in the Pacific. Documentary evidence was "old history, a scholarly abstraction composed of archival records, argumentative books, and...fading images on black and white film." Living history came from veterans.

One of the vets Ringle quoted was Grayford C. Payne, who had been a prisoner of war in Japan from 1942 to 1945. With tears in his eyes, Payne said he was sure that the atomic bombs had saved his life. If an invasion of the home islands had taken place, he and his buddies would have been executed.

Powerful flesh-and-blood stuff; documents compete poorly with human interest. Ringle's piece seemed to imply that the opinions of the veterans he interviewed were a more accurate guide to what happened in the war than histories of the war based on archival materials. Subsequent editorials in the *Post* gave explicit support to that view.

In an August 7 op-ed piece in the *Post*, Martin Harwit, director of the Air and Space Museum, defended the original script as well as his efforts to placate critics. Nevertheless, he wrote, "We have found no way to exhibit the *Enola Gay* and satisfy everyone."

A week later, the *Post* responded editorially, suggesting that Harwit and the curators assumed their critics had less "intellectual sophistication." This, said the *Post*, "naturally rankles with veterans and other groups that offered detailed and substantive criticisms of the initial plan which they said was emotionally rigged to create an anti-nuclear perspective and to present Japan overwhelmingly as a victim country fighting only to preserve its 'culture.'"

The *Post* charged that the curatorial failings reflected an "inability to perceive that political opinions are embedded in the exhibit or to identify them as such—opinions—rather than as universal, 'objective' assumptions all thinking people must necessarily share. This confusion is increasingly common in academia and owes much to the fashionable and wrong academic notion that objectivity is unattainable anyway and that all presentations of complex issues must be politically tendentious."

The editorial made me wonder if any member of the *Post* staff had actually read the script. The personal experiences of individuals are important to historians. But they *are* just some of the pieces in a puzzle that has many different kinds of pieces. That's a basic point, but one that seemed to elude most journalistic observers.

By August 1994, it was clear that the Air Force Association and the American Legion didn't have a better hand than Harwit and the curators—but they had the *upper* hand. They were adept at working with the press and putting their particular flag-waving, human-interest spin on the story.

As early as May, the Air and Space Museum curators had begun negotiating the content of the exhibit and the wording of the labels directly with representatives of the Air Force Association and the American Legion. The advisory board, which had met just once—in February—was simply out of the picture.

From the start, the Air Force Association and the American Legion exploited early lapses in judgment by the curators. These were lapses that the advisory board had noted at its February meeting, and which surely would have been fixed in the normal course of events without much hassle. For example, the board objected to a first-draft label that ended with the following passage:

"For Americans this [Pacific] war was fundamentally different than the one waged against Germany and Italy—it was a war of vengeance. For most Japanese, it was a war to defend their unique culture against Western imperialism."

To critics of the proposed exhibit, that passage was the smoking gun, and it was widely disseminated to the press. The *Post* editorial I quoted a moment ago referred to it, as did countless newspapers. But the passage had been ripped from its context. The full label said:

"In 1931 the Japanese Army occupied Manchuria; six years later it invaded the rest of China. From 1937 to 1945, the Japanese Empire would be constantly at war.

"Japanese expansionism was marked by naked aggression and extreme brutality. The slaughter of tens of thousands of Chinese in Nanking in 1937 shocked the world. Atrocities by Japanese troops included brutal mistreatment of civilians, forced laborers and prisoners of war, and biological experiments on human victims.

"In December 1941, Japan attacked U.S. bases at Pearl Harbor, Hawaii, and launched other surprise assaults against Allied territories in the Pacific. Thus began a wider conflict marked by extreme bitterness. For most Americans, this war was fundamentally different than the one waged against Germany and Italy—it was a war of vengeance. For most Japanese, it was a war to defend their unique culture against Western imperialism. As the war approached its end in 1945, it appeared to both sides that it was a fight to the finish."

That is solid history, not an absurdity. The label wasn't wrong; it just needed fine tuning. The contempt that both countries had toward each other during the war has been well documented, for example by John Dower in *War Without Mercy*. That contempt was fully explored in the original script. Nevertheless, the advisory board suggested that the "imperialism" paragraph be recast to emphasize the role of Japanese militarism.

The meaning of many other labels was badly distorted by the critics. Air Force Historian Hallion, who had found the first-draft script so praiseworthy at the advisory board meeting, decided later, after the initial attacks by the Air Force Association, that the curators had "resisted addressing basic deficiencies of the exhibit even during subsequent 'grudging' revisions." He told *Post* reporter Ringle that Harwit and the curators insisted on focusing on the devastation of Hiroshima and Nagasaki and resisted portraying Japanese aggression and atrocities.

Hallion also told a *Washington Times* reporter, Josh Young, that "the information [in the exhibit] is biased. It doesn't permit the visitor to reach an informed conclusion. The visitor comes away with the impression that the bomb should not have been dropped. It doesn't take into account the severity of the war or the complexities of the decision."

Some of the artifacts that were to be displayed in the exhibit also unhinged critics. The exhibit that I helped put together for the Smithsonian's National Museum of American History in 1985 went to great lengths to avoid shocking the viewers, but the proposed 1995 Air and Space Museum exhibit was confrontative in its choice of photos and artifacts.

Among the more unsettling artifacts, loaned to the Smithsonian by the Hiroshima Peace Memorial Exhibit, were items belonging to a group of schoolmates: a student's lunch box containing the carbonized remains of sweet peas and polished rice; a water bottle; and a wooden clog revealing, by blast-induced darkening, the outline of a foot. Photos depicted the devastation of the city and badly burned people. Critics charged that such displays were designed to evoke sympathy for the Japanese. The exhibit, they said, should contain artifacts and photos depicting Japanese atrocities. In fact, the curators were simply trying to show the effects of an atomic bomb. Those effects were real, and they are hard to face up to. The Hiroshima bomb detonated over a hospital, not a tank factory or an ordnance works. Nearby schools were in session, filled not with soldiers but with children. Two bombs killed upwards of 200,000 people immediately and over the following weeks and months. Most were civilians. That is history; that is context.

"Critics charged that such displays were designed to evoke sympathy for the Japanese."

Many of the critics believed that the contents of the labels should be limited to artifact identification. Paul Tibbets, the pilot of the *Enola Gay*, said that history would be best served by that approach. Many museum curators around the nation would agree with him. There is a long-standing debate among museum curators over the context issue. Some curators say that artifacts should speak for themselves, and they cite the traditional role of bare-bones labels in art museums, which usually identify the artist, the year the work was completed, and the title of the work, if it has one.

But works of art are not the same as museum artifacts. The essence of art is that it is a subjective expression of an artist. That is why it is "art" instead of a mailbox or a screwdriver or a paper clip. A work of art has as many subjective meanings as it has viewers. But in this context, the fuselage of the *Enola Gay* and the carbonized remains of a child's lunch are not *objets d'art*. They are *evidence*—surviving fragments of past events.

By the end of 1994, on orders from Harwit, the curators had done four revisions of the script, the last two in close consultation with American Legion critics. In the first revision, a "pre-exhibit" display occupying some 4,000 square feet was added, containing 50 photos, some of which depicted Japanese atrocities early in the war. The pre-exhibit also would have displayed a U.S. carrier-based fighter plane.

The final two revisions involved line-by-line consultations between representatives of the American Legion and the curators. Among the changes: the removal of archival documents showing that some government officials and military leaders did not believe the bomb should be used, and that some highly placed U.S. officials thought the target city should at least be warned. The curators were also forced to eliminate some artifacts and photos. The lunch box, for instance, had to go.

The most difficult issue was the question of American casualties. The Air Force Association and the American Legion argued that the bombs were used to end the war quickly, thus avoiding the need for an invasion of the Japanese home islands, which would have produced perhaps a million or more U.S. casualties. Few historians who have looked closely at the documentary record believe that any high-level military planner actually thought that in 1945.

Harwit and the American Legion representatives eventually *negotiated* a figure—229,000—for the expected number of U.S. casualties, if Project Olympic, the invasion of Kyushu planned for November, had taken place. Then—in mid-September—the American Legion pronounced the exhibit flawed, but passable. The Air Force Association was still unhappy.

Agreeing to a figure of 229,000 was a mistake. Those of us on the advisory board who were familiar with the documentary evidence knew the casualty figure was still high. The generals and admirals who were actually planning the invasion were projecting lower numbers for the invasion of Kyushu. Barton Bernstein, a Stanford historian who has looked at the question for years, persuaded Harwit that, in light of the available evidence, 63,000 casualties was a better figure. And on January 9, Harwit informed Legion officials that the script was being changed accordingly.

That was the final insult, insofar as the American Legion was concerned. From the perspective of the Legion, Harwit had broken his word. The Legion—backed by several members of Congress—called on Smithsonian Secretary I. Michael Heyman and President Clinton to take the exhibit out of the hands of Harwit and his curators, at the very least. But what they really hoped for, they said, was that the Smithsonian would cancel the exhibit altogether.

As William M. Detweiler, the commander of the American Legion said, the museum leadership had managed to antagonize everyone on all sides of the issue.

ACT THREE: The Cave-In

On January 30 of this year, Smithsonian Secretary Heyman announced the cancellation of the original *Enola Gay* exhibit. In its place, he said, would be a simple display of the front portion of the *Enola Gay*'s fuselage and perhaps some videotaped interviews with surviving crew members.

"I have taken this action, for one overriding reason," Heyman said. "I have concluded that we made a basic error in attempting to couple an historical treatment of the use of atomic weapons with the fiftieth anniversary commemoration of the end of the war. But we need to know which of many goals is paramount, and not confuse them.

"In this important anniversary year, veterans and their families were expecting, and rightly so, that the nation would honor and commemorate their valor and sacrifice. They were not looking for analysis, and frankly, we did not give enough thought to the intense feelings such an analysis would evoke."

The scaled-down exhibit will open in June instead of the middle of May, as originally planned. Many historians said they were relieved by the cancellation of the full-scale exhibit, arguing that it had been so eviscerated that it was better not to mount it at all. I don't share that view. Yes, each new draft of the script bore the scars of censorship. But even in its damaged state, the exhibit would have challenged viewers to rethink their comfortable notions about Hiroshima and Nagasaki, the end of the war, and the origins of the Cold War.

"Many historians said they were relieved by the cancellation of the full-scale exhibit..."

In recent months, I have privately discussed the stillborn exhibit with some members of the American Legion. And it is clear that the motives and concerns of the Legion and the Air Force Association were, in some respects, fundamentally different.

Air Force Association press releases as well as the remarks of individual members of the association suggest that their campaign to discredit the *Enola Gay* exhibit was designed, in part, to embarrass the Smithsonian and force the resignation of Harwit. Under that scenario, he would have been replaced with someone whose idea of a good museum was strictly celebratory—and therefore congenial with the Air Force Association's views.

For the American Legion, the issue was much different. From a Legion perspective, the exhibit appeared to slight the contributions that veterans of the Pacific war made to victory over Japan. When *Post* reporter Ringle interviewed Grayford C. Payne, the prisoner of war quoted a moment ago, Ringle noted that the curators had said the question of whether it was necessary and right to drop the bombs still "continues to perplex" the nation.

To Payne, the curators sounded as if they were saying "that the thousands of Japanese killed by those bombs were somehow worth more than the thousands of American prisoners in Japan.... After all we'd been through? ...What about the women and children I saw bayoneted and buried alive...by the Japanese in the Philippines? What about the hundreds of thousands of Chinese hacked to pieces in the Rape of Nanking?"

Perhaps it is no overstatement to say that for the American Legion, the issue was sentiment. But for the Air Force Association, the issue was power. It wanted "its" museum back.

The Fallout

Some say that the big loser in the *Enola Gay* flap was the public, not the Smithsonian. There's some truth to that. Ordinary men, women and children have been denied the opportunity to assess different interpretations—supported by artifacts and documents—regarding the end of World War II, which have emerged from an intense study of the documented views and actions of the major actors who shaped the events in the Pacific in the summer of 1945.

In this fiftieth anniversary year of the end of the war, there is no dearth of information about the bombings. There has been an explosion of articles, books, and television specials about the first and only uses of atomic weapons in warfare, each presenting a distinctive and sometimes unique interpretation of the evidence concerning the motives behind the decisions of our leaders. Unfortunately, if someone wants to see an interpretation accompanied by actual artifacts that bear on the story, he or she will have to visit Hiroshima or Nagasaki.

The public *was* a big loser. But so was the Smithsonian. Last year, the administration of the Air and Space Museum forced the curators of the exhibit to negotiate directly with representatives of lobbying groups like the Air Force Association and the American Legion.

Meanwhile, 28 members of Congress signed a letter to the secretary of the Smithsonian denouncing the exhibit and urging him to intercede. Director Harwit was confronted by 21 members of Congress, some of whom wanted to know why the curators were being so un-American. Sen. Christopher "Kit" Bond, a Republican from Missouri, wrote a letter to one of the curators, accusing the curator of being un-American. Bond said he would keep his eye on the curator.

As the controversy unfolded, I suggested to Harwit and the curators that the advisory board could play a useful role as a buffer between the curators and the critics. That idea got nowhere.

In September, I resigned from the advisory board, as a protest. I was outraged that the museum administration had exposed the curators to the direct pressure of organizations such as the Air Force Association and the American Legion. And I was thunderstruck when members of Congress became actively involved.

The fact that a significant portion of the funds for the Air and Space Museum comes from public sources no more entitles members of Congress—or anyone else—to censor the conclusions of sound historical scholarship than does the fact that public monies support other kinds of research and writing projects.

That kind of thought control should have no place in a government committed to democracy. I believed that that issue had been settled in the 1950s, when McCarthyism was laid to rest. Apparently I was wrong.

Fifty Years Under a Cloud[3]

Just after noon, Honolulu time, on September 2, 1995, President Bill Clinton stepped up to a podium at Hawaii's National Memorial Cemetery of the Pacific to mark the fiftieth anniversary of the end of World War II. Speaking to CNN's cameras and a crowd of aged veterans of the war, the President invoked a half-century-old moment when "[we] found...unity in a shared mission, strength in a common purpose."

Although clearly meant to call up memories of an ascendant America, Clinton's speech had an abiding post-Vietnam ring to it. It emphasized the war's destructiveness ("it ravaged country-sides...[c]ost in total the lives of 58 million people...civilians and prisoners felled by disease and starvation...[m]illions wiped out in the gas chambers"); made covert passing reference to the atomic bombings of Hiroshima and Nagasaki ("it destroyed whole cities...[left] children buried in the rubble of bombed buildings"); replaced the unified melting-pot platoon of wartime propaganda with a multicultural list of races and ethnicities ("...the whites, the blacks, the Hispanics, the Asian Americans who served including Japanese Americans, the Native Americans including the famous Navajo code talkers..."); and in place of an enemy left a blankness.

The contrast between this almost funereal V-J Day remembrance and earlier World War II commemorations was striking. The story of American triumph that came so easily to Ronald Reagan, for example, in his 1984 D-Day speech at Normandy, was one that Clinton, in 1995, seemed unable to evoke. The oddly wistful tone of Clinton's speech could be traced in part to his own tenuous position: though he spoke of his generation as "heirs" to the veterans' "legacy," he was addressing a military that had mocked him as a draft dodger. But there were deeper currents at work as well.

If the President's speech caught not an old and familiar American ethos but rather a confusing new national mood, it was because the final moments of the war had proved to be very much alive in public memory. In fact, they held a rawness startling for events so long past. Peter Jennings anchored an ABC documentary questioning the American decision to drop the atomic bomb; Ted Koppel defended it on ABC's *Nightline*. Countless talk-radio programs, magazine and news articles, editorials, books, and book reviews argued the minutiae of policy-making in 1945 with a kind of passion and vitriol more often associated with fast-breaking news events; and increasingly upset World War II veterans struggled to reassert to an oddly

---

[3] Article by Tom Engelhardt, author of *The End of Victory Culture*, and co-editor of *History Wars: The Enola Gay and Other Battles for the American Past*, from *Harper's* 292:71-6 Ja '96. Copyright © 1996 Tom Engelhardt. Reprinted with permission.

resistant nation the victory story they believed was their right. What had changed was the place of that victory in a once-familiar American story. The great narrative arc of triumph that used to lead from an embattled New World wilderness to V-J Day and an American century now seemed to stop short in a state of collapse on August 6, 1945, the day of the atomic bombing of Hiroshima.

The first clue that the history lesson of 1995 was not going to be the one we expected came in January, when the Smithsonian Institution abruptly announced the cancellation of an exhibit at Washington's National Air and Space Museum on the last days of World War II. Meant as an exploration of the end of a boiling hot war and the beginning of a cold one, the proposed four-room show was to be centered around an iconic object, the fuselage of the *Enola Gay*, the plane that had dropped the first atomic bomb. Based on three decades of sober research by historians little known to the public, the planned exhibit had for months been the target of escalating attacks in the media, in Congress, and by veterans' organizations.

The first draft of the exhibit's script was entitled "The Crossroads: The End of World War II, the Atomic Bomb, and the Origins of the Cold War." The "roads" crossed at Hiroshima, an ominous X on the Smithsonian's map. The organizers of the show, most of whom grew up on the postwar side of August 1945, had an encompassing and generous vision: to take the stories of a global victory beyond imagining and a global terror beyond comprehension, and create from them a single narrative that all could visit and partake of. They assumed, somewhat naively, that the triumphalist story of the war in the Pacific could be yoked, in a single space, to the nightmarish postwar tale of a burgeoning nuclear arms race and a M.A.D. (as in Mutual Assured Destruction) world. The Smithsonian's planned exhibit would have linked the unlinkable: the burnished plane with the human suffering it caused and continues to cause; smiling shots of boisterous young airmen with unbearable images of seared victims; the consciousness of those who fought in World War II with the consciousness of those who grew up in the penumbra of World War III; the celebratory with the crematory; the just with the unjust; victory with defeat. This was a show that would begin at the end and end at the beginning, celebrate that end and deplore that beginning. As an icon, the plane's gleaming fuselage would be both world redeemer and world destroyer.

The idea of presenting such an exhibit in the National Air and Space Museum seems, in retrospect, a kind of inspired folly. Yet in its judicious approach to controversies that in academia had swirled around the *Enola Gay* for decades, the draft script, critiqued both by official Air Force historians and by "revisionist" historians, clearly was an effort in consensus exhibition-making, a remarkably careful, not to say bland, summary of decades of historical research and argument about the decision to drop the bomb.

The script's shock lay not so much in what it said as in what it didn't say. Despite years of laborious work restoring the *Enola Gay* to a pristine state, there was no hint of the celebratory feeling that had once been so inextricably linked to triumph in the Pacific. The writing remained almost entirely unemotional as it dutifully described and praised the plane's crew; its pilot, Colonel Paul W. Tibbets; all American veterans who fought in the Pacific; and the various political, scientific, and military figures involved in the decision to make and use the first atomic bombs. It remained uninflected, in fact, until it reached the crossroads: the moment a visitor to the exhibit would have left the *Enola Gay*, turned a corner, and entered a gallery marked "Ground Zero: Hiroshima, 8:15 A.M., August 6, 1945/Nagasaki, 11:02 A.M., August 9, 1945."

The first objects to catch that visitor's attention would have been two smashed wristwatches and a wall clock from Hiroshima, stopped at "the precise moment of the explosion of the atomic bomb," followed by Japanese photos of the mushroom cloud as seen from the ground and the first testimony of survivors. ("My strongest impression when the bomb fell was of the clouds...chasing me...like a black hand stretched out...covering everyone so that I too would eventually be crushed by it.")

The show was to include some of the most forbidding images of the nuclear age: a dead schoolboy's tattered jacket; a fused rosary; and a lunchbox belonging to Reiko Watanabe, a first-year student at Hiroshima's Municipal Girl's High School, with "the carbonized remains of sweet green peas and polished rice, a rare wartime luxury" inside. ("No trace of Reiko Watanabe was ever found.") It was also to have included photographs of hideously burned victims in the ashes of Hiroshima, as well as of those who lived on, having experienced "temperatures so high that the dark, heat-absorbing pattern of their clothing was burned into their flesh."

Keloid-scarred and disfigured *hibakusha* ("explosion-affected persons") were to be seen not only in frozen images from 1945 but in a present-day video. ("Only they can tell you what it is like to survive an atomic explosion.") Like the crew of the *Enola Gay* encountered earlier in the show, they would testify to their experiences. ("[O]n the following morning I bandaged my head...and went to the work site. Many of the students'...eyeballs had popped out, all the way out...the girls' school uniforms were burned off completely; they were completely stripped...naked. It was just like, well, a scene in hell.")

These scenes of atrocity and slaughter were to be placed near the central icon of what had previously been a triumphant American tale about a Good War. So it is no wonder that the planned exhibit excited such a fury. Even after being heavily revised, the draft script drew an unending stream of criticism.

From the *Washington Post* to the *Wall Street Journal,* from the Air Force Association to the American Legion, from Rush Limbaugh to a string of Republican presidential hopefuls, the lineup of those eager to condemn the show's curators for "hijacking history" grew.

Perhaps the most anguished reaction to the show came from retired Brigadier General Paul Tibbets. Despite the Smithsonian script's respectful and lengthy treatment of him (labeled a "hero") and of the 509th Composite Group, which he commanded, he saw in the planned exhibit only betrayal and defeat. In a tone commensurate with fifty years of disappointment, he denounced the show-to-be as a "package of insults," insults that, for Tibbets, did not begin or end in the museum. "I suggest, " he said, "that few, if any, of the articles, books, films, or reports have ever attempted to discuss the missions of August 6 and August 9 *in the context of the times.* Simply stated, the Enola Gay and the 509th Composite Bomb Group have been denied a historically correct representation to the public. Most writers have looked to the ashes of Hiroshima and Nagasaki to find answers for the use of those atomic weapons. The real answers lay in thousands of graves from Pearl Harbor around the world to Normandy and back again." Nor, in his eyes, had he, a man who had been, "to the best of my ability, doing what I could to bring the war to a victorious conclusion," been portrayed in a reasonable fashion. "Too many have labeled the atomic missions as war crimes in an effort to force their politics and their opinions on the American public and to damn military history."

In Tibbets's statement, one can hear not just anger but an old man's plea to be allowed—finally—to pilot the *Enola Gay* out of the mushroom cloud of destruction and confusion that had dogged him for most of his life, out of a world in which his story had the power to scare a generation of children into nightmarish sleep and into the one that he (and many others) believed America deserved. "What about the airmen who flew those strikes and lost their lives?" he asked. "And those who survived. Are they to be denied recognition for their efforts? Something is wrong with this scenario.... [L]et me urge reconsideration and let the exhibition of the Enola Gay accurately reflect the American spirit and victory of August 1945."

To truly understand the weight of Paul Tibbets's bitterness, one must imagine him in the cockpit of the *Enola Gay,* sitting on a runway on the island of Tinian on that August morning in 1945. He is at the controls of a B-29 Superfortress, the latest development in aviation, the most powerful plane ever built. It has taken the construction of a virtual city in an American desert, two billion dollars in government funds, and years of intense work by an army of scientists and technicians to create, produce, and deliver a single bomb to his plane's specially reconfigured bomb bay. The new weapon represents the very latest development in the long history of destructive technology.

The journalists, movie cameramen, and photographers swarming around the bomber at the behest of the Department of War are uncertain of exactly what they are recording, but sense that they may be close to the final moments in a global war already brought to its triumphant conclusion in Europe. Tibbets, who has spent the last year commanding the 509th Composite Group, has been assured in secret briefings that this mission will help end the grim war in the Pacific expeditiously.

Although we cannot know what he is imagining, he is certainly well aware of the honor roll of air-power pioneers whom he might soon join. They are his history, as are the heroes of the Argonne, San Juan Hill, Gettysburg, Bunker Hill, and the frontier wars against the Indians, who brought his nation to this possible moment of ultimate triumph. He has every reason to believe that, if success is his, his plane, his crew, and his exploits will someday be part of a glorious story of the Air Force, as well as of a larger national tale of triumph that his children and theirs will invoke with pride.

As the *Enola Gay* lifts off from the specially lengthened runway built for it on Tinian, it carries not only a bomb weighing more than four metric tons but the full weight of American optimism, of the sense that life has progressed for untold millions of years from the primordial soup to this moment: that tens of thousands of years of development have taken Man from the discovery of fire to the mastery of flight; that hundreds of years of expanding freedoms have led from the Magna Carta to a prospective U.N. charter; and that from the first tentative landings on a new continent, more than three hundred years of American history have led to this potential prelude to an American century.

But as the past year of confusing and contentious non-celebration showed, something happened to American society when the *Enola Gay* dropped its payload. As the bomb detonated and a fireball incinerated Hiroshima, Tibbets made a long-practiced sheer turn away from the destruction. And there, in the sky over Hiroshima, at that largely unacknowledged disjuncture in history, the American frontier—the one that remained deep in the national imagination—truly closed.

The world that Paul Tibbets returned to was, superficially, the same one he had left. The postwar economic boom seemed to confirm the ineluctable nature of the tide of victory that Americans had ridden for centuries. American officialdom, though, sensed early on that America's "trumph" at Hiroshima was not a simple victory and moved quickly to suppress all evidence of its catastrophic human cost. The cities of Hiroshima and Nagasaki were made off-limits to American reporters, all images of and information about the nature of the human destruction there disappeared into the inaccessible files of the occupation authority in Japan, and evidence of atomic danger in the United States, where the weaponry had been—and continued to be—tested, was carefully kept from the public. With the war over, President Truman requested in the name of "the highest national security" that the media consult the War Department before writing about most nuclear matters. Even the nicknames of the two bombs dropped on Japan, "Little Boy" and "Fat Man," remained classified information.

But why hide the effects of the atomic bomb? Why suppress images of the ultimate American victory? Because although it could never be publicly acknowledged, when Paul Tibbets dropped his bomb America's culture of victory was suddenly fused to an incipient culture of defeat. And the evidence was there on the ground in Hiroshima. To see what happened to tens of thousands of people in that single instant was to experience not the glories of immediate triumph but the horrors of possible future loss.

Not to look, however, provided only partial protection. Even with just the carefully crafted information on Hiroshima released by the government the day of the bombing, many Americans quickly grasped the implications of the new weapon. What could not be seen was transmuted into a riot of imaginings about ever more terrifying finalities. Long before the possibility existed for any nation but the United States to launch devastating atomic attacks, Americans began to imagine themselves, their cities, their nation, the world, obliterated.

These first fantasies about a post-Hiroshima world had all the trappings of "reality," even if the reality was one whose time had not yet come. In these scenarios, which could be found in newspapers, magazines, radio shows, and private imaginations, millions of people in America and tens of millions elsewhere died horribly in a few days of "battle." In private, in silence, in a world in which most of the time few people were conscious that the bomb was even on their minds, fears and anxieties grew, and a sense of the future narrowed.

Among the hundreds of films that Hollywood would make about World War II in the postwar years, only two would include the most famous B-29 of all time: *The Beginning or the End* (1947), a semi-official explanation of the Hiroshima bombing, vetted by President Truman and his advisers; and *Above and Beyond* (1953), about Tibbets himself. (He was hired as a consultant on the film.)

Each of these films failed to meet the requirements of the genre, and each failed to draw a significant audience eager to see the war end again in such a triumph. Both lacked emotional payoff, partially because neither could put onscreen the moment that was always the end for the enemy and the beginning for us. Hollywood simply could not show the enemy dropping in the tens of thousands. This scene of victory in battle, so essential to the American war film, would have been in this case an unviewable atrocity. To put it onscreen would have meant acknowledging that something new and terrifying had occurred; and yet not

"To see what happened to tens of thousands of people in that single instant was to experience not the glories of immediate triumph but the horrors of possible future loss."

to be able to show the winning weapon at work, destroying people even President Truman had called "beasts," was implicitly a defeat, an admission that Tibbets's flight was, in fact, not the beginning of something triumphantly American and hopeful.

As children, my postwar generation always sensed that this was so. As much as we played at, dreamed about, and imagined ourselves a part of our fathers' story of wartime triumph, as much as that story enveloped us in movies, on TV, and in comic books, we knew that the culture of victory was not really ours. We felt instead a secret culture of despair growing all around us, and in the postwar division of spoils, we came to understand that it was *that* culture—horrifyingly and thrillingly—that was ours. Much, in fact, that was then dark and frightening was experienced first by the young. When we flocked to the movies, we could see with a certain pleasurable clarity the dark shape of things to come. Even if John Wayne would never pilot the *Enola Gay* into battle heaven, that plane, along with its weapon and crew, mutated into spaceships, horrifying rays, and radioactive monsters, migrating from the war film that couldn't be made into the horror and science-fiction movies being made just for us. In those films, monstrous beings and alien creatures did to our cities and towns what we had done to Hiroshima and Nagasaki, and crowds of Americans onscreen screamed and fled and were crushed or mangled, burned or consumed.

> *"...the United States was a victorious society that lacked a defeat to make tangible its deepest despairs and anxieties."*

For those who fought or lived through the war, what it was like to be born into a secret culture of despair amid vistas of wealth and seeming promise, in a world filled with stories of victorious fathers, was too unsettling to grasp. For their children, who would huddle under their desks with sirens howling, hands over heads, while adults warned them that soon their eyes might pop out and their ears burst, living with triumphalist despair was normal.

Most of the wartime generation never came to grips with either the final acts of the Pacific war or the postwar view from under those desks. Their children, however, imagining ashes where there were burgeoning suburbs, would try to find thrills and excitement in a developing underground culture of defeat, while at night, in their dreams, the mushroom cloud rose again and again.

For more than two decades, the United States was a victorious society that lacked a defeat to make tangible its deepest despairs and anxieties. When that defeat finally came, in Vietnam, it provided a kind of confusing relief, for it gave Americans a chance to release long-suppressed doubts and fears. The defeat, though, was blamed on the generation that grew up under those desks. The young, in a collapsing army in Vietnam or protesting at home, "blowing their minds" with drugs or fleeing the city for "the land" as though the bomb had already fallen, were seen (and sometimes defiantly saw themselves) as the losers, the betrayers of an American dream.

Although a culture of defeat came into existence when the *Enola Gay* was a few miles from Hiroshima, it had taken almost three decades to work its way through American society and take a form that might be confronted. The frantic patriotism of the Reagan and Bush years that followed was only another attempt to push that culture from view. The Gulf War, in particular, was intended to banish once and for all the "syndrome" of defeatism that Vietnam had come to represent. But though the war washed over the public in a flood of blood-pumping, all-channel TV coverage, it left almost no cultural residue. The most successful American military venture since the landing at Inchon, Korea, some forty years earlier did not produce a single movie or toy fighting figure, comic book or TV series.

In such a world, the Smithsonian's *Enola Gay* exhibition, even in collapse, should be seen as a salutary, if not a healing, event, one for which we can thank the museum curators and historians involved. For it addressed a moment that Americans could still hardly bear to consider, and exposed the slow-motion collapse of the traditional narrative that had been going on for fifty years.

If, as in a science-fiction fantasy, we could create a personalized virtual-reality museum on the capital's Mall, then both stories might be able to inhabit the same moment in 1945 without contradiction. Paul Tibbets could have his show: his plane, polished to a fine shine; his crew, honored for their task; his war, successfully concluded due to his mission. The bomb would once more fall toward a distant bridge, the victory cloud would once again rise, and the *Enola Gay* would fly away into history and into glory.

But that cloud, concealing events below, sooner or later enveloped us all—soldiers and civilians, parents and children. Those, like Tibbets, still dreaming of a victory culture in the mid-1990s found themselves in confused and angry mourning over the fact that their children and grandchildren were incapable of telling that victory story, and that they could no longer tell it with conviction themselves.

Among Tibbets's generation there has been an increasingly strong urge to scream about the desecration of that story. Many feel that historians now tell no tale about them in which they recognize themselves or their country. Even those now in power, who want to return the country and its history to an imagined state of grace, find themselves in a strangely oppositional stance. They challenge, often with hysterical vitriol, any tale told, any exhibit mounted, any standards suggested that do not strike them as familiar. But they themselves are unable to tell the tale, mount the exhibit, write the textbook. They know that they are incapable of creating a story that might take Americans successfully from the victory cloud to the present moment. Their *Enola Gay* show must always stop at 8:15 A.M. on August 6, 1945, because they cannot pilot that plane into the postwar world.

This is what it is like for the generation of victors (and their putative successors) to find themselves living in a culture of

defeat. Even the postwar body of thought meant to suppress literal defeat—the endless varieties of deterrence theory that came
with a two-superpower world—has been relegated to the junk
heap. Yet the weapons, in all their theoretical uselessness, remain
no less horrifying and dangerous. Little wonder that some from
the aging generation of victors have the urge to lash out rather
than reflect. For them, each familiar tale now seems to exist only
as an isolated pool of embattled memory, hardly extending
beyond personal experience. Each tale can be challenged, amend-
ed, dismantled, but not placed back in a narrative stream.

It is not surprising, then, that defeat in the *Enola Gay* controversy was first implicitly acknowledged not by museum officials
but by the plane's pilot. In a June 1994 press conference, Tibbets
proposed what would become, after the Vietnam Wall, the second memorial to defeat in the nation's capital. Instead of the
"package of insults" the Smithsonian was planning, he urged the
museum to display the *Enola Gay* the way it "displays any other
airplane. Look at Lindbergh's airplane. There it sits, or hangs, all
by itself in all its glory. 'Here is the first airplane to fly the
Atlantic.' Okay. 'This airplane was the first one to drop an atomic bomb.' You don't need any other explanation. And I think it
should be displayed alone."

On January 30, 1995, Smithsonian secretary I. Michael
Heyman concurred, announcing the cancellation of the planned
exhibit. "We made," said Heyman, "a basic error in attempting
to couple a historical treatment of the use of atomic weapons
with the fiftieth anniversary commemoration of the end of the
war." Opening instead in June 1995 was a minimalist show
somewhat like the one Tibbets had suggested. Along with the
Enola Gay's impressive fuselage, other bits and pieces of the dis-
assembled plane—engines, a vertical stabilizer, an aileron, pro-
pellers, radar antennae—were scattered throughout the empty
space that was to have been occupied by "Crossroads." It was a
technician's exhibit. Two of the four rooms were filled with
upbeat accounts of the plane's restoration and restorers
("They're saving it...for your grandchildren and...that's why
they have the smile on their face when they come to work"); a
video of surviving crew members giving testimony was repeated
twice ("...a great group of patriotic men...we succeeded in bringing that carnage to an end and everybody got to go home"); and
copious statistics were offered about B-29s. The horror story of
what had happened under the mushroom cloud had disappeared
entirely from these dull rooms, but the old tale of triumph in the
Pacific was almost as hard to find.

In the end, in a year of confusion rather than celebration, there
was no story Americans could agree upon that would cross that
crucial divide of August 6, 1945. We could only strip away all stories, leaving little more than the gleaming plane itself, open to
whatever story a visitor might bring to it. In front of it, you could
weep for almost any kind of loss. You could move close to that

highly polished metal, look into it, and, if you were a veteran of the war, perhaps see those young airmen smiling, and you might weep for them and their now inexpressible story. Or perhaps you would see the scarred face of one of the children of Hiroshima and weep for a very different kind of loss; or see a child crouched hands over head under a desk and weep for the ludicrousness of it all. Or perhaps what you would see would not coalesce into an image at all, and you would know that, in the end, there is no way, not in Washington, not in Hiroshima, to adequately memorialize the nuclear age, or to capture in any exhibit anywhere that moment in August 1945 when it all began. Perhaps, finally, you would weep for all the lost selves of the nuclear age, and even for a nation that made the very weapon with which it was defeated in a moment of triumph, more perhaps than any nation could bear.

History Lesson[4]

Lynne Cheney wasn't gone long. The head of the National Endowment for the Humanities under Ronald Reagan and George Bush has jumped back into the news with her attacks on the National Standards for History, a guide for elementary and high school teachers. Ironically, though, her mode of return may have its benefits, for it shows how a false story, with the help of the right-wing media, can enjoy a fine run in the public forum.

The National Standards make for an unlikely victim. To begin with, they were financed by the Bush administration and were well underway by the time Cheney left the endowment. Moreover, they were put together not by some leftist coven, but by teachers, administrators, scholars and parents—along with organizations ranging from the American Association of School Librarians to the National Education Association. The standards express a consensus that the teaching of history, long in neglect, should be the centerpiece of the social studies curriculum. This should include coverage of the experiences of ordinary people as well as elites, and treatment of nations and cultures throughout the world.

So what's the problem? In her first attack, launched in a *Wall Street Journal* op-ed on October 20, a week before the American History Standards were released, Cheney said the issue was simple: not enough white men. Harriet Tubman, the African American who led slaves to freedom before the Civil War, was "mentioned six times," while George Washington "makes only a fleeting appearance," and Thomas Edison gets ignored altogether.

A few days after Cheney's article appeared, Rush Limbaugh had it on the air. Limbaugh yelled that the standards were the work of a secret group and should be "flushed down the toilet."

Thereafter, more respectable journalists began picking up the story. *The New York Times* ran an Associated Press article on October 26, the day the standards were officially released. (Headline: "Plan to Teach U.S. History Is Said to Slight White Males.") The story did not describe the standards or give examples. Instead, it reported on Cheney's laments: "They make it sound as if everything in America is wrong and grim."

Two days later *The Washington Times* weighed in with an article complaining that the project took "$2.2 million of taxpayers' money." On October 28 *USA Today* columnist Joe Urschel wrote that the commission's purpose was "to mislead and bully elementary and high school instructors." A *Washington Post* story devoted seven paragraphs to Cheney's criticism.

On November 4 Charles Krauthammer published an essay in

---

[4] Article by John Wiener, professor of history at the University of California, Irvine, CA, from *The New Republic* 212:9-11 Ja 2 '95. Copyright © 1995 *The New Republic*. Reprinted with permission.

the *Post* titled "History Hijacked"; it cited Cheney on Tubman and Edison. *U.S. News & World Report, Time* and *Newsweek* also participated. *Newsweek* even offered some original reporting—its article concluded with a quote from a black teacher backing the standards. Black children, the teacher said, have been "brainwashed" to "celebrate white heroes...and values," and "what needs to happen now is a reverse brainwashing." The statement did little to undermine Cheney's critique.

On November 8 *The Wall Street Journal* editorial pages ran letters under the headline, "THE HISTORY THIEVES." The first of these declared that national standards were "developed in the councils of the Bolshevik and Nazi Parties, and successfully deployed on the youth of the Third Reich and the Soviet Empire." Soon thereafter, *The New York Times* op-ed page featured an article by John Patrick Diggins of the CUNY Graduate Center, the only historian to write in support of Cheney. Nothing in his essay indicated he had read the standards. "At a time when people from all over the world are flocking to America," Diggins wrote, "students are told that they must study precisely that from which people are fleeing?" Don't study the rest of the world, he was arguing—a position more extreme than Cheney's.

"Nothing in his essay indicated he had read the standards."

On November 11 *The Wall Street Journal* broadened its attack by going after the World History Standards. It quoted Albert Shanker, president of the American Federation of Teachers, who had been swept up in the Cheney critique. "It's a travesty," Shanker said of the standards. It's "leftist point-of-view history. Everything that...has to do with white people is evil and oppressive, while Genghis Khan is a nice, sweet guy just bringing his culture to other places."

That day—three weeks after Cheney's initial broadside—a national news story reporting on the actual contents of the standards finally appeared. The article, page 1 of *The New York Times*, noted that the standards "keep William the Conqueror...but also give emphasis to non-European hallmarks like China's powerful Song dynasty." The guidelines, the paper added, "ask students to go beyond rote memorization and explain, analyze and explore historical movements around the world."

Even a cursory look at the standards suggests the assault by Cheney and Co. was flawed. When I purchased a copy at the National Center for History in the Schools, located a few blocks from UCLA, I met project co-director Gary Nash, a UCLA history professor. I asked him whether white men had been neglected. "The fact is there are white males on every page of this document," he replied. Sure enough, there they are. Flip to page 76: for the revolution of 1776, "Analyze the character and roles of the military, political and diplomatic leaders who helped forge the American victory." If you don't discuss George Washington, you flunk. Page 138: for the period 1870-1900, "How did inventions change the way people lived and worked? Who were the great inventors of the period?" If you don't discuss Edison, you're in trouble.

What about Cheney's claim that "not a single one of the thirty-one standards mentions the Constitution"? Well, page 84 says students should be able to "analyze the fundamental ideas behind the distribution of powers and the system of checks and balances established by the Constitution." And, it turns out that the person mentioned most often is not Tubman, but Richard Nixon. Ronald Reagan comes in second.

Cheney complained about the preferential treatment of women and minorities, but it's hard to see why. High school students should be able to explain "the arguments for and against affirmative action" and "for and against ratification of the Equal Rights Amendment." They should be able to evaluate "the Warren Court's reasoning in *Brown v. Board of Education.*" Politics is treated in a similarly unbiased and resolutely middle-of-the-road way: students should be able to "demonstrate understanding of the origins and domestic consequences of the cold war" and to analyze "the Kennedy, Johnson and Nixon administrations' Vietnam policy."

Shanker's anger that the standards portray Genghis Khan as a softie also runs into problems when compared with the text. The two pages on the Mongol empire say students should be able to "describe the destructive Mongol conquests of 1206-79 and assess their effects on peoples of China, Southeast Asia, Russia and Southwest Asia"; in grades seven and eight, students are asked to examine Genghis Khan's statement, "Man's highest joy is in victory: to conquer one's enemies, to pursue them, to deprive them of their possessions, to make their beloved weep."

Cheney made a particularly big deal out of one of the suggested high school teaching exercises on the rise of big business: "Conduct a trial of John D. Rockefeller on the following charge: 'The plaintiff had knowingly and willfully participated in unethical and amoral business practices designed to undermine traditions of a fair and open competition for personal and private aggrandizement in direct violation of the common welfare.'" She thought this was outrageous, but it is one of the older chestnuts of American history teaching. Those who went to college in the '50s and '60s may remember *John D. Rockefeller, Robber Baron or Industrial Statesman?* published in the Heath Problems in American Civilization series, which presented the pros and cons of the industrial era, and on which countless papers and exams were based.

What comes next? Although the standards project began during the Bush years, the Clinton administration adopted it as part of its "Goals 2000" program of educational reforms. The standards are supposed to be submitted for certification by a bipartisan National Education Standards and Improvement Council, whose yet unnamed members are to be nominated by the president and confirmed by Congress. Certification would encourage textbook publishers and school systems to adopt the standards. But they would remain voluntary.

The battle likely will rage beyond the standards and the people appointed to approve them. Indeed, the flap could grow into a Republican effort to scrap the NEH. Don't be surprised if the halls of Congress, newly populated by a GOP majority, resound with denunciations of the endowment. And don't be surprised if the Clinton administration fails to put up much of a fight. Undersecretary of Education Marshall S. Smith told the *Post* that the president "had nothing to do with those folks" who drafted the standards. That doesn't sound good.

What Johnny Still Won't Know About History[5]

To the accompaniment of a fair amount of ballyhoo, the National Standards Project released in April a revised version of its National History Standards, thus signaling the start of Round Two in a fight over whether and how our American and Western heritages ought to be taught in our schools.

The original project, it may be recalled, had been mandated in the early 90's under President George Bush, in the hope of reversing our children's scandalous slide toward historical illiteracy. Lynne Cheney, then the head of the National Endowment for the Humanities, assigned the task to UCLA's National Center for History in Schools, under the direction of Gary Nash and Charlotte Crabtree. But no sooner did the two volumes of Standards appear, comprising outlines respectively of world history and American history, and accompanied by some 2,600 sample lessons, than a long list of critics including Cheney herself (by then no longer in office) denounced them as a brazen exercise in political correctness.

The Standards provoked scores of op-eds and letters, and a 99-1 vote in the U.S. Senate condemning them as anti-American. The World Standards, the critics argued, had given short shrift to Western civilization, accentuating its darker chapters while ignoring its achievements. The U.S. Standards, they said, set aside the traditional political narrative of American history in favor of tendentious assaults on our heritage—a heritage not of liberty and prosperity but, allegedly, of racism, sexism, environmental destruction, and foreign adventurism.

My own contribution to the debate was an essay in these pages ("Whose History? Whose Standards?" May 1995), concluding that whereas some of the attacks were generalizations based on a few damning examples, the critics were on target regarding the Standards' pedagogical agenda. The world-history lessons, to begin with, did repeatedly hold Europeans up for censure, while granting a moral pass to other cultures (even those of Genghis Khan and the Aztecs). The rise of totalitarianism went unexplained, and Communist holocausts unmentioned. Nothing in the voluminous outline would have helped students to understand why science, industrialization, and ideas of liberty and human rights (not to mention socialism and feminism) emerged in the West, and not elsewhere. The distinction drawn between "Core" and "Related" standards was unfathomable. Above all, the lesson plans, lauded as "treasures" by the *New York Times*, were often tendentious (underscoring, for instance, the oppres-

---

[5] Article by Walter A. McDougall, Pulitzer Prize-winning historian at the University of Pennsylvania and co-director of the Foreign Policy Research Institute's project on the teaching of history, from *Commentary* 102:32-6 Jl '96. Reprinted with permission. All rights reserved.

sion of women in all times and places), repetitive, way above the heads of students, or just weird.

The U.S. Standards, I concluded, were at least explicit in their bias. The authors invited students to conclude that the American Revolution had left an unfulfilled "agenda" that defined the rest of American history. Hence, the reforms of the Jacksonian, Civil War, Progressive, New Deal, and Great Society eras were uniformly to be extolled (except insofar as they did not go far enough); the cold-war era was defined by unconscionably dangerous "swordplay" between the United States and the Soviet Union; the post-1968 era claimed "precedence" for its "struggle to carry out the environmentalist, feminist, and civil-rights agendas"; and so forth. In foreign policy, the U.S. Standards mocked Woodrow Wilson, all but blamed the United States for the rise of fascism and Pearl Harbor, and repeatedly questioned *Allied* conduct during World War II.

In the face of the criticism leveled at the National History Standards, a nonpartisan body, the Council for Basic Education (CBE), was called in as referee. It concluded that the Standards were indeed flawed, but nevertheless worth saving. The CBE offered a series of stern recommendations: make the Standards voluntary, not mandatory; delete the teaching examples altogether; discourage present-mindedness and moralizing; give more emphasis to science, technology, medicine, and economic and intellectual history; discuss social groups (e.g., women and ethnic minorities) in their true historical contexts, and stress the diversity within as well as among them; make the World Standards reflect a truly global perspective instead of a congeries of regional ones; make the U.S. Standards acknowledge the opportunities, not just the bigotry, that immigrants found in America; and stress the origins and development of American democratic ideals, chief among them the pursuit of *e pluribus unum.*

So the UCLA group, supported now by private foundations—the feds had cut off all funds—went back to work and, lo and behold, completed its revisions in just a matter of months. To anyone aware of the project's elaborate procedures, that in itself should have been grounds for suspicion. What with focus groups, task forces, curriculum committees, advisory boards, forums, councils, and panels, some twenty bodies and over 400 persons had supposedly helped to shape the old standards. How was such rapid "improvement" possible? Were the critiques so compelling that the scales miraculously fell from the eyes of Nash and Crabtree, causing them to see the substance and purpose of history in an entirely new light? Had the 400-odd experts been merely sloppy the first time around, and therefore pleased to have their grand project rewritten? Or were, perhaps, the masters of the project simply bending with the political breeze, having purposely staked out a far-leftist bargaining position in the original Standards so that a merely leftist revision might win approval?

Whatever the authors' private motives, it is a fact that few of the pugilists who leapt into the melee over the original Standards have seemed eager to answer the bell for Round Two. In fact, two of the original critics, Diane Ravitch and Arthur M. Schlesinger, Jr., co-signed a long op-ed article in the *Wall Street Journal* (April 3, 1996) calling for the bout to be stopped. The revised Standards, they wrote, meet all the CBE recommendations and are now "rigorous, honest, and as nearly accurate as any group of historians could make them." Hence they hope that

> critics of the original version will declare victory and lay down their rhetorical weapons, as we have done. Any fair-minded reviewer must conclude that everything objectionable in the original documents has been excised.

Not so, replied Lynne Cheney (thereby flunking the Schlesinger/Ravitch litmus test for fair-mindedness). In her own *Wall Street Journal* article (May 2, 1996), Cheney insisted that the revised standards still "take sides" in subtle ways, and opined that we would be better off leaving history curricula up to individual states. The next day Schlesinger weighed in yet again, in the *New York Times*, although he now said he found the whole debate "distracting and irritating." He, too, had been "troubled" by certain tendencies in the original standards, but he also considered the criticism that *others* had leveled at them a "vociferous overreaction," and the Senate's 99-1 condemnation "absurd." In his opinion, the ranks of those against whom the Standards now need to be defended include "militant monoculturalists of the Right."

Whether Schlesinger really believes the UCLA team would have made all the praiseworthy changes it did in the absence of that "vociferous overreaction" is a matter best left to speculation. What is more, those critics whom I recall reading measured the Standards against yardsticks of objectivity, historicity, comprehensiveness, relative emphasis, and simple honesty; they did not demand that some "monoculturalist" agenda of their own dominate the revision. But Schlesinger's was not the last word. In another op-ed in the *Times* (May 16, 1996), the historian John P. Diggins resoundingly retorted that whatever cosmetic changes they had made, the authors of the Standards had still gotten the basic things wrong.

In an attempt to decide where the truth lies, I have scrutinized the revised standards as I did the original ones. But I too grow weary. Consider this my parting right cross.

In the World History Standards, the first big change has been the elimination of the sometimes impossible, often tendentious, and always too numerous study lessons. What is left is a long list of what students should learn, not a guide to how they should go about learning it. The other big change is the elimination of the rubrics dividing the outline into "Core" and "Related" standards. All subjects now are born equal, although it remains obscure how much time a teacher should devote to each one.

These two great subtractions have swept away most of the targets of the critics. But according to some of the high-school teachers who participated in the generation of the original volumes, they have also destroyed most of the utility the Standards had for the classroom. What good does it do for a ninth-grade teacher in Grand Rapids to be told her students should learn about "Japanese government in the Kamakura and early Ashikaga periods," without being given any advice on how to do that? As it happens, the UCLA center is said to be planning to issue a fat book of study lessons, under separate cover from the Standards themselves. If so, does that mean that material judged harshly by the critics may find its way back into play after all? The answer is not hard to guess.

There is also one noticeable thematic change in the revised World Standards: the muting of feminist influence. References properly abound to the position of women in all times and cultures, but they no longer sport the "in-your-face" quality of the original. Thus, in place of the separate sub-standard on women in ancient Greece, there is now one that describes the "social tasks that men and women of different classes performed"; similarly, the sub-standard on the "changing image and status of women in early Christian and Buddhist societies" has been replaced by one describing the importance of "both men and women in monastic life." In other cases, women are distinguished by social class and thus no longer treated as if they were a uniform (and uniformly put-upon) group.

The new World Standards also try harder to compare contemporaneous developments in all parts of the world through sections on "major global trends" which range back to the dawn of civilization. Also on the plus side, Russia receives noticeably fuller treatment, as do science and technology. And perhaps most importantly, the weak 20th-century section has been expanded and divided into two much stronger chapters that stress, as the original Standards did not, the rise of ideologies like fascism and Communism and their "elaborate forms of authoritarian repression."

Unfortunately, however, Communist-inspired holocausts still go unmentioned in the World Standards: Stalin's first Five-Year Plan is said only to have "disrupted and transformed Soviet society." And it should also be noted that the great majority of the Standards covering world history *before* 1900 have been left virtually untouched. Thus, although slavery is now recognized as a universal phenomenon, many other anomalies—like the failure to mention the Aztec practice of human sacrifice—still perdure.

But all in all, the revised World Standards retain a good regional and chronological balance, fill a number of the gaps noted by critics, and downplay the double standards and judgmentalism that pervaded the original. A curriculum based on the World Standards would still be extremely ambitious for teachers, not to mention pupils, but they do comprise a learned outline of history.

The revised U.S. Standards are more problematical. They, too, exclude the old, obnoxious study lessons—so, for instance, the pejorative treatment of John D. Rockefeller and "big business" is gone, and the suggestion that Ronald Reagan was a "cheerleader for selfishness" has likewise disappeared down the memory hole.

As in the new World Standards, the authors have also watered down the language that made the struggle by minorities and women against a white patriarchy seem to be the central theme of American history. Thus, where one passage used to say that the postwar era took on "deeper meaning when connected to civil-rights and feminist movements," it now reads, "when connected to politics." And in place of a reference to the founding of the National Organization for Women, the Standards now "explore the range of women's organizations" and "the issues currently dividing women." In similar fashion, the authors have replaced their description of the cold war as morally neutral "swordplay" with passages that acknowledge Soviet espionage and Communist ideology, and that grant the successes of containment. An entirely new sub-standard focuses on U.S. relations with Israel.

"The revised U.S. Standards are more problematical."

Nevertheless, the original "agenda" of the Standards is unchanged. Although "individualism" now gets an occasional nod, the larger context is always the struggle for group identity and equality on the part of women, racial minorities, and "gays." (It is as if the authors were trying to appease Newt Gingrich *and* his lesbian sister.) So readers who leap to the very end of the story in hopes of catching its drift will be pleased (or piqued) to read of "the continuing struggle for *e pluribus unum* amid debates over national vs. group identity, group rights vs. individual rights, multiculturalism [vs. what?], and bilingual education [vs. what?]." Not only does that awkward formulation put poor *unum* at rather a disadvantage, it concludes a section which has asked students to assess the plight, assertions, grievances, and civil rights of immigrants, the disabled, racial and ethnic minorities, and the gay-liberation movement, all of whom, we are told, base their demands on "recurring reference to the nation's charter documents" and "invocation of democratic ideals."

The philosophical passages that introduce the U.S. Standards have also been altered, but the results are decidedly mixed. For instance, two long paragraphs now elaborate on the notion of historical causation, but the example chosen to illustrate this theme—the "devastating demographic effects" and "enslavement of indigenous people" caused by the European discovery of America—is only too predictable in its spin. One big concession is the elimination of a sentence insisting that history "involves *more than* the passive absorption of facts, dates, names, and places" in favor of a new sentence stating that history *"rests on knowledge of facts, dates, names, places, events, and ideas"* (emphasis added in each case). At the same time, however, the new Standards delete an excellent sentence, which formerly concluded the passage on how to teach value-laden material: "The best approach is to open these issues to analysis grounded in historical evidence and allow a variety of perspectives on the problem to emerge." The Left giveth; the Left taketh away.

On balance, the new U.S. Standards are fairer and more objective than the originals. But do they restore the quest for individual freedom and fulfillment to the center of the American experience, while making due reference to the freedom denied certain citizens in the past? That is a matter of judgment. Lynne Cheney and John P. Diggins are undeniably correct in stressing that the authors still approach their task with an ideological chip on their shoulders and a partisan interpretation of the American experience. But with the removal of the offending study lessons, less now depends on the language of the Standards themselves than on the quality and predisposition of teachers and the textbooks and teaching aids they employ.

Diane Ravitch and Arthur M. Schlesinger, Jr. are also right to prefer these Standards to having none at all. Uniform standards and classroom materials could be a great boon to school districts that lack the funds for new library and textbook purchases, or even a budget for xeroxing. Then, too, national standards indicating what subjects ought to be taught, and when, can ensure against teachers sticking only to what they like or know, or against students being taught the same material two or three years in a row (it happens). Finally, and perhaps ironically, uniform standards that pay as much attention as these do to "marginalized" people in American history may provide a good argument for eliminating the tiresome, wasteful Black History and Women's History Months that currently interrupt each year's curriculum.

Lynne Cheney now regrets the part she played in supporting the idea of national standards. But thanks to her project, the educational establishment tipped its hand, and that is no small thing. Parents now *know* what most of the people who teach their children, write the textbooks, and control the National Education Association think of American history and values. The angry generation may continue to preside over our classrooms, but, thanks to the controversy over the Standards, the days of its *quiet* conquest may at last be over.

There is also reason to take Schlesinger's and Ravitch's advice that we drop the debate over these Standards altogether. For the fact is that we have far more serious educational issues to tackle. Many of our schools are beginning to resemble "failed states," where all authority has collapsed and violence, drugs, and tru-

"But with the removal of the offending study lessons, less now depends on the language of the Standards themselves than on the quality and predisposition of teachers..."

ancy rule. In one district (Chester, Pennsylvania), schools are so chaotic that a federal investigating team has recommended simply placing them in receivership.

The fundamental problem that inspired the Standards is, moreover, as dire as ever. Most of our young people are plug-ignorant. According to a 1994 national sample of 22,500 fourth, eighth, and twelfth graders, no more than half of white and Asian students, and no more than a fifth of Hispanics and blacks, meet even a minimal level of historical knowledge. That means that most students cannot place the Civil War in the 19th century or name the cold war as the main theme of U.S. foreign policy after 1945.

Under these circumstances, learned debate about which precise adjectives to attach to the Progressive movement is (if the analogy may be permitted) like quibbling in the 1960's over which model of rural development to try out on a Vietnamese village being racked by intimidation, propaganda, and diurnal warfare. Currently we are doing no better—perhaps even worse—at pacifying our own urban schools than we did in the Vietnamese boondocks. I doubt that Schlesinger, Nash, Diggins, or myself, sent into the fray with our own ideal standards and our pockets bulging with federal money, would make so much as a dent.

However important curricula are, they are powerless to improve education in the absence of security, discipline—and, above all, excellent teachers. Maybe one day we shall have a real "Education President" who will roll back the culture of license, coddling, and "self-esteem" and figure out a way to improve our deteriorating, demoralized teaching corps. But the last in particular will take more than presidential fiat. Indeed, perhaps the final irony in this whole sorry story is that nothing in our time has done as much damage to the quality of teaching, especially at the grade-school level, as the loss of all those intelligent women who once upon a time stayed home with their children or took low-paying jobs as teachers, but who now pursue careers in government, business, the universities, and law. Amid all the other blows it has suffered, American education is reeling from the side-effects of the very feminist movement celebrated in the National History Standards.

Culture Wars: The GOP's Version of American History Is "Don't Worry, Be Happy"[6]

America's children are being taught the "propaganda of an anti-Western ideology," warns Republican presidential candidate Patrick Buchanan, "their minds...poisoned against their Judeo-Christian heritage, against America's heroes and American history, against the values of faith, family and country." Buchanan, like so many conservatives, is furious about the recent release of a set of voluntary curricula guidelines for teachers and textbook authors called "National Standards for United States History." Sen. Bob Dole, speaking before the American Legion Convention in Indianapolis last month, called them part of the government's "war on traditional American values." Newt Gingrich said the curricula were "beyond the pale." Republican Sen. Slade Gorton of Washington labeled the standards a "perverse document" and persuaded his colleagues to condemn them by a vote of 99 to 1. Former National Endowment of the Humanities (NEH) chief Lynne Cheney hates the standards so much, she even asked Congress to "kill my old agency, please."

With the Republican presidential race heating up, what Buchanan calls "the war for the soul of America" has started to draw blood. Dole and conservative guru William Bennett have Hollywood and the rap-music industry on the defensive over the unpleasant realities depicted on film and in song lyrics. The House has already voted to zero out the National Endowment for the Arts by 1997, and the House Appropriations Committee wants to cut the NEA's budget next year by 40 percent. With massive cuts planned for America's tiny $620 million culture budget—not even enough to pay for a new B-2 bomber—Congress may very well cut off all federal funding for the arts and humanities. And now the right is trying to wrest control of just what American teenagers should be taught about their nation's history.

The conservatives' real enemy is multiculturalism in all its forms. Gary Nash, the UCLA historian who headed up the standards project, says, "There is tremendous conservative fear because the monopoly has been broken and property in history is being redistributed. What passed in the past as official history was much to the advantage of certain Americans, and now they can't put Humpty Dumpty back together again." Indeed, Gingrich honestly feels that young people should be taught to believe in an

---

6 Article by Eric Alterman, contributing editor and senior fellow at the World Policy Institute, from *Rolling Stone* 45-6 + O 19 '95. Copyright © by Straight Arrow Publishers Company, L.P. 1995. Reprinted with permission. All rights reserved.

America that resembles "the Norman Rockwell paintings of the 1940s and 1950s." Partisans of the '60s counterculture have, according to Bennett, "Marxized, feminized, deconstructed and politicized" America's public culture. Conservatives want their story back. Emboldened by their 1994 election victory, they are aiming their fire at anyone who seeks to tell it differently.

History teachers in public schools found themselves in the crossfire of culture warfare even before the standards came into being. According to People for the American Way, one school board in Lake County, Fla. ruled that its students had to be taught that American values were "superior to other foreign or historic cultures." Another Florida school district faced objections to teaching about the Holocaust. Opponents were concerned that the bill might open the way for tolerance training and, hence, the acceptance of homosexuality.

The attack on the new history curricula has as much to do with the decades-long nationwide right-wing jihad against art and public culture as it does with standards. Cheney consistently manages, when discussing the history standards, to bring up the NEA's funding of "artists who submerge a crucifix in urine and hang out in morgues" as if the two were somehow of a piece. (Artist Andres Serrano, who created *Piss Christ*, received $15,000 in NEA funds as an award from the Southeastern Center for Contemporary Arts; Joel-Peter Witkin, who once received an NEA grant, graphed decapitated bodies in morgues.)

Conservatives have always been suspicious of federal participation in cultural and educational issues. But when the right-wingers had control of the purse strings, they managed to keep their objections pretty quiet. Just three years ago, then chairwoman Cheney said of her NEH co-workers, "No federal agency, to my mind, has so many capable professionals so thoroughly dedicated to the idea of excellence." Bennett, plucked from obscurity by neoconservative godfather Irving Kristol, rose from being a college professor to his current status as a Republican kingmaker after serving as NEH chairman and later as secretary of education. In 1991, following the selection of Kristol's wife, conservative historian Gertrude Himmelfarb, to deliver the prestigious annual Jefferson Lecture at the Library of Congress, conservative pundit George Will called the NEH "the best part of the government."

But when the party in the White House changed, noted art critic Robert Hughes in *Time*, so did the conservatives' party line. Earlier this year, Will warned, "If Republicans merely trim rather than terminate [the NEA and NEH], they...will prove that the Republican 'revolution' is not even serious reform."

While art, literary criticism, gender studies and inquiries into race and class are all under conservative attack, history has emerged as perhaps the most hotly contested ground of all. Partly this is because parents care so deeply about what their children are taught in school. Partly it's because of an explosion in the country's interest in its past. Shows like Ken Burns' *The Civil War* enraptured millions of PBS viewers. Cable now has a history channel. More than 47 million people, according to the National Park Service, visited the nation's historic sites in 1993.

No less important, however, is the idea of "America" that will be taught to the next generation of the country's leaders. Honest but critical history has always bedeviled America's superpatriots. Back in 1913, the famed Columbia University historian Charles A. Beard published his revolutionary work, *An Economic Interpretation of the Constitution.* The *Marion Ohio Star* announced the news with the headline SCAVENGERS, HYENALIKE DESECRATE THE GRAVES OF THE DEAD PATRIOTS WE REVERE. The story informed readers that "if correctly represented" by reviewers, Beard's book was "libelous, vicious and damnable" and that all patriotic citizens "should rise to condemn him and the purveyors of his filthy lies and rotten aspersions."

The problem for conservatives is not so much liberalism; not all historians are liberals. The problem is history itself. Historians believe that America's story is a complex one, fraught with moral ambivalence and ambiguity. Right-wingers fear that a national history that allows for America's failings as well as its successes, that treats an unknown slave with the same respect it accords a general, will—like dirty song lyrics—corrupt the minds of America's youth and undermine the psychological foundations of our society.

Given such stakes, it's no surprise that a major-league controversy should arise almost every time conservative pundits and politicians get a whiff of what their sons and daughters are being taught in the nation's great universities. In recent years tempests have brewed in teapot after historical teapot. When the Smithsonian attempted to display the history of the American West by focusing on the unhappy experience of American Indians and the despoiling of their land and culture, Will accused the institution of portraying the county's westward expansion as "an alloy of only three elements—capitalist rapacity, genocide and ecocide." The quincentennial of Columbus' landing in the New World was similarly marred across the country by angry conservatives' accusations of political correctness, an epithet that seems to apply to any work that does not hew to Gingrich's view that American history should be taught as one long Horatio Alger story. More recently, right-wing attacks forced the Smithsonian to censor a historical exhibition featuring the *Enola Gay*, the plane that dropped the atom bomb on Hiroshima in 1945. The conflict, as the historian Anna K. Nelson told the *Chronicle of Higher Education*, is one between "history and memory."

Despite the confusion engendered by the controversy, the authors of the new history standards insist that their work is in no way intended to substitute for a regular American-history textbook. The curricula do not constitute a new "version" of American history that will hitherto be shoved down students'

"More than 47 million people, according to the National Park Service, visited the nation's historic sites in 1993."

throats regardless of the views or beliefs of any given teacher or school district. Rather, the standards seek to outline the kinds of issues with which students might be expected to grapple at various points in their studies. While the standards do not bear much resemblance to the kind of history that most American adults learned when they were in high school, they do approach a consensus among historians and high school teachers. Columbia University historian Alan Brinkley believes they represent "a very centrist view of American history."

What the standards do reject is the notion that there can be a single patriotically correct view of that history and that the past can be understood through the rote memorization of the names and dates of famous battles and personages. The emphasis instead is on critical thinking, alternative interpretations and the lives of everyday people. The standards ask students to challenge what they read and hear. While some legitimate objections can easily be raised to some of the interpretations implied in the thousands of historical examples offered, in most instances the authors go the extra mile to try to encourage the understanding of all points of view. With regard to the Vietnam War, for example, students are asked to "measure the impact of saturation bombing on North Vietnam and the effect of the invasion of Cambodia on the anti-war movement in the United States." By the same token, they are also asked to consider "the proposition that national security during the Vietnam War necessitated restriction of individual civil liberties and the press. To what extent did voicing public dissent hinder the American war effort?" Jeannie Lang, a 16-year-old high school senior from Scarsdale, N.Y., insists that the teaching of the moral ambiguities of American history makes the story both more interesting and more credible. "Nothing in real life is cut and dried," Jeannie notes, "so to learn history that way makes it seem unreal."

That the history standards have raised the ire of conservatives is almost funny. The curricula were originally planned and funded by conservatives in the Bush administration, directed by none other than Lynne Cheney. The idea for a set of standards for high school students had been brewing for a long time—the mathematicians drew up theirs in 1989—when Cheney's NEH approved the initial $1.75 million grant. Beginning in early 1992, Gary Nash and the National Center for History in the Schools organized thousands of teachers, administrators, scholars and parents, along with groups ranging from the American Association of School Librarians to the National Education Association, to join in the effort. Cheney now accuses Nash and Co. of staging "a kind of intellectual shell game." Earlier drafts, she insisted, emphasized "individual greatness" and "managed a tone of affirmation."

Now a consistent complaint by the standards' critics is that they emphasize "the sad and the bad," skimping on America's white male heroes to glorify a bunch of nobodies simply because

"The emphasis instead is on critical thinking, alternative interpretations and the lives of everyday people."

they were black or female. Cheney found too many mentions of ex-slave Harriet Tubman (six) and not enough of Ulysses S. Grant and Robert E. Lee (one and zero, respectively). When the authors of the standards responded that they were intended to inspire students to think about issues that would naturally call to mind the great white men of American history, and, anyway, you can't judge a book by its index, Cheney and her fellow attackers seemed to switch tactics. When I spoke to her recently, Cheney said that the "most serious" problem with the standards is the way they "scanted science so seriously." Gary Nash now accepts this criticism and promises to rectify it in the next edition.

Ideology, not science, is the heart of the matter, however. The right-wing Family Research Council put together an alternative to the history standards called "Let Freedom Ring: A Basic Outline of American History." The booklet, Cheney says, "is more in the mainstream of what history is" than the historians "version" and can be taken to express the conservatives' idea of how American history should be taught. It covers the history of the Cold War without mentioning President Harry Truman's internal security program, the CIA-directed coups in Guatemala and Iran and the agency's secret war in Laos. The booklet's entire description of the counterculture is as follows: "beatniks to hippies; drug culture; Woodstock." In its VIP section on the era, the FRC mentions conservative heroes like the philosopher Russell Kirk and a famous segregationist, Sen. Strom Thurmond, but manages to exclude Bob Dylan, Abbie Hoffman and Dr. Benjamin Spock. Many of the texts it recommends are, significantly, more than 30 years old.

No one would argue that the content or even the very idea of national standards should not be debated. Both the concept itself and the nature of the guidelines represent a significant departure from the way history has been taught—and is still taught—in many parts of the country. FRC head Gary Bauer makes the thoughtful criticism that the primary problem with the national standards is their existence. "It is dangerous, in our view," Bauer says, "for government or an agency of the government to come up with an official, ideal version of how to teach about the past. Our hope would be that our adversaries would be as nervous about that as we are." He has a point. Eric Rothschild, a high school history teacher who chaired the focus group of the Organization of American Historians that recommended the adaptation of the standards, noted that when the issue was debated, "There were as many people on the left as on the right; they saw [the standards] as a national instrument." Nash replies that this criticism would be more troubling were it not for the fact that the standards take an "explicit anti-official stance—the centerpiece is historical analysis and interpretation."

Just where the standards will go from here is hard to say. Twenty thousand copies have been produced, and Nash says there are plans to present a revised edition. The standards will remain optional for local school boards as part of the Clinton administration's "Goals 2000" program. Yet President Clinton has, surprise, surprise, shown little stomach for the entire controversy. Referring to Nash and Co., Undersecretary of Education Marshall S. Smith insisted that Clinton "had nothing to do with those folks."

The concern about the standards most frequently voiced by those who will be implementing them is not that students will be brainwashed or depressed but that they will be overwhelmed. Hannah Holborn Gray, former president of the University of Chicago, says "If students graduating from college, let alone high school, knew as much and thought as well as the standards prescribe, we could die happy and...confident about the future of Western civilization." Indeed, any student who managed to master all the material in the standards would know more American history than most senators and congressmen.

Here, perhaps, lies the greatest irony of the entire battle: Conservatives are counting up mentions of generals and slaves in voluntary history standards that most students will probably never see. We are currently in the midst of an educational crisis that threatens the very foundations of young people's future. The dropout rate among high school students in big cities like New York is more than 50 percent. Many who do graduate cannot read and write above an elementary-school level. If the right-wingers paid a fraction of the attention to figuring out how to keep kids learning in school that they do to trying to censor what they're taught there, then one day future historians might look back and see a real American revolution in what is now a failing educational system.

IV. Multiculturalism and National Identity

Editor's Introduction

Perhaps what lay at the core of the debate and conflict which surrounds the multi-cultural movement is the fundamental realignment of national identity multicultural-ism can be understood to evoke. Many perceive this to be a potential result of adher-ing to a multicultural agenda. The articles in this section take a step back from the controversy so much a part of the articles in the three previous sections of this com-pilation. In doing so, the writers contained herein assess the United States as whole, and attempt to define the identity crisis which multiculturalism is often considered a symptom of.

In "Kitchens and Rivers," J. Patrick Dobel, declares that the melting pot and the mosaic should be abandoned as metaphors for American identity. In their place should be American cuisine and rivers, according to Dobel. American cuisine, often an entic-ing blend of dishes from other nations, allows for the differences in other foods to "blend in juxtaposition." The result is a unique and satisfying concoction unlike any-thing offered by other countries. In a similar vein, Dobel views massive American rivers, such as the Missouri or the Mississippi, as a "concert of movement" that is the result of many rivers coming into one. The river, like the United States, is ever chang-ing, adopting the characteristics and peculiarities of that which flows into it.

Patrick A. Hall, writing in *America*, points out that the integration of different cultural groups challenged an entire generation of Americans to confess the fears that differences in skin color and language arouse. Such integration, as it was espoused by the civil rights movements of the 1960s, provided African Americans with a wider variety of "social choice" and fostered a sense of similarity between the races. It is this integrationist phi-losophy that Hall believes should come to encapsulate the American identity.

The differences that Hall believes integrationism circumvents are the focus of "Sweet Land of Liberties" by Jerry Adler. In this article, Adler reports that multiculturalism has brought about "the unpleasant discovery of a whole new set of fault lines running through American society." In essence, Adler believes that the American society is so rapidly dividing, a binding center, being a "national character," is difficult, if not impossible to define.

Christopher Clausen, writing in *The American Scholar*, counters Adler's views, not-ing that America is in a "post-cultural" state, being "a strange mixture of freedom and nostalgia." There is no culture, according to Clausen, only a liberty and a lack of those entities, including "family, religion, ethics, manners," which are the traditional mark-ers of a defined culture. Clausen feels that this is owed, in part, to the cultural rela-tivism so inherent to multiculturalism. Yet, according Clausen, it is also the conse-quence of a technology and a television culture which does not adhere to the fixed norms of external reality so necessary for a solid culture.

Kitchens & Rivers[1]

Americans are always trying to figure out who we are. The current battles over multiculturalism and identity politics simply extend that debate. Sometimes this never-ending renegotiation of American identity revolves around metaphors.

Our first such national identity metaphor was *E pluribus unum.* It drew from the poet Virgil's description of a wonderful salad where all the flavors blend into one. In the recent clamors over multiculturalism and identity politics, two metaphors have come to frame the debate: the melting pot and a mosaic. Each is useful but oversimplifies reality and has polarized the discussion. We need new metaphors that better capture the moral and social realities of American life.

The image of the melting pot, popular since the great European immigrations of the last century, suggests that whatever characteristics a given national or ethnic group brings to American life must be reduced by heat and melded into one gooey, indistinguishable mass society. We become a national stew where nothing remains of the original individual ingredients, and where distinct cultural identities are obliterated. Yet the metaphor nicely captures the dynamism of American life arising from the interactions of social and economic change. It hints at the passionate forces that simmer beneath everyday life, and it reminds us that born identities need not be forever: that we can come to share a new common destiny by virtue of physical proximity and a common environmental, economic, and political future.

America as mosaic has emerged as the preferred metaphor to *the melting pot,* especially for today's multiculturalists, identity politicians, and some communitarians. Its proponents argue that individuals come from distinct communities and that their differences deserve respect as constituent elements of the nation. Mosaics can stun with their beauty and their power: their collage of colors and textures yields a majesty greater than the sum of the individual tiles.

The attractiveness of this metaphor cannot conceal its problems, however. Each community or culture subsists in a complex and larger, multi-hued composition, yet each remains a segregated unit, hard and impervious as the proverbial individual tile. Further, glazes seal off each stone from outside influences. Nothing common exists between individual segments except the rigid mortar that maintains their separation.

It is time to jettison *both* metaphors. For starters, I would suggest two others, each of which offers a better balance between the individual and the communal, and better reveals the joy,

---

[1] Article by J. Patrick Dobel, associate dean of the Graduate School of Public Affairs at the University of Washington, from *Commonweal* 124:11-12 F 28 '97. Copyright © 1997 by the Commonweal Foundation. Reprinted with permission.

diversity, chaos, and order of American life. I am thinking of a Great Northwestern Halibut Taco and The Big Muddy River.

The first, in keeping with Virgil's insight, reminds us that the future of American identity lies in its kitchens. Two years ago I had dinner in a New York City restaurant that billed itself as Cuban-Italian-Chinese. The stir-fried rice tasted of Caribbean spices, Italian marinated chicken, and fried sesame oil. The food revealed a marvelous if impure mixture of flavors, identifiably Caribbean, Asian, Mediterranean, and profoundly American. In Seattle, where I now live, the food—we call it cuisine—melds many different cultures. One of my favorite dishes takes Alaskan halibut mingled with Italian garlic, Thai chili, and peanut sauce wrapped in a whole-wheat tortilla with a side order of mixed greens using cilantro and romaine covered with honey Dijon dressing. Thailand, Italy, Mexico, France, Alaska all rolled into one American meal. American cuisine—with its hyphenated experimentation and concoction of enticing new combinations—represents a truer identity metaphor than the melting pot. The new creations I am thinking of offer tastes that are not only distinctive but pleasing because they cohere. Their achievement lies in the fact that their differences *have not been obliterated but blended in juxtaposition*.

Some might call this metaphor a recipe for mongrelization, even the ultimate debasement of distinctive national cultures. But to me the image captures something quintessential about American identity that emerges from the interaction of new tastes, colors, combinations, and textures, never before envisioned.

This also helps explain why the mosaic metaphor fails. That image implies that cultures and communities exist as static, self-contained, impervious units. Beneath this view lies the moral claim that personal identities should be determined by their culture. It enshrines a vision of individuals as embedded in groups, perpetually strangers to outsiders, who are bound only by the forced cement of proximity. In real life, people are *thrown* together. They work, mix, argue, love, fight, talk. And in many American families, love binds and connects despite differences in race, culture, religion, geography, income.

The kitchens of America reflect this reality. In homes across the land, millions of individual chefs experiment, cross boundaries, hybridize, create new dishes, and fashion new identities. An even more durable and noteworthy reality occurs when intrepid souls from various tribes meet, connect, love, form families, and raise children who represent new flavors, new possibilities. Think of it: Puerto Rican-Irish, Finnish-Filipinos, African-Poles, Jewish-Catholics, Mexican-Chinese, Methodist-Hindus. Each one forms new, evolving identities, not bound by molds, that would be unimaginable elsewhere.

My other metaphor has to do with rivers. Growing up in the Midwest, I watched the great Missouri as it flowed near my city.

From high above, it resembled a broad brown expanse, meandering steadily through lush fields and past great cities. Up close, the Missouri is a river of rivers, formed by a concert of movement. It is filled with wide, deep currents of distinct hues, speeds, temperatures. Each time a new stream or tributary enters, the composition of the mainstream alters. Upon entering, some of the larger tributaries remain seemingly intact for hundreds of miles, yet even here the eventuality of change is manifest in subtle differentiations of color, temperature, speed. On the various channels' fluctuating boundaries, water molecules leach into the mainstream, changing its chemistry and altering their own. Some streams disappear quickly into the enveloping larger river; others form roiling eddies before finally joining in. And the river is replenished by rainfall from above, by runoff from fields and highways, and by subterranean springs. Still, it is one, ever changing, ever complex, constantly recasting itself.

Since we Americans lack the foundational bonds of race, blood, religion, geography, and even long-enduring political covenants, we need metaphors to help define ourselves. Our kitchens and rivers provide a key. They embrace the tension between community and individuality while underscoring the energy and openness of life. In them, we better become one.

Footnote from an Integrationist[2]

Twenty years ago I was a high school instructor teaching Yupik Eskimos in northwestern Alaska. I can remember the day I arrived in the village of St. Mary's along with several other teachers. We pulled up to the school on the back of a flatbed truck that had shuttled us from the airfield. All of us were buzzing with enthusiasm for our new jobs, and we found the Yupik people to be kind and giving. Since the school was a boarding school, the environment fostered a close relationship between students and teachers. And because we lived in the dorms, the students saw us as not only as teachers during the daytime, but at night in the role of surrogate parents.

As time passed, I began to look beyond the ephemeral realities of skin color, language and social custom. I discovered that even though I had grown up as a young black man in a U.S. urban environment during the 1950's and 60's, I shared more commonalities with these people than differences.

It has become far too fashionable, in the current climate of multicultural awareness, to stress differences over commonalities. In today's world of ethnic awareness and diversity, no one would be caught dead identifying himself as a card-carrying integrationist, now that the term has been hopelessly distorted by political constituencies on both left and right. The fact is that the idea in its heyday stood for something we as a nation desperately need. Integration meant open dialogue among different groups. It challenged an entire generation of Americans to face and confess the fears that our skin color, language and class associations arouse in one another. In more practical terms, integration meant opportunity for millions of Americans of African descent who previously had very few choices in the way of jobs, housing, education and freedom to go anywhere in this country without running into the ugly specter of segregation.

When I was a child in the 1950's, we often visited our relatives in the South, and I enjoyed the long road trip through the northern and southern states. Since there were 13 children in our family, our trips took on a caravan atmosphere. We would stop to eat and rest along the side of the road or picnic in a park, which I thought was great fun. But even as a child, I noticed that my parents and older siblings were less than enthusiastic about these extended road trips and the roadside picnics. As most blacks over 40 will attest, you couldn't just stop at the Holiday Inn or restaurant; we simply did not have that choice as Negroes. Throughout the South and parts of the North, rest facilities were

---

[2] Article by Patrick A. Hall, coordinator of instructional services at the library of the University of Notre Dame, IN, from *America* 176:16-17 My 10 '97. Copyright © 1997 America Press, Inc. Reprinted with permission.

legally (or illegally) segregated. The civil rights movement and its early integrationist philosophy, therefore, gave many Americans, both black and white, more social choices. This does not mean that we inhabit a world free of racism. We certainly do not; but things have changed radically in my 46 years of life. My seven children can now live in an America that, despite our continuing racial discord, is much freer and offers the liberty that my 86-year-old mother could only dream about in her youth.

Sadly, I am very aware that this message will not play well with members of the present civil rights leadership who betrayed the early integrationist philosophy two decades ago by substituting group entitlements for individual rights. Integrationism in its truest sense was synonymous with liberty, so that as an individual, not a black person or a white person, I have the inalienable rights our Constitution so eloquently describes. This is not to say that as an integrationist I am obligated to associate with whites, blacks, Asians or Native Americans. But it has always implied that I have the freedom to do so if I wish, without hindrance from either individuals or government.

"Integrationism in its truest sense was synonymous with liberty..."

Years ago I remember seeing the Rev. Martin Luther King Jr. on news programs speaking of the need for Americans to find commonalities and not exaggerate differences. As the years have passed, I find myself admiring the simplicity and yet profound challenge of his words. It is far easier to express hate or dislike of a person or group than it is to see how similar we all are. The latter takes effort, and most of us—including black folks—would rather harbor prejudices, because that seems the easier road. In reflecting back on my experiences with the Eskimo people, I realize that it was during the day-to-day routines of living and working together that it became possible for us to begin to see one another fully as human beings. As an integrationist, I believe that as human beings we will always be more similar than different.

Sweet Land of Liberties[3]

Like millions of Mexican-American teenage girls, I still remember where I was when I learned that Selena had been shot. I was on my way to work, and I saw the story in the *Times*, and I said, Gee, never heard of her, and turned the page.

And then I thought: Wait a minute, this happened in America, not Bangladesh! She was the biggest star in tejano music, and I'd never heard of that, either! And after reading a description of it as "a fast-paced mix of accordion, guitars and lyrics...with roots both in the oompah music of European settlers in Texas and in Mexican ballads," I still don't know what the hell it is, except that millions of other Americans were practically throwing themselves out of windows because the queen of it was dead. If it was this big, why hadn't I heard about it on National Public Radio?

"... it remains to be seen whether any society can endure if even a fraction of its people believe that their own government was capable of planting the Oklahoma City bomb."

Perhaps we're just too big, too diverse to hold together. Thomas Jefferson surely would think so, although he probably would have thought so a hundred years ago, too. The great centrifugal engine of American culture turns faster and faster, spinning off fashions, slogans, ideologies, religions, artistic movements, economic theories, therapeutic disciplines, cults and dogmas in fabulous profusion. In America even fringe movements seem to number their adherents in the millions. Everyone's identity is politicized—not just in terms of race, ethnicity, religion and language (as in the nation formerly known as Yugoslavia, say) but also gender, sexual behavior, age, clothing, diet and personal habits. To smoke in public is a political act; to consume as much as a leaf of arugula is to make a potent statement of one's class and outlook.

Is our national identity really threatened by this? A substantial minority of Americans seem to think so, predicting that the United States will cease to exist in recognizable form some time in the next century (*Newsweek* Poll, p. 151). If so, 1995 may turn out to be a turning point—not because of Selena, but owing to the other big news that also broke last spring, that right-wing militias were arming themselves against federal law-enforcement officials. America will survive tejano just as it endured zydeco and klezmer, and it will work its way into the mainstream in the form, most likely, of a jingle for Taco Bell. But it remains to be seen whether any society can endure if even a fraction of its people believe that their own government was capable of planting the Oklahoma City bomb.

Not that fanaticism is a new development in American politics. If someone accused Bill Clinton of personally driving the bomb to Oklahoma, it wouldn't be much worse than what was said about Franklin Roosevelt, Harry Truman, Lyndon Johnson, Richard Nixon—or George Washington. Our standard for civic comity remains the placid 1950s, the decade most commonly cited by Americans, especially white Americans, as a time when "people in this country felt they had more in common...than Americans do today" (poll, p. 151). But the three-and-a-half decades of chaos that followed should have given Americans the idea that upheaval and turmoil is in fact their country's normal condition. Nor was the 1950s as empty of conflict as we like to recall. This year's rebels—Western ranchers who aren't about to let government bureaucrats tell them where their cattle can step—had their counterparts 45 years ago in a Montana draft board that took it upon itself to withhold inductions unless Gen. Douglas MacArthur was given *nuclear weapons* to use against North Korea. Later in the decade, America didn't seem like an especially harmonious place to black children who needed federal troops to protect them on their way to elementary schools in the South. Perhaps unsurprisingly, a plurality of blacks in the *Newsweek* Poll chose the *1960s* as the nation's halcyon era. But both groups—as well as Hispanics—agreed by wide margins that the American "national character" has gotten worse since 20 years ago (poll, p. 151).

Over the centuries, various institutions have held America together against the centrifugal tug of its sheer size and diversity. In successive generations these have been the Protestant religion, the English language, the Constitution, the shared experience of war, the three television networks and Disney World, of which only the last remains a universal, unchallenged touchstone of national identity. The Constitution is still in effect, naturally. But in the May decision striking down term limits a forceful minority on the Supreme Court seemed intent on radically reinterpreting it as a compact among sovereign states rather than the people—an inherently separatist view that has been out of favor at least since the Union won the Civil War.

From the 1950s to the 1970s, the belief in shared prosperity was a powerful, if not exactly inspirational, unifying force in American society. But more recent economic trends have called even that basic tenet of Americanism into question. Housing data analyzed by Paul A. Jargowsky, an economist at the University of Texas at Dallas, show what he calls "a pronounced trend toward increasing economic segregation" since 1970. It was in those years that millions of people left their homes in cities—notorious for letting poor people poach on the same census tracts as rich ones—for suburban developments whose walls and gates enclose a population self-selected for income compatibility. Many people, although not economists, were shocked to discover a few months ago that the United States now has the *least* equitable income distribution among all developed countries, including those, like England, with a hereditary aristocracy.

As common purpose and shared interests have declined, national unity has increasingly become a matter of symbols. We have symbolic enemies—Japanese auto manufacturers, invoked by President Clinton to represent the global economic forces behind the stagnation in real American wages. And symbolic heroes—Scott O'Grady, whose success in hiding in the woods for six days stood in for the war we didn't fight against Serbian genocide. We even have symbolic symbolism, in the form of a proposed amendment that would unleash the awesome power of the United States Constitution against "desecration" of the American flag, which has been occurring at the epidemic rate of around 10 times a year. This retroactive slap at the 1960s doesn't get at the contemporary problem of emigration by rich Americans (still a trickle, but an increasing one) who decide they'd rather salute the flags of nations with lower income taxes.

Many of the issues that divide Americans are familiar ones. One of the most widely discussed books of 1995 has been "Alien Nation," in which journalist Peter Brimelow sounds the alarm that if present trends in birth and immigration continue, some time in the next century white Americans will be outnumbered by those of black, Hispanic and Asian descent. Brimelow acknowledges that even to raise the subject is to risk condemnation as a racist, but he's willing to take the chance. A naturalized American of English birth, he evidently holds a fairly narrow view of who qualifies as white, leading him to the ludicrous observation that "when you leave Park Avenue and descend into the subway...you find yourself in an underworld that is not just teeming but is also almost entirely colored...where do all these people get off and come to the surface?" Leaving aside the fact that he's wrong (according to the Metropolitan Transportation Authority, whites make up roughly 45 percent of New York's subway riders), it is hard to think of another time in the last 25 years when a white writer would have felt free to make such a dismissive generation about the "colored."

But in fact immigration seems to be making one of its periodic resurgences as a divisive political issue. In part this is driven by economics. Brimelow's book conclusively demonstrates that contrary to myth, not all immigrants win the Nobel Prize after they get here; some drive cabs their whole lives, and quite a few wind up on welfare. Many Americans seem to have figured out the same thing for themselves. By a small but significant margin (52 percent to 40 percent), Americans in the *Newsweek* Poll (poll, p. 151) were more likely to agree that "immigrants are a burden on our country because they take jobs, housing and health care" than with the view that "immigrants strengthen our country because of their hard work and talents." Psychologically, "multiculturalism!" has also changed the terms of the debate, by dropping the presumption that immigrants come here in order to assimilate. The sentimental argument for immigration has been that newcomers "enrich" American society. But how can they do that, if they never even join it? If Selena was so great, why should Mexican-Americans (and, apparently, mostly just those who had settled in southwestern Texas, not the ones in California) have had her all to themselves? Brimelow is not the only one to ask why America should admit almost a million immigrants a year merely for them to re-create self-sufficient national enclaves on our shores.

But this is a variation on an old debate. The 1990s has been marked by the unpleasant discovery of a whole new set of fault lines running through American society, superimposed on the familiar ones of race, religion and ethnicity. Gun control and grazing rights are not important issues, but no one 20 years ago could have predicted that they would become rallying cries for a militant right-wing separatist movement, fueled by the class resentments of the one group that wasn't supposed to have any, white men. Nor did most people expect the relation of intelligence to race to surface suddenly as a divisive issue in American society. Educated people who suspected that whites were smarter than blacks, or vice versa, kept it to themselves; the unspoken consensus was that television was reducing us all to morons at about the same rate anyway.

The common thread here is *class*, another issue that supposedly was put to rest in America two generations ago. The upper class, which no one expected to recover from its betrayal by Franklin Roosevelt, has risen again, but in a different form, consisting of a self-perpetuating elite of managers, professionals and marginal hangers-on such as journalists and artists. Two influential new books—*The Next American Nation* by Michael Lind, and *The Revolt of the Elites* by the late Christopher Lasch—describe this group, which seems to include many of the same people who a decade ago were semi-affectionately known as Yuppies. Lind goes out of his way to make the generally unacknowledged point that Americans have sorted themselves out partly on religious lines. He writes: "If you are Episcopalian or Jewish, have a graduate or professional degree from an expensive university...watch MacNeil/Lehrer on PBS and are saving for a vacation in London or Paris, you are a card-carrying member of the white overclass...If you are Methodist, Baptist or Catholic, have a B.A. from a state university, work in or for a small business or for a career government service, watch the Nashville Network on cable and are saving for a vacation in Las Vegas...you are probably not a member of the white overclass, no matter how much money you make."

The creation of such a class must constitute a significant development. Obviously there have always been subcultures in America, and rich people were more likely to vacation in Europe than poor ones. But until fairly recently most "managers" and "professionals" probably thought of themselves as part of a broad middle class, together with civil servants and the owners of small businesses, with shared aspirations and tastes. Some people smoked and others didn't, but the choice didn't signify anything about one's social status, as it does today; in 1990 people earning between $10,000 and $20,000 were 50 percent more likely to smoke than those making $50,000 or more. In William Manchester's compendious history of mid-20th-century America, "The Glory and The Dream," he reports a 1954 survey that found that the overwhelming choice of most Americans for dinner, cost no object, would be fruit cup, vegetable soup, steak, french fries and apple pie à la mode. What's interesting is not the absence of arugula from this menu, but the very assumption that a meaningful consensus could be arrived at. A comparable exercise today would undoubtedly result in what statisticians call a bipolar distribution, defined by the presence or absence of truffle oil as an ingredient. Conversely, the phrase "à la mode" can stand in for all the other tests by which Lind distinguishes the "white overclass"; it's virtually vanished from their vocabulary.

The larger point Lind and Lasch make is that white wine and aerobics aren't just neutral choices about lifestyles, but essential badges of privilege in contemporary America. And, according to these authors, the widespread suspicion on the part of middle- and working-class white Americans that the overclass condescends to them is absolutely correct. Having arranged society for their own convenience, the privileged class is now busily siphoning off an increasing share of the national wealth. They use it not to advance the general welfare, but to erect ever more barriers between them and the kind of people for whom "oil" brings to mind "Quaker State" rather than "extra-virgin olive." They "have made themselves independent not only of crumbling industrial cities but of public services [schools, transit, hospitals...] in general," Lasch wrote. "In effect, they have removed themselves from common life...Many of them have ceased to think of themselves as Americans in any important sense...Their ties to an international culture of work and leisure...make many of them deeply indifferent to the prospect of American national decline."

This is a pretty serious indictment. Americans of this class are presumably not about to express their disaffection by building bombs (and if they did, they would be more likely to blow up a Kentucky Fried Chicken or a Dairy Queen than a federal office building). But their alienation is in some ways even more dangerous. It's hard to imagine a real scenario in which the "Aryans" of the Northwest actually secede from the Union, but the investors of Wall Street and the screenwriters of Brentwood can secede just by getting on a plane. It would be ironical if America survived civil war, black separatism, white separatism, international terrorism and domestic terrorism only to become the first nation to fall victim to a revolt by its Yuppies.

For that matter, we can't really afford to lose anyone. For the social contract to work, it must bind us all, irrespective of skin color, native language, IQ or the percentage of fat in our diet. The forces of separatism are on the rise in many parts of the world, and it would be naive to think we are beyond their reach. Right now, before setting off for London, Paris or Las Vegas, would be a good time for all Americans to rededicate themselves to the proposition that we are all in this nation together. Or else Selena will have died in vain.

NEWSWEEK POLL

Has the American national character changed in the last 20 years?

Changed for the better

BLACKS	WHITES	HISPANICS
19%	**12%**	**9%**

Changed for the worse

BLACKS	WHITES	HISPANICS
41%	**63%**	**51%**

Stayed the same

BLACKS	WHITES	HISPANICS
34%	**23%**	**32%**

THE NEWSWEEK POLL, JUNE 19–25, 1995

POPULATION BY RACE
IN MILLIONS

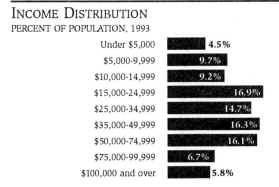

SOURCE: U.S. CENSUS BUREAU

INCOME DISTRIBUTION
PERCENT OF POPULATION, 1993

Under $5,000	4.5%
$5,000-9,999	9.7%
$10,000-14,999	9.2%
$15,000-24,999	16.9%
$25,000-34,999	14.7%
$35,000-49,999	16.3%
$50,000-74,999	16.1%
$75,000-99,999	6.7%
$100,000 and over	5.8%

SOURCE: DEPARTMENT OF COMMERCE

Welcome to Post-Culturalism[4]

Writing recently in the *New Republic* about the Internet, Gary Chapman described its adepts as "the intellectual vanguard for an internationalist, libertarian world-view of global, amoral, stateless capitalism" and contrasted this vision with "the nativist, patriotic 'family values' apparently ascendant in the American middle class." Chapman, director of the 21st Century Project at the University of Texas, believes that the increasing use of computer networks has greatly strengthened the first of these outlooks and weakened the "parochialism" of which the second is a rationalization. Politicians, he maintains, have failed to grasp either the "culture" of the Internet or its implications for the politics they practice.

"The relationship between cultural change and its expression in politics is not always what one would expect."

Apart from pointing out the difficulty of regulating cyberspace, Chapman has little to say about what those implications might be. Readers who are not "digerati" may suspect that, like other enthusiasts, he exaggerates the importance of computers on the way most people think or behave. He has, however, neatly encapsulated two frames of mind (neither quite systematic enough to be called an ideology) that increasingly dominate political and cultural controversy, not only in the United States but in much of the world. On one side are libertarians, free traders, optimistic space travelers through the modern world whose lifeblood is "information" in the various senses of that protean buzzword. On the other are neo-isolationists, nationalists, advocates of restricting trade and immigration, religious believers who demand that the state use its power to enforce traditional prohibitions against illegitimacy, abortion, and many forms of incivility. As has often been pointed out, Muslim fundamentalism offers a counterpart to the latter set of positions in much of the non-Western world.

My concern here is not with political controversy as such but with the unfolding cultural history that it dimly reflects. The relationship between cultural change and its expression in politics (whether electoral or academic) is not always what one would expect. For example, a libertarian, internationalist vision of the world ought in theory to be just what the doctors of diversity and multiculturalism ordered. On the Internet or in a world of permeable borders, different cultures should flourish side by side in relationships unmarked by either dominance or submission. In practice, however, such an environment rapidly breaks down not merely boundaries but cultures themselves. This process began long before computers were invented, and, whether we label it modernity, cultural imperialism, the technological revolution, or

---

4 Article by Christopher Clausen, author of *My Life with President Kennedy,* professor of English at Pennsylvania State University and columnist for *The New Leader,* from *The American Scholar* 65:379-88 Sum '96. Copyright © 1996 Christopher Clausen. Reprinted with permission.

the inexorable logic of capitalism, no culture is immune to it. The result is a United States—and increasingly an entire world—fast approaching a condition that can best be described not as multi-cultural but as post-cultural.

Notice that Chapman referred to the "culture" engendered by the Internet. The word *culture*, when used anthropologically rather than honorifically, refers to the total way of life of a discrete society, its traditions, habits, beliefs, and art—"the systematic body of learned behavior which is transmitted from parents to children," as Margaret Mead summarized it in 1959. For a traditional culture, Ruth Benedict pointed out in her immensely influential *Patterns of Culture* (1934), "outside of the closed group there are no human beings." The culture of Inca Peru or of Anglo-Saxon England varied over time but had certain constant features, including a language, that differentiated it from other cultures in other times or places. A culture is defined by those differences and exclusions. The "culture" of the Internet is another story altogether and requires a different kind of telling. Used metaphorically, *culture* is everywhere these days. The latest edition of *Books in Print* contains three and one-half columns, in minuscule type, of titles such as *The Culture of Addiction, The Culture of Biomedicine, The Culture of Childhood,...of Complaint,...Disbelief,...Protest,...Science,...the University,* and *The Culture of War*. A *New York Times* story last year about a company that makes preppy clothes for a black clientele paraphrases the owner, Charles Walker, Jr., to the effect that Ralph Lauren and Tommy Hilfiger "didn't make clothes that reflected blacks' lifestyles or culture," and adds that Walker's new line of gear "allows the wearer both to dress in preppy style and to express cultural pride." Around the same time, the news from South Africa included a controversy about whether Zulus should be allowed to carry such "cultural weapons" as spears and machetes in political demonstrations. Today the press is full of stories about the "culture" of the Defense Department, the Central Intelligence Agency (John Deutch, the new director, is trying to change it), Congress (Speaker Newt Gingrich is said to have already changed it), and any large corporation that happens to be in the news. *GQ* even describes opera as being characterized by "the culture of booing." Has the word *culture* acquired the same cultural status as a cough?

Yes and no. Clearly, most of the time *culture* is a lazy, trendy substitute for a more specific word. Sometimes the writer really means common attitudes, sometimes fashion, sometimes behavior. The concept of culture carries with it, however, two serious implications in most contemporary usage. First, whatever is cultural is presumed not to be biologically determined, despite the frequent sloppy equation of culture with race. Cultural determinism, together with its corollary cultural relativism, is an entrenched academic dogma in the humanities and social sciences, popularized though not invented by such widely read anthropologists as Mead and Benedict. "By the time [a child] can talk," the latter declared memorably, "he is the little creature of his culture, and by the time he is grown and able to take part in its activities, its habits are his habits, its beliefs his beliefs, its impossibilities his impossibilities."

William Connolly reflected this implication of the world, though with a curiously flexible notion of determinism, when he complained in the *New York Times Book Review* about "the cultural demand for heterosexuality." If heterosexuality is only a "cultural demand," not a matter of biology, its normative status ranks as a mere prejudice and can be changed, as Connolly obviously thinks it ought to be. Culture has become a familiar whipping boy, particularly where sex is involved. "I'm no longer willing to call it an illness, the kind of promiscuity I engaged in between 1960 and 1970," Jeffrey Masson recently told the *Philadelphia Inquirer*. "But it was probably cultural."

On the other hand, "culture" can equally be an excuse, a rhetorical device to place some taste or practice beyond criticism. "The principle of cultural relativism," the eminent anthropologist Alfred Kroeber wrote in 1952, "has long been standard anthropological doctrine. It holds that any cultural phenomenon must be understood and evaluated in terms of the culture of which it forms part." The Zulus of South Africa feel that their "cultural weapons" should be exempt from bans that apply to other weapons; otherwise their culture is being discriminated against. (Some residents of the American West make the same argument about their favorite firearms but get little sympathy from the news media.) *Cultural* is not being used here with the implication that carrying spears, like demanding heterosexuality, is a vestige of less enlightened times and should be discontinued. Quite the opposite. To deprive Zulus of their spears is to attack their culture. And to attack a culture these days will sooner or later inspire a charge of genocide, another growth stock on the lexical market.

Describing something as the product of culture can therefore imply either of two contradictory things about it: that it is not genetically fixed and can (usually should) be changed, or that it exists in an autonomous realm that, because of the doctrine of cultural relativism, is immune to criticism from outside. In contemporary polemics, what the American Indian activist Russell Means castigates as "Eurocentric male culture" is often attacked from the first perspective (as a collection of prejudices to be overcome), while non-Western or minority "culture" is often defended from the second (as a precious inheritance that should be beyond criticism). At the United Nations World Conference on Human Rights in 1993, China, Iraq, and other Asian dictatorships invoked cultural relativism to contend that Western complaints about their human-rights abuses represented a form of imperialism. Forcibly suppressing dissenters, the argument went, may violate European and American norms, but the ancient cultures of the East have the right to follow their own customs. In some versions of this defense by the Chinese and Singaporean governments, the modern police state becomes an expression of traditional Confucian morality. Besides the fact that this whole line of argument depends on Western anthropology for its underpinnings, it grossly libels the very cultures it ostensibly defends by implying that individual rights have no place in them.

The claim that every "culture" and all of its expressions should be equally respected is too sentimental for anyone to follow consistently, though it gets a lot of play in the abstract. Even Kroeber felt that his anthropological colleagues were insufficiently attentive to the possibility of "fixed, pan-human, if not absolute, values." What cultural relativism often means in practice today is that only those aspects of non-European cultures that seem compatible with Western feminism and some notion of human rights are held up as examples of diversity. Few American multiculturalists are enthusiastic about the treatment of women in Saudi Arabia (the fact that they aren't allowed to drive cars led to outrage in the media during the Gulf War), while female circumcision in parts of sub-Saharan Africa has lately illuminated another boundary of cultural relativism in the West. Similar criticisms of traditional practices were made by many speakers at the 1995 United Nations Conference on Women held in China. The multiculturalism festivals held in many American towns and universities are sometimes reduced, like movie travelogues of the 1940s, to celebrating little more than the traditional foods and costumes that Third World peoples haul out on special occasions. Meanwhile the "cultural diversity" practiced in university hiring and admissions has almost nothing to do with culture but offers a justification, in academically familiar language, for affirmative-action categories that are really based on physical characteristics or ancestry.

"The multicultur- alism festivals held in many American towns and universities are sometimes reduced..."

What these contradictory uses of *culture* suggest is that the objects the word used to identify, which were always more fluid and slippery than many anthropologists liked to admit, are now close to moribund. A culture capable of determining its members' thoughts and behavior to the extent that Ruth Benedict, for example, asserts can do so only by keeping them isolated from countervailing influences. Cultures in that isolated sense, however, have been growing rarer for several centuries. When real cultural conflict erupts today, as in Lebanon or the former Yugoslavia, the spectacle is so atavistic and unexpected that the rest of the world is reduced to impotent horror.

The doctrines of cultural relativism and determinism derived from anthropologists' study of tiny, exceptional groups, mostly living on islands in the farther reaches of the Pacific, on Indian reservations in western North America, or in remote parts of Africa. Those cultures were fast losing their distinctness even as they were being studied. The steamship, the telegraph, and the newspaper had already gone a long way toward breaking down cultural separation in most of the world fifty years before the jet plane and nearly a century before the Internet. The result was the first stage of post-culturalism, in which technology begins the long process of displacing custom. The spears of the Zulu can be described as "cultural weapons" precisely because they represent quaint survivals from a vanished way of life. If they could be used effectively as weapons in modern warfare, nobody would call them cultural.

In contrast to the now-fading traditional life of the Zulu, the "culture" of the Internet has none of the characteristics of a real culture. It is not a total way of life; it did not evolve among a distinct people; nobody inherited it or was raised in it; it makes no moral demands and produces no art. The same is true, in slightly different ways, of the "culture" of the CIA, the press, or General Motors. The word has come to be used so loosely because those who use it have no organic relationship to a real inherited culture and no clear conception of what such a relationship would be like. Apart from WASPs and the children of immigrants, hardly any Americans grow up knowing their ancestral languages. Intermarriage has given most Americans multiple ancestral languages. Except on the most superficial level, few Americans inherit traditions that are distinct from the ones that other Americans of different ethnic backgrounds inherit equally. One result is what Michael Ignatieff aptly calls "the narcissism of minor differences." Many black Americans exaggerate and sentimentalize their connections to a homeland across the sea—Kwanza, after all, was invented in Los Angeles—but Italian-Americans and Irish-Americans do exactly the same thing. More significantly, in an era when identity is more fluid and elusive than ever before, everyone at a given level of affluence has access to the products (electronic and otherwise) that now help to define it from moment to moment.

Put in its simplest terms, the ideal of multiculturalism is the laudable one that people from drastically different backgrounds should live together in harmony and respect for each other's cultural heritages. Some multiculturalists go further and equate the sacredness of life with the sacredness of culture. In *Multiculturalism: Examining the Politics of Recognition*, edited by Amy Gutmann (Princeton University Press, 1994), the ecologist Steven Rockefeller expresses this concept at its most grandiose:

> It may be argued that human cultures are themselves like life forms. They are the products of natural evolutionary processes of organic growth. Each, in its own distinct fashion, reveals the way the creative energy of the universe, working through human nature in interaction with a distinct environment, has come to a unique focus. Each has its own place in the larger scheme of things, and each possesses intrinsic value quite apart from whatever value its traditions may have for other cultures.

Problems arise, however, when one examines the assumptions underlying this formulation. First, what is it that one is respecting when one respects the "intrinsic value" of another culture? Something different from one's own inheritance, or an echo of something already familiar? If, like many young people in the 1960s, I find Buddhism admirable because of its emphases on peace and equality, am I embracing something genuinely "other" (a favorite word of multiculturalists) or merely finding confirmation for ideals I already hold? Or is the point of consistent multiculturalism, as Rockefeller implies, to honor those aspects of other cultures that really are "other," such as caste in traditional Hinduism, *Bushido* in pre-1945 Japan?

The deeper question has to do with what features of a culture survive in the kind of society that is described as multicultural. If cultures are like life forms, they must eventually grow old and die, but few advocates of multiculturalism take this possibility into account. On the contrary, the philosopher Susan Wolf describes some of the joys of the new dispensation:

> Every time I go to the library with my children, I am presented with an illustration of how generations past have failed to recognize the degree to which our community is multicultural, and of how the politics of recognition can lead, and indeed is leading, to a kind of social progress. My children tend to gravitate toward the section with folk stories and fairy tales. They love many of the same stories that I loved as a child—Rapunzel, the Frog Prince, the Musicians of Bremen—but their favorites also include tales from Africa, Asia, Eastern Europe, and Latin America that were unavailable to me when I was growing up.... [B]y having these books and by reading them, we come to recognize ourselves as a multicultural community, and so to recognize and respect the members of that community in all our diversity.

It goes without saying that the books Professor Wolf has in mind are all in English, all published in England or North America, all written for an audience of English-speaking children. The "culture" that produced these books for its own purposes is Western. As in the stereotypical economy of imperialism, only the raw materials come from Africa, Asia, or another poor region of the globe—fossil souvenirs, at least in the American context, rather than expressions of profound cultural variation.

In the same book, Charles Taylor discusses a minority culture in North America that is determined to survive in a more robust sense: French Canada. Whether the government of Quebec can be counted as multicultural, however, is open to doubt.

> For instance, Quebec has passed a number of laws in the field of language. One regulates who can send their children to English-language schools (not francophones or

immigrants); another requires that businesses with more than fifty employees be run in French; a third outlaws commercial signage in any language other than French. In other words, restrictions have been placed on Quebeckers by their government, in the name of their collective goal of survival, which in other Canadian communities might easily be disallowed by virtue of the Charter [the Canadian equivalent of the Bill of Rights].

The premise of such legislation is obvious: that without these protections, the French language and the culture it embodies would continue to die out as French-speaking Canadians join the more numerous and prosperous Anglophone civilization on both sides of the forty-ninth parallel. Harmony and mutual respect are seen as a recipe for assimilation; to survive even in its stronghold, French requires exclusivity enforced by law. Whatever one thinks of the Quebec government's policies, this analysis is probably correct.

"E pluribus unum, the motto of the United States, means 'Out of many one...'"

Even these laws to safeguard their language are not enough for many French-Canadians, who seek nothing less than an independent state. When a referendum on Quebec sovereignty narrowly lost in October 1995, the province's premier blamed the result on outside money and the "ethnic vote"—a notorious expression of the xenophobia that is probably inseparable from any vigorous effort to preserve much more of a culture than its food and folk tales.

For all but a tiny proportion of the North American population— Vietnamese or Cuban immigrant families in certain enclaves, religious minorities such as the Old Order Amish or the Lubavitchers, French Canadians in rural districts—the connection with an ancestral culture is now so vestigial that whether to assert or ignore it has become entirely a matter of choice. Taco salad, pizza, stir fry, or a Big Mac? Take your pick. The universal familiarity of these dishes indicates not that many cultures flourish here but that innocuous morsels of each are now part of something else, something which is often called American culture—dynamic, inclusive, a melting pot despite the recent unpopularity of that term—but which is not a culture at all in the traditional sense of the word. If it were, it would exclude more, and at the same time take more for granted. In a living culture neither E. D. Hirsch nor anyone else would write a book called *Cultural Literacy*, which tries to teach people things they would already know if they were part of such an organism.

E pluribus unum, the motto of the United States, means "Out of many one," but the one is a wholly different kind of entity from the many, especially since the melting pot became a microwave. This post-cultural quality of American life was previsioned as long ago as the eighteenth century, when universalism was a widely shared ideal and Enlightenment thinkers dis-

missed any local forces that stood in their way as mere provin-
ciality. If all men are created equal, with certain unalienable
rights, and Congress shall make no law respecting an establishment of religion, and the golden door remains more or less open,
there is not much chance for any culture to preserve its unique
qualities by repelling outside influences. Apart from the survival
(more or less) of the English language, this loss of distinctiveness
applies just as much to the WASP-derived American culture of
the nineteenth century as to more recent immigrant cultures
from outside Europe. In contrast to societies of the pre-industri-
al past, the contemporary United States has neither one big culture nor a number of smaller ones—only a strange mixture of
freedom and nostalgia.

The American political tradition places individual liberty ahead
of nearly every other goal, thereby (among many other benefits)
reducing occasions for intergroup conflict. The libertarian universalism that Gary Chapman describes is one of the permanent
trends in American life and comes closer to realization with
every advance in communications. But the freedom that lies
beyond culture may be a mixed blessing—in some respects a liberty that not even John Stuart Mill could love. The escape from
restraint that the Internet represents derives not from an ideal of
human fulfillment but from the narcissistic experience of one's
own personality, strengthened by its reflection in the computer
screen, as the only significant reality. The major constituents of
real cultures—family, religion, ethics, manners, impersonal criteria for distinguishing between truth and falsehood—have shrunk
almost to the vanishing point as authorities over individual
behavior. This inflation of personality at the expense of external
reality did not begin with the computer age; Christopher Lasch
chronicled its rise in a book entitled, naturally, *The Culture of
Narcissism* (1978). Computers and their sibling, cable television,
have, however, greatly accelerated the process.

One consequence increasingly visible since about 1965 is the
almost total subjectivism of American popular and academic
"culture" today in matters of value. Contrary to the intentions of
the anthropologists who gave it currency, cultural relativism has
evolved to the point where the particular claims of all cultures
are simply ignored. Western monogamy and traditional Muslim
polygamy are morally equal in the eyes of Chapman's "digerati,"
not because their sympathy for other cultures is greater than that
of previous generations, but because virtually all cultural
demands on individual behavior have come to seem equally out-
dated and meaningless. Why marry at all if you think some other
arrangement would suit you better? Nothing is good or true
unless it satisfies me at this moment.

The old liberal distinction between self-regarding and other-
regarding conduct has little significance if one inhabits a world
made up primarily of bytes and images. Like television itself,
which exists only to reach the largest possible audience, such a

world has no fixed norms; like the Internet, it welcomes virtually any content from any source. Every expression, however violent, pornographic, or merely shallow, is equivalent to all other expressions. "The First Amendment," proclaims Michael Eisner, chairman of the Walt Disney Company, "gives you the right to be plastic."

As it continues to evolve, one can only hope that this expanding post-cultural world will become safer for human beings, because the alternatives to it look perilously weak. Family values, as Chapman says, have some salience with Americans today—polls and other evidence suggest that most people regard the breakdown of the family with dismay—but no form of government action is likely to restore that institution's health. The same applies to other imperatives that used to be central in American life, from politeness to patriotism. The problem is not so much competition from other ideals or cultures as the fading away of all normative standards of behavior and achievement, no matter what their source. In the contested suburbs of social ideology, the multiculturalism of the Left and the authoritative community of the Religious Right are both expressions of longing for a past—differently interpreted, of course—that is probably beyond recall. We seem likely to go on traveling in a post-cultural direction for a good while.

"Be not disheartened," Walt Whitman, the prophet of a libertarian America freed from the historic demands of culture, wrote just before the Civil War, "affection shall solve the problems of freedom yet." It would be nice to think so. Meanwhile the age-old problems of freedom have been drastically intensified by the decline of culture. A painfully acute question for the early twenty-first century is whether, once most of the traditional guideposts are gone, individuals who have been freed by technology from everything but their own personalities can rediscover some basis for the harmony and respect that many cultures treasured before anyone dreamed of either computers or multiculturalism.

Bibliography

An asterisk (*) preceding a reference indicates that an excerpt from the work has been reprinted in this compilation.

Books and Pamphlets

Abalos, Daniel T. Strategies of transformation toward a multicultural society. Praeger '96.

Abrahamson, Mark. Urban enclaves: identity and place in America. St. Martin's '96.

Amott, Teresa L. A multicultural economic history of women in the United States. South End Press '96.

Arthur, John and Shapiro, Amy, ed. Campus wars: multiculturalism and the politics of difference. Westview '95.

Banks, James A. and Banks, Cherry A. Handbook of research on multicultural education. Macmillan '95.

Belcove-Shalin, Janet S. New world Hasidim: ethnographic studies of Hasidic Jews in America. State University of New York Press '95.

Bennett, Christine I. Comprehensive multicultural education: theory and practice. Allyn and Bacon '95.

Bernstein, Richard. Dictatorship of virtue: how the battle over multiculturalism is reshaping our schools, our country, and our lives. Vintage '95.

Bowser, Benjamin P. Toward the multicultural university. Praeger '95.

Braaten, David and Moran, Robert. International directory of multicultural resources. Gulf '96.

Brandon, Lee. Celebrating diversity: a multicultural reader. Heath '95.

Brogan, T. V. F. The Princeton handbook of multicultural poetries. Princeton University Press '96.

Campbell, Duane E. Choosing democracy: a practical guide to multicultural education. Merrill '96.

Cenkner, William. The multicultural church: a new landscape in U.S. theologies. Paulist '95.

Christiansen, Paul and Young, Michelle. Yesterday, today, and tomorrow: meeting the challenge of our multicultural America. Caddo Gap '96.

Clegg, Luther B., et al. Celebrating diversity: a multicultural resource. Delmar '95.

DeWitt, Howard A. The fragmented dream: multicultural California. Kendall/Hunt '96.

Diamond, Barbara and Moore, Margaret. Multicultural literacy. Longman '95.

Dinnerstein, Leonard. Natives and strangers: a multicultural history of America. Oxford University Press '96.

Disch, Estelle. Reconstructing gender: a multicultural anthology. Mayfield '96.

Dove, Rita. Multicultural voices: literature from the United States. Scott Foresman '95.

Ellis, Roger. Multicultural theatre: scenes and monologues from new Hispanic, Asian, and African-American plays. Meriwether '96.

Fay, Brian. Contemporary philosophy of social science: a multicultural approach. Blackwell '96.

Fine, Marlene. Building successful multicultural organizations: challenges and opportunities. Quorum '95.

Fullwider, Robert F. Public education in a multicultural society. Cambridge University Press '96.

Fusco, Coco. English is broken here: notes on cultural fusion in America. New '96.

Gay, Kathlyn. I am who I am: speaking out about multicultural identity. F. Watts '95.

Gish, Robert. Beyond bounds: cross-cultural essays on Anglo, American Indian, and Chicano literature. University of New Mexico Press '95.

Gitlin, Todd. The twilight of common dreams: why America is wracked by culture wars. Metropolitan '95.

Gordon, Avery and Newfield, Christopher. Mapping multiculturalism. University of Minnesota Press '96.

Gottlieb, Alan M., et al. Politically correct environment. Merrill '96.

Grant, Carl M., ed. Educating for diversity: an anthology of multicultural voices. Allyn and Bacon '95.

—— and Gomez, Mary. Making schooling multicultural; campus and classroom. Merrill '96.

Green, Michael K. Issues in Native American cultural identity. P. Lang '95.

Harris, Dean A. Multiculturalism from the margins. Bergin & Garvey '95.

Hawley, Willis and Jackson, Anthony. Toward a common destiny: improving race and ethnic relations in America. Jossey-Bass '95.

Henderson, George and Olasiji, Thompson. Migrants, immigrants, and slaves: racial and ethnic groups in America. University Press of America '95.

Hirschberg, Stuart. One world, many cultures. Allyn and Bacon '95.

Hollinger, David A. Postethnic America: beyond multiculturalism. Basic '95.

Hollins, Etta R. Transforming curriculum for a culturally diverse society. L. Erlbaum '96.

Ingoldsby, Bron and Smith, Suzanna. Families in multicultural perspective. Guildford '95.

Joseph, James A. Remaking America: how the benevolent traditions of many cultures are transforming our national life. Jossey-Bass '95.

Julia, Maria C. Multicultural awareness in the health care professions. Allyn and Bacon '96.

Kahn, Joel S. Culture, multiculture, postculture. Sage '95.

Kammen, Michael G. Contested values: democracy and diversity in American culture. St. Martin's '95.

Kenton, Sherron and Valentine, Deborah. Crosstalk: communicating in a multicultural workplace. Prentice Hall '96.

Kesselman, Amy, ed. Women—images and realities: a multicultural anthology. Mayfield '95.

Kingwell, Mark. A civil tongue: justice, dialogue, and the politics of pluralism. Pennsylvania State University '95.

Knippling, Alpana. New immigrant literatures in the United States: a sourcebook to our multicultural literary heritage. Greenwood '96.

Kymlicka, Will. Multicultural citizenship. Oxford University Press '95.

LaBelle, Thomas J. and Ward, Christopher R. Ethnic studies and multiculturalism. State University of New York Press '96.

LaGuardia, Dolores and Guth, Hans. American voices: multicultural literacy and critical thinking. Mayfield '96.

Lee, Courtland C., ed. Counseling for diversity: a guide for school counselors and related professionals. Allyn and Bacon '95.

Lester, James D. Diverse identities: classic multicultural essays. NTC '95.

Lind, Beth. Multicultural children's literature: an annotated bibliography. McFarland '96.

Lind, Michael. The next American nation. Free '95.

Lutzker, Marilyn. Multiculturalism in the college curriculum. Greenwood '95.

Manning, M. Lee and Baruth, Leroy G. Multicultural education of children and adolescents. Allyn and Bacon '96.

McLennan, Gregor. Pluralism. University of Minnesota Press '95.

Michaels, Walter Benn. Our America: nativism, modernism, and pluralism. Duke University Press '95.

Michener, Dorothy. Cresting connections: learning to appreciate diversity. Incentive '95.

Miller, David and Walzer, Michael. Pluralism, justice, and equality. Oxford University Press '95.

Minkoff, Debra C. Organizing for equality: the evolution of women's and racial ethnic organizations in America, 1955–1985. Rutgers University Press '95.

Morris, Libby and Parker, Sammy. Multiculturalism in academe: a source book. Garland '96.

Moser, Edward P. American history revised: politically correct tales of the American experience. Crown '96.

Nagel, Joane. American Indian ethnic renewal: red power and the resurgence of identity and culture. Oxford University Press '96.

Nieto, Sonia. Affirming diversity: the sociopolitical context of multicultural education. Longman '96.

Olesky, Elzbieta. American cultures: assimilation and multiculturalism. International Scholars '95.

Olson, Carol. Reading, thinking, and writing about multicultural literature. Scott Foresman '96.

Parrillo, Vincent N. Diversity in America. Pine Forge '96.

Platvoet, Jan and Toorn, K. Pluralism and identity. Brill '95.

Ponterotto, Joseph G. Handbook of multicultural counseling. Sage '95.

Powell, Richard R., et al. Field experience: strategies for exploring diversity in school. Merrill '96.

Press, Petra. A multicultural portrait of immigration. Benchmark '96.

Rensberger. Susan. A multicultural portrait of the great depression. Benchmark '96.

Richardson, Richard C. and Skinner, Elizabeth. Achieving equality and diversity: universities in a multicultural society. Oryx '96.

Richer, Stephen and Weir, Lorna. Beyond political correctness. University of Toronto Press '95.

Rico, Barbara and Mano, Sandra. American mosaic: multicultural readings in context. Houghton Mifflin '95.

Rogers, Mary F. and Ritzer, George. Multicultural experiences, multicultural theories. McGraw-Hill '96.

Rosenblum, Karen and Travis, Tono-Michelle. The meaning of difference: American constructions of race, sex and gender, social class, and sexual orientation. McGraw-Hill '95.

Royal, Robert. Reinventing the American people: unity and diversity today. Eerdmans '95.

Roy, Donald H. The reuniting of America: eleven multicultural dialogues. Peter Lang '96.

Shusta, Robert M. Multicultural law enforcement: strategies for peacekeeping in a diverse society. Prentice-Hall '95.

Sklar, Morty and Barbato, Joseph. Voices from the heart of the new America. Spirit

That Moves Us '96.

Sleeter, Christine E. Multicultural education as social activism. State University of New York Press '96.

Spickard, Paul N. Japanese Americans. Twayne '96.

Spring, Joel H. The interaction of cultures: multicultural education in the United States. McGraw-Hill '95.

Tayeb, Monir H. The management of a multicultural workforce. John Wiley '96.

Thomas, Gail E. Race and ethnicity in America. Taylor & Francis '95.

Thomas, Rebecca. Connecting cultures: a guide to multicultural literature for children. R. R. Bowker '96.

Timm, Joan, Four perspectives in multicultural education. Wadsworth '96.

Tsongas, Paul. Journey of purpose: reflections on the presidency, multiculturalism, and third parties. Yale University Press '95.

Valdivia, Angharad N. Feminism, multiculturalism, and the media. Sage '95.

Verderber, Kathleen, ed. Voices: a selection of multicultural readings. Wadsworth '95.

Whang, Gail. Literature study circles in a multicultural classroom. Stenhouse '96.

Wiener, Harvey S., ed. Side by side: a multicultural reader. Houghton Mifflin '96.

Zell, Fran. A multicultural portrait of the American revolution. Benchmark '95.

Additional Periodical Articles with Abstracts

For those who wish to read more widely on the subject of multiculturalism, this section contains abstracts of additional articles that bear on the topic. Readers who require a comprehensive list of materials are advised to consult the *Readers' Guide to Periodical Literature, Readers' Guide Abstracts* and *Full Text, Education Abstracts* and *Full Text, Humanities Abstracts* and *Full Text,* and *Social Sciences Abstracts* and *Full Text.*

Sorry, Emma Lazarus. Vincent Carroll. *The American Spectator* 29:50-1 Mr '96

Multiculturalism and affirmative action have fueled the immigration backlash in American public opinion. These policies are based on the argument that a different racial heritage justifies not only preferences in government contracting but also in college admissions and hiring and promotions throughout much of the labor market. Such favoritism poses a question of the starkest self-interest for nonminorities who oppose these trends but who also historically have welcomed generous immigration quotas because of their presumed economic benefit. These people question why they should sustain their enthusiasm for immigration when the overwhelming number of immigration slots are taken by people who will immediately possess a panoply of official and unofficial advantages over their own families.

Quit the Babel-ing. Charles W. Colson. *Christianity Today* 40:72 Ja 8 '96

In the aftermath of the O.J. Simpson trial, the writer likens the situation in America to the biblical story of the Tower of Babel. He explains that the cultural fabric, composed of a shared language and a common culture, appears to be in danger of unraveling. He rejects the postmodern idea that language can only express the culture-bound perspective of the speaker, positing instead that human language can express ultimate truth and that the universal message of salvation is meant to be received and embodied by an endless variety of individuals through their local cultures.

Digging for our roots. Abigail McCarthy. *Commonweal* 123:6-7 Mr 22 '96

The diversity of American society implies a certain strength, but it also raises the question of how common roots might be found. The key lies in the particular treasures of the past and the particular expectations for the future that might be shared by all Americans. Concepts of work and time and combined effort from the past are subtly built into the self; so too is the American sense of space and the possibility of physical mobility. Even angers and discontents have a common source in what Seymour Martin Lipset called the key American values: equality and achievement. These values, however, are threatened in the growing split between rich and poor and by the effects of globalization and the shrinking job market. The solution lies in the values noted by de Tocqueville: Americans must strive for their objectives and not accept their lot.

Surrendering to the multiculturalists. Thomas Sowell. *Forbes* 159:72+ Je 16 '97

We Are All Multiculturalists Now, by Harvard professor Nathan Glazer, will be welcomed by the Left as a defection, if not to the Left's way of thinking, at least away from the views held by its opponents. In the book, Glazer notes that multiculturalism is already present throughout the curriculum in schools and colleges across America. Nonetheless, it is surprising that he goes beyond this assessment to offer apologies for multicultural deception. Moreover, Glazer asserts that the United States' racial problems are caused by Americans' basic refusal to accept blacks, citing low rates of intermarriage in support of his argument.

Pride and prejudice. Brian Bergman. *Maclean's* 107:32 + N 7 '94

Part of a special section on immigration in Canada. Montreal-based novelist Neil Bissoondath has stirred a debate with his recently published polemic *Selling Illusions: The Cult of Multiculturalism in Canada*. Bissoondath, who grew up in an East Indian family in Trinidad, dismisses the federal multiculturalism policy as a cynical "instrument to attract ethnic votes" that encourages immigrants to believe that where they came from is more important than where they have settled. He further contends that the nation's liberal elites ignore popular expressions of discontent with multiculturalism. Bissoondath's critics protest that he is being unduly alarmist.

After Reaganism. John O'Sullivan. *National Review* 49:56-62 + Ap 21 '97

Although the Left should be more confused than the Right by the ideological flux of the post-cold war world, the former is moving more rapidly to reinterpret the ground rules of the new political game. Throughout the advanced world, politics now consists largely of a liberal New Class trying to broaden its control of society by regulation and law while freeing itself from democratic accountability by shifting decisions from elected bodies to bureaucratic or judicial ones shaped by its values. There has, however, been no sustained critical response by American conservatism, politicians, or intellectuals to this challenge. Conservatism under Ronald Reagan, the use of multiculturalism by liberals to impose their values, and the reasons for the conservative failure to respond are discussed.

America's identity crisis. John O'Sullivan. *National Review* 46:36-8 + N 21 '94

Conservative supporters of immigration are wrong to maintain that America is an idea rather than a nation. This view holds that there is no common American culture or American ethnicity to unite the country's citizens, that they are instead bound by an allegiance to a set of liberal political principles embodied in the Constitution. If this is true—if America is no more than an ideological experiment—then Americans will eventually wage wars over the meanings and applications of the very ideas that supposedly define them. In fact, America does have a national identity. It is a nation that stands as the universalization of the British culture from which it derived. Despite the use of phrases like "nation of immigrants," it has always been important for new arrivals to assimilate to a WASP norm. High immigration and the multiculturalism that it feeds threaten to dissolve bonds of common nationhood and shared destiny and bring about a Balkanized America.

Country time. Clynn Custred. *National Review* 49:39-40 Je 16 '97

Part of a special section on immigration and American politics. Immigration, particularly at high levels, has a tendency to disrupt the cultural consensus, rendering the political process less effective and destabilizing the social order. High immigration fosters ethnic enclaves where immigrants retain their original language and culture. This trend provides ethnic pressure groups with seemingly reasonable grounds for bilingual arrangements in schools, voting, and the workplace. Ordinary Americans initially consider these arrangements as temporary concessions to immigrants adjusting to American life, realizing only late in the day that they are the permanent rules of a balkanized society. Moreover, the elites in business, government, and education either accede to or actively promote this balkanization.

The empty creche. Richard John Neuhaus. *National Review* 48:29-31 D 31 '96

Multiculturalists have tried to strip Christmas of its meaning. The greatest virtue in civic religion is to cause no offense, and, so not to offend, anything in public must include all the public. So the knowledge-class prelates of the civic religion have banned any generalizations that might suggest that there is an American Christian culture and not a gorgeous mosaic of multicultural diversity. The Christian West has now become the culture that dares not utter its name. The best way for Christians to put Christ back into Christmas is to observe Christmas in a Christian manner, forgetting about the culture wars for a moment and fixing their attention on God Incarnate.

Politics is job #1. Georgie Anne Geyer. *National Review* 48:56-7 + S 16 '96

By providing significant funding to radical organizations, the Ford Foundation is fostering Hispanic separatism and attacking American democracy. With assets in excess of $4 billion, the foundation is the leading financial backer of groups that advocate replacing the rights and duties of citizenship with the rights and privileges based upon one's ethnic background, real or imagined. The assault on majoritarianism, which has always protected and defined American citizenship, is underlaid by the new philosophy of group rights under the rubric of multiculturalism. Proponents of multiculturalism talk about becoming citizens not of America but of ethnic and other interest groups. Multiculturalism therefore amounts to nothing less than an alternative to citizenship. The writer discusses the Ford Foundation's funding of La Raza and the Mexican-American Legal Defense and Educational Fund.

Classroom booksploitation. Gabriel Brownstein. *The New Leader* 80:12-13 May 5 '97

Multicultural readers safeguard the needs of institutions at the expense of the writing they anthologize and the students they hope to instruct. Not too long ago it seemed that composition was a battlefield with leftist intellectuals promoting multiculturalism and right-wing academics defending institutional values. The war appears to have been won not by the revolutionaries or the reactionaries but by commercial concerns and a creeping bureaucratic conservatism. The new multicultural readers symbolize not so much a challenge to the established academic order as a way of managing that challenge. The books are a corporate answer to an academic problem.

For identity. Michael Walzer. *The New Republic* 215:39 D 2 '96

The debate regarding multiculturalism must be understood in the context of the fact that the majority of Americans favor one so-called correct code of behavior. Most Americans believe that there is one way of worshiping one God, one correct form of political allegiance, and one cultural ideal. America has always been a multicultural nation, however, from the earliest times, Americans were differentiated with regard to religion, ethnicity, race, and region. Contemporary America is notable for the fact that multiculturalism is asserted by those groups that previously fearfully denied accusations of difference.

Who's to judge? Gish Jen. *The New Republic* 216:18-19 Ap 21 '97

Many minority writers, once marooned by prejudice, are now marooned by identity politics. Asian-American authors used to be quite profoundly nobody, but multiculturalism validated "being between worlds" as a suitable topic for a story, and Asian Americans could suddenly speak for themselves and make themselves seen.

Multiculturalism has also brought identity politics, though, which sees the truth in external, rather than internal, definitions of the self. This is a problem for writers, who are generally devoted to the inner life that identity politics denies. It has therefore become necessary for some writers to brand themselves as anti-politically correct, as politically correct multiculturalism has left them no choice. Diversity is still an issue in the literary world, however. The writer discusses judging the PEN/Hemingway award and multiculturalism as a publishing phenomenon, among other topics.

Wounded. Alain Finkielkraut and Linda Asher. *The New York Times Magazine* 49 Je 8 '97

Part of a special issue on how the world views America. A paradigm shift has occurred in U.S. universities with the decision to designate intellectual disciplines by their subjects rather than their methods. From now on, learning will exist not in order for people to increase their understanding of subjects but to heal white heterosexual males of their superiority complex and restore pride to others. The aim of the humanities in the age of multiculturalism is thus to bring down the offenders and exalt the offended.

Reflections on multiculturalism. Alan Singer. *Phi Delta Kappan* 76:284-8 D '94

Most of the debates about multiculturalism in American education have more to do with who will hold power and shape education policy than with the nature of history, the relative merits of different types of art and literature, or the way these are taught. Still, there is a social cost if educators reject multiculturalism and maintain school curricula the way they are. If educators want to respond to what they feel are historical misrepresentations and prejudices in Afrocentric and other ethnocentric philosophies, they must also address current societal issues such as growing racial divisions, the widening economic disparity between social classes, and the increasing disaffection of our youth. The writer discusses criticisms of multicultural education, Afrocentrism, black anti-Semitism, and ten ideas that he believes provide a basic foundation for a multicultural curriculum.

Crossroads cities. *The Unesco Courier* 50:8-37 Mr '97

A special issue on multicultural cities. So-called crossroads cities are cities where successive waves of immigrants have settled to create a rich and diverse life and a shared sense of belonging. Such cities can be more unpredictable and intense than others, but each has managed to cope with its internal violence, even drawing vitality from it. Crossroads cities have a creative energy formed by a very wide spectrum of thinking and imagination, and this energy diffuses into the surrounding country. These cities also act as laboratories for the future for their nations as they face the challenges of globalization. Articles discuss Tangier, Morocco; New York, America; Bombay, India; Marseilles, France; La Paz, Bolivia; Vancouver, Canada; and the spirit of diversity found in crossroads cities.

The spirit of diversity. Anissa Barrak. *The Unesco Courier* 50:36 Mr '97

Part of a special issue on multicultural cities. So-called crossroads cities have evolved through the centuries due to population shifts and voluntary or forced migrations bringing together diverse cultures and ethnic groups. Located in economically important areas, these composite cities have benefited from the diverse contributions made by the people who settled in them, and some people regard this ethnic and cultural intermingling as a source of mutual enrichment. Others, however, see it as a source of cultural impoverishment through a fusion that produces uniformity and a leveling down. This dilemma reveals the paradox that is at the core of all crossroads cities, the question of whether the pursuit of cultural intermingling as an ideal in plural cities is in fact anathema to their very pluralism.

It takes many cultures to make one faith. *U.S. Catholic* 62:14-17 Ap '97

An interview with Jesuit father Marcello Azevedo. Azevedo is director of the John XXIII Center for Social Research and Action and of the Brazilian Institute of Development in Rio de Janeiro. A long-time student of American culture and society, he has taught and lectured widely and has published 12 books and numerous articles on faith and culture. Among the topics Azevedo discusses are whether religion and culture are related, the purpose of evangelizing, and how to foster unity through diversity of cultures.

Your mission, should you choose to accept it. Charles Johnson. *U.S. Catholic* 61:31-2 Jl '96

The words "diversity" and "values" mean a lot for people who think of themselves as missionaries. The call for each Christian to be engaged in mission for the sake of the gospel takes us beyond limited parochial attitudes and perspectives, and missionaries are people who feel this call and respond to it. The call to mission is a task many people are not comfortable with, but if we open ourselves to deeper meanings of life and God's creation, we are able to understand diversity and differences not as trendy words but as hallmarks of humanity. It is through sounding these depths of the mystery of human life that we can encounter the more profound meaning of our faith, which can guide us in how we live with the rich possibilities that diversity has to offer. The Christian call to mission is based in values that are nourished by the gospel, and, in short, these values impel people to go to the other and the different. At the same time, we go entirely aware that Christ has preceded us.

The intellectual bankruptcy of multiculturalism. Thomas J. Famularo. *USA Today* 124:42-4 My '96

Multicultural education, which strongly opposes the concept of an identifiable and definable American culture that might form the foundation of a core curriculum, is undermined by two fatal flaws. First, the more the school curriculum consists of a multicultural test based on so-called exposure to diversity, the more shallow and superficial learning becomes. Second, multicultural education, by its nature, precludes the single most important element of a successful education—coherent means to a discernible end. By denying the existence or value of a distinctive American culture, thus rejecting the idea that public education must help in the process of assimilation, multicultural education makes itself aimless and rudderless. Moreover, multicultural curricula, which are overtly committed to diversity and difference, almost always concentrate on underlying, dormant, and often dogmatic themes.

Multiculturalism is driving us apart. Linda Chavez. *USA Today* 124:39-41 My '96

American society is currently undergoing a "reracialization" in the name of multiculturalism. The idea that the United States is a multicultural nation implies that Americans differ with regard to race, values, mores, temperament, customs, and language—thereby bringing into question the concept of an American people. This process of reracialization is a regression to the America that existed before *Brown v. Board of Education* and the passage of the major civil-rights laws of the 1960s. Allowing race and ethnicity to determine public policy invites the kind of cleavage that will set one group against another in ways that cannot be beneficial either for the groups themselves or for American society as a whole. The more diverse the United States becomes, the more vital it is that Americans commit themselves to a shared, civic culture.

It's the culture, stupid. John Leo. *U.S. News & World Report* 117:30 N 21 '94

Morality and culture were crucial concerns for the voters in the November 8 elections. The public has not become much fonder of the Republicans, but it does tend to associate the Democratic Party with moral and cultural decline. According to a poll by People for the American Way, a clear majority of Americans feel that moral decline is at the heart of the nation's problems. A poll by *Times Mirror* also noted that cultural conservatism is more important than economic conservatism as a source of Republican appeal to voters, many of whom feel estranged from the Democrats on moral issues. Much of the estrangement is related to the rise of multiculturalism, which denigrates traditional American values and common American identity. White males in particular have felt themselves targeted; squeezed by race and gender quotas, they can be expected to continue their Republican drift.

The terrible toll on college presidents. Thomas Toch. *U.S. News & World Report* 117:82 D 12 '94

Harvard President Neil Rudenstine's indefinite leave from his post highlights the crushing demands of the job. Harvard announced that Rudenstine, who had headed Harvard since 1991, was taking his leave at the insistence of his doctors to recover from "severe fatigue and exhaustion." As state and federal largess has slowed and the public has revolted against tuition hikes, college presidents have become almost full-time fundraisers. They have also been besieged by a number of contentious nonfiscal issues, ranging from multiculturalism in the curriculum to campus safety. Aside from handling the day-to-day responsibilities of a modern university with 19,000 students and 2,200 faculty, Rudenstine was charged with carrying out an unprecedented five-year, $2.1 billion fund-raising campaign, and he has had to quell faculty and student protests.

Appendix

Listed below are related e-mail addresses, websites, and phone numbers of organizations who can provide additional information on the subject of multiculturalism.

AFL-CIO Civil Rights Department
815 16th St., NW
Washington, D.C. 20006
Tel: (202) 637-5000
www.aflcio.org

Alliance Working to Achieve Racial Equality (AWARE)
jfmcdo00@www.uky.edu

American-Arab Anti-Discrimination Committee
4201 Connecticut Ave., NW, #300
Washington, D.C. 20008
Tel: (202) 244-2990
www.adc.org

American Civil Liberties Union
125 Broad St.
New York, NY 10004
Tel: (212) 944-9800
www.aclu.org

American Friends Service Committee
1501 Cherry St.
Philadelphia, PA 19102
Tel: (215) 241-7000

American Jewish Committee
Institute of Human Relations
165 E. 56th St.
New York, NY 10022-2746
Tel: (212) 751-4000
ajc.org

Anti-Defamation League of B'nai B'rith
823 UN Plaza
New York, NY 10017
Tel: (212) 490-2525
www.adl.org

Anti-Racist Action (ARA)
P.O. Box 291
Stn.B, Toronto, Ontario
M5T 2T2, Canada
Tel: (416) 631-8835
www.web.net:80%7Eara/

Artists Against Racism (AAR)
P.O. Box 54511
Toronto, Ontario
M5M 4N5, Canada
Tel: (416) 410-5631
www.vrx.net:80/aar

Arts Censorship Project
American Civil Liberties Union
125 Broad St.
New York, NY 10004
Tel: (212) 944-9800
www.artsusa.org

Asian American Legal Defense & Education Fund
99 Hudson St., 12th Fl.
New York, New York 10013
Tel: (212) 966-5932

Center for New Community
6429 W. North Ave.
Oak Park, IL 60302
Tel: (708) 848-0319

Center for Women Policy Studies
1211 Connecticut Ave., NW, Suite 312
Washington, D.C. 20036
Tel: (202) 872-1770

Center for the Applied Study of Ethnoviolence
712 W. Lombard St.
Baltimore, MD 21201
Tel: (410) 706-5170

Coalition Against Anti-Asian Violence
Break the Silence
P.O. Box 2165
San Francisco, CA 94126
Tel: (415) 751-3924

Coalition for Human Dignity
Portland Office
P.O. Box 40344
Portland, OR 97240
Tel: (503) 281-5823
Fax: (503) 281-8673

Facing History and Ourselves
16 Hurd Rd.
Brookline, MA 02146
Tel: (617) 232-1595

Gay & Lesbian Advocates & Defenders
P.O. Box 218
Boston, MA 02112
Tel: (617) 426-1350

Idaho For Human Dignity, Inc.
P.O. Box 797
Boise, ID 83702
Tel: (208) 336-5160

International Gay & Lesbian Human Rights Commission
1360 Mission St., Suite 200
San Francisco, CA 94103
Tel: (415) 255-8680
www.progway.org

Japanese American Citizens League
1765 Sutter St.
San Francisco, CA 94115
Tel: (415) 921-5225

Mexican American Legal Defense & Education Fund (MALDEF)
634 Spring St., 11th Fl.
Los Angeles, CA 90014
Tel: (213) 629-2512
www.latinoweb.com:80/maldef/

Minority Activist Apprenticeship Program
Center for Third World Organizing
1218 E. 21 St.
Oakland, CA 94606
Tel: (510) 533-0923

National Association for the Advancement of Colored People (NAACP)
4805 Mt. Hope Dr.
Baltimore, MD
Tel: (410) 358-8900
www.wh.org/naacp/

National Organization for Women
1000 16th St., NW, Suite 700
Washington, D.C. 20036
Tel: (202) 331-0066

National Network for Immigrant and Refugee Rights
310 8th St., Suite 307
Oakland, CA 94607
Tel: (415) 465-1984

One World
www.oneworld.org

Organization of Chinese Americans
1001 Connecticut Ave., NW, Suite 707
Washington, D.C. 20036
Tel: (202) 223-5500

Third Force Magazine
Center for Third World Organizing
1218 E. 21 St.
Oakland, CA 94606
Tel: (510) 533-0923

UAW Civil Rights Department
8731 E. Jefferson Ave., 3rd Fl.
Detroit, MI 48214
Tel: (313) 926-5361

Index

	DATE DUE		